PENGUIN BOOKS

FORGOTTEN WARS

Christopher Bayly is Vere Harmsworth Professor of Imperial and Naval History, University of Cambridge, and a Fellow of St Catharine's College, Cambridge. His books include *Imperial Meridian, Indian Society and the Making of the British Empire* and *The Birth of the Modern World, 1780–1914*.

In June 2005 Christopher Bayly won the Wolfson Prize for History for his 'distinguished contribution to historical writing'.

Tim Harper is a Senior Lecturer in History at the University of Cambridge and Fellow of Magdalene College, Cambridge. He is the author of *The End of Empire and the Making of Modern Malaya*.

Christopher Bayly and Tim Harper jointly wrote the highly praised *Forgotten Armies: The Fall of British Asia, 1941–45* which is a prelude to this book.

CHRISTOPHER BAYLY
AND
TIM HARPER

Forgotten Wars
The End of Britain's Asian Empire

PENGUIN BOOKS

PENGUIN BOOKS

Published by the Penguin Group
Penguin Books Ltd, 80 Strand, London WC2R ORL, England
Penguin Group (USA) Inc., 375 Hudson Street, New York, New York 10014, USA
Penguin Group (Canada), 90 Eglinton Avenue East, Suite 700, Toronto, Ontario, Canada M4P 2Y3
(a division of Pearson Penguin Canada Inc.)
Penguin Ireland, 25 St Stephen's Green, Dublin 2, Ireland
(a division of Penguin Books Ltd)
Penguin Group (Australia), 250 Camberwell Road, Camberwell, Victoria 3124, Australia
(a division of Pearson Australia Group Pty Ltd)
Penguin Books India Pvt Ltd, 11 Community Centre, Panchsheel Park, New Delhi – 110 017, India
Penguin Group (NZ), 67 Apollo Drive, Rosedale, North Shore 0632, New Zealand
(a division of Pearson New Zealand Ltd)
Penguin Books (South Africa) (Pty) Ltd, 24 Sturdee Avenue, Rosebank, Johannesburg 2196, South Africa

Penguin Books Ltd, Registered Offices: 80 Strand, London WC2R ORL, England

www.penguin.com

First published by Allen Lane 2007
Published in Penguin Books 2008
1

Typeset by Rowland Phototypesetting Ltd, Bury St Edmunds, Suffolk
Printed in England by Clays Ltd, St Ives plc

978-0-141-01738-9

Contents

List of Illustrations

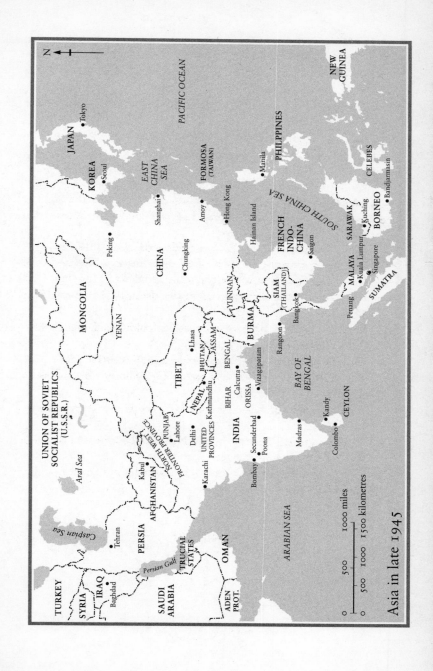

Asia in late 1945

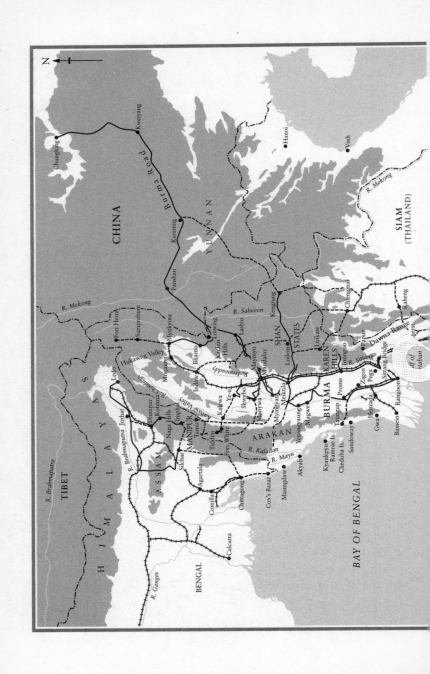

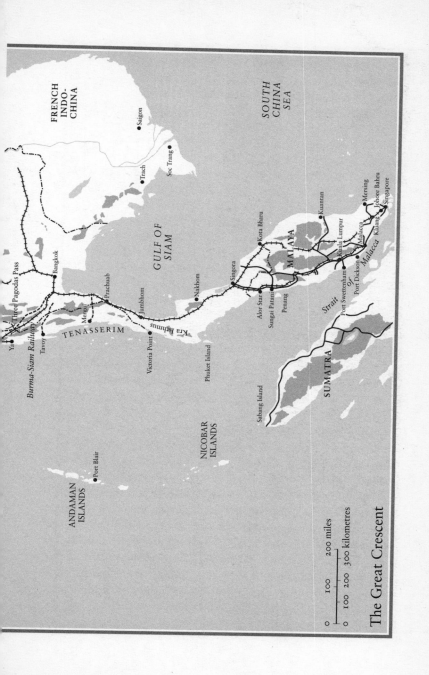

The Great Crescent

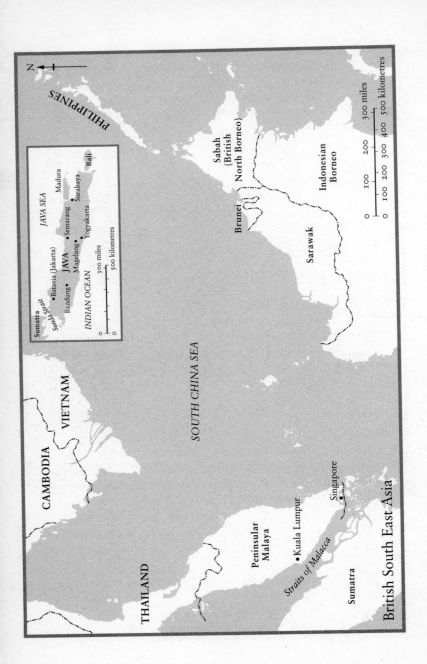

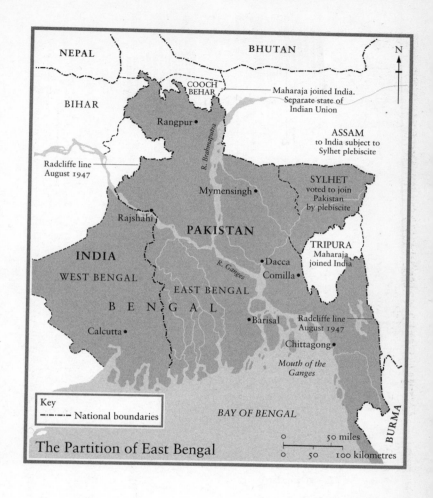

NEPAL

BHUTAN

N

BIHAR

COOCH
BEHAR

Maharaja joined India.
Separate state of
Indian Union

Rangpur •

R. Brahmaputra

ASSAM
to India subject to
Sylhet plebiscite

Radcliffe line
August 1947

Mymensingh •

SYLHET
voted to join
Pakistan
by plebiscite

Rajshahi •

PAKISTAN

TRIPURA
Maharaja
joined India

INDIA

R. Ganges

• Dacca

WEST BENGAL

Comilla •

EAST BENGAL

B E N G A L

• Barisal

Radcliffe line
August 1947

Calcutta •

Chittagong •

Mouth of the
Ganges

Key

National boundaries

BAY OF BENGAL

BURMA

The Partition of East Bengal

0   50 miles

0   50   100 kilometres

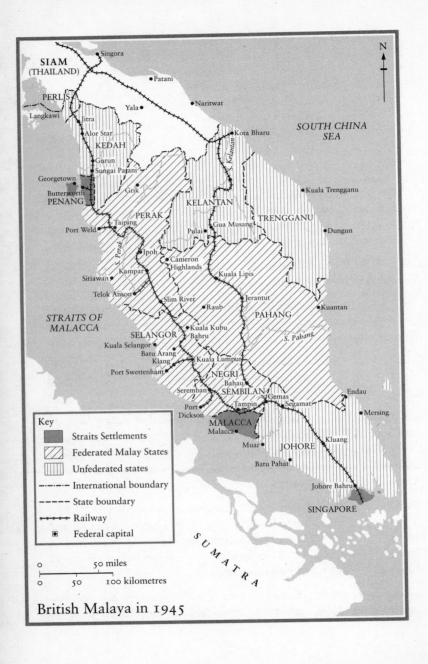

British Malaya in 1945

Some Key Characters

Abdul Razak bin Hussein (b. 1922). Malay politician. Served in the war as a district officer; studied law in London, where he became a close associate and political ally of Tunku Abdul Rahman. Succeeded him to become second prime minister of Malaysia, 1970–76.

Amery, Rt Hon. Leopold, MP (b. 1873). Conservative politician. Secretary of state for India and Burma, 1940–45.

Attlee, Rt Hon. Clement Richard (b. 1883). Labour politician. Deputy prime minister, 1942–5; prime minister, July 1945–1952; defence minister to 1946.

Auchinleck, General Claude (b. 1884). Commander North African Front, 1940–42, Commander-in-Chief, India, 1943–7; co-ordinated India base for the Burma campaign.

Aung San, Thakin or **'Bogyoke' (General)** (b. 1916). Leading Burmese revolutionary. Commander of Burma Independence Army, 1942; defence minister under Ba Maw, 1943–5. President of Anti-Fascist People's Front Freedom League; member of Governor's Executive Council 1946–7. Assassinated July 1947.

Ba Maw (b. 1893). Lawyer, politician and prime minister of Burma, 1937–9. Emerged as main collaborator with Japanese in 1942 and became 'Adipadi' (first man) of independent Burma in 1943. Fled to Tokyo; imprisoned by Allies 1945; returned to Burma in 1946; interned following 1947 assassinations.

Boestamam, Ahmad (b. 1920). Born Abdullah Sani bin Raja Kechil. Malay novelist, journalist and politician. Founder and leader of

Angkatan Pemuda Insaf, 1946–8. Detained 1948–55. Founder Partai Rakyat and leader of Socialist Front in parliament after 1959. Detained again during 'Confrontation' with Indonesia.

Bose, Subhas Chandra (b. 1897). Bengali politician and radical leader within Forward Bloc of Congress. Arrested by British 1940, fled to Berlin 1941. Took over leadership of Indian National Army and Free India government 1943. Retreated from Imphal with Japanese in 1944. Presumed dead in plane crash, August 1945.

Burhanuddin al-Helmy, Dr (b. 1911). Leader of Malay Nationalist Party, 1945–7. Detained after Nadrah riots and on release became leader of Parti Islam Se-Malaya. Detained again during 'Confrontation' with Indonesia.

Chiang Kai Shek (b. 1887). Chinese nationalist leader and 'generalissimo' of Chinese armies fighting Japan since 1936; drawn into fighting in Burma during 1942 to keep the 'Burma Road' open. Pressed for Allied campaign against Burma, 1943–4. Fought and lost civil war with Mao Zedong, 1946–9.

Chin Peng (b. 1924). Party name of Ong Boon Hua. Communist liaison officer with Force 136 in Perak, Malaya. Secretary general of the Malayan Communist Party from 1947 and led rebellion against the colonial government 1948–60. Resident in China from 1960. Signed a peace accord with the Malaysian government in 1989.

Christison, Lt General Sir Philip (b. 1893). Commanded 15 Indian Corps in Burma. Took surrender of Singapore and commanded in Indonesia. Later became ADC to King George VI.

Creech Jones, Arthur (b. 1891). Labour Colonial Secretary, 1946–50, having earlier headed the Fabian Colonial Bureau.

Cripps, Sir Richard Stafford (b. 1889). Labour politician. As Leader of the House of Commons in 1942, visited India to treat with Indian National Congress (the Cripps mission), and again with Labour government's Cabinet Mission in 1946. Chancellor of the Exchequer from November 1947.

Davis, John. A policeman in Perak before the war; senior Force 136 officer in Malaya, 1943–5. Afterwards a district officer in Malaya; escorted old comrade Chin Peng to the abortive Baling peace talks in 1955.

Donnison, Colonel Frank S. V. (b. 1898). Civil servant. Secretary to Burmese government, 1939–41 and its representative in Delhi, 1942–3. Commissioned, joined Civil Administration Secretariat (Burma) during re-conquest, 1944–5; later wrote official history of the war and military administration in the Far East.

Dorman-Smith, Sir Reginald (b. 1899). Governor of Burma, 1941–6, escaped from Myitkyina 1942. Exiled in Simla. Returned as civil Governor of Burma autumn 1945. Replaced by Attlee government May 1946.

Eng Ming Chin (b. 1924). Joined the Malayan Communist Party in Perak in 1940 and played a leading role as a women's activist in the 'open' organization of the party after 1945. Took to the jungle in 1948, and assigned to the Malay 10th Regiment. In 1955 married Abdullah C. D. and took the name Suraini Abdullah.

Furnivall, J. S., ICS (b. 1878). Retired Burma civil servant and Fabian socialist, well connected with radical Burmese Thakins. Advised on reconstruction of Burma in Simla, 1943–4; returned to Burma after independence as an economic adviser.

Gandhi, Mohandas Karamchand (b. 1869). Symbolic head of Indian National Congress. Apostle of non-violence. Headed the anti-British Quit India movement of 1942. Jailed by the British for much of the rest of the war, during which time he staged a hunger strike. Assassinated January 1948.

Gent, Sir Edward (b. 1895). Colonial civil servant. As head of Eastern Section, played a major role in devising Malayan Union Plan. Governor of Malayan Union, 1946–8. Killed in an air crash on recall to London after the outbreak of the Emergency in June 1948.

Gracey, General Douglas (b. 1894). Commanded 20th Indian Division, 14th Army at Imphal and Kohima 1944. Occupied Saigon,

French Indo-China, August 1945 to February 1946. Effectively handed back southern Indo-China to French colonial government. Chief of Staff of Pakistan Army, February 1948 to January 1951.

Gurney, Sir Henry Lovell Goldsworthy (b. 1898). Career colonial servant; formerly Chief Secretary in Gold Coast and Palestine before replacing Sir Edward Gent as High Commissioner in Malaya, 1948. Oversaw the early stages of the Emergency until his assassination by the communists on the way to the hill station of Fraser's Hill in October 1951.

Hirohito, Showa, Emperor of Japan (b. 1901). Implicated in aggressive Japanese policies in China and Southeast Asia. Remained on throne 1945, under American tutelage.

Hussein bin Onn (b. 1922). Malay politician. Son of Onn bin Jaafar. Served in Indian Army during war; then led UMNO Youth until 1951 when he left with his father to form the Independence for Malaya Party. Joined UMNO in 1968 to become third prime minister of Malaysia, 1976–81.

Ibrahim, Sultan of Johore (b. 1873). Independent-minded sultan of peninsular Malaya's southernmost state; ruled from 1895 until 1959.

Ishak bin Haji Mohamed (b. 1910). One of the leading Malay novelists and journalists of his generation. Leader of the Malay Nationalist Party after Dr Burhanuddin and played leading role in PUTERA-AMCJA. Detained 1948–54.

Khatijah Sidek (b. 1918). Women's activist and politician. Born in west Sumatra, where she led a women's paramilitary organization during the Indonesian revolution. Took struggle to Malaya, but detained in 1948. Led UMNO's women's wing, but was expelled for radical views and later joined the Parti Islam Se-Malaya. Died in poverty in 1982.

Khin Myo Chit (b. 1915). Socialist radical, Buddhist and literary figure. Women's official in Ba Maw's government, 1943–5. Teacher in Rangoon University after the war.

Knight, Sir Henry (b. 1886). Joined Indian Civil Service in 1909.

Acting Governor Bombay, 1945, Madras, 1946, and Burma, June–August 1946.

Lai Teck (b. 1900?). Best-known alias of the Vietnamese-born secretary general of the Malayan Communist Party. Exposed as a British and Japanese agent in 1947; fled to Bangkok, where he was assassinated later the same year.

Laithwaite, Sir Gilbert (b. 1894). Assistant undersecretary of state, India Office, 1943; undersecretary of state, War Cabinet, 1944–5; deputy undersecretary of state for Burma from 1945.

Lee, H. S. (Hau Shik) (b. 1901). Industrialist and leader of the Selangor Chinese. Active in the Kuomintang (he held the rank of colonel) and then the Malayan Chinese Association. Brokered the MCA's first electoral alliance with UMNO in the Kuala Lumpur municipal elections of 1952. First finance minister of independent Malaya.

Lee Kong Chian (b. 1894). Rubber tycoon and philanthropist. Son-in-law to Tan Kah Kee and leading spokesman of the Chinese of Singapore.

Lee Kuan Yew (b. 1923). Singaporean politician. A student at the elite Raffles Institution in Singapore in 1942. Worked as a translator for the Japanese during the war, then studied in Cambridge and at the London Bar. Founded the People's Action Party in 1954; prime minister of Singapore, 1959–90; after stepping down, continued to exercise a leading political role.

Leyden, John L. (b. 1904). Joined the Burma Frontier Service in 1927. Well connected with Kachins and Chins; involved in covert operations 1942–3. Returned to Frontier Areas Administration 1946.

Liew Yao (b. 1918). Leading military commander of the MPAJA. An early casualty in the Emergency when intercepted at Kajang, Selangor, June 1948.

Lim Chin Siong (b. 1933). Charismatic Singaporean left-wing trade unionist and politician. Detained 1955–7 and again 1963–9. After release went into exile in England; later returned to Singapore but never re-entered politics.

Listowel, 5th earl of (William Francis Hare) (b. 1906) Labour politician. Parliamentary undersecretary for India and Burma, 1944–5; secretary of state for India and Burma from April 1947 and for Burma only from August 1947. Visited Burma 1947.

MacDonald, Malcolm John (b. 1901). Governor general, 1946–8, and commissioner general, 1948–55, in Southeast Asia. Son of Ramsay MacDonald. Served as a reforming colonial secretary, 1935, 1938–40, and dominion secretary, 1935–8, 1938–9. Later high commissioner in India, governor of Kenya and special representative in East and Central Africa.

Mahathir Mohamad (b. 1923). Malay politician. A medical student in Singapore after the war, and author of occasional newspaper columns on Malay affairs. Later joined UMNO and became fourth prime minister of Malaysia, 1981–2003.

Mahomed Ali Jinnah (b. 1876). President of the All-India Muslim League, 1916, 1920 and from 1934. First Governor General of Pakistan from August 1947. Died 1948.

Marshall, David (b. 1908). First chief minister of Singapore, 1955–6, on a Labour Party platform. Of Baghdadi Jewish background, he was a noted trial lawyer and human rights campaigner.

Maung Maung, Bo (b. 1920). Young recruit to Aung San's BIA who took part in the anti-Japanese revolt in 1945 and went on to a career in the Burmese military after 1948.

Mountbatten, Admiral Lord Louis (b. 1900). Supreme Allied Commander, South East Asia Command, 1943–6. Rebuilt army morale 1943. Overall director of Imphal–Kohima campaign, 1944. Cultivated relations with Aung San's Burma Defence Army in 1945 and aided its rebellion against the Japanese that March. Viceroy of India 1947, then governor general of independent India.

Mustapha Hussain (b. 1910). Malay nationalist. Vice-president of the Kesatuan Melayu Muda. Accompanied the Japanese advance to Singapore, but soon became disillusioned with them. Detained briefly after the war, and narrowly defeated by Tunku Abdul Rahman in UMNO's presidential election of 1951.

Ne Win (b. 1911). One of 'Thirty Comrades' of the Burma Independence Army. Military commander of Burmese Defence Forces, 1943–5. Commander of Burmese armed forces in 1948. Later dictator of Burma.

Nehru, Jawaharlal (b. 1889). Indian Congress Socialist leader. Favoured the Allies over the Axis, but went to jail following the Quit India movement in 1942. First prime minister of independent India, 1947. Architect of Bandung Conference and Non-Aligned Movement.

Nu, Thakin (later **U Nu**) (b. 1907). Burmese student activist and devout Buddhist. Minister in Ba Maw's government 1943–5; AFPFL, 1945–6. Became head of government for independent Burma following the assassination of Aung San in 1947, and its first prime minister in 1948. Architect of Bandung Conference, 1955.

Onn bin Jaafar, Dato (b. 1895). Leading Malay of Johore. In 1946, headed the United Malays National Organization. Left UMNO to form multi-racial Independence for Malaya Party, 1951–4, known from 1954 as Party Negara. Failed to win seat in 1955 election, but elected MP in 1959.

Paw Tun, Sir (b. 1883). Conservative Arakanese politician. Prime minister of Burma 1942. Exiled to Simla in India with Dorman-Smith. Member of Governor's Executive Council 1945–6.

Pearce, Major General Sir Charles Frederick (b. 1892). Governor's secretary, Burma, 1939. Commissioned into the army, he became a key figure in Civil Administration Secretariat (Burma) during reconquest, 1943–5. Counsellor to Governor, 1946.

Pethick-Lawrence, 1st Baron (Frederick William Pethick-Lawrence) (b. 1871). Secretary of state for India and Burma, 1945 to April 1947. Member of Cabinet Mission to India, 1946.

Purcell, Victor (b. 1896). Civil servant in Malaya and a key figure in its post-war planning. Returned there as adviser on Chinese affairs in 1945. Later critic of Templer regime; historian of the Chinese in Southeast Asia and Cambridge University lecturer.

Rance, Major General Sir Hubert (b. 1898). Served on Western Front,

1939–43. Director of civil affairs in Burma, 1945–6. Governor of Burma, August 1946 to January 1948.

Saw, U (b. 1900). Minister of forests for Burma 1939; prime minister, 1940–42. Flew to London in 1941 on goodwill mission. Imprisoned in Uganda during war for contacting Japanese. Returned to Burma 1946. Convicted of assassination of Aung San 1947. Hanged 1948.

Shamsiah Fakeh (b. 1924). Malay radical and leader of AWAS women's movement. Took to jungle in 1948 and active in the 10th Regiment of the MNLA. Married briefly to Ahmad Boestamam.

Sjahrir, Sutan (b. 1909). Indonesian socialist born in West Sumatra and educated in the Netherlands. Experienced imprisonment and internal exile by Dutch, 1934–41. First prime minister of Indonesia, 1945–7, he led negotiations with British and Dutch.

Slim, General (later Field Marshal), Sir William (b. 1891). Commander 1st Burma Corps, 1942, during retreat with Gen. Harold Alexander. Main figure in rebuilding 14th Army and success of its Burma campaigns 1944–5. Commander Allied Land Forces South East Asia, 1945. Later governor general of Australia.

Smith Dun, Colonel (b. 1906). Karen military officer who fought with 14th Army in Burma campaign, became commander-in-chief of Burma's armed forces 1948, but was speedily dismissed.

Soe, Thakin (b. 1905). Communist leader. Set up 'base area' in Burma delta, 1942–5. Broke with Anti-Fascist People's Front government and led Red Flag communists in rebellion against British and independent government of Burma, 1946–55.

Stevenson, Henry Noel Cochrane (b. 1903). Joined Burma Frontier Service in 1926. Organized Chin levies, 1942–3. Served in Civil Affairs Secretariat Burma, 1944–5. Director Frontier Areas Administration, 1946 to February 1947, when he was replaced for being too close to minorities leaders.

Suhrawardy, H. S. (b. 1892). Bengali Muslim politician. Minister of labour, Bengal, 1937. Minister of supplies in Bengal government during 1943 famine. Chief minister, Bengal, after 1946 elections. Implicated in Great Calcutta Killing, 1946. Founded East Pakistan Awami League.

Sukarno (b. 1901). First president of Indonesia, 1945–66. Presided at Bandung Conference, 1955. Declared martial law and 'guided democracy' in 1957. Removed by Suharto after failed military coup in 1965.

Tan Cheng Lock (b. 1883). Straits Chinese leader, businessman and legislator. Fled to India on Japanese invasion of Malaya. Figurehead leader of left-wing United Front in 1947; founding president of the Malayan Chinese Association in 1949. Knighted 1952. His son, **Tan Siew Sin** (b. 1916) succeeded him and was a minister in independent Malaya.

Tan Kah Kee (b. 1874). Leader of the Overseas Chinese; headed the China Relief Fund, 1937–41. Spent the war hiding in Java, returning to Singapore to head China Democratic League. Returned to China in 1949.

Tan Malaka (b. 1897). Sumatra-born leader of Partai Kommunis Indonesia and Comintern. In hiding in Singapore on outbreak of war, and later escaped incognito to Indonesia. Revealed himself in 1946 to lead calls for social revolution. Died at hands of republican soldiers in 1948.

Templer, Sir Gerald Walter Robert (b. 1898). High Commissioner of Malaya, 1952–4. Earlier served in military government of occupied Germany and as director of military intelligence. After Malaya became Chief of the Imperial General Staff, 1955–8, and retired a field marshal.

Than Tun (b. 1911). Student leader. Minister of agriculture under Ba Maw, 1943. Joined anti-Japanese resistance. Led Burma Communist Party in 1945. Broke with AFPFL in 1946

Thein Pe Myint (b. 1914). Burmese communist who escaped to India in 1942. Author of *What happened in Burma*, an attack on the Japanese occupation. Sent to Chungking, China, but maintained links with Burmese resistance to Japanese. Secretary of the Burma Communist Party, 1945–55. Broke with AFPFL in 1946.

Tin Tut (b. 1895). Barrister and Burmese member of Indian Civil Service. Accompanied U Saw to London in 1941. Joined Dorman-Smith in Simla, 1942. Left ICS and became financial adviser to AFPFL government. Accompanied Aung San to London, January 1947. Assassinated 1948.

Tunku Abdul Rahman (b. 1903). Malay prince of Kedah. Served as a district officer during war. As head of the United Malays National Organization led Malaya to independence in 1957; prime minister until 1970.

Wavell, Field Marshal Sir Archibald (b. 1883). Commander-in-chief, India, 1941–3. Viceroy and Governor General of India, 1943–7.

Yeung Kuo (b. 1917). Malayan Communist Party leader. In Penang in 1946, aided Chin Peng in exposure of Lai Teck and was viewed as Chin's deputy. Killed in the jungle shortly before the 1955 Baling peace talks.

Preface

In August 1945 the US dropped atomic bombs on Nagasaki and Hiroshima, so bringing to an end the Second World War. Yet in Asia the Second World War was only one intense and awful phase of a much longer conflict: 'the defeat of Japan would not end war in Asia', as one Indian newspaper mused when news of the Japanese surrender leaked out. This long and savage war had begun in 1937 with a full-scale attack on China by the Japanese imperialists. It continued after 1945 in a range of intense and bloody wars, both civil and against a revived European colonialism. These conflicts, variously called the Indonesian revolution, the First Indo-China War, the Partition of India, the Burmese civil war, the Malayan Emergency and the Vietnam War, surged on into the 1970s and beyond. It was not really until the 1980s, with the economic renaissance of Japan, the rise of Singapore and Malaysia and the beginning of the transformation of Asian communist regimes towards free-market capitalism, that Asia began to claim its place in the sun as the dominant continent of the twenty-first century.

This book is the story of the first and most intense period of the birth pangs of this new Asian world. It concentrates particularly on the great crescent of territory between eastern India and Singapore which had once been the commercial heart of Britain's Asian empire and which a revived and self-consciously 'constructive' British Empire now wished to reclaim as its own. The book focuses on the years between 1945 and 1949 and is a sequel to our earlier work, *Forgotten Armies: Britain's Asian Empire and the War with Japan* (Allen Lane, 2004). British troops, including a large contingent of Indian and African soldiers, poured into Burma from northeastern India, reversing the humiliating defeat which they had suffered at Japanese hands three years earlier. The British went on to occupy Thailand, much of the former French Indo-China and Dutch Indonesia, ostensibly in order to disarm the Japanese. But this revivified British Empire attempted to recreate itself in conditions vastly different from those that had prevailed a few years earlier. The British now faced a variety of powerful, armed and embittered nationalist leaderships determined to claim immediate independence.

Forgotten Wars tells the story of how Burmese resistance and the collapse of the British Raj in India brought Burma to independence in 1948, but how that independence was corroded by inter-ethnic conflict and the irresistible rise of the Burmese army which remains dominant in the country today. It shows how Britain was able to maintain its grip in Malaya and Singapore only because it garnered and received the support of conservative Malay and Chinese leaderships which feared the powerful Malayan Communist Party whose cadres Britain itself had helped to arm during the conflict with Japan. It charts the beginning of the long Indo-China war which culminated in the American defeat in southern Vietnam in 1975 and the bloody and little-understood lurch towards Indonesian independence after the fall of Japan. In the process, the book analyses the emergence of the Cold War in Asia. To the north of the region, China became a communist monolith. To the east, North Vietnam seized independence from the French. But to the south, Britain's rigorous campaign of counter-insurgency against the Malayan communists determined that the future states of Singapore and Malaysia would remain pro-Western and capitalist. These events sowed some of the seeds of East Asia's great economic miracle which was to blossom in the 1990s. Meanwhile, Burma took a unique road to isolation and stagnation as its leaders battled both communist insurgency and the demands of minority peoples for autonomy.

This book describes the struggles of proconsuls, colonial military commanders and nationalist leaders. But, like *Forgotten Armies*, it also tells the story of many ordinary people, both Asian and British, who were swept up in the violence of insurgency and counter-insurgency, communal rioting and renewed economic privation. The four years after the fall of Japan were Asia's time of revolution. Amid the turmoil, people still looked forward to an age of plenty when they would 'dance among showers of gold and silver', according to a Burmese verse. This bright future was still long decades away in the year 1949. Many people are still waiting.

In writing this book we have accumulated many more debts than we can possibly recount here: research has been undertaken in many places and over a long period of time. Historical research depends on dedication and specialist expertise, and the staffs of archives and libraries in Asia and Britain have consistently provided both. We would like to mention Kevin Greenbank of the Centre of South Asian Studies, Cambridge, and Rachel Rowe of the Centre and the Royal Commonwealth Society Collections in the Cambridge University Library. Our thanks to the librarians and archivists in the British Library, the National Archives at Kew, the Imperial War Museum, the National Army Museum, the Liddell Hart Centre in King's College, London, and the library, archives and Burma Star Collection in the School of Oriental and African Studies, London, and the Netaji Research Bureau, Calcutta. In Southeast Asia, the Perpustakaan Universiti Malaya, the Arkib Negara Malaysia, the National Archives of Singapore, the National Library of Singapore and the Institute of Southeast Asian Studies in Singapore have been particularly helpful.

We owe a special debt of thanks to Simon Winder, who has not only been a patient and indulgent editor but has also plied us with historiographical queries like the most genial of research supervisors. Katherine Prior once again contributed the index and helped us to clarify important questions. Thanks are due also to Chloe Campbell, Michal Shavit and Trevor Horwood for their editorial help over the two volumes and to Sophie Brockley, Bruce Hunter, Dr Romain Bertrand and Stuart Martin for their support and encouragement. Many other debts have been incurred. Sunil Amrith, Chua Ai Lin, Neil Khor, Gerard McCann, Emma Reisz, Felicia Yap, Lim Cheng Tju, C. C. Chin, Ronald Hyam, Christopher Goscha, Dr Syed Husin Ali and Professor Jomo K. S. all provided us with new material or insights. We owe special thanks to Professor Robert Taylor and Professor Robert Anderson for their helpful comments on portions of the manuscript. Any errors that remain are, of course, ours.

Magdalene College and St Catharine's College in Cambridge; Ms Véronique Bolhuis and the Centre Asie, Institut d'Etudes Politique, Paris; Oommen George, Yeo Seok Lian and many others in Kuala Lumpur all provided wonderful conditions in which to write. Our most unfailing supporters have been Susan Bayly and Norman and Collette Harper. We are very grateful to everyone who has helped us.

Prologue: An Unending War

As a little girl, Kimura Yasuko was evacuated from the city of Hiroshima to the countryside. When the war ended on 15 August 1945, group evacuations were abruptly ended and children began to return to their homes. The children of Hiroshima really had nowhere to return to. All the same, the authorities decided to send them back to where their homes had once been, if they thought a single relative had survived the atomic bomb. Kimura heard that her father was still alive and so she went back to the city in a truck with thirty or forty other children. She remembered:

We arrived in the early evening. The reddish setting sun hung in the sky. The ruins from an ordinary fire are burned black, aren't they? But the ruins of Hiroshima were brown, the colour of unfired pottery . . . The city didn't look as if it had been burned. Yet it was flattened. In the middle of the ruins two buildings, a department store and the newspaper [office] stood all alone. There my father met me . . . I remember the tears in his eyes when I met him . . . I knew Mother had died.[1]

The dropping of the atomic bombs on Hiroshima and Nagasaki was the defining event of the twentieth century. Everywhere the news was received with deep ambivalence. The leaders of the USA and Britain had been determined to save Allied lives by bringing the war to a rapid conclusion, but now they were assailed by guilt and doubt. In London Sir Cuthbert Headlam, a Conservative politician and robust supporter of Winston Churchill, rejoiced that the war was over, but he stood aghast at 'this new and fearful form of bomb' and the wanton destruction it had caused. The bomb would mean 'either the end of war or the end of civilisation'.[2]

The Japanese themselves were torn by mixed emotions. In Hiroshima itself, some American prisoners of war who had survived the explosion hidden in a cellar were found and beaten to death. But the majority of Japanese viewed the disaster as they would a great calamity of nature.[3] Kimura Yasuko later recorded that the bomb did not make her hate the Americans. In the two years before the bomb, life had been horrible and heartbreaking as city after city across Japan had been consumed by incendiary attacks.[4] Some 3 million Japanese had been killed since the attack on Pearl Harbor in 1941 and millions more had been wounded, bereaved or made homeless. The country was so utterly devastated that the incoming victors were astonished that it had held out for so long. The bomb finally ended that resistance. Some Japanese fainted when the high-pitched voice of Emperor Hirohito was heard over the radio, conceding defeat in stilted, formal Japanese. A few militarists and patriots committed suicide, while many other Japanese were shamed to the bottom of their hearts by their country's defeat and awaited the coming of the Americans with trepidation. Others quietly rejoiced in the knowledge that the imperial house and the nation had at least survived. Hundreds of thousands of their young men would now escape almost certain death on the battlefields of East and Southeast Asia.

The first Allied witnesses to this recessional were some of the Allied prisoners of war who had been sent to toil in the mines and heavy industries of Japan. Constantine Constantinovich Petrovsky was a White Russian doctor who had escaped the revolution to Singapore via China, and, like so many ambitious and talented people in Asia, found a home in its cosmopolitan world. In 1939 he had volunteered to fight for the British Empire. His war took him to Europe, then back to Singapore, where he experienced the trauma of its fall in February 1942. With the rest of the garrison he was herded into the prison camp at Changi, then sent to work on the Burma–Siam railway; he survived its horrors only to be embarked on one of the 'death ships' to mine coal fifty or so kilometres away from Hiroshima: of the 50,000 who began this journey, 11,000 perished. On the morning of 6 August 1945 there was an air-raid warning, as there had been most days that summer, 'and suddenly *phew!* Like earthquake. And black smoke . . . a column of this coming up like mushroom, spreading out, black and so on. I said "My God! They shot one plane, one bomb, they got oil tanks" ... They were all shuddering.' The next day the Japanese guards came and announced that everyone in Hiroshima was dead.[5] The bomb had killed a microcosm of people caught up in the terrible conflict: prisoners of war, Koreans and Chinese labourers, students from Malaya on scholarships, and perhaps 3,200 Japanese American citizens who were stranded in the city after Pearl Harbor.[6] Later, American planes flew over again, but this time they dropped food and medicines. Some of these supplies landed near Petrovsky's mine. Petrovsky and his fellow prisoners of war passed their supplies to the Japanese, who suddenly had nothing to eat. They realized that something quite extraordinary had happened when they noticed that all the flies and the bed bugs had disappeared. The prisoners were put to work digging a trench. They were told that it was an air-raid shelter; only later did they realize it was to be their own grave: if the Americans invaded, they were to be lined up beside it and shot.[7]

Across their empire, the Japanese were still killing prisoners, and orders had been given in Taiwan, Borneo and elsewhere to exterminate whole camps. But there was, in the end, to be no mass slaughter.[8] After the initial confusion, a strange mood of equanimity and freedom prevailed. Allied prisoners in Japan travelled without restraint, 'commandeering' cars and trucks, disarming Japanese servicemen on trains, entering houses in search of food and looking for women. There was an epidemic of venereal disease. Some prisoners even went into business, one Australian opening a hotel in Kyoto, where he sold *sake* and Asahi beer. There was remarkably little violence. The Japanese had all along feared this vast captive army, but now it was too weak to take its revenge. Many Allied servicemen visited the ruins of Hiroshima. They understood little of what had happened there: some thought the city had been a huge ammunition dump. In the words of one Australian major, they 'did tours with cut lunches and hot boxes etc. and on a picnic. All parties boiled the billy, had their lunches, picked up souvenirs and generally picked around the debris and the ruins.' There was little feeling of elation. The Japanese had, in every sense, been humbled. As an Australian private in Kobe recalled: 'our former enemies became polite, likeable, respectful people, only too pleased to help wherever possible'. But, equally, the men felt little

3

guilt or even compassion: 'they had seen the shelters dug into the hills by them to be [put] into and set alight'. Then, on 9 August, came the bomb at Nagasaki, and the whole valley around it felt the fury of the impact; afterwards 'not a sound. No birds, Not even a lizard. Just brown, treeless soil like cocoa, no grass, and twisted girderwork . . .'[9]

The day before the first bomb was dropped, most military commanders in mainland Asia believed that the war would go on for many months more. The British 14th Army had pushed down into Burma since their defeats of the Japanese at Imphal and Kohima on the borders of Assam in June and July 1944. The British took Rangoon, the country's capital, in May 1945.[10] But Japanese troops were still numerous in Burma's southern peninsula, Tenasserim, and in the recently liberated areas the mood was tense. Long-range B-17 bombers were pounding Singapore. The Japanese continued to occupy Thailand, Indo-China, Malaya and Indonesia. Despite the island-hopping advance by General Douglas MacArthur's forces in the Pacific, the Japanese had held on to the main islands of the Philippines, and pockets of resistance remained in Borneo. The Japanese army was also engaged in a huge and bloody war of attrition with the forces of nationalist China to the north of the capital, of Chiang Kai Shek's republican government at Chungking. Across this vast area, the pursuit and killing of Japanese troops came to a halt only slowly. The political outlook was uncertain, while food and clothing were alarmingly scarce.

Malaya and Burma had borne the brunt of the fighting in Southeast Asia. Here, as word of the bomb spread through the bazaars and villages, the mood was ambivalent and the air full of new menace. It first arrived as 'black-market news'. The past three and a half years had been a time of virtual isolation and rumour ruled: now there was rumour of a secret weapon, of an American invasion, that the Chinese were coming.[11] In Malaya, when parachutists from the British Special Operations Executive began to break cover, in all their garb of modern warfare they seemed like visitors from another world. This was the first of a series of strange new wonders, along with jeeps, penicillin, walkie-talkies and atomic power. The news of the surrender was confirmed by radio broadcasts from the Allied headquarters in Ceylon. Only a few days before, to be caught listening to Allied radio would have meant arrest, torture and possibly even death, but the Japanese no longer had the will to enforce their diktats. In the camp for women internees in Singapore, Sheila Allan, the Eurasian daughter of a British mining engineer, kept a secret diary of a youth in captivity. On 10 August she marked her twenty-first birthday by writing: 'Baby born to crippled Jewess – prophecy concerning her – a Jewess Rabbi dreamt that when a crippled woman gave birth to a boy we'll hear of Peace!' The next day she heard one of the POWs bringing the news by singing, 'The war is over'.[12]

Then came other portents: war businesses liquidated overnight; the gambling syndicates and lotteries that had flourished in the occupied lands cashed in their assets. There were celebrations that ranged from the quiet consumption of hidden bottles of brandy and whisky in Malaya to outright rejoicing in Burma. In the mountainous forest fringes of Malaya, the Chinese peasants who taken shelter there slaughtered their pigs and fowl. In the towns, Chinese papermakers and tailors prepared flags of the four victorious powers: Britain, the United States, Russia, and Chiang Kai Shek's China. Then, in a sudden rush of confidence, Malaya burst into light. The blackouts during the Allied bombing had created 'cities of dreadful night'; but now light bulbs appeared on verandas and the 'five-foot' walkways of shop-houses.[13] The great 'Worlds' – the amusement parks where the towns-folk came to play and to trade in one of the great spectacles of local life – turned on their show-lights and resumed their gyre. People went on a spending spree with freshly printed Japanese notes bearing their distinctive 'banana' design. But the mood was soon deflated. Inflation spread like a virus. Famine loomed. Everywhere people were anxiously on the move, to reach their families, or to get to the port cities where a sudden bounty of food and clothing was expected. And there were others – Taiwanese auxiliaries, mistresses of Japanese officers, informers, police and profiteers – who took to the shadows, fearing the reckoning that was to come.[14]

Only slowly were these rumours and portents confirmed by the behaviour of the Japanese themselves. In August 1945 there were around 630,000 armed Japanese across the whole region. Much of the rank and file was too young to have been complicit in Japan's lurch towards militarism in the 1930s. Many of the over 100,000

Japanese civilians had lived in Southeast Asia before the outbreak of the war, and called it home. They were all victims in a sense. Their conditions varied. Many of the soldiers who had been involved in the fighting in Burma were diseased and malnourished. Those surrendered in Malaya, Indo-China and Indonesia were likely to be relatively healthy and better fed. There were emotional announcements in camps and work places. Many felt humiliated by the terms of Japan's surrender. In Singapore the regional commander, Lieutenant General Seishiro Itagaki, announced that he would resist the Allies. He had laid plans for guerrilla warfare. His supreme commander, Field Marshal Count Terauchi, stated that he would submit only to a personal order from the emperor. A prince of the ruling house, Haruhito Kanin, flew with it to Terauchi's headquarters in Saigon on 19 August, and Itagaki was summoned to receive it. Only then was the Imperial Rescript published in the Singapore press, together with Itagaki's emotional appeal to his men that the imperial command was now 'absolute and irrevocable'.[15]

Many Japanese officers – 300 in Singapore alone in one account – saw the surrender as a racial apocalypse, and took their own lives: some in the lounge of the luxury Raffles Hotel where they heard the news from Itagaki.[16] Others who submitted to surrender and the prospect of imprisonment were anxious as to whether they would receive the protection of the Geneva Conventions, which Japan itself had not observed. Books on military law were at a sudden premium. The officers disposed of their plundered goods, burnt archives and, in some cases, killed witnesses to their atrocities. In the end the bulk of the Japanese garrison at Singapore marched itself into internment at Jurong, in the west of the island. British and Allied prisoners of war remained concentrated in the east, at Changi. But after the surrender Japanese units were ordered off the island and across the short causeway to the Malay peninsula. At Kranji, where the Commonwealth war cemetery now stands, they first met the Allied forces: Gurkha paratroops from Special Operations Executive. As one local POW observed: 'It went full circle – we saw the whole lot, thousands and thousands, marching their way to Woodlands, past our camp.'[17] These were the beachheads the Japanese had stormed in February 1942. They headed into the desolate, deserted rubber estates of the interior, and there amid a wrack of military machinery and surrounded by the spoils of war – furniture, bedding, refrigerators, carpets – they sat waiting for the end. They became 'Japanese surrendered personnel', a term of art introduced by the British in order to avoid implementing the Geneva Conventions' protocols towards prisoners of war. Although a few remained arrogant and uncooperative, the majority were compliant and patient. But it was still unclear what was happening to the more remote garrisons. Some of Itagaki's officers tried to flee to Sumatra, where there was rumoured to be last-ditch defiance. One Japanese officer of the Imperial Guard in northern Sumatra, who had fought down the length of the Malay peninsula and into Singapore in late 1941, wrote that after the announcement the mood was so mutinous that it was dangerous for officers to walk in the barracks.[18] As the Allies brought ahead plans to reoccupy the region, it was still unclear whether or not large numbers of Japanese would fight to the death.

These events can no longer be viewed as a minor theatre of a global war centred upon Europe. This was the Great Asian War: a connected arc of conflict that claimed around 24 million lives in lands occupied by Japan; the lives of 3 million Japanese, and 3.5 million more in India through war-related famine. The Great Asian War was longer and ultimately bloodier than Europe's civil war. The number of European, American and Australasian casualties – substantial, tragic as they were – was perhaps 1 per cent of the total. The first skirmishes began in 1931, erupting into open war in China in 1937, and in 1945 it was not yet at an end. Its impact was all the more dreadful for the fact that many of these societies had not known war on any large scale, still less the full ferocity of modern mechanized conflict. The Great Asian War was the most general conflict in Southeast Asia since the Mongol invasions of the thirteenth century, and the most intense since the great struggles for primacy on the mainland of Asia in the seventeenth century. And it had its serial holocausts, in the extermination of civilians, the coercion of slave labour, and mass rape.

For Asians, the horror of the bomb was accentuated by the fear that their war had merely paused. The Europeans, Americans and Japanese had ceased fighting, but Asians would be embattled with each other and, from time to time, with Europeans and Americans for the next generation or more. None of the fundamental causes of the Great Asian War had been eradicated. Imperialism, grinding poverty and ideological, ethnic and religious conflict continued to stalk the land. In many ways, they had been strengthened by the destruction and butchery of combat. It was plain to see that the war was continuing under another guise. Those huge forgotten armies of malnourished soldiers, prisoners of war, guerrilla bands, coolie labourers, sex slaves and carpetbaggers were still on the march. They were to march on for decades more as the British Empire dissolved and new nations were born amid racial and religious strife. A new 'great game' of diplomacy and subversion broke out between communism and capitalism, and provoked some of the most tragic, and forgotten, wars of the twentieth century.

The pivot of this long struggle was the crescent of land that stretched from Bengal, though Burma, the southern borderlands of Thailand, down the Malay peninsula to Singapore island. It was the hinterland of the Straits of Malacca, one of the world's greatest arteries of oceanic trade that separates the Indian Ocean from the South China Sea. In 1941, this vast crescent was under British control: the apex of a wider strategic arc that encompassed Suez and Cape Town in the west and Sydney and Auckland to the south. Even the independent kingdom of Thailand had for a hundred years been under the sway of the British diplomats and the expatriate business community in Bangkok. In the late nineteenth century, imperial visionaries had dreamed of blasting a new Suez Canal through the narrow isthmus of Kra, and after war broke out Churchill raised the possibility of 'some sort of protectorate' over this area, rich in tin and rubber. This was encouraged by the expatriates, many of whom were signed up for British secret-service operations in the region.[19] At this point the imperial gaze extended even further afield. If the neighbouring empires of the French in Indo-China and the Dutch in Indonesia had survived until 1941 largely unchallenged, they had done so under the sufferance of British power. And it would be British power that would restore them.

The crescent was one of the great frontiers of modern history. For centuries it had drawn in millions of people in search of a livelihood, particularly from the ancient agrarian civilizations that bordered it. The advent of the imperial economy had created new opportunities.

Waves of Chinese migrants, mostly from the hinterland of the southern seaboard, had come to the Nanyang, or the 'South Seas', as traders and artisans. They pioneered the plantations and mines of Malaya, and still provided the bulk of their labour force. South Asian communities were to be found in an infinite variety of specialist trades: Muslim shopkeepers, Malayalee clerks, Chettiyar money-lenders, Sikh policemen, Ceylonese lawyers. The train service of Malaya was known as the 'Jaffna railway' because of the monopoly by Tamils from Ceylon on the post of ticket-collector. The large-scale European rubber enterprises in Malaya pulled in another three-quarters of a million Tamils from the hinterland of Madras. Many more Indians made the shorter journey from eastern Bengal and Orissa into the rural economy of Burma. Migrations from Java and Sumatra kept alive a sense that the Malay peninsula was the heart of the Islamic civilization of the islands, that dated back to the fifteenth-century empire of Melaka. The traditional Malay rice, fishing and trading economy survived in the midst of some of the most advanced and regimented systems of wage labour on earth.

The main points of arrival for most of these pioneers were the great port cities such as Rangoon and Singapore: dynamic and diverse, they were built for play as much as trade or government, and their citizens were obsessed by their own modernity. They were glittering outposts of the West, where the colonial elite enjoyed a lifestyle they could never aspire to at home. Yet the lives of the Europeans, contained by their gross obsessions with race and hierarchy, barely touched the complex Asian worlds around them. The cosmopolitanism of a place like Singapore, for example, was built by Chinese, Indian, Arab, Armenian and Jewish merchants and professionals, many of whose own businesses were now regional in scope. Not least among them, and concentrated in new 'modern' sectors, were the Japanese: as dentists, photographers, and shopkeepers. Like the British before them, they saw Southeast Asia first as a frontier for private commerce, and then as a field for empire. In 1942 they renamed it 'Syonan-to', or 'light of the South'. Singapore was the Paris, or even the New York, of the East, and more of a global city than either. Its fall seemed to herald the collapse of an entire civilization and all its certainties. But the colonial city was enveloped by another, invisible city; an Asian metropolis of artisans and labourers, prostitutes and players, itinerants and peddlers, teachers and preachers, artists and writers, spies and revolutionaries: people of all communities who began to interact and explore the commonality of their lives and ideas. In the years after 1942, the invisible city would come into its own.

There was a curious insubstantial quality to Britain's Asian empire. Its political topography baffled the layman: as colonial power stretched to the south and east, the great traditions of the Raj gave way to complex arrangements of indirect rule. Even the 80 million people of Bengal, the oldest British possession in India, were governed at a distance. Assam to the northeast was an uncertain border region. Burma had been part of British India until 1936, and although the predominant Burmese population of the lowlands was governed on a Raj model, the ethnic minorities of its hill regions enjoyed a good deal of autonomy. British Malaya was a cluster of Islamic sultanates; there was no central government as such: British rule rested on the treaties of 'protection' that had been signed with Malay rulers from 1874 to 1914. The British governed, but they did not, strictly speaking, rule. The Straits Settlements of Singapore, Penang and Malacca were older outposts of the islands: models of Anglo-Saxon municipal management with oriental trappings. To all this the war gave a flaking veneer of coherence. If there was an 'imperial system' it really functioned only in wartime: men and materiel were mobilized across the crescent: Indian soldiers for the garrisons of Malaya, Chinese labourers for the Burma Road that supplied Chiang Kai Shek's war effort. But in Malaya, the mobilization and the defeats of 1941 and 1942 exposed all the inadequacies of an administration that was 'more suited to the days of Clive'.[20] The final, squalid exodus from Singapore laid bare the complacency and racial arrogance of its colonial masters. When the city fell on 15 February 1942, General Yamashita Tomoyuki's armies shattered the myth of white invulnerability, and broke the mandate of 'protection'.

This loss was catastrophic to Britain's global prestige and material strength. As India became a drain on the domestic balance of payments, Southeast Asia had emerged as one of the Empire's prize assets. The region exported two-thirds of the world's tin, and British Malaya alone provided half the world's production of rubber. Most of it passed through the port of Singapore. These industrial colonies were a major buttress of the sterling area: before the war, rubber exports to the USA were running at $118 million a year; tin, another $55 million.[21] Even Burma, although something of backwater, had oil and rich reserves of timber, and its export economy was intimately tied to the rest of the crescent. The frontier economies of Southeast Asia were dependent on the food production of the basins of the great river systems of the mainland, particularly the 3.7 million tons of padi exported annually from the Irrawaddy delta: Burma was the rice bowl of Malaya.[22] Japan's blitzkrieg to the south in 1941 had as its principal target the oilfields of British Borneo and Sumatra, and the iron and bauxite mines of Malaya. The assault on Burma and India was dictated by the need to throttle the supply route over the 'hump' of northern Burma to Yunan in China. The economic resources of Southeast Asia were seen by Britain as so vital to its domestic recovery that it was willing to expend an unprecedented amount of blood and treasure in its reconquest.

The Japanese had sought to impose their vision upon the crescent by incorporating it, with their other conquered territories, in a Greater East Asian Co-Prosperity Sphere. It was a dream of a new Asian cosmological order, with Japan at its political and economic core. This vision left a powerful legacy in the minds of all who were exposed to it. However, the Japanese conquest states were hamstrung by conflicts between officials, chiefly men of a civilian background who wanted to give substance to Japan's dream of 'Asia for the Asians', and military commanders who saw only the imperatives of the war effort. Japan did not manage to make its colonies serve its economic needs. A brief phase of constructive imperialism in 1942 soon gave way to the politics of scarcity and plunder. Japan's military ascendancy was short lived, and the resurgence of Allied naval power after the Battle of Midway in mid 1942 meant that strategic goods from Southeast Asia could not be shipped back to Japan in any meaningful quantity. The great rubber estates of Malaya became virtual wastelands in which the remaining labourers scraped a subsistence by growing food on roughly cleared ground. The campaigns in Burma left behind large regions of scorched earth. When rice exports from Burma and Thailand dried up in 1943 and 1944 the rest of the region faced desperate food shortage and its attendant scourges of malnutrition and disease. The old trading links to South Asia and China were severed. After August 1945 the peoples of the region scrambled to reconnect their world.

The great crescent was to be forged anew. The instrument for this was South East Asia Command (SEAC), and the tribune of the new imperial vision was its supremo, Admiral Lord Louis Mountbatten, a cousin of the British king-emperor, George VI. Created in 1943, Mountbatten's new command was the first expression of 'Southeast Asia' as a distinct geopolitical entity. It was a partner to the Pacific vision behind General MacArthur's South West Pacific Command, but there was little love lost between the two unequal allies. To Americans, Southeast Asia was an 'unnecessary front'.[23] To wits, SEAC stood for 'Save England's Asian Colonies'. There was much truth in this: 'Here,' Winston Churchill thundered in September 1944, 'is the Supreme British objective in the whole of the Indian Ocean and Far Eastern Theatre'. But the resources necessary to achieve it were a long time coming. In the interim Mountbatten, unable to wage war directly, encouraged others to do so on his behalf, using covert methods for which he exhibited a puckish enthusiasm. No fewer than twelve clandestine or semi-clandestine organizations operated in the theatre. Not for nothing was SEAC also known as 'Supreme Example of Allied Confusion'.[24] Only after the fall of Germany were the materials of conventional war released for Southeast Asia, and it was not until August 1945 that Mountbatten was in a position to take the war back to the Japanese through a series of massive amphibious landings on the coast of Malaya. However, the bombs on Hiroshima and Nagasaki denied him the opportunity to restore Britain's martial pride in the region. The main task of South East Asia Command was to begin only after the surrender of Japan. But there were new tasks at hand: at the final hour, in addition to the Asian mainland, Mountbatten was given responsibility for the vast Indonesian archipelago. This marked the beginning of a final era of British imperial conquest.

The pre-Hiroshima war plan had required a massive build-up of men and materiel in India at Bombay, Cochin, Vizagapatnam and Madras. Mountbatten's personal staff at Kandy in Ceylon numbered over 7,000. The war plan – Operation Zipper – demanded the landing in Malaya of 182,000 men, 17,750 vehicles, 2,250 animals and 225,000 tons of stores, and half the men had to be disembarked in the first eight days. It was 1,050 miles from Rangoon to the nearest airbase in Malaya. Even after VE Day, the reconquest been delayed owing to a shortage of shipping, repatriation of personnel and uncertainty of conditions of the ground. This had allowed the Japanese, who were well apprised of Allied intentions, to pour more troops into Malaya. The received wisdom of amphibious warfare was that, for landings to be successful, a superiority in numbers of three to one was needed; in August 1945 Mountbatten had an advantage of only eight to five, and a high proportion of his men had yet to experience combat. Mountbatten returned from a visit to London on 14 August to learn that, following Emperor Hirohito's formal capitulation, the operation was to be launched immediately. And it was still not clear whether or not the Japanese would obey their emperor's order to surrender.[25]

I

1945: Interregnum

THE NEW ASIA

The great force that now embarked on reconquering British Asia saw itself as the new 'forgotten army'. British India provided the bulk of its manpower. The subcontinent was seething with discontent, directed and channelled by the Indian National Congress whose leaders the British had reluctantly released from jail as the war drew to its close. Official monitors reported that local people were relieved that the fighting had ended but were too exhausted and apprehensive about the future to indulge in anything more than perfunctory celebration. Indians, Burmese and Malayans were also horrified by the barbarity they had witnessed during the war's ending and the future dangers it portended. The Bengal press adviser reported to the governor that people believed 'the situation did not call for such indiscriminate havoc; and that the readiness to use such means has lowered the moral prestige of the United Nations'.[1] The fiery nationalist apparatchik Sardar Vallabhbhai Patel, general secretary of the Indian National Congress, commented that: 'Entire cities, children, the old, animals and all have been wiped out. What a demonstration of the limitless cruelty of Western civilisation.' Ominously, he went on to link Western barbarism with what he saw as the British attempt to perpetuate differences between Hindus and Muslims in India.[2] Lord Wavell, viceroy of India and Patel's main sparring partner, agreed about the atomic bomb: 'It is not a weapon that any thinking man would willingly have put into the hands of the present-day world.'[3]

Indians asked themselves what was the point in condemning German and Japanese atrocities if the Allies themselves were prepared to massacre civilians on such a massive scale. Others were as concerned with the political as with the moral implications of the atom bomb. Would its existence so hugely increase the imbalance of power between the West and Asian peoples that the mirage of independence would once again vanish? A Bengali newspaper wondered if 'the Asiatic people would not pass from the hands of one group of pirates to another'.[4] Aung San, leader of Burmese resistance against first the British and then the Japanese, vowed that 'no atom bomb can stop our march toward freedom'.[5]

What the British did not immediately appreciate was the extent to which Asian nationalism had been transformed by the war. Before it there had been movements of civil disobedience across India and Burma: peasant farmers had been goaded into revolt by the sufferings of the Depression of the 1930s; terrorist movements had flickered in Bengal and pan-Islamic ideologues had stirred the passions of the faithful throughout Asia; the Comintern had sponsored fledging communist parties in Burma and Malaya, where trade unions had flexed their muscles in its industrial areas. The Japanese war, however, had given nationalism a new face – a youthful, militaristic one. Before the Second World War Burma had been granted a form of semi-independence by the British. It had its own flag and its own prime minister, but it had no proper army. What passed for Burma's defence forces comprised recruits almost exclusively from minority peoples, the Karen, Kachin, Shan and Chin, along with resident Anglo-Burmese, Gurkhas and Indians. Burmese Buddhists had effectively been excluded from the army since the final British conquest of the country in 1886. The reason given was that Buddhists were too pacific, a fiction contradicted by Burma's impressive military traditions; the real reason was that soldiers from the minorities were cheaper and friendlier to the British Raj.

During the war all this had changed. With Japanese support, Burma had created its own army, the Burma Independence Army, renamed first the Burma Defence Army (BDA) after the Japanese invasion, and then the Burma National Army (BNA) after Japan's installation of a nominally independent Burmese government in August 1943. One day in March 1945, the BNA had revolted against the embattled Japanese forces, hoping finally to secure real independence before the

British reoccupied the country. By now the Burmese had military heroes as well. The young and intense former student leader, Aung San, had become 'Bogyoke', the general.[6] He was the first Burmese commander since General Mahabandula in 1826 to embody the military spirit of the Burmese people and to be known and admired across the country. Aung San and his 'Thirty Comrades' had marched into Rangoon with the Japanese in early 1942. The contrast between these young men in uniform and the civilian politicians of the British era, Ba Maw and U Saw, was obvious to all Burmese youth. Volunteers signed up in healthy numbers. Moreover, the war forged new links between the cities and the countryside as the army was billeted on the villages. When the British moved back into north Burma in 1945 they were faced with a militarized countryside populated by volunteer levies, many of whom identified with the socialist or communist thinking of the metropolitan radicals.[7]

Further down the crescent in Malaya, an inchoate Muslim Malay nationalism was on the move. It had its roots in movements of reaction to the notion – endlessly reiterated by British officials, scholars and educators – that the Malays were custom obsessed, docile and passive. This 'myth of the lazy native' was challenged in the 1930s by movements of religious and community uplift and by a phenomenal expansion of newspapers and periodicals that debated the future of the Malay race. Malay martial pride was rekindled, even as the Malay Regiment all but perished in an heroic last-ditch defence of Singapore. The Malay rulers were not the effete figureheads – 'pitiful Neros, squalid and insignificant' in one description – that most British imagined them to be, and they guarded their privileges jealously, not least their status as the heads of the Islamic religion. A wealthy State such as Johore, just across the causeway from Singapore, could embark on its own programme of modernization; Sultan Ibrahim, who had ruled Johore since 1895, had looked to Meiji Japan as a model, as had his father before him. Initiatives were also coming increasingly from commoners, especially the new caste of clerks and school teachers. The more radical of these looked to Japan as well, but as a nation-state and an anti-Western force. In 1937 they founded the Kesatuan Melayu Muda, or League of Malay Youth, which, led and orchestrated by the civil servant and journalist Ibrahim Haji Yaacob, ran an underground intelligence network for the Japanese military. Ibrahim used Malay prostitutes in the northeastern town of Kota Bahru to coax information about the coastal defences from their British clients.[8] It was here that Yamashita had made his initial landings, on Pantai Cinta Berahi – The Beach of Passionate Love – on the northeast coast of Malaya in December 1941. When the British rounded up 150 supporters of the movement shortly afterwards, they included fifteen bartenders and cabaret 'taxi-dancers'.[9] The Malays who assisted the Japanese were not to receive the same rewards as Aung San and his Thirty Comrades. The Japanese held a similarly patronizing view of the Malays to that of the British, but the Malay youths received the same kind of training as the Burmese and the Malay nationalism that emerged from the war would have the same radical potential. In the words of one of the central figures of these years, Mustapha Hussain: 'although the Japanese Occupation was described as one of severe hardship and brutality, it left something positive, a sweet fruit to be plucked and enjoyed only after the surrender'.[10] This was also a nationalism that did not necessarily recognize the old colonial boundaries. Mustapha Hussain and Ibrahim Yaacob had dreamed of merging their people into a greater Malay nation that would include the vast population of Indonesia.[11]

The much larger and older forces of Indian nationalism had also been galvanized by the war. The leaders of the Indian National Congress, the main nationalist movement, had witnessed the surge of popular anti-colonialism during the Quit India movement of 1942. Gandhi's largely non-violent mass protest against the continuing British presence had been particularly intense in Bengal and the eastern areas of the country, where people had experienced real hardship during the war and had seen with their own eyes the humiliation of the British Raj by the Japanese invaders. They felt, perhaps for the first time, a sense of mass nationalism, unifying student and shopkeeper, peasant and small landlord, man and woman. They had ample time to ponder on the lessons of the movement: 14,000 of the 60,000 demonstrators and political activists arrested in August and September 1942 were still in jail in 1944 and the leadership remained imprisoned until nearly end of the war. When they were finally released on 15 June 1945, Nehru, Patel and their socialist colleague Jayaprakash

Narayan emerged determined to make up for lost time. At a speech in September 1945, an impatient Nehru threatened to set the country alight. For his part, Patel resurrected the spirit of 1942 as soon as he was released. A final push was necessary to force the British out of Indian and this time, unlike 1942, the armed forces, police and lower government servants, all on the verge of striking for better pay and conditions, were also determined to see the back of the British.

THE LAST JOURNEY OF SUBHAS CHANDRA BOSE

Increased militancy among the Congress and its supporters owed much to the Indian National Army (INA). This force had been recruited from Indian civilians in Malaya and from Indian Army soldiers who had been captured by the Japanese in Singapore in 1942. The racism of British expatriate society in Malaya, the tide of nationalism among Indians in the region and the apparent invincibility of the Japanese had encouraged many Indian soldiers to throw in their lot with the Axis powers. In 1943 leadership of the INA and the civilian Indian Independence Leagues had passed into the hands of the Bengali politician Subhas Chandra Bose who, on escaping from a Calcutta prison, had made his way to Singapore via Berlin. Bose had been among the most radical of the senior Congress leaders. An inveterate foe of the British, he was willing to accept military and political help from any of their enemies. The INA had fought alongside the Japanese in their great campaign to invade India during the spring and summer of 1944. When that thrust was defeated, Bose's force had pulled back into Burma and finally retreated into Thailand and Malaya. As the British captured INA personnel, they categorized them into three groups – 'whites', 'greys' and 'blacks' – according to how seriously they rated their offences against the British crown and their former comrades. Opinion among Britain's Indian troops was mixed. Some believed the INA men should be tried, while others thought of them as misguided patriots, but most civilians in India believed that they should not be tried for treachery or desertion as the British apparently intended.

The captured INA personnel posed a real problem for the British. Local commanders were inclined to view them with hostility. Colonel Balfour Oatts, who had fought with tribal hill levies in northwest Burma, hated the INA even more than he hated Aung San's forces. After interrogating many of them he concluded that there was nothing to be done with these feral, 'red-eyed' deserters and traitors. Some officers gave them grudging respect in view of their fortitude during the clash with the 14th Army near Mount Popa, while others acknowledged that in Rangoon INA men had helped administer the city before the British returned in force, saving it from yet further despoilation. There was also the delicate question of allegiance and of not alienating loyal soldiers in the Indian Army. Some rank and file sympathized with the INA because their British officers had virtually abandoned them in 1942. The British themselves were uneasily aware that the status of Bose's Azad Hind (Free India) government and its army was unclear under international law. Was Bose's government, headquartered in the Andaman and Nicobar Islands, tantamount to a sovereign power, like the United States after 1776? Certainly, Eamon de Valera and the government of Eire thought so, because they had exchanged diplomatic notes with it. If so, the INA, however detestable, must have been a legitimate military force, no more 'traitors' indeed than the old Burma Independence Army, most of whose officers and men had never sworn an oath to the king-emperor and could not be held to have acted treasonably. The British in the 1940s were still an imperialist nation and many of them were unabashedly racist in their attitudes, but they had a deep respect for the rule of law and its demands. Many agonized about the legitimacy of prosecuting the INA men. For this reason they quite quickly fell back on the issue of the violence and torture exercised by INA officers against those Indian soldiers who would not join their rebel army. Trials of INA men would hinge on charges of violence against fellow Indian officers and men, rather than the more nebulous question of treachery to the king-emperor. Slowly the meaning of this retreat came to be understood among the British and Asians for what it really was: an acceptance that King George was no longer the legitimate sovereign of India.

In the meantime, the practical issue of the fate of captured INA soldiers could not be avoided. Some of them were cooped up for long periods in internment camps in different parts of Southeast Asia. Others were repatriated under guard to India and then dishonourably discharged from the ranks without pay or provisions. Here the qualms of the civil administration came into view. There was a danger that these soldiers would return to their villages and form cells of virulently anti-British nationalists. The authorities began to fingerprint them in order to trace their diffusion into a countryside already seething with economic woes, political disquiet and communal tension. The auguries were poor. When INA men began to be repatriated to India under guard, there were many demonstrations of popular support. People met them at stations, garlanded them and gave them sweets. On his release from prison the Congress strongman Sardar Patel proclaimed that 'Congress recognises the bravery of the INA people', though during the war Congress leaders had generally distanced themselves from the INA.[12]

Up to the very last minute Subhas Bose had hoped that Japan would resist the Allies' resurgence long enough for his Azad Hind government to secure something from the expected peace conference. If that did not succeed, he would approach the Soviet Union, which appeared increasingly antagonistic to Britain as the war ended. As their own nemesis approached in August 1945, the Japanese commanders finally agreed to help him make contact with the advancing Soviet armies in Manchuria. The dropping of the atom bombs and the Japanese surrender forced him to move fast. He was touring Malaya, after laying the foundation of the INA Martyrs' Memorial at Connaught Drive on Singapore's seafront. On 17 August he issued a final order of the day, dissolving the INA with the words: 'The roads to Delhi are many and Delhi still remains our goal.'[13] He then flew out of Singapore on his way to China via French Indo-China. If all else failed he wanted to become a prisoner of the Soviets: 'They are the only ones who will resist the British. My fate is with them.'[14] But as the Japanese plane took off from Taipei airport its engines faltered and then failed. Bose was badly burned in the crash. According to several witnesses, he died on 18 August in a Japanese military hospital, talking to the very last of India's freedom.

British and Indian commissions later established convincingly that Bose had died in Taiwan. These were legendary and apocalyptic times, however. Having witnessed the first Indian leader to fight against the British since the great mutiny of 1857, many in both Southeast Asia and India refused to accept the loss of their hero. Rumours that Bose had survived and was waiting to come out of hiding and begin the final struggle for independence were rampant by the end of 1945. A later British interrogation of a Japanese civilian associated with their Southeast Asian secret-service organization, the Hikari Kikan, hints at the rumours' source. This operative recorded that when news of Bose's death was reported in Rangoon on 19 August 1945, several Japanese officers went to offer their condolences to one of Bose's senior officers, Bhonsle. He had not been altogether in Subhas Bose's confidence and told General Isoda that 'he had a feeling that Bose was not dead, but that his disappearance had been covered up'.[15] Despite denials from the Japanese, who had received more details on the fatal crash, INA personnel remained unconvinced and passed on this feeling to Indian civilians. When the news of Bose's death reached India, about a week later, many did not believe it and dismissed the report as British propaganda. In Tokyo young INA leaders studying at the Japanese Military Academy were also unconvinced by the account of his death and disturbed by the hasty cremation. They guarded Bose's ashes around the clock.[16] There are still some in India today who believe that Bose remained alive and in Soviet custody, a once and future king of Indian independence. The legend of 'Netaji' Bose's survival helped bind together the defeated INA. In Bengal it became an assurance of the province's supreme importance in the liberation of the motherland. It sustained the morale of many across India and Southeast Asia who deplored the return of British power or felt alienated from the political settlement finally achieved by Gandhi and Nehru.

Of those Indians who did accept that Bose had perished, most eulogized him as a great patriot and military leader, even when they took the official Congress line that he was mistaken in allying with Japanese 'fascism'. Even Gandhi thought kindly of him. To Amrit Kaur he wrote: 'Subhas Bose has died well. He was undoubtedly a patriot, though misguided.' Typically, however, the Mahatma immediately changed the subject and reverted to avuncular advice, adding: 'Your gum has caused me much trouble. I blame the dentist.'[17] Bose's martyrdom most directly traumatized the many young men and women from the Indian civilian communities of Malaya and Singapore who had rushed to enlist. Fearing British reprisals, the INA officers in Tokyo sought sanctuary in the USA from the new military ruler, General MacArthur.[18] Bose's exit further dramatized the issue of the legitimacy of the INA and the problems that the British would face in dealing with it. They had already decided to try as many as 300 of its officers, but their gradual retreat from this position over the next two years was a further demonstration that the Raj was moving inexorably towards its end.

NATIONS WITHOUT STATES

Alongside these big nationalisms – Indian, Malay and Burmese – the war had mobilized and militarized a host of minority peoples across the vast swathe of South and Southeast Asia. It was not only the leaderships of easily recognizable minority groups, such as the Karen of Burma, who were asserting their claims to autonomy in the autumn of 1945. Other older and more shadowy entities seemed to be rising from the grave of history to plague both the would-be new imperialists and the new nationalists who were on the point of grasping independence. Strange as it may seem today, in 1945 many Bengali leaders, Hindu and Muslim alike, were contemplating a separate 'Banglistan', a Bengal outside of or only loosely affiliated to any future Indian federation. Some Hindus, for instance, were unhappy with any political settlement that might put the rural Muslim majority of the province into a position of unassailable power. Some Muslims in the province would have preferred partial separation from India to subordination to all-India politicians such as Mahomed Ali Jinnah.[19] Across the border in Arakan, the northwestern coastal strip of Burma which had been the scene of heavy fighting during the war, similar ideas of separation were in the air. The Muslims of the region had been violently at odds with their Buddhist neighbours since the 1930s. They had already signed up for a vague idea of a Pakistan embracing the Muslims of eastern Bengal and those of Arakan. Even the Buddhists here harboured dreams of autonomy. Arakan had only been annexed to Burma in the 1780s. Arakanese Buddhists always thought of themselves as a different sort of Burmese. Some of them had leaned more to the British than had the Burmese of the Irrawaddy valley and the south. Others again had fantasies of re-founding the ancient state of Arakan which had been a major force in the region in the sixteenth and seventeenth centuries. In the autumn of 1945 public meetings in Akyab, the seaport capital, and other Arakanese towns pressed the case for their homeland.[20] Even in Rangoon a meeting of Arakanese immigrants demanded local autonomy for Arakan within Burma. As for India: 'the Government of Burma would have to ensure that the annexed portions of Arakan are returned or the rights of Arakanese within India are safeguarded'. Symbolically, the meeting also insisted on the return to the homeland of the ancient gilded image of Buddha Mahamuni that was housed in a pagoda in Mandalay. The image had been seized in the eighteenth century by the empire-building Burmese king Bodawpaya when he first conquered the region for the Ava monarchy.

Then there were national visions that transcended territory. Just as the INA had placed a new responsibility for the freedom of India upon the Indian communities of Southeast Asia, so too, after 1937, did the National Salvation movement bring together the Overseas Chinese, as never before and as never since. Led by the 'Henry Ford of Malaya', Tan Kah Kee, a self-made millionaire philanthropist, it drew on the wealth of the Nanyang capitalists to provide as much as one third of the war expenditure of Chiang Kai Shek's government. But it was also unprecedented in the way it mobilized labourers, food hawkers, rickshaw men, school students and prostitutes into Anti-Enemy Backing-Up Societies to collect subscriptions and boycott Japanese goods and shops. It united for a time the Kuomintang in Southeast Asia with the Malayan Communist Party, whose support was overwhelmingly Chinese, and allowed them to extend their organizations in a way that had not been possible before. Of all the communities of the crescent, it was perhaps the Chinese who paid the highest price for their resistance to Japan. Yamashita's soldiers saw the Malayan campaign as a theatre of the China war, and after the fall of Singapore began the systematic screening and execution of Malayan Chinese. The *sook ching*, or 'purification by elimination', claimed perhaps 50,000 lives. It was the biggest single atrocity of the war in Southeast Asia: in the words of the Japanese administrator in Singapore, Mamoru Shinozaki, who had tried and failed to stop it, it was 'a crime that sullied the honour of the Japanese army'.[21]

These sufferings, and the sense of place fostered by these new sites of memory and mourning, contributed to a stronger Southeast Asian identity for those of Indian or Chinese origin. This had begun long before the war. In Malaya and Singapore, locally born Chinese had taken on a distinctive Peranakan (Straits) identity, and adopted the Malay language whilst also taking advantage of English mission schools. Their graduates formed the core of the growing professional classes of the towns. The response by more recent settlers to cultural and intellectual change in China had, by the late 1920s, brought with it a growing awareness that there was a distinctive 'Nanyang' style of politics.[22] Many writers and artists who fled China in 1937 came to Malaya; a community that had been built by traders and labourers now possessed a growing intelligentsia. They saw the region as an artistic utopia and argued that their work needed to take in 'local colour' and adopt a proletarian bias. After 1945 the old links to distant homelands were difficult to re-establish. The urgency of the local political situation in Burma, Malaya and elsewhere, catalysed far-reaching debates: where did the Overseas Chinese or Indians call 'home'? What stake might they be allowed in their places of abode? Was Burma to be for the Burmans, Malaya for the Malays? And who precisely were the 'Burmese' or the 'Malays'? The British had tended to see the ethnic divisions of these 'segmented societies' in stark terms, and see racial groups in eternal conflict with each other: never more so than in what British writers termed the 'plural society' of Malaya. But this was not a true reflection of the ethnic diversity that existed within 'Malay', 'Chinese' or 'Indian' communities. Nor did it recognize their increasingly complex interconnections, or address the new solidarities of class that were being preached by the communists. This raised further questions: to what extent was a composite, multi-racial 'Malayan' identity emerging? And what was to be its foundation? In the years to come these debates would engage the minds of nationalists, communists and colonialists alike.

So the British faced newly energized nationalist movements, both great and small, which limited their room for manoeuvre in the longer term. But it was not only Asian thinking about empire that had changed. Many young Britons, though not yet the Tory and Labour leadership, had come to see empire as an anachronism during the war. Not only did it divert valuable manpower and resources from where they were needed at home, it also threatened domestic liberties and seemed likely to blow Britain's new socialist government off course. At an almost unconscious level, the complaints of the 'forgotten army' in the East and its even more radical RAF comrade, the 'forgotten air force', represented a deep desire for change in the British social order as a whole. Before the election Churchill had been disgusted to hear from Sir William Slim that 90 per cent of the troops in the East were going to vote Labour and the other 10 per cent would not vote at all. Now those Labour supporters, heartily tired of dysentery, malaria, ENSA humour and poor pay, wanted to see the brave new world that their left-leaning tutors in the army education corps had promised them. Morale slumped and would soon lead to small-scale mutinies among British forces from Karachi to Singapore. Months after the surrender of Japan, British troops were incensed to find themselves fighting and suffering casualties in what seemed like completely unnecessary wars against nationalists in Indonesia and French Indo-China.

This mood was picked up and articulated by radical newspapers in Britain and political discussion groups at army and air-force bases. A newspaper such as the old Labour broadsheet, *Reynolds News*, was typical. It was written for working people, but most of its correspondents and columnists were British middle- or upper-class communists and socialists, free to inveigh against the country's archaic society and the dominance of 'monopoly capital' now that wartime censorship had been lifted. Major Woodrow Wyatt, a socialist with an interest in the 'Indian problem', demanded a pro-Congress policy and the abolition of the India Office in London.[23] Harold Laski, Labour's most prominent left-wing intellectual, urged that the viceroy's executive council be turned into a 'national government'.[24] These radicals made common cause with Asian nationalists. Indonesian nationalists argued in *Reynolds* against any attempt by the British government to reinstate the Dutch capitalists who were accused of exploiting and impoverishing the Indonesian peasantry.[25] All the while, the paper's editorials demanded the swift demobilization of the eastern army and justice for Britain's miners, steelworkers and textile workers, many of whom were now on strike. The Labour government and the political establishment at home found itself fighting on three fronts, in Asia and the new United Nations and among its own supporters at home. The news was full of reports of the trial and execution of French collaborators, concentration-camp guards and Japanese militarists. Repression was harder and harder to justify.

One of *Reynolds* columnists was Tom Driberg MP, a colourful and maverick British politician who came to play a small but representative role in the history of the crescent. His *Times* obituary thirty years later stated with surprising candour that he was 'a journalist, an intellectual, a drinking man, a gossip, a high churchman, a liturgist and a homosexual',[26] while many at the time also hinted that he had worked for the KGB. Before the war Driberg gloried in the sort of circles portrayed in Evelyn Waugh's *Vile Bodies*, but at the same time he rejected the British establishment represented by his late father, a former Indian civil servant in Assam. Frank Owen, the journalist who ran Lord Louis Mountbatten's propaganda sheets for South East Asia Command, told Driberg that the men in the East thought of themselves as the 'forgotten army' and thirsted for coverage of their exploits and demands to be demobilized. Driberg wrote to Mountbatten at the end of July 1945 asking to visit South East Asia Command. At first, suspicious of his position as an MP, Mountbatten hesitated. Then, under the influence of Owen, Mountbatten changed his mind and agreed to meet him. Driberg's biographer Francis Wheen writes: 'he and Tom hit it off at once and discovered they had much in common, including a sexual preference for men', although it has to be admitted that the jury is still out on this last point. Mountbatten, Wheen goes on, was 'a royalist and a snob who nevertheless held left-wing views; Tom was a left-winger, who nevertheless loved the monarchy.'[27] By early September Driberg was embarked upon a grand tour of South East Asia Command which would take him to Kandy, Singapore, Rangoon and Saigon. In all these locations he wrote despatches to *Reynolds News* which subtly influenced Labour opinion in favour of the conciliatory policy towards the Asian nationalists preferred by

Mountbatten. He met many of the region's nationalist leaders, notably Aung San, and reckoned later that he played a minor role in the early independence of Burma.

So the leaders of nations and would-be nations continued their pirouettes of bargains, threats and violence. Meanwhile, across the whole vast crescent that stretched from the plains of India to Singapore and beyond, to Sumatra and the northern shores of Australia, millions of people dislocated by war, famine and disease tried to rebuild their lives. There were many tragic stories of loss, brutality and dispossession and these grew in strength as the interrogation of Japanese personnel for war crimes uncovered more horrors. Sometimes, however, fate was charitable. Take the case of the appropriately named Sweeper Pissoo, a low-caste Indian sanitation orderly, once attached to the British forces in Burma. As a non-combatant enrolled in the Indian Army, he had been left behind during the scuttle from Rangoon in 1942. He had gone to ground and survived the war as a humble sweeper. After the war he began to parade his military credentials again and turned up at a number of British military camps in Burma. Burma Command eventually signalled GHQ (India) and it was discovered that he had been formally reported missing. Burma Command began to make arrangements for his repatriation to Aurangabad, India. 'This,' said a British officer, 'we did with a happy smile, wondering just how much pay Sweeper Pissoo would get before his demobilization.'[28] With four years' back wages due, he would be wealthy beyond his wildest dreams.

THREE WEEKS IN MALAYA

For so many people, the fortunes of war would be decided in the interregnum that followed the Japanese surrender. Many of the definitive political events of the war occurred in the power vacuum between two empires. In these few short weeks bids for freedom were made in Burma, Malaya, Vietnam and Indonesia. This was also a time of some of the most horrific internal violence within these societies, the memory of which continues to scar the collective consciousness of the nation-states that emerged. Nowhere, perhaps, was the political future so open as in Malaya. It was here that the Japanese had devolved the least power to their Asian subjects. It was here too that imperial power was about to be reasserted with the greatest resolve. But on 15 August 1945 Mountbatten's army of re-occupation was still in India. Its vanguard reached Malaya only three weeks later. In this hiatus of anxiety and anticipation, most of the people there did not know who or what to expect. In the towns of the Malay peninsula the flags that flew most prominently were those of China, bearing the name of the communist-led Malayan Peoples' Anti-Japanese Army as they fluttered from triumphal arches erected across the streets. As its fighters came down from the mountains, a struggle began for control of Malaya.

The central battleground of the peninsular war was the frontier to the west of the densely forested central range. Here, Malay and Chinese peasants had been caught in a cycle of raids, reprisals and extortion. Mustapha Hussain was a witness to this. He was one of the most prominent Malay radicals who had marched in the baggage train of the Japanese army in 1941. However, he had been disillusioned by the betrayal of Malay hopes. As they marched into the capital, Kuala Lumpur, Mustapha told his young Malay followers: 'This victory is not our victory.' Deeply traumatized by the violence he had seen in the wake of the fall of Singapore, he withdrew from public life. Before the war, Mustapha had been a lecturer in a government agricultural college; now, like many educated townsfolk, he returned to the land, at a village in northern Perak. Life for him and his family became a hard struggle for survival. Yet Mustapha was persuaded to return to politics in mid 1945, when the Japanese began to lay plans for a declaration of independence for Malaya. Mustapha helped draft a constitution for a free republic. But again, he and his friends were cruelly disappointed. As nationalist leaders gathered in Kuala Lumpur to realize their dream, the news of the surrender broke: the collapse of Japan had forestalled the declaration of independence for Malaya by just forty-eight hours. Ibrahim Haji Yaacob fled with the Japanese to Indonesia, the lost leader of the greater Malay nation. Mustapha, disillusioned and ill, and fearing the wrath of the British and the resistance army, had returned to his village. But it was no longer a sanctuary. All around him were rumours of violence; Malay policemen had been attacked by Chinese guerrillas in a nearby town.

'The heat closed in on us', he wrote, 'when we saw a Chinese banana seller emboldened into giving a speech. A normally timid Chinese buffalo herder was openly declaring: "All Malay heads must be shaven!" '[29]

The resistance army was dominated by young armed Chinese. It had mobilized out of the remnants of National Salvation movement in late 1941 when, at Singapore's eleventh hour, it was armed by the British. It was given the name 'Dalforce' after John Dalley, the policeman who acted as its liaison officer, but in local memory it was the Singapore Overseas Chinese Volunteer Army. It was the first forgotten army of the Great Asian War. Some 2,000 townsfolk, men and women together, fought fiercely in their makeshift uniforms to resist Yamashita's final assault on the island. The Malayan Communist Party also sent some of its most committed cadres to be initiated into the black arts of clandestine warfare at British 'jungle training schools' in Singapore and Kuala Lumpur. As the Japanese advanced, they infiltrated the jungle to become the nucleus of the Malayan Peoples' Anti-Japanese Army (MPAJA). In many places the mobilization of patriotic young men and women was already well advanced, having been accomplished by unlettered labourers and a sprinkling of graduates of the Chinese schools of the small country towns. The nominal leader of the British 'stay-behind' forces was the mountaineer and explorer Major Freddy Spencer Chapman, whose heroic but lonely war is portrayed in his memoir, *The Jungle Is Neutral*, a tropical *Seven Pillars of Wisdom*. More 'left-behind' than 'stay-behind', the few Europeans who made it into the forest were utterly dependent on the guerrillas. Chapman whiled away the months trying to contact other Europeans and providing basic military training to the MPAJA. The communists even exploited the expertise of a stranded civil servant and anthropologist, Pat Noone, who had gone native with one of the aboriginal communities of the forest, the Temiar, and began to win their trust. In these years, the jungle was red.

Little of this was known to Allied commanders in India. Special Operations Executive, the British secret warriors, only began to launch their own operations from Bengal in May 1943. Two British officers, John Davis and Richard Broome, who had briefly contacted the communist forces in February 1942 before escaping to India in an open boat, returned by submarine, together with some Chinese agents. Part of what later became styled as 'Force 136', the Chinese were recruited chiefly from Kuomintang circles; many were students from Malaya who had been stranded by the war in Chiang Kai Shek's capital, Chungking. They were, by definition, staunch enemies of the communists, but on landing in Malaya they passed into the hands of the MPAJA and operated out of their camps, chiefly from Blantan, 2,000 feet above the towns of Bidor and Tapah, in the state of Perak. It was a mining area with some of the densest concentrations of Chinese in Malaya, and a bastion of MPAJA support. The resistance laid networks of supply and intelligence, particularly among the tens of thousands of Chinese workers and peasants who had taken refuge on the jungle fringes to grow food. The war years had seen a massive move of Chinese pioneers into the hinterland of the towns, mines and estates. They had begun to migrate in the Depression years when wages were low, and workers moved between farming and industry as conditions dictated: a reserve army of the proletariat. But during the war many had become established peasant farmers, with *atap* (thatched) dwellings, vegetable plots and pigs. The squatters provided the MPAJA with food, intelligence and recruits. Their ramshackle settlements were a screen from Japanese policing, and provided lines of communication. A hut or a coffeeshop was used as a staging post, and behind it a trail would lead into the hills. In the undergrowth, the trails would connect to jungle tracks, running up watercourses and mountainsides. The central range was a matrix of such paths. Outside the jungle, couriers on bicycles linked these networks.[30] At Blantan, Davis and Broome finally made contact with Freddy Spencer Chapman, but they were as isolated as Chapman had been before their arrival; they had no radio contact with India until January 1945. Their attempts to set up an independent intelligence organization with their Kuomintang Chinese agents in the towns ended in disaster when it was betrayed in March 1944. Its leading personality, a Singapore businessmen turned secret agent, Lim Bo Seng, died of dysentery in a Japanese jail. He was Force 136's only casualty of the war, and was to become Singapore's national martyr.

The fragile alliance between the British and the MPAJA was sealed by an agreement, sketched on a page torn from a school exercise book, at Blantan on 26 December 1943. The communist leadership was represented by a new arrival in the camp, a man the British called 'the Plen', and who signed the agreement as 'Chang Hong'. It placed the MPAJA under South East Asia Command and promised communist 'co-operation' in what 'Chang Hong' insisted was to be called 'the retaking' of Malaya. Future relations between the British and the Malayan Communist Party were not discussed. But at a further meeting, in mid April 1945, when agreement on practical arrangements had become pressing, it seems that the British officers went further in promising that, in return for support, the Malayan Communist Party would be able to operate legally as a political party after the war. This was later disavowed, but most communists assumed that the concession had been won, and so too did many British officials. In the wake of this second agreement, British officers began to parachute into the Malayan jungle in greater numbers. On the day of the Japanese surrender the head of the Malaya section of Special Operations Executive, Innes Tremlett, a Singapore Special Branch officer, summarized the situation for Mountbatten. There were 308 Force 136 men in Malaya: 88 British officers, with their Gurkha guards. The British had supplied around 2,000 guns and other weapons to the MPAJA. This was but a small part of the MPAJA's armoury, which was stocked with pickings from the battlefields of 1942. The force had between 4,000 and 5,000 men and women in arms, organized into eight regionally based regiments; there were several thousand more workers in the towns and villages and the number was rapidly rising. The British had some information on the workings of the Malayan Communist Party, but only a hazy view of its higher command. There did not, Tremlett reported, seem to be a standing committee in any one place; leadership was in the hands of a man known as 'Mr Wright', the party's 'most secret and revered personality. He is known to Davis, myself and one or two others. He is a shrewd and clever man but no fanatic.' Then there was 'Chang Hong', the man who led the negotiations in the jungle.[31]

It seems that Davis and his friends failed to recognize 'Chang Hong', and did not realize that he and 'Mr Wright' were one and the same person. But Freddy Spencer Chapman had met him, masked with dark glasses, along with Tremlett in December 1941, in a room above a charcoal dispensary in the Geylang area of Singapore. It was the secret rendezvous where they had negotiated the arming of the Malayan Communist Party. 'Chang Hong' had appeared at their jungle meetings without dark glasses, and at the second meeting was wasted by illness, and leaning heavily on a stick. He was a man of many guises, a political phantom whose name, background and motivations remain deeply obscure to this day. From the best available accounts, his given name seems to have been Hoang A Nhac, and he was born in Nghe Tinh province in Vietnam, of Chinese or Chinese-Annamese descent, though he could neither read nor write Chinese. In 1945 he was perhaps in his early forties.[32] Only a Special Branch photograph of him survives; it shows a lean-faced man of ambiguous ethnicity, with large deep-set eyes, marks of dissipation perhaps. He is staring at the camera with thin-lipped severity, later to be recalled as cold callousness, 'like the treacherous villain in a Chinese opera'.[33] He came to prominence in Singapore around 1934, a rising star in the Malayan Communist Party. His growing mystique derived from his claim to be a representative of the Comintern. Few communists in Malaya were so well travelled, so well informed on world affairs. Of the many aliases he used in this period, the name that has endured is Lai Teck: it seems the British thought this was merely a Chinese mispronunciation of the English name 'Wright', and so 'Mr Wright' became yet another layer of pseudonymity.[34]

Lai Teck's early career is an extraordinary journey across the underground of the port cities of Asia; the stuff of the cloak-and-dagger fiction so popular in the region at this time. Lai Teck liked to surround himself in its aura. He became a convert to communism in Saigon in the 1920s, but then he joined the French navy, only to flee when faced with arrest for disseminating communist literature among his fellow sailors. He reappeared in Hong Kong and from there travelled through the revolutionary circles of Shanghai and Tientsin. In 1931, in a strange sequence of events, he was arrested at Mukden on the Soviet border, apparently en route to Moscow, and was imprisoned in a Chinese jail, only to be released in a general amnesty when the Japanese invaded Manchuria. He then retraced his steps to Shanghai, where he was again arrested in the French concession and deported to Vietnam. Given a choice between prison and co-operation with the Sûreté,

Lai Teck chose the life of a double agent. His career was short lived: in 1934, whilst working undercover in Annam, he was exposed and, useless now to the French, Lai Teck was gifted to the British in Hong Kong. Special Branch supplied Lai Teck with communist documents they had seized in raids in Hong Kong and Shanghai. These were to authenticate a cover story that he was a Comintern agent sent to advise the Malayan Communist Party. He was then introduced into Singapore as an informer. His betrayals over the next few years assisted his rise in the Party's secret hierarchy. By 1939 he had been elected Secretary General, and was known by the rank and file as 'Ah Le' – 'Our Lenin'.[35]

When Singapore fell, Lai Teck did not take to the jungle. He thrived in the cosmopolitan underbelly of the city: it was said that he had two Vietnamese wives, one of whom owned a coffee shop on bustling Orchard Road, as well as a Chinese mistress. But he was arrested in the security sweep that followed the Japanese takeover. Faced once again with a choice between death or betrayal, he bartered his release by agreeing to supply information to the Japanese secret police, the Kempeitai. The fact of Lai Teck's arrest could not be hidden from Communist Party circles, but such was the power of his personality cult that it was believed he had charmed his way out of jail. In a curious way, the very audacity with which he conducted his business over the next few years, cycling around Singapore on his red sports bicycle, driving to the peninsula in a Morris 8 saloon given to him by the Japanese, preceded by a string of female couriers, all helped support the myth of his invincibility and mastery of clandestine struggle. At the same time his betrayals tore apart the Party leadership in Singapore and southern Malaya. His motive of self-preservation in this seems clear, but he was also carefully consolidating his hold on the Party and, by the end of the war, was effectively a one-man central committee. In August 1942 he enacted his greatest betrayal, when he alerted the Japanese to a meeting of senior commanders of the MPAJA near Batu Caves, a Hindu temple complex just outside Kuala Lumpur. On 1 September the delegates and their bodyguards were ambushed: twenty-nine of them were killed and fifteen more arrested. Lai Teck claimed that he had been delayed in attending the meeting by the breakdown of his car; in fact, he had remained in Singapore. Of the pre-war leaders of rank, only a few now survived in isolated parts of the peninsula, just leaving the younger men who had made their reputations fighting with the MPAJA. By this time, some of the communist leaders imprisoned by the Japanese had begun to suspect Lai Teck. However, as a smoke screen, a number of them were released by the Kempeitai, in the sure knowledge that their former comrades would eliminate them immediately as turncoats and bearers of misinformation. This had the effect of dampening down and discrediting any evil rumour surrounding the Secretary General. But Lai Teck did not betray all he knew. He did not fully expose the Force 136 agents; nor, it seems, were the Japanese aware of the agreement he had signed with the British. As the war changed its course, Lai Teck tried to play all sides and win. In August 1945 only a few communists and some Vietnamese émigrés in Singapore had begun to suspect that 'Mr Wright' was not all he seemed.

One of the new leaders to emerge out of this was the liaison officer with Force 136 in Perak, known by his Communist Party alias, Chin Peng. Like much of the new-generation leadership, he had been introduced to the Party through the anti-Japanese movement which had taken hold of the Chinese Middle School students after 1937. Chin Peng was born as Ong Boon Hua, in Sitiawan in Perak, where his parents ran a bicycle shop. As a schoolboy, he dreamed of enlisting to fight in China and began a process of self-education in the works of Mao Zedong. He was recruited to the Malayan Communist Party organization in 1940, aged only fifteen, by a charismatic fellow-student, Tu Lung Shan, who was best known by his *nom de guerre*, Lai Lai Fuk. Tu Lung Shan had extraordinary influence in Perak, by making party work seem a natural extension of the close-knit, multi-ethnic networks of friendship in a small town. As one prominent Malay recruit, Rashid Maidin, put it, he 'usually began with conversations on topics which touched on everyday happenings. He did not bring books or pamphlets. Probably, at that time, the party was not rich enough to produce books'.[36] Trilingual in Chinese, Malay and English, Tu Lung Shan personified the kind of Malaya-born Chinese men and women who were to take the Malayan Communist Party in a new direction; although they still looked for inspiration to the struggle for China, their revolutionary patriotism was rooted in a

Malayan context, and made emotive by their sacrifices there. Chin Peng was to mourn the loss of Tu Lung Shan, beheaded by the Japanese in Taiping jail in 1943.[37] Chin Peng also had many near arrests, but through his underground work as state secretary in Perak he developed his own following. As John Davis reported, he was: 'Physically robust with round boyish face. Courage marked and commands natural respect without fuss or formality. Quiet character with incisive brain and unusual ability. Frank and reliable. Very likeable.'[38] It was a source of ironic pride to Chin Peng that the British officers acknowledged that it was 'entirely due to him' that South East Asia Command possessed armed and trained guerrilla allies in Malaya. Yet Chin Peng was also unflinching in the use of violence to attain his objectives. Lai Teck, too, identified him as a useful man.

Chin Peng had arranged the Blantan meetings, and was present at a gathering of party cadres in October 1944 in the jungle near Serendah, some miles north of Kuala Lumpur, at which Lai Teck announced the alliance with South East Asia Command to the surviving MPAJA hierarchy. However, this agreement, he told them, was not to be honoured. The MPAJA was to be split: an 'open' army would work with the British, as agreed at Blantan, while the rest of the forces would remain underground. When the Allied invasion came, it would rename itself the National Liberation Army and seize control. Since it would not be possible to hold on to the big urban centres of Singapore, Penang, Kuala Lumpur and Ipoh, the small country towns were to be the base areas of the liberation struggle. 'It was', Chin Peng remembered, 'a rousing call to revolution. Our spirits soared'.[39] As this directive filtered through to the jungle, British Force 136 officers in the camps sensed that they were being kept in quarantine, away from many guerrilla units. But there was little they could do about it. These were the first intimate encounters between British soldiers and Asian revolutionary fighters, and they made uneasy comrades. The Europeans experienced the culture shock of a relentless routine of Marxist education, community singing and self-criticism sessions in the camps. Some viewed it in a sympathetic spirit. The sister of a tin miner in Pahang, Nona Baker, who spent most of the occupation hiding with the local guerrillas, wrote an improvised life of Lenin for propaganda purposes.[40] But many of the Force 136 recruits had been civilians in

Malaya before the war, businessmen or, more often than not, policemen. Although they admired the self-discipline and sacrifice of the guerrillas, they struggled to come to terms with the sight of a rubber tapper or house-boy in arms. A former rubber planter in Kedah stepped down from Force 136 in the field, claiming he could not be party to a policy of co-operation with communists, 'as I intend to spend many more years in Malaya'.[41] Major I. S. Wylie's assessment of the commander of the 700-strong 5th Independent Regiment of MPAJA in Perak, the formidable Liao Wei Chung, or 'Colonel Itu', is typical in its condescension: 'a man of lowly origins', he reported, 'advanced to a position of power and authority which he was not properly fitted to fill'.[42] The leader of the 1st Regiment of the MPAJA in Selangor, Liew Yao, might sign off letters to his liaison officer, Major Douglas Broadhurst, formerly of the Singapore Special Branch: 'chins up and keep smiling, Cheerio', and end a request for money and arms (and an English–Chinese dictionary), 'your loving firend [sic], Ah Yeow'.[43] But Itu and Wylie, Liew Yao and Broadhurst, would soon be on opposing sides in a new and bitterly personal war.

The MPAJA was primed for revolution, but the sudden surrender of Japan took everyone by surprise, not least Lai Teck. In the days that followed he executed a dramatic *volte-face*. He summoned Chin Peng to Kuala Lumpur, but did not meet him personally. By the time the younger man arrived on 19 August, Lai Teck had just left for Johore and Singapore in the south. Chin Peng instead met another of the Party's new generation of leaders, Yeung Kuo, who – in some distress – informed him that the MPAJA would not, after all, fight the British. Lai Teck had drawn up a new policy: an 'eight-point programme'. Its first two points were support for the Allies and the pursuit of an open democratic struggle. It was bland enough to receive the endorsement of the British high command: Mountbatten's Foreign Office adviser, Esler Dening, called it 'irreproachable'. 'The Communist Party have rather stolen our thunder', he complained.[44] Lai Teck ordered both the 'open' and the 'secret' MPAJA to disband; the only concession to armed struggle was that the Party would hold on to its secret caches of arms. To Chin Peng, and to all who had fought and suffered in the jungle, this was 'a devastating blow'. To his surprise he learned that Lai Teck had made him responsible for implementing the new policy, by appointing him to a new three-man Central Military Committee, together with Lai Teck and the Selangor commander, Liew Yao. Chin Peng was only twenty years of age. Despite his private misgivings, he submitted to Lai Teck's directive – after all, he later reflected, 'he was the Comintern's man' – and Chin Peng was swayed by the belief, shared by many in the MPAJA, that they had already won legal recognition from the British. He also assumed that the full Central Committee was behind the decision not to fight. In fact Lai Teck was covering his tracks, and had acted on his own.[45]

It was unclear to the British what the peacetime role of the MPAJA was to be. Mountbatten's initial bland directive – 'Victory is now at hand and your contribution has been important and is appreciated' – did not impress the guerrillas. Nor did his stipulation that the MPAJA should avoid towns and districts where the Japanese were present. There was, as John Davis radioed the supremo four days after the surrender, 'a serious risk of disastrous anti-climax'. To Davis, the status of the MPAJA as soldiers under SEAC was crucial: they 'must be given full share in the honour of victory'. 'Orders for them to remain half-starved in the hills while the Allies leisurely take over the administration from the Japs will not be reasonable.' Davis was also worried that, if they remained in the jungle, all control over them would be lost.[46] Davis was overridden by Mountbatten's advisers. General Sir William Slim carried the day by arguing that the guerrillas could upset the delicate ceasefire with the Japanese. Mountbatten relented slightly by allowing the guerrillas to move into towns if they could avoid clashes with the Japanese. He had for months urged the British cabinet to trumpet its liberal intentions for Malaya in order that the tensions of reoccupation might be eased, but to no avail. In London Davis's views were dismissed as part of a pattern whereby liaison officers in the field went native and 'become rather imbued with the views of the resistance movement to which they are attached'.[47] Already, vague wartime understandings were being repudiated.

The MPAJA met its moment of revolutionary crisis in a state of confusion and with no central direction. Some jungle companies received Lai Teck's new directive, others did not. Some who did receive the orders fought on anyway. As the Japanese began to withdraw from many settlements, MPAJA fighters wearing their new

SEAC jungle green with three stars on their forage caps, moved to capture village police stations and arms and supply dumps. The Japanese military claimed that in the fifteen days after the surrender there were 212 attacks on its troops. The MPAJA seized transport, and for the first time enjoyed swift mobility. In many areas they began to set up skeleton administrations in the form of 'people's committees': according to one estimate, 70 per cent of rural towns were under their control.[48] There they took over public buildings, and in some instances burned land-office records. The ability of Force 136 officers to restrain their allies varied dramatically. In Chin Peng's sphere in Perak, where MPAJA units were perhaps at their most disciplined, the very night that Force 136 officers gathered to celebrate the surrender, with Scotch whisky and Highland reels, Colonel Itu ordered units of the 5th Independent Regiment into the towns that had been abandoned by the Japanese.[49] The hidden networks that had sustained the resistance suddenly revealed themselves. Chin Peng's female comrade, Eng Ming Chin, turned underground workers into a highly effective propaganda troupe of singers and actors. The MPAJA took over the Perak Chinese Amateur Dramatic Association in Ipoh as their headquarters: 'neighbours could hear night after night the squealing of pigs and the death throes of poultry as these were prepared in the kitchen for the enjoyment of the hundreds of jungle fighters . . .' They were presents from the poor farmers. Even local capitalists fêted the communists: 'white skin', it was said, 'red hearts'. The coffee-shop owners of the town of Pusing gave the guerrillas free meals for a month.[50] In the northern states, which had been placed under the nominal government of Japan's ally Thailand, both the British and the Japanese were thin on the ground, and the guerrillas had an even freer hand. The occupation of Kuala Trengganu was largely uncontested and in Kedah, the local 8th Regiment, who had not heard the new orders, made an all-out takeover bid; it took Chin Peng's personal intervention to bring them into line. In Johore in the south, Major H. H. Wright of Force 136 reported that the people's committees 'were all-powerful in those small towns'. By the end of October there were 233 guerrillas in his patrol alone, well-armed with Brens, Stens, carbines and rifles. There were no British troops in the area. Wright compared them to the partisans in Albania, with whom he had spent nine months: 'they were the masters and not me'. The local commanders were unhappy at Lai Teck's policy. As they marched into the towns, they left their jungle camps intact behind them.[51]

Around the main garrison areas in Perak and Kedah, senior Japanese officers, impressed by the strict military discipline of the guerrillas, made it clear that they would not stand in the way of the MPAJA if it chose to fight. Japanese police in Kuala Kangsar, Perak, agreed to pass arms in a silent trade, by vacating the police station and leaving weapons behind, including machine guns taken from disarmed French soldiers in Indo-China.[52] On one rubber estate in Johore, a Japanese military HQ shared an office with the MPAJA.[53] These negotiations were broken off only when news of the new directive was received. This perhaps averted a crisis within the MPAJA: its leaders were deeply split on the issue of co-operation with the Japanese. Some felt that their surrender had changed everything and revealed the true enemy: British imperialism. Others were still governed by their deep hatred for the Japanese. Chin Peng would later estimate that around 400 Japanese went over to the communists.[54] Many of them disappeared when they realized that the MPAJA was not to fight. But some remained.

There was another crucial dilemma for the MPAJA. The local armies that the Japanese had raised could now act freely. The Malay radicals, abandoned by their patrons, sent out feelers to the MPAJA. Ibrahim Yaacob later claimed to have initiated the contacts. A 280-strong Malay militia from Singapore moved up towards Kuala Lumpur. It was intercepted by the MPAJA in northern Johore, where it threw the local communist leadership into confusion. With the new policy in mind, it decided not to arm them and the group disbanded into the neighbouring *kampongs* (villages). Some Indian National Army garrisons in Malaya also approached the MPAJA. There had been mounting tension between Malayan Indian recruits and the north-Indian regulars. The local men were disenchanted by their appointed role in defending Japanese imperialism, and there were many desertions. In Sungei Siput, Perak, a resistance heartland, INA men supplied a great deal of intelligence to the local guerrillas.[55] In Kuala Lumpur, M. K. Ramachandra Naidu, the chairman of the board of the largest Hindu temple in the town, the Sri Maha Mariamman, was approached by emissaries who wanted to hand the INA over to the MPAJA. Naidu attempted to mediate, but the local communists refused the offer and merely accepted some transport in exchange for guaranteeing the safety of the large Indian community in the city.[56] In Party folklore these incidents would later be seen as catastrophic missed opportunities, but they reflected an overriding constraint on the Party: its lack of mass support outside the Chinese community.

As the Japanese pulled back, the MPAJA unleashed brutal revolutionary terror. Suspected collaborators, officials, policemen and profiteers were hauled before kangaroo courts where they often faced an angry crowd. Eyewitness accounts are chilling: denunciations would ring out, a voice from the crowd would cry for the death penalty and the accused would be taken into the jungle or behind a building, to be executed with a single bullet or hacked and mutilated with knives. Sometimes those accused were cut down by the mob there and then.[57] In Perak, Force 136 officers observed that it was often the guerrillas' helpers from the towns, and not the more disciplined armed bands, who took the lead in this. Ho Thean Fook, a former teacher in an English school, was a non-communist who had fought with the MPAJA in the vicinity of his hometown of Papan. He realized that there was a turf war beginning in the town between the 'uniformed' MPAJA and 'non-uniformed' men, who were opposed to the Lai Teck policy. 'These blighters', he wrote, 'were more ruthless than the Japanese.' He saw a stout, elderly Chinese gentleman dragged off and tied to a telephone pole merely for being overzealous in carrying out his duties in the Ipoh traffic office. Only the intervention of a family connection who was a communist state committee member saved him. In disgust, and denied the triumphal homecoming of which he had dreamed, Ho Thean Fook returned to a jungle hideout until a force of uniformed MPAJA with SEAC liaison officers arrived to restore order in the town.[58] British officers made speeches urging restraint. However, they were delivered through communist interpreters and often went unheard. 'They were most annoyed', reported Major Wright in Johore, 'when I told them not to take the law into their own hands, after they had beheaded three so-called collaborators in [the] Kulai area.'[59]

After the Japanese in Singapore had pulled back into camps on the west of the island, guerrillas from the 4th Regiment of the MPAJA in Johore moved over the two-kilometre causeway that linked the island to the mainland and marched into the urban area. They seized the premises of the old Japanese Club on Selegie Road as their head-quarters. A period of 'whispering terror' began. Particular targets were the local business and community leaders whom the Japanese had strong-armed into an Overseas Chinese Association, extorting from them a $50 million 'gift' as 'guilt atonement' for supporting the Allied cause. Most had the means to make themselves scarce, but smaller fry were hauled away and killed. Mistresses of Japanese officers were paraded shaven headed round the town. Areas such as Chinatown became 'completely lawless'.[60] As one Chinese school-teacher wrote: 'We could not find it in our hearts to condemn this wild justice, which we were too squeamish to mete out ourselves. Indeed, we were thankful to our guttersnipes for doing it for us.' Some older men seemed to be directing operations on bicycles, blowing whistles.[61] Much of the killing was merely the settling of old scores, but in some areas it began to develop into an ethnic war.

Mustapha Hussain evokes the mood of the Malays in northern Perak: 'Abductions and killings were rampant. *Kampong* folks, sud-denly drawn into chaos, moved in indescribable fear.'[62] The three stars of the guerrillas – the Bintang Tiga – had become a sign of terror for the Malay community. For several months there had been Sino-Malay clashes in Perak and in parts of Johore during which hundreds had been killed. The MPAJA blamed gangsters and the machinations of the Japanese. Both of these elements were certainly present, and in many areas unlicensed bands extorted and killed in the MPAJA's name. But Malay village headmen and policemen were often targeted by MPAJA guerrillas. The killings were concentrated in certain locales, on the plain of the Perak river and the coastal area of western Johore. Both these areas had seen recent settlement from Indonesia, especially of Banjarese with a reputation for the tenacious defence of their honour. In many ways the conflict went against the grain of inter-ethnic relations in the Malayan countryside, which were gov-erned by complex links of interdependence and carefully observed forms of trust. Whatever its longer-term causes, a common theme of first-hand accounts was that violence was provoked not by a general breakdown of day-to-day dealings but by the sudden transgressions of armed outsiders: an arrogant demand for food, taxes or labour; abductions and insults to women. The spark was often an incident in or near a mosque – a demand to move the time of Friday prayers, for example – or involving pork, which is unclean to Muslims. Not only the killings, but their method – the mutilation of corpses, say – inflamed Malay sensitivities. And, of course, rumour abounded, often sparking more violence. For the Malays, the occupation was a time of religious uncertainty. The Japanese had played propaganda games with the mosques, and had tried clumsily to liken their war effort to a *jihad*. It was under the banner of Islam that Malay resistance to the MPAJA began to mobilize.[63]

When the times were so out of joint, leadership within Malay rural society could slip away from the established elite. In the Batu Pahat area of Johore, where violence had begun in the middle of the year, the cult leadership of a village headman, Kyai Salleh bin Abdul Karim, came to the fore. A *kyai* is a local leader of an order of sufis, the mystic brethren of Islam, and sufism was strong in Malaya. This was a tradition of religious leadership that lay outside the established Islamic hierarchy, and had been influential in propagating Islam in the Malay world. As a local religious scholar, Syed Naguib al-Attas, wrote a few years later: 'Never has the Malay mind soared to [such] heights of sublimity in the realm of abstract thought as when it was steeped in sufism.' Kyai Salleh, he noted, 'sports a goatee and has small beady eyes that can at times glow with boyish mischief, or glare with a fury that has been known to strike terror into the hearts of his enemies'. Kyai Salleh's reputation extended across Malaya, and carried with it the claim that he possessed supernatural powers, such as invulnerability to bullets and weapons. Deputations from Indonesia came to seek his help and sanction. His famous *parang panjang*, or long sword, was said to have severed 172 heads. He claimed that the medieval founder of the Qadiriyyah sufi order appeared to him in a dream, dressed in black, to warn him of an attack by Chinese 'bandits'.[64] Kyai Salleh's powers derived from the disciplines of prayer, fasting and recitation of the Quran, particularly the Yasin, the chapter that is read to the dying. An initiate could use these powers only in times of danger and by following an upright path. If the powers left him, it was a reflection on his faith and piety, and his appointed time for death had come. The 'invulnerable' wore a cloth of red at their neck and armed themselves with *parang panjang*, bamboo spears, and the *kris* – a Malay dagger potent with symbolism. Calling his movement Sabilillah – or the Path of God – Kyai Salleh and his Malay fighters began raids on Chinese villages, and in August and September he spearheaded resistance to the MPAJA.[65]

The fighting threatened to engulf large areas of the Malayan countryside. There was a connected incident much further to the north, in Sungai Manik in the Perak river basin, where many of the Banjarese settlers were recent arrivals from Johore and had witnessed the fighting there. In one Sino-Malay clash in this area, over 150 people died. Again, religious men organized the defence of their *kampongs*. The first British officer to reach the scene recorded that the leader of the Banjarese, Imam Haji Bakri, was said 'to have given some sort of dope to his men prior to action'.[66] The MPAJA saw the fighting as a cynical attempt by the Japanese to divide and rule. There is no doubt that the Japanese supported the Sabilillah bands once their conflict with the MPAJA was underway. They followed up Kyai Salleh's raids with their own operations, and supplied arms and men in Perak. The fighting gathered intensity as Malays began to fear that the Chinese were taking over their country. An ill-timed airdrop of leaflets in Malay by the British in Johore, promising punishment to those involved, underlined the fact that SEAC was allied to the MPAJA, and this led the Malays to fear British reprisals. Sultan Ibrahim of Johore was said to have met Kyai Salleh and kissed his hand, asking him to 'guard our country'.[67] The cycle of violence continued into the following year.

Armed bands of all kinds had been set loose in Malaya. In the far north, operating out of remote lairs in Upper Perak and Kelantan, were a number of smaller Chinese guerrilla groups, mainly comprising small-town racketeers who had moved in on the lucrative smuggling trade across the Thai border. Styled the 'Overseas Chinese Anti-Japanese Army', they professed loyalty to Chiang Kai Shek's Kuomintang and were identifiable by the single star on their caps. Some British 'stay-behind' agents had made contact with them, and they tended to find their loose-living picaroon style a refreshing change from the puritan regime of the communist camps. The two groups fought for the allegiance of the Chinese hill farmers. By the end of the war J. K. Creer, a former official who had spent the entire conflict in the forest in Kelantan, reported that the state was 'at the mercy of Chinese guerrillas of two warring factions'. Creer eventually occupied the capital, Kota Bahru, with an Overseas Chinese Anti-Japanese Army force of around 170 men and repelled MPAJA attempts to enter the town. He felt that his men had fought the Japanese harder than the MPAJA had ever done.[68] But Chin Peng saw them as nothing more than 'Kuomintang bandits': 'they spent their money freely on drugs and women. When they ran out of funds they began to loot, pillage and rape.' He held the large unit in Upper Perak responsible for the abductions and killings of Malay villagers.[69]

The distinction between patriotism and criminality was merely one of perspective. The end of the war also saw a resurgence of the triads, the Chinese secret societies that combined protection rackets with popular sanction as defenders of their communities. At the beginning of the occupation the Japanese had executed any man they found with triad tattoos. Triad members from Penang took refuge in the Chinese fishing villages of the mangrove swamps on the west coast; they too profited from smuggling and low-level piracy, and used their gains to propitiate both corrupt Japanese officials and the guerrillas in the hills. But in August, under the shadow of the revolutionary wrath of the MPAJA, a new brotherhood was formed to unite the secret societies. It was known as the Ang Bin Hoay – the Brotherhood of the Ang [or Hung] People – a name which denoted kinship with a long lineage of societies in China that claimed to uphold the true ethos of the Chinese people. One fishermen described his initiation rite: 'We were gathered together and invited to save ourselves against the invasion of communists. There were no prayers. There were joss sticks, and we took our oaths that we would be punished by Heaven if we did wrong.' They fought to keep the MPAJA out of their villages, and made common cause with the Banjarese Malays in the Lower Perak disturbances. In Singapore and elsewhere, similar gangs claimed to act in the name of the MPAJA, and terrorized locals under names such as the Exterminate Traitor Corps, Blood and Iron Corps and Dare to Die Corps.[70]

South East Asia Command's search for allies, and its bonanza of arms, extended to the Malays as well. There were anti-Japanese groups in Perak and Kedah that called themselves Askar Melayu Setia – the Loyal Malay Soldier – and in the wild west of Pahang, Wataniah – For the Homeland. They had their own Force 136 liaison officers, and the British parachuted in to them some Malay agents: mostly former civil servants or pilgrims to Mecca who had become stranded by the war in the bazaars of Cairo and Bombay. As the tide of war turned, these movements obtained covert support from Malay courts and district officers, not least to counter-balance the influence of the MPAJA. For the British their importance was not so much military as political: they were vital to dispel the idea that the Malay majority were disloyal to the Empire.

American agents of the Office of Strategic Services, the forerunner of the CIA, were also becoming increasingly interested in Malaya, and had parachuted in at a late stage. On direct orders from Colombo, and working with Wataniah, a small party captured the Sultan of Pahang en route to Kuala Lumpur, and placed him under armed guard. The sultan was kept in a squalid jungle camp together with a huddle of fractious Chinese refugees for over three weeks. This was ostensibly to prevent him falling into the hands of the communists; it was also to stop him acting as titular head of the independent Malay government that was about to be formed in the capital. But the rumour was put about that the communists had taken him, and this raised ethnic tensions in the state.[71] In the event, few of the royal houses were molested. In Kedah, the defence of the Sultan of Kedah's palace and of Malay villages was orchestrated by a youth organization, known as Saberkas, a co-operative society formed in the state capital in 1944. Among its patrons was a middle-aged prince from the ruling house of the state, Tunku Abdul Rahman, who had before the war enjoyed a reputation as something of a playboy. Like many Malay aristocrats he had lain low in the occupation, working as a district officer and, with quiet acumen, tried to deflect some of the worst excesses of Japanese rule away from the population. In the interregnum he managed to use his influence with Malay young men to recruit four lorry-loads of Malays for Force 136 and to keep racial violence at bay.[72] These acts would give him good credentials for the defence of Malay interests when, some six years later, as a somewhat unlikely contender, he would emerge as a major political force.

The Malay elite had lost ground in the war, and now struggled to reclaim their position. At the height of the violence in Batu Pahat in Johore, Sultan Ibrahim appointed a fifty-year-old local notable, Onn bin Jaafar, as district officer, after the incumbent was assassinated by the MPAJA. Over the years Onn had enjoyed a stormy relationship with his royal patron; he had been raised at court, and his father had been the sultan's chief minister, but his family had fallen from grace and Onn had made his own way in Singapore as one of the first full-time Malay journalists. In 1928 he was accused of *lèse majesté* and treason after he wrote a series of articles called 'Tyranny in Johore' for an English-language newspaper, attacking the sultan for abuse of power, extravagance and corruption ('His motor car deals would excite the envy of a Lombardy Jew').[73] However, a talented man of letters was too influential to overlook, and Onn was rehabilitated by Sultan Ibrahim shortly before the war. Onn had stood quietly to one side as the Japanese conquered Malaya; his son, Hussain – a later prime minister of Malaysia – served in the Indian Army. But like other prominent Malays, he had been implicated in Ibrahim Yaacob's movement for independence in 1945. As the violence in his district reached a head, and Kyai Salleh's supporters massed to attack the Chinese town of Batu Pahat, Onn made a decisive intervention by opening negotiations with the MPAJA and the Sabilillah fighters. When the talks hung in the balance, Onn is said to have confronted Kyai Salleh in front of some 1,600 of his armed supporters. In a melodramatic account of the incident by an early biographer, Onn bared his chest to the holy warrior, saying: 'Plunge your dagger into it if you do not wish to obey me.' Kyai Salleh was overcome by the power of his words.[74] In other versions, Onn is said to have flattered Kyai Salleh, warning him that the British were about to arrive in force, and so perhaps offered him an honourable way out by bringing him some local Chinese to sue for peace. But from any telling of this, Onn bin Jaafar's reputation grew, and Kyai Salleh became one of his most devoted political supporters.[75]

During the war communities had learned to defend themselves, and after the surrender of Japan they did not give up this prerogative lightly. All local pretenders to power along the crescent would need to come to terms with these forces of violence, and even cultivate them for a time. For the returning British, however, the central task was to contain and neutralize them. This set in motion a central dilemma of Britain's Asian crisis as it now began to unfold. Throughout the history of British imperialism, conquest had been legitimated by the argument that without colonial rule, territories would be in a state of perpetual civil war. After the Second World War, British statesmen would argue that Asia could not be free until it was at peace. To this the nationalists would reply that peace was all well and good, but not better than life itself, and that there would be no peace until Asia was free. In national memory, the communal violence of this period remains a dark and eternal point of reference; a time when the bonds of the region's plural societies were tested to the absolute limit. Although the tragedy in Johore was only one small incident among so many others, it was not untypical, and still hundreds had perished while thousands more were forced to flee their burning villages. It was a prelude to other communal bloodlettings that would play out across the crescent on an even larger scale. Significantly, in Batu Pahat local leaders had restored social peace before the British soldiers arrived. By 2 September, the end of Ramadan, traditionally a time of reconciliation, an uneasy calm prevailed in the area. A short distance up the coast lay the beachheads for Operation Zipper, and the second colonial conquest of Malaya was heralded by the dropping of leaflets announcing the abolition of the Japanese 'banana' currency and by the spraying of insecticide from the air.[76]

THE FALL OF SYONAN

On 1 September 1945 a large Royal Navy flotilla appeared off the northwest coast of Malaya. As the island of Penang, Britain's oldest possession in Southeast Asia, came into view, a 'Singapore curry' was served to the officers and men on the command ship, HMS *Derbyshire*. Its taste was unrecognizable to many of the old Malaya hands present, who remembered the real thing. The landings had been delayed, by order of General MacArthur, until after 9 a.m. on

2 September: the moment when he was to receive the surrender of the Japanese High Command on USS *Missouri* in Tokyo Bay. At this ceremony, positioned directly behind him, was Lieutenant General Arthur Percival, the man who had commanded British forces in Malaya in 1942. He had been released from Japanese internment on Taiwan and was shortly afterwards to witness the capitulation in the Philippines of his arch-nemesis, General Yamashita. Like many Japanese senior commanders, Yamashita would be tried and executed as a war criminal. Percival would return to London finally to write his despatch on the fall of Singapore. The whole series of events was carefully choreographed to impress on the peoples of Asia that Japan had been defeated by force of arms, and to erase the memory of the earlier Allied capitulations.

The original battle plan had called for a series of co-ordinated landings: first, a strike at the Thai island of Phuket to capture forward airbases, and then an assault in larger force on two main landing grounds in Malaya, at Morib beach in Selangor and the resort of Port Dickson, some miles to the south. The original codenames signalled martial resolve: Mailfist – the push to the south to Singapore, a replica of the Japanese blitzkrieg of 1941–2 – and Broadsword – a sweep northwards from Kuala Lumpur to secure the rest of the peninsula. Mountbatten had estimated it would take him until the end of the year to fight his way to Singapore, and likely longer if a large garrison was mustered to hold it. However, the operation was now Tiderace: a dash to occupy Singapore. The first landings at Penang were designed to probe the intentions of the Japanese, but no resistance was encountered. After some delay, and a failure to attend an earlier meeting, the Japanese local commander, Rear Admiral Jisaku Uzumi, came aboard HMS *Nelson* on the evening of 2 September, wearing the DSC he had earned as Britain's ally in the 1914–18 war, and surrendered the garrison. He fainted and was rushed to hospital; the military policemen who carried him there took his sword as a souvenir.[77] The next morning, led by the town band, a detachment of Royal Marines marched to the Eastern & Oriental Hotel. The E&O had been the hub of the pre-war colonial elite, the place where the entire British community had gathered secretly on the night of 16 December 1941 to abandon the island. It had been left to the Ceylonese editor of the local *Straits Echo*, M. Saravanamuttu, to lower the Union Flag at Fort Cornwallis and surrender Penang to the Japanese. In September 1945, Saravanamuttu once again gathered together the representatives of the Asian communities, this time to pass the administration of their home back to Britain. As the Royal Marines marched they threw Senior Service cigarettes into the crowds. Those who managed to grab them sold them at exorbitant prices to buy food. Across the island, hunger riots were breaking out.[78]

On the morning of 4 September the armada passed the old Raffles Lighthouse, at the southern entrance to the Straits of Malacca. After 1,297 days as a Japanese city, 'Syonan' was to fall to the British without a shot. As they approached the island the soldiers noted that the Japanese defensive dispositions were remarkably similar to those adopted by Percival in 1941. The first, tense encounter between British and Japanese officers was aboard HMS *Sussex*. There were still rumours that General Itagaki had defied Hirohito's orders and ordered a die-hard defence of Malaya. The navy feared Japanese attack boats. Itagaki was furious that the humiliating task of surrender had fallen to him. (His superior, Count Terauchi, had suffered a stroke in Vietnam.) Accompanying Itagaki was one of the architects of the attack on Pearl Harbor, Vice Admiral Shigeu Fukudome. Itagaki was received aboard by the senior British officers, Lieutenant General Sir Philip Christison and Major General E. C. R. Mansergh. The contrast between the two delegations was striking. The Japanese were in immaculately starched ceremonial rig, with their swords at their side. The British officers wore crumpled battledress. They had left India at short notice, with no change of clothes; there was no water to wash with on ship, and their skin was stained by the malaria preventative Mepachrin. A Japanese officer was reported to have remarked: 'You are two hours late,' only to be met with the reply, 'We don't keep Tokyo time here.' The main issue at the meeting was responsibility for law and order on the island. Then Itagaki was given an agreement to sign. He shut himself with his aides in an anteroom for four hours to translate it. The only concession Itagaki secured, and that only temporary, was the right of his officers to keep their swords. He left the meeting in tears.[79]

The next morning advance parties of British and Indian troops landed on the southern islands, and at 11 a.m. reached the docks at Tanjong Pagar. One of the first men ashore was O. W. Gilmour, a civil engineer who had been one of the last to leave in February 1942. 'Two Indians and a Chinese boy, looking very dazed, appeared from a near-by shed. They were the only people in sight and I addressed them in Malay, getting no response but a stupefied stare. Walking to the Station Buildings, we passed two more Chinese, and exchanged a subdued "Tabek" (good-day), which, in the circumstances, seemed an inadequate greeting.' The mood was one of 'overwhelming desolation'. Two hours later Gilmour joined a small convoy of three jeeps that sped through the residential areas of Chinatown, along New Bridge Road. Crowds lined the route, Union Jacks appeared at windows, but as the British crossed Singapore river the ceremonial and municipal heart of the city around the Padang was empty of people. There were no more than a dozen spectators to the hoisting of the Union Flag above the Municipal Building at around 13.45 hours. The Japanese officers assigned to witness the event were nowhere to be found. They were indeed still on Tokyo time, as the whole of Singapore had been for three and a half years. They had come and gone two hours earlier. One of Gilmour's first tasks was to put the public clocks back two hours.[80] On Saturday 8 September the first British libertymen came ashore, including seventy sailors from HMS *Cleopatra* who marched through the streets to Jalan Besar stadium for a game of football.[81]

If the main British landings on the Malay peninsula had been opposed, there is a strong possibility that they would have been swept into the sea by the Japanese. Despite the intimate knowledge of the terrain professed by many British officers, the sites chosen were entirely unsuitable. The first landings at Morib on 9 September were a disaster. On the first day, fifty trucks and tanks sunk or were mired in the sand and very few made it to the beach without being winched out. There was hardly any room on the beachhead and only one good road leading away from it. Vehicles were hemmed in by drainage ditches and a raised water pipe; this meant that the off-road area required to de-waterproof tanks and lorries was not available and the beach road flooded. '"Zipper"', according to 17 Squadron's war diary, 'seemed to come slightly "Unzipped".' If the 6,000 Japanese at

Kuala Lumpur had attacked in concentrated force, British commanders would have had little option but to withdraw their forces.[82]
Chin Peng stood beside John Davis and watched from the Japanese
lines: it was 'an anticlimax – a dramatic scene – but an anticlimax
nonetheless'. He recalled his feelings many years later: 'We are letting
them back unimpeded to reclaim a territory they have plundered for
so long.' Then, in a final humiliation, Force 136 was ordered to break
cover and ask the Japanese for transport to allow British troops to
move inland.[83] The other landing zone at Port Dickson was choked
by sightseers. 'It was', according to another Force 136 witness, 'a
circus atmosphere. A carnival with roadside stalls, puppet shows and
entertainers.'[84]

For the next few days the British grip on events was uncertain.
Detachments did not reach Malaya's largest state of Pahang for a
further three weeks: along the entire east coast the colonial government was represented by a handful of Force 136 officers. The first
British troops reached Kuala Lumpur on 12 September to find the
streets deserted. 'If the populace were happy to see us,' remarked one
officer of the Royal Devon Yeomanry, 'they proved adept at conceal-
ing their emotions.'[85] The jungle fighters of the Malayan Peoples'
Anti-Japanese Army were already established in the capital. Chin
Peng, together with the military commander, Liew Yao, moved into
a commandeered bungalow in the elite white suburb of Kenny Hill.
Chin had been travelling widely, enforcing the peace between the
British and the MPAJA. His mood was bleak. 'I had been required to
calm and pacify, restrain and arrest. I was mentally and emotionally
drained.'[86] There were confrontations between the MPAJA and the
north-Indian troops of 5 Division, who took them to be Japanese.
The Indians did not received a warm welcome; they had no linguistic
common ground with the people of Malaya, and after nearly four
years of war, all men in uniform were viewed with suspicion. Recognizing this, the local British commander staged a ceremony in front
of the Royal Selangor Club, the 'Spotted Dog' of pre-war days, at
which the MPAJA were allowed to take centre stage.[87]

Over 70,000 Japanese remained on Singapore island, another
reminder of the fragility of the British position. Many of them were
still armed, and the people of Singapore watched in furious incompre-

hension as the officers continued to wear their swords. But over the next few days the Japanese were paraded and stripped of their valuables. British forces took these piles of 'souvenirs' as the legitimate spoils of war. There were few reprisals, however. Many of the troops were newly arrived to Asia, and had not been a part of the bitter fighting in Burma. Those who had were less charitable to the Japanese rank and file. In a public spectacle designed to repay the humiliations of 1942, the captives were put to work levelling the turf of the ceremonial ground of the Padang in preparation for Mountbatten's arrival. Some turned up to work in white gloves and refused to take them off. A crowd gathered to watch. People jeered and cheered when a European ex-prisoner of war stepped forward, and in mockery of the martial style of Nippon, slapped the face of a Japanese officer.[88] Across Malaya most of the Japanese were put to task in grim conditions. In Perak three Japanese died after they had been given the job of dredging a dry dock using empty seven-pound jam tins.[89] One Japanese prisoner in Singapore, Shikimachi Gentarō, described how 2,000 of them were cooped up in warehouses near the piers and made to work twelve hours a day. 'The worst indignity was cleaning out the sewers of the town where Chinese, Indians and Malays lived together. We were told to dredge by hand the dead rats and human excrement that flowed down . . . if we disobeyed our captors at all we were beaten with rifles and kicked. There were those who went crazy and those who died from malnutrition.' It was two years before he was sent home. 'I am not excusing the conduct of the Japanese,' he said in recounting this years later. 'War makes all of us lose our humanity.'[90]

The anger of British troops deepened as they began to liberate POWs from the camps on the island. They were appalled by evidence of starvation, and worse horrors were soon to be exposed along the Death Railway in Thailand: it was estimated that there were 100,000 POWs to be recovered.[91] Hitherto, their condition had been kept secret, so as not to distress their kin. For the prisoners, the last days had been an agony. In Changi Mountbatten was known as 'Longer Linger Louis', or invoked in ironic prayer: 'How much longer, O Lord?' For five days after the surrender the Japanese continued to transport labourers to the construction sites of the great tunnels they were boring in the central heights of the island, but did not put these men to work. In the words of one POW, an Armenian from Singapore's volunteer force: 'we just hung around staring at them and they staring at us'. But the men were in better shape than they had been for months. As the news of surrender began to filter through the wire, so too did food from former Asian employees and friends. Some men succumbed to sudden plenty, or to illicit liquor: a tale did the rounds that two Australians had died gorging on bully beef and butter.[92] In addition, there were 16,109 Indians in Singapore and 2,664 on the peninsula who had not joined the INA. They had, wrote one witness to their liberation, 'a cowed look on their faces as if they were ashamed to be alive and were unsure of their reception'.[93] They were not a priority. By 11 October, at Neesoon camp in Singapore, forty-five men had died in the space of three weeks.[94] In Thailand it was left to the individual efforts of a former rubber planter from Kelantan, freshly released from a POW camp, to stay on to provide relief for over 70,000 Malayans who had been sent to work there. Here the military agency for Recovery of Allied Prisoners of War and Internees (RAPWI) was known as 'Retain All Prisoners of War Indefinitely'.[95]

For the British, some of the most moving scenes were at the civilian internment camp at Sime Road. There 3,160 men, 1,020 women and 320 children were liberated by former colleagues of the Malayan Civil Service, men who had got out of Singapore before the fall and were now in uniform. One of them was O. W. Gilmour:

A number of my friends were unrecognisable, on account of the great beards which adorned their faces and the deteriorations of physique, while others were equally unrecognisable for the latter reasons only. Some had grown old beyond what the years could account for, and worst of all, a number had obviously changed completely; the change having started in frustration of mind and worked outwards.[96]

The women and children had been interned separately from the men and had run their own affairs. The world they had created was abruptly dissolved. Sheila Allan had been a motherless child of sixteen when she was imprisoned, and like many young internees had come of age in captivity. Before the war she had lost her Malayan mother;

in Changi she had also lost her father. Her diary records a flood of powerful new impressions: the sudden plenty of Red Cross parcels – 'powder puff, face cream, lipstick, toilet papers and sanitary towels' – dances, the sexual attentions of soldiers and, above all, the loss of the close-knit community of the camp. 'I don't think', she wrote, 'that anyone really knows what he or she is going to do . . .' Like so many others, Sheila Allan would have to begin her adult life with no resources of her own.[97]

The former civil servants were crushed by the sight of a new administration. They had expected to return immediately to their jobs, and over the long years had drawn up elaborate contingency plans, even down to leave rosters. Whilst the military commandeered the best hotels and the clubs, the internees were left for several weeks in their squalid camps, without even fresh linen. One Malayan civil servant, Sjovald Cunyngham-Brown, was liberated from a camp near Pekanbaru in Sumatra. There the POWs cleared a landing strip. A plane circled and landed, and Cunyngham-Brown ran to meet it. He lost his loincloth, his only scrap of clothing, in his excitement. A striking and smartly dressed woman disembarked. 'I say,' he said, 'I do apologize.' The lady opened a gold cigarette case; 'What you need is a cigarette!' As he led her to his camp, he asked her name. 'I am Lady Louis Mountbatten.' In her work for the Red Cross, Lady Edwina covered 33,000 miles and sixteen countries, visiting camps in an attempt to accelerate the relief work. Later that day Cunyngham-Brown managed to fly to Singapore, where he presented himself to the island's chief civil affairs officer, P. A. B. McKerron. There his reception was very different. McKerron refused to meet his eye and told him: 'To tell you the truth, we don't want you around.' Cunyngham-Brown ignored this and made it to his former post in Johore, where later that evening he was put in charge of the northern part of the state. His case was exceptional. The civilians carried with them the stench of the failure of 1942; their physical dilapidation impeded the restoration of white prestige. As Cunyngham-Brown acknowledged, 'we embarrassed everybody'. He bristled at the new arrivals 'worming up to us as though we were lunatics, speaking in baby-talk and offering us their nauseating pity'.[98]

Some internees made it upcountry to visit their homes. One

long-time Ipoh resident, John Lowe Woods, drove north giving a thumbs-up sign – a gesture new in Malaya but popularized by the war elsewhere – to the locals. He travelled through a series of Arcs de Triomphe: 'at least two in every small *kampong* (one at each end), lots of odd ones along the road at estate entrances, solitary *kedais* [shops] and so on, aping the dignity of a large village or small town; quite a number, one for each community and a few private efforts as well'. North of Kuala Lumpur, the mood changed. It was 'more Arcs and rather fewer thumbs'. He had driven into the triumph of the MPAJA as it progressed from town to town through the Perak countryside.[99] Europeans such as Woods showed steely resolve in reasserting the privileges and protocols of their former life. As the first internees departed from Singapore by sea, they complained that cabins were allocated alphabetically, and not by official precedence. A story did the rounds: 'I used to pass a certain senior civil servant in the camp each morning', reported an internee, 'and he always greeted me with "Hullo, Tom, old man, how are things going?" One morning he changed his greeting to "Good-morning, Brown, how are you?" so I knew the war was over.'[100]

Military medicine was ill-equipped to deal with the physical and psychological toll of captivity. The depth of anguish was slow to emerge: at the liberation of the camps, army psychiatrists spoke of surprisingly high morale, but they were misled by the initial euphoria of release. If the number of overt cases of psychological illness was 'remarkably low', it was perhaps because the most vulnerable people, especially the loners, had perished. Among the survivors, it was noted that if someone left a group, temporarily, there was collective anxiety and exaggerated relief on his return. They meticulously hoarded and shared food, even when it was in abundance. Ragged and ill, they were desperately tongue-tied with women. When nurses responded by jesting that they had seen half-naked men before, their embarrassment deepened. As one woman relief worker noted: 'It was we who had changed and become more frank, not they.' This soon gave way to concern about detainees' 'elation' and 'over-activity', and a worrying sign that 'the thought of returning home was not greeted with as much enthusiasm as one might expect'. It was clear the normal means of demobilization would not meet the needs of men who had spent nearly four years in horrific conditions in prison camps, with the long-term health problems that such prolonged periods of deprivation had created. Army psychologists now warned that a delayed reaction could set in – even nine to twelve months after release. Of the first 1,000 repatriates from Malaya and Singapore, 600 showed 'some degree of anxiety'; over 500 were suffering from 'mild apathy and depression'.[101] Above all, internees and POWs had to come to terms with a 'Rip van Winkle effect' of their lost years when confronted with unexpected bereavement, infidelity or estrangement, and public indifference. They had been allowed, at most, five messages in three and a half years. One of the few provisions for psychological support was a series of pep talks: 'things – and people – have changed . . . It's on the whole a good thing too – mostly they are wiser and bigger people'. But above all, the POWs were told, it was women who had changed. 'She'll be more independent, more used to managing on her own (which you may not like).' They were also warned to expect disappointment on resuming their lives, but reassured: 'The Forgotten Army is not forgotten now.'[102]

Many of the forgotten witnessed the formal end of Japanese rule at the Singapore Padang on 12 September. Still in scraps of uniform, they stood between the pillars or on the roof of the Municipal Building. It was here, just two years previously, that Premier Tojo and Subhas Chandra Bose had reviewed the Indian National Army. Now with sixty-one Allied warships moored in the harbour, Japanese commanders were made to walk with bowed heads to meet Mountbatten and over a hundred officers of the various components of South East Asia Command, and dignitaries ranging from the Sultan of Johore to Tom Driberg. It was Mountbatten's finest moment as supremo. Yet, to his bitter regret, his great rival, Field Marshal Count Terauchi, had pleaded illness and was absent. Mountbatten sent his own doctor to verify this. Unlike MacArthur in Tokyo Bay, who let the Japanese keep their swords, Mountbatten wanted to take Terauchi's. He made it clear that he would allow Itagaki to deputize only on the understanding that Terauchi would make his personal submission to Mountbatten as soon as he was well enough to do so. As he told the Japanese delegation: 'As I speak, there are 100,000 men ashore. This invasion would have taken place on 9th September whether the Japanese had resisted or not. I wish to make this plain: the surrender today is no negotiated surrender. The Japanese are submitting to superior force, now massed here.' To impress this on the local population, there was a ceremonial march past of newly arrived troops, in neat dress order. As part of the guard of honour, just inside the Municipal Building, was a double file of men from the MPAJA.[103] In a fifteen-minute ceremony, General Itagaki signed each copy of the surrender document, stamped it with an official chop, and then, with great deliberation, applied his personal seal. Once he had finished, the Japanese officers were each tapped lightly on the shoulder and left the building. As they marched away, multiple chants broke out from the crowd of *Bakaro! Bakaro!* – Bastard! Bastard![104] Shortly afterwards Itagaki left for Japan, there to face his trial and execution as a war criminal.

In the days that followed the people of Malaya took to the streets to celebrate the second coming of the British. There were 'loyal' processions of the Chinese and the Indian Muslims of Singapore. The Kuomintang raised a pavilion in front of the Singapore Cricket Club and Chinese firecrackers were set off. The British read too much into these demonstrations of loyalty. The release of tension and the initial good will mediated some of the problems of peace. But not for long. In most peninsular towns it was the MPAJA that dominated the proceedings. In their stronghold of Ipoh in Perak, the 5th Independent Regiment paraded 1,000 strong. Eng Ming Chin rode with Colonel Itu in a convoy of cars, followed by hundreds of MPAJA supporters on foot, and behind them the representatives of the business community. 'Before the war', she explained, 'the *towkays* [bosses] always walked in front in public processions, but now poor people like us led the way . . . the world had changed.'[105] The Kuala Lumpur victory parade included a number of local worthies who had been known to work with the Japanese. The British officers ignored them. The treasonous shadow of Roger Casement hovered over them, and the charge of 'adhering to the King's enemies'. The fear was greatest among the Indian civilians who had supported the Indian National Army. Some had done so under duress, others from long conviction; their shops still displayed images of Subhas Chandra Bose. Within a week many of them were arrested and detained in the notorious Pudu jail.[106]

One of the first acts of 5 Indian Division on 6 September was to pull down the INA memorial beside the Singapore Padang on the Esplanade; Bose had laid the foundation stone only two months previously, and after his death it had become a shrine to his memory, albeit only for a few days. (Jawaharlal Nehru visited the site six months later: a temporary wooden replica was erected in its stead.[107]) Other symbolic moments followed in which the British attempted to erase the war memory of the vanquished. The Chureito, the wooden obelisk raised up on top of Bukit Batok hill, overlooking Bukit Timah, the final line of defence in the battle for Singapore, was an immediate target of the British. However, the obelisk had already been demolished by Japanese troops – so the engineers of 5 Indian Division blew up its base. The great Shinto shrine constructed on a forested side of the central reservoir and dedicated to the Amaterasu Omikani, the Sun Goddess, had also been destroyed by the Japanese using traditional Shinto purification rites. With less ceremony, the British cleared what remained because it took up land formerly occupied by the Royal Singapore Golf Club, which the military were impatient to reopen. It remained, as British visitors recognized, a beautiful spot. It was approached by a bridge of red and yellow timbers across the reservoir and the shrine itself had been exquisitely crafted in wood, and landscaped with black and white pebbles and rows of lanterns.[108] But for many victims of the Japanese there was no known resting place. Chinese families were unable to perform the mourning rituals that Confucian rites demanded, the offerings of food and burnt paper goods that would prevent their ancestors becoming 'hungry ghosts' in hell. Rumours spread across the island that the ghosts were wailing from their unmarked graves.[109] It was many years before they would be laid to rest.

2

1945: The Pains of Victory

BURMA INTRANSIGENT

The night of 12–13 August 1945, three days after the second atomic bomb fell on Nagasaki, marked the high point of good relations in Burma between the returning British and the local population, proudly led by their new army. That night news and rumours that the Japanese emperor had offered to surrender spread like wildfire through Rangoon. Streets were soon filled with cheering crowds. Jeeps bulging with people roared up and down the main highways. Ships' sirens blared forth the victory sign. Very lights stabbed the blackness of the night. The next day's *Rangoon Liberator*, the administration-sponsored newspaper, carried the banner headline 'Japan Surrenders. Rangoon goes wild with joy'.[1] In fact, the formal surrender did not come until two days later. Even then no one in Burma was quite sure that the fighting was finally over because units of the Japanese forces were still active in Tenasserim, the southern peninsula, and the southern Shan hills. The atom bomb also stoked fears about the future. Yet most people of whatever background now believed they would survive the war. That shrewd leader of the 14th Army, General William Slim, soon to become commander of Allied land forces, South East Asia Command, had once been worried by the possibility of conflict between Aung San's forces and the British army.[2] Now he congratulated Aung San on his fighters' patriotic resistance. Relations between the powerful Buddhist priesthood, the Sangha, and the Allied liberators remained cordial, too. Friendly contact had been established two months earlier. A hundred chief monks under the leadership of the Venerable Alatewa Sayadaw welcomed Mountbatten as supreme

commander, and thanked the administration for the excellent breakfast prepared for them that day. The meeting also established a committee to advise the British administration on all matters connected
with the monks.[3]

In the countryside, Japanese forces had been fighting on, pursued
by the British and the Burma National Army.[4] Slowly the news filtered
through to the remotest places. Maung Maung, one of the leading
soldiers of the BNA, remembered: 'One night in August the camp
of the Indian Brigade broke up in light and noise. Guns boomed,
searchlights danced, flares went up to send out showers of stars.'[5] The
war began to end here, too. Delicate negotiations were in train as
captured Japanese officers and Japanese-speaking British liaison personnel tried to convince the pockets of desperate Japanese troops that
the emperor had told them to lay down their arms. Some soldiers
surrendered with resignation; others 'would crumble to the ground
weeping and tearing the ground with frantic hands'.[6] A few attempted
suicide. One man blew himself up with a grenade in front of the
victors. Maung Maung recorded that the strange and ambivalent
comradeship between the Japanese and the old Burma Independence
Army flickered to life again, despite the mutual killing of the previous
four months. Even in the despair of their defeat, the Japanese were
easier to deal with than the British, many of whom still seemed
'snobbish', determined to reassert their superiority over what they
saw as a gaggle of Burmese youths.[7]

The British were themselves caught between feelings of relief and
horror at the magnitude of the task of reconstruction that faced them.[8]
Ironically, their only advantage in this was the large number of docile
and disciplined Japanese POWs they now held who could be assigned
tasks previously reserved for the meanest Indian coolie. The authorities hurriedly tried to improve Rangoon's conservancy department,
which had no more than a handful of sweepers to cleanse the latrines
of hundreds of thousands of dwellings. House owners were exhorted
to collect and properly dispose of rubbish rather than throw it into
the shattered drainage system. There was an ever-present danger of
disease. Slowly the city began to creep back to a basic level of normality. The *Rangoon Liberator* of 27 September carried a letter redo-
lent of the sweet old days of trysts in the shade of the Sule pagoda: to

'H. H. Princess of Magnolia. My most sincere apologies for the indiscreet note – pray remember memories of Radio – darling, forgive me – meet me at the "MARINA" – always awaiting you there – "S."'[9] Perhaps this was a plant by the secret services to improve morale. More convincing was the advertisement of Tong Hin Co. of 705–7 Dalhousie Square announcing a lottery. The prizes included 'a piece of silk for making Lady's Shanghai dress' and a bottle of hair cream and a box of face powder, all rare commodities in the battered metropolis. Alarmingly, the Lightning Chemical Institute of 314 U Wisara Road announced in the same issue: 'The old order has changed. Our Lightning Brand gin helped to bring in the new.'[10]

Within days new strains began to emerge. People had been prepared to bear privations in the months following the city's liberation, but now the world war was supposedly over they began to wonder why they were still dressed in rags, why prices were rising and why new supplies of cloth and other essential commodities had not been brought in.[11] Someone should wave a magic wand and put things back to where they had been in 1942. There was disgruntlement about the employment policies of the civil affairs secretariat set up by the military administration. Many Burmese complained that former Burmese members of the middle and lower civil service had not been re-employed. Instead, 'second-rate' Anglo-Burmans, Anglo-Indians and Indians, who had been hangers-on at Simla, where the Burmese government had been in exile during the war, were flooding back into the country.[12] On the other hand, the British seemed remarkably careless in screening those few Burmese who did regain government employment. Only four Burmese officers who were known to have been particularly active collaborators with the Japanese had been refused employment and those who had not collaborated were enraged that in many cases the sins of the occupation had apparently been washed away. All this fed into a wider disaffection about pay scales and ranking in the new order. Worse, individual civil servants found themselves caught between a resentful people and an administration determined to get back on top with punitive measures.

Balwant Singh, a young Burmese-born Sikh, observed all this first hand. He had joined the Burma civil service in 1942 and had survived the war working on the railways, having first learned basic Japanese.

In 1945 he rejoined the civil service and became assistant to a Burmese township officer. He found himself forcing rigid price and commodity controls upon an uncomprehending population, and was often shocked by the harsh sentences his superiors handed out for breaches of them. Even forced labour continued after the Japanese occupation: 'Life was full of hardship in a country now being occupied for the second time and for people struggling to survive under conditions of chaos. It was bewildering for men such as me who were new to the administration.'[13]

Another man who resumed a job interrupted by war was the medical missionary Gordon S. Seagrave. He had been born in Burma but educated in the United States and his ancestors included some of the earliest American missionaries in Asia, who had arrived in Burma before the first Anglo-Burmese war of 1824–6. 'Dr Cigarette', as he was affectionately known to local people because of his chain-smoking, had worked among the Kachin people of the far northeast frontier adjoining China.[14] His medical work and mission had been savagely disrupted by the Japanese invasion. He had been commissioned as a medical officer in 'Vinegar Joe' Stilwell's American and Chinese forces as they pushed through on their arduous and disease-ridden march to the Myitkyina airfield in 1944. Now Seagrave returned to his hospital at Namkham to face a medical and social emergency of unequalled proportions.[15] In their own way, the frontier regions had suffered even more from war than Burma's cities. The Japanese and returning Allied troops had done massive damage to an already parlous infrastructure. Food and medicines were virtually unobtainable. Bacillary dysentery had wiped out whole villages throughout the north. Plague was 'going strong'. Lepers had gone untreated. Cattle had been eaten by the Japanese army. On top of all this, many of the frontier peoples still distrusted Western medicine. The Sawbwa or local prince tried to stop Seagrave's hospital from reopening. He was quite happy poisoning himself with Shan medicine, according to the doctor.[16] At the time of Seagrave's return, stray Japanese troops were still taking pot shots at passing vehicles. Worse, here as elsewhere, the war had armed and militarized the minorities, presaging further tension and conflict, not only with the returning British but with any potential independent government in Rangoon.

Over the next few years the life of an American medical missionary was unlikely to be much easier than that of a junior Burmese administrator of Sikh origin.

In Burma the most important political development during the autumn of the victory year was the rapid souring of relations between Aung San and the British. At his first meeting with Slim, Aung San made it clear that he expected to be treated as the military commander of a provisional Burmese government. He had repeatedly asked that the civil wing of the Burmese patriotic or defence forces, the clumsily named Anti-Fascist People's Freedom League (AFPFL), should be regarded as the sole legitimate body politic in Burma. In early September at Kandy, Mountbatten's headquarters in Ceylon, a temporary accommodation was reached. Aung San had to accept a period of British administration as a 'necessary evil'. Neither the British nor Aung San could go it alone. The Japanese were still to be disarmed in southern Burma, Malaya and Indo-China, and the British needed the support of the BNA and particularly the information it could command.[17] The BNA, for its part, was too ill equipped and too small to have inflicted any strategically significant defeat on the British. The agreement between Mountbatten and Aung San stated that about 5,000 men from the BNA would be absorbed into a new British-led Burma Army, with a few more thousand kept up as reserves.[18] This did not solve the looming unemployment problem but it did put to rest concerns about 'rebellion against the king'. Everyone was well aware that Burma desperately needed supplies of cloth, oil, chemicals and food. All but the most radical Burmese politicians accepted that, for the foreseeable future, these could only come from British and American sources. Just as the Malayan communist leader Chin Peng was meeting senior British commanders in Malaya, so his cautious, 'snub-nosed, square-headed' Burmese counterpart, Than Tun,[19] warily seated himself around a table in Kandy with Mountbatten and Reginald Dorman-Smith, the returning governor. Yet less than two months after the atomic bomb had fallen on Hiroshima, the truce broke down at a political level. In the words of Mountbatten, Aung San chose to become a Churchill rather than a Wellington. He resigned his military commission to become political leader of the AFPFL.[20] There began a long and ill-humoured struggle between the two rivals for civil legitimacy, Aung San and Dorman-Smith. Ironically, and to Dorman-Smith's enduring disgust, the Burmese people never accepted Aung San in civilian guise. To them he would always be Bogyoke – the General.

The ill will should have been expected, but the politicians in London and even in Simla had never really grasped the depth of the change that had overtaken Burma's politics since the Japanese invasion. As almost one of its last acts in the early months of 1945, Churchill's wartime coalition government had published a White Paper, a political briefing document, on the future of Burma. This had had the singular effect of making even Dorman-Smith seem like a moderate. He might have been dismissed by Churchill as 'the man who wants to give Burma away', but the governor-in-exile was hardly looking to a quick transition to independence for the country. He considered that another five years of pre-war-style British administration would be needed before Burma even qualified for dominion status.[21] But the White Paper drawn up by Churchill and his secretary of state for India and Burma, Leo Amery, was light years behind this thinking. It had no time scale at all for independence. It seemed to be retrogressive, even by the standards of the 1936 arrangements that had given the country very limited local autonomy. Worse, to Burmese nationalists, it threatened to create a Balkans-type decentralized state in which tribal and minority areas would remain more or less permanently under British tutelage. Dorman-Smith was less sure of the document's import; he judged it 'infuriatingly vague'.[22]

The AFPFL had set their sights on the White Paper while they were still fighting the Japanese. One thing they particularly noted was the much higher priority given to India in the political discussions that took place as the war drew to its end. The viceroy, Lord Wavell, was forever trying to conciliate India's fractious politicians, while in Burma a substantial element in the civil affairs administration, represented by pre-war civil servants such as Frederick Pearce and Frank Donnison, seemed determined to keep Aung San at arm's length. This was despite the fact that Aung San, unlike India's Congress leaders, had latterly come to the aid of the Allies. Nor was it just a matter of Churchill's old antipathy for Burma's aspirations; the AFPFL expected to be sold down the river by Clement Attlee's new Labour government, too. At worst, they felt Labour were conniving at the return of a Tory governor; at best, Attlee seemed to be concentrating his efforts that autumn on labour unrest in Britain and other domestic problems. Sir Stafford Cripps, Labour's elder statesman of Asia, was tied down by Indian problems. Frederick, later Lord, Pethick-Lawrence, the new secretary of state for Burma, was not exactly a big hitter within the Labour movement and was derided by the opposition as 'Pathetic Lawrence'. Despairing of progress, the AFPFL and the BNA decided to flex their muscles. In every village and on every major urban building fluttered the 'victory flag', the red and white-starred banner of Burmese nationalism. Huge demonstrations began to take place in the burned-out ruins of Mandalay and around the Shwedagon pagoda, the great temple at Rangoon's heart.

One thing that crystallized the nationalists' hostility was the physical reappearance of Dorman-Smith. Mountbatten and Slim they could just about abide, but on 20 June Dorman-Smith made a quick visit on HMS *Cumberland* to what remained of Rangoon harbour.[23] He did not step ashore because he had no jurisdiction there until mid-October, when the civil government was due to resume some of its functions, but he invited many of the Burmese old guard on board, including Sir Paw Tun and Htoon Aung Gyaw, lately pensioners at the viceroy's pleasure in Simla. The governor noted that he would be returning to a politically transformed Burma and spoke of the huge task of reconstruction. Yet here he was courting the old gang all over again. The nationalists were deeply suspicious. Even a moderate like the high-court judge U Ba U warned Dorman-Smith not to try to return Burma to the status of a 'third-class crown colony'. But, perhaps despairing of Dorman-Smith's capacity for change, the judge also buttonholed Mountbatten, inviting him to speak in the newly opened Orient Club in September.[24] Nationalism was not explicitly on the menu: the dinner consisted of 'Orient soup', baked fish and a tactful 'victory pudding'.[25]

Above all, Dorman-Smith's reappearance brought to the surface the underlying conflicts between the British and the nationalists in Burma. The British had refused to set a date for Burmese independence. In their minds – and the Burmese knew this – independence was not really to be full independence anyway. Burma would still be under the crown, a symbolic issue of great importance for both sides. Worse, the great Anglo-Indian trade nexus was set to engulf the country again. British firms were already pressing the administration to recommence their Burmese operations and Rangoon's Indian Chamber of Commerce and evacuees in India were demanding the return of their lands and installations. The economic exploitation of Burma by foreign interests was an article of faith even for moderate Burmese politicians. They had in their minds wildly inflated estimates of the real wealth that British companies had sucked out of the country during the Depression years and after. Communists and socialists alike were convinced that 'British imperialism' and Indian capital were hovering in the wings waiting to pounce. Some of the British understood this. They had read enough Marx and Lenin to know that the British connection would have to take on a different complexion from now on. 'We Burmans today are not the Burmans of 1942,' Aung San warned them.[26]

In August 1944 Mountbatten himself had said that he favoured some kind of policy statement that the returning British would safeguard Burma from outside exploitation, 'and particularly from Indian moneylenders'. He acknowledged that under the Japanese 'a great burden of debt must have been lifted from the shoulders of the Burmese cultivator and I should be very sorry to think that its reimposition would synchronise with our return.'[27] An old Burma hand, R. M. MacDougall, had also advised Dorman-Smith that however illusory the Japanese-sponsored 'ten anna' independence of 1943 had been, it 'powerfully affected the imagination of the Burmese'.[28] Ba Maw's tenure as president or 'Adipadi' of Burma from 1943 to 1945 had had its Gilbert and Sullivan moments, notably some fanciful official dress and obscure titles, but ultimately the Japanese had pulled the strings. Even so, MacDougall believed it had been 'an honest attempt' to restore normal life to the country. Dorman-Smith, however, had retained close connections with both the Indian and the British business communities in Simla. In spite of MacDougall's warning, he seems to have felt that only foreign private capital could revitalize the Burmese economy. His return to Rangoon on 18 October to take up the civil administration heralded the reappearance of impatient British and Indian firms in the Burmese market.

Aung San had already turned politician by the time Dorman-Smith returned. His political creed, however, was ambiguous. In 1941, when he was being trained by the Japanese, he had written 'Blueprint for Burma'. This pamphlet spoke of the supremacy of the state and adopted the eugenicist's language of 'advanced' and 'backward' peoples: all the trappings of quasi-fascism, in fact. But it was probably designed for circulation within the Japanese Army and it may well have been Aung San's enemies who published it for a wider audience in 1946.[29] Judging by his speeches and writings after the war, he was a kind of populist democrat, a non-doctrinaire socialist, who believed in 'one man one vote', but only insofar as it delivered a government in the people's interest. This proviso, of course, left room for political intervention by strongmen. Later military dictators exploited this aspect of Aung San's legacy though, on the whole, Aung San seems to have had a higher regard for democratic values than many contemporary political leaders in Southeast Asia. He must have realized that, as the senior Burmese commander within the newly constituted British Burmese Army, he would have little room for manoeuvre. As head of the AFPFL, however, he would command a wide range of political cadres and working-class activists as well as the numerous members of the People's Volunteer Organizations, paramilitary bodies that were now becoming home for those members of the BNA who were rejected by or resisted joining the British-officered force. The PVOs, a loose melange of armed men biding its time on the fringes of the state, and sometimes hostile to it, inherited the traditions of the paramilitary nationalist volunteer groups of the 1930s. It also prefigured the emergence after independence of armed bands of dubious loyalty prowling the countryside.[30] On resigning his military role, Aung San had written to Mountbatten that he would have preferred to continue as a military officer, but his colleagues had decided he would have to lead the AFPFL as a civilian. Striking a warning tone, he told the British supremo that he 'would always retain an affectionate corner in my heart in spite of all the vicissitudes that may or may not arise between Burma and Britain in the political sphere in the future'.[31]

Aung San had some contact with people on the left of British politics, notably Tom Driberg. The MP and war correspondent first met him and other members of the newly recognized Patriotic Burmese

Forces at Mountbatten's headquarters in Kandy in early September 1945. Driberg had formed a good impression of Aung San, describing him as 'a slight, boyish figure with a surprisingly deep voice; physically and mentally agile with an irrepressible sense of humour and a gift for cynical wisecracking which he exercised impartially at the expense of his Burmese friends and of the British.'[32] Soon afterwards Driberg flew into Rangoon with Mountbatten. He had a vivid impression of swooping down to central Burma's 'flat green, soggy plains overwhelmed by angry monsoon clouds' in unbearable heat. He visited the Shwedagon pagoda and was surprised to find that the numerous book and trinket shops that filled the temple's lower levels were still selling Japanese military propaganda magazines.[33] The state of the city appalled him; it was as bad or worse than anything he had seen in Calcutta. Even Burmese employees of the civil affairs administration lived in 'wretched shacks 6 foot by 6 foot with bamboo walls, palm thatching' and no latrines. Driberg was invited by Aung San to sit on the platform with him at a political rally in a central Rangoon park attended by some 10,000 people. The rally had become a huge picnic for the city's workers. Even the few remaining buses had forsaken their normal routes to bring people there. The lawns surrounding the large central meeting hut were 'jammed and strident with musicians, red banners, sweetmeat vendors and family parties. The heat was overpowering.'[34] Driberg had plenty of time to absorb the atmosphere: Aung San and others made characteristically lengthy speeches in English, which were then translated into Burmese, Tamil and Urdu.

Driberg's less public encounters left an equally strong impression on him. At a dinner in the Rangoon Orient Club, Driberg joined Mountbatten, Dorman-Smith and Burmese politicians of the older generation, the latter catching his attention with their 'dainty pink and mauve head dresses'. Aung San was there too, but he had been relegated to an obscure corner of the room and his presence was not recorded on the menu card.[35] Mountbatten refused to go along with the slight. He told the dinner's organizers that he would not speak unless Aung San was moved to the top table and invited to speak too. This had an immediate effect and Driberg was left admiring the 'acumen of this prince of Battenberg' who understood so well 'the new nationalist forces' in Asia. The deep divisions among the British on how to proceed were brought home to him, too. He spent a 'fascinating evening' with Mountbatten and Dorman-Smith, noting the governor's fury over the way that the supreme commander was now courting Aung San just as he had courted Nehru. The two men bickered over copious quantities of drink: 'Each time one of them went out of the room to pee, the other would say: "Take no notice of what he's saying. He's just a hopeless reactionary" (or an "irresponsible radical", as the case may be).'[36] Driberg wrote off Dorman-Smith as 'a blimp of the old school', an opinion that was not entirely justified. But he was certainly right about the nationalist leadership. He wrote in *Reynolds News* of Burma's young leaders: 'You will hear more of these men.'[37] He compared them to the Greek socialists who had fought against the Nazis and applauded Mountbatten for engaging with the AFPFL, whereas in Greece the British had begun to suppress the radicals.

While in Rangoon, Driberg had several private meetings with the AFPFL leadership in which he urged them not to attend the ceremonies welcoming Dorman-Smith back to the country in case they should appear to be angling for jobs with the new administration. He also told them to demand at least equal treatment with India in the matter of constitutional reform. And he assured them that, whatever problems they had with the civil affairs administration, they could believe that Hubert Rance, its effective head, was their friend. Later a copy of a letter from Driberg about his consultations with the AFPFL found its way to Dorman-Smith, who reacted furiously. The acrimonious and ultimately violent developments on the path towards the end of colonialism in Burma over the next two and a half years were in some degree a consequence of the fact that the British, as much as the Burmese, had broken down into contending factions.[38]

Driberg did not drop Burma on his return home. Through the Orwellian-sounding Union of Democratic Control, a London-based pressure group, he used the many contacts he had made on his trip to link up disgruntled British forces personnel and Asian nationalists with left-wing opinion in Parliament and the press. As conditions neared mutiny in several stations, soldiers from India and South East Asia Command wrote to him denouncing their 'filthy conditions' or marvelling that 'the terrible Jap Rat is quite a good fellow when defending European imperialism'.[39] Colonel John Ralston wrote complaining that the 'Bollinger Bolshevik' had built up a huge and unnecessary staff in Singapore.[40] This pained Driberg, who had thought Mountbatten 'genuinely progressive'. Driberg had obviously made himself known widely, if somewhat imperfectly. From Burma a 'poor cultivator in Sangyaung' wrote to 'Mg. Drie Budd, P. M.' to complain of agricultural distress and the return of a dreaded class of Indian landowner-bankers: 'I am unable to plough the field now. It is not easy . . . Lands are in the hands of "Chettyers".'[41]

While the nationalists took an increasingly dim view of the machinations of Dorman-Smith, none of them appears personally to have disliked him. It was widely recognized that he was not responsible for the mess that was Burmese administration before the war. At Simla, however, he had got too close to what they regarded as the sleazy old order, particularly Paw Tun, the exiled Burmese prime minister. There was a feeling too that U Saw was lurking in the wings. U Saw had been the dominant politician in Burma in the late 1930s. A big, jovial and ruthless man, he had charmed many British officials. He held great parties, he was forever surrounded by pretty women and, above all, he was nothing like the ice-cold intellectuals of Indian politics whom so many of them disliked. He had seriously blotted his copy-book in 1941 after Pearl Harbor when he had contacted the Japanese and offered to help them invade Burma. Reports of his treachery were deciphered by British codebreakers at Allied intelligence and he had been sent off to exile in Uganda.[42] Now, he was about to return, with a brand-new German 'wife', who was very much the talk of the town as he already had a wife and a clutch of mistresses there. The British seemed to be prepared to forget, or at least forgive, U Saw's overtures to the Japanese. Besides, everyone knew that Dorman-Smith had a soft spot for him. The AFPFL suspected that the governor would use U Saw to try to build up a kind of pro-British centre party in order to bypass them. In December Aung San said as much to Montagu Stopford, now GOC Burma Command, who duly passed it on to Mountbatten. The British military, Aung San was reported as saying, simply had no idea how corrupt Burmese politics had been before the war. There was graft and favouritism in all departments. Aung San 'knew who the crooks were' and wanted Burma to be a free and decent country. The problem was that there were a lot of crooks already in the army's civil affairs secretariat and the return of the governor had simply made matters worse.[43]

The animus and suspicion beneath the surface was revealed in early October by a controversy involving the *Rangoon Liberator*. In spite of their official sponsorship, the Burmese editors of this newspaper carried an article headed 'Major-General Aung San speaks'.[44] The British were immediately irritated because by this stage Aung San had formally surrendered his military rank. Worse still, Aung San used the article to denounce an earlier editorial that had called the failure of the BNA and other partisan units to hand in their weapons a betrayal of Mountbatten. Not so, he stated: all nations had the right to keep arms for their own defence and in Burma it was particularly necessary because the British appeared to be arresting people on suspicion and violating their civil liberties. He went on to reject charges that he had planned a coup in 1938–39 and ridiculed rumours that the plans for this could be found in a hostel on the south side of the Shwedagon pagoda. This was a fabrication put about by the British security services, he said, implying that they were paving the way for his arrest. Put under pressure by the British, the editors of the *Liberator* temporized. They argued that just as the American commander, Douglas MacArthur, had accepted the Philippines nationalist army as genuine allies of the Americans, so too the British should accept the BNA. On the other hand, Aung San had to ensure that his forces did not impose their views on the people, for this would be 'fascist'.[45] This, at least, was a line with which many British civilian and military personnel agreed. For them, Aung San's was indeed a fascist organization and they had not fought for six years to see it win out in 'their' Burma. The year ended in deadlock. The AFPFL demanded the immediate creation of a dominion-style governor's council in which they would run the lion's share of the ministries.[46] This was to be accompanied by the announcement of a forthcoming election with a universal franchise. Aung San pleaded for peace but prepared for war. Dorman-Smith acknowledged the influence of the AFPFL but formed an executive council from members of other political parties. He adhered rigorously to the long timetable of Churchill's White Paper; what he had once found 'infuriatingly vague' now turned out to be rather convenient.

In the long term, Burma's fate, still in the balance in 1945, was to be determined mainly by big, impersonal considerations. How many troops could the British Empire deploy around the world while rebuilding the home front? How deeply entrenched in the countryside were the Burma defence forces and the volunteer armies of communists and nationalists? What ultimately was the value of Burma's teak, oil and rice to businessmen and governments in London, Madras and Bombay? Yet Burmese political society was a small and intimate one compared with India's. Personalities mattered a lot and their mutual clashes went a long way towards determining the form, if not the wider outcome, of Burma's struggle for independence. In turn, the fact that Burma gained that independence not only outside the Commonwealth but also outside the influence of communism was to be of great significance for the future of the crescent and indeed the whole of South and East Asia.

As 1945 drew to a close the big players of Burmese politics manoeuvred to gain a tighter hold on their opponents. Dorman-Smith, embittered by the British failures of 1942 and out of sympathy with his new Labour masters, was less genial than he seemed on the surface. Two men in particular seemed to stand in the way of his desire for a moderate Dominion of Burma under the British crown. One was Aung San, a national leader, but one still being pressured by his own communist allies and at times seemingly doubtful of his political touch. His rhetoric became more violent towards the year's end as the provisions of the detested White Paper still seemed to be in place. The governor, he claimed, had become 'fascistic', ironically the AFPFL's most derogatory term of abuse.[47] The other obstacle to Dorman-Smith's plans was 'Dickie' Mountbatten, whom he instinctively disliked as a royalist radical, too flippant for high imperial office. Then there were the other big egos flitting in and out of this little political world. U Saw's imminent return was to be followed in mid 1946 by that of the ex-Adipadi Ba Maw, released from detention in Tokyo by the British. Who knew how much political support he could muster among those who still had a pang of nostalgia for the Japanese days? Would Thakin Nu, Buddhist nationalist and minister under Ba Maw, return from religious retreat to strengthen the nationalist centre against the old politicians and the left? And what of the communists?

Thein Pe, the communist leader who had fled to India in 1942, was anxious to reassert his influence over the young comrades drilling and polishing their weapons in the villages. Thakin Soe, who was even more hard line than Thein Pe, was already dug in, Mao Zedong-like, into his 'base areas in the countryside'.

Across the country, in the hills and minority areas, dozens of spokesmen for newly armed peoples were waiting to stake their own claims for power and autonomy in Burma's dimly prefigured future.[48] The 'frontier areas' had always had a separate administration since the onset of British rule and, whether deliberately or not, this had fostered a sense of difference between Kachin, Shan, Karen and Chin peoples and 'ethnic' Burmese. The war had made the difference starker. The British had clung on in the northern hills, whether in the guise of Chindits, Force 136 or lone British officers, such as Hugh Seagrim who had died trying to shield the hill peoples from Japanese atrocities. British special forces had also released thousands of weapons to guerrilla armies of the hills, viewing the BNA askance even when it had come over to the Allies. The situation with the principal minority of the Burmese plains, the Karen, was similar. Many of the 1.5 million Karens had been Christian since the nineteenth century, an enduring source of suspicion to their Burmese neighbours. They were widely literate in English and often spoke it at home or sang English hymns in their Baptist churches. In some cases they even praised God in Welsh. Many wore clothes typical of the respectable people of the English countryside, floral skirts or grey flannels, rather than the traditional Burmese longyi. For generations they had lovingly tended and passed on a special history which asserted that they had been Christian even before they received the Gospel. Persecution by the Burmese Buddhist kings reinforced this consciousness of being a separate people. The British, who had commercial interests in the Karens' teak forests as well as the rice-producing plains, cultivated this sensibility. They fostered conservative Karen notables such as Sir San C. Po, author of the pre-war *Burma and the Karens*,[49] and awarded the community special constitutional recognition. The war had brought particular hardship. In 1941 gangs on the fringes of Aung San's Burmese Independence Army had mass-acred several hundred Karens in the delta. Isolated Japanese and

Burmese atrocities against them and other minorities continued throughout the war. When the British returned the Karens received them with enthusiasm, inviting British soldiers into their churches and homes. For their part, the British applauded the formation of the Karen National Organization in 1945 and put substantial amounts of money into the hill and minority areas. The Seagrim Hospital was founded as a memorial to the heroic special operations officer who had led them. Christian priests even gave the Karens a kind of national anthem: 'You've been persecuted and enslaved as well/ The white brother liberators, God sent them back!'[50] At this stage only a few Karen, Kachin, Shan or Chin radicals were talking about political separation from Burma, but with partition in the air all around – in India, Palestine, Ireland and Poland – expectations had been raised to a dangerously high level. The confused military settlement between Aung San and the British had made matters worse. At the negotiations at Kandy in September 1945 little attempt had been made to merge the armed minorities with the armed Burmese. Instead there was to be a 'two-wing army', one wing consisting mainly of Kachins, Karens and Chins officered by British regulars, the other mainly of Burmese elements in the British army and 6,000-odd BNA men. The officer corps of this second wing was to be 'Burmanized'. This, of course, was a recipe for long-term ethnic conflict, particularly in view of the existence of tens of thousands of other Burmese who were organized into the PVOs and had access to illicit arms.[51] Southeast Asia's bloody conflicts had merely paused for a few months in the afterglow of the atomic bomb.

INDIA: THE KEY

During the two years between the atom bomb and Indian independence, Indian concerns drove British policy in Southeast Asia. The availability or otherwise of the Indian Army to suppress dissidence determined events not just in Burma and Malaya, but even in Indo-China and Indonesia. Public perceptions of the East were shaped above all by events in India, much to the dismay of nationalist leaders in Burma and Malaya who wanted to get their concerns to the top of the agenda. Even after 1947 India cast a long shadow over the region, though the new prime minister, Jawaharlal Nehru, scrupulously tried to avoid the perception that 'greater India' would now replace the British Empire east of Bengal. British policy towards India over these years was formed by a set of assumptions and sensibilities that went far back into the past of the Labour Party and the Indian National Congress. Attlee, Cripps and Nehru had a long and tumultuous history of mutual admiration and mutual distrust. Attlee had served on the Simon Commission of 1927–9, an all-white committee of constitutional enquiry which Indian nationalists believed had hijacked their country's future and perpetuated British power by a policy of divide and rule. Nehru and Cripps, old socialist thinkers, had parted company with bad grace in 1942 after the failure of the Cripps mission to find a solution to the constitutional tangle.[52] Nehru and many other Congressmen had spent most of the rest of the war years in British Indian jails.

This long history was no less apparent in the case of Lord Pethick-Lawrence, Labour Party elder statesman and the newly appointed secretary of state for India and Burma in the Labour government. Pethick-Lawrence and his wife had been involved in Indian issues since the 1920s. Burma, by contrast, hardly entered their consciousness. In September 1945, as her husband took up his job, Lady Pethick-Lawrence wrote to Nehru's sister, Vijaya Lakshmi Pandit, about her early days as a suffragette. 'As long ago as 1909/10 Indian students were in the habit of attending our suffrage meetings in great numbers and I had many personal conversations with them.'[53] They had associated the movement for women's votes with the liberation of India and she now knew 'how faithfully that promise has been kept'. Even when Pethick-Lawrence had been a member of the 1929 Labour government, his wife had remained a member of the pro-Congress India League.[54]

The Labour Party of the 1940s was still essentially the political arm of a movement of moral, and specifically Christian, reform. Likewise the Congress was suffused with Gandhi's neo-Tolstoyan and semi-Christian ideology, while even the socialism espoused by Jawaharlal Nehru was influenced by the rhetoric of Hindu and Christian moral uplift movements in India. But these religious influences were not necessarily recognized by the British, let alone applauded. In late 1943 Pethick-Lawrence had discussed the role of holy men in politics with the novelist Aldous Huxley, proposing that Gandhi's 'spiritual conception of Indian independence' made him 'intolerant of compromise'. He had, Pethick-Lawrence thought, displayed intolerance towards the untouchables in India in the 1930s and had worsened India's problem of over-population by his stubborn opposition to birth control. Worst of all, he was unable to offer an 'olive branch to the Muslims'. Indeed, 'I think Gandhi himself has envisaged the breaking out of a civil war.'[55] Pethick-Lawrence was inclined to agree with a friend who felt that 'the neglect of human suffering is typical of Eastern mysticism'.

Despite the apparent overlap of their ideals and political language, then, there was still a fundamental lack of trust on the part of the Labour government's leaders towards the Congress and still more towards the Muslim League. The same was true on the other side. The Congress leaders had been let down by successive British governments, Labour politicians included, once too often. Right up to independence and beyond they expected to be sold down the river again. Somehow the chains would remain in place. Nehru wrote to Cripps in friendly terms in December 1945. He said he felt 'a dull pain' when he thought about Cripps's actions in 1942, when the two leaders had failed to strike a compromise between the British government and the Congress. He must understand, Nehru went on, how vastly India had been changed by war: 'People have grown desperate and it is no easy matter to hold them in check . . . There must be no prevarication' by the Labour government in its Indian policy.[56] At Christmas, as a new Labour mission set out for India, Gandhi wrote to Pethick-Lawrence summoning up 'the Prince of Peace'. He drew the secretary of state's attention to an event nearly fifty years earlier when King Edward VII had supposedly played a 'benign role' during the peace negotiations between the British and the Boers at the close of the South African war.[57] He hoped Pethick-Lawrence would exert a similar statesmanlike influence. But India must move immediately to independence. Through the dew of Gandhi's Indo-Christian piety, the message was clear: there were at least two potentially armed and bitterly opposed forces. For Boer and Briton read Indian and Briton.

Yet the speeches of nationalist leaders were only the surface wind.

The real lessons were to be learned from the Indian Army itself, which had already metamorphosed into a genuinely national force. One fact that became increasingly clear in the autumn of 1945 as demobilization began was that the Indian Army would never be the same again. Even before VJ Day, commanding officers had noted that the troops were saying in their letters that the world must change. One army electrician writing in Urdu expressed his sense of shame when 'an Italian peasant' – presumably a POW or a volunteer – asked him why education was not compulsory in India. 'I resolved in my mind that I will do my best to start a primary school in my village after the War.'[58] Indian commissioned officers were even more vigorous in their political determination. They told their British colleagues in no uncertain terms that the INA's aim of liberating India was entirely right.[59] The only thing that was wrong was their method. The British must leave India immediately, now that it was under no threat of attack from Japan.

By October 1945 the issue of the INA had risen to the top of the national political agenda and it became a key point of controversy between the newly released Congress leadership and Wavell's government.[60] Many people in India believed that Subhas Chandra Bose and the INA were wrong to join the Japanese, but even so they felt that the INA officers and men were true patriots. Whereas the British reserved particular contempt for the INA men they called the 'blacks', men who had tortured and flogged Indian Army soldiers who had refused to join them, most Indians made no distinctions between members of the INA. They agitated for the release of all of them. One comparison developed by members of Bose's old party, the Forward Bloc, was between the INA and the Free French under General de Gaulle. The INA, too, had rebelled against a government of occupation and had been sentenced to death in their absence. Not surprisingly, this view was not popular with the British and the Americans, but went down wonderfully among ordinary Indians. A national defence fund was instituted and some of the best lawyers in the country, including Jawaharlal Nehru, came forward to act as defending counsel for INA men put on trial. In England, the Cambridge University Indian student association, the Majlis, set up an INA Defence Fund. V. D. Savarkar, Hindu ideologue and historian of the Indian freedom struggle of 1857, sent a telegram to Attlee.[61] It demanded a general amnesty for all INA prisoners. It was signed, not with Savarkar's name, but with a date, '1857', the year of the Great Mutiny.

At first the British resisted the campaign to free the INA men. Wavell was quite clear that the INA 'blacks', estimated at about 7,000 men, would have to face trial. Their 'rebellion against the king-emperor' and violation of their oath put these men in quite a different category from, say, those Tamil estate workers in Malaya who had joined the Japanese. Nor was there a comparison with the BNA, for the Burmese had 'redeemed' themselves by ultimately rebelling against the Japanese. Even the cautious General Sir Claude Auchinleck, commander-in-chief India Command, was insistent that INA men who had personally beaten and tortured their former comrades must be held to account. Otherwise the army would be guilty of disloyalty to its own men. The British made a lot out of those enlisted men who were hostile to the INA. Not everyone was cowed by the public adulation of Bose. One R. A. Hassan of Lahore wrote to the *Statesman* in October denouncing him as 'selfish, vain, ruthless'. He had eaten four-course meals every day while slowly killing the POWs who would not join him.[62] A British officer, W. L. Alston, was moved to compose a little ballad on how he thought a penitent INA man might feel:

> It makes me shudder when I think
> That once I lent a hand,
> To help that squat barbarian,
> To take my native land.[63]

Alston sent his doggerel to Auchinleck, but did not receive a reply, perhaps because his verses went on to indict the Labour 'cranks' for betraying the Empire.

The INA was a prickly issue for the Congress too. Despite their public denunciations of the British for even considering trials, the Congress leaders were privately in two minds, concerned that a new national army should be loyal and not divided by factions that had originated in the war. Nehru had always referred to the INA as 'misguided men', but had then gone on to say that 'whatever errors and mistakes they had committed', they had been real patriots. The issue of the oath meant little to civilian Indians, but the atrocities against other Indian troops were more difficult to dismiss. The British picked up some of the Congress's disquiet through a returned POW, Captain Hari Badhwar. Badhwar, who was well acquainted with the accounts of atrocities, met Asaf Ali of the Congress Working Committee and found that he had been deputed by Congress to test opinion in different parts of the country.[64] Badhwar reported that Ali had found a widespread feeling amongst ordinary Indians that the British must not try even the INA 'blacks'. Congress was well aware of the INA atrocities and deplored them. It was also worried about the future of the army. But Congress dare not take a line against the INA 'as they would lose much ground in the country'. There was an implicit suggestion in Badhwar's report that if the government of India were to abandon the plan, Congress might be prepared to put them on trial when it came to power.

The British themselves were already backing down a little. Everyone was aware that a campaign of 'mass glorification' of the INA was going on, particularly in Bengal. The idea that the ordinary 'white' rankers, the INA men who had escaped British censure with no more than a dishonourable discharge, would simply be quietly absorbed into the villages was exploded. Instead, provincial Congress committees arranged receptions as the men passed through railway stations on their way home. They were garlanded, eulogized and treated like conquering heroes. One thing that particularly worried the authorities was the way in which the issue might become communal. Though Muslim soldiers had joined the INA, some soldiers from the Muslim peoples of the northwest regarded Bose and his followers as traitorous Hindus. With communal tensions beginning to build up again as the war ended, the British did not want the INA issue to feed into Hindu–Muslim disagreements.[65] The authorities reached a consensus at a conference of provincial officers held in November 1945. They agreed that, since there was so much sympathy for the INA among army rank and file and ordinary people, the only safe policy was to confine prosecution to those INA officers specifically accused of brutality against fellow soldiers. It took a while for full import of this decision to sink in, but the fact that so many officials were prepared to overlook the charge of rebellion against the king-emperor was a tacit admission that the imperial game was up.

BENGAL ON THE BRINK

The fallout from the INA and the animosities of the war's end combined in a noxious way in populous and impoverished Bengal. Calcutta had always acted as the northern hub of the crescent just as Singapore acted as its southern hub. It remained so even when the governments of Burma and Malaya returned to their reconquered territories. Intelligence activities in Indo-China were organized in Calcutta and, however poverty stricken its inhabitants, Calcutta remained the centre of British business for the whole Bay of Bengal. In the second half of 1945 the city of more than 2 million was a place of rising tension that was soon to spill over into an almost perpetual state of violence. In Burma, conflict between the armed representatives of ethnic groups took place mainly in the peripheries of the country; in Bengal it affected the province's heart. Calcutta began to resemble Thomas Hobbes's nightmare vision of 'a war of all against all'.

Bengal, unlike the Punjab, was not home to many soldiers' families, but war and famine had brutalized a large section of its population. Since 1942 it had sheltered many of the displaced, the refugees from Burma and Malaya. Survivors of the famine of 1943 still eked out a livelihood on its streets. As the war came to its end, new dangers arose. Labour in the city was restive throughout the autumn. Business firms and state enterprises took the opportunity to reduce the 'dearness allowance' that they had paid during the wartime emergency. There were postal strikes, steel workers' strikes and strikes in the Railway Press, one of the major printing houses. People went about in rags because there was a 'cloth famine', a consequence, it was said, of profiteering and corruption in the wartime rationing system. Worse, there were eerie echoes of 1943. Floods were afflicting large areas of northern India while other parts of the same region suffered a drought: 'spontaneous hunger marches and the influx of rural people into the towns had started and the price of rice and paddy were steeply rising'.[66]

Since the city had been near to the fighting in Burma, a lively trade in contraband arms, ammunition and explosives had grown up. Troops sold their weapons to Calcutta people and many were stolen. The police later indicted the military for 'carelessness' in allowing so much war materiel to fall into the wrong hands.[67] These arms would be used to deadly effect over the next two years. There were also the men around keen to use these illicit weapons, not people with some military training, as was often to be the case in the Punjab, but those whom the British and the press called *goondas*. These were gang bosses and thugs who ran prostitution and drugs rackets. They had always flourished on Calcutta's streets, but during the war many had been locked up under the Defence of India Rules. Much as they would have wished to keep them behind bars, the authorities had to let them out when wartime restrictions were lifted: '2,000 persons of the goonda variety' were released between July and December 1945.[68]

Then there were the issues to stir the city's inhabitants to political demonstration and violence. Since before the First World War there had been a tradition of anti-British terrorist violence, with sporadic assassinations of policemen and bomb attacks on symbols of British rule. Revolutionary communism was popular among the educated youth of the city and strikes at the jute mills had sometimes ended in violence and mass protests. This inheritance had been given new meaning by the events of the Second World War, and especially by the exploits of the INA, which had been watched with admiration in Bengal. A relatively small percentage of INA troops had been Bengalis. This was because of the predominance of men from the Punjab and North West Frontier Province in the Indian Army troops captured by the Japanese in 1942. The civilians who joined the INA were mostly Tamils, because they had dominated Malaya's plantation workforce. Yet, because the INA's revered leader, Subhas Chandra Bose, was a Bengali and his brother, Sarat Chandra, had spent much of the war in British jails, Bengalis identified strongly with the INA. Almost from the moment that the British allowed normal political life to resume there were demonstrations, public meetings and pamphlet campaigns demanding the release of the INA men. These grew to a climax in November as the British began the trials at the Red Fort. Bengal rallied to the call of K. N. Katju, one of the men's defence team, when he declared, 'they are the soldiers of freedom,' and, 'for a subject people the law of treason has no moral sanction behind it'.[69] The Bengal Provincial Congress Committee set up a defence fund, declaring that the men's only crime had been to love their country. As detainees were released and soldiers returned, an old rumour that the British had summarily executed some of the INA men was given a new lease of life. Freed from a Bengal jail, the president of the UP provincial Forward Bloc, Bose's old party, stated that he had seen Sardar Singh of Jullunder being led to execution shouting 'Jai Hind!' (Victory to India!) and 'Inquilab Zindabad!' (Long live the revolution!).[70] Stories of the execution of the 'soldiers of freedom' merged with new speculation and evidence about British atrocities during the 1942 Quit India campaign. Tamluk, a subdivision of Midnapur district with a forty-year history of anti-colonial resistance, had been the scene of numerous examples of police firing on crowds, village burnings and rapes by the security forces. The victims could now come forward to tell their stories, as they were in Nuremberg. Indians did not waste the opportunity to make some inflammatory comparisons: Britain's record in Bengal was every bit as bad as that of the Nazis at Belsen; 'will the UN have the courage and the fairness to hold trials in India?'[71]

Emerging legends about the INA were closely bound up with a fever of speculation about the fate of Subhas Bose himself. In November an 'authoritative source' had confirmed to a Press of America reporter that Bose had died at 9 a.m. on 18 August at Taihoku hospital, Formosa (present-day Taiwan). Bose's staff officer had asked the Japanese to take his body to Tokyo, but the coffin was too big for the small plane available. The body had therefore been cremated and Bose's aides had carried his ashes to members of the Indian community in Tokyo, who had performed a small ceremony in the Renkoju Temple, Suginami.[72] This account seems to have been substantially true, but since the source could not be identified and none of the Tokyo Indians could be contacted, it did little more than fuel the frenzied speculation that Bose was still alive and would return to claim his legacy of freedom. It is not hard to see why this myth proved attractive in the apocalyptic conditions of Bengal in 1945 when the atomic bomb had followed the mass evacuation from Burma, cyclone, famine and cholera. As the INA trials opened on 5 November, the press carried dozens of pictures and souvenirs of the men under trial and of various INA units, including the all-female Rani of Jhansi Regiment, parading before Subhas Bose. Sarat Bose declared 'Azad Hind Week' and hundreds of thousands of rupees were collected for INA defence and rehabilitation costs. Released INA men were fêted enthusiastically and, almost inevitably, many of the Calcutta demonstrations in their honour tipped over into violent protest and riots against British rule. On 7 November 1945 at least 100,000 people staged a mass rally at Shraddhananda Park in the centre of the city. Later the same month, the police fired on student demonstrators, killing sixteen and injuring 125.

Bose and the INA were not, however, the only political trigger in Bengal over these months. There was a much wider apprehension that 'imperialism' was rampant once again, despite people's sacrifices during the war. The press and politicians dwelt on the deployment of British and British Indian, French and Dutch troops to suppress national movements in Indonesia and Indo-China and action against nationalists and trade unions in Burma and Malaya. American 'commercial imperialism' was denounced. An All-India South East Asia Day of demonstrations was declared and vigorously celebrated in Calcutta. The word went out that 'Indians' conditions throughout Malaya is [sic] helpless. Prominent lawyers, doctors, merchants and missionaries have been confined in solitary cells for over a month without trial.'[73] The people on the receiving end of this wave of Bengali sympathy were members of the former Indian Independence Leagues. But brotherly solidarity with the subject peoples of Southeast Asia did not inhibit another type of agitation about the region. This was the movement for the return of Indian nationals who had fled Burma at the beginning of the war, a cause that was by no means popular among Burmese, Malays or Indo-Chinese. In October the Burma government's Civil Supplies Board announced that, come the following March, it would begin repatriating half a million of these refugees from Calcutta, Chittagong and Vizagapatnam in the south. Moreover, it promised that: 'all Indian merchant refugees returning to Burma would be granted retail trade licences. If their shops were occupied by Burmese or if they had been destroyed or damaged, the government would help the merchants in reoccupying or rebuilding their premises.'[74] Calcutta may have been pleased, but announcements such as this had the effect both of distressing many inhabitants of Southeast Asia and also of raising unrealistic hopes amongst the refugees, many of whom were desperately poor.

While economic unrest and hatred of the British surged through the cities of Bengal, a more insidious and ultimately more murderous passion was slowly gaining force: Hindu–Muslim hostility. Ironically, Hindus and Muslims in Bengal had more in common than they had in most parts of India. They all spoke Bengali and there was no superficial written-language division based on the difference between Sanskrit- and Persian-derived scripts as there was over much of the subcontinent. In the countryside, despite the efforts of preachers who tried to insist on the practice of pure Hinduism or Islam, there was still not a lot to distinguish a Hindu from a Muslim peasant, particularly if he or she was from the plebeian but hard-working Namasudra caste numerous in many of the eastern districts. Most Bengalis were followers of popular devotional sects that blurred the boundaries between Hinduism and Islam, and some of these, notably the Bauls, had both Hindu and Muslim adepts. Yet over the years economic differentials, the play of sectarian politics in British-founded institutions and the activities of unscrupulous or purblind leaders had fractured relations between members of the two religious traditions. There had been a spate of serious Hindu–Muslim riots in the 1930s when peasant protests against landlords and moneylenders had become infused with the inflammatory language of religious revivalists. Those divisions might have narrowed during the war, but with the fighting in Burma unnervingly close, the British authorities had been happy to let attempts at religious coalition fall by the wayside. Incensed by Congress's opposition to the war effort, they preferred to keep in power a conservative Muslim ministry which had a loose alliance with Mahomed Ali Jinnah's Muslim League in all-India politics. Muslims on the whole were more favourable to the British war effort and it was important to keep recruits flowing into the army. For their part, the Hindu leaders of Bengal, whether formally members of Congress or not, were more inclined to think in communal terms than in many other parts of India. The old gentry class, the *bhadralog* or 'respectable people', dominated Hindu politics. Though fiercely anti-British, they were fearful of domination by the Muslim majority in the province. These fears were only heightened as the probability of a British withdrawal increased in the aftermath of the Labour election victory of the summer.

Meanwhile, the Bengali autumn festival of Durga Puja, celebrated in honour of the province's great mother goddess, proceeded with much gusto as a kind of peace returned to India. A series of incidents in which Muslim bands attacked Hindu images and scuffles and retaliatory shooting by police erupted outside mosques presaged a dark future. The great crescent, so recently violently unified by the successes of the British and Indian armies, was soon to be fragmented again. Hindu would fight Muslim in Bengal. Self-selected leaderships of the Nagas and other people of Assam and the eastern hills would agitate and later fight for the autonomy which they believed they deserved because of their services during the war. To the south, in Arakan, Buddhist would fight Muslim. Christian Karen would fight Burmese Buddhist. Chinese and Malay Muslim gangs continued to skirmish in rural Malaya. The malevolent spirit of the war hovered above the crescent even as millions of soldiers returned to their homes.

THE RECKONING

Across the world these last months of 1945 were months of retribution. In Europe the Nuremberg trials of Nazi leaders were being prepared. In Rangoon and Singapore Japanese officers were arraigned as war criminals. Dozens passed through the Gothic central prisons of these cities, interrogated persistently, aggressively, week after week, but without the benefit of whips, bamboo splinters beneath the fingernails, or bastinadoes, as had been commonplace with the Japanese secret police, the Kempeitai. In Tokyo Allied judge advocates prepared the trials of bigger figures in the war. Emperor Hirohito escaped, but the chain of events had been set in motion that led inevitably to the hanging of Hideki Tojo and his associates, sacrifices for the imperial house. In this atmosphere the British were determined to bring the INA to some kind of reckoning.

The first arrests were in Malaya and Singapore, where the INA was not merely a scattering of renegade military units but a citizen army. The arrival of Subhas Chandra Bose in Singapore in July 1943 had created an unprecedented wave of mobilization among the Indians of Southeast Asia. Many INA personnel were Malayan residents who had never seen India but identified with it as their great national community. The sons of middle-class families joined up; so too did the daughters, by enlisting in the Rani of Jhansi Regiment, named after the heroine queen of 1857. The civilian organization – the Indian Independence League – supplied propagandists and administrators of Bose's Azad Hind government; virtually the whole Indian business community was co-opted in one way or another, as were Ceylonese professionals, in spite of the island being peripheral to Bose's vision. The INA had connected the educated townsmen to the largely illiterate Tamil masses on the rubber estates as never before.

On reoccupying Singapore, Penang and Kuala Lumpur, the British threw most of the leaders of the Indian Independence League into jail. This included some of the most educated and prominent personalities of the pre-war era, such as the London-educated lawyer, N. Raghavan, in Penang and S. C. Goho, a Singapore barrister who had quasi-diplomatic status before the war as the official 'agent' of the government of India. Not all of them had been unequivocal in their support for Bose. Journalists were a particular target, such as the most senior Asian editor of the pre-war era, Francis Cooray, a Ceylonese who ran the Kuala Lumpur daily *Malay Mail*. In the cells they were given a form on which to declare their work for the INA. But the pattern of arrests seemed hasty and arbitrary. The British, Cooray complained, 'acted no better than the Japanese did on the uncorroborated evidence of accomplices and informers, who had axes to grind and grudges to pay off.'[75] The treatment of the troops of the INA was also haphazard. The 1,940 soldiers of the INA captured in Thailand were truculent and uncooperative. British interrogators complained of the 'brazen insolence' and 'outward veneer of bravado' with which they boasted of their defeats of Allied troops, and of the false statements they made to annoy them.[76] But the around 2,500 INA personnel in Malaya were more mildly treated. They merely had to await repatriation until 'loyal' Indian soldiers were sent home and, like the Japanese, were put to work in the interim.[77] The young British historian Eric Stokes and his mountain artillery regiment was sent to escort members of the INA back to internment in India. The local INA recruits melted away. One Indian from Singapore garrisoned in Perak was told simply: 'If you want to go, you are free to go.' Some of the more educated recruits were even employed by the British military.[78] Mountbatten did not see himself as bound by policy in India, and he did not want responsibility for the INA. He tried to slow the process down: 'There are', he ordered, 'to be no executions without my approval.'[79]

The decisive moment came in the autumn when the Indian government and military authorities decided to try a group of INA officers. Indians in the army recruiting areas in the northwest told British officials 'if only they had been shot in Rangoon or Singapore everyone would have been pleased',[80] but they warned that a show trial in India would be a political disaster. Why did the British proceed? The desire for retribution was strong but more than that, many officials including the viceroy believed that Congress was going to use the INA as a 'spearhead' in some forthcoming revolt.[81] So Captain Shahnawaz Khan, Captain P. K. Sehgal and Lieutenant G. S. Dhillon were arraigned. These three young Punjabi officers of the INA were all graduates of the Indian staff college. They were accused of torturing and executing INA soldiers who had tried to return to their British allegiance very late in the war, in March 1945, at the INA camp near Mandalay, Mount Popa. Subhas Bose, defeated but still defiant, had urged his officers to root out treachery and backsliding as Slim's advance into Burma gathered pace. The three officers had carried out Bose's orders.

On 5 November 1945 three 'smart young men, unbadged, but with a sense of command', were ushered into a military court in the great Moghul Red Fort of Delhi. The British may have thought that the date of the trial, the 340th anniversary of the gunpowder plot against the English Parliament, was appropriate. The venue, however, was not. Among Indians, the Red Fort still echoed with memories of the previous British show-trial staged there, that of the last Moghul emperor, Bahadur Shah Zafar, after the rebellion of 1857–8. It was earth from the tomb of Bahadur Shah, who had died in exile in Rangoon, that Bose's men had intended to convey in a silver casket on their ill-fated march from Burma to India in 1944.

The arguments between the prosecution and defence were hurled back and forth for days. The Indian public hung on every word. Court transcripts were published daily. One proclaimed: 'This trial is far more sensational than the trial of Jesus Christ and many other trials around the world.'[82] Vallabhbhai Patel, general secretary of the Congress, got in a shrewder blow. The man who should really be on trial, he asserted, was Lord Linlithgow, the former viceroy, for sentencing 3 million Bengalis to death by famine in 1943. Points of fact arose: were the INA deserters actually executed and, if so, by whom? The British judge advocate general belittled the INA as a Japanese quisling army. The men who had joined it were either traitors or they were forced by bad treatment into its ranks. In rebuttal, the defence team argued that the INA was Indian-officered and led. Were the British quislings to the Americans simply because General Eisenhower was supreme commander in Europe? The accused exculpated their personal actions. Shahnawaz Khan said that he had sacrificed 'my life, my home, my family and its traditions' for his country.[83] Dhillon is supposed to have said that the Japanese were 'leaders of the Buddhist religion' which was born in India. Indians should therefore work with the Japanese.[84]

The most telling arguments, though, were those that brought international law into the scales. The British, the defence argued, had abandoned their status as a government in Malaya and Burma. Four years before in Singapore, as the garrison surrendered, Colonel Hunt had told captured Indian troops that they should 'obey the orders of the Japanese in the way that you obeyed the British government. Otherwise you will be punished.'[85] Other evidence seemed to suggest that the Singapore commander, General Percival, had endorsed this position. So, said the accused, P. K. Sehgal: 'In return for the loyalty of the Indians, the British representative handed them over to the Japanese like a flock of sheep. Thereby the British had cut off all our bonds of allegiance to the British crown.' Buoyed up by the public reaction to this claim, the defence went on to argue that Bose's Azad Hind government was an independent administration created by war. It controlled its own territories, even if they were only the sparsely populated Andaman and Nicobar Islands. It had an effective and autonomous army, and its government had been recognized by, among others, the government of Eire.[86] The Azad Hind government enjoyed exactly the same status as the United States of America after the declaration of independence in 1776. The fact that Bose had failed was neither here nor there. The INA soldiers were officers of an independent army. The floggings and executions they administered in Burma and Malaya were perfectly compatible with the British Army Act of 1911.

What was striking about this line of argument was that it had been put together not solely by the three determined Congressmen among the defence lawyers, Nehru, Bhulabhai Desai and Asaf Ali, but by several hoary old Indian liberals who had been decorated by the British government and were widely regarded as loyalists by both British and Indians.[87] If such men were arguing that the independent Indian nation already existed, how could it be otherwise? The three young officers were ultimately convicted, but only of the lesser charge of rebellion against the king-emperor. The sentences passed were never imposed. Wavell later acknowledged that the first trials should have been of men who could actually be convicted of brutality or murder.[88] The three were later released from jail and given dishonourable discharges from the army. But the British Raj had already suffered a lethal blow. Its legitimacy, long questioned, was now seeping away. Even Ajit Rudra, a senior Indian officer who had once believed passionately that the INA had betrayed their loyalty to the king-emperor, had second thoughts.[89] If the British had willingly released the Indian troops from their allegiance, how could they be classed as traitors?

The effect on soldiers and civilians up and down the crescent was electrifying. As the debate over the INA raged on, hundreds of thousands of Indian troops remained in Southeast Asia under British command. By far the majority were scattered over a demoralized and devastated Burma, suspicious of the BNA and doubting the intentions of the British. Nehru and other Congress politicians had already warned Auchinleck, the army's commander-in-chief, that it would be impossible to use Indian troops to put down nationalist rebellions in fraternal countries. This hamstrung Dorman-Smith in his attempt to bring the BNA to heel over the next nine months. As Wavell reminded the cabinet on 17 October: 'SEAC depends almost entirely on [the] loyalty and discipline of Indian troops'. Yet Attlee brushed aside his objections to the despatch of fresh levies of men from India in the face of new tasks confronting the British.[90] It caused new difficulties as the British tried to rebuild their rule in Malaya. Indian troops were also in French Indo-China, attempting to reassert French authority in the face of communist and nationalist rebellions. And such was the drain on manpower that Britain had to risk sending 5 Indian Division from Malaya to Indonesia, where they would fight alongside British troops against the Indonesian nationalists in what was to be the bloodiest of the first wars of peace.

In Burma and elsewhere the INA issue raised the temperature of politics. There never had been a question of treating the BNA in the same manner as the INA, except among the most intransigent old British civil servants. If the INA were not really guilty of rebellion, Burmese thought, the BNA must surely be the legitimate military wing of their national movement. There was, however, one exception to Britain's relatively prudent approach to the BNA: early in 1946 Dorman-Smith tried to bring against Aung San a charge of murder very similar to those which the British authorities had sought to pin on the 'blacks' of the INA. The resulting showdown ensured that either Aung San or Dorman-Smith had to go. The witch hunt against Indian civilians in Southeast Asia rapidly lost all moral force. The full weight of South Asian public opinion made itself felt in Malaya. In November a new 'agent' of the government of India arrived in Singapore. S. K. Chettur, an Oxford graduate and Madras civil servant, carried himself as if he were the representative of a friendly, independent power. Urbane and at ease in colonial circles, he put pressure on the British authorities to release the detainees, especially by engaging a legal team on the Red Fort trial model, and by drawing the attention of Indian public opinion to the conditions of solitary confinement of the detainees held in Kuala Lumpur.[91] There were dark hints of racism when an Indian defendant and his Indian lawyers came in front of white judges and prosecutors. By early December 1945 this issue was causing so much difficulty in India that it led Wavell to plead with Mountbatten to either try the men or release them.[92] The prosecutions unravelled: by the end of the year, of the 114 arrested, only three were accused of treason; of the fifty-eight cases handed to the magistrates, thirty-one accused were provisionally released and nineteen conditionally released, with the rest in abeyance.[93] Chettur argued that all those who were innocent of violence should be freed. Any suggestion of this in November, he observed, would have thrown the British 'into a fit'. But by January 1946 Mountbatten was willing to agree.[94]

There was even less clarity as to British treatment of others who had worked with the Japanese. Mustapha Hussain was one of the many Malay radicals arrested. Fully expecting to be tried by the British, he surrendered himself to a local Force 136 officer, Colonel Peter Dobree, who was attached to a group of Malay fighters of the 'Loyal Malay Soldiers' in Perak. Mustapha discovered that his name was on an 'arrest on sight' list. Confined in the local police station, he warned the Malay soldiers not to be duped by the British, and found them to be already disenchanted. '*Tuan* Dobree used to eat wild-growing fiddle-head ferns with us in the jungle,' they told him. 'Now that he is dining with the Sultan, he hardly remembers us.' Mustapha was moved to another police station then to Batu Gajah jail. It had a black reputation in these years: many prisoners of the Japanese, including the Force 136 agent Lim Bo Seng, had died there. Mustapha spent long months in grim conditions in a lock-up with a rag-bag of aristocratic Malay officials, former policemen and their narks. Their fates varied dramatically. Mustapha was released without trial in 1946, after an appeal from 400 former Malay Regiment soldiers for whom he had interceded after the fall of Singapore. But others with him in Batu Gajah faced imprisonment or even death. Many arrested spent nearly two years in jail without trial. Some later took their own lives. Nominally a free man, Mustapha found himself shunned by his community, sacked by the British from his old job as a lecturer, prohibited from re-entering politics and subjected to further interrogations on the history of the Malay radicals.[95] It was but a short step from the retribution of war to the preventive detentions of counter-insurgency.

By this time there were around 1,392 complaints under investigation, but most were withdrawn through lack of evidence. Roughly half the cases that came before the special courts were dismissed. Of the 385 Malayans detained, most were released, some conditionally. At the end of January 1946 the British announced that they would accept no more complaints.[96] A defining moment was the trial in

Singapore of a Eurasian, C. J. Paglar. He was a respected medical practitioner who, for the lack of any other candidate, had acted as a figurehead leader of the Eurasian community and made a number of broadcast messages, for example on Emperor Hirohito's birthday. He was one of the few people charged with treason. The principal defence witness was a Japanese civilian administrator in Singapore, Mamoru Shinozaki. During the war he had taken upon himself the protection of vulnerable Anglophone groups, such as the Eurasians and the Straits Chinese. Shinozaki argued that Paglar acted upon instructions, and under the compulsion of protecting his community. The Japanese regime, he said, was 'like a stepfather after the real father, the British, left their children behind. The stepfather was brutal ... Now, alas, the real father has returned and is blaming these leaders for obeying their stepfather.'[97] The trial was adjourned *sine die*. The trial divided public opinion, but most Eurasians took the view that 'somebody had to stand up for the people to be representative.'[98] The Muslim president of the Indian Chamber of Commerce, R. Jumabhoy, a man who had spent the war in India, reflected on the prosecutions: 'Had I been here I'm not certain that I would not have done the same to save myself and my family.'[99]

It was bitterly ironic that these vendettas struck hardest at those key groups the British needed to rebuild their authority. The police force was shattered by the war, and by the stigma of working with the Japanese. In Malaya, the British discharged 500 Sikh policemen, and 400 others enlisted by the Japanese. It would be many years before public trust in them would be rebuilt. This denunciation of a Chinese police inspector was not untypical:

The Wildebeeste of Syonan and the Black Snake Spitfire of Gestapodom, fit to rank with the street sweepings and organized gangsters. His very name spells doom and anathema ... He experimented with the barbaric cruelties of the Spanish Inquisition. By jingo & the heavens! He was a bad egg, rotter and wicked blighter in his heyday.[100]

Yet the British desperately needed experienced officers, and tended to listen to pleas from those who had worked under duress: 'If I had really collaborated with the Japanese', petitioned one officer, 'I would have arrested hundreds of persons and not only twenty.'[101] The British were caught in a bind. On the one hand, many Malayans felt that old-style colonial retribution could have no further place in a territory where so many – above all the British themselves – had played morally and politically ambivalent roles during the war. Yet equally, the sight of known collaborators and profiteers on the streets alienated popular opinion. Above all, it was the unevenness and inconsistency of British justice that was the source of lasting anger. A sharp distinction emerged between colonial justice and popular justice. As soon as the newspapers began to publish again, denunciations crowded their pages: of the schoolmaster for removing the word 'Britain' from text-books, 'thereby treating Britain as an enemy'; the arrogant mistresses who had escaped arrest; charges of 'fawning on the Japanese without shame'; even of pushing a Japanese officers' car when the engine broke down.[102] Reputations were blackened by dark innuendo, and this fed undercurrents of corruption, blackmail and extortion. Men with guilty consciences turned to the triads for protection. As the vengeful fury of the British began to subside, a long, slow internal reckoning was only just beginning, and for many it would never be complete.

3

1945: A Second Colonial Conquest

In 1945 imperialism was down but not out. Japan's dream of a great East and Southeast Asian empire had been crushed flat in the ruins of Nagasaki and Hiroshima. But the British seemed determined to retain a dominant influence in the region. As British armies fanned out across Burma, Malaya, French Indo-China and Indonesia, a more intrusive and authoritarian form of administration seemed to be taking shape in place of the distant paternalism of the old Raj. Yet not all the signs seemed to favour renewed imperialism. A new British Labour government had been voted into office by a landslide as the European war ended in mid 1945. Prime minister Clement Attlee and Stafford Cripps, its dominant personalities, had always displayed an interest in India's independence, or at least dominion status under the British crown. But both men were paternalists rather than liberators, and in the dangerous new world which followed the bomb many of their colleagues believed that a powerful military position in Asia was essential to guarantee Britain's worldwide security. Clement Attlee personified his party's awkwardness about imperial authority. In 1945 he made a speech to Americans insisting that British 'socialists' were not 'against freedom': 'We in the Labour Party', he said, 'declare that we are in line with those who fought for Magna Carta and *habeas corpus*, with the Pilgrim Fathers and the signatories of the Declaration of Independence.'[1] But this freedom was not to be of an untrammelled nature; elsewhere he lamented the fact that 'man's material discoveries have outpaced his moral progress'. By implication, most people would benefit from a strong and morally assured guiding hand. Such beliefs flowed from his sense of the injustice of poverty, which far more than any belief in the principles of scientific socialism had drawn him into the Labour Party.

Attlee and his generation were really nineteenth-century Whigs and their colonial policy was conceived in this vein. By no means convinced of the inherent value of territorial empire, they were none the less sure of the doctrine of the white man's burden. Pondering the possibility that Britain might be forced to take over some of Italy's colonies after the war, Attlee wrote: 'Why should it be assumed that only a few Great Powers can be entrusted with backward peoples? Why should not one or other of the Scandinavian countries have a try? They are quite as fitted to bear rule as ourselves. Why not the United States?'[2] The even-handedness of this thinking towards Europeans is as striking as its insistence on the category 'backward peoples'. In a similar exercise of doublethink, Herbert Morrison, the rumbustious foreign secretary, had declared: 'we have ceased to be an imperialist race', whilst adding in the same breath that Labour was a great friend to the 'jolly old Empire'. Arthur Creech Jones at the Colonial Office reckoned that the continuation of British imperialism was not problematic because America effectively had an empire in the West Indies, Hawaii and the Philippines, 'not to mention her internal race problem'.

Labour's paternalism was not undiscriminating. Government ministers took it for granted that Indians deserved more respect than other Asian peoples, especially Burmese and Malays, let alone Africans. They had mixed with the likes of Jawaharlal Nehru and Krishna Menon, the Indian National Congress's roving ambassador, who were Fabian socialists like themselves. Stafford Cripps was committed to constitutional change in India, since this had been the message during his abortive mission in 1942 when he had sought to bring the Congress into the wartime government. Attlee's connections went back even further. He had been a member of another ill-fated constitutional investigation, the Simon Commission of 1927–9, which had similarly ended in mass civil disobedience. Yet even in the case of India, the Labour ministers still seem to have expected that the country would remain a dominion of the crown, and one with which Britain had continuing military ties. As for other peoples – Burmese, Malays, Arabs and Africans – they might well require decades more imperial tutelage before they could emerge into the light of freedom and democracy.

In the two years following the end of the Second World War socialist paternalism was in the ascendant in Britain. But other, more conservative shades of British opinion also helped maintain a fragile imperial consensus. This was the era of moral rearmament and Christian service was to be an ever-present if often unacknowledged motivator of the Empire's war against communism and radical nationalism in several parts of the globe in the later 1940s and 1950s. The adjutant-general of the post-war Indian Army endorsed a paper on 'Religion in the army' by its chaplain-general. It was essential to teach religion to British personnel in India because, it stated, the 'effect on the spirit of empire as a whole will be immense'. On Christianity would depend the 'future of our race'.[3] In the Colonial Office, civil servants contemplating the rebuilding of empire in Southeast Asia invoked 'the Stewardship which God has entrusted to our Nation'. Was not the British Commonwealth an expression of the 'Brotherhood of Man'?[4] Secular reform was couched in terms of a 'civilising mission'. But there were problems with this kind of language. In 1945 the British Empire governed more Muslims than any other power in history.

The Conservative opposition to imperial retreat was even more adamant. Churchill, the valiant fighter for the free nations of Europe, had never believed that that freedom should extend to the coloured races. Privately he had specifically excluded them from the Atlantic Charter of 1941, that great Anglo-American clarion cry for freedom which had so raised expectations across the colonial world. Churchill had mused to Wavell about the possibility of dividing the Indian empire into 'Pakistan, Hindustan and Princestan', the last an amalgam of India's princely states. The first and the third of these entities would remain within the British Empire no matter what happened to the 'Hindoo priesthood machine' and its commercial backers.[5] Churchill's parting shot to Wavell, on the viceroy's visit to London in August 1945, was 'keep a bit of India!'[6] Anthony Eden, a powerful Conservative foreign relations expert, feared that the loss of Malaya with its rich resources of tin and rubber and of Hong Kong with its strategic position would reduce Britain to the status of a 'bagman' east of Suez. Far from believing that British rule in India was inevitably coming towards its end, many Conservative politicians, quite apart from the obdurate Churchill, believed that the Raj should continue to function in one way or another. Harold Macmillan, a man later considered a moderate Tory, thought that national servicemen might be sent to hold India. He recorded in his diary his astonishment that the viceroy considered that British rule could be re-established in the subcontinent with a mere five divisions of troops and 1,000 extra administrators. This was nothing to what the British were doing in 'Germany, Trieste, Greece and Palestine', where large new administrations had been put in place.[7]

With many Labour and Liberal MPs undecided and the Conservatives generally opposed, the political consensus in 1945 for Indian independence was fragile. Only with hindsight has it seemed a sure thing. This helps to explain why the Indian National Congress was so suspicious of British intentions, a suspicion that ultimately led them to accept the partition of India rather than trust British good offices. Even if successive British cabinets had made vague promises about freedom after the war, the senior leadership of the Congress, especially Jawaharlal Nehru and Vallabhbhai Patel, were wholly unconvinced. They believed that the British were still playing a game of 'divide and rule' and that Wavell was privately building up Mahomed Ali Jinnah's Muslim League against them. The result would be a 'Balkanization' of India into a host of fragments that the British could easily manipulate: some kind of Muslim 'Pakistan', semi-independent princely states with treaties with the British crown and, possibly, an independent Bengal.

If Britain's grip on the subcontinent should weaken, the great arc of empire could still be anchored in Southeast Asia. On this, if nothing else, the consensus in Westminster was solid. The region was now crucial to Britain's Great Power status. Malaya was the 'dollar arsenal' of the sterling area, and Singapore was destined to become more of a 'fortress' than ever it was before the war. But reconstruction was not seen in solely material terms. Britain had to rebuild her moral authority: the humiliation of 1942 was to be redeemed by the creation of new model colonies. For over a decade Malaya and Singapore were to be subjected to some of the most ambitious projects of political development and social engineering in British imperial history. As a first step, reform-minded civil servants in Whitehall seized the opportunity to realize a long-cherished ambition: the ten different authorities which constituted British Malaya were to be ruled directly for the first time. A Malayan Union was to be created, under the British crown, and united by a common citizenship. At a stroke, this overturned the founding principles of British Malaya: that of the sovereign independence of the Malay rulers and the privileged position of the Malays. With the memory of the final squalid exodus from Singapore never far from the surface, the new watchword was 'multi-racialism'.

One of the few senior Malayan civil servants to be included in these discussions was Dr Victor Purcell. Aged forty-nine, he was an influential voice in the Malayan Planning Unit in London that developed the new policy from mid 1943, and adviser on Chinese Affairs to Mountbatten's military administration. 'The rigid pro-Malay attitude', Purcell wrote, 'was more often than not a paternalistic feeling towards the Malays (and occasionally it was homosexual)', but it was not universally shared. The Malayan Civil Service was 'virtually split . . . into two camps'.[8] Purcell was a scholar-administrator of a special kind: as a cadet he was sent to Canton to learn Chinese dialects and put to work in Malaya as a 'protector' of Chinese. This was a personage unique in British colonial history; the protector acted as *tai-jin*, a great panjandrum to every level of Chinese society: banqueting with tycoons, suppressing secret societies and traffic in women, even mediating in marital rows. From Purcell's perspective, the 'fiction of a "*Malay*" Malaya had become a farce'. At the last census of the peninsula in 1931, of a population of 3.79 million, 49 per cent were classified as Malays, as against 34 per cent Chinese and 15 per cent Indians. If the overwhelmingly Chinese city of Singapore was included, the Malays were reduced to only 44 per cent of the population. They were, as Malay poets lamented, a minority in their own country. British patronage, Purcell argued, was a 'gilded insult' to the Malays and held them back. The system whereby the Malays were governed through sultans, and the Chinese and Indians hardly at all, merely encouraged their 'separatist tendencies'. As one of the leading advocates of change put it: 'We want to fully develop the plural society.'[9] Assuming that Mountbatten would have to fight his way back into Malaya, the Colonial Office for the first time was making an active bid for the support of the non-Malays.

The Malayan Union was seen as a first step to 'self-government', if not full independence. The time-scale of what Labour ministers called colonial 'partnership' was entirely open ended. It was axiomatic to the British that before the war there was no local patriotism in Malaya. Dressed in the borrowed robes of nationalism, the British would now create it. After 1945 the fashioning of a 'Malayan' national identity became the lodestar of imperial policy. Until this point the term 'Malayan' had no legal status; it was neither a census category nor a synonym for 'Malay'. Yet the word had taken on a more fixed meaning in the inter-war years to refer to those people who were locally domiciled and who did not perhaps retain any overriding loyalty to their country of origin, and it was adopted in particular by English-educated Eurasians, Straits Chinese and some Indians.[10] As the future of Malaya was debated in London, the European ex-residents of the Association of British Malaya also staked their claim: 'For all intents and purposes we are Malaya.'[11] What was now called 'nation-building' was taken up with an evangelical fervour by a post-war generation of British officials and educators.

But it was unclear as to what a 'Malayan' nation might be founded upon. The idea seemed not to relate to any one ethnic group, but had to encompass all of them. The British tended to see it, as they preferred to see all colonial nationalism, in terms of the culture of a responsible middle class, united by English education and the values it carried. The language of Shakespeare, the King James Bible and the Atlantic Charter was the key to multiracial harmony and to colonial peoples' continuing loyalty to the British Commonwealth. This vision was to collide violently with other nations of intent. But it was a bold experiment: Victor Purcell was adamant that the 'utmost freedom' be allowed so that political parties could emerge and 'achieve a balance of power amongst themselves'. The draconian laws that controlled speech, publication, assembly, societies and trade unions, were all to be suspended. This was to herald Britain's liberal intentions. But, as Purcell made clear, it was also to honour the bargain struck in the jungle between John Davis and 'Chang Hong'. For the first time in its history the Malayan Communist Party was coming out into the open.

'BLACK MARKET ADMINISTRATION'

The British Military Administration (BMA) of Malaya was a khaki-clad revolution in government, the most direct form of rule that Malaya had experienced in its history. It united Malaya and Singapore as never before and took on functions that were entirely novel in a colonial context: refugee and relief work; food rationing and nutrition; social welfare and public relations. Yet for 208 days after 4 September 1945, the BMA operated in conditions where in many places the apparatus of state had all but broken down, or where people had opted out of it entirely. Ralph Hone, former head of the Malayan Planning Unit and now Chief Civil Affairs Officer, was to claim that 'no single problem arose when Malaya was occupied which had not already been considered by the planning staff'.[12] Yet he was desperately short of resources and expertise. Hone himself, although he had been legal adviser to a government of occupation in Italy's African colonies, which he took as a model, had never visited Malaya, nor had much practical experience of administration. His team was reinforced by junior army officers, who were also new to empire and to Asia, and who had received only a crash course in local topography, the Malay language and the Indian penal code at a police college in Wimbledon.[13] By this route, in the final years of British Asia, new kinds of men and women entered imperial service, who had a different class and educational outlook to the 'high born' civil servants of the pre-war days. But the local knowledge that was acquired in the first few weeks began to drain away once demobilization began in November; the new temporary drafts were often disinterested and disillusioned by their role. And by its very nature, military government proved to be a wholly inadequate agent of liberal, democratic reform.

The charter of the BMA was to prevent the outbreak of 'disease and disorder'. But it was overwhelmed by the magnitude of Malaya's crisis. The devastation began at the dockside. The naval base at Sembawang in Singapore lay in ruins, incinerated in the Allies' scorched-earth retreat of 1942. The 50,000-ton floating dock was lying on the bottom of the Straits of Johore with a tanker sunk inside it: it would take over five years to rebuild it.[14] Inland the landscape was, at every turn, scarred by war. Fearing the escalation of air raids on Singapore, the Japanese had burrowed tunnels deep into ridges and hillsides. All available land – the public parks, playing fields and tennis courts – was given over to vegetables and rows of tapioca, the ubiquitous, despised staple food of the war years. Other open areas had become vast dumps for looted or destroyed equipment. There were hoards of incongruous commodities. As the civil engineer O. W. Gilmour made an inventory of the island, he discovered in a rubber plantation some sixteen brick warehouses, each 100 feet long, by 24 feet wide and 20 feet high. They were full of leather saddles, bridles, straps, holsters and harnesses, enough 'to equip all the cavalrymen and cowboys left in the world, and that in a country where a horse is a curiosity'.[15] As the Japanese struck camp, few buildings were left guarded, and looters moved into abandoned houses and offices. Upcountry, the pickings were richer: stockpiles of food, rubber and tin were collected by armed gangs.

Peninsular Malaya had taken a step backwards from the industrial age. None of the great tin dredges were working; Chinese mine-owners complained that their businesses were stripped of machinery and motors. Much of the rubber plantation land was overrun by either food production or weeds. At the liberation Guthrie, one of the largest rubber companies, had only six experienced planters to husband over 155,000 acres of rubber trees.[16] Electricity supplies would not meet demand until 1949 and transportation had all but broken down. The east coast was cut off from the rest of the country because the railway line from Kuala Lumpur had been stripped of track to lay the Burma–Siam railway. This left Kelantan virtually isolated in the monsoon season. Outside the towns, the roads were pitted and unsafe. Cars and lorries were at a premium; the army was forced to issue orders that its men should not drive out alone, because so many of their vehicles were immediately stolen when left unattended. For most people cheap Japanese-made bicycles were now the only viable form of transport. The British estimate of war damage was a staggering £127 million, the total costs incalculable.[17]

At every turn, the British were confronted by the human debris of war. Thousands of people were without shelter, or stranded far from home. Javanese *romusha* (forced labourers) haunted Singapore, they gathered around the railway station, in the eyes of one witness, 'half-dead like skeletons . . . like in Germany, half-starved like. And some of them, their legs dangling, sitting down, their legs hanging down the sides of the train, and load[ed] like sheep inside.' By the end of 1945, there were still 18,000 of them in Malaya.[18] Singapore was dangerously overcrowded, and life was a constant scramble for space. Even before the war its urban population density had been between 500 and 900 persons an acre; now it took 'tea money' of $100 to secure a lease for a room, $1,000 for a house. And still more people were arriving, as Chinese fled from ethnic fighting in Johore and Indonesia.[19] Soon after his arrival in Singapore, the agent of the government of India, S. K. Chettur, made a 'hurricane tour' of the west coast of the peninsula, visiting rubber estates and interviewing Indian labourers by the wayside. After the general collapse of industrial exports Indians had been easy prey for Japanese forced-labour schemes. Of the estimated 72,204 labourers sent from Malaya to Burma and Thailand, 29,634 were reported to have died and 24,626 'deserted'; many of this number were lost in the jungle, or disguised in the statistics of fatalities in the camps. The impact on small estate communities was traumatic: over 40 per cent of the labour in rubber areas such as Selangor had vanished, and everywhere Chettur reported the absence of menfolk who either 'never returned or returned broken men'.[20] A 'citizen's advice bureau' in Singapore, staffed by local community leaders, was inundated with thousands of appeals from desperate families; it despatched Chinese businessmen with experience of trading in Thailand to locate refugees. But by the end of 1945 there were still believed to be 6,500 Malayans in South Thailand and another 23,000 around Bangkok.[21] Some took years to return.

The missing haunted the post-war years, their suffering unrecorded in the official documents. It is clear that the British were aware of forced sexual slavery in Japanese-occupied Malaya and Singapore: escapees spoke of it, as did reports from local police officers.[22] Soldiers began to find more evidence, but the Japanese were covering their tracks. At the hill resort of the Cameron Highlands, for example, some girls were found in a former convent: the Japanese colonel passed them off as convalescent pulmonary tuberculosis cases, but it was clear that they were there under coercion as 'comfort women'. In cases like this, British soldiers would transport the women to the main towns, but then they often disappeared from view. Press pictures sent home to Britain of Malayan women and their babies liberated in the Andaman Islands had a description of them as 'comfort women' excised by the military censor.[23] Half a century later, the full story of the 'comfort women' had yet to be told. Many of the girls, recruited locally, could not return to their families for shame of what had happened to them and fear of rejection.[24] The social welfare officers who arrived with the BMA were aware of these women, but the military were unable to discern the nature of the 'comfort women' system, and unequipped to deal with mass rape. They saw the problem as one of 'rehabilitation' of prostitutes. But an attempt to use welfare homes run by the Chinese community for the 'reclamation' of fallen women, the Po Leung Kuk, collapsed because victims were repelled by the stigma it carried. The British fell back on the view that those who were not going into prostitution had rehabilitated themselves and that the others were already prostitutes.[25] This abandoned many young girls to the insidious free market in women. As Victor Purcell acknowledged, 'the facts, as known, would bring the government into grave disrepute. Girls of 10–15 are suffering from venereal disease.'[26]

The experience of war was etched in people's faces. With the collapse of food exports from Burma and Thailand, Malaya's rice bowl was broken. The British shouldered the massive responsibility of distributing and rationing supplies, through relief in cash and kind and public canteens on the lines of the spartan wartime 'British restaurants' at home. But the government failed in one of its most fundamental tasks: it could not import enough rice to feed its people. By December the average individual ration was a mere 4.5 ounces a day, and not everyone received it. The British, like the Japanese before them, campaigned to get people to eat more tapioca and grow more food. But as it was, Malay peasants said that they could not bring in the harvest as the women who did most of the work had no clothes to wear. The opening up of new land often meant encroaching on the forest, and the forest could strike back: marauding boars and elephants ruined rice crops. The rare Malayan tiger was more often seen. In one village in Malacca, eighteen people were taken by crocodiles in one year. Pioneers opened up badly drained areas where the *Anopheline malculatus* mosquito thrived and malaria was endemic. There was, doctors warned, little point asking people to open up land for food crops 'if it was merely to provide a grave for the occupants'. In the towns the need for food was such that there was even a brisk market in 'night soil' – human waste – as fertilizer for vegetable farms. Fragile mechanisms of disease control were breaking down: there were outbreaks of cholera and doctors felt a rise in tuberculosis might be 'the worst aftermath of war'.[27] S. K. Chettur enraged local opinion by reporting back to India that famine did not exist in Malaya. This was technically true, but the full effects of the shortages were disguised. Nutritionists reported that Indian labour was incapacitated by beriberi and tropical sores. Malaya escaped the horror that was visited upon Bengal in 1943, but by a narrow margin, and lived with its effects for many years. The growth of an entire generation was stunted – little difference could be discerned between children aged 6–9 and those aged 10–14 – and there was 'permanent damage to the working capacity of the population as whole'.[28]

The military now demanded vast regiments of local labour for the docks, airfields and roads. But families could not survive on wages set at a pre-war rate, when cheap food had been taken for granted. European employers complained that workers had lost the habit of toil, and turned to old methods of recruiting and disciplining them, particularly by engaging them through labour contractors. This was bitterly resented: contractors took a cut of their workers' pay, and ensnared them in debt for the supply of their basic necessities. People remembered the contractors who dragooned labour for the Japanese, but the BMA took them on with few questions asked.[29] By the end of the year it had become the biggest single employer Malaya had ever seen, with some 102,000 people on its books in Singapore alone.[30] Such was the demand for labour that 1,500 Indian, brought back to Singapore from the Burma–Siam railway by the military, were classed as 'essential persons' and put back to work in the shipyards.[31] As an incentive to toil, the BMA took the extraordinary step of importing 50 million grains of opium into Malaya for issue over a six-month period. This was classed as 'a military necessity'. The opium appeared in early October in the form of distinctively coloured tablets, marked as a government monopoly.[32] This was a clear breach of international

agreements; the Tokyo War Crimes Tribunal would put great emphasis on Japanese culpability in the Asian narcotics trade. The illegal
traffic also revived. In mid November one smuggling syndicate staged
several days of theatrical shows in thanksgiving for the arrival of three
ships bearing over 3,000lb of opium. 'There is a sigh about the lack
of rice', a Chinese newspaper correspondent commented, 'but the
"black rice" which is strictly forbidden by the government seems to
be able to come in continuously . . . This is indeed Heaven helping the
lucky man.'[33]

Fortunes were lost and made overnight. One of the British government's first proclamations was to announce that the Japanese wartime
currency would not be recognized. This was an exceptional step,
intended to sow confusion behind Japanese lines; it reaped chaos for
the people of Malaya. In the interregnum, the Japanese money kept
some of its value as people hurriedly sold off hidden hoards of Straits
dollars to pay off debts in the Japanese 'banana money'.[34] But when
Japanese themselves offloaded their freshly minted notes, it soon
became worthless: 'Everywhere', one Chinese trader observed, 'you
find the Japanese notes everywhere – along the roadside, five-foot
ways, people just throw them away.'[35] A petition to the government
described the resulting hysteria: 'Many civilians have registered their
names with the lunatic asylum, commit suicide and daylight robbery
due to the non-recognition.'[36] The Malayan Communist Party was
reported to have lost most of its funds. Mountbatten was furious: the
policy was, he said, 'un-British and disastrous to our reputation for
fair play'.[37] The British put Straits dollars into circulation by issuing
cash relief and advances on salaries, and a surprising amount of
pre-war money came out of holes in the ground. The transience of
wealth was inseparable in the popular imagination with the prolifera-
tion of open gambling in the streets. But a more abiding legacy was a
lingering suspicion of paper money, particularly among peasants who
were reluctant to part with their rice crops for cash at the low official
prices; they bartered or put it on the black market. Weimar-proportion
price inflation resulted: rice was now at thirty to forty times its pre-war
price, and banana and sweet potato skins were sold as staples in the
markets.

The black economy eclipsed the old colonial economy almost

entirely. It was a parallel world that reached from maritime trade to industrial production on the forest frontier. Quiet tropical islands such as Karimun, just southwest of Singapore, suddenly became chaotic 'free ports' for the smugglers' trade from Thailand, Sumatra and Java. Pirates staged audacious raids on Penang island. Taking advantage of the liberal policy towards societies, the Ang Bin Hoay brotherhood united the notorious gangs of Penang and, by the end of the year, mass initiation ceremonies – involving hundreds at a time – were held in the Relau hills. Lorries cruised through the streets of George Town, picking up men with cries of 'This way for the Show!' and 'Any more for the hills?'[38] During the BMA period, 600 murders were reported and 470 instances of gang robbery, as against thirteen in 1939. Before the war the British had governed this volatile world at a distance. Labour had been controlled principally by employers and contractors. But the European managers had disappeared and many Chinese industrialists fled abroad. Those who remained had found it difficult to refuse to join Japanese-sponsored community organizations, and now carried the stain of collaboration. They lost considerable prestige; some retired from public life altogether, or had to struggle to regain their standing in the community. The power of the *towkays* was weakest in the countryside, where, for a time, the rule of the bosses was broken.

The production of strategic commodities such as rubber, tin and timber was taken over by the informal economy. Rubber was collected on a 'self-tap, self-sell' basis. An everyday sight around mining pools was large numbers of women panning for ore, a process known as *dulang* washing. There were violent confrontations when the police tried to stop it. Gangs of 'democratic workmen' elected their own bosses and demanded logging rights. Chinese peasants moved onto disused plantation land or forest reserve. The first British visitors to reach these areas were grudgingly impressed. 'Although these people may be given to gang robbery', a forester wrote in his diary, 'they are nevertheless remarkably good gardeners.'[39] Townsfolk were almost entirely dependent on their terraces of vegetables and tobacco. Many labour and forest departments and district and land offices had ceased to function. But to the British these people were illegal 'squatters', and as order slowly returned they came into conflict with the colonial regime and European rubber planters. Foresters were 'constantly being threatened with calamity', and in October two were killed trying to prevent some Chinese from felling timber.[40] For the first time the squatters – slash-and-burn farmers, freewheeling tappers and loggers, 'wild rat' miners and charcoal burners, illicit distillers and wild-game hunters – had political muscle and military backing. Kuomintang guerrillas still controlled most of the routes across the Thai border, and in the squatter hamlets and small towns it was the fighters of the MPAJA who were the law. Those *towkays* brave enough to restart their business paid them 'taxes'. Large tracts of the peninsula – including much of the central range – were no-go areas for Europeans: a state within a state. There were around half a million 'squatters' in Malaya, one in five of the population.

The British were desperate to put the legitimate economy back to work. They flew in leading Chinese financiers from exile in India as 'sponsored civilians' to reopen the banks. The European businessmen who were still awaiting repatriation resented their head start. The old network of Teochew merchants revived the junk trade with Siam. Although loans were scarce, for a businessmen with cash there were tremendous new opportunities. By the age of twenty-five, the Chinese trader Ang Keong Lan had acquired $50 million by trading pigs for copra and castor oil with the Japanese. He was slow to sell on his 'banana' currency, and had to exchange it at $10,000 to the Straits dollar. Still he managed to bounce back: he obtained a motorboat and, with the connivance of customs men, was able to trade flour and cigarettes from Singapore to Penang, where they fetched a much higher price. It was slow business, but in this way Ang laid the foundation of a business empire – the Joo Seng Group – that would extend from trade to banking and insurance.[41] The Japanese military government was staffed by businessmen and run for profit, and had brought the worlds of money and administration closer together. After the liberation, commercial success remained conditional on squaring police officers and customs officials.

The BMA evolved into a form of what was later to be called 'crony capitalism'. In its transit camp in India, officers were overheard to regret the delay of Operation Zipper because 'there would not be any loot left'.[42] Wherever British and Commonwealth troops were deployed, graft followed them. The Sydney police warned British commanders in Japan that Australian criminals were enlisting solely to get at the black market opportunities.[43] Ralph Hone himself later admitted that his officers were among the systematic offenders. Many British businessmen from the pre-war days were now in uniform, and in this, as one Penang newssheet remarked acidly, 'they have found an ideal combination'. New arrivals cheerfully accepted treating and pleasing from local businessmen, and some connived in local scams. Military stores and 'rehabilitation' goods disappeared en route to Malaya, or were landed in the wrong place; in the docks, goods vanished, invoices never appeared, or when they did, charges were paid three times over. This was known locally as 'the multi-million scandal' and, when an audit report finally appeared two years later, the scale of the losses from short deliveries, looting and pilfering was over $15 million. The BMA officers' mess at Fu Court in Singapore was, reported one old Malaya hand, H. T. Pagden, 'full of such loot'.[44] The British practice was to give a commodity to a company to distribute, and there were kickbacks right down the line to the distributors' agents and salesmen.[45] Competition between suppliers forced up the price of sweeteners. Even when BMA supplied its own transport to move vegetables to break the black market, food control officers charged for access to the lorries, and the drivers charged 'tea money' to the suppliers. Yet traders were still willing to pay as there were profits of 1,000 per cent to be had.[46] The NAAFI was notoriously venal; one case alone – which was prosecuted – involved the robbery of £20,000 worth of cigarettes; service goods were sold openly in the market at Petaling Street in Kuala Lumpur, and Indian soldiers levied a toll on the transport of pigs and other foodstuffs to Singapore.[47] It was reported in Ipoh that merchants could not even get their calls connected at the telephone exchange without being asked for a 'loan' by the operators.[48] The notoriety of the 'banana colonels' and 'banana majors' of the BMA struck a savage blow at the reputation for clean, impartial government that the British were so anxious to maintain. It gave further encouragement to people to avoid government altogether. As the Chinese proverb observed: 'Don't enter a government office with no money even if you are right.'[49]

At a fundamental level, British rule had lost its legitimacy. The first men ashore put a great deal of store in the spontaneous celebrations and the loyal processions that had greeted them. O. W. Gilmour rejoiced to be welcomed at his old house in Singapore by his gardener, his driver and his cook. That the leaden paternalism of the British was preferable to the arbitrary violence and psychological trauma of Japanese rule was a point few Malayans, of the middle classes at least, would dispute. For this reason, most of them deferred to the old hierarchy. But Asian civil servants resented that the fact that they had stayed at the posts, when the Europeans had not, was interpreted by their British masters as unquestioning 'empire loyalty'. Malayans who had kept basic services going were roughly pushed aside. One leading Chinese doctor, Benjamin Chew, who had kept a tuberculosis ward going at Tan Tock Seng hospital in Singapore, was told by a British medical officer, 'Chew, your cases can go into the streets.' Dr Chew left the government service in disgust.[50] The 'colour bar' was restored at its pre-war level. One of 'sponsored civilians' brought in from India by the BMA was the Selangor mining tycoon H. S. Lee. He was one of the first of the China-born *towkays* to be educated at Cambridge University, and had the honorary rank of colonel in the Nationalist Chinese Army. But on his first arrival back in Malaya he experienced crude racial affronts. As a BMA officer he was entitled to buy NAAFI goods at a service price, but was refused them on the grounds that he was Chinese. 'I can hardly believe', he wrote to Victor Purcell, 'that racial discrimination still exists.'[51] The general responsible was challenged on this. He did not deny the discrimination, his argument being, Purcell was told by a sympathetic colleague, 'that whisky is not a natural part of the standard of living of a Chinese. I agreed with him that they preferred brandy, but as that is not obtainable they are prepared to put up with whisky as a second-best.'[52] These slights would never be forgotten by the individuals who suffered them.

The second colonial conquest was more aggressive than the first. 'The army', wrote H. T. Pagden, 'behaved as if they were in conquered territory.' Singapore became a staging post for hundreds of thousands of men in uniform shipping to points further east, and this soon deflated any sense of elation that war was now over. At the beginning of December, at huge expense, Mountbatten moved the HQ of South East Asia Command to Singapore. He took the city's landmark skyscraper, the Cathay Building, as his offices. It had many associations with the war, as a Japanese headquarters and where, in its auditorium, Subhas Chandra Bose declared a government of Free India. The supremo's personal staff was regal in scale: the previous year it reached 7,000 people. The military requisitioned 2,227 houses and 51 institutions and clubs, and they took the best: navy officers messed in the Adelphi Hotel and the RAPWI organization at the Goodwood Park. Even the luxury department stores in Raffles Place – Little's and Robinson's – were taken over by the NAAFI; the elite Singapore Cricket Club became the Army YMCA. By contrast, Raffles Hotel was a dismal haunt for European refugees and ex-internees. The military soon became unpopular with the locals for forcing up prices still further. But the good life for which the Singapore garrison had been famous in 1941 began to revive: roadside cafés sprang up, with 'singers and young girls acting as waitresses; and beer drinking. There were no holds barred.'[53] The senior civil affairs officer on the island called the extravagant public entertainments 'nothing short of criminal', and Mountbatten was compelled to issue draconian standing orders for a curfew on other ranks, the closure of service bars and clubs by midnight, a ban on meals or drinks in civilian-run establishments and detailed checks on bad traffic discipline.[54] This was mostly on the part of Indian drivers who had learned to drive in the desert of North Africa or the dirt-tracks of Burma, but it seemed to symbolize the arrogance of the new regime. In the words of one Chinese newspaper, people saw military vehicles 'as snakes and scorpions, and streets and thoroughfares as hells'.[55]

Attlee took a personal interest in the morale of army personnel. The BBC Home Service was urged to broadcast encouragement to people to keep a constant flow of letters posted to serving men who now had time on their hands, time to brood. One of the first units into liberated Malaya was an advance party of ENSA, the armed forces' entertainments association. By the fourth day of reoccupation they were giving an impromptu performance to the POWs in Changi: Gracie Fields appeared there on 1 October. They reclaimed the Victoria Theatre on Singapore's Esplanade – killing around 5,000 swallows who had roosted there throughout the Japanese occupation – for John Gielgud to perform his *Hamlet*.[56] But what was on offer fell far short of what was desired by weary, frustrated men. Malaya's allocation of 15–16,000 barrels of beer a month was well below the target of 25,200 for the NAAFI canteens.[57] Soldiers turned to other diversions. One unit in Ipoh discovered an antiquated provision in the King's Regulations for fodder for horses, and they used this to resurrect the Perak Turf Club. The first race meeting was on Boxing Day 1945. It drew a bigger crowd than the victory parades, and made a considerable profit for the British 'owners' of the horses.[58] But such events made a mockery of the BMA's calls for people to be patient in the face of scarcity. 'We ask for bread', the Malaya Tribune remarked, 'and we are given . . . horse-racing!'[59]

Men gravitated to the dance halls and to the kupu-kupu malam, the 'night butterflies', who were everywhere to be seen in Malayan towns. The dramatic post-war increase in prostitution was rooted in coercion, trafficking and poverty. It was perpetuated by a lack of education and alternatives, and aggravated, particularly within the Malay community, by chronically high levels of divorce.[60] It was now seen by military commanders as 'a real danger to the health of troops'. In 1943, casualties from VD within SEAC were sixteen times greater than those in battle. By early 1946 the rate of infection in the military peaked at 7.2 per cent. Some service chiefs wanted to revive the nineteenth-century Indian Army remedy of regulating the trade in controlled lal, or 'red' bazaars, but welfare workers argued that the only course was to raid the brothels and bring more women to treatment.[61] There was some success in this, but in the long term, police officers were unwilling to take responsibility for it because 'there was too much money to be made by junior police officers'.[62] Women were often the first victims of war, and now among the first casualties of peace. People noticed that there was a discomforting continuity between the sexual violence of Japanese occupation and the new red-light economy and air of sexual predation in the garrison towns. From October the Chinese press published a catalogue of reports of robberies and rapes around Ipoh, Kuala Lumpur and Klang. Stalls were attacked and taxi drivers beaten up by drunken soldiers. Many of these incidents involved British servicemen, but the worst of the accusations fell on common outsiders: Indian soldiers. They were increasingly unpopular, especially when the British used them to break strikes. Indians called in to maintain the coal mine at Batu Arang were accused by the communists of molesting women as they tended to their food crops.[63] There were other reports: for example, of a man shot trying to stop a rape in Morib; women attacked cutting timber, and of a reported 'unnatural offence' against a young boy in Ulu Salong.[64] Near Taiping, it was said that a Chinese girl was taken in a lorry and repeatedly raped in a barracks. She, like others it seems, was afraid of coming forward.[65] By the end of the year only one case of sexual assault had gone to courts martial. Victor Purcell confronted military commanders with this, and warned them that the incidents were being covered up.[66] The public came to their own bitter conclusions. As the leftist Kuala Lumpur daily *Min Sheng Pau* put it: 'Now there is no distinction between Japanese fascists' outrages and those of the present Indian soldiers.'[67]

As the reputation and moral authority of the military regime began to disintegrate, it established the first 'public relations department' in Asia. Initially it was used to monitor press opinion and to dispel rumours. Letters to Malay village headmen in the 'best Malay traditional style' helped damp down ethnic tensions. Then it launched campaigns of mass education to improve people's diets and combat inflation: 'A dollar is always a dollar. It becomes smaller because people are spending it in a *ti-da-apa* [carefree] way.' The accompanying slogan – 'Goods are coming. Don't buy now!' – was an easy target for satire: a better message, one Chinese newspaper suggested, might be: 'Don't eat now!' or 'Don't live now!'.[68] As the British became more aware of the impact of three and a half years of Japanese anti-Western indoctrination, they responded with exhibitions and lectures on the war, reading rooms, public address vans, travelling theatre and Chinese story-tellers, and even a film studio. Victor Purcell himself had run a smaller information bureau before the fall of Singapore. Many old Malaya hands, he complained, disapproved, calling it 'meretricious, loud and ungentlemanly (which of course it was)'. This was a dramatic change in the way colonial rule manifested itself and 'PR' was now a permanent arm of government. The British saw themselves as impresarios of public opinion and in active competition with the local press and political parties. By early 1946 the department had distributed 140,000 posters and notices of a 'political nature'.

But the senior Malay officials involved felt they were a waste of effort. The people of Malaya were speaking very different languages of politics.[69]

A WORLD UPSIDE DOWN

'When we arrived', O. W. Gilmour observed, 'everything had stopped. There was no money, no public transport, no Post Office services, no newspapers, no trade, no courts of justice, and to all intents and purposes no police protection.' The Asian banks opened on 12 September and the British banks on 1 October. The Post Office ran a free letter service from 17 September – even the Singapore Museum reopened on 12 September. Much of this, as Gilmour claimed, was to the credit of the BMA, and achieved at the price of the 'sickness and partial breakdown' of many of its officers. When, on 5 September, he first turned on the switches and taps in the Singapore Municipal Building, there was light and water but the electrical power supply in Singapore was strained beyond capacity, and as Gilmour investigated further, he discovered that an entirely new system had come into being:

Inside many houses, long lengths of flex made spider's webs connecting every type of electrical gadgets, wires in hundreds emerged from windows and doors to hawkers' stalls and outside lights of every description. Many hundreds or thousands of people had connected their supplies to the mains outside the meters, and, over all consumption, there was a light-hearted irresponsibility. Wires lights and gadgets entwined buildings in the town with a gay abandon and one judged that many a suburban house had been combed to make a down-town display.[70]

A transfer of power had taken place, in all senses. For three and a half years, Malaya had its own form of black market administration.

The invisible cities that had arisen in the shadow of the old colonial towns had come into the light. During the war, the focus of much of urban life had gravitated towards the new Asian urban settlements on the fringes of towns such as Singapore, Kuala Lumpur, Penang and Ipoh. They were at a safer remove from the settlements of Japanese, and closer to opportunities for small-scale cultivation and trade. They were worlds of constant change and movement, a place where migrants – often young, unmarried men and women – might lodge and begin to make their way in the towns. There was poverty, risk and danger here – armed men still roamed the streets – but also opportunity. The new middle class of clerks, skilled labourers and entrepreneurs could acquire some property and standing; in the war urban land was the surest form of investment. These settlements were villages within the city, but entirely adapted to it. For Mustapha Hussain, Kampong Baru, the Malay 'New Village' near the heart of Kuala Lumpur where he brought his family to live in a small room after he lost his job with the British, eking out a living as a seller of *sotong bakar* (highly-spiced grilled dried squid), was a place to regain some freedom. Although these village-cities were often a patchwork of ethnic enclaves, settlement demarcations became blurred. This was a rich environment where communities met, often for the first time, and with no language in common, learned to communicate, borrowing services, forging trust and, over time, sharing a popular culture.

One of the first writers to attempt to describe this was Chin Kee Onn, a Chinese schoolteacher from Ipoh who had worked for the Japanese military administration in Perak. His *Malaya Upside Down*, published in 1946 and reprinted twice in its first year, was a darkly humorous account of the tragedies, absurdities and social transformations of the war. It recounted events which people had witnessed only in fragments or heard through rumour. The war years, Chin wrote, were 'a muddled hallucination conjured by some super-surrealist imp in which hordes of dwarfs suddenly became bloodcurdling ogres, turning everything topsy-turvy . . .' Men of high standing, civil servants and lawyers, had joined the ranks of the urban poor. The emblem of bourgeois status, the neck-tie, was abandoned. In the Japanese regime, those who made money were not the tycoons 'of the Rolls-Royce type. They were humble-looking and inconspicuous rice importers, fishermen, tobacco manufacturers, oil millers, hardware dealers and gambling-stall owners!' Now status was entirely precarious: war was a great leveller. 'The prevailing style of dress for men in this period', Chin wrote, 'consisted of an open-collar shirt with breast pockets, "shorts" or long trousers and rubber sandals or slippers, without socks.'[71] This simple style was adopted by a new generation of young urban activists; and the open-necked, short-sleeved shirt became a uniform for would-be politicians. In the war, there was little privacy; in a time of informers, solitude invited suspicion; in a time of hunger, survival demanded that life be lived in the open. Thousands of women – refugees, mothers and children without a male provider, homeless Cantonese *amahs*, house servants and housewives – took to hawking in the streets and parks. Once it would have been shameful for a bourgeois to be seen eating in public; now everybody ate by the wayside, and mingled in the impromptu markets. People of all ranks approached one another with ease. The cosmopolitan energy of the village-city was turned inwards, and new solidarities were being formed across Malaya's 'plural society'.

And in late 1945, after the years of fear and austerity, and despite the continuing shortages, the cities and towns came dramatically to life. The barometers of urban life in Malaya were the Worlds, the amusement parks that were to be found in all the major towns. The oldest and most spectacular was the New World of Singapore: an open labyrinth of fantastical halls and pavilions, connected by alleyways of restaurants, hawkers and sundry stalls. There were theatres, nightclubs, dances, and open-air cinema that played continuously through the evenings. The crowds could wander from each to each, and impresarios would attract their attention by *entr'actes* of boxing, magic and other 'special turns'. The Worlds were a playground for all ethnic communities and income groups, a place of high and vulgar culture; a place of escape for the poor. The Worlds were a fantasy of Asian modernity, enacted nightly for the invisible city, in a walled enclave within the colonial town, but outside its order and exclusions.[72] During the war the Japanese had allowed gambling farms to operate in the parks, but they generally stayed away from them. Here, in the absence of Western movies, local culture such as the Malaya opera experienced a revival: a new scripted form called the *sandiwara* became 'the drama of modern daily life'. The troupe of a Malay radical, Bachtiar Effendi, the Bolero, took the lead in attacking the corruptions of the age, and popularized new political languages.[73] After the war there was a boom in entertainments. Theatres screened continuously the movies people had missed. In this free and democratic time, the Worlds became showgrounds for the new spectacles of mass politics.

As the Malayan Communist Party emerged from the undergrowth in which it had hidden so long, it embedded itself in this urban landscape. In most towns an MPAJA 'Anti-Japanese Union' office became the nucleus of a cluster of communist-led organizations. Its fighters, many of whom were now unemployed, moved into the informal economy. After its first triumphs through the streets, the MPAJA adopted the Worlds as a platform for its work; the cabarets in the daytime became used for political 'tea parties' and even schools and crèches. In the evening they staged fund-raising events with 'glory tickets' for workers at $1 or de luxe 'emancipation tickets' for businessmen at $100.[74] Theatre groups such as the Mayfair Musical and Drama Society, which had around 300 members, raised awareness of the communist cause in China and elsewhere. The Worlds were sites for many of the great rallies and commemorations that marked the first weeks of peace. It began on 2 October, with the birthday of Mahatma Gandhi. In Singapore Indian soldiers fraternized with a crowd some 7,000 strong. The slogans were Long Live the Independence of India! Long live Mr Gandhi! Long live the Communists in India! Long Live the Malayan Communist Party![75] A week later, the national day of China – the 'Double Tenth' – was celebrated for the first time in four years in Singapore, by a procession five miles long led by the communists and Kuomintang, sometimes in unison but increasingly separately. In Penang there was a grand parade, with bands and lion dances, but also three minutes' silence for the war dead: the day was also the first anniversary of some of the most brutal Kempeitai arrests and tortures. Afterwards, 20,000 copies of the 'Eight Principles' of the Malayan Communist Party were distributed.[76] A few days later, the Russian revolution was celebrated by the arrival of the 8th Regiment of the MPAJA in Wembley amusement park in George Town, and there were events and film shows elsewhere. In the months that followed, appalled by the anarchy on the streets, the British would attempt to seize back urban space; they rounded up hawkers and prohibited processions, but as they cleared the streets the revolution continued in the Worlds.

With Lai Teck's decision not to oppose the British by force of arms, the MCP embarked on the 'democratic' path to power. For the first time it began to acquire a public personality. In Singapore the chosen voice of the MCP was Wu Tian Wang, a Party organizer from Ipoh. To the British he stood apart because of his fluency in English; Victor Purcell described him as 'an elegant young communist intellectual with eyes gazing into utopian space'. His ease in colonial circles would earn him the resentment of his comrades upcountry. The other 'open' representative, Lee Kiu, had been a propagandist for the MPAJA during the war: 'a young Chinese coolie girl of 26 with a neo-Jacobin toilette', recorded Purcell, somewhat perplexed, but 'energetic, indomitable'.[77] Wu Tian Wang and Lee Kiu put Britain's 'democratic' policy on trial by repeatedly testing the extent of recognition the British were prepared to give the MCP. Lee Kiu outmanoeuvred the churches and charities to bring a substantial part of the relief work of the BMA in Singapore under the aegis of the MPAJA; by late September eight of its eighteen relief centres were run by the resistance organization, and the British officer who worked most closely with her praised her highly.[78] These were some of the first direct encounters between senior colonial mandarins and the new Asian revolution. These autodidactic young Marxists were at a long remove from the new 'Malayan' leadership that men like Purcell were hoping to promote, and so too was their vision of democracy.

In the jungle, a book widely read by Communist Party leaders was Mao Zedong's 1939 tract *On New Democracy*. It spoke of two stages of revolution: the first demanded a broad alliance across society before the second, full communist revolution, could be accomplished. It was a product of Mao's need, in his base areas in the border regions in China, to consolidate his political control with policies that would appeal across a diverse social landscape. In Malaya the MCP had not seized the moment to create their Yenan, but, by analogy, New Democracy seemed well-tempered to Malaya's plural society.[79] The vanguard of New Democracy was the generation that had come to consciousness during the war, young people who had perhaps been too young to serve in the MPAJA, but were in awe of its patriotic mystique. The MCP targeted school students, many of whom, because of the closure of the Chinese middle schools, were now re-enrolling as young adults, experienced well beyond their years. Successive British governors were severely taxed by having to explain to ministers why their colony seemed to be continually under threat from school-children. The Party's principal open organization, the New Democratic Youth League, absorbed a giddying panoply of groups into its ranks: the Penang branch included propaganda, singing and theatrical parties, school unions, basketball and volleyball clubs, hairdressers and barbers, coffee-shop keepers and lion dance troupes.[80]

New Democracy for the first time brought young women leaders to the fore. Chin Peng's comrade, Eng Ming Chin, became the leading light of the movement in Perak, and Lee Kiu led a Chinese women's organization in Singapore which, by the end of the year, claimed 20,000 members. The war had made women more visible in the labour force and in trade; it had taken them out of the home. This was not always to their benefit, but it had shown their resilience and exposed their oppression. The experience of 'comfort women' and prostitutes was a spur to organization among women of all communities. One of the first resolutions of the MPAJA's Johore People's Assembly contained demands for women's equal rights to inheritance, to equal wages and crèches in the workplace, and for an end to polygamy, prostitution and the keeping of 'slave-girls'.[81] Many Chinese women were attracted to the Communist Party by this preaching of an end to feudalism. For them, this meant a rejection of patriarchal Confucian thought. Party life could be an escape from oppressive households or bad marriages, and it often split families. Above all, perhaps, it was seen as a road to self-development. The MPAJA had shown itself willing to arm women as fighters.[82] One Perak newspaper caught the mood: 'Now Spring had returned to the world we must go hand in hand to unite together, no matter whether we are mistresses or paid-servants, or *nonya* [Straits Chinese matrons] or labourers or *dulang*-washers . . .'[83]

The MCP built support by tapping into the anarchical self-help of the occupation years, and by making it heroic. By all accounts its success was dramatic and this, for a time, seemed to vindicate Lai Teck. There was a sense that the organization was caught in the full, unstoppable flood of history; in Lai Teck's words, a 'revolutionary high tide' that would bring in its wake the birth of a 'New Age'. This mood of expectation was taken up by the press with unprecedented freedom. Apart from Japanese propaganda in English and Malay newspapers, the war years were a period of complete isolation and silence. News in Chinese vanished entirely. But in the months after the surrender there was a rush of information from outside that gave local events an almost apocalyptic ring. Although newsprint was in short supply, old newspapers revived quickly with small print runs and the MCP was able to invest in its first mouthpieces: in Singapore the *New Democracy* and in Kuala Lumpur the *Min Sheng Pau* – The People's Voice – the editor of which was Liew Yit Fan, a English-educated Jamaican-born Eurasian Chinese and one of the Party's most able cadres. Even the older *towkay*-backed Chinese newspapers, such as *Nanyang Siang Pau* and the *Sin Chew Jit Poh*, had editors who were active in the resistance movement, and gave significant coverage to the left. The New Democratic Youth League churned out pamphlets – Victor Gollancz of London was the universal model – ranging from catechisms for the MCP to a best-selling self-help book (*How to treat people*). Literary periodicals revived, stimulated by the poetic offerings of MPAJA veterans, in the mode according to one British reader, of 'reminiscences under a sombre sky, then the eternal "running dogs" of the Japanese'.[84] Writers celebrated the lack of censorship by launching a kind of guerrilla journalism against the BMA. This was duly translated daily by the government PR department for the military to read. They were incensed at the public ridicule. Papers countered with teasing apologies: 'We are surprised at your Honours being offended by our remark that your Honour is oppressive, cruel, unjust and insincere, and we hope that your Honour will forgive our ignorance.'[85] The soldiers were not amused.

Not only the British were alarmed at the headway the communists had made, so too as they began to resurface were Chinese businessmen, most of whom were instinctive supporters of the rival Kuomintang. The nationalists' few Force 136 fighters were marginalized by both the British and the MPAJA. The Kuomintang attempted to set up its own youth groups and make its presence felt. Senior nationalist leaders, businessmen and opinion-makers began to drift back from exile. The one man whose moral authority transcended the political cleavages among the Overseas Chinese was Tan Kah Kee. On 6 October, he returned to Singapore from Java, where – as Japan's

Public Enemy No. 1 – he had spent the war in hiding. In the traditional manner, a party was given the next evening to greet him in his old residence, the 'millionaires club', the Ee Hoe Hean. At seventy-one years of age, Tan Kah Kee was now a great patriarch. Victor Purcell attended the gathering; the spectrum of guests, he noted, was 'unprecedented': there was a full turn-out of dignitaries from the various Chinese clan and commercial associations over which Tan Kah Kee had once held sway, but the guests now included Wu Tian Wang and Lee Kiu, as representatives of the Malayan Communist Party. Tan Kah Kee made a speech criticizing the low price of rubber and made a plea for the abolition of opium and cabarets, his old bugbears. Surveying the crowd, Purcell speculated that Tan Kah Kee could well turn out to be 'the George Washington of a Nanyang Chinese independence movement'. But Purcell also noted that, although Tan Kah Kee's anti-Japanese credentials were unimpeachable, he was in very many ways out of touch with local conditions. His theme, Purcell recorded, remained 'the drawing off of Malayan wealth for China' and 'Malaya for the Chinese'. In the propaganda of the communists, Purcell observed, 'there is no mention of any one race'. The Party was beginning to turn away from its core Chinese support base and becoming more 'Malayan' in its outlook. But, at the same time, its peaceful co-existence with the British was coming rapidly to an end. As the meeting to welcome Tan Kah Kee drew to a close, it was disturbed by news of police raids on the nearby premises of the New Democratic Youth League.[86]

LIBERAL IMPERIALISM AND NEW DEMOCRACY

The new freedom to meet and to march had raised political expectations to fever pitch. Victor Purcell, together with a number of other 'wise Britishers', was for a short time lionized by the Chinese press for having endorsed the 'Eight Principles' of the Malayan Communist Party. He was now facing intense criticism from his British colleagues: a senior policeman wrote to Mountbatten demanding that Purcell be removed from his post with immediate effect.[87] But Purcell reiterated in a radio broadcast that 'Liberty of speech is allowed which extends to the right to criticize government measures of policy in the strongest terms.'[88] A few days after Tan Kah Kee's return, Purcell left Singapore to travel around the peninsula to take in the political air. His impressions were recorded in an irreverent personal journal, which he circulated to senior members of the BMA. Intended to rally support for the liberal experiment, it began to chart its demise.

Purcell went first to Malacca, the ancestral home of Malaya's largest community of Straits Chinese. It was, he observed, 'still the same old Sleepy Hollow'. But surrounded by antique Chinese mansions and an air of decline, Purcell saw how the Straits Chinese elite had lost a great deal of their wealth and influence to newer men. At Malacca's 'Double Tenth' celebrations, the triumphal arches for the occasion were those erected to welcome the MPAJA a few weeks earlier; they had merely been reinscribed. As he moved north, the political atmosphere became heavier. Kuala Lumpur 'had an unquiet air': Purcell noticed the constant passage through the streets of MPAJA men. The centre of this frenzy of activity was the People's Assembly which had been set up in the Selangor Chinese Assembly Hall. Here the communists had gone furthest in attempting to maintain a shadow local government, including a Treasury and a Department of Civil and Cultural Affairs. Although its core support remained Chinese, the Assembly had representatives from all the main ethnic communities.[89] It was led by a hardened ex-guerrilla leader, Soong Kwong, who discarded the MPAJA's preferred banditti battledress style of the previous weeks and cut a flamboyant figure in a pristine white linen suit.

Purcell arrived at a tense moment. The editors of the Min Sheng Pau had been rebuked by the military for criticizing arrests made in the police raids in Singapore a few days earlier. Then, on 13 October, 6,000 workers went on strike out at Malaya's only coal mine at Batu Arang. This was a serious challenge to the British: before the war the mine had been the scene of Malaya's most dramatic industrial unrest, and of the MCP's first attempt to set up soviets. Purcell visited the mine and implored the workers to be patient. 'The men's reply was that they could not work on empty bellies. There was a deadlock.' This triggered a wave of industrial action: in the small-town strongholds of the MPAJA there were processions led by guerrillas, with ardent young Chinese as flying pickets. In Singapore, on 20 October, 7,000 harbour workers protested at the return of the contractor system. But the strike here took on an entirely new dimension: British troops were embarking from the docks for Indonesia, and the labour gangs refused to load materials of war. The British declined to listen to what they perceived to be political demands. It was reported that the European manager threatened the men with arrest and three years' imprisonment under military law. 'If you people don't want to work', they were told, 'we have British soldiers and Japanese prisoners of war.' The BMA drafted in 2,000 Japanese surrendered personnel, and over the next few days the strikes spread through the city to other transport and municipal workers, including the collectors of night soil and firemen; even 300 cabaret girls stopped dancing. At a vast rally of 20,000 workers at Happy World amusement park, fifty unions turned out in solidarity. Japanese troops were now out cleaning the streets and fighting fires.[90]

These disputes set the pattern for three years of deepening industrial conflict. With communist support, the General Labour Unions of the pre-war period began to revive. Where before they had been underground movements, they now set up offices in resistance organization buildings. They were not confined to single trades; they amalgamated workers in artisan or service industries who were employed in small, dispersed clusters and who saw the need to form larger combines. The Singapore General Labour Union, inaugurated at the 25 October Happy World rally, claimed a membership of 100,000 workers from over seventy individual bodies, most of whom earned a mere 50¢ to $1 a day. The General Labour Unions brought together smaller unions of hawkers and trishaw riders to fight British attempts to clean up the streets, and unions of shop assistants and waiters whose livelihood was threatened by government food control measures. They represented the invisible city and gained support through its defence of the informal economy. As shortages worsened in December, the strikes engulfed hospital attendants, taxi and bus drivers, clerks, mechanics, telephone workers, postmen and government clerks. The unions were formidable combinations of workers, and stoppages in one sector could easily escalate to become general strikes.

The British claimed that the MCP was orchestrating these campaigns by intimidation; certainly few labourers dared oppose them. But much of the labour organization was spontaneous. Subhas Chandra Bose's great achievement in Malaya was that, in S. K. Chettur's words, 'he infused dignity and self-respect' into Indian labour. His loss had caused widespread demoralization but, by the end of 1945, independent Indian unions were being formed and the Azad Hind movement was reassembling on the rubber estates. Desperate to encourage moderate trade unionism, the Labour government created an entirely novel government position. At the end of December a 'trade union adviser' arrived in Singapore. 'Battling Jack' Brazier was a cockney railwayman who had driven the *Bournemouth Belle*. A product of Ruskin College Oxford, he was a passionate socialist and anti-colonialist, but also a committed anti-communist, probably from religious conviction, and he adopted the view that unions should restrict themselves solely to economic matters, and play no political role.[91] Purcell demurred. 'There is', he wrote, 'no need to sniff about political agitators to explain a refusal to work when the cost of living at the lowest pre-occupation standards is higher than wages.'

The distinction between rice and freedom was incomprehensible to local unionists. There seemed to be no other forum in which political issues could be debated. At Purcell's suggestion the MCP was allowed representation on the official Advisory Councils. But if they hoped to use this to make speeches, they were disappointed; the agenda was strictly apolitical and the membership dominated by local worthies. Purcell witnessed the frustration at first hand in Kuala Lumpur. The day before Purcell's visit, on 12 October 1945, the leader of the People's Assembly, Soong Kwong, was arrested by RAF police on a charge of extortion. There is little doubt as to Soong Kwong's guilt. His Chinese victim was a known Japanese informant who was imprisoned in a basement for a week by Soong Kwong and his followers and released only after he agreed to produce a 'fine' of $300,000. But there was a large rally of Soong Kwong's outraged supporters on the Kuala Lumpur Padang on 15 October. The issue at stake was the status of the MPAJA. The extortion had occurred before the surrender when Soong Kwong was a guerrilla leader and a combatant under the command of SEAC. The BMA had earlier decided to overlook the violent episodes of the interregnum, but it seems that the RAF police had acted on their own initiative. On the afternoon of the rally, Soong Kwong was released on bail. He confronted Purcell and other British officers: 'Did not the BMA realise that he, Soong Kwong, was the people's leader?' Purcell was not impressed, describing him as 'a bit of a dandy. His is a common type among Chinese "intellectuals" of the semi-cooked variety – vain, grinning, dealing in impertinences with ingratiating smirks and yet with a slight sneer behind the grin . . . He will', Purcell foretold, 'court a comfortable martyrdom from the British.' 'Chan Hoon and Wu [Tian Wang]', Purcell noted, 'are quite different types and quite reasonable.'

The reference to 'Chan Hoon' (i.e. 'Chang Hong') is telling. Purcell had met 'Chang Hong' and other senior British officers in Singapore on 24 and 25 September; they had discussed co-operation with the BMA and 'Chang' had then introduced Wu Tian Wang and other Singapore Party leaders. But it seems that the British did not discern Chang's true identity, and he then disappeared from view. Of the man the British knew as Lai Teck there was now no sign. Rumours about him continued to circulate, and they broke into print in the Penang newspaper, *Modern Daily News*, in October. An anonymous article accused an unnamed official of the MCP of betraying comrades to the Japanese. It called for a public investigation at which the author would appear and give evidence. It was written by Ng Yeh Lu, who had been perhaps the most prominent public spokesman of the MCP before the war. It was he who had represented the Party in discussions that led to the British arming the Chinese for a last-ditch defence of Singapore. Although he was never a Central Committee member, he was English speaking and a formidable polemicist. After the fall of Singapore, Ng Yeh Lu was arrested by the Kempeitai; he was detained and then worked for the Japanese as a court translator. It was at this point that he became aware of Lai Teck's treachery, but Ng Yeh Lu's own record discredited his testimony in the eyes of most Party members. It seems that he had been kept alive by the Japanese for this very purpose. Yet it was Lai Teck who had remained at large and in a position to expose his comrades. Ng Yeh Lu – or 'Yellow Wong,' as he was now known – never regained standing in the MCP. There was a report that Lai Teck attempted to have him assassinated by the Singapore Party, but the local leaders stayed their hand.[92]

There were signs of dissent within the Party. A flurry of statements by various MCP organs appeared in the press enquiring after the health of 'Mr Light' or 'Mr Wright' and paying glowing tributes to his leadership. Eng Ming Chin, at a tea party in Ipoh in late November, made a speech in which she 'exposed the conspirators against Lai Teck'.[93] But other leading Party figures began to act on their suspicions. Yeung Kuo, the Party leader in Selangor, disenchanted with the moderate policy followed in August, managed to orchestrate the exclusion of Lai Teck from the MCP's key organizing committee. But Lai Teck still possessed an aura of invulnerability, and fought back. It is unclear how much the British knew about all this. The first hard evidence seems to have come to H. T. Pagden, an etymologist by training, who was working as a Chinese-affairs officer in Singapore. He was given a detailed report, written by Ng Yeh Lu, which itemized Lai Teck's treacheries including the massacre of the MPAJA high command at Batu Caves in 1942 and the betrayal of Force 136 officers. Among the latter was the Chinese Kuomintang agent Lim Bo Seng. In December Lim's remains were exhumed from the grounds of Batu Gajah prison in Perak, where he had died at the hands of the Kempeitai. There was a public funeral in Ipoh, from where the cortège proceeded to Kuala Lumpur and then Singapore for a moving commemoration ceremony. He was, observed Victor Purcell, 'already a legend'.[94] Around this time Pagden was visited by a senior Kuomintang leader, a close friend of Lim Bo Seng, who threatened that, if the British did not bring Lai Teck to trial, 'certain people would probably make it their business to put the matter in the limelight'. Pagden took the matter to the head of the Malayan Security Service, A. G. Blades, a pre-war policeman who had known Lai Teck. Pagden suggested that Lai Teck's Kempeitai controller, Satoru Onishi, now imprisoned in Changi, be interrogated. 'As an etymologist, however,' he wrote some three years later, 'I was not in a very strong position.' Pagden was told in no uncertain terms to drop the matter and the Kuomintang, he believed, were pressured into silence and told to leave matters to the police. But Pagden sowed seeds of doubt: 'The Malayan Security Service', he told the Colonial Office, believed they knew 'more about

[Lai Teck] than anyone, but I am not sure that they do. They probably find him useful, but one wonders how useful this association with him may be to the other side.'[95]

By December 1945 the British were aware that Lai Teck was still alive. Once again, his story becomes obscured by a lack of sources, and by misinformation at every turn. But, from scraps of evidence in the official papers, it appears that knowledge of Lai Teck was confined to a small circle of initiates within the Malayan Security Service. A field security officer, Major R. J. Isaacs, opened a file on 'The Wright Case' and began to interview MCP members to discover what had happened to him, and to investigate his wartime activities. Members of the Kempeitai in British custody were asked to write down all they knew about the Malayan Communist Party. According to Onishi, Issacs visited him to seek his opinion.[96] Then a key witness committed suicide at Isaacs's house. With an impending inquest there was a danger that Isaacs and other witnesses might be put on the stand, and that information might come to light that would compromise the Security Service. It would also embarrass the British officers of Force 136 who, although they had known nothing of Lai Teck's relationship with the Japanese, now had to confront the probability that they had inadvertently passed on military information to the Japanese. Force 136, too, was now a legend. At this point, the 'Wright Case' quietly dropped from view. It appears that it was not until early 1946 that Lai Teck was once more in contact with the British.[97]

The 'secret' army that Lai Teck had promised the Party in August did not exist. Everything was now staked on the 'Eight Principles'. A further statement on the 7 November anniversary of the Bolshevik Revolution extended these to nine, with a demand for 'self-government'. But the underlying article of faith remained the same: 'We still believe in the good things which the British government has promised us.'[98] Notwithstanding any machinations on the part of Lai Teck, this credo still held good for many in the Party. Secret conversations between agents of the United States Office of Strategic Services and Party leaders in Singapore and Kuala Lumpur revealed that the MCP leadership believed that the moral authority of the San Francisco Declaration, the UN's founding charter, together with world opinion 'would force [the British] to change their policy'.[99] But at this point, and not for the last time, frustrated rank-and-file took the responsibility of revolution into their own hands and went on the offensive. The catalyst was the closure of two leftist newspapers in Perak. The local military were so antagonized by hostile press reports of corruption and rape by troops that they argued it constituted a threat to the safety of its men, as defined in the proclamation of the BMA. On these grounds newspaper staff were arrested, tried in a military court and given sentences of up to seven years' rigorous imprisonment; even the compositors were held guilty.

In the wake of this, on 21 October there were hunger marches in the main towns of Perak. One of the largest was in the small town of Sungei Siput, where a crowd of 5,000 assembled in the New World amusement park and marched to keep a midnight vigil outside the government offices. The British commanders, rough-handled by the crowd, feared for their own safety and ordered it to disperse within five minutes. The order was ignored and, for the first time in postwar Malaya, troops were told to fire on civilians: one person was killed and three others were wounded. The following day there was a general strike throughout the state, and again troops fired on demonstrators: three more were killed in Ipoh and four in Taiping.[100] Chin Peng would later claim these casualties as first blood in the Malayan Emergency.

Victor Purcell travelled to the scene of the Perak disturbances in early December to meet the local MCP leadership. He spoke with Eng Ming Chin, whose propaganda troupe and speeches at Ipoh had roused the crowd into an uncompromising mood. With Lee Kiu in Singapore in mind, he recorded in his journal that Miss Eng 'has decidedly more sex appeal ... Her most remarkable features are her eyes. At one moment they are flat, brown and dull, at the next revealing in baleful flashes the smouldering fires of fanaticism if not of actual insanity, at another melting into a smile of something suspiciously like coquetrie.'[101] But such contacts were becoming less common. Although the MCP had allowed women leaders such as Eng Ming Chin to take centre stage, it was less willing to expose its leading men. Although Chin Peng now worked from a well-appointed party office in Kuala Lumpur, living with his wife on the affluent Ampang Road, he had adopted the cover of a businessman. The lesser-ranking 'open' leaders in the public eye allowed much of the rest of the Party to slip back into the shadows.

On 1 December the MPAJA formally disbanded. It did so in an acrimonious mood, its commanders outraged at the humiliations they had received at the hands of Allied military leaders. 'The British treated us like coolies,' Wu Tian Wang told the Americans.[102] Lai Teck organized the men into ex-servicemen's associations. 'We might not have an army now', Chin Peng reflected bitterly, 'but at least we had a club.' Many ex-comrades found it hard to settle back to peace and to work or study. Many found that, on presentation of their demobilization certificates, managers were unwilling to take them on. A year after the war's end, the MPAJA commander Liew Yao estimated that over half of his men were unemployed. He even asked the Office of Strategic Services for help in setting up an import–export business to bring in US goods.[103] The Chinese veterans of Dalforce, who had defended Singapore to the last, were ignored. They had been given only $10 each when the British disbanded them in February 1942, and many were later slaughtered by the Japanese.[104] Their commander, John Dalley, freshly released from internment, campaigned in London for benefit payments for them. The dispute dragged on until 1950, when the government buried the issue by pointing out that many of the veterans were untraceable as they were back in the jungle.[105]

Passing-out parades were held across Malaya. They were carefully stage-managed. In Alor Star, in Kedah, Ho Thean Fook, a non-communist who had fought with the guerrillas, stood proudly on the podium as the interpreter for the occasion. The representatives of the other resistance organizations were there, even of the Kuomintang fighters whom, Ho recalled, 'we used to call "bandits"'. The proceedings began with 'God Save the King', and a message from the British commander, General Messervy, was read out promising the guerrillas training as motor mechanics or licences as hawkers. The MPAJA men did not surrender their weapons publicly but later, in the barracks, 'throwing them into a heap as if they were old brooms'. The guerrillas were each given $350 – in Messervy's words, to 'tide [them] over' – of which $200 was taken by the MPAJA for political funds. With his share Ho Thean Fook bought some waxed duck, a local delicacy for which Kedah was famous, to take back to his home town in Perak. 'The copy of General Messervy's speech, campaign ribbons, medals and flashes, we burnt . . . We could not buy a cup of coffee or exchange them for a plate of *mee rebus* [spicy noodle soup], could we?' Ho had been promised a scholarship to study in England; it never materialized. He was shocked to discover in the weeks that followed that most of the European officers of Force 136 had reappeared in police uniforms; they had, he believed, been planted deliberately to make use of their knowledge in peacetime. Ho retired from politics, deeply disillusioned. He believed that most of his comrades, even the most fanatical communists, now wanted above all to get a job, take a wife and raise a family. Ho had lost some of the best years of his life. For him, the demob parade 'represented the culmination of over three years of wasted struggle, the risks we had taken and the suffering we had undergone.'[106] The MPAJA, Purcell believed, 'had been treated like interlopers . . . without regard to their rights or dignity'. The British deliberately played down the communists' role in the jungle war. Purcell had argued unsuccessfully for a bigger bounty for them; if it would have prevented what was to follow, he later observed, it would have been 'cheap at the price'.[107]

'MALAYA FOR THE MALAYS, NOT THE MALAYANS'

As wartime alliances disintegrated in Malaya, on 10 October the Labour colonial secretary, George Hall, rose to his feet in the House of Commons to announce the grand plan for a Malayan Union. Mountbatten had urged the government to release its plans long before this, to give an unequivocal signal that the British intended to reward the Malayan Chinese for their loyalty. But by the time Hall's statement came, if the British still expected plaudits from the Chinese they were bound to be disappointed. Reaction was at best lukewarm or indifferent, at worst hostile. The news that Singapore was excluded from the Union astonished most non-Malay observers: it was Malaya's natural capital, and the heartland of 'Malayan' sentiment. But the British were anxious not to jeopardize Malay opinion too far, and wanted to keep a tight grip on their 'fortress'. Singapore's precise constitutional status was entirely undecided. In the longer term, this separation was to be the most enduring legacy of the grand design.[108] Suspicion mounted when it became known that the next step towards the implementation of the Malayan Union would be consultations in private with the Malay rulers. Homer Cheng, a Chinese civil servant working under Victor Purcell, summarized the problem: the local-born Chinese, he wrote, 'claim to have as much right as the Malays to be regarded as the sons of the soil. They contend that the Malays are technically and anthropologically as much immigrants and intruders as the Chinese.' The indigenous people of Malaya were the aboriginal Orang Asli. The Malays had forfeited their claim to preference in the war. 'Malayan nationality was an insult', Cheng concluded. 'Few would feel proud of being the subjects of Sultans.'[109] The terms of the debate had moved on a long way from the question of citizenship. 'The Union will go through without opposition or enthusiasm from the Left,' Victor Purcell wrote. 'Their interest is solely one of representation.'[110]

The Malay rulers were approached first in order to sign new treaties that gave the British crown the necessary legal jurisdiction in their states to establish the Malayan Union. In one of the first acts of the BMA, a former Malayan Civil Service legal officer, H. C. Willan, was to instruct field security officers to investigate the record of individual rulers during the Japanese occupation, and label them as 'white', 'grey' or 'black'. Only five of the pre-war sultans remained in office, four others who had acceded during the Japanese occupation had yet to be recognized by the British government. The Malay courts well remembered the deposition by the British of the Sultan of Perak in 1874, an act that precipitated the first conquest of the Malay states. Mountbatten had all along worried about the propriety of this. It would, he warned, be 'psychologically questionable' to secure the rulers' agreement under the shadow of 'overwhelming force'.[111] But, once again, the nature and extent of the local reaction took the British entirely by surprise.

Willan broke the news to the rulers like a bank manager refusing credit. He first called upon the senior ruler, Sultan Ibrahim of Johore, who had reigned since 1895 in a proud and independent manner, retaining his own army, administrative service and many of his own European advisers. He was, according to Sir George Maxwell, the only sultan who really governed his state. Ibrahim had a reputation for sympathy for the Japanese before the war, receiving imperial honours for his protection of Japanese business interests in his state; he had hunted big game with princes of the Japanese royal family. A vigorous man who sired a child in his seventies, between 1898 and 1927 Ibrahim had no fewer than thirty-five tiger kills to his name. Willan travelled from Singapore over the short causeway to Ibrahim's capital at Johore Bahru. But Willan had some difficulty in finding him; his sumptuous palaces seemed deserted. Eventually Willan ran to ground Ibrahim and his Romanian consort at one of his minor residencies. He found the sultan in emollient mood: the Japanese had ousted him from his principal palaces and he resented them bitterly for it. Allied intelligence appraisals accepted that his relations with the Japanese had been driven solely by a desire to protect the independence of his state, and that they had soured swiftly during the war. With rare humility, Ibrahim offered to serve under the BMA. The British placed tremendous weight on Ibrahim's acquiescence in the new constitutional agreements, and there was much relief at his state of mind. The sultan asked for permission to fly the Union Flag on his car on his way to the surrender ceremony in Singapore, and for assistance in taking passage as quickly as possible to his other residence, at Grosvenor House on London's Park Lane, where he had cut a colourful figure in happier times.[112]

The life of the Malay courts came to a standstill as they awaited the verdict of the British. To the surviving rulers of the pre-war period, Willan gave nominal recognition but to Japanese appointees he was, on occasion, unforgiving. In Selangor the Japanese had deposed the reigning sultan, Alam Shah, and installed his elder brother, Musa Uddin, a man who had been disinherited by the British in 1933 on the grounds of 'personal misbehaviour'. Musa Uddin foresaw what was coming: in a speech on 10 September he warned that 'the air has been thick with rumours' about the future for him and his state.[113] Three days later he was taken away by Indian Army officers and, with three servants and two suitcases, sent to his Elba, the Cocos and Keeling Islands, a remote Allied staging post in the southern Indian

Ocean. The state regalia and Rolls-Royce were returned to Sultan Alam Shah. As news of these events circulated, some Malay courts acted to anticipate the British. In Trengganu, the legitimate sultan had died during the occupation and his eldest son, Raja Ali, had taken over. But before the war, it was said that Raja Ali had alienated both the British and local opinion through a misalliance with a woman of low reputation. During the war, he had entertained Japanese officers at his palace, and had shocked the local notables by asking them for 'presents' and by leasing out land for an amusement park where heavy gambling took place. Seeing their opportunity, the Trengganu State Council, using the authority of the state's constitution, deposed Raja Ali. But many Malays would be increasingly uneasy that the *adat*, or customary law of succession, was not being followed.

These tensions came out into the open with the arrival in Malaya on 7 October of Sir Harold MacMichael, a former high commissioner of Palestine, as His Majesty's special representative. He carried with him full powers to sign the treaties and to make or break kings by granting or withholding British recognition. His mission began, like Willan's, in Johore and ran from 18 October to 21 December. It was conducted in a slow, stately fashion and, as MacMichael admitted, subject to careful 'stage-management'. Accompanied by a small retinue, he again began with Sultan Ibrahim. Impatient to leave Malaya, it seems, Ibrahim handed MacMichael a list of concerns relating to his personal status and that of his state, but in the end raised little objection to the terms. Pointedly, he did not consult the leading Malays of the state. After signing, MacMichael reported, the sultan heaved a sign of relief and MacMichael responded in turn with 'Praise God' in Arabic. It was, he wrote to London, 'reasonably plain sailing . . . The contrast to Palestine is quite remarkable!'[114]

But MacMichael soon ran into troubled waters. In Kedah the regent, Badlishah, was in a compromised position. He had succeeded during the war and needed recognition from the British. MacMichael met him on 29 November, and his first impression was rather dismissive: 'the small shy and retiring "failed BA type", unstable and inclined to be introspective and lonely'. However, the regent told MacMichael that he found the surrender of power 'very devastating'. MacMichael responded tartly that an independent Kedah was not feasible. He raised the alternative of Thai control – a spectre from Kedah's past history – and remarked that it was 'fortunate that Labour ministers had not concluded that Sultanates were altogether out of date'. It was clear that the regent faced the choice of giving his signature or losing his throne. He signed only after a final meeting at which he and his state council made it clear they submitted 'because there was no alternative'. At this point MacMichael stood and, on behalf of King George VI, formally acknowledged Badlishah as Sultan of Kedah. The sultan then rose and said that 'this was the most distressing and painful moment of his life. Henceforward he would lose the loyalty, the respect and affection of his subjects, and he would be pursued with curses towards his grave by the ill-informed. He called on Allah to witness his act and to protect him for the future. He would sign because no other course was open.' Although perhaps MacMichael was more polite, Badlishah wrote shortly afterwards, his manner was 'not unlike the familiar Japanese technique of bullying'.[115] Badlishah thought that MacMichael was acting upon London's specific instructions, but later came to believe that MacMichael was not in fact authorized to deal with the rulers 'in such a brutal manner'. Mac-Michael had, as one old Malaya hand put it, 'blackmailed them all'.[116] The term 'MacMichaelism' entered the vernacular.

The king's special representative's past connection with Palestine now took on a deeper significance. In Badlishah's capital, Alor Star (now Alor Setar), posters appeared that showed a Malay walking sorrowfully out of the town into the country, carrying a small bundle of possessions, with the caption: 'The meaning of equal rights'.[117] There was a mood of crisis within the Malay community. The memories of the communal violence was still fresh, and in parts of Perak and Negri Sembilan there was renewed fighting. Not only had MacMichael trespassed against the *adat* of succession, but the ancient constitutions of Malay states had been transgressed by the rulers themselves. A writer in the Malay newspaper *Majlis*, or 'Assembly', of Kuala Lumpur, described the situation: 'the entire Malay community will stand solidly behind the Rulers . . . But the majority of our Sultans ignore the interests of their loyal subjects in this vital matter . . . Our Sultans should not be surprised if the Malays ignore them in the future.'[118] There was a deepening sense that the new treaties were *tak sah dan tiada halal*, 'illegitimate and unlawful'. The citizenship proposals were also coming under attack. In Kedah and elsewhere slogans circulated: 'Malaya for the Malays, not the Malayans'.[119]

During these weeks the Malay elite was paralysed by the uncertainty surrounding the courts. This was an opportunity for commoners to seize the political initiative. The first post-war Malay political party was founded in Ipoh, which was fast emerging as a centre of radical politics. A group of journalists who had worked together in the occupation period took over the offices of the local Japanese daily, and created a new paper called *Suara Rakyat*, 'The Voice of the People'. The leading personality was the 24-year-old Abdullah Sani bin Raja Kechil. Like many writers of the day, he was better known by a *nom de plume*, Ahmad Boestamam. Before the war he had been a precocious talent in Malay journalism, working for *Majlis* when it was edited by the leader of the Kesatuan Melayu Muda, Ibrahim Yaacob. On the eve of war, Boestamam was arrested by the British in a pre-emptive sweep of Malays suspected of being sympathetic to Japan. This was the first, and by far the briefest, of Boestamam's three periods in preventive detention. Released after the fall of Singapore, his life in wartime was low-key and quite typical for a young Malay radical of the time: he was schooled in propaganda techniques and underwent officer training in a Japanese militia. But he was to emerge after the war to become one of most charismatic political personalities of his day.

Boestamam and his friends were visited by another young man who said he wished to speak with them. At first Boestamam thought he was a Special Branch man. He introduced himself as Mokhtaruddin Lasso, and calmly announced that he was with the MPAJA guerrillas. He was smoking English Craven A cigarettes; these had been unattainable for years. 'We didn't know where he had got them, and we didn't want to ask either.' But this seemed to vouch for his authenticity. Like many voyagers of the Asian underground, little was known of his origins, both at the time and now, even by local communist leaders like Chin Peng. He came from Sumatra, it was said, where he had been active in the communist movement. He had been a schoolteacher, and had a nickname in Javanese: Lang Lang Buana, 'The Traveller'. But through him, the MCP began to extend its links with the Malays, and young radicals would be introduced to Malay cadres of the MPAJA. Mokhtaruddin used his communist connections to acquire money for the new paper; eventually $50,000 was invested in this project by the Malayan Communist Party.

It was, as Boestamam realized, 'tantamount to an ultimatum'. But he took it and gathered his own supporters into the venture to retain the upper hand. They argued down pressure from Mokhtaruddin and his friends to form a socialist party, and on 30 November 1945 a first meeting was held in Ipoh town hall of the Partai Kebangsaan Melayu Malaya, or the Malay Nationalist Party. It was a fresh venture for Malay radicalism. It announced a very different claim for the sovereignty of the Malays to that of the rulers; that of a *bangsa Melayu*, a Malay nation. To signal its opposition to the courts, the new party voiced tentative support for the Malayan Union. But it was also a challenge to the synthetic nationalism of Malayan Union, and it reached far beyond its borders: its ultimate aim was to create a greater Indonesia, an *Indonesia raya*.[120] As the British completed their second colonial conquest, they were encountering a world of interconnected protest of a kind they had never witnessed before. The champions of liberal imperialism were beginning to learn that imperialism was never so vulnerable to attack as when it attempted to reform itself. To many of its subjects it had never been so invasive. These attacks became more ferocious and unyielding when, in late 1945, British and Indian armies extended the boundaries of the British Empire to encompass the vast entirety of colonial Asia. Rarely had Britain's benevolent intentions been so tested, and by so many people.

4

1945: The First Wars of Peace

THE CRESCENT REGAINED

In the last months of 1945 the troops of the British Empire reconstituted the great crescent of land that Britain had occupied before 1941, and then fanned out beyond it. As in the First World War, the scope of empire actually increased as the formal fighting ended. The British had finally come to dominate the entire great area that curved from Bengal through Burma and Thailand on to Singapore. Indeed, in 1945 and 1946 the British military empire in Asia stretched triumphant over an even wider territory, from the Persian railhead at Zahedan to New Guinea and the Australian seas. For a time, British armies and administrators occupied half of French Indo-China and large parts of Indonesia. The vision would have dizzied even Lord Curzon. Certainly, to India's Congress, the British seemed alarmingly reluctant to surrender control over the Indian Army that had served them so well against the Germans, the Italians and the Japanese. In 1945 South East Asia Command was apparently determined to deploy Indian troops not only in Burma, Malaya and Singapore, but also in Thailand and what had been French Indo-China and Dutch Indonesia. If they got their way, Salisbury's great barracks in an Oriental Sea would be spilling blood for the British Empire for years to come. Indian journalists scanned the speeches and press comments of British ministers for any signs of a change of heart. Why had the king's broadcast to the nation, the first of Attlee's administration, not mentioned Asia? One newspaper remarked: 'Perhaps messages of freedom, democracy and lasting peace, liberal as they are, will have application to no wider an area than Europe.'[1] Another gloomily and correctly concluded that 'the war in the East will not come to an end with the defeat of Japan'.

Tired veterans of the war in Europe headed east in cramped troop-ships: a new forgotten army. A young captain, Derek van den Boe-garde, had witnessed the long push from Normandy into Germany, and as the war in Europe ended he had witnessed the horror of the Bergen-Belsen concentration camp. On 1 July, he departed from Liverpool on the SS *Carthage*, a new passenger liner, for the build-up of the liberation of Southeast Asia. It was a grotesque parody of the stately voyages that had connected Britain's Asian empire before the war. Later he would recall his arrival at the Gateway of India, where his ship was greeted by waving men being demobilized back to Britain. Bombay seemed squalid: 'The stench was heavy: oil, bodies, dirt; somewhere, faintly, spices.' Then, immediately, came the long rail journey to Bengal. 'The India I saw, from that terrible train, was sere, desolate. It was a fearful let-down ... I had expected story-book splendour. Instead we trailed for days across stony, beige desert.' He detrained at Calcutta to see an Indian porter being beaten by 'a fat, ginger-haired, moustached, red-faced stocky little major from Transport. Screaming. Thrashing at the cringing Indian with his swag-ger cane ... My first sight and sound of the Raj at work.' Fifty years on, he wrote that the memory of 'the cowering humbled body' in the crowded Seddah station repulsed his mind even more than the desolation of the bleak heaths and pines of Germany. In Calcutta van den Bogaerde was put to work memorizing maps and photographs of the beaches and mangroves of the Malay peninsula.[2] In the event the only action that occurred in his time in India came after a screening of the film *Objective, Burma!* when the Royal Enniskillen Fusiliers returning from the Arakan front took umbrage at the sight of Errol Flynn liberating Burma single-handedly, and set fire to the cinema.[3] Years later, Dirk Bogarde, as he styled himself after the war, would come under attack for his own portrayal of one of his commanding officers, Mountbatten's chief of staff, Frederick 'Boy' Browning, in the film *A Bridge too Far*.

After celebrating VJ Day in Calcutta, chaotic with deserters, he left for Southeast Asia. Five weeks after the Japanese surrender he arrived in Singapore. The harbourside was still in ruins, and the city had the odour of defeat, which 'meandered through the paint-peeling streets of Singapore like a slowly dispersing marsh gas, lying in pockets here and there, loitering in rooms and corridors, bitter, clinging, sickening'. Ex-prisoners of war still haunted the hotels and bars; internees told terrible stories of the chaos and incompetence of the fall. Yet colonial society was coming to life, with all its attendant snobberies. Van den Bogaerde noted that, as in 1941, the memsahibs of Singapore refused to speak to mere soldiers. The city was 'a white-washed bastard Tunbridge Wells – with palm trees'. Inching across the sea in a landing ship, his detail passed south, across the equator and into the Java Sea towards Jakarta. It was a cramped, nauseating journey for the soldiers. Van den Bogaerde landed in Tanjong Priok harbour amid a bustling scene of Javanese dock labour, Japanese prisoners of war – 'naked except for their boots, peaked caps and flapping loin cloths' – and turbaned Indian soldiers. The air reeked of burnt rubber, from a smouldering store, after a bomb attack by armed revolutionaries. Three and a half months after the surrender of Japan, van den Bogaerde had arrived in the middle of a combat zone.[4]

This vast new deployment placed a colossal burden on South East Asia Command, which by the end of year had become, in the words of Mountbatten's political adviser Esler Dening, 'more and more a purely British Indian affair'.[5] India had to find troops, not only for Burma, Malaya and Singapore, but also for Thailand and what had been French Indo-China and Dutch Indonesia. The British were even readying to send detachments of the Indian Army to occupied Japan; this was the first and the last 'British Commonwealth' force of its kind. Some of the first forces to enter were the 536 British and Australian sailors and marines who landed in Tokyo Bay in MacArthur's triumph. They were the advance guard of a Commonwealth contingent force that was to be 37,000 strong. These were war-weary men. The senior Indian officer, Brigadier Thimayya, had seen his brother – a staff officer in the INA – captured by his own brigade at Rangoon. For his Indian officers, the occupation was unlikely to lead to any career advancement. It was to be the last adventure of the Raj: the final Indian soldiers left Japan on 25 October 1947.

The Commonwealth troops were given an area that included Hiroshima. It was believed at the time that this was because the Americans did not want to be so closely associated with the devastation their bomb had wrought: a headline in the *Australian Army Journal* read: 'Australia takes the Ashes'. The Americans denied having any ulterior design; the area had been chosen on climatic grounds, that the north was too cold for the Indians and Australians. The effects of radiation were unknown at this time, but many of the men who served in Hiroshima would die at a comparatively early age. After the first sight-seeing they stayed away from the city: it brought doubt and depression. Some men spat at the wharfside on disembarking, but most were saddened by the poverty and wrack of war. As General 'Punch' Cowan, who had himself fought and lost a son in the Burma campaign, asked: 'How can I blame these children and their families for what has happened?'[6]

BRITAIN'S FORGOTTEN WAR IN VIETNAM

Even before the British reoccupied the Malay peninsula they were planning a strike to the east against Japanese forces in French Indo-China, the territories that are today Vietnam, Laos and Cambodia. The main target was the headquarters in Saigon of the ageing and ailing Field Marshal Count Terauchi, who had suffered a stroke earlier in the year. The British intervention in Indo-China is almost forgotten now, but it was to have major repercussions for the whole of Southeast Asia during the period of the Cold War. Why did British politicians and commanders commit forces to what might have appeared to be the sideshow of a sideshow, when everyone was worried about 'imperial overstretch'? Why not leave it to the Chinese nationalists with American assistance, as happened in Hanoi and the northern region?

War brutally exposed the limitations of empire, but to the imperially minded it also offered tantalizing glimpses of further expansion. Up in the heights of Simla in 1943, Dorman-Smith had been in correspondence with Leo Amery, secretary of state for India, and the foreign secretary Anthony Eden about not only the recapture of Burma but also the establishment of a new British protectorate in Thailand. In 1945 most British politicians saw no reason to doubt that Burma, Malaya and Hong Kong would remain theirs. For empire to be re-established, however, it was imperative to set it amid friendly powers, and in Asia in the mid 1940s this meant imperial powers. Certainly, this was what Winston Churchill believed. Quite apart from this, the prime minister felt obligated to the Free French and Dutch regimes that had been his strong allies during the war and which showed no sign of wishing to give up their colonial territories in Indo-China and Indonesia. Churchill had several spats with Franklin D. Roosevelt about this in 1943 and 1944. The US president, brought up on British and Dutch history, heartily detested French imperialism and was keen to install a United Nations protectorate in Indo-China after the war. Then, at a stroke, the political scene was unexpectedly transformed. FDR died and his successor, Harry S. Truman, seemed prepared to give the British their head in southern Indo-China and Indonesia, provided that Chiang Kai Shek and the Chinese nationalists, now close allies of the USA, were allowed a controlling influence in the north. Shortly afterwards Labour came to power in Britain, ostensibly committed to policies of colonial independence. On the ground Mountbatten had established good relations with Indian and Burmese nationalists.

It could not be assumed, therefore, that the British would take the line that they did. This was effectively to restore the French and Dutch empires in Indo-China and Indonesia at the very time that they were coming to realize the limitations of their own tenure in India and Burma. In Indo-China in particular the consequences were momentous. In 1970, at the height of the American war in Vietnam, George Rosie, a radical journalist, wrote *The British in Vietnam: how the twenty-five year war began*. Rosie built up a formidable case against General Douglas Gracey, commander of the 20th Indian Division, which intervened in Indo-China in September 1945 on the orders of South East Asia Command. Gracey, the book argued, had greatly exceeded his orders. While claiming that he would not intervene in the politics of Indo-China, Gracey purposely allowed the French to rearm and stage a coup against the communist-led Viet Minh national front government in Saigon on 23 September 1945. He then used the Indian Army and surrendered Japanese forces to suppress a legitimate nationalist rebellion. Rosie concluded that the British 'as a nation, bear some measure of responsibility for the tragedy of Vietnam'.[7] Now that official and private papers are open, it is possible to consider anew many of Rosie's assumptions and also to show how the beginning of the brutal war in Indo-China impacted on Britain's policies in Southeast Asia more broadly.

Indo-China had been conquered piecemeal by the French after 1850. In the deltas of the Mekong to the south and the Red River to the north, their rule was direct and intrusive, even though they maintained the fiction of Vietnamese sovereignty in the form of a client emperor, based at the old royal city of Hue. By the 1930s French land companies owned much of Cochin China (southern Vietnam) and Vietnamese labour was exploited on rubber and coffee estates across the country. In the hills and forests away from the river valleys, in Laos and Cambodia, the French allowed more authority to native rulers. The Depression had a devastating effect on the Indo-Chinese countryside. Hardship fuelled peasant risings. The French had suppressed mainstream Vietnamese nationalism. Inevitably, clandestine communist movements filled the vacuum. French forces carried out savage punitive campaigns during the 1930s. But the shadowy communist leadership, headed by Nguyen Ai Quoc, 'Nguyen the patriot', alias Ho Chi Minh, slipped to and fro across the Chinese border and infiltrated the homelands of the Moi, the tribal peoples of the northern hills.

When the Japanese invaded Southeast Asia in 1941–2, they preserved the rule of their French Vichy ally while clamping down hard on any sign of restiveness among the large French expatriate populations of Hanoi and Saigon, which numbered nearly 100,000. But the French settlers offered relatively little resistance; it was the Vietnamese who really suffered. There was the usual face-slapping and brutality on the part of the Japanese. As the Japanese lost control of the air, Allied bombing made impassable the difficult roads which brought rice from the south through the central hills to the food-deficient tracts of the north. In 1943 and 1944 scarcity degenerated into full-scale famine. Tens of thousands died of starvation; today older people still remember pushing the dead bodies of victims away from their doors each morning. The Vichy regime nevertheless gave the Indo-Chinese peoples a new sense of identity as they attempted to counter Allied propaganda, while the Japanese stimulated national feeling across Vietnam in the same way they had done in Burma and Malaya. The

French language was discouraged while Buddhist and Confucian rites flourished. Vietnamese youth was mobilized through the Buddhist Vanguard movement and martial arts associations.[8]

As long as pro-Axis Vichy rule lasted in France the French in Saigon and Hanoi had offered little opposition to the Japanese. Even after the fall of Paris to the Allies in 1944, local French administrators collaborated fully with the Japanese, helping to put down local Chinese and communist revolts and tracking Allied special forces. Paul Mus, a French special forces operative and sociologist who had been brought up in Indo-China, prepared a report for the Free French authorities in Calcutta in March 1945. In it he deplored the lack of effective 'resistance' among the French expatriate community. But as Burma fell to the 14th Army, the settlers and the local French forces began finally to refuse Japanese orders and make secret contacts with the special forces. At this stage, the Japanese were still expecting to hold their perimeter in southern Indo-China, Tenasserim and Malaya. They were in no mood to compromise and on 9 March 1945 they reacted with ruthless efficiency, ousting and imprisoning the former Vichy regime overnight and clamping much tighter controls on the hitherto largely untouched French settler lifestyle.

There were 60–70,000 Japanese soldiers in southern Vietnam and another 30,000-odd north of the 16th parallel. It was impossible for them to control this large and complex domain without Vietnamese help. Very late in the day, therefore, they instituted the sort of local government that had existed in Burma since 1943, installing in Hanoi a regime of moderates under Tran Trong Kim, some of whom were secretly sympathetic to the Viet Minh. Indo-Chinese members of the former French armed forces signed up with the new state. In Saigon, capital of the southern province, huge parades were held at which the motley collection of local political parties and religious groups handed out leaflets asking civilians to show their gratitude to the Japanese. A large placard proclaiming 'Vietnam' was erected outside the city's cathedral. At first the new regime, though nationalist, was technically responsible to the Bao Dai emperor in Hue, the old client ruler of the French. But its writ did not run very far. In the countryside, armed bands of communists and followers of local religious sects ruled the roost along with bandit gangs.

Before the Japanese surrendered in August, their last political act was to recognize a more radical government in Hanoi led by Ho Chi Minh. The incoming Chinese forces of Chiang Kai Shek also preferred a friendly independent Vietnamese government to the re-establishment of colonial rule. From the balcony of Hanoi's baroque opera house, Ho proclaimed the Democratic Republic of Vietnam under the leadership of the Viet Minh nationalist coalition. He mixed the language of the American Declaration of Independence with violent invective against the French: 'They have built more prisons than schools. They have mercilessly slain our patriots; they have drowned our uprisings in rivers of blood . . . To weaken our race they have forced us to use opium and alcohol.'[9] For nearly nine months the new regime was to act as a sovereign power, organizing elections, redistributing land to peasants and trying to combat the dreadful poverty that followed the famines. The ruling groups that emerged in distant Saigon were formally subordinate to the new regime in Hanoi. The two major leaders in the south were the communists Tran Van Giau and Dr Pham Ngoc Thach, the heads of the shaky local Viet Minh coalition which jostled for power with other armed popular groupings.

The nationalists in Saigon tried to persuade Count Terauchi to arm them: 'You are defeated, now it is our turn to fight the white imperialists.'[10] Terauchi refused to surrender Japanese arms, but seems to have allowed French ones to find their way to the Viet Minh. The situation was extraordinarily tense. The new government had some arms but had little sway beyond the outskirts of Saigon. In Cholon, Saigon's twin port city, French and Chinese business communities subsisted uneasily with a mafia-like organization called the Binh Xuyen. Up towards the mountain-goddess shrine of Tay Ninh on the Cambodian border it was the Cao Dai, a religious sect armed by the Japanese, who held power. Inside Cholon, the large French population was restive. Colonel Jean Cédile had parachuted into the country and represented Free French authority until the arrival of a French commissioner. He established strained relations with the Viet Minh authority, which was itself split between moderates who were prepared to co-operate and radicals who wanted an immediate attack on the returning colonialists. When the surrendered Japanese representatives visited the British headquarters in Rangoon in late August they said frankly that they could not control the population of southern Vietnam.

Into this minefield moved General Gracey's 20th Indian Division, a crack unit of the 14th Army, with some trepidation and little knowledge. French Indo-China had never figured strongly in the British mental map of the East, even though it adjoined Burma and Malaya and was home to substantial numbers of Indians and the same southern Chinese communities who traded in Singapore and Rangoon. British minutes of 1945 waffled about the 'Annamite character' with its 'ceremoniousness' and 'veneration for age'.[11] Nor, apparently, were the British very interested in replacing these comfortable stereotypes with more solid information about the roots and nature of Vietnamese identity. Earlier in the year Paul Mus, the soldier sociologist, had been parachuted into Vietnam in an extension of Force 136 activities. In a rice field he had a sudden vision of a resurgent Vietnam in which Ho Chi Minh, bearded father of his people, appeared to him as a true representative of Vietnam's ancient culture and long tradition of independence. Mus seemed to have understood before many of his compatriots that the Japanese had destroyed the illusion of French power and that it could never be repaired. He prepared an eloquent sociological minute on the issue for a British general in Calcutta. The latter dismissed it brusquely as 'nothing important, just ideas!'[12] The British therefore entered the country with fixed assumptions and simple tasks in mind. Their first objective was to secure Japanese forces attached to Count Terauchi's Southern Army HQ in Singapore. They had to release Allied prisoners of war and civilian internees. They had to arrest 'black' and 'grey' Japanese 'war criminals' and notorious French Vichy collaborators including local mayors, merchants and purchasing agents. They were to maintain the 'writ of law' in the south and this quite soon came to be seen as a French writ, not a Vietnamese one. This whole operation was to be carried out in isolation from events in Hanoi and the north where Chiang's forces and their American advisers were much more inclined to respect the authority of Ho and the Viet Minh.

The first of General Gracey's troops to arrive from Rangoon was a detachment of Gurkhas. They were accompanied to Saigon by a Polish photojournalist, Germaine Krull. She contrasted the banners welcoming the Allies, but pointedly not the French, with the empty streets where 'a few sullen, stormy-eyed Chinese and Annamites [Vietnamese]' watched them furtively. The French population mobbed them, seeking news of France. They had been out of touch for four years and reported that since March relations with the local population had become even worse. 'How much longer do we have to put up with this Annamite trash?' someone asked.[13] The Japanese still maintained the fragile truce. The 14th Army was well aware that the Japanese in French Indo-China did not regard themselves as a defeated army, even though they had received a direct order from the emperor to surrender unconditionally. As in Burma immediately after the dropping of the bomb, some local resistance was expected from 'dissident units or individuals'.

One of Gracey's first orders was to stop Japanese soldiers from wandering around in search of entertainment in the port city of Cholon as they had been wont to do. On the other hand, these were 'surrendered personnel' and not prisoners of war. As such they were to keep their own officers. The British took this point seriously. It was made quite clear that Japanese commanders from Count Terauchi downwards should maintain strict discipline. They were expected to provide men for 'labour tasks such as reconstruction, rehabilitation and general maintenance, as required by commanders'.[14] They became in effect a huge coolie labour force. This was the reality of total defeat. Later, they were again required to risk their lives as frontline troops when the British war with the Viet Minh broke out. British commanders were advised to tell their forces to hold the Japanese at arm's length. There was to be no camaraderie, drinking sessions or musing over the events of the Burma campaign. The Japanese were a defeated enemy and were to be constantly reminded of this until they were sent back to Japan at the expense of the Japanese taxpayer. All the same, a degree of tacit co-operation took place between British, Indians and Japanese, occasionally directed against the French. The Japanese did not regard the French as victors in war and 'viewed them with veiled contempt'. In one incident Major Hagimura, a Japanese officer in control of medical stores, gleefully apprised his British opposite number that a French officer had come in search of stores: 'French officer look stores. No authority. Me throw officer out.'[15] Despite the

British order against fraternization, there were cases where officers swapped memories of the great battles at Imphal and Kohima in the previous year.

The trouble the British expected from the Japanese or the French never came. Instead, it was the Vietnamese who caused them grief. The situation deteriorated even before Gracey had got much of his force on the ground. On 2 September the Viet Minh hopefully celebrated Independence Day. People listened to Ho's speeches from the north and marched proudly down Paris Commune Street in Saigon. Suddenly shots rang out. The Vietnamese were convinced that French *agents provocateurs* had fired into the crowd.[16] Whatever the truth, Vietnamese radicals beat up many French people in retaliation. Vietnamese wives or mistresses of Frenchmen were also targeted: 'the enemy was yesterday's houseboy and coolie seeking revenge on his former masters'.[17] A French professor who had once sympathized with Vietnamese aspirations told Krull that his domestic servant had suddenly hit him over the head with a stick: 'I would never have believed it possible. I can understand revenge, but not this blind, wild fury,' he said.[18] There was a serious riot in Rue Catinat at the elegant heart of Saigon. The head of the Viet Minh police tried to calm the situation by arresting people he deemed troublemakers, such as Trotskyites or members of the Cao Dai and other armed religious sects. But the French settlers were already dangerously on edge.

When Gracey's main force arrived the city was draped with nationalist banners proclaiming 'Welcome British and Americans, but we have no room for the French'.[19] On 17 September the Viet Minh closed down Saigon and Cholon with a strike. This was an impolitic move since it gave the green light to bandit elements in Cholon to stage further attacks on French property. Gracey bluntly declared that the 'Annamite government was a direct threat to law and order through its armed Police Gendarmerie and its armed Guard Civile'. On 21 September he issued a draconian declaration of martial law, warning wrongdoers that they would be 'summarily shot'. This applied not simply to Saigon but to the whole of southern Indo-China. Mountbatten was especially shocked by its harshness. Gracey also closed down the Vietnamese press, which he believed was being stirred up by communists, announcing that 'all newspapers at present published in Saigon–Cholon in any language will be suspended immediately'. This was more drastic than the press restrictions imposed on frontier areas in India at the height of the war. It grated with the many European and American journalists in Asia who had been under the impression that the war had been fought for democracy and free speech.[20]

The Viet Minh were enraged, rightly feeling that they had lost everything gained over the previous months and that their legitimate authority was being swept aside. They immediately made plans for armed resistance. But Gracey outmanoeuvred them. On the prompting of Jean Cédile, the Free French representative, he surreptitiously armed more than a thousand French POWs and internees and stood back while they staged a coup against the Viet Minh People's Committee. On Sunday 23 September 1945 the French suddenly moved. Vietnamese guards were shot, committee members were imprisoned and some were hanged. Many nationalists were savagely beaten, while one French woman who sympathized with the Viet Minh had her hair shaved off like those who collaborated with the Germans in mainland France. Germaine Krull was disgusted by the violence of the disorderly mob of non-uniformed French soldiers who 'wandered through the streets as if celebrating 14 July, their guns slung over their shoulders, cigarettes dangling from their lips'.[21] On Rue Catinat she 'saw soldiers driving before them a group of Annamites bound, slave-fashion to a long rope. Women spat in their faces. They were on the verge of being lynched.'[22] This meant war, she thought.

The violence achieved little other than to inflame the situation. Cholon witnessed a counter-massacre of French residents and looting of their businesses by the bandit Bin Xuyen. At least 150 French men, women and children were brutally murdered there and in Saigon, setting in train a pattern of vicious French revenge. A British journalist reported that the terrified French population of one part of Saigon retreated to the Continental Palace Hotel as sniper bullets flew through the streets. The Vietnamese cooks and servants had run away so some Dutch former POWs, who had been imprisoned in Saigon by the Japanese, undertook to give the refugees a meal: 'Hot soup and stew was provided for hundreds of people in the hotel. As there was no light except a few candles the scene with crashing rain outside was ghastly and rather dramatic.'[23] Soon French, Indian, British and Viet Minh forces were engaged in scattered firefights across southern Indo-China. Still weak in numbers, the British rearmed and deployed their erstwhile enemies, the Japanese, against what most Vietnamese saw as the legitimate forces of a national government. General Philippe Leclerc, the French commander, wired his government that 'any signs of weakness or lack of agreement [among the Allies] would play the game of the Japanese and lead to grave consequences for the future of the white races in Asia'.[24] Leclerc was the tough Free French general who had liberated Paris from the Nazis along with General de Gaulle the previous year. Leclerc and other French officers believed that the Japanese were still surreptitiously aiding the Viet Minh. Though there is little evidence that this represented any kind of policy of Terauchi or his commanders, some Japanese deserters were probably fighting alongside the Vietnamese.[25]

Fighting went on until early in the new year of 1946, by which time most Viet Minh resistance in the south had been driven underground. There were several attempts at negotiation and several truces, all of which broke down. One of the first was made by the irrepressible Tom Driberg, who decided to spend a weekend in Saigon before flying back to Britain for the new parliamentary session. He quickly sized up the situation. The French, he wrote in *Reynolds News*, had behaved with 'maximum ineptitude and considerable cruelty'.[26] Not only had their municipal police fired on the local population amid 'disgraceful scenes of vengeance against helpless Annamites', but 'equally trigger-happy French degenerates haunt the opium dens'. Driberg later boasted that he had nearly prevented the Vietnam War. What he had actually done was to use his old London communist connections to try to arrange a meeting between the British authorities and the Viet Minh. Driberg had written to Mountbatten about this but the letter had reached South East Asia Command in Singapore only after Mountbatten had left for London. Driberg was convinced that Gracey had deliberately held it back.[27] Over the next two years Driberg continued to argue the case of the Vietnamese nationalists in Parliament, in the press and even in Paris.[28] Through Vietnamese connections in Paris he contacted Ho Chi Minh. But he could do little to influence events.

Later attempts by the British to end the fighting were equally unsuccessful. On 10 October, for instance, Gracey and his commanders attempted to explain themselves to Dr Pham Ngoc Thach and 'Mr Kien Cong Cung', who called themselves the 'heads of the civilian resistance'. 'The British have no interest in the politics of the country as between you and the French,' Gracey stated. But he went on to threaten the rebels with 'armed cars, guns, mortars and aircraft', adding that the British troops 'are today the finest trained troops in the world . . . You are fools if you think your troops can oppose them successfully.'[29] In response 'the Annamites said (with some justification) that, although we say we have no political interest in this country and are impartial, we are in fact being used to cover the concentration of large French forces'. The next day a Viet Minh spokesman said that the nationalists had no wish to impede the British in their laudable aim of disarming and repatriating the Japanese. 'Our only purpose,' he added, 'is to forbid French people or soldiers to get out of the region of Saigon or Cholon. So we beg you not to mix in your army any French soldiers, who after returning back to your bases, would occupy by force our towns and villages, as they did some days back in Saigon.'

On this occasion, Gracey claimed that the Viet Minh broke the truce. They staged marches and 'PT [Physical Training] parades' in the city. He admitted that the demonstrations were peaceful and that when they encountered massed British forces the demonstrators did little more than salute and turn about. What really concerned him was the possibility that armed insurgents were moving back into the city under the cover of the civilians who were slowly returning from their villages following the panic induced by the French coup. Gracey's letters give the impression that, while these events were unfolding, he was concerned above all with the lives of his own soldiers and then with the security of the European population of the city. These practical concerns apparently drove his actions from the declaration of martial law through to the final withdrawal of the 20th Indian Division in early 1946. But his hard line against the Viet Minh also had a doctrinaire aspect to it and this became clearer as he pondered the operation after it had finished. He saw himself very much as a representative of 'the Allies', not just a British commander, and 'the

Allies include the French', as he told the Viet Minh. A new France 'had fought gloriously to free their own country' and this was unknown to the 'Annamites'. Indo-China was without 'legal writ' and the only legality at hand was that of the French. He considered the extremist and hooligan reaction sparked off by Viet Minh demonstrations as barbaric and was soon asking for permission to 'bump off' – after summary trials – the perpetrators of 'flagrant' cases of murder.[30] He was also enraged that Hanoi Radio was broadcasting more and more anti-British and anti-French propaganda. He tried to get General Wedemeyer, the American commander of the Chinese forces in the northern sector, to have the nuisance stopped.

Mountbatten's position is clearer than when George Rosie wrote his diatribe in 1970, though his private papers – now open to researchers – are not particularly revealing. Mountbatten was clearly taken aback by Gracey's declaration of martial law on 21 September, above all by its catch-all character. He also rebuked Gracey for making the proclamation apply to the whole of southern Indo-China and not simply Saigon. He resented the fact that Leclerc had apparently gone back on his personal undertaking to him that he would not attack the Viet Minh without authority. Mountbatten was, however, a realist. He had always given his local commanders such as Slim and Leese a good deal of room for manoeuvre. He was aware that the 20th Indian Division was heavily outnumbered by resentful French and Japanese. To intervene and attempt to rein in Gracey might actually result in a sharp deterioration of the situation on the ground and lead to the loss of British and Indian lives, and the tying down of soldiers who were badly needed in Malaya, Borneo and India itself. Ultimately, he resolved, 'since you have taken this line and you are the man on the spot, it is my intention to support you'.[31] Moreover, Mountbatten had his doubts about the Viet Minh. They were probably communists, he thought, stirred up by the Chinese. They had been put in power by the Chinese nationalists and Japanese respectively. They had not fought against the latter as had the Burma Independence Army. There was, at least in southern Vietnam, no Aung San equivalent, only a group of distant and inscrutable politicians whom the French regarded as bandits.

Mountbatten was not happy, though. Always acutely aware of how events might be interpreted, he deprecated Gracey's uncompromising tone. He must have worried not only about the radical British press but also about the distant fulminations in Tokyo of his alter ego, Douglas MacArthur, against the perfidious English and the brutal French. He chided Gracey: 'I must say that it would be most indiscreet for a British Commander to put on record [as Gracey had done] that "tanks, ships, aircraft and guns" are massed against virtually unarmed people and that "useless misery" might ensue.' He was also 'distressed to see that you have been burning down houses, and in congested areas, too! Cannot you give such unsavoury jobs (if they really are military necessities) to the French in future?' Gracey replied with characteristic bluntness that he had to maintain 'a proper standard of British prestige' and that force was necessary because the Viet Minh had not the slightest intention in practice to make any distinction between British and French troops. British and Indian lives were at stake, so the threat of overwhelming force was appropriate. As for burning down Vietnamese houses, 'getting the French to help would result in the complete destruction of not 20 but 2,000 houses and probably without warning to the inhabitants'. Mountbatten's objections became more muted after this exchange. It is clear, though, that he remained frustrated and continued to see himself as the friend of national liberation movements. On 4 October he wrote to Driberg: 'I can assure you that if I was left as free a hand in French Indo-China as I was left in Burma, I could solve both problems by the same method', that is bringing the Viet Minh into a national government. The problem, he believed, was that the French, like the Dutch in Indonesia, were intransigent and refused to give any ground whatever to the nationalists.[32] Driberg used this letter along with his own observations on the ground when he attacked Paris and The Hague in Parliament later in the year. Mountbatten also benefited from the gamble of taking Driberg into his confidence. While he remained in Singapore or later as viceroy of India, he could always count on the arrival of detailed and gossipy letters from the roving correspondent about the state of parliamentary or popular opinion.

The muted argument continued among the British in Saigon, Rangoon and Singapore. Slim told his superiors in London mildly but firmly that their orders were 'somewhat contradictory'.[33] Later, a report of the Saigon Control Commission up to 9 November went the rounds of the commanders for comment. One note, not in Gracey's handwriting, recorded that the Saigon situation was 'an almost exact parallel with Burma. If only the French would promise progressive sovereignty to be complete at a very much earlier date (say two or three years) AND the Annamites would be equally ready to meet them, the situation might clear up.' One note said simply 'Good'. Another hand, possibly Gracey's, added, 'Waffle'. Perhaps this was the British officer who had dismissed Mus's reportage as 'just ideas'. More perceptively, someone had responded to a comment that it was 'inevitable that the French should re-establish control' with the query: 'Can they control any better than Annamites?'[34]

Despite the parallels that some wished to draw, the Indian Army soldiers faced quite different problems in Saigon and the surrounding countryside from the ones they encountered in the newly reconquered cities of Burma and Malaya. The French settlers, the '*colons*', were extremely ambivalent about them. As Mus pointed out, there had been little resistance to the Japanese and the population had embraced Vichy and 'Pétainisme' with complacency. Relatively speaking, the *colons* had suffered little from the war even during the scarcities of 1943–4. They wanted French troops back and, after the coup that Gracey sanctioned, they had arms themselves. The British were merely unwelcome birds of passage. Gracey had to fire off a letter to General Leclerc, the French officer commanding during the British occupation, insisting that he tell the settlers and French forces some home truths. The Indian Army had come to their rescue. As for arming the Japanese and putting them back on the streets, if the Japanese had not faithfully carried out Gracey's orders, 'there would have been a disaster of the first magnitude in Southern French Indo-China with a massacre of thousands of French people and the destruction of vast amounts of French property'. What irked Gracey particularly was the attitude of some of the French to the Indian troops. He insisted that Leclerc explain the 'camaraderie' that existed between the white officers and the Indian and Gurkha soldiers: 'Our men of whatever colour are our friends and are not considered "black" men. They expect and deserve to be treated in every way as first-class soldiers, and their treatment should be, and is, exactly the same as that of white troops.' In treating such men as 'black', the French had misunderstood 'our Indian Army traditions'.[35] This was an interesting reflection on differing racial attitudes in the two colonial systems. French settlers did not always subscribe to France's racially blind ideal of a civilizing mission among the non-white races. The French in Indo-China had been humiliated by Asians twice over, once by the Japanese and then by the Vietnamese. Many were not prepared to concede equality of any sort to Indians. Yet British attitudes were only superficially liberal. However friendly working relations appeared to be within the Indian Army, eating and socializing away from the front were still racially segregated activities. Indian officers had had to struggle hard to achieve a degree of equality with their white counterparts. Gracey, though, was sincere. He personally was little concerned with race and it was this that made *Chacha* ('Uncle') Gracey an acceptable commander-in-chief of Pakistan's army after independence.

Saigon and Cholon were elegant and prosperous cities fallen on hard times. Even after the French *estaminets* and cinemas reopened, there was little entertainment for the troops. Narain Das, a local Indian merchant, opened an Indian Other Ranks Club at the Cercle Hippique. A Canadian social worker from northern India, Mr Love, set up two YMCA clubs, one each for British and for Indian personnel. The more friendly of the French residents allowed British officers into the Cercle Sportif Saigonnais. But time hung heavily on their hands in the tense atmosphere of the city. The men began to amuse themselves in other ways. The French army and civilians had never had much of a problem with prostitution. There were no anti-vice leagues or distant fulminations by the Archbishop of Canterbury to close down brothels as there had been in India. The French organized them for easy access and checked the women's health regularly. But during the Japanese occupation the medical inspections had stopped. Indian and Gurkha troops began to contract VD in significant numbers. British medical officers tried to trace the source of disease. The men were deliberately vague about where they had picked it up, mumbling disclaimers such as 'in the Punjab four years ago'. The French were unhelpful, except 'in one way', as a medical officer put it sardonically: 'their troops so often filled the brothels that ours could not get in'.[36]

Infection of a political sort threatened the Indians and Gurkhas. During October and November Viet Minh and communist cadres tried to win over Indian Army men to their side. English and Vietnamese leaflets appeared denouncing the British: 'Indian Soldiers, You are our friends because your country is under British imperialism. You and your countrymen are struggling for independence as we are doing. Why are we struggling against each other?'[37] Indian and Vietnamese nationalism were the same emotion, one broadsheet explained lyrically: 'Viet-nam has once been brilliant and sparkling beneath the Asia-sky with its heroic and everlasting history.' Vietnamese would soon throw off the French yoke. Why were Indian soldiers spending their blood for 'evil capitalists'? Another, more politically astute message told the Indians that the San Francisco Broadcasting Station had reported that one 'Mr Nonon' had wired Prime Minister Attlee objecting to the use of Indian soldiers in the suppression of the Vietnamese people.[38] The 'Nonon' in question seems to have been a composite of Nehru and Menon. Both were indeed trying to rouse international public opinion against British and French actions in Vietnam and Indonesia. American opinion was receptive. General Douglas MacArthur called British and French action in Indo-China a betrayal of trust. Gracey was not too worried. He believed that the propaganda had little effect on his men, many of whom expressed their disgust at the communists' brutal attacks on the French and on Vietnamese women associated with them. But Gracey may have been over-confident. Tom Driberg recorded that some Indian soldiers were indeed worried at having to put down resistance among another Asian people, and particularly resented the use of Japanese troops to restore order.[39]

One side effect of the appearance of Indian soldiers in Saigon was the deterioration of relations between local Indian civilians and the Vietnamese. These had previously been quite good, though Indian moneylenders had come under attack in the 1930s. Whereas in Malaya, and particularly Burma, large and growing Indian populations had sparked resentment among local people who felt they were losing their jobs and livelihoods to them, this had not happened in French Indo-China. The 2,000-odd Indian residents here were grouped in the major cities, especially Saigon–Cholon, where they formed a quiet and prosperous merchant community. On the whole, they did not bring their families with them, unlike their contemporaries in the British territories and Thailand.[40] They stood out less as a community, partly because they were fragmented into local religious groupings. This absence of a single community identity had frustrated the Japanese during the occupation, when they had tried to foster branches of Bose's Indian Independence League in Saigon and Hanoi. When one finally did appear, it seems to have functioned chiefly as a protection racket, siphoning off funds from the big merchants, Chettiyars from southern India, into the pockets of the League's officers. But the local Indians' relative anonymity evaporated when Gracey arrived with the 20th Indian Division. Vietnamese resentments bubbled up when Indian soldiers appeared to be helping the British and, through them, the French to regain power. Half a dozen local Indians were murdered during the September outbreak and nearly seventy were kidnapped by militants. Indians presented huge compensation claims to the British authorities against the Vietnamese rioters, to add to their numerous headaches.[41]

Despite all this, the 20th Indian Division did not waver when, in late December and January, the Viet Minh tried one last push from Bien Hoa down towards Saigon. The poorly armed Vietnamese were mowed down by machine-gun fire as they encountered disciplined Gurkha and Indian soldiers. As the occupation came to an end, Gracey issued a 'Divisional commander sahib ki paigam'. This was an eloquent Urdu address in which he praised his soldiers for their steadfastness and bravery, saying that the name of the 20th Indian Division 'would shine throughout the world' (20 Hindustani Division ka nam tamam duniya men roshan hai). But the end was near for the Indian Army as an instrument of British world power. In October 1945 Lord Wavell, viceroy of India, had urged that Indian soldiers should be withdrawn from Indo-China as quickly as possible as Nehru and Patel inveighed against their use abroad. As 1946 wore on it became apparent that the leadership of the Indian National Congress was emerging as a regional and even international power. Further British action against national liberation movements with Indian soldiers would be impossible. This began to limit severely British options in both Burma and Malaya.[42]

The year 1945 drew to an end amid antiquated but highly symbolic ceremonial. On 30 November Mountbatten, inspecting Allied forces in Saigon, accepted Count Terauchi's sword as a formal signal of surrender. Earlier Gracey had worried that in the disturbed conditions of Indo-China this might seem to indicate that all authority had been abrogated. He urged instead that the ceremony take place in Singapore, where British power was fully re-established. Mountbatten also had had qualms: 'I do not wish to drag an invalid man of sixty-seven through a humiliating ceremony.' The Japanese field marshal was still suffering the after-effects of his stroke. Mountbatten concluded that the scale of Terauchi's humiliation should be limited by inviting few guests and reporters. Yet the surrender must be completed. Mountbatten required one sword for himself and one for his king-emperor. Terauchi duly sent an aide to retrieve his finest swords from his home in Japan and transport them to Saigon. At the ceremony, a *Times of Saigon* reporter noted, they were 'encased in draped boxes which according to Japanese tradition enhanced the act of presentation'.[43] Terauchi died shortly afterwards in Singapore, where his ashes were interred in the Japanese cemetery.

The *Times of Saigon* was a cyclostyled broadsheet with an issue of 500 daily. On 15 January 1946 it published its last issue. This recorded one final, slightly bizarre ceremony that had taken place the previous day. General Gracey and General Leclerc took the salute in the shadow of Saigon's French cathedral. The march-past took place to the music of the Dogra Pipe and Drum Band, a curious amalgam of Scottish bagpipes and the music of the Kashmir hills. The band's favourite tunes included 'Killiecrankie' and 'Scotland the Brave'.[44] It was accompanied by a French military band playing the battle music of the French Republic. Then the two generals went off to Government House, where the British handed over two further surrendered Japanese swords to the French. These weapons had previously belonged to the deputy Japanese commanders in the area. One sword was accompanied by a scroll that proclaimed that it was 650 years old. It is clear from other correspondence that Gracey regarded the swords as the symbol of Japanese sovereignty over Indo-China by right of conquest. He was now symbolically handing back that sovereignty to France, which he believed held it according to international law.

Standing alongside Leclerc during these hybrid colonial ceremonies was Admiral Thierry D'Argenlieu, France's new high commissioner for Indo-China. D'Argenlieu was a former monk. He followed General de Gaulle's orders to the letter, believing that it was his mission to bring back Indo-China, with its substantial population of French, Eurasian and Indo-Chinese Catholics, into the fold of Christian civilization. One of his staff observed privately that he possessed 'the most brilliant mind of the Twelfth Century'. Within a short time D'Argenlieu began an attack on the base of Viet Minh power in Hanoi and Haiphong to the north. This was to set the scene for thirty years of savage fighting which ended only with the fall of the American-backed government in Saigon in 1975. Douglas Gracey saw clearly what would happen. He had written to Slim on 5 November 1945 that the French troops moving out from Saigon had left a trail of atrocious destruction behind them. This would 'lead to such resentment that it will be progressively difficult for them to implement their new policy, and, I am convinced, will result in guerrilla war, increased sabotage and arson, as soon as we leave the country.'[45] Yet Gracey also believed that the restoration of French power was 'inevitable' and, no less important, necessary to protect the retreat of his own soldiers. He stuck to a politically barren doctrine of sovereignty and seemed unable to understand the post-war power of national liberation movements. Mountbatten and Slim were too distant to moderate his position. As Germaine Krull had observed back in September 1945: 'The Annamites will win their independence because they are ready to die for it. We must recognise this inevitable fact.'[46]

BRITAIN AND THE BIRTH OF INDONESIA

This lesson was forced home in the Dutch East Indies, and at a bloody cost in Indonesian, Indian and British lives. The Allied reoccupation was a strung-out affair. British troops landed in force only towards the end of October 1945. General MacArthur, in whose command the region originally fell, had not felt the need for an immediate intervention in the former Dutch colony. He feared resistance from the 250,000-odd Japanese who remained in the theatre, and demanded that action wait upon the formal surrender of the Japanese in Tokyo Bay. The transfer of responsibility for Indonesia to Mountbatten's command came on 15 August, with MacArthur's warning: 'Tell Lord Louis to keep his pants on or he will get us all into trouble.' At a stroke of the pen, the area under South East Asia Command was increased by half a million square miles, and another 80 million people were added to its responsibilities. Mountbatten's already strained communications were strung out another 2,000 miles across a vast archipelago. South East Asia Command had become the largest single administrative apparatus on earth.

Indonesia lay at the final stretch of the great strategic arc of control from Suez to Sydney harbour: it was the 'Malay barrier' that had broken with such dire consequences in early 1942. By 1945, British interests in the region were chiefly economic: pre-war British investments in the Dutch colony totalled £100 million, and this included a 40 per cent stake in Royal Dutch Shell with its large refineries in Sumatra and Borneo.[47] In August 1945 a highly secret agreement had been signed by the Dutch granting the British and Americans access to thorium deposits – vital for nuclear processes – on Singkep island, south of Singapore.[48] But by the end of 1945 Britain had been drawn into the fire of a national revolution that threatened to overwhelm its own possessions in Southeast Asia.

The British were once again the proxy for a defeated power of Europe. To the Dutch, the reconquest of Indonesia was vital to their credibility as a nation. In the words of the wartime Dutch prime minister, Pieter Gerbrandy: 'The Netherlands nation is far more than a small part of the European continent. We have a stake in four continents. Our overseas interests condition our very existence.'[49] The will to empire was intensified by an emotive nostalgia: the Netherlands East Indies was 'Holland's Atlantis'.[50] Pre-war Dutch administration was admired by British colonial officials for its technocratic achievements, but known also by its unflinching authoritarianism: the *Rust en Orde* – tranquillity and order – that it took as its motto. But the Dutch had never fully controlled the archipelago. Their power was felt in ever-decreasing circles around core areas of control: the world's most densely populous island, Java, the plantation belt around Medan in northern Sumatra, and the Christianized island trading posts of Maluku in the east. Most of the archipelago was governed only lightly through local authority, such as the Islamic sultanates of east Sumatra, southern Borneo and Sulawesi and other tiers of subordinate native officials or tribal chiefs. Even at the epicentre of empire on Java, the royal courts of Yogyakarta and Surakarta still possessed aura and authority, and the proud *priyayi* aristocracy had carved out a role for themselves as a native administrative elite. It was a kaleidoscopic society, shaped by influential minorities such as the wealthy communities of Chinese and Arab traders and governed by an elaborate and legally entrenched racial hierarchy. At the apex of this world stood a large community of Dutch settlers and officials. In the villaed suburbia of cities such as Jakarta, Bandung and Surabaya they had enjoyed a privileged lifestyle that made the social excesses of pre-war Malaya and Indo-China seem modest by comparison. At its margins was the Indo-European community. For many generations it had been the custom of the Indies Dutch to take 'temporary wives' locally and create families that remained behind in Indonesia when a father was repatriated to the Netherlands. In 1945 the Dutch settlers and Eurasians who emerged from the Japanese internment camps were to face the most uncertain of futures.

In the years after the First World War, the façade of *Rust en Orde* had been crumbling. To describe this era as one of 'national awakening' does inadequate account to the maelstrom which confronted the British in late 1945. For Indonesians, the first decades of the century were the time of *pergerakan*, the age of movement: of dramatic experiment, particularly in journalism and letters in the Malay medium, which was fashioned by writers into a new Indonesian national language. It was also a 'world-upside-down': old hierarchies were challenged by a level of popular mobilization that was not to be found in Britain's Southeast Asian colonies. Different streams of thought and action emerged, sometimes in synthesis, sometimes in competition.[51] Global currents of Islamic resurgence swept through Indonesia, and re-energized an old tradition of religious learning at a village level. In Sumatra, from where many of the new intellectuals heralded, in Java and then beyond, arose 'wild schools', independent of the Dutch system, whose graduates created a series of Islamic associations that both the Dutch and the Japanese hesitated to repress. Then came the internationalism of Marxism. The Partai Komunis Indonesia (PKI), founded in 1920, was the first in Asia. It had emerged, in part, out of the Islamic movement, and some of its key intellectuals sought to equate the struggle for Islam with the struggle against colonialism and capitalism. The PKI was repressed savagely by the Dutch after abortive uprisings in 1926 and 1927. As many as 13,000 people were arrested, and 1,308 of them sent to a purpose-built 'isolation colony' at Boven Digul in New Guinea. However, they left behind them a spectre that haunted European power throughout the Malay world after the war: that of Islamic social revolution.

By the 1930s a more secular nationalism had taken centre stage. Parties were formed and were dissolved in fierce disputes as to how Dutch rule, and its insipid efforts to reform itself, might best be challenged. The dominant personality was Sukarno, a Dutch-trained engineer who sought to build on the legacy of the *pergerakan* by synthesizing the different ideological currents and movements in the name of national unity: his 1926 credo was entitled *Nationalism, Islam and Communism*. His oratorical style, which appealed to Javanese mythology and to the symbolic language of the shadow-play theatre, was utterly beguiling to an Indonesian audience, and incomprehensible to most Europeans. In 1945 Sukarno would emerge as the charismatic centre of the nation. Yet in the relative calm before the storm of the Japanese conquest of Indonesia, the Dutch seemed to have neutralized the threats of nationalism, Islamism and communism, and that of Sukarno himself. He was arrested for sedition in 1933, exiled to Flores and then Bengkulu in south Sumatra, where he disappeared entirely from public view. The other leaders of national stature, the Sumatran-born intellectuals Muhammad Hatta and Sutan Sjahrir, were sent to the malarial jungle fastness of Boven Digul. Given that they were the most educated Indonesians of their day, this was a damning testimony to the failure of Dutch rule. The PKI remained underground; its leaders spread their influence in a self-imposed exile in British Malaya and Singapore, where many of the Malays were recent migrants from other parts of the archipelago. Through these links, the vision of a vast, free Indonesia was kindled.

When the Dutch fled the islands in 1942, few Indonesian leaders held any illusion that co-operation with the colonial power was possible. All the pent-up ideological ferment and popular frustration found expression in a world and a time out of joint. To this, the Japanese invasion brought a sense of millennial expectation: in Java it seemed to herald the fulfilment of the prophecy of the twelfth-century King Joyoboyo that the rule of the white man would end with the coming of the dwarfish yellow men who would reign as long as 'a maize seed took to flower'.[52] There was genuine popular enthusiasm for the Japanese in many parts of Indonesia, and the impact of Japanese social policy was very marked. But the promise of Japanese rule was not sustained and it soon generated deep resentments, as the state trespassed into areas of neighbourhood and family life which the Europeans had wisely steered clear of. The moment the Japanese ordered people to bend in prayer to the Imperial Palace in Tokyo was, as the Sumatran writer Hamka termed it: 'the day of the severest trial for Muslims'.[53] The great crimes of the Japanese occupation were perhaps committed most freely in Indonesia: *romusha* forced labourers were sent to projects in the outer islands, and further afield in Singapore, Burma and Thailand, and women were enslaved for the 'comfort houses'. These and other policies, such as food requisitioning, discredited many of the traditional authority figures, who were associated with them as Japanese underlings. By 1945 the situation was explosive: the people of Indonesia were living in conditions of dire poverty and nursing bitter resentments against authority of all kinds.

But a vital and enduring legacy of Japanese rule was what one historian has termed its 'ideological, fanatical romanticism'.[54] This created a new sense of the possible for many young Indonesians. In particular, the Japanese led an assault on the Dutch language and in the war years Malay, or more strictly *bahasa Indonesia*, gained credence as a 'national' language. By the end of the war a self-proclaimed 'Generation of 1945' spearheaded a literary revolution in the service of national struggle. The iconic figure of the time was Chairil Anwar, the Medan-born poet. His urgent, intense language distilled the revolutionary personality, and was fired by a sense of the power of words to shape events, no more so than in the 1943 poem, '*Aku*' – 'I':

Surrendered Japanese troops in Burma, August 1945

Japanese troops clearing the Singapore Padang before the surrender ceremony,
12 September 1945

Lt General Seishiro Itagaki signing the surrender, Singapore, 12 September 1945

Mountbatten announces the surrender of the Japanese in Singapore, September 1945

A forgotten army: surrendered Japanese in north Malaya,
November 1945

Seagrave's return, 1945

Leclerc and Gracey with Japanese
sword of surrender, Saigon, 1945

Soldiers of the Parachute Regiment, Java, 1945

Bengal sappers and miners watch the reprisal burning of the village of Bekassi,
Java, 1945

Imperialism's return? Christison in Java, 1946

Sukarno addresses an 'ocean' rally, Java, 1946

Charisma and revolution: Sukarno, Java, 1946

Nehru's arrival at Kallang Airport, Singapore, April 1946

Macdonald inspects the Malay Regiment, Kuala Lumpur, 1946

Dorman Smith leaves Burma, June 1946

Muslim rioters and the corpse of a Hindu, Calcutta, August 1946

India's interim government at their swearing in, Delhi 1946

When my time comes
No one's going to cry for me,
And you won't, either
The hell with all those tears!

I'm a wild beast
Driven out of the herd
Bullets may pierce my skin
But I'll keep coming,
Carrying forward my wounds and my pain
Attacking
Attacking

Until suffering disappears
And I won't give a damn
I want to live another thousand years.[55]

Chairil Anwar lived fast and died young, in 1949, of tuberculosis. His influences were diverse, modern, and often European. In the words of the Generation of 1945's 'Testimony': 'we are heirs of world culture'. But Chairil Anwar also became an archetype of the kind of figures who gave the Indonesian revolution its distinctive character: they were known as *pemuda*, a word which translates as 'youth', but conveys much more than this: a spirit that challenged the poised bureaucratic finesse of the older elite generation. It was a claim to lead in troubled, dislocated times, to take responsibility when others had failed. These elements of *pemuda* identity had deep roots in Javanese culture.[56] The *pemuda* were not a party as such, nor a clear class. They were vague coteries of young, mostly single men who took upon themselves the responsibility for the Indonesian revolution. They were marked by their attire; their simple clothes and long hair, and a semi-military swagger; they chose to speak in a staccato, commanding Indonesian, or a low form of Javanese, ignoring affectations of status: all men were *bung* – brother – or *saudara* – comrade. At times the world of the *pemuda* would overlap with the criminal world of the towns, the social banditry of the countryside, and the anger of the ordinary folk. Their watchword was *Merdeka!* or Freedom! But again this word had deeper connotations: derived from the term for the free men of early colonial Java – the *mardijkers* – it evoked freedom from slavery and, after 1945, political independence. But it was also something to be lived: a freedom of the spirit, a freedom from fear of death. The cry *Merdeka!* would be answered with a raised fist and *Bebas!* – Unchained! In the dark days of 1945, it would be answered also by the shout of *Mati!* – Death! By the end of the Japanese occupation, the *pemuda* would drive forward events, goading on the more moderate nationalist leaders. As they were to acknowledge: 'These long-haired youths, these armed fighters whose names were not known, were the strength of our Revolution.'[57]

As in India and elsewhere, the Japanese war had divided the older nationalists. Sukarno, Hatta and Sjahrir were brought out of exile. Back in Jakarta, they adopted complementary strategies. Hatta co-operated with the Japanese regime in the hope of ameliorating some of the effects of occupation. Sutan Sjahrir, a socialist internationalist, was to organize an underground. Sukarno himself saw the war as a contest between empires and was more open to exploiting its political opportunities. He did so by aligning himself with some of the Japanese initiatives and manipulating them for his own national purposes. With a formidable Japanese propaganda machine behind him, Sukarno honed his oratorical skills, and although he was not immune from criticism for his association with unpopular policies, he managed, by subtle shifts in message that were never really translatable to the Japanese, to project his claim to embody the nation. He played to the messianic mood: independence, he said, was a 'golden bridge' to a glorious future. Politics became a form of theatre, in which the main actors were the Indonesian auxiliary forces that the Japanese recruited and armed. These took multiple forms and, as in Burma and Malaya, a generation of young men became deeply militarized. By the last months of the war the Japanese were losing control of these forces; at the surrender they were dissolved into a host of local militias. When the Japanese surrendered, they unleashed revolution.[58]

The initial events were dramatic enough, but, in the light of what was to come, relatively peaceful. In mid 1945 the war effort was at a point where Sukarno and Hatta found the Japanese more receptive to the idea of a declaration of independence for Indonesia. This was hammered out at a meeting in early August between the Indonesians and Field Marshal Count Terauchi at his headquarters in Dalat in Vietnam. On their return on 12 August, Sukarno and Hatta stopped in Malaya at Taiping airport. There the Malay radical Ibrahim Yaacob met them to try to persuade them to include Malaya within a greater Indonesia: an *Indonesia raya*. The provisional date for the declaration of independence was 7 September, and the first meeting of the planning committee was scheduled for 18 August. But events moved faster than this. The sudden surrender of Japan precipitated a crisis. Sukarno and Hatta well realized that the good will of the Allies was vital to the success of Indonesia's freedom. But there were other, more radical voices, not least those associated with the socialist underground. On 17 August – in a dramatic foreshadowing of the shape of things to come – Sukarno was kidnapped by his own armed *pemuda*. They were determined that the new nation should not be seen as a Japanese puppet regime. Sukarno was compelled to seize back the initiative. In the courtyard of his house in Jakarta he read out the prosaic formula: 'We, the people of Indonesia, hereby declare Indonesia's independence.'[59] There was no mention of Malaya, or of *Indonesia raya*, but in the minds of many Malays their destiny still was bound up with that of the new nation.

Such was the force behind this idea that spontaneous declarations for the new republican government, and of loyalty to President Sukarno, were made throughout the islands. But the new government was not universally embraced: many local administrators were suspicious; many local aristocrats feared its levelling rhetoric; others were simply bewildered by the pace of events and uncertain where their loyalties should lie. In many areas it was young partisans who seized the initiative in the republic's name. In the face of this, Japanese troops as often as not withdrew into their secured perimeters, leaving the streets, key buildings and installations in the hands of the Indonesians. Soon the key royal houses, such as Yogyakarta, and local governors in Java and the outer islands declared for the republic. By September it possessed a relatively stable bureaucracy and, with the assistance of many sympathetic Japanese officers, the core of a well-equipped army. This was a massive shift in initiative, and one that was to reverberate throughout the Malay world. At the same time, however, the Indonesian revolution unleashed all the social frustration and political anger of decades of colonial rule and Japanese oppression. It was unclear how far this could be controlled by the new political elite in Jakarta.

This first phase of revolution reached a crescendo with a series of massive 'ocean' rallies in Indonesia's major cities. On 19 September a crowd of 200,000 gathered in Ikeda Square in Jakarta under the watchful eyes of a cordon of Japanese troops. Many in the crowd were armed with sharpened bamboo staves. Sukarno, increasingly worried about provoking the Japanese or the Allied armies that were poised to take their place, had tried and failed to prevent the assembly but, in a moment of supreme political theatre, demonstrated his control over the crowd by taking the rostrum, persuading it to disperse peacably. Not everyone was impressed. A silent witness to this event was Tan Malaka. One of the first leaders of the Partai Komunis Indonesia, he had been in exile since 1922, living under a string of pseudonyms, working as an agent of the Comintern, avoiding the colonial police. It was a life that was lived, as the title of his memoirs has it, 'from jail to jail'. He was perhaps the most travelled Indonesian of his age: a legend, like Lai Teck in Malaya, a figure for the cloak-and-dagger novels of the day, Patjar Merah, the Scarlet Pimpernel of the Asian revolution. He had returned to Indonesia only in 1942, incognito, working as a clerk in a Japanese coal mine in Java, a stranger in his own country. In August he revealed his identity to the revolutionary leaders, though not to the public. Such was his mystique that Sukarno even signed a secret document stating that Tan Malaka should assume the leadership of the revolution were Sukarno to be incapacitated. But the veteran revolutionary felt that his time had not yet come. The Ikeda Square demonstration had been his suggestion: a way of testing the will of the revolutionaries. He was disappointed in Sukarno, who had come not to inspire the crowd to action, 'but to request the masses to "have faith" and "obey" and to order them to go home'.[60] He was appalled at the concessions Sukarno was prepared to make to the imperial powers. He bided his time, waiting to reveal himself and seize his moment as had Ho Chi Minh in Vietnam. Perhaps a more telling comparison would prove to be Subhas Chandra Bose. In 1945 there were to be reports and sightings of various 'Tan Malakas' throughout Java and Sumatra. In Malaya, some – including British intelligence – believed that the mysterious founder of the Malay Nationalist Party, Mokhtaruddin Lasso, was none other than the 'Scarlet Pimpernel'.[61]

The British and Dutch heard little of events in Java. During the war there had been virtually no intelligence gathered about Indonesia, an information gap which British secret warriors were now tasked to fill. Even as Special Operations Executive was being rapidly wound down in Europe, Mountbatten retained a force of not less than 2,500 for peacetime tasks. The need for information about Indonesia was desperate.[62] There were a few Dutch officers at Mountbatten's HQ at Kandy, but most Dutch who knew anything about Indonesia were either in Japanese prison camps or in Australia, as part of a government-in-exile at Camp Columbia just outside Brisbane, where their shipping – known as 'Flying Dutchmen' to port workers – choked the harbour. A formal Anglo-Dutch agreement on civil affairs was signed only on 24 August. It gave authority to a British commander working through a Netherlands Indies Civil Affairs Administration. The British were to take responsibility for Java and Sumatra; the outer islands would be looked after by the Australians. Dutch political planning for the future of its vast Asian empire was founded upon a speech made by Queen Wilhelmina on the first anniversary of Pearl Harbor: it reaffirmed the 'indivisibility of the Kingdom'. As a sop to United States opinion it called for a conference with national leaders, but the proposal was no advance on the last major programme of Dutch colonial reform in 1918; arguably, it promised less. When it was announced in Indonesia, it was met with scorn: 'ridiculous', a leader in West Java recalled, 'as if Hitler and Japan had done nothing to the world of men'.[63]

The first landings on the isolated Dutch territories of New Guinea gave no foretaste of conditions elsewhere. The first British officers to parachute into Java and Sumatra added little to the picture: they landed on 8 September and reported a reasonably peaceable situation. They met the moderate Indonesian leaders, and not the *pemuda*. In any case, their principal task was to begin to locate the 100,000-odd prisoners of war and civilian internees in Indonesia. They were mostly Dutch, but included British women detained in remote locations after their ships had been sunk in the 'Dunkirk'-type small-ship exodus from Singapore a few days before its fall. Their conditions were dire. It was at this point that tensions began to mount. Like their British counterparts, the former Dutch officials in the internment camps fully expected to return to their Indonesian homes and resume their old jobs and, unlike the old Malaya hands, the opportunity was there for them to do so. They were, therefore, bitterly angry on hearing the first broadcast announcements of South East Asia Command ordering them to stay in their camps. Many now hated the Indonesians for what they saw as betrayal. Many defied SEAC and began re-enter the towns to reclaim their old privileges.

The returning Dutch found a new world, one that now belonged to exultant Indonesians. The red and white flag of the republic flew from public buildings, shops and houses. Graffiti were scoured on walls and banners spanned the streets. They saw everywhere the word *Merdeka!* and also citations – in English, the language of the Atlantic Charter – from the preamble of the United States Constitution, even of Abraham Lincoln's Gettysburg address. Many Indonesians fully expected to enlist the support of the Allies behind the revolution. The ex-internees were entirely unprepared for such scenes. Emaciated and in rags, many were treated sympathetically by the Indonesians they met, but refused to abandon the arrogance and swagger they had shown during the pre-war era. Antagonism erupted into violence. Dutch men and women were murdered as they tried to reclaim their businesses and homes. Men of military age were especially vulnerable. Derek van den Boegarde was deeply scarred by the memory of domestic murder in Bandung, where he was stationed with the British forces: Dutch internees had returned to their homes, 'trying with what remained of their looted belongings to restart their lives, only to lose them in acts of hysterical hatred and violence'.[64] Hotels and clubs became battlegrounds. As in French Indo-China, there was an obsession with symbols of sovereignty. In many towns and cities there was a 'war of the flags'. One incident at the focal point of European community life in Surabaya, the Oranje Hotel, was to assume a much wider significance. On 19 September young Dutch and Eurasians crowded round the hotel, then principally housing journalists and still bearing its Japanese name, the Yamato. In an atmosphere almost of schoolboy rivalry they entered the hotel and raised a Dutch tricolour. Angry Indonesian youths stoned the building, fatally injuring a Eurasian lawyer. They scaled the walls of the hotel and ripped the blue stripe from the flag, leaving the red and white of the republic flying.[65] The Eurasians were incensed. In the words of the writer Idrus, an acerbic witness to events in the city: 'They remembered how things had been three and a half years before, and they remembered their fathers, who had been real Dutchmen. And they felt insulted, as though their own fathers had been stripped naked.'[66] A mêlée ensued. In Jakarta, Indonesian medical students responded by electrifying the flag poles.[67]

The first major British landing was in Jakarta on 15 September, a month after the end of the war, when HMS *Cumberland* docked in Tanjong Priok harbour. The first regiment ashore was 29 Seaforth Highlanders. The regiment had served in the last British occupation of Java: Thomas Stamford Raffles's conquest of 1811. Raffles had sought to reform and reverse the corrupting effects of Dutch rule on native society. In 1945 British officers were to invoke his memory. The bulk of 23 Indian Division disembarked on 25 September in an eerie calm. It was not a scene of chaos. 'The trams ran regularly up Koningsplein, the trains steamed out of the main station to Bandung with innumerable passengers.'[68] The tensions rose as Dutch began to arrive in the baggage-train of the British. The first senior official on the scene was Charles van der Plas, the pre-war governor of East Java: the vanguard of the Netherlands Indies Civil Affairs administration. He was met with a poster: *Nèr Plasje – Indonesia maoe kaoe tjatoet – Djenggolmoe nanti koe tjaboet!* It was a cruel play on his name; loosely translated, it read: 'Hey piss-puddle – If you try to wipe out Indonesia – I'll pull your beard!'[69] His first broadcasts to the people of the islands were a disaster: he spoke of ruthless retribution for traitors and collaborators, by which he clearly meant Sukarno and Hatta. In his first reports he gave Mountbatten no hint of the difficulties that were to be met: 'The Indonesians', he informed the supremo, 'are too nice a people to fight really hard.'[70] The Dutch military commanders were ill-equipped to comprehend the magnitude and the meaning of the events that had taken place in Jakarta. They disliked the British; they resented the precedence that seemed to be given to French interests in Indo-China.[71] They had spent the war living a grotesque colonial fantasy in Camp

Columbia, where racist attitudes were, if anything, worse than in the pre-war Indies, and the Indonesians were openly called *bangsat* – 'son of a bitch'.[72] The two senior military men were Admiral Helfrich, a disciplinarian who thought the antidote to nationalism was corporal punishment, and General van Oyen, 'so fond of his wine, his food and his women', according to a 1946 British official report, and 'universally disliked by his countrymen, particularly by the ladies who rightly or wrongly believed that he flew out of Bandung in March 1942 with his mistress, leaving his wife behind'.[73]

When the lieutenant governor, Dr Hubertus J. van Mook, arrived on 1 October, he too was welcomed by a crowd waving placards. Very short-sighted and unable to read them, he turned to his secretary: 'What do they say?' There came the answer: ' "Death to van Mook", Your Excellency.'[74] Van Mook viewed the Indies as his homeland; he was born in Java. So too was van der Plas, probably of a mixed marriage. A celebrated scholar of Islam, van der Plas had been taunted by hardliners as an *Inlander liefde*: a lover of the natives. Van Mook and van der Plas personify many of the contradictions of the reforming imperialisms of the end of empire. They shared a vision of 'association', in which the Indies Dutch, with a privileged status, gave cohesion to the ethnically diverse society of the archipelago under the tutelage of the Netherlands – a kind of tropical Canada. But it was a politically barren vision that would compel the Indies Dutch to fight like Boers in southern Africa to maintain their primacy. To men like van Mook and van der Plas, 'Indonesia' was merely a geographical expression. Their vision of a multiracial society was sincerely held, but it led them to despise nationalism, which they saw as ethnic chauvinism. They did not recognize the republic's leaders, they put their faith in old hierarchies and they saw no possibility of departure from the governing obsession with *Rust en Orde*.[75] Above all, they could not comprehend that the coming conflict was to be a war between nation-states.

As in the case of Indo-China, the British intervention was seen, both by its critics at the time and by historians since, as a calculated war of imperial conquest. Like Indo-China, the forces shaping policy were more complex and driven by the pace of events on the ground.[76] But more than this, it was a definitive encounter with nationalism. There were important differences in approach between the two territories. The British commander was Lieutenant General Sir Philip Christison. A baronet and former medical doctor, he had won the first British victories against the Japanese in Burma and had been knighted in the field by Lord Wavell – the first such event since the Middle Ages. Like Gracey in Vietnam, he was told by Mountbatten that he was to be a politician, and ultimately to 'carry the can'. But he was perhaps better equipped for this task than Gracey, and more instinctively sympathetic to nationalism. Attlee counted himself 'lucky to have a soldier-statesman there'.[77] Although for both men the safety of their troops was an overriding concern, the British paid for their presence in Indonesia with vastly more casualties than in Indo-China, and this shaped Christison's attitude to the Dutch. He was appalled by their intransigence and, in the face of it, was less cowed by constitutional niceties than was Gracey in Vietnam. In any event, the British could more easily afford to offend the Dutch than the French. Although the question of Dutch sovereignty was unquestioned at the diplomatic level, there was a wide difference between the capacity of the Dutch and the French to restore their own authority on the ground. It was not until March 1946 that Dutch troops landed in Java in any numbers. The earlier arrivals gave major provocation to the Indonesians without contributing to security. Their Indonesian auxiliaries, mostly Christian Ambonese, were a liability. Many felt that their trigger-happy entry into Jakarta was an attempt to provoke the British into more decisive moves to save the Dutch empire. But Christison embargoed the introduction of more Dutch troops: if any were landed, he told Mountbatten on 13 October, civil war was inevitable. They were diverted to the outer islands, which were under the jurisdiction of Australian forces, and a much milder political climate.[78] Faced by an armed revolution, British troops would bear the liability for the bitter-ender mentality of the Dutch. Both Christison and Mountbatten viewed this prospect with horror.

There were now clear limits to what British soldiers were prepared to take. Morale, Mountbatten told the chiefs of staff in mid October, was good. But there was every likelihood it would deteriorate. His men were war weary, and many of them had slogged through the worst of the Burma campaign. They were obsessed with demobilization and did not understand their role in Indonesia. It would be a 'grave mistake', Mountbatten warned, to give any impression that 'they are about to become involved in putting down local independence movements on behalf of other governments in countries they are liberating'.[79] The Indonesia campaign was the last outreach of the Raj, and carried with it all the signals of its imminent dissolution. Only four of the thirty battalions at Mountbatten's disposal were British. It was not clear how willing the Indian troops would be to fight another Asian nationalist movement. Congress supported the new republic. Nehru asked to visit Java to assess the situation, but Mountbatten could not guarantee his safety. Reports on SEAC units in the early part of 1946 spoke of a 'growing sympathy' for the INA and a deep dislike of the Dutch, who treated sepoys 'like . . . native[s]'.[80] For their part, Dutch internees had little faith in the Indian soldiers' ability to protect them.[81] Indian Muslim soldiers came under a barrage of republican propaganda. Indonesian nationalists believed many of them to be sympathetic to their cause. The West Java leader, Abu Hanifah, witnessed an Islamic militia attacking a small British convoy crying *Allahu akbar!* God is Greater! The Indian Muslims escorting it then put out a white flag. 'What do you want from us?' they asked, and supplied the fighters with tinned food and cigarettes, rifles and ammunition.[82] By the end of the year, there were reports of desertions to the republican forces, some lured by pan-Islamic propaganda, others by promises of women and plenty.[83]

Mountbatten limited the British mission in Indonesia to the preservation of law and order in key areas; the disarming and repatriation of the Japanese and the release of prisoners of war and internees. On 10 October Mountbatten decided to focus on the key port cities of Jakarta, Semarang and, fatefully, Surabaya. The hill towns immediately behind, where many of the internees were believed to be, were to be occupied if possible. In the interim Mountbatten had informed Count Terauchi that the preservation of peace in Java was the responsibility of the Japanese. There were, at the surrender, 65,000 Japanese troops in Java alone. But such was the magnitude and multitude of the tasks facing the British that the Japanese were deployed in a much wider role. The British were warned against this by Sukarno, who, struggling to control the *pemuda*, feared that reprisals would be taken against Dutch internees.[84] An early flashpoint was Bandung, the major inland city of West Java. Japanese commanders in the city were keen to reassert their authority and, with at least the tacit encouragement of British liaison officers, Bandung was reoccupied on 10 October. This was a major humiliation to the local revolutionary leaders: they were sent lipsticks by their comrades in East Java. In Semarang the local British officer, fearing attacks on internment camps, turned to the Japanese for aid. Their local commanders too were incensed after the detention and killing of Japanese civilians by *pemuda* forces, and struck back on 15 October – 'fighting mad', in one British account – giving no quarter to Indonesians in arms. About 2,000 Indonesian and several hundred Japanese lives were lost. In these areas the use of Japanese troops went far beyond the minimal defensive requirements of the peace agreement and, in Semarang and elsewhere, they were incorporated into the command structure of the British and Gurkha forces who began to arrive in the cities after the worst of the fighting was over. The Japanese commander in Semarang, Major Kido, was recommended for a DSO. In East Sumatra Japanese troops were used on a large scale after attacks on British forces and their own men: at the market town of Tebing Tinggi a Japanese operation in mid December left between 2,000 and 5,000 dead. Whilst the British government struggled to justify the use of Japanese troops even to rescue internees, in Sumatra, in conditions of some secrecy, the Japanese were used to guard key economic installations until as late as November 1946. Mountbatten, on an official visit to Palembang in April 1946, was shocked to be greeted by a 1,000-strong Japanese guard of honour, the officers saluting him with their swords.[85] Yet individual Japanese field commanders saw their role in very different ways. As one Japanese officer in Sumatra put it: 'Most of us had no earnest desire to prevent the flow of arms.' They would stage mock battles as cover and leave 'presents' of ammunition behind. By the end of 1945 perhaps 1,700 Japanese in Java, 350 Japanese in North Sumatra and 100 more in Aceh had defected to fight with the revolution. Most of them were killed in battle.[86]

From their first arrival until the departure of the British over a year later the Dutch protested at lack of support from the British. They were furious at Christison's first statements on landing in Jakarta, which promised good will and co-operation with the Indonesians. They argued that it amounted to a 'virtual recognition' of the republic. Such was the mood in The Hague that it was considered treasonable even to talk to the nationalists. From early October Mountbatten's political adviser, Esler Dening, attempted to mediate in Jakarta. Whilst Britain wholeheartedly desired the return of the French and the Dutch to their positions, he argued, it was vital not to prejudice Britain's own position in the Far East. Both French and Dutch had to be saved from themselves to ensure that they did 'not to imperil the general position of European power in the Far East'.[87] With increasing frustration, he urged the Dutch to talk. The first meeting between the British – Christison and Dening – and the new Indonesian government took place in Jakarta on 24 October. The republic was represented by Sukarno and Hatta. Dening was impressed by Hatta, but less so with Sukarno: 'not a man of remarkable character'. Both men were struck by the extent to which the Indonesians felt that the Dutch were in thrall to pre-war attitudes.[88] By this time van Mook was visibly under strain. Mountbatten demanded that more authority be given to van Mook to bring the republican leadership to talks, but the main stumbling block was Sukarno, whom the Dutch saw as an arch-collaborator and with whom they would not negotiate. A South African officer, Laurens van der Post, later to win fame as a travel writer and spiritual guru to the present Prince of Wales, was flown to The Hague to meet with the die-hards in the Dutch government. He had been a prisoner of war in Sumatra and was the first eyewitness to events in Java to reach the Netherlands. He also saw Attlee, and although he was dismissive of Sukarno, on the assumption that his reputation had been ruined in the war, he told the British prime minister that the Indonesian president must be included in the negotiations. The Dutch government, however, insisted that Sukarno was a traitor and was not representative of the Indonesian people. 'My reply', Mountbatten telegraphed the British cabinet on 14 October, 'is that his case is similar to Aung San, traitor or patriot according to point of view ... the Dutch by dealing with him now could avoid having to deal with extremists later'.[89] He had been urged to take a hard line against him in Burma, but found that the alternative leaders had no support. 'It is as though [the Dutch] refuse to recognise any British government which did not contain Mr Baldwin or Mr Chamberlain.'[90] But events were unfolding in the east of Java that demonstrated to all observers that Indonesian nationalism was an unstoppable and revolutionary force.

FREEDOM OR DEATH IN SURABAYA

Surabaya was the largest naval base in Southeast Asia after Singapore. The city had been rather quiet during the early days of the republic, at least until Ramadan drew to a close on 7 September, and the riot at the raising of the Dutch tricolour at the Oranje Hotel. Now Indonesian flags flooded the city. Families sewed white and red patches onto their clothes, and even the *becak* (trishaw) riders decorated their vehicles. When Dutch internees began to step off the train, towards the end of August, they were, as one former colonial official put it, 'looking completely into a dark room'. Frantic to re-establish their lives, they collided with the new Indonesian authorities in a host of ways. This fed resentment and unease. A sense of menace intensified after 28 September with the arrival of a Dutch naval officer, P. J. G. Huijer, who, as a face-saving concession to the Dutch, had been despatched to the city in advance of Allied troops. Ostensibly he was there to look after prisoners of war and internees, but as ex-internees attached themselves to him, many Indonesians thought he represented the reappearance of the Dutch regime, and that the internees had arrived by ship. Exceeding his orders, and with only five men under his command, Huijer tried to reoccupy the city. In Surabaya, at least, the Japanese would surrender to a Dutchman. The Japanese vice-admiral commanding the city was only too happy to relinquish the responsibility. Bizarrely, the terms of the agreement stipulated that republican forces would act as custodians of the Japanese arms; but this was to recognize the reality of republican forces' control, and they were delighted to accept the responsibility. Huijer's car was then stolen, and he could not get to the airport to return to Jakarta. When he headed for the train – which was still running – he was detained by the republican forces and locked up for his own safety. Former internees were rounded up; some were imprisoned, interrogated and beaten in the Simpang Club, another of the pre-war playgrounds of the colonial elite.[91]

When the 49 Infantry Brigade Group of 23 Indian Division arrived in Surabaya on 25 October they found themselves confronted by Indonesians in possession of Japanese heavy artillery, tanks and armoured cars. Idrus described the mood:

People were drunk with victory. Everything had exceeded their dreams and expectations. All of a sudden their valour emerged like a snake out of a thicket. All their self-confidence and patriotism bubbled over like the foam on a beer. Rational thinking declined, people acted like beasts, and the results were eminently satisfactory. People no longer had much faith in God. A new God had arrived, and he was known under various names: bomb, machine-gun, mortar.[92]

The *pemuda* of Surabaya scented an historic opportunity. This found expression in the figure of Sutumo, the 25-year-old son of a clerk, who had worked as a journalist for the Domei news agency and was known universally by the revolutionary honorific of 'Bung [Brother] Tomo'. He was a model *pemuda*: jaunty military attire, a handgun, a Napoleonic bearing. He refused to cut his hair, and swore not to touch a woman, until Indonesia had gained its freedom. With a Japanese transmitter he created his own radio station: Radio Pemberontakan, 'Radio Rebellion'. British soldiers were astonished to hear on it the voice of a Englishwoman. She was a Manx hotelier from Bali, interned by the Japanese and best known by her Balinese name, K'tut Tantri. She was one of the first of many Westerners to be caught up in the spirit of this revolution and to serve it. The forces and press named her variously Modjokerta Molly, Solo Sally, Djokja Josy and, finally, in a nod to the Bertolt Brecht and Kurt Weill hit song 'Surabaya Jonny', she achieved worldwide notoriety as 'Surabaya Sue'.[93] But it was the raw charisma of Bung Tomo that catalysed the resistance of the city. 'His voice was loud and harsh,' wrote Idrus, 'the man himself small and pretty. His eyes sparkled like the rays of a light-house far out at sea.'[94] He was able to offer on air, talking directly to the people, a kind of spiritual leadership that transcended any political organization. Speaking in the unmistakable accents of Surabaya, he drew into the youthful rebellion of the *pemuda* the gritty opposition of the urban poor:

It is the masses in their thousands, starved, stripped, and shamed by the colonialists, who will rise to carry out the revolt. We extremists, we who revolt with a full revolutionary spirit, together with the Indonesian masses, who have experienced the oppression of colonialism, would rather see Indonesia drowned in blood and sunk to the bottom of the sea than colonized once more! God will protect us! *Merdeka!*[95]

These phrases would be repeated like a mantra across the region.

As the British were about to land, the Indonesians in control of the docks signalled that they should await orders from Moestopo, the former dentist who was now nominally in control of the city administration. The British commander, Brigadier A. W. S. Mallaby – a long-serving Indian Army staff officer with no recent field experience – responded curtly: 'We take orders from no one!' Nevertheless, the initial British entry into Surabaya was quite peaceful, if tense. The British impressed on the Indonesians that they were there to evacuate the 16,000-odd POWs and internees held in and around the city. But the situation deteriorated swiftly as Mallaby tried to rescue the luckless Huijer from imprisonment. Then, on 27 September, there was an ill-advised airdrop of leaflets demanding that the Indonesians surrender their arms within forty-eight hours or be shot. This was made without Mallaby's knowledge, and in contravention of local agreements, but it now had to be enforced. This was seen by the Indonesians as base treachery. They were now convinced that the British were preparing to reoccupy the city for the Dutch. The leaflets unravelled the ceasefire negotiations on the ground, and the Indonesian soldiers and militias fell on Mallaby's forces. The next day there was fierce fighting throughout the city. The 6,000, mostly Indian, troops of the brigade were scattered and set on by an estimated 20,000 trained and armed regulars and 120,000 civilians brandishing knives, clubs and bamboo spears. In the midst of this, evacuees – including women and children – were attacked with machine guns, grenades and swords. 'Bestial scenes', recalled one British observer, which 'rivalled the vilest moments of the French revolution'.[96] The British garrison, Whitehall was forced to announce, was 'more or less besieged'. The losses during the next four days were appalling for a peacetime operation: 16 officers and 217 other ranks.[97] On 29 October Sukarno, Hatta and the republic's defence minister, Amir Sjarifuddin, were flown into the city to negotiate a truce. They landed in a hail of bullets.

As the fighting abated British Indian soldiers were left adrift in isolated pockets throughout the city. In the afternoon of 30 October Brigadier Mallaby drove into the city to explain the ceasefire, and to visit the locations in which his troops had washed up. He was warned against this by his second-in-command, who knew about the danger of an angry crowd from a spell as a policeman in India. Mallaby, it seems, felt that only he could undertake this task. His last words on leaving his HQ were: 'If any of us get killed, splash it all over the world.' Travelling in an ordinary car in convoy with Indonesian nego- tiators, and with only three British aides with him, Mallaby went first to the Internatio Bank in Union Square, where a company of 6th Mahrattas were holding out, confronted by a hostile crowd of 500 or so Indonesians. Mallaby, with the aid of the Indonesians, tried to broker a ceasefire and to disperse the crowd, but the crowd was in no mood to listen. Mallaby's car was surrounded and, as armed Indonesians threatened to overwhelm the Mahrattas in the bank build- ing, their Indian officer, seemingly unprompted, gave the order to fire. The volley of Bren-gun fire and grenades killed perhaps 150 Indonesians. In the British accounts, Mallaby's car came under fire in front of the bank. No one was hit, and Mallaby and the two officers in the car with him lay inside it playing dead for about two hours. Then two Indonesians came to the car window. One touched Mallaby on the shoulder; the brigadier stirred and demanded to see the Indo- nesian commanders. The men went away, as if to confer, and when they returned one of them shot Mallaby who died almost instantly. General firing started up again, and the two Indonesians ducked behind the car. The two surviving officers seized the opportunity, and as Mallaby's killer was about to open fire again one of them lobbed a grenade. It is unclear exactly where the grenade exploded, but it almost certainly killed the assailants. The officers escaped from the car and dived into a nearby canal. Hidden between barges and pon- toons, and ducking under floating corpses, they made it back to the burning warehouses near the naval base. It took them several hours.[98] The Indonesian version was that Mallaby was hit by a mortar shell fired by the Indian troops in the Internatio Bank. This version was relayed by Tom Driberg to the House of Commons. Mallaby, Driberg argued, was killed in action and not by 'foul murder'; the charge was a slur on the Indonesian people.[99] The details of the episode remain confused and disputed. What is clear is that by scattering his command and exposing himself personally, Mallaby made fatal errors of judgement. Military historians have tended to reach a verdict of death by misadventure. Mallaby's brigade had been all but overwhelmed and the defenders of Surabaya claimed victory. An Indonesian news photographer captured the scene: the burnt-out Lincoln sedan in the square and, behind it, a banner: 'Once and forever – the Indonesian Republic'.[100]

The British response was immediate and unflinching. Christison issued a chilling proclamation to the defenders of Surabaya: 'I intend to bring the whole weight of my sea, land and air forces and all the weapons of modern warfare against them until they are crushed.'[101] Sukarno and Hatta were told that Major General E. C. R. Mansergh would arrive with a full infantry division and tanks. Sukarno himself now made a radio address: 'A tiny grain of arsenic is enough to ruin a glass of water', he pleaded. 'So also in a nation.' This created sufficient calm for the withdrawal of around 8,000 internees, and for the British counter-attack. Over the next few days 5 Indian Division massed in the docks. On 9 November Mansergh ordered the surrender of all arms by the following daybreak, on pain of death, and all women and children were to leave the city by the following nightfall. 'Crimes against civilization', his ultimatum stated, 'cannot go unpunished.' The republican leadership in the city was divided: there was little realistic opportunity for the ultimatum to be obeyed and, as the British officers well knew, it gave the city leadership no alternative but to fight.[102] The surrounding countryside was awash with calls for jihad; students from the religious schools poured into the city. Sukarno, pressured to intervene once more, left the issue to the city to decide. In this mood the *pemuda* prevailed. The airwaves were used to dramatic effect by Bung Tomo that evening. Radio Pemberontakan urged the people of Surabaya to brace themselves: 'Our slogan remains the same: freedom or death.' He closed with the invocation he used to begin all his broadcasts: '*Allahu akbar! Allahu akbar! Allahu akbar!*'

The next morning the city was at war with one and a half British divisions: 24,000 troops, supported by twenty-four tanks and twenty-four aircraft. The battle of Surabaya remains one of the largest single engagements fought by British troops since the end of the Second World War, and it was the last use of Indian soldiers in combat by the British Empire. There was little doubt in the minds of the city's defenders that the British were fighting Surabaya to avenge Mallaby. The Indonesians felt that they had brought the British to their knees, and this further inflamed the situation. The British fought for the city as if it were a full campaign of the Burma war, and not a peacekeeping operation. They opened with a tremendous barrage from the sea and from the air: perhaps 500 bombs were dropped in the first four days. RAF Thunderbolts and Mosquitoes strafed republican buildings and, according to Indonesian reports, refugees on the road south. British troops fought slowly and methodically to minimize their own casualties, street by street, house by house. *Pemuda* rushed Sherman tanks with spears and knives, and there were suicide squads with explosives. At night women came to claim the men's bodies. The fighting was most furious in the first few days, but resistance continued until the end of the month, the first fury giving way to a more disciplined core of Indonesian troops.[103] The British attempted to point to the hidden hand of the Japanese, but admitted privately that, apart from a couple of Japanese bodies recovered, there was no evidence that they were engaged in the fighting.[104] By the time the British reached the city perimeter at Wonosobo bridge on 28 November, Surabaya was in ruins:

Smoke came off the scorched beams like the smoke of Zipper cigarettes; and from people's mouths came the moans of death. The air stank of cordite and of human and animal carcasses; the hospitals stank of ether and rose-water. Now and then an explosion could be heard, followed by black smoke billowing up into the sky. The rain was full of a dirty black dust which hurt the eyes and the heart alike.[105]

In a private letter to Sir Archibald Nye of the general staff, Christison estimated some 10,000 casualties and a loss of 600 Allied troops. It was, he said, 'a most tricky party . . . One false step . . . would have brought a mass slaughter of Europeans and Eurasians in comparison with which the notorious Armenian massacres of forty years ago would have been small beer.'[106] Local estimates of casualties were higher at perhaps 15,000 dead. The decision of the Indonesians to fight British tanks was a tactical disaster, but it was a national epiphany. It is commemorated each year as Hari Pahlawan, Heroes' Day, and the monument in the heart of the city remains a point of assembly for young protesters. In August 2001, in a rare gesture, the British government made a statement of apology.

The wake of the battle washed across Indonesia. East Java was flooded with refugees from the city. They brought a new level of instability to the villages, and a struggle for food and other resources. The women, in particular, had a terrible time. Tan Malaka had left Jakarta in disgust at the temperance of the republican leadership there. He arrived in Surabaya to witness the desperate resistance and the exodus from the city. The veteran revolutionary was at once inspired and appalled by the undisciplined fury of the fighters: the Indonesians must, he wrote, 'harness holiness with reins we made ourselves'.[107] But the radicals regrouped at Malang and Bung Tumo resumed his broadcasts. Fighting broke out again in Semarang and the British managed to regain control of the city only with the use of air power and Japanese troops. The Gurkhas were forced to abandon the central Javan town of Magelang. The *pemuda* were galvanized to action further afield in Medan and elsewhere in Sumatra. This era in Java was known as the *bersiap* time, from the cry *'Siaaap!'* – 'Get ready!': the perpetual call to vigilance and to arms in the towns and villages. It was a time of revolutionary violence in the name of the sovereignty of the people or the defence of the revolution. It manifested itself in attacks on Christians, Japanese and British stragglers, Chinese, Eurasians and in an obsessive search for spies. It also built on local traditions of fighting: as in Malaya, cults of amulets that conferred invulnerability to their wearers flourished, and the figure of the *jago* – literally 'fighting cock' – the martial-arts champion of the village, on whom Javanese tradition conferred legitimacy as a protector figure in times of crisis. Some Western-educated local leaders, who saw their revolution as an extension of the French revolutionary principles of 1789, were deeply shaken by what they witnessed. But in many Indonesian accounts of the time, the violence seemed inevitable, even morally neutral.[108] Many of the more organized and politicized *pemuda* militias made common cause with the underworld of large cities such as Jakarta to draw on the expertise of men experienced in violence.[109] The *bersiap* amounted to social revolution in some areas – in north and east Sumatra the old aristocracies came under bloody attack – but in Java much of the republican leadership fought shy of its implications; here the social revolution remained a feral populism, without programme or direction. In many places it simply meant the struggle for scarce resources or settling of old scores. 'The Indonesia revolution', admitted the Islamicist leader Abu Hanifah, 'was not totally pure.'[110]

British horror and incomprehension at the violence came to a head at the village of Bekasi, in west Java. The area was notorious for containing what Abu Hanifah, who was based there, termed the 'lairs of the wild men of the district. They of course had their own leaders, their own heroes and strongmen. In the beginning there was nothing the republic could do about it.'[111] On 22 November a military Dakota crashed in its vicinity, and its twenty-three British and Indian crew and passengers were taken prisoner, stripped and hacked to pieces. When patrols disinterred the remains, the bodies of Indian and British soldiers could not be distinguished from each other. There was little exceptional about this incident in the midst of so many. What was exceptional was the swiftness and ferocity of British response. Around 600 houses were burned, including sixty occupied by neutral Chinese that caught light as the flames spread in the wind. The attack engendered lively public debate in Britain. It was perhaps the first occasion when the British people had to confront a crucial dilemma of the end of empire: how far should terror be met with terror? Mountbatten did not defend the action, but justified it on the grounds that 'we must realise the feeling of our regiments who suffer casualties every day at the hands of these terrorists and who on this particular occasion had to bury the dismembered bodies of their comrades'.[112] Already in northern Sumatra a young Dutch officer, Raymond Westerling, was developing a reputation for cold-blooded killing. Raised in Istanbul and known by the sobriquet 'Turk', he had been trained by the British in the dark arts of commando warfare. In Sumatra he cultivated an Indonesian fighter's mystique as 'The White Tiger'. His memoirs, published in England in 1952, portray northern Sumatra as a 'convulsed society . . . in the grip of terror' and show him abandoning the collective policing methods employed by the British for a very personal kind of war. The 'method of execution' was all. In the East, 'To execute a criminal behind prison walls has absolutely no effect on the population. To execute him in the marketplace does.' Westerling's legend and methods were to spread, a grisly omen of the drift towards colonial white terror.[113]

In the wake of events in Surabaya and elsewhere, the leadership of the republic changed hands. On 14 November Sukarno, whilst remaining president, passed power to a new cabinet headed by Sutan Sjahrir as prime minister. He was the obvious choice: his opposition to the Japanese enabled him to negotiate with the Dutch; his support amongst the Jakarta *pemuda* gave him the radical credentials the times demanded. Under Sjahrir's direction, the earlier working committee for independence reconstituted itself as a parliamentary government, and political parties were founded. Sjahrir was also the author of one of the key attempts in 1945 to analyse and direct the revolution, a pamphlet published as he came into power, entitled *Perjuangan Kita*, 'Our Struggle'. Without naming Sukarno, it attacked the running dogs and henchmen of Japanese. It traced the psychological impact of the war on the young, a tragic legacy of confusion and hatred, and repudiated the millennial fire of battles such as Surabaya: 'Many of them simply cling to the slogan Freedom or Death. Wherever they sense that freedom is still far from certain, and yet they themselves are not faced with death, they are seized with doubt and hesitation. The remedy for these doubts is generally sought in uninterrupted action.' Sjahrir instead set the Indonesian revolution firmly in an international context. 'Indonesia's fate', he wrote, 'ultimately depends on the fate of Anglo-Saxon capitalism and imperialism.' He argued the need for allies, and for the political maturity necessary to gain their respect, a sign of which would be Indonesia's treatment of its ethnic minorities. There were no fewer than four Christians in Sjahrir's cabinet.[114] It was a bold move, in which Sjahrir repudiated the social revolution that had largely brought him to power, and heralded a long process of diplomacy that would drag on for the rest of the British occupation of Java and Sumatra.

In the wake of the fighting, war reporters began to arrive in

Indonesia. The old scourge of the colonial establishment and 'whisky-swilling planters' of pre-war Singapore, Ian Morrison, was an eyewitness to events in Java for *The Times*. Martha Gellhorn reached an even wider audience with her vivid report on the 'seedy ruin' of Dutch imperialism and new political style of the 'adolescent guerrillas' of the *pemuda*. Like many Western journalists she was drawn into the circle of young dandyish intellectuals that had formed around Sutan Sjahrir. She shared a train journey with a young, delicate, bird-like poet named 'Johnny'. As they talked she became charmed by 'the place [the Indonesians] give a boy like Johnny; they know he is good for nothing except to write poetry once in a while but everyone loves him and respects him . . .' It seems that 'Johnny' was Chairil Anwar, himself a protégé and distant relative of Sjahrir.[115] These witnesses did not always understand well what they saw. When the *New York Times* reported the appointment of the new prime minister, it gave him a royal name: 'Sultan Charir'. In common with many Javanese people, Sukarno had only one name. It was an American journalist who gave the Indonesian president a first name he did not possess: 'Achmed'. It stuck.[116]

This revolution of artists and poet-philosophers fascinated Western observers. Some of its camp followers such as 'Surabaya Sue', K'tut Tantri, were part of the generation that 'discovered' Indonesian art and culture before the war, and it was what Sukarno termed the 'Romanticism of revolution' and its primordial energy that cast a spell. But others were drawn more to the rationalist internationalism personified by Sutan Sjahrir. His old friends and acquaintances in Europe mobilized support for the new republic, particularly among the British left. One prominent supporter was Dorothy Woodman, long-time companion of Kingsley Martin, the editor of the *New Statesman and Nation*. A great and well-connected artisan for Asian independence, she was under intense Secret Intelligence Service surveillance at the time as a suspected Soviet agent.[117] Another convert to the cause was John Coast: a POW in Thailand, he had fallen in love with Indonesia after hearing the lilting popular music of the *kronchong* played by Dutch fellow prisoners, and he began to learn the Malay language. Repatriated to London, where Indonesian students introduced him to Woodman's circle, he set up a kind of unofficial information bureau for the republic. He translated Sjahrir's *Our struggle* into English, and distributed it to United Nations delegates at their meeting at Westminster Hall. With the patronage of John Maynard Keynes, he also invited a Balinese dance company to perform in London. Coast worked his passage back to Southeast Asia and would serve Sjahrir's government for several years.[118] The republic also had supporters at the heart of the British operation: in December in Jakarta, two British NCOs produced a critical news sheet, *News from Indonesia*, and assisted in the publication of an English-language weekly, *Independent*. The British were conducting their war in an unprecedented glare of publicity. It was no longer possible to suppress colonial subjects in private.

For this reason, both the Dutch and the British governments welcomed the Sjahrir administration, but they remained bitterly divided on how to move forward. To Dening, the Dutch failure to appreciate reality was 'astonishing'. The Dutch, he told Mountbatten, were 'mentally sick ... one cannot help wondering whether in that condition they are really in a fit state to resume control in this vast area'.[119] That said, Dening's attitude to the Dutch was more conciliatory than Mountbatten's and he attempted to resign at the end of November in frustration at the supremo's 'open advocacy of the Indonesia cause ... and his harmful utterances against the Dutch'.[120] Christison talked of sending the Dutch on a new Great Trek to the outer islands and the empty interior of New Guinea. This echoed an earlier colonial fantasy of the Dutch themselves; there was in the Netherlands a plan to send Nazi collaborators there.[121] Christison was determined to ease the burden on his troops. At the end of November he talked of letting central and eastern Java 'go to ruin – temporarily'. But the British had obligations, not least a new category of person: IFTU, or 'Inhabitants Friendly To Us', the Eurasians, and Chinese – in Surabaya alone, 90,000 of them – and the smaller numbers of Arabs and Indians who were now dependent on British protection. In the exodus from Magelang, many Eurasians who had taken refuge there were abandoned. It was mid 1947 before some of them were released in Dutch-held territory.[122] In the event, the cities remained occupied, but the weight of Christison's forces fell back on to Jakarta and attempted to establish a safe perimeter around the city in which normal government could resume and negotiations take place. A new kind of pacification mission began to clear the city of armed men by stages: first to the city limits, then to surrounding villages that were centres of *pemuda* violence, and then, finally, to secure the triangle between Jakarta, the hill station of Buitenzorg and the major city of Bandung. There was still heavy loss of life. On 10 December a convoy was attacked and seventeen men were killed and another eighty-eight wounded.[123] On 27 December, in the first stage of what was now a counter-insurgency operation, 743 Indonesians were arrested and a cordon placed around Jakarta. However, the situation in the city remained tense. Perhaps the main threat to peace there was the Dutch themselves. Although there were only 2,000 Dutch on SEAC strength, there were five times that number present, mostly embittered men from the internment camps, armed and in makeshift uniforms.[124] Even Sjahrir himself was beaten on the streets, and he and Amir Sjarifuddin were the target of Dutch bullets. In the face of this, at the end of 1945, Sukarno and Hatta withdrew by special train with most of the government to Yogyakarta. The republic now had an alternative centre in the spiritual heartland of old Java.

For the British, Jakarta was now a major fortress, a new thorough-fare of empire and a strange enclave of calm and normality in the sea of violence. British officers took over the old centre of the British community, the Box Club; the YMCA turned the once elite Harmonie Club into a centre for other ranks. 'It was', recounted the official history of the 'Fighting Cock', 23 Indian Division, 'not uncommon to be dancing in the evening after dodging bullets. There was a plentiful supply of beer, although even this was subject to revolutionary mood, when the Indonesian brewery threatened to withhold it after they learnt that supplies were reaching the Dutch. There were no lack of Dutch and Eurasian dancing partners.'[125] They supplied the secretarial staff for a growing establishment, and supplied their country with information on British intentions. Marriages were contracted with Eurasian girls, who, as van den Bogaerde, now ADC to Major General Douglas Hawthorn, described them, 'had only the vaguest idea of what England or Europe might be like, and who would have to face the grey north, and new habits and customs in places like Swindon, Manchester, Macclesfield or Croydon'. His own general drew comment about the female entourage he gathered around him in his house in Bandung. The Christmas and New Year of 1945, the Division's fourth in the field, was celebrated in high style in Jakarta, with the pipes and drums of the Seaforth Highlanders; the Patialas in *tamasha* to honour the maharajah's birthday, and a soccer match against the Indonesians. At midnight drunken British officers let loose a massive salvo of gunfire into the air: it was answered by a return of fire across the city which took an hour to subside.[126]

The dawn of 1946 was marked by another momentous event. On 3 January, at a large 'people's congress' in Purwokerto, central Java, Tan Malaka chose to reveal himself to the public for the first time in twenty-three years. In his speeches, and in writings produced at the time of the struggle in Surabaya, he announced a 'minimum programme' for the revolution. It was based on the call for '100 per cent *Merdeka*'. Its radicalism was a yardstick for freedom movements in the region, calling for the immediate departure of all foreign troops from Indonesia, the establishment of a people's government and the people's ownership of the economy. It was seen as a major challenge to Sjahrir. A battle for the soul of the Indonesian revolution was underway, which pulled its leaders toward different paths of diplomacy and struggle. This was a dilemma that all Asian nationalisms would face. In Indonesia it seemed that the *pemuda* had finally found their leader. But in early 1946 Tan Malaka lacked any organization or power base beyond his own mystique. By mid March, in a bitter struggle for power, he was arrested and imprisoned, and the path of diplomacy took precedence for a time. By the time of the British withdrawal, its prospects were uncertain. One of Britain's most senior diplomats, Sir Archibald Clark Kerr, had arrived in February 1946 to act as an honest broker – he was the first Allied leader to call on Prime Minister Sjahrir at his home – and there were abortive talks in Holland in April and May. The British deadline for an agreement was the end of November 1946, when South East Asia Command would wind up its activities. At the eleventh hour, on 15 November, a first diplomatic understanding was reached between the Dutch and the Indonesians, led by Sukarno and Sjahrir, at the hill resort of Linggajati outside Jakarta, to be ratified in March of the following year. It was an agreement for a ceasefire, it recognized de facto republican authority in Java and Sumatra and it spoke of co-operation in the creation of a united Indonesia. But it left the vital issue of sovereignty vague – it was a long way from '100 per cent *Merdeka*' – and the agreement did not last. By the end of July 1947 fighting had erupted again, with the first of the savage Dutch 'police actions' that would, after much bloodshed, finally lose them their empire.

Mountbatten, Christison and others had expended much effort in pushing the Dutch into talks. They recognized the power of Indonesian nationalism, but they had not won its trust. Most British observers, even the most liberal, still thought of nationalism in Asia in very limited terms, as an affectation of a small, Westernized elite. As such, it might be easily pacified with concessions. But in Indonesia, and later elsewhere, nationalism was revealed as something more elemental: a profound and dangerous perturbation of spirits. It seemed to be without an ideology. To the British it was 'extremist', 'fanatical', 'terrorist' – all words that would now dominate the vocabulary of empire, but which betrayed a fundamental lack of comprehension. Nor could nationalism in Indonesia be dismissed, yet, as communist conspiracy; ironically it was to the socialist, but quintessentially Westernized, Sutan Sjahrir that the British looked to discipline the movement, and for the salvation of a negotiated withdrawal. They could not understand Sukarno's continuing and growing hold on his people. British witnesses to Surabaya wrote of Bung Tomo as if he were a wild beast. The British were entirely unprepared to face the full implications of Tan Malaka's '100 per cent *Merdeka*'. In Indonesia, as in Vietnam, British soldiers had seen the meanest folk articulate their freedom, and fight to the death to defend it, and it had terrified them. So too had the behaviour of the French and the Dutch. It raised the as yet unanswerable question: how far would Britain be willing to go to keep its Asian empire? These dilemmas were now to be confronted closer to home in India, in Burma, in Malaya and in Singapore. The British wars in Vietnam and Indonesia did little to re-establish Britain's imperial confidence, nor its martial reputation. They disillusioned profoundly many of the British who fought there, and few of them wished to celebrate their achievements. In all, there were 2,136 British and Indian casualties. As the last British troops finally departed from Tanjong Priok docks in Jakarta at the end of

November 1946, the Seaforth Highlanders, who had been among the first to arrive, taunted the fresh Dutch conscripts disembarking to face their own colonial war with raised fists, and the cry, '*Merdeka!*'[127]

5

1946: Freedom without Borders

Colonial Asia was now a connected arc of protest. Everywhere local nationalists borrowed the words and emulated the deeds of neighbours, and the language of the Atlantic Charter and the San Francisco Declaration became a common tongue for all. In early 1946 Indonesia's struggle was first raised in the United Nations, and this made it a test case for the rights of fledgling nations everywhere. In British Asia, nationalists followed events in Indo-China and Indonesia as if their own future were being decided, which it effectively was. In Malaya the cause of the Indonesian republic captivated not only the Malays, who felt tied to it by kinship and language, but the whole of Malayan society, whose trade unions, youth and women's movements all took up its slogans. The Chinese population caught up in the fighting in Semarang and Surabaya appealed directly to the community in Malaya, and many fled there as refugees. Harold Laski's campaigning articles from *Reynolds News* were immediately translated into the Tamil newspapers in Singapore. They were united in their opposition to the use of Indian troops, stating, 'We [the British] have no business in Java.'[1] This larger 'we' was reinforced by the British servicemen in Singapore – corporals mostly, it seems – who wrote polemical articles for publication in the vernacular press. Surabaya was a turning point for everyone: the British argument that force was necessary to bring a large Asian rebel army to heel seemed to be a harbinger of a new Armageddon. 'Battle for Surabaya', announced the *New Democracy* in banner headlines. 'Cause of a Third World War?'[2] Would this, the campaigning Malay newspaper *Utusan Melayu* speculated, 'become a strong argument to use the atomic bomb on the Indonesians whose only sin is to attain their independence?'[3]

The battle of Surabaya was fought in unlikely places. Southeast Asian students in Japan demonstrated on the streets of Tokyo. In a bizarre twist of fate, many of the most hardened veterans of anti-Dutch resistance were to be found in Australia. Japan had failed to occupy the Dutch territories of the island of New Guinea, and in mid 1943, Charles van der Plas, then the senior Dutch official in Australia, secretly moved 507 exiles and their families from the Boven Digul isolation colony to Bowen and Sydney, where they were placed in a guarded camp together with Axis internees. Many were members of the Partai Komunis Indonesia, imprisoned after the uprisings of 1926–7, including Sarjono, the party's former chairman. The Digul families were the first convicts to land in New South Wales for over a century, and when two notes dropped by Indonesians at the quayside and on a train platform were picked up by Australian workers, their plight attracted wide sympathy. The exiles were released and, notwithstanding the 'white Australia' policy then in force, were assimilated into the Australian workforce. They included graduates and skilled craftsmen, and such was the Dutch military's own desperation for personnel that some of them even found employment with the government-in-exile. But biding their time, the Indonesians organized, formed strong links with the Australian left and in 1944 set up their own independence committees. When Japan surrendered there was a wave of strikes by Indonesian seamen who refused to return to pre-war conditions of employment. In six days after 24 September, 1,400 of them came ashore. When Indian workers were drafted in as replacements, they joined the strikers. The Dutch, desperate to ship men and materials to Java, were thrown into panic.[4] As ex-detainees began to resign from Dutch service they were arrested as illegal immigrants by the Dutch authorities, who prepared to send them back to Digul camp. This was an extraordinary use of their extra-territorial privileges. By April 1946 820 Indonesian mariners and soldiers were interned in Australian jails.[5] The Australian unions joined the protest, declared that 'everything Dutch is black' and boycotted Dutch ships. On 11 November at Morton Bay there was a mutiny on a RN auxiliary vessel at Woolloomooloo. The sailors draped slogans on their ship: 'Food for Britain before troops for Java'. The Australian government's decision to repatriate some exiles and their families (which now included some Australian Aboriginal wives) in October 1945 inflamed the controversy. The Dutch were unwilling to have so many seasoned radicals land, and wanted to take them into custody. Mountbatten felt unable to guarantee their safety. But many evaded capture and, in the event, only nineteen 'extremists' and eight of their family members were despatched on the *Esperance Bay* and landed at Kupang in Timor. They took with them a large Indonesian flag, embroidered with the words, 'To Dr Soekarno from Queensland Trade Unionists'.[6]

The Vietnamese and Indonesian revolutions drew upon networks of support across the region. Bangkok was a huge arms bazaar, stocked by supplies from surrendered Japanese garrisons and from SEAC's airdrops to the Free Thai resistance. 'Buying arms in Thailand', the veteran southern Vietnamese revolutionary Tran Van Giau joked, 'was as easy as buying beer'. The Filipinos and Burmese also offloaded guns onto the Thai market, and Chinese, Swedes, Czechs and Americans – idealists, freebooters and demobbed special forces – all got involved in the trade. Jim Thompson, a Princeton-educated ex-OSS man, invested his profits in a silk business that still bears his name.[7] Vietnamese exiles in Singapore tried to recruit fighters from Malaya, and they approached the Malayan Communist Party for 500 guns from its secret stockpile in Johore. It became impossible to ship them by junk to Cochin China, but the contacts were important in other ways: through them, Chin Peng and others began to learn more about the secret lives of Lai Teck.[8] Malaya was the armoury of the Indonesian republic. The British dumped as many as 2,000 tons of surplus arms at sea south of Singapore, and they easily found their way into Indonesia through the Riau islands. The first major republican supply operation was orchestrated in September 1946, by a Chinese lawyer, Captain Joe Loh, who had served in Force 136. He used his British connections to acquire – with no advance payment – 1,400 Lee Enfield rifles, six anti-aircraft guns, a field hospital, a field kitchen and army clothing, and ran them past the Dutch navy to the republican forces in Java on a wooden vessel called the *Mariam Bee*. This was enough to equip a battalion: the goods were marked in the log at the Changi naval base as 'One lot of surplus goods dumped and destroyed.'[9] In Pekanbaru, on the Sumatran mainland, some 1,000 republican soldiers paraded in British uniforms. This caused real confusion when they then attacked a nearby Dutch garrison.[10]

Chinese intermediaries dominated the arms trade. In Indonesia, although the community was precariously placed, and often targeted for attack by nationalist mobs, businessmen borrowed the authority of political organizations as a shield, and used it to seize the lucrative import–export trade from European firms. When the Dutch navy intervened to stop this illicit trade, Singapore merchants and trade unions united in their attacks on Dutch 'piracy'. Tan Kah Kee, who had spent the war hidden in exile in Java, used his influence to strengthen sentiment in favour of the revolution, and this very quickly developed into an attack on local British authority. When, in early 1946, the BMA in Malaya banned the use of sugar in coffee-shops because of shortages, the connection was immediate: 'Java produces sugar. Let the British armies leave Java and allow it independence then sugar will be plentiful.'[11] Sweeping boycotts of Dutch shipping and trade were launched. Although Overseas Chinese politics never achieved the cohesion and purpose it possessed in the anti-Japanese movement before the war, it still remained a force to be reckoned with.

The cause of Indonesia was kept alive in Malaya by the presence of the 15,000 Dutch soldiers and ex-internees who were based in Singapore by the end of 1945, and some 2,000 more upcountry.[12] The refugees were traumatized and bitter: they were the first of some 300,000 lost children of empire who would travel into exile in the Netherlands, and then on to the United States or Australia.[13] As SEAC prepared to wind up its operations by the end of November 1946, the Dutch shipped in 75,000 men to keep order in Java and Sumatra, and many of them came through Singapore. Eventually, over 140,000 Dutch were mobilized for *De Grote Oost* – an extraordinary commitment for a nation that had a population of only 1,750,000 men of military age – and there were Dutch camps in Malaya until 1948.[14] The main civilian settlement in Singapore, Wilhelmina Camp, was a substantial township with its own radio station, cinema and orchestra. But it was adjacent to the Malay settlement of Geylang, and in mid 1946, as Dutch operations intensified in Indonesia, there were Dutch–Malay clashes in the neutral ground between the two areas: the Happy World amusement park. There was fighting in its bars, cabarets and even at the Bolero Malay Opera. An NCO, his wife and another Dutchman were killed. Tensions between Menadonese and Amboinese troops and local Malays nearly escalated out of control, as the Malays threatened to call in compatriots in the services to 'stage a real battle'. The violence was usually triggered by soldiers' improper conduct towards respectable Malay women, although Dutch intelligence suggested that its origins were political, and that it was orchestrated by local Indonesians.[15] Dutch agents were at work across Malaya; Mustapha Hussain was approached by a European and offered $1,000 a month to spy on 'pro-Indonesia' supporters in Perak.[16]

In this way Indonesia's struggle became part of the daily lives of Malays. Geylang was a place of transit for many refugees; it was also close to the camps of *romusha* labourers. It was a crowded and volatile world – poor Indonesians were still dying on the streets – but compared with Java it was a safe haven. One of the first political organizations to be founded in post-war Malaya was an Indonesian Labour Party, that worked to organize and repatriate the labourers. It set up an office in the Arab Street area, near the palace of the last, exiled ruler of the Johor-Riau empire that had once held sway across the colonial borders of the region. There was a short-lived attempt to revive the sultanate, and Singapore remained a symbolic centre of the entire Malay world: a crossroads for traders and craftsmen, scholars and writers, religious teachers and pilgrims, especially after the *hajj* to Mecca began to revive. With the arrival of Mountbatten Singapore became an important diplomatic centre and home to the Republic of Indonesia's main external office.[17] One of the many arrivals in 1946 was the 27-year-old Khatijah Sidek, a spirited, independent Minangkabau woman, educated at Padang Panjang in western Sumatra, a dynamic centre of modernist Islamic learning. She was one of the leaders of the controversial Puteri Kesatri, the women fighters of the revolution, who had challenged traditional roles in a dramatic way. On the prompting of exiles from Malaya, Khatijah decided to take her message of emancipation to Singapore. She arrived without funds but, with the help of local associations, travelled around Malaya lecturing to women of all communities, from the wives of the urban elite to peasant women in the Malay *kampongs*. The British were becoming increasingly alarmed by the activities of such people. 'When-ever we made a speech', Khatijah wrote, 'the police and the Special Branch were there too, and the Malay people themselves advised us not to make our speeches too strong or too "hot" because Malaya was different from Indonesia; and it was not only the common people who advised us thus, but also the leaders . . . in those days they were very afraid to hear the word *Merdeka*, which we from Indonesia spoke of constantly.'[18]

But it was a two-way traffic. Many Malay radicals travelled to Indonesia and fought in the revolution, and what the British now began to describe obsessively as 'Indonesian influence' was often an expression of a local vision of a greater Malay nation.[19] Young leaders such as Ahmad Boestamam cultivated the *pemuda* style. Malay ora-tors took Sukarno as a model – 'that Ox and Lion of the Indonesian podium' – although Boestamam himself, perhaps the most effective platform speaker of his generation, claimed that his greatest inspi-ration was Subhas Chandra Bose.[20] On 17 February 1946, the six-month anniversary of the Indonesian revolution, Boestamam founded the Angkatan Pemuda Insaf – the Generation of Aware Youth. It was known – as were many Malay associations in this period – by its dramatic acronym, API, which meant 'fire'. Within the space of a few days he and his friends assembled around 500 young Malays, many of whom had received Japanese basic military training, and paraded at Jubilee Park, Ipoh, in red and white armbands that mirrored the Sang Saka Merah Putih flag of Indonesia. Although it kept its separate identity, API became the youth wing of the Malay Nationalist Party, and supplied many of its activists. The MNP was now a national force. Shortly after the foundation of API it moved its office to a shophouse in Batu Road, Kuala Lumpur, and the young radicals began to live in a communal fashion in a rented house in nearby Kampong Bahru which became known as 'Hotel Merdeka'. Here they were joined by a young woman from Negri Sembilan, Shamsiah Fakeh, another graduate of a religious school, who slept next to the stove and took over the women's section of the party. She created a sister organization to API: the Angkatan Wanita Sedar – Generation of Aware Women – or AWAS, 'look out!' With this cry, its members would raise their clenched right fist with the index finger extended as a warning sign. The women goaded the men, and encouraged wives of non-politically minded husbands to go on strike from their domestic duties.[21]

The Malay Nationalist Party also began to attract the support of leading Malay intellectuals of an older, pre-*pemuda* generation. Mockhtaruddin Lasso, a shadowy figure to the end, disappeared suddenly in early 1946, and little other than rumour was heard of him again. The new chairman, Dr Burhanuddin al-Helmy, was forty-five years of age; he had been schooled at the Penang *madrasah* of the great Malay modernist reformer Syed Sheihk al-Hadi, and then spent a long sojourn in India, training in homoeopathic medicine at Ismaileah Medical College in Hyderabad, and the Anglo-Muslim College at Aligarh. In India, he had met Jinnah, and became very interested in the cause of Palestine.[22] 'Pak Doktor', as he was dubbed, possessed an Islamic cosmopolitanism that was unequalled among Malay political leaders, and his nationalism was religiously grounded. Within the MNP different traditions of radical thought were beginning to assemble under the same banner. Malay cadres of the Malayan Communist Party were also regular visitors to 'Hotel Merdeka'. The most prominent of these were two Perak Malays, Rashid Maidin and Abdullah Che Dat. Rashid, aged twenty-eight, had worked for a mining company as an electrical technician whilst taking a correspondence course in English. He had been recruited into the MCP by Tu Lung Shan, Chin Peng and Eng Ming Chin's mentor, and had worked as an underground publicist during the war. The 23-year-old Abdullah C.D., as he was known in the party, had attended Clifford School, an English school in Kuala Kangsar. He had been a member of the Kesatuan Melayu Muda but left the movement in protest at its co-operation with the Japanese and instead worked among the Malays for the MPAJA. In the dark days of communal violence, Rashid Maidin and Abdullah C.D. toured the Perak river with Eng Ming Chin's propaganda troupe to allay Malay fears and broker local understandings. Over the next two years the communists would invest a tremendous amount in the Malay Nationalist Party: it symbolized its growing commitment to 'Malayanization' and substantiated its claim to patriotism. In the MNP, Abdullah later wrote, there were 'branches of many *aliran* [flows of consciousness] – nationalist, religious, socialist, communist. Yet by taking our *aliran* out of the equation, we were able to set aside differences, able to unite and cooperate. This was for the sake of a patriotic front that was anti-imperialist, anti-colonialist and loving independence, freedom.'[23]

THE PASSING OF THE
MALAYAN SPRING

The first weeks of 1946 were a period of unprecedented political freedom and experiment that would later become known as the Malayan Spring. The phrase was coined by Han Suyin, a novelist who came to Malaya in 1952. She calculated that around fourteen books of poetry, ninety-six novels – a new form in Malayan Chinese literature – and forty-eight books of essays appeared in Chinese in this period, though by the time of her arrival six years later the parameters of open public debate had shrunk dramatically. To her eyes, intellectual life seemed to have been obliterated entirely, and 'Special Branch was The Power'. She found that much that had been written in the immediate post-war years was no longer available; the authors could not be traced or, if they could, denied that they had ever written anything.[24] But at the time the Malayan Spring was a significant shift in mood, and perhaps more enduring than Han Suyin realized. One writer, styling himself 'Fu-sheng', or 'Revival', described the change in an essay in *New Democracy* that marked the fourth anniversary of the Japanese invasion of Malaya, or 'Twelve-Eight', as it was now called. Before the war, he wrote, the Chinese in Malaya were 'just an overseas Chinese and nothing more'.

Then the British lost Malaya in just two months and a week, and the duty of beating the Japanese and regaining Malaya fell on the Malayan people, especially on us Chinese. And so Malaya was reborn thanks to the blood of the Chinese and other revolutionary warriors. The fates of Malaya and our mother country are related. We fight for Malaya and our mother country, while the people of our mother country fight for the country and for Malaya. The mother country is ours, but in Malaya also we have our share. There is a testimony of blood which no one can gainsay.

The local landscape was now poignant with memory; the local situation a microcosm of Asian history and current politics. In the past, Fu-sheng wrote, three races – China, India and Indonesia – had ruled half the globe and now they came together in Malaya. The 'three big races' of Malaya – the Chinese, Indians and Malays – were like the three Great Powers at Yalta. They had a shared destiny. 'Peace is indivisible; so is the fate of Malaya, China, India and Indonesia.'[25] Whilst Chinese writing in Malaya tended to claim a leading role for the Chinese in the political struggle in Malaya – for Chinese rights as 'pioneers' – it remained divided on how far this struggle was for Malaya. But through the prism of the resistance struggle, Chinese writers and intellectuals explored their surroundings with a new emotion and purpose, and debates on identity and emancipation were conducted with a new urgency.

One of the key figures in this revival was the writer and journalist Hu Yuzhi. Educated in Paris and a leading luminary of the Shanghai intellectual scene, he had, along with many other 'refugee writers', fled from China to Singapore in 1940. This influx of sophisticates was a minor revolution in a society that for the most part comprised labourers and traders, and, for their part, the writers saw the Nanyang as an artistic utopia. Hu Yuzhi later admitted that he was secretly a member of the Chinese Communist Party sent to Singapore to intensify propaganda work in the Nanyang. He spent the war in hiding in Sumatra, running a wine-brewing factory with a fellow-exile, the celebrated modernist novelist and poet Yu Dafu. Yu was killed by the Japanese in the interregnum: he was witness to too many of their brutalities. This loss would haunt Chinese writing in Malaya after the war, and writers composed multiple laments for his passing. Hu Yuzhi – 'a little homunculus of a man with bright eyes like a marmoset', wrote Victor Purcell – returned to Singapore to work with Tan Kah Kee to build unity among the local Chinese.[26] He edited the most prominent literary magazine, *Feng Hsia* (Land Below the Wind), which ran to 132 issues between December 1945 and June 1948, and achieved an unprecedented quality of output. Hu Yuzhi's wife, Shen Zijiu, published Malaya's first journal for women, *New Woman*, and many newspapers now began to carry literary supplements. Hu Yuzhi became a vocal critic of the Malayan Communist Party's propaganda:

he felt it lacked power and depth. The people were in a state of 'semi-feudal *towkay*-ism'. Bosses controlled the newspapers, would-be intellectuals such as students became clerks and were 'shoved into a shop'; teachers became 'mere wage-earners'.[27] 'We do not require tanks, guns and hand-grenades now,' wrote Hu Yuzhi. 'Our weapons are pen and paper only.' The struggle was against a 'servile culture'. The problem was 'thinking too highly of foreigners and belittling ourselves. This is a common psychological phenomenon among the Malayan people. It needs to be conquered, because it makes it easy for the rule of imperialism.'[28] This touched upon a nagging difficulty for the Malayan Communist Party. After its losses to the Japanese in the war, it lacked experienced and educated leaders; Chin Peng's schooling had ended when he was fifteen years of age, and in this he was not exceptional. To broaden its support, the leftist movement began to cultivate the intelligentsia.

The war made anti-imperialists out of British rule's natural supporters, the very middle-class 'Malayans' the British hoped to cultivate. For them a defining issue was 'back pay' for civil servants. After the liberation, the Europeans in Changi and Sime Road were quietly paid the thousands of dollars in salary they had accrued over three and a half years; they were given 90 per cent of it in cash before being repatriated, and even a generous clothing allowance to replace their wardrobes. This 'internment bounty' incensed Asian civil servants, who, although they had not been incarcerated, had been singled out for pay cuts and persecution by the Kempeitai. For them, 'Singapore was one large prison camp'. For the first time, the middle classes marched in protest. They were eventually made a raised offer of three and a half months' pay, but the damage was done.[29] As one former student at Singapore's elite Raffles College observed: 'My education in the unfairness and absurdities of human existence was completed by what I saw in the immediate aftermath of the war. If three and a half years of Japanese occupation had earned me my degree in the realities of life, the first year in liberated Singapore was my postgraduate course.' The young Lee Kuan Yew would soon sail for England to complete his formal education at Fitzwilliam House, Cambridge. He would return to dominate the island's politics for over fifty years. The attitude of his generation of colonial students would be dramatically different from an earlier elite generation who had returned, in Lee's words, 'overawed and overwhelmed by English values'.[30]

The 'English-speaking brain-workers', as they termed themselves, now began to organize, and a circle of them established Singapore's first political party, the Malayan Democratic Union, in December 1945. The MDU included some of the most privileged young Malayans. Its first secretary, Lim Hong Bee, was educated at Cambridge on a King's Scholarship, together with another member of the party, Lim Kean Chye, a son of one of the oldest and most illustrious Straits Chinese families of Penang. An older London-trained lawyer, the Guyana-born Eurasian Chinese Philip Hoalim, was chairman, and his money seemed to keep the small party afloat. The Malayan Democratic Union set up an office above the Liberty Cabaret in New Bridge Road, and the dance floor became a setting for political debate.[31] The intellectuals' vision of 'Malaya' was formed out of the cosmopolitan urban world of Singapore. It was inclusive and internationalist. Its manifesto announced that the MDU did 'not take the stand that Malaya should break away from Great Britain. Indeed, Malaya with full democratic self-government will benefit most if she remains within the British Commonweath . . .'[32] This was, by the standards of the time, a very moderate platform. But it attracted little sympathy from the British. Many of the Union's leaders, including its most well-known figure, the lawyer John Eber, came from the Eurasian community, and they were subjected to condescending racial prejudice. Eber's anti-colonialism, it was muttered, was grounded in resentment that while his English mother could mix with the colonial elite, his Eurasian father could not. But Eber had been largely brought up by his mother's relatives in England, educated at Harrow and Cambridge, and on returning to Singapore had joined the exclusive Tanglin Club and Singapore Golf Club. As his friend and fellow Cambridge graduate Lim Hong Bee put it, he was 'in no way seen to display any of the obsessional traits of inferiority . . . He had no need to.' The British reaction to him was pathological and hostile, Lim suggested, because Eber was 'an acute embarrassment – so much like them in form, yet so different in substance'.[33]

The leaders of the Malayan Democratic Union were inspired by a socialist critique of imperialism. They argued that the British had created communal tensions in Malaya by building up the non-Malays as middlemen, and they looked to overcome this by a programme of nationalization and rural development. A central concern was to develop a system of 'social security' on the New Zealand model. In education, they looked beyond their own anglophone bias to the creation of four national language streams; the Malayan Democratic Union's newspaper, *The Democrat*, gave unprecedented coverage to Malay affairs and to the Malay Nationalist Party. Again, and as Victor Purcell later admitted, this was no more dangerous than the socialism of Sutan Sjahrir or Aung San, but the party's relations with the British were distorted entirely by its relationship with the MCP. The Malayan Democratic Union was never an organized political party as such; most of its 300 'members' were civil servants and its leaders were acutely aware of their need to reach out to the masses, but also of the obstacles to them doing so. They shared the Liberty Cabaret with a consumers' co-operative society, which was an important means of local self-help during the economic crisis. Eber built up his political reputation by working for them and for trade unions as a legal adviser. He was active in the back-pay issue and, as a senior local lawyer, was prepared to be co-opted to government committees. But Eber and the other leaders saw co-operation with the communists as their route to the masses. The MCP's open leader in Singapore, Wu Tian Wang, attended the inauguration of the MDU on 19 January 1946, the same ceremony at which a Friends of Indonesia Association was founded. The MDU's organizing secretary, Gerald de Cruz, was a Party member, and Lim Hong Bee, who returned to the United Kingdom at the end of the year, would act as its unofficial roving representative overseas. One of the MDU's most gifted figures was Eu Chooi Yip, a bilingual writer whom Hu Yuzhi singled out for praise 'as a scholar and as a writer of the modern school'. He had worked for the Chinese Protectorate and as a government inspector of mines and possessed a formidable knowledge of the labour scene. The sympathies of young intellectuals such as Eu Chooi Yip for the MCP would very soon place them in an acute dilemma, and the British would exploit this to 'expose' the Malayan Democratic Union as a communist Trojan horse. But the MDU was a diverse and independent organization, and the Malayan Spring was a moment before such difficult and irreversible ideological choices had to be made. The question of who was and who was not a communist was of interest only to the Malayan Security Service. But police paranoia about what they rather sinisterly termed the ESI – English-speaking intelligentsia – was already beginning to dominate and distort British attempts to build a 'Malayan' nationalism.

The Malayan Democratic Union was to assume an importance far beyond its numbers, and would later be seen as an historic lost opportunity of Malayan politics. It arose at a moment when a broad-based multiracial patriotism seemed to be within reach; an authentic Malayan nationalism that might absorb the various *aliran* of the time. It was evidenced in popular culture and drew on the unstructured and flexible networks of the informal economy. Local papers now stressed the close cultural and economic connections between the Chinese and Malay communities. Through shared campaigns for the protection of journalists from harassment and for freedom of speech, a stronger sense of the 'left' was emerging, and in Malay the equivalent word, *kiri*, was increasingly used. It was a time when neither English-speaking intellectuals nor the MCP believed they could work alone and when both hoped to widen the scope of colonial reforms. The MCP seized the moment to launch a Malayan United Democratic Front. On 21 January, the anniversary of Lenin's death, the Party held its first plenary meeting since 1941. At it, Lai Teck vigorously defended his position and on a surge of support was re-elected general secretary. In his speech, he reviewed the history of the Party, and its present position. 'The colonial problem', Lai Teck argued, 'can be resolved only in [one of] two ways: liberation through a bloody revolutionary struggle (as in the case of Vietnam and Indonesia) or through the strength of united front'. He argued that both the internal conditions – the need to win support outside the Chinese community and the promise of colonial reform – and the external situation – particularly events in India and Burma – made this a time to wait and to watch, and to take the opportunity to expand the Party's mass support.[34] 'Only through racial unity [could] the colonial conditions in Malaya be wound up . . .'; only through this could the Party 'discharge the sacred mission entrusted upon them by history'. Lai Teck did not even mention independence as an immediate objective. Yet the policy commanded wide support and would be the foundation of the Party's strategy for the next two years. The stated aim was the 'hundredfold strengthening of the unity of the three races and the coalition of various parties and factions'.[35]

But the Malayan Communist Party and the BMA headed for confrontation. Just prior to the plenary conference Chin Peng and seven other comrades – including Colonel Itu and Liew Yao – were invited to a special ceremony in Singapore to receive their campaign medals, the Burma Star and the 1939/45 Star, from the supremo. They acknowledged Mountbatten with a clenched-fist salute. Lai Teck was still lying low. The MPAJA men were accommodated in the luxury of Raffles Hotel. At a gala cocktail party at Government House, Mountbatten greeted them with some words in Mandarin he had memorized for the occasion, Chin Peng chatted with General Messervy and Lee Kiu charmed Victor Purcell by her fascination with the royal portraits: 'With a different hair-do', he announced in his journal, 'I believe she could give Miss Eng Ming Chin a run for her money.'[36] The next day they were to be given a VIP tour of the Royal Navy and RAF bases and the Alexandra barracks. Unwilling to be used in this way, the MPAJA leaders, after an all-night discussion, refused to attend in protest at the continued imprisonment of the Selangor guerrilla leader Soong Kwong. The British reaction was, in Chin Peng's account, emotional. John Davis, his comrade from the jungle, arrived suddenly at the Party's office in Kuala Lumpur with a prepared, typed apology and demanded that Chin Peng and his friends sign it. Lai Teck was in the room, but made no protest. The younger men duly signed the letter, which was never published. Ahmad Boestamam was also asked to sign series of similar pre-typed letters to the BMA to prevent his newspaper being closed down. On the face of it these were minor enough incidents, but powerful undercurrents of pride governed the relations between these young fighting men. The rookie officers of the BMA were troubled by the ignominy of 1942, and were acutely sensitive to criticism and perceived slights. The wounded *izzat* of the Raj collided with the determination of Asian leaders to maintain their honour and 'face' in the eyes of their people.

The episode looms large in Chin Peng's account of the breakdown of the relationship between the MPAJA and the British, and of his growing frustration with the leadership of Lai Teck. But Lai Teck's betrayals were closing in on him. In February a leader of the Partai Komunis Indonesia, Alimin, came to Kuala Lumpur with the leader of the Thai Communist Party, Li Chee Shin. Alimin was a legendary figure and a well-known Comintern agent, but was travelling under an assumed name. Lai Teck did not recognize Alimin, and was himself unknown to either communist visitor. His claim to be the Comintern's man was weakened considerably.[37] About this time, too, it seems that Lai Teck resumed his meetings with the British. It is not clear how frequent they were, or precisely what transpired at them. The few accounts by writers who have seen unreleased British records suggest that the allegations of Lai Teck's treachery made by Ng Yeh Lu were discussed, as well as caches of arms hidden at the end of the war. Lai Teck seems to have enlarged on published Party pronouncements, and stressed that the MCP's policy was one of peaceful pressure on the British than rather than violent confrontation.[38] Although this may have reassured the British, it is not clear how else they benefited from their relationship with Lai Teck. He was increasingly compromised, and his natural life as an agent was drawing to a close.

Immediately after the plenary meeting, a general strike was called for 29 January. It was to mark the establishment of a pan-Malayan General Labour Union and its demands focused on the release of labour activists and ex-MPAJA men. By March 1946, 70 per cent of MPAJA veterans in Selangor were unemployed; thirty-three had either been convicted of or were being tried for various offences.[39] The case of Soong Kwong now dominated public debate, in a way that Aung San's did in Burma. His trial was a confrontation between the unbending logic of colonial law and the new demand for government by the popular will. It deepened local outrage that the British were not pursuing collaborators with the same energy as they were targeting their former allies. In the words of a poet:

> Soong Kwong, Soong Kwong,
> You have taken the wrong path.
> Why didn't you make a fortune out of the Japs,
> Instead of taking up anti-Jap activities, in the tropics?

An old saying goes:

The Good and Loyal are always tortured.
The Evil and Bad are praised in temples.

Another old saying runs:
The cunning rabbits are dead,
The excellent fox remains.

You have taken the wrong path.[40]

Soong Kwong's trial was riddled with inconsistencies: it was held in a military court under civil law; if military law had been used, Soong Kwong's defenders argued, there would be no case to answer as their man was a belligerent. There were three separate trials; at the first, the British judge was overruled by the two Asian assessors and ordered a retrial; at the second, when the judge was again overruled, he ordered a third trial. On this occasion the Asian assessors were dispensed with altogether, and replaced by two British military judges, on the grounds that no Asian judge could withstand intimidation. Soong Kwong was found guilty and sentenced to four years' imprisonment. At the final hearing, he threw his slippers at the judge.

The general strike was Malaya's first and the largest trial of strength yet between the left and the British regime. In the eyes of Philip Hoalim and other Malayan Democratic Union leaders who gave it their support, it was a strike for civil rights. A few days earlier the British had further provoked the Chinese community when British national servicemen wrecked the offices of Chinese associations and tore down pictures of Chiang Kai Shek. Local hawkers protested bitterly at one incident in Senai, Johore: 'although we are merely hawkers who know nothing, our national flag represents our country. And they insulted our flag in such a manner!'[41] The strike threatened to cripple the colonial economy. The first confrontations began on 21 January at the Singapore Harbour Board, where 7,000 stevedores again refused to load shipments of arms bound for Java. On 29 January between 150,000 and 170,000 workers downed tools in Singapore, another 60,000 in Selangor and more in Penang, Perak and elsewhere. In Singapore the markets came to a standstill and the British reported that 3,500 pickets and supporters were out on trishaws and lorries enforcing the stoppage. The Kuomintang and Chinese business leaders claimed that if the British could break the strike, they could get the city back to work within hours, but in the event the strike was abruptly called off at its peak, on the eve of Chinese New Year, just before support threatened to drop away. The General Labour Union claimed a major victory. Soong Kwong was released, his sentence remitted, on 4 February. Mountbatten had wanted to do this before the strike, but had been unwilling to be seen to capitulate to pressure. The effect was the same. In the words of the BMA's police adviser, René Onraet: 'never in the History of Singapore have all sections of the diverse Asiatic community been so overawed and subdued'.[42] The 'January 29 Strife', as it became known in Communist Party annals, was a political strike, and the British justified their punitive reaction to it on these grounds. But in private they acknowledged that they were fighting unrest based on hunger. 'The administration cannot have a clear conscience in fighting a general strike on such as basis', warned the chief civil affairs officer in Singapore. 'The next strike might be effective ... If force were to be used, it would be disastrous for here and for the empire as a whole.'[43]

Despite such warnings, British opinion hardened. Mountbatten observed in his diary that officials were now calling for 'more flogging' and the death penalty.[44] Even the architects of the liberal policy wavered. As Richard Broome, who with Force 136 had spent many months in the jungle with Chin Peng, told Mountbatten: 'they are after revolution for the sake of revolution ... The great majority of the leaders are after nothing else but trouble, and gratification of the lust for power that the stirring up of trouble gives them. They are therefore an evil force ...' A series of monster demonstrations was now planned in support of human rights. But the timing of them provoked the British beyond all endurance. The unions demanded a public holiday on 15 February, the fourth anniversary of the fall of Singapore, and asked to hold a mass rally at Happy World to mark National Humiliation Day. Enraged, Mountbatten suggested an alternative public holiday on 27 February to commemorate the *sook ching* massacres of Chinese.[45] BMA officers pressed Mountbatten to revive pre-war mechanisms for control of associations and speech, and suggested that powers of banishment be used against the organizers. At this point, the supremo hesitated. He objected to the idea of 'banishment'; always quick with an historical analogy, he pointed out that the banishment of Mussolini's opponents to Lipari had kept the flame of anti-fascism active. Lenin himself had been banished by the tsar of Russia, and this had increased his prestige. And where would people be banished to, Mountbatten asked? Most were of long domicile in Malaya, and would qualify for the new Malayan Union citizenship. Should the new state choose its citizens on criteria of 'desirability'? In the end, at Purcell's own suggestion, Mountbatten was persuaded to use old legislation that allowed him to 'expel aliens'; a much less loaded term. Mountbatten took the unusual step of despatching his trade-union adviser, John Brazier, to London to explain personally to Labour ministers that the General Labour Unions were not 'legitimate' trade unions and were out 'to embarrass us by every means and . . . hoping to arouse contempt for the administration'.[46] At 4 p.m. on 13 February a warning was issued that anyone who attempted to organize strikes 'to interfere with the due course of law' may be 'repatriated to the country of their origin or their citizenship'. On the following evening Purcell and Broome were present at a series of pre-emptive arrests on the premises of the General Labour Union and other bodies. On 15 February the monster meeting in Singapore did not materialize, but there was a gathering outside St Joseph's Institution, in the heart of the city. Police and troops went in with lathis and were seen by journalists to beat men lying on the ground. Two of them died and their bodies were paraded by demonstrators through the streets. Over 5,000 people attended the funeral of 18-year-old student Lin Feng Chow at the Khek Cemetery in Bukit Timah. Upcountry, the repression was more severe: in Labis, Johore, fifteen people were killed and forty-eight wounded when troops opened fire on a crowd. At Mersing, where the protests were against the original killings, another seven people were killed and twenty-six wounded.[47]

The 'February 15th Incident' marked the end of the Malayan Spring. There was public outrage at the deaths, which were reported in the British and international press. But the arrests continued. The British now had in custody many senior union leaders, including the chairman and vice-chairman of the Singapore General Labour Union, and the secretary of the MCP in Singapore, Lim Ah Liang. The British baulked at deporting Lim Ah Liang: he was jailed for four years. But Mountbatten sought permission from the Chinese government to deport ten of them. The reply came back that 'suitable arrangements' would be made for their reception. This stopped Mountbatten in his tracks. He was now worried that they might be 'bumped off' on arrival; he had heard that, fearing this, many convicted communists before the war had begged for life imprisonment rather than banishment. Purcell responded that this had not been known to happen since 1929. In that year, 850 people had been banished. Nor was the Colonial Office moved. But the supremo, now in Australia, where he failed to persuade Australian trade unionists to call off their blockade of goods for Indonesia, refused to endorse the deportations. 'I am not thinking of my own name, or even of the good name of the military administration, I am solely imbued with the desire to act in a manner which I consider in the true interests of HMG, and which history in ten years' time will vindicate.'[48] The civil government, due to take over at the end of March, must deal with the issue. The problem was, as the growing number of hardliners – now including Purcell and Hone – well realized, that although civil government could reintroduce banishment it would also have to reintroduce *habeas corpus*. 'It is', Mountbatten concluded, 'precisely because the civil government is unable to detain these people legally that I am being asked to take action.'[49] The general feeling of the British in Malaya was that Mountbatten was determined 'not to let himself in for any unpleasant political consequences'.[50] He wished to be remembered as a liberator. 'I do not really think he believed that the Chinese communists were really communists,' Hone reflected later. 'He thought that they were just decent left-wing chaps who valued freedom of speech and freedom of association as much as we did and that if they were properly handled by the administration generally, they were 100% British.'[51] On the first day of civilian rule, Hone reported, in one of its first acts, the new government 'despatched ten little nigger boys homeward'.[52]

Victor Purcell was also about to depart. His own progress had been extraordinary: from tribune of the liberal imperialism to one of the leading advocates of preventive detentions. A personal turning point, he recalled twenty years later, had been on 29 January when the servants in the residence he and Ralph Hone shared refused to serve them. It was clear then that 'we must prevent them taking charge of the country or abdicate'. The illusions of liberal imperialism were exploded. Purcell was, like many British officials, unable to live with the consequences of his own policy. Democratic opinion that had emerged in the Malayan Spring appalled him, so too had the very idea of 'the people'. 'The ideal human being boils down to the moronic', he wrote in one of the last of his journals, 'the adenoidal, the unwashed, the scrofulous, the naked, the illiterate, the dumb and, above all, the passive and the victimised.' This was not a 'people', Purcell seemed to say, on which a progressive colonial policy could be based: 'until Malaya produces her own leaders and her own sense of civic responsibility (which sometimes seems a thousand miles away) we must continue to accept the responsibility of governing'.[53] For Malayans, the Spring was a chance to explore the meaning of freedom, and most had rejected the freedom that was on offer from the British.

Apparently, the democracy demanded by the people in the past few months differs a great deal from the democratic system as specified by the British Army. Hence 'democratic' tragedies have occurred incessantly. Perhaps the BMA may accuse the people of abusing 'freedom' over the past few months, but they must reflect on that which they promised the people. How may the people use the freedom so as to conform to the government specifications? There is no definite statement, and so the random use of force is inevitable.[54]

Over the coming months, 'the laws of 1941' would begin to return. The Malayan Spring was an epochal and tragic moment. It was a period when the people of Malaya, for the first time under colonial rule, began to taste political freedom and debate the meaning of their *Merdeka*. Never again in Malaya's history would intellectual and political activity be subject to so few legal restraints.

HANG TUAH AND HANG JEBAT

It was at this stage that the greatest political challenge came from where it was least expected. On 22 January the British government published its White Paper on the Malayan Union. Beset on all sides, Mountbatten urged caution, to allow time for the British to take soundings of local opinion. To impose a constitution from on high, he argued, would be 'stigmatised as a return to the old type of colonial government and a denial of democratic principles'.[55] He was overruled by the cabinet: the policy was to be implemented by order-in-council before the return to civil government on 1 April 1946. But the scale of the Malay backlash took everyone by surprise and shook British power throughout the Far East.

The Malays were still defending their *kampongs*, and the cycle of communal violence of the interregnum was not yet at an end. In late 1945 there were large-scale disturbances in Kuala Pilah in Negri Sembilan, in which forty Chinese were killed, many of them women and children. In Lower Perak, in an area north of the town of Telok Anson, there were Chinese attacks on Malays and reprisals throughout the first weeks of the year. Many bodies were never recovered; there was no police station in the area and little reliable evidence as to who was responsible. It was estimated that sixty Chinese and thirty Malays perished. In the village of Batu Malim, in Pahang, on 11 February there was a clash in the market involving 200 Malays and 150 Chinese: thirty people died, including ten children.[56] Perhaps the most troubled area was the Perak river region. In early March there was grievous violence in Kuala Kangsar district. One young BMA officer described the scene around Bekor: 'We poled down the river in sampans ... There were dead men, women and children, all Malay, lying everywhere for about a mile and a half along the river-side, and several houses burnt down. I counted 22 bodies, but the total was 56.' A number of Chinese were arrested and three more were killed by troops: 'Inquests were rather tricky', the officer reported, 'when soldiers shoot.'[57] Against this background, the disquiet among the Malays which had greeted the rulers' signing of the MacMichael treaties became a battle for ethnic survival.

It began when the Kuala Lumpur newspaper *Majlis* called for a united front of leadership, and for Malay associations to petition the rulers and to defend the Malays where the sultans had failed to do so. But in Johore there was an attempt to dethrone the ruler himself. Many of the State's elite had fallen foul of Sultan Ibrahim over the years, yet they had a powerful sense of their privileges, fortified by Johore's strong administrative tradition, and the State possessed the largest concentration of Malay graduates. Dissidents appealed to the constitution of 1894, which the sultan's signing of the MacMichael agreement seemed to flout. The leader of the Johore rebels, Dr Awang bin Hassan, telephoned Onn bin Jaafar to invite him to a meeting at Abu Bakar mosque on 5 February. Onn at this time lived in comparative obscurity as district officer in Batu Pahat. But he agreed to attend and even discussed the possibility that they could, in Onn's words, 'get the Old Man down'. At the meeting the cry rang out (in English): 'Down with the sultan'. Onn arrived in the midst of this, but then confounded the organizers by making a speech that called for calm and caution. There was much speculation about Onn's motives; it might have been that he was intercepted by the British or, as is more probable, he now felt that the English-educated elite were courting disaster.[58]

Word of this meeting reached the old sultan at Grosvenor House in London, where he had arrived in January. He reacted with predictable anger, but he also made a swift *volte-face*. As he told the British in private, 'I have to say that they have led me to doubt whether, in my great satisfaction at the return of the British administration, I gave the scheme the close scrutiny for which it called.'[59] On 22 February Ibrahim received a telegram: 'Malays in Johore have no more faith now stop Not worthy you let us all down and ran away without explanation stop No longer your subjects stop Johore Malays'.[60] British observers felt that Ibrahim had only himself to blame. Sir George Maxwell, a pre-war official close to the Malay elite, believed he had been enticed by a pre-war promise of a major-generalship. 'Ibrahim's love of decoration', Maxwell wrote, 'is as childish as that of Goering.'[61] Now the sultan appealed to the Colonial Office in extreme consternation and revoked his support for the Union. This did not appease his critics. Another telegram arrived: 'Your own confession now proves your disloyalty and breach of trust of the Johore Malays stop We can fight our battle stop No need for you any more God's help and protection sufficient for us'.

This was an unprecedented public attack on the authority of a ruler who, for the Malays, whatever his personal failings, was God's vice-regent on earth. It was treason, or *derhaka*. But the elites responded that the rulers, by signing the treaties, had betrayed a

God-given trust as defender of their subjects. As *Majlis* put it, it was 'the *raja* who has committed *derhaka* against the people'. The ruler held his position by virtue of his role as protector of the Malay people. If the ruler failed in his duties, it was legitimate for subjects to rebel, to protect the community. The Malay community – the nation – took precedence over the ruler.[62] A central point of reference for Malay political thought was the fifteenth-century golden age of Melaka. The Malayan Union crisis called to mind the prophecy of its great warrior, Hang Tuah: *Tidakkan Melayu hilang di-dunia!* – 'The Malays shall not disappear from the World!' Hang Tuah was the champion of the Sultan of Melaka and his people; the leader of a legendary band of fighters. His virtues were the steadfastness and loyalty of the Malay people. In the tale of Hang Tuah, he is slandered to the sultan and forced to go into hiding. His friend Hang Jebat comes to court to avenge him, and in an act of rebellion against an unjust ruler drives the sultan from his palace. But it falls to Hang Tuah, who is then recalled, to fight and kill Hang Jebat, because – as Hang Tuah tells his dying friend – loyalty to the ruler, however unjust, and duty must come before all else. Hang Tuah is the hero of the tale, but the story was also used to illustrate a ruler's convenant with his people: Hang Tuah represented an absolute loyalty to a ruler and Hang Jebat the right to rebel when he transgressed. The meaning could be more ambiguous: Hang Tuah's loyalty could been seen as feudal, even slavish; Hang Jebat's rebellion as wild and self-seeking. In the years to come, Malay radicals began to adopt the cause, and invoke the name of Hang Jebat as the 'herald of a new age . . . a leap forward from the absolutist to the democratic plane'.[63] The MNP and API dropped their earlier support for the Union, and voiced virulent opposition to the rulers: the time had come for the nation – the *bangsa* – to stand forth against feudalism and imperialism.

Not everyone was prepared to go so far. Onn bin Jaafar now began to appeal to a national audience with his call for a 'Movement of Peninsular Malays', that transcended State loyalties. The movement began in his district of Batu Pahat where, by touring the *kampòngs* and addressing large rallies of Malays, Onn built on his personal prestige as a defender of the Malays in the weeks of communal violence during the interregnum. The *Majlis* of Kuala Lumpur began to canvass his name as the potential leader of a general conference of the Malays. Onn remained throughout these events a fiery and complex figure. In his youth, his politics seemed to be in the mould of Kemal Ataturk in Turkey: secular, modernizing and with a hint of republicanism. Now his message was of Malay unity, but his attack sheered away from the rulers and focused more on the British. And it was not a demand for independence, but solely an attack on the Malayan Union, in which Britain had broken faith with the Malays. Malaya, he argued, was 'not yet ready' for independence. He made this argument from deep patriotism and for the defence of Malay primacy. The Malays needed continued British protection to strengthen themselves to ensure their survival. Onn was also an aristocrat and, at a time when across the Straits in northern Sumatra, the revolutionaries were slaughtering aristocrats, he baulked at the thought of an Indonesian-style revolution in Malaya, a revolution he could have quite easily led.

On 1 March a gathering of some 200 Malays took place at the Sultan Suleiman Club in Kampong Bahru, Kuala Lumpur. They were representatives of some forty-one Malay associations, including the MNP and API. The meeting concluded that the interest of the Malays could be defended effectively only by a national umbrella organization of Malay bodies. The United Malays National Organization (UMNO) was founded, and it would dominate Malay politics for the next sixty years. It had no institutional structure, no membership, no broad political platform, but there were few voices of opposition to Onn as its leader. Under his direction, UMNO began to distance itself from the anti-feudal radicalism of the MNP. It was, quite deliberately, an 'organization' and not a 'party'. Dato Onn had even wanted to drop the word 'national' and call it UMO, presumably to evoke UNO, the United Nations Organization. Onn, in what one British observer called his 'perfect, even donnish English', pronounced it 'Amno', which was some way from the vernacular.[64]

In the name of UMNO, a boycott was announced of the installation of the new governor of the Malayan Union. Sir Edward Gent arrived in Kuala Lumpur on the afternoon of 31 March. He had been a career civil servant in the Colonial Office, where, although a specialist in Far Eastern affairs, he had worked entirely within Whitehall. The appointment was a surprise even to Gent himself. In London he had been a leading advocate of the new policy. As he took residence in King's House, the rulers gathered for the installation ceremony in their full princely regalia in the Station Hotel, a many-turreted Moorish fantasy of a building. A crowd gathered outside, shouting loyal slogans. But they were, as instructed by the Malay Congress, wearing white bands over their *songkoks* – the black velvet fez-like caps worn by the Malays for prayer – as a symbol of mourning. Onn bin Jaafar persuaded the rulers to go onto a balcony to acknowledge the crowd. This was an entirely unprecedented gesture: by identifying themselves publicly with the people in this way, the rulers seemed to endorse a subtle shift in the Malay body politic. The Sultan of Kedah was in tears. Onn was worried that violence might erupt, and the rulers saw that they must throw in their lot with UMNO. The meeting ended in patriotic fervour with expressions of allegiance to the sultans. In Onn's words: 'The Rulers have become the People and the People have become the Ruler.' In one sense, this meant that peace had been restored between them; in another, it acknowledged that the rulers now held their position only in so far as they held it in trust for the people. In the words of the Sultan of Pahang, the man who would have headed the independent Malay nation in August 1945 had it been declared: 'I am one of the people and, therefore, for the people.'[65]

The rulers asked to see Gent. With much self-effacement at the breach of the protocol, the Sultan of Perak asked that the Union constitution be set aside pending full consultations in Malaya. They adjourned, only to return again shortly before midnight to announce that they would not be attending the swearing in of Gent the next morning, nor even an informal meeting the following day. Although attended by Mountbatten and other worthies, the inauguration of the Malayan Union was, in the words of the *News Review*, 'as flat as the local beer'.[66] A few days later the rulers announced their repudiation of the MacMichael agreements and their intention to travel en masse to London to demand that their rights be protected in a looser federal constitution. From Park Lane, Sultan Ibrahim asked to see his fellow-monarch, George VI, ostensibly on a social call. The rulers found allies in the creators of British Malaya. A Malay, Ismail Moh'd Ali, who had written to *The Times* to defend the Malay rulers, had invoked the spirit of the 'late Sir Frank Swettenham'. 'May I point out', shot back the reply, 'that, if late, I am still in time to be your obedient servant, Frank Swettenham'. Swettenham's career was outstanding in British imperial history in that it lasted so long and was made in one place. He was involved in the initial British acquisition of rights in the peninsula in 1874; he presided over the creation of the Federated Malay States in 1895, and had largely created the term of art, 'Malaya'. He died, aged ninety-six, in early June 1946, engaged in an impassioned defence of the Malay sovereignty he had done so much to undermine.[67] As Malay protests escalated, Swettenham and other 'old Malaya' hands warned the Colonial Office that if there was delay in revoking the Union: 'we would have Indonesia'.[68] On 12 April a further 'Proconsul's letter' was published in *The Times*, in which the surviving architects of 'British Malaya' spoke with a rare authority and unanimity. They deplored the lack of time for consultation and argued that some of the rulers had merely seen the document as an affirmation of loyalty after the occupation.[69] They were preparing the ground for a visit of the sultans to London. The Colonial Office viewed the arrival of these colourful figures and their entourages with mounting trepidation. In the House of Commons, even Tom Driberg, while admitting that he cared little for sultans, announced that he could not support the Union.

The spectre of Indonesia loomed large in the mind of the British in Malaya. There were continual intelligence reports, not all of them accurate, of Indonesian-style militias crossing into the peninsula. Sir Edward Gent was now alarmed that Malay non-cooperation might paralyse the police, with its overwhelmingly Malay rank and file, at a time when the British regime was facing threats on every side. He was under no illusion about the scale of the protest: it was not orchestrated by the Malay elite, he concluded; the sultans were facing genuine popular pressure. On 4 May Gent sent a remarkable telegram to George Hall which urged the secretary of state to accept the federal proposals, in the face of 'surprising but real' Malay unity on the issue, and the threat proposed by Malay civil disobedience. Hall was astounded: 'I confess that your sudden and fundamental change of attitude has come as a great shock to me.' Gent was seeking to overturn a policy that been agreed by both cabinet and Parliament and sealed by binding treaties. Hall demanded further and fresh assessments of the situation. He asked two MPs who had been on a mission to Sarawak to divert to Malaya: David Rees-Williams, a former Penang lawyer, and the Conservative and unofficial 'Member for Malaya', Captain L. D. Gammans. Gammans journeyed up the west coast to Onn's stronghold of Batu Pahat and along the way was met with several well-orchestrated demonstrations in which women played a prominent role. Both men attended a conference of UMNO and the rulers at Kuala Kangsar and were deeply impressed by its resolve. But more decisively, in May 1946 Attlee appointed another senior imperial statesman to try to knock British Southeast Asia into some kind of shape. Malcolm MacDonald, son of former Labour prime minister Ramsay MacDonald and previously High Commissioner of Canada, was, under the new constitutional arrangements, to be the first Governor General of British Southeast Asia. It was an unprecedented position. MacDonald was to co-ordinate policy across the region, but had the power to direct governors. Although he was reluctant to be seen to be superseding Gent's authority, MacDonald was instructed to adjudicate the fate of the new constitution. Within five days of his arrival in Singapore on 21 May, MacDonald had come to the conclusion that it must be abandoned and quickly. Malay opinion was 'solid'. He praised Gent's 'courage, honesty and capacity'. But what was perhaps most persuasive was MacDonald's fear of the protests 'being swept into Indonesian anti-European currents'. He told Hall that Britain's international prestige was now at stake. As a palliative, he observed that 'it is the will of the people expressing itself'.[70] In private, Onn bin Jaafar had played on the security fears of the British. He offered them a quick way out, and MacDonald insisted they took it.

The controversy had unified the Malays to an unprecedented degree; the British had created a peninsular 'Malay' community which before the war had been barely conscious of itself. But the MNP and API never accepted Onn's argument that Malaya was unripe for independence. They rejected the new federal proposals, which seemed to entrench the old aristocratic order and prevent the full expression of this new nation. The MNP's opposition to the Union was not opposition to a unitary state, nor was it support for the sultans, but for the *rakyat jelita*, 'the common people' and 'their sovereignty and dignity'.

Its newspaper, *Pelita Malaya* – The Lamp of Malaya – was printed at a Chinese press, and used its first issue to define for whom it spoke: 'It is for such common people – peasants, small farmers, and domestic animal rearers, hawkers, fishermen and rubber tappers – that this paper is meant.' It rejected leaders who 'are usually district officers or some high-ranking officials who do not understand their feelings and do not know what are their desires. They are only good for making speeches at tea-parties, and nothing more than that.'[71] This was also a rejection of UMNO. There is a sense in which UMNO merely appropriated the language of nationalism in order to head off the challenge of common people. Its leaders had little faith in nationalism, and wanted nothing to do with its democratic implications. When the Malay Congress reconvened in June, the MNP and API walked out when it refused to adopt the flag of Indonesia. They now adopted the cry of Tan Malaka: 'On the ruins of this Malayan Union a "One Hundred Percent Independent *Merdeka*" must be erected.'[72]

BRITISH AND INDIAN MUTINIES

The British in Southeast Asia were now extremely vulnerable to any threat to internal security which might demand the use of British or Indian troops. The Allied Land Forces South East Asia were now demoralized and potentially mutinous. Many had had a very long war, and the resultant mental strain was now a major problem. Military doctors had noted the effects of this as early as 1942. By 1945 there were around 100 full-time psychiatrists in the theatre who were running between forty and fifty psychiatric centres in India, Burma and Ceylon. The troops of ALFSEA appeared to be suffering from massive psychological dysfunction. Army doctors suggested that the 'sudden change' in stresses of many soldiers – and particularly of the staff officers deeply concerned with the planning and liberation of Malaya – was responsible for this. They reported that Indian troops were particularly at risk: many had been in continuous service for three and a half years, with no leave for two. There were cases of suicide on disembarking in a new theatre, with a hostile climate and no prospect of return to deal with domestic problems.[73] In October

1945 there was a minor mutiny on HMS *Northway* in Singapore, when sailors left their dinner uneaten on mess tables, following what the enquiry called 'a schoolboy grouse about food'. The men were particularly aggrieved at having fish (herring in tomato sauce) for breakfast three times a week.[74] But if this incident was relatively minor, it was one of a growing number, and it could not be attributed solely to inactivity. Across the theatre fraternization created a series of incidents, each relatively short lived, but increasingly connected. At the height of the crisis in Indonesia Mountbatten had seen the limits of what he could ask British and Indian troops to do. There was deep disillusion among British troops about the reconquest of Indonesia, and about their continued presence in Malaya. Soldiers attended political rallies and Malayan Democratic Union meetings, and much of the Malayan Communist Party's library in Singapore was donated by servicemen.[75] An 'East and West Society', begun as an Army Education Centre project, started actively to foster these links.[76] At the time of the 29 January General Strike, there were reports in the leftist press that troops at Bukit Timah threatened to come out in support for the Malayan workers, and would refuse to put down the strike.[77] This was perhaps wishful thinking, but at the same time a larger protest by British servicemen was already underway.

At the end of January there was a series of protests at Royal Air Force bases across the crescent. They involved perhaps fourteen stations and 50,000 men. It seems to have begun at Drigh Road, Karachi. The immediate case was poor food and living conditions, and a return to peacetime discipline, with all the kit inspections and parade in 'best blue' uniforms. But the underlying tension was the delay in demobilization. Men of the 'forgotten armies' were deeply worried about being disadvantaged in jobs or being denied places in higher education. In the petitions of the men, the use of the army in India and Indonesia was deplored, as it was seen as a central obstacle to demobilization. Men with a Labour or Communist Party background founded their own discussion groups and made contacts with the Indian Communist Party. When protests began, the 'strike committees' were run by men with trade-union experience; their news-sheets were run by conscripted journalists who had links with the local press. The incidents stretched across the widest arc of the British Middle East and Asia: from Gibraltar, Cairo and North Africa, to India, and through to Seletar, in Singapore, where more than 4,000 men were involved in the strike. It began with a meeting in the canteen, which was filled to capacity, on the evening of 26 January and the next day spread to Kallang aerodrome. The press reports and the incessant movement across the theatre through airbases created the sense of a connected protest across Asia. There was even some condoning of it by officers, who obstructed the enquiries into the events. Those at the forefront of the protests maintained that they were spontaneous, that their own leadership was unpremeditated and moderating.[78] But the main figures, such as Arthur Attwood in Karachi and D. C. Brayford at Manipur, became the subject of high-profile trials. They were in correspondence with Tom Driberg, who engaged D. N. Pritt – then riding high as an independent MP – to defend them. But investigating officers felt the strikes were a communist conspiracy, 'the work of an organisation which remained in the background and controlled both the Indian and the Middle East to suit its own ends'.[79] This was the kind of charge the British were applying to Asian trade unionism in Malaya and Singapore.

By May 1946 the incidents spread to frontline troops. Men of the Parachute Regiment stationed at Muar in Malaya, recently returned from Java, protested at their living conditions. After a meeting in a canteen on 13 May, with the lights out, there was an assembly by the sea wall the next morning at which they refused to attend parade. They had been instructed to turn out clean, but it was impossible in the tropical mud, and there was insufficient water for washing. The men gathered in an angry mood and twice refused to obey the commanding officer's orders to return to their companies: 258 men were taken into custody and brought to trial en masse at Kluang airfield on 12 August, where they had been detained. Some were brought in handcuffs, having slipped over the wire to buy cigarettes and necessities in the town. They termed it a strike, but were rebuked by the judge advocate: 'The word "strike" is not in Army vocabulary,' he said. 'It is Mutiny or nothing else.'[80] Of the 258, 243 were sentenced to three or five years' penal servitude (later commuted to two years' hard labour), and discharged with ignominy. Their defence was that men had protested similarly elsewhere and had not been punished. There were questions in Parliament and public petitions in their support. Eventually, all convictions were quashed, due to irregularities in the trial. Churchill himself condemned the conduct of the court martial in the Commons: 'I unhappily presided over the Army when there was a shoal of mutinies, and no one ever attempted to bring large masses of the rank and file to a mass trial.'[81] It was the British Army's Red Fort Trials. To the military it was a 'complete bombshell'. It seemed as if the new Labour government was capitulating to public opinion. The battalion was immediately despatched to a transit camp and posted out of Southeast Asia.[82] Field Marshal Montgomery was compelled to write to all field commanders. 'No criticism must be allowed against our new Secretary of State or against the Government . . . He handled the problem in a brave and determined manner.'[83] The commander of the Parachute Regiment, who had been in Java at the time of the 'mutiny', saw that it indicated a fundamental problem of peacetime operations. The local commander was a rugby international and a 'real live wire'. But his troops were men who 'had *not* the responsibilities of soldiers'. They were merely 'civilians in uniform': 80 per cent of those involved were aged eighteen to twenty-one, forty-five of whom had not seen active service, and included forty-seven out of fifty newly drafted from the UK.[84] It was becoming dangerous to try to defend the empire with a conscript army.

Not all soldiers were so politicized. A special section of the Royal Army Medical Corps – the No. 1 Biological Research Section – distributed a questionnaire to British troops in 1946. Its results could not have been surprising to commanders, but they were nevertheless perturbing. Servicemen expressed their resentment of 'wasting time, their sense of losing time' – what the psychologists called 'disuse atrophy'. The phrases that cropped up repeatedly were soldiers' anger at 'red tape' and 'bullshit'. The army struggled to interpret this latter term. The report stated that it 'may be defined pedantically as "excessive insistence, in military administration, on the specious and showy, rather than on things really contributing to military efficiency"'. Encouraged by this, the authors of the survey expanded eloquently on what, for the serviceman, complaints at 'messing around', might mean:

Drafts of men roam about the country like droves of armed sheep, but more articulate – the Transit Camp, that slaughterhouse of hope, looming menacingly before them. All this fluidity gives an impression of administrative efficiency, so different from the stable, peaceful and well-oiled bureaucracy of Great Britain.[85]

One of the symptoms of the collapse of morale, according to the army doctors, was the high rate of venereal disease. This was the era of Brian Aldiss's 'Horatio Stubbs'; a young man set loose in the 'great whoring cities of the East'.[86] The cabarets were now a huge industry. Dancing classes proliferated to train the 'taxi-dancers', who were often in debt for the cost of them and for the hire of their seats in the cabaret. In May the Penang Cabaret Girls Association was founded at the City Lights cabaret. A Miss Tseng Pi Chi spoke: 'We are marching ahead in society . . . but although we are mere dancers we have our country behind us . . . We don't want to be dancers all our lives; we want only to make a living from dancing. We are waiting till we shall be the equals of men when we shall quit dancing and seek other opportunities of making a living.' There was a confrontation with the military over their plans to make standard the price of dance coupons.[87] The behaviour of British troops continued to have a deep effect on locals. There was fighting in Penang when a British serviceman threw an ashtray at a Chinese boy, killing him. Civilians avoided the cabarets and girls walking with soldiers were shied with watermelon skins.[88] In the eyes of a young Malay woman, British troops 'were often drunk and disorderly, consorting openly with women of the streets . . . They flaunted their bad manners before the shocked eyes of the Asian population, and we winced at the filthy language we heard. Even to us, the new generation of Singaporeans, it was clear that these soldiers did not belong to the same world as their pre-war countrymen . . . The picture of the English gentleman was shattered.'[89]

Eric Stokes, a British subaltern, wrote to his sister at the end of the war that, walking along a Calcutta street, he felt 'rather like a Nazi officer must have felt walking along a Paris boulevard'.[90] The hatred of the clerks and professional people for him was palpable. Whatever the politicians in London and the administrators in Delhi thought, most ordinary British soldiers and businessmen in India already knew that the game was up. In 1946 the British Raj in India died and its death lay heavily on the British in Burma and Malaya. The Raj's obsequies were not finally said until August 1947, by which time more than a million Indians were doomed to perish in a frenzy of communal killing and many millions more had fled their homes. It was in 1946, however, that the underpinnings of British rule, which had survived even the Quit India movement of 1942 and the disillusionment of 1945, finally came apart. War's end always brings crises. India's huge war effort had left it exhausted. More than a million army personnel needed to be repatriated to their villages. Many of these men, particularly the officers, were convinced that self-rule should come immediately. The war had awakened them to politics. If, as they had been told, they were fighting in Southeast Asia for the self-determination of Burmese, Thais, Indonesians and others against Japanese rule, why should India not be free? If most of the Burmese villages they had seen had once had schools and clean water, why should not India's? Economic hardship drove the point home. Inflation roared away, goods were scarce and military pay did not keep pace with prices. Simmering racial tensions damped down by fear during the war flared up. A younger generation of Indian officers and men would not now put up with casual racial abuse and disdain, especially from Johnny-come-lately British officers who had not fought through the war as they had done. In the Royal Indian Navy a full-scale mutiny broke out in February 1946, fuelled by a combination of racial tension and economic frustration. A white officer had apparently called an Indian subaltern a 'black bastard'. The fleet went on strike off Bombay. Parties of men from the ships invaded the city centre carrying Congress flags and demanding independence.[91] Local Congress volunteers joined them, and the police, already sullen and resentful because of their own lack of compensatory pay, seemed on the point of going over to the mutineers. Wavell acknowledged that the experience of the RAF strikes had encouraged the men.

The trouble quickly spread across the country with the Congress leadership now going for the kill. Tension mounted before the March provincial elections which Wavell had announced the previous autumn. Anti-British riots convulsed Calcutta, where Subhas Bose's brother and old allies joined the communists in demonstrations of solidarity with the INA internees. Cars were burnt out. Areas such as leafy Park Street, which had been quiet even in 1942, were invaded by crowds of youths. Shop windows were smashed. When the British authorities released Sher Khan, a colonel in the INA, he received a nearly hysterical reception in Calcutta. Denizens of the august Bengal Club looked out from the veranda in dismay as he and other reprieved officers of the INA were paraded past in triumph.[92] The white man's *izzat* or charisma had finally evaporated. Arthur Dash, a senior Bengal civil servant, recorded that Britons and Anglo-Indians walking in Calcutta's streets were waylaid and abused. A favourite game was to purloin their regimental or club ties and *topis* (pith helmets) in a sort of ritual humiliation. If they resisted, they were beaten up.[93]

DORMAN-SMITH'S WATERLOO

This atmosphere of crisis spread across British Asia, in part because the nationalists were aware of each other's actions. In Rangoon Aung San's speeches became more inflammatory after the New Year. In India Nehru was threatening the British with mass civil disobedience, but in Burma it was the threat of military force that loomed. At the Shwedagon pagoda in early January 1946 Bogyoke, as Aung San was popularly known, denounced Dorman-Smith as a Tory imperialist who was misleading Labour and was in cahoots with British capitalists. There were calls for the resignation of the 'fascist governor' and cries of 'Rise! Kill! Kill!' On 19 January Aung San surpassed himself with a three-hour speech, during which even he had to sit down for a time as a result of exhaustion. In the course of this marathon he insisted that Britain was no longer great. It was indebted to the USA and even to its own colonies. The British were attempting to reintroduce their commercial interests into the country and 'the Emergency Laws in Burma and [the] British Judicial system are similar to those of the Kempeitai', the hated Japanese secret police.[94] Amidst the ranting, however, he enunciated three demands that would resonate throughout the year. First, he insisted that the White Paper of May 1945 which seemed indefinitely to postpone Burma's independence should be torn up: power should be transferred to a wholly Burmese ministry.

Second, he called for full adult suffrage to be introduced and, third, he demanded an immediate passage to Britain to talk to Attlee's government.

In January 1946 all this sounded like the wishful thinking of a firebrand. Dorman-Smith certainly maintained his haughty demeanour to the young fellow. Yet by the end of the year Aung San had achieved every one of these aims. This was testimony both to the rapid weakening of Britain's international position and to the approach of a social crisis in Burma itself. In this same speech, Aung San went on to demand the immediate nationalization of business, the exclusion of British, Chinese and Indian firms and the seizure of their assets, and government control of padi exports. Again, every one of these aims was in the process of being achieved two years on when Burma became an independent country and left the Commonwealth.

To the British it might have seemed that these speeches were cynical attempts by Aung San to restore his credibility with his restive left wing. Yet there was no hiding the fact that the AFPFL spoke directly to the fears of many, if not a majority, of Burmese.[95] British business was obviously re-establishing itself in the teak forests and oilfields. Indians were trickling back into the country and the governor, along with Indian business representatives, was putting strong pressure on his fairly tame executive council to allow the 1942 evacuees to return, promising only to retain some of the restrictions on immigration agreed in 1940. It was true that the Americans had withdrawn from the north of the country. But it was Indians and Chinese, not Burmese, who were making vast fortunes by buying up and selling off US war surplus. In the cities, the Anglo-Burmans and the Chinese were setting up lucrative and semi-criminal businesses. Even though the 'Black Market Administration' was more or less over, a few unscrupulous British officers were still on the make. Meanwhile, Karen and Kachin separatists and their missionary friends thought their day had come and were intent on biting off large chunks of the country.[96] To ordinary Burmese people who had not known security since the Depression, impoverished and without savings, it seemed that the whole nightmare of occupation and dispossession was to be played out again. However foolish Ba Maw and his gaudy satin pants had been, there had at least been some hope of independence in 1943.

Now his partial or 'ten anna' independence seemed to have been devalued to five annas. The Pegu Club had even reinstated its colour bar, as if it were still 1939, or perhaps even 1889. So Aung San sparked a bonfire of resentment when he spoke of the 'fascist governor' and his business cronies. He also expected his message to find some sympathetic British listeners. Mountbatten's old aides were still on the ground in some places and the Army Education Corps had done a good job of converting a lot of men to Fabian socialism. Word filtered through to the governor of the existence of an East and West Association, a British officers' club whose members courted Burmese nationalists and made anti-government pronouncements.[97]

The RAF seemed particularly radical in this respect. Dorman-Smith called it the 'Red Air Force'. His judgement seemed to be borne out by an incident that took place in April. The previous December Aung San had told Reuters that he was planning an Asiatic 'Potsdam Conference' at which 'Asiatic liberties' would be discussed and guaranteed by a small group of senior nationalist leaders. He added that the plans for this would be discussed with Pandit Nehru during his 'forthcoming visit' to Burma. Dorman-Smith immediately dashed off a telegram to the external affairs department of the government of India, insisting that they should give no facilities for a visit to Burma by Nehru. There was too much loose tinder lying around, not least a thousand increasingly restive INA men still held in Rangoon. Yet Nehru did fly to Singapore at the end of March 1946 to meet Mountbatten. En route his RAF plane developed 'engine trouble' and had to land at Rangoon just at a time when the governor was absent in Mandalay. As Dorman-Smith later described it, Nehru was greeted ecstatically by 300 Indians at the Strand Hotel 'who Jai-ed him Hind and anything else they could Jai'.[98] ('*Jai Hind!*' – 'Victory to India!' – was a standard nationalist slogan.) He also met Aung San for two and a half hours and planned with him an East Asian 'subject nations' conference. This was eventually to take place in March and April 1947. All this confirmed Dorman-Smith in the view that the 'engine trouble' had been a put-up job. The 'good old RAF have rather too many red gentlemen within their ranks for my liking', he asserted. What was more, why was Nehru ferried to Singapore in the first place and fêted by Mountbatten? 'Yet, damme, Dickie put him up at

Government House and drove with him plus Mrs Dickie to show him the Town, etc.'

In fact it was Wavell who told Mountbatten that Nehru was to be treated as a future prime minister of India. When the BMA could find no transport for him, Mountbatten lent his own, and travelled with him. The sight of Nehru by Mountbatten's side was a political sensation. Nehru's first engagement was a visit to a welfare centre for Indian troops in Singapore in the company of the Mountbattens. They were mobbed together with Nehru and had to escape. A vital political friendship was born. Nehru was fêted by representatives of all communities. A crowd of 100,000 people gathered outside the Adelphi Hotel where he was staying.[99] Tan Kah Kee led a delegation of Chinese and they feasted him at their 'millionaires' club', the Ee Hoe Hean Club. Wherever he stopped, the local MCP representatives came to see him. When confronted by MPAJA veterans, he retorted: 'Army? You have not come here armed have you?'

Nehru had agreed not to intervene in local politics, but made twenty speeches in eight days to around 60,000 people. His themes were pacific and pan-Asian rather than the specifics of the struggle in Malaya.[100] The police were worried that support for the INA would resurface. Guards of honour were provided, and it was agreed that they would not wear INA badges, although many wore their old uniforms: they had no other decent clothes. One of his first acts was to visit the Indian political detainees in jail, dispensing good advice on how to keep body and soul together in prison.[101] Congress sent a medical mission under an ex-INA officer that during a ten-week period treated over 17,000 labourers. But there were complaints that some of Nehru's gifts of clothing did not reach the poor people, for whom they were intended.[102] This was one of the last interventions of Congress nationalism in Malayan politics and many local Indians were disappointed by the statesmanlike moderation of the Pandit's language. At a big rally at Jalan Besar Stadium in Singapore in front of around 10,000 people, including over 3,000 INA personnel, there was a cry of 'Blood!' Nehru rebuked the crowd: 'He agreed that Netaji had done great work, but stated that the fighting spirit called for then was now out of date.' The veterans in the crowd began to melt away.[103] Behind the scenes, in Penang, Indian community leaders gathered to confront him about the fate of the gold that Bose had collected in Malaya. Nehru had been seen as slow in coming to the defence of the INA men on trial at the Red Fort. It was felt that in having cocktails with Mountbatten, Nehru had himself become a 'sahib'.[104]

But none of this washed with Dorman-Smith, to whom Dickie – 'rot him!' – was the root of all the troubles in Burma because he flattered and built up Aung San. 'Let's face it, our Dickie may be a first-class military commander, but he is a damned poor politician. If he ever became Governor General of anywhere I would expect a spot of bother because he just cannot keep his hands off politics . . . Probably Dickie will get the order of the White Rabbit from the first Government of Free India.' Dorman-Smith saw plots all around him, most of them originating with Attlee or Mountbatten. He had recently met Edward Gent and felt he was facing similar trouble. Gent told him that there was an agreement between the British government and Ceylon that the colony would have its freedom in five years' time. 'I only hope my people [the Burmese] do not get to know of this!' Dorman-Smith commented. In London, the civil servant to whom this long lament was addressed, Sir David Monteath, minuted loftily that he had a lot of sympathy with Dorman-Smith, even if his letter was 'phoney' in parts.

For the time being, the governor thought he had a few cards left to play. He continued to tinker with building a coalition of the old pre-1941 politicians. The friendly rogue, U Saw, was on the way back with his Myochit party. Ba Maw was heading back too, having escaped prosecution in Tokyo,[105] while poor old Sir Paw Tun hung on, gamely trying to put the clock back. From Dorman-Smith's point of view, any of the flotsam and jetsam of the pre-war years was better than the BNA firebrands. Besides, like many other observers, he sensed that Aung San himself did not know what to do, caught as he was between the British and the old guard on the one side and Thakin Soe and the communists on the other. Military intelligence later reported that Aung San was 'severely terrified of U Saw, who is really dangerous' and whose return to power was propelled by 'criminal gangsters'.[106] Aung San lived in perpetual fear of assassination but, according to the assessment, 'has much personal courage, unlike U Saw'. His courage was perhaps not always matched by his judgement;

Aung San had poured out his woes to 'a motherly type of woman' who just happened to be a British informant: 'He did not know what to do; all his life he had been without real friends and now everything he tries goes wrong.' He was 'beginning to doubt his ability to live up to the position which he has now acquired', Dorman-Smith para-phrased with satisfaction.[107] All the same, the governor was sensible enough to realize that Burmese opinion was largely on Aung San's side. Burma wanted to 'gallop down the road without any help'.[108] The 'middle classes', such as they were, seemed weak and their rep-resentatives were likely to be wiped out at the next election. Dorman-Smith had had a 'heart-warming trip' up to Myitkyina and the north, where the Kachins and other minority groups remained staunchly pro-British. Yet the minorities could not really provide a bulwark for continued British government in Burma. Though he was often accused of playing divide-and-rule politics, Dorman-Smith was sus-picious of a strongly pro-minority stance. Perhaps his Irish back-ground helped here: 'resistance groups are awkward things to handle as they may go on looking for something to resist', he wrote, adding that these 'special arrangements for minority groups only lead to trouble in the long run'.[109]

Then, quite suddenly, Dorman-Smith began to overplay his hand. In October 1945 he had been prepared to give Aung San the benefit of the doubt and even at his bitterest he still had some time for the man. At the turn of the year, as Aung San's rhetoric intensified, Dorman-Smith's tone soured. In mid December Ralph Michaelis, a radical journalist who published an 'independent newsletter', reported that the governor was so obsessed by his trial of strength with Bogyoke that he was losing his grip on the fragile administration. Rather than answering Aung San's charges of delaying Burma's independence, the governor had chosen to reopen the old Rangoon Yacht Club, a 'pre-war stronghold of the futile snobbery of the British colony in Rangoon to which no Burman was admitted'. Yachts, Michaelis's pamphlet noted, were once again being built at the club and were being guarded at the expense of the British taxpayer.[110] Dorman-Smith's political touch seems to have been deserting him. His dysentery, which flared up in the miserable conditions of post-war Rangoon, was getting worse. His view of Aung San became darker and darker. By April he was talking about 'Aung San and his band of thugs', by whom he meant the rapidly proliferating network of paramilitary People's Volunteer Organizations. Loosely administered by the AFPFL, the PVOs now effectively controlled large parts of the countryside. Dorman-Smith could almost feel British power draining through his hands into the swamps of the Burmese delta.

As the administration began to lose the propaganda war in Burma, Dorman-Smith searched for a way to stop what he viewed as the country's slide towards 'fascism', a sorely overused term in Burma at the time. One issue on which Aung San seemed to be vulnerable was the persistent rumour that he had murdered a village headman with his own hands during the Burma Independence Army's advance on Rangoon in early 1942.[111] This rumour had been relayed to London in 1945, but had wisely been shelved by the Burma Office. When Dorman-Smith was scouting around for politicians to appoint to his newly constituted executive council in early 1946, he approached Tun Oke, an old rival of Aung San. Tun Oke then used the more public forum of the legislative council formally to accuse Aung San of murder. This was a proceeding of dubious merit, not only because it tied the attack on Aung San to Dorman-Smith's political manoeuvring, but also because Tun Oke was himself wanted by the American military police for atrocities against Allied troops in 1942. According to one account he had had the heads of three British soldiers cut off and impaled on stakes outside a village, posting a notice beside them that read: 'The dirty, cunning English people came to Burma and not only committed the crimes of thieving brigands but cut off the heads of so many of our Burmese people ... What I have done is revenge for that.'[112] By working with Tun Oke, Dorman-Smith therefore managed to offend not only Aung San's followers but the British military too. One of Tom Driberg's correspondents described the reaction: 'There are several thousand British troops in Burma who are not at all keen on dying to defend a government which is close to such men as Thakin Oke.' Why, asked Driberg in exasperation, 'does Labour choose ex-ministers of the Chamberlain government as agents of its colonial policy?'[113]

Nevertheless, Tun Oke's allegations against Aung San gained momentum. In March newspapers in Rangoon, India and Britain began to report on the case and the police apparently had some success in digging up pertinent evidence. Determined to rid himself of the troublesome young nationalist, Dorman-Smith wrote to London seeking permission to arrest him. At this stage the British government had not thought through the implications of trying Aung San. While attending a conference in Singapore Dorman-Smith received a note from Whitehall ordering him to proceed with the arrest. He rushed back to Rangoon. The CID was alerted but, at the last minute, a telegram arrived countermanding the order. India had reasserted its primacy again. On 27 March Mountbatten had written to the government of Burma that, although he no longer had any responsibility for Burma, he was deeply perturbed at the proposal to arrest Aung San. Aung San's antics might have been disturbing but he had 'played the game by me' and, given his youth, he was bound to play a major part in Burmese politics for many years to come.[114] Three weeks later, as Dorman-Smith was beginning to hope that Mountbatten's intervention would be ignored, Cripps and Pethick-Lawrence telegraphed Burma urgently from Delhi, where they were on Cabinet Mission duty. They were trying to resolve the increasingly intractable stand-off between the Congress and Muslim League over the structure of a future government of independent India. The Indian issue thrust Burma to the margins. 'Solely from the point of view of our mission here, we must repeat to you the great risks we see in the arrest of Aung San at this juncture.'[115] It would be a 'disastrous' move and would derail the whole Indian constitutional process. To a long private letter to Attlee about the Indian deadlock, Pethick-Lawrence added a postscript on the possible arrest of Aung San: 'My personal feeling is that if we start probing into what happened during the Japanese occupation, we shall stir up mud which may well give us a lot of trouble.'[116]

The arrest warrant was duly intercepted between the chief secretary and the CID. Another hour and Aung San would have been behind bars. This would almost certainly have been the signal for a mass Burmese uprising against the British which could well have brought about the sort of bloody denouement that the British faced in Indonesia that very year. In Surabaya, they tried to suppress a well-entrenched nationalist movement. Many British and Gurkha soldiers who had survived the campaign against Rommel and the bloody fighting at Imphal and Kohima died for no good reason. In his memoirs Dorman-Smith was unrepentant. This was a nettle that the British had refused to grasp, he insisted. It discouraged the loyal and encouraged illegality. Ultimately, he implied, it set Burma on the path towards authoritarian government.

This attitude was to prove his undoing. The British position was now too weak. As one official put it, it might have been possible to arrest and shoot Aung San a year earlier, but it was too late now. Quite apart from the demands of the Cabinet Mission, the Indian situation frustrated Dorman-Smith at another level. The Indian Army was no longer available to suppress any popular movement that might have developed in response to the detention of Aung San. The Indian authorities had already made it clear that Indian troops could not now be used to put down Burmese nationalists. Congress would not wear it and the Indian Army would anyway probably have mutinied. Watching bitterly from the fringes, Dorman-Smith noted that a meeting of 'Dickie, Archie [Wavell] and the Auk [Auchinleck]' in Delhi had decided that the governor of Burma would have to govern in such a way as to avoid a popular uprising. 'Struth! Old Archie does not seem to be able to manage his show so as to avoid the use of British troops and Indian troops, while friend Dickie seems to be using troops of all sorts in Malaya.'[117] This refusal to deploy the Indian Army in Burma was, as he later put it, 'a bit of a facer', an insoluble problem, especially as he felt sure that Indians would be among the first to suffer in any AFPFL uprising.[118] But he was not ready to give up yet; he still hoped that he could persuade London to go ahead with the arrest and trial of Aung San.

What were the facts about the murder of the headman? Given the years of mayhem in Burma and the slaughter of hundreds of thousands, why did it matter so much? The key point was that the man killed by Aung San was a Muslim of Indian descent, one Abdul Rashid, who had been loyal to the British and opposed the nationalists.[119] He was headman of a village near Moulmein on the southern coast where tension between Muslims, who were mostly of Indian origin, and Burmese Buddhists had been very high since the Depression. In 1942 the incoming BIA had been immediately drawn into settling local scores as the British fled to the north. In her petition for the trial of Aung San, Abdul Rashid's widow gave a vivid account of his brutal last days. Denounced by the villagers, he had been thrown into a locked cart with a pig and starved for eight days. Though there is no independent evidence of this, the story's very existence, with its emphasis on an insult carefully tailored for a Muslim, illustrates the depths of the hatreds involved. Then, the widow continued, Aung San 'took him to the Thaton football ground and in the presence of thousands of people, speared him to death with his bayonet after crucifying him to the goal post'.[120] Aung San did not deny the killing, though he later told Dorman-Smith that he had been incapable of the degree of resolution alleged by the widow. He had certainly intended to kill the man himself, because it was his order that had condemned him, but he had bungled it 'and almost collapsed after the first stroke'. His subordinates had to finish off the headman.[121]

In early April, Aung San gave a lengthy response to these accusations in the legislative council.[122] The context, he said, was the mass looting and murder which accompanied the BIA's entry into southern Burma in 1942. He had tried to stop the score settling, but neither he nor Suzuki, the senior Japanese liaison officer with the BIA, had been able to do so effectively. Aung San said that it was important to try to restore order by punishing those who really had been guilty of abuses under the old regime. He claimed that British administration had failed and therefore it was incumbent on the nationalists to form an administration. Besides, 'in such slave countries as Burma, it cannot be said that conformity with the law is justice'. Abdul Rashid was one who had abused the slave people. He was a 'wicked man who had ill treated the villagers' and had indulged in despicable looting 'for his own stomach'.[123] Aung San declared that his conscience was clear, but as he made his statement, he appeared to lose his way, muttering, 'I forget, I forget . . .' He also added: 'To confess the truth, however, though this measure is not at all regular, yet it was rough and ready justice to suit the time and the conditions prevailing in the country.' This statement earned him some respect from the more open-minded of the British officials.[124]

Despite the governor's desire to act decisively, other British authorities in Burma were in two minds about prosecuting the case. For a start, there were procedural problems. Only six people of the 500 or so present at Abdul Rashid's killing had come forward to give evidence, and they were all Indians. Also the government doubted its ability to shield Indians from the inevitable reprisal attacks should the case come to trial. Even the archdeacon of Rangoon, George Appleton, who doubled up as the government of Burma's director of public relations, could partially excuse Aung San. He should perhaps have been 'arrested and executed' a year ago, but once Mountbatten had treated him 'respectfully', the British had effectively condoned his crimes. His arrest now would have 'repercussions comparable to those of the INA trials in India'. Besides, added Appleton, there were racial factors involved: 'In Burma people do not generally think in terms of justice and reason, but in terms of personalities and relationships.' Aung San's crime, and certainly his version of it, was 'understandable' and less heinous than many committed during the war, especially given that he was 'an emotional and in some ways fanatical man'.[125]

Dorman-Smith, however, refused to relent. This was a struggle of wills between his authority, the AFPFL and London. Once the petition of Abdul Rashid's widow was in the public domain, he decided on a struggle to the death, effectively handing victory to Aung San. Why was he so inflexible? It was this phase in Dorman-Smith's career that was to tar him as a Tory reactionary, the character he plays in Aung San Suu Kyi's memoir of her father and also in Fergal Keane's 1990s television documentary on Aung San's assassination. Certainly the Dorman-Smith of 1946 was not the genial Irish observer of nationalist movements who had soothed Tin Tut's ruffled feathers in Simla three years before. His health was rapidly deteriorating. He was in the grip of his fourth attack of amoebic dysentery since his return to Burma. The season was terrible and conditions were poor even for a governor. He had difficulty in understanding the massive changes that had over-taken Burmese politics since 1942, used as he was to the likes of Paw Tun and U Saw. He was also truly horrified by what was now coming out about Axis atrocities. He was haunted by images of the *sook ching* massacres of the Chinese in Malaya by the Japanese in 1942, their torture of Major Seagrim and the Karen special forces in 1944, the Burma–Siam railway and, more distantly, the Holocaust. He was horrified by the brutal treatment of the Burmese and Anglo-Indian

Christians of Rangoon, among whom he had once felt at home. Aung San and his colleagues were indelibly painted in his mind as JIFS, Japanese-influenced forces, as 'quislings' and 'fascists'. He was also deeply at odds with the Labour ministers in London, pining for his old expansive relationship with his 'wonderful boss',[126] Leo Amery, rather than the stiff and self-righteous left-wingers who now held power. Attlee's government seemed to embody dither and interference in about the same degree. Dorman-Smith once drafted a telegram to Attlee: 'I had a dose of Eno's [liver salts] last night. May I please be allowed to go to the lavatory tomorrow?'[127]

Some weeks after the plans to arrest Aung San were shelved, the security of the country deteriorated markedly. Aung San was building up his strength in the villages and small towns, aware that he might still need to stage a show of force against either the British or his communist 'allies'. The drilling, marching and counter-marching of more than 80,000 volunteers became feverish in the weeks after the first anniversary of the BNA's revolt against the Japanese. Then came the crisis. On 18 May a fatal shooting took place at Tantabin in Insein district, a small town with a mixed Burman/Karen population. A band of local volunteers was moving through the town protesting against the Defence of Burma rules. These prohibited quasi-military marching and arms drill, even when carried out with dummy weapons. The exact sequence of events is unclear, as defence and prosecution witnesses flatly contradicted each other,[128] but there had evidently been ill feeling for some time between local leaders of the PVO and the police sub-inspector, Maung Gale. The authorities believed that the nationalists were collecting arms. Some people deposed that leaders of the crowd were carrying dummy weapons. The *yebaws*, or volunteers, allegedly told people to resist the police if they attempted arrests during the demonstrations: 'Let the masses surround the authorities and forcibly take back the persons arrested.'[129] On the day of the shooting, things had got out of hand as people converged on one of the main teashops in the town. The police started to beat members of the crowd with their rifle butts. The crowd attacked the police with bamboo poles. The police then discharged at least sixty live rounds, killing five people and wounding many others before the crowd retreated. Three hundred *yebaws* were arrested, but it was never clear if the order to disperse was actually given to or understood by the crowd before the firing began.[130] As in so many incidents in British imperial history, from Ireland through Egypt to India and beyond, a relatively minor but bloody police action galvanized people's perception of British rule as irredeemably repressive. An ominous feature of the situation in Tantabin was that the crowd was composed of villagers, not students or 'agitators'. They were protesting because of demands for the repayment of agricultural loans in a terrible season of shortage and hardship. Tantabin was an indication of the strength of the bonds that had been forged between the *yebaws*, the volunteer corps of the old BIA, and the villages in 1942. It was a portent of a major revolt.

The government of Burma set up a commission to investigate the incident while Dorman-Smith urged London to take a hard line against nationalist leaders whose speeches stirred up popular demonstrations of the sort that ended with the Tantabin firing. Once again he seems to have had Aung San in mind. When news of the incident had broken, Aung San put all the blame on the British government. According to Aung San's agreement with Mountbatten at Kandy some eight months previously, members of the BNA were to be absorbed into the British Burma Army and more men would be recruited to turn it into a truly national force. But the British had not even begun to honour this pledge. Many former BNA personnel were unemployed and resentful, while village youths were pressing to enlist. Aung San was uncomfortably aware that people of this sort could easily shift allegiance to clandestine communist cadres unless the nationalist elements of the AFPFL moved fast. Besides, he asked, why was drilling by the volunteers illegal in the first place? Who had deemed it so?[131]

As it turned out, Aung San had already won the game. Attlee had finally begun to take a closer interest in Burma, aware that a flare-up there would do enormous damage if it came at the same time as mass demonstrations in India and Malaya. He had decided that Dorman-Smith was becoming erratic. This was not without reason. In early May, shortly after resuming his demands for the arrest of Aung San, the governor made an apparent *volte-face* by holding out the possibility of recruiting some new blood into his old-fashioned executive council, perhaps even Aung San himself. He also finally conceded the need to review the White Paper. By 7 May Attlee had concluded that the governor 'changes his policy from day to day' and was 'losing his grip'.[132] He would have to be relieved on the grounds of ill health. Attlee's conclusion was only confirmed by Dorman-Smith's vacillation and indecision after the Tantabin shootings. Blowing hot and cold, he first called for strong action against those who had fomented the agitation, only to reverse his policy in favour of a general amnesty for these and other political prisoners, a recommendation that infuriated senior police officers and civil servants.

On 14 June Dorman-Smith's recall was made public and Sir Henry Knight became acting governor pending the arrival of Sir Hubert Rance, who would take over in August. Knight was an impeccable old India hand who had previously been acting governor in both Madras and Bombay. This change in personnel reflected a much deeper policy switch, for Rance had been Mountbatten's right-hand man. The conservatives in the Burmese civil service were appalled. As Dorman-Smith left, Frederick Pearce, counseller to the governor, sent him a note of commiseration. He had been right all along, Pearce said. He had been unfairly made to carry the can in 1942 because military morale was too fragile to be told the truth. He had tried to defend the Burmese civil administration against the false accusations of the war correspondents. Finally, his policy had been undermined 'by the wilfully blind conceptions and pre-emptive conclusions of that Heaven-inspired politician Dicky M.'[133] For Pearce himself, the bitterest blows were to find himself accused of mismanaging the military administration and having his old boss replaced by Rance. Pearce hinted and Dorman-Smith believed that Mountbatten was covertly responsible for the governor's sacking. They were probably right. True, Mountbatten had not been Dorman-Smith's only handicap – a Chamberlain appointee was never likely to reach a meeting of minds with Labour ministers who disliked his politics and personal style, and Attlee quickly lost patience with him – but it does seem likely that Mountbatten played a key role in ejecting Dorman-Smith and choosing his successor. Certainly Tom Driberg, thought so. He believed that Mountbatten had privately briefed against Dorman-Smith and had impressed Attlee with the idea that only a rapid move towards independence could avoid the sort of situation that had arisen in Indo-

China, where the French were desperately fighting to suppress the Vietnamese resistance.[134] For his part, Driberg kept up the pressure on Mountbatten, relaying to him the fears of Aung San and other local politicians who valued him as one of their few direct links to domestic British opinion. On 12 June Aung San wrote to Driberg of 'the blind prejudice and stark policy of bureaucratic intransigence he had encountered'.[135] He alone, he claimed, was trying to restrain his infuriated followers from attacking British interests. Driberg duly passed this on to Mountbatten.

It is unsurprising that Dorman-Smith, Pearce and the hardliners of the military administration loathed Dickie and his men. But their poisonous hatred of Aung San, whom they regarded as a creature of Dickie's, was dangerously infectious. It entered the bloodstream of Burmese politics and fed the festering resentment of U Saw and his followers towards Aung San. Naively, Dorman-Smith disassociated his own actions from U Saw's machinations. Till the end he retained some regard for Aung San as a strong man and military hero. Did he see in him an Asian Daniel O'Connell, The Liberator of Burma, perhaps? At any rate, having tried for three months to have the man hanged, he left a surprisingly emollient assessment of him for Sir Henry Knight. Aung San was 'Burma's popular hero and . . . I look upon him as a sincere man . . . He has enough sense to realise that an uprising can only mean added misery.'[136] Dorman-Smith did not extend this benediction to Mountbatten, however. Back in England, he poured out his bile. He railed against the impression that Dickie's 'sea-green incorruptibles' had replaced 'our old corruptibles', adding in a deplorable piece of word-play that one of his own senior officials had been pushed out 'unhonoured and Aung San'.[137] He always knew he was persona 'not very grata' to Attlee, he said, but he really felt it when he arrived back in London. Unlike the old days when Leo Amery used to meet him at the railway station, there was no one waiting at Euston this time. He duly turned up at Whitehall. 'Then I saw the Pathetic One [Pethick-Lawrence] – "Out you go" . . . So that was it. Exit Smith.' Pethick-Lawrence had consulted him on nothing, had not enquired after his health – the alleged reason for his recall – and had not even bothered to get up from his chair to shake hands when he entered the room. Now he was sure that Mountbatten had plotted against him. He got wind of rumours that Mountbatten was destined for 'some monumental appointment in the East'. Surely not the vice-royalty of India? But that would explain a lot. As viceroy Mountbatten would want to have his own man in Burma: 'I HATE Dickie having a finger in the Burma pie because I think he is so unsound.'[138] None of this would have mattered very much except that it encouraged the former governor to stick his own fingers in the pie. Over the next two years he remained dangerously close to Saw, the rogue element in Burmese politics, and he cultivated the radical Karen separatists, irrec-oncilables who were almost to blow apart the future Union of Burma.

Almost all the pieces were now in place for the endgame of British Burma and the emergence of the new republic. But one other tangled set of events in the early part of 1946 set the scene for the country's future and arguably for much of the rest of Southeast Asia. This was the implosion of the Burmese Communist Party, an event that ensured, in the long term, the relative isolation of Burma from the Cold War. Like the creaking British administration, the communist split was very much a matter of personalities. Since the beginning of the war, the communist hard man Thakin Soe had been quietly building up his cadres in the countryside. Soe took a dim view of erstwhile comrades such as Thakin Than Tun who had spent the war in ministerial office under Ba Maw, or skulking in Simla or Chungking. In the quaint lexicography of contemporary leftist abuse, Soe accused Than Tun and others of 'Browderism' or compromising communist purity by making deals with 'imperialists'. Browder was an American commu-nist leader who had preached a gospel of accommodation with capi-talism.[139] Worse, Soe accused Than Tun of corruption, in particular the misappropriation of a large quantity of gold that had been accumu-lated by the left for the purpose of anti-Japanese resistance during the war. An open split occurred at a conference in March 1946 when Than Tun and other communists who did not favour immediate armed struggle hit back with a lurid assault on Soe's personal integrity. They accused him of extending his disdain for private property to other men's wives and daughters and produced a lengthy charge sheet, detailing 'how Thakin Soe had forcibly taken to himself the sister of his first wife; how he had deserted both the sisters and married a third wife; how he again left her and appropriated to himself a young woman recruit to the Party from the hands of one of his lieutenants'.[140] After this conference, the main aim of Soe's 'red flag' or Trotskyite communists became the extermination of the 'white flag' or Stalinist communists led by Than Tun. Soe went underground and continued to build up a following of Karen and Burmese communists in the Irrawaddy delta districts, occasionally engaging in dacoit-like attacks on the police and their rivals. This disunity among its future enemies was one important reason for the survival of the AFPFL government in the dangerous years immediately after independence.

A NEW WORLD ORDER?

A year on from the end of the European war and the death of Hitler, the world seemed no closer to reaching lasting peace. In Britain prosperity remained elusive. As a winter of bitter cold and gnawing food shortages drew to a close, labour disputes reached a crescendo. To no avail: the socialist millennium was indefinitely postponed. Abroad, British troops were spread thinly in Germany, as relations between the Allies and the Soviet Union deteriorated. They were also spread desperately thinly across Southeast Asia. Acute shortages of manpower eventually resulted in the British garrisons pulling out of Indonesia and Indo-China. This brought relief to the British alone, for as soon as they withdrew bloody fighting erupted between the nationalists and the Dutch in Indonesia and the Viet Minh and the French in Indo-China. Moreover, the British troops released from Indonesia and Indo-China faced likely redeployment in the region. Burma and Malaya were seething with ethnic and industrial conflict. In the one, Dorman-Smith's unceremonious exit had left a dangerous vacuum that the perennial administrative 'Mr Fixit', Governor Knight, was scarcely able to fill. In the other, Sir Edward Gent's plan for a Malayan Union ran into ferocious constitutional opposition from Malays at the very time that Chinese and Indian labour unions were flexing their muscles.

It was by only a small margin that the communists in Burma and Malaya failed to take to arms in early 1946. A fair wind seemed to be blowing for revolution as Mao Zedong and his red cadres declared all-out war against Chiang Kai Shek and capitalized on their gains during the war. If Southeast Asian communists had followed the Chinese, the British would have been in an impossible position. British troops had to be demobilized to kick start the home economy in a period of desperate financial crisis. That old standby, the Indian Army, could no longer fill the gap as Nehru and Patel were demanding that Indian troops be brought home. In India itself, the results of the March provincial elections led to an impasse between Hindus, Muslims and Sikhs worse than anything the gloomy and mordant Wavell had predicted. Calcutta daily inched closer to riotous violence and mass murder. Meanwhile, Sarat Bose and other Indian radical politicians played up the issue of the INA detainees for all they were worth. Ironically, Britain's real saviour in these dark days of the eastern empire was the Japanese army. 'They have been carrying out their "defeat drill"', Esler Dening told Ernest Bevin, the foreign secretary, 'with the discipline and determination which characterised their aggression.'[141] Deprived of British and Indian troops, the British authorities used Japanese POWs to put down Indonesian and Vietnamese insurgents, police a restive Burma and build a real Fortress Singapore.

Though Attlee was beginning to tire of Wavell's pessimism, it was to be several months before he confirmed the rumours of Mountbatten's 'monumental appointment in the East'.[142] Mountbatten and Malcolm MacDonald had similar views about the future of empire, although they approached the issue from a different social perspective. Mountbatten was a high aristocrat with a popular touch, a military man who could deal with nationalists, who saw himself as a kind of latter-day Lord Durham, turning the old empire into a commonwealth of free nations. MacDonald, a member of the Scottish socialist elite who tended towards liberal Toryism, had a similar vision, but none of the military or royal charisma of Mountbatten. While Mountbatten delighted in state pageantry, MacDonald opted for the more intellectually respectable ceremonial of university degree days. He much preferred attending meetings in an open-necked shirt and was famously denounced by the colonial press in Singapore for not possessing a tailcoat or dinner jacket. Mountbatten seems to have got on with Indian leaders precisely because he was a royal, but formed few intimacies. MacDonald reportedly had a string of Chinese and Eurasian girlfriends and adopted a Dayak family in Borneo. When the Sultan of Johore loaned him what his frequent guest, the Eurasian writer Han Suyin, called the 'Walt Disney fantasy castle' at Bukit Serene, MacDonald had some Dyak friends to stay. The sultan was incensed: 'Why', he expostulated, 'should I have his damned Dyaks with their backsides in my chairs and in my bed?' He cut off the water supply to the swimming pool.[143] Yet MacDonald did not find India's intense and intellectual politicians entirely to his taste. Like Mountbatten, who had accompanied the Prince of Wales on his unhappy tour of India in 1921–2, MacDonald had had an earlier introduction to Indian politics. He had acted as a go-between for his father with Gandhi when the latter had visited London for the second Round Table Conference in 1931. MacDonald found the Mahatma to be both charming and perplexing but remembered particularly his strangely shaped set of false teeth.[144] MacDonald's own rather prominent teeth left much to be desired, but, like the handsome Mountbatten, he nevertheless delighted in the company of stage and screen celebrities. He was to remain in the region in high office for eight years. He oversaw, though never directly managed, the exit of Burma from the Commonwealth and the Malayan Emergency. He underestimated the strength of communism in Indo-China, but helped to lay the foundations of the economic rise of Singapore and Malaya. The British Empire had entered a new and final phase.

6

1946: One Empire Unravels, Another Is Born

For one last time events in India changed the situation in Burma and sent shock waves speeding towards Malaya. Following the Congress's great victories in the March 1946 elections, it had become obvious to Wavell and Auchinleck that the Indian Army could not be used to put down a revolt in Burma. This conclusion had already been forcibly impressed on Dorman-Smith. Now, as the impasse in Indian politics deepened, it also became clear that the British withdrawal from the country would be faster than anyone could possibly have predicted. The political outcome of the elections in the Punjab in the spring had left the Muslim League deeply embittered, although it had done rather well in several other provinces, notably through its proxies in Bengal. Sir Stafford Cripps, now President of the Board of Trade, A. V. Alexander, First Lord of the Admiralty, and Pethick-Lawrence on their Cabinet Mission failed to find any common ground between warring politicians in Simla or Delhi.[1] Congress refused to allow the Muslim League 'parity' of power in a future independent central government.[2] The only alternative for Jinnah and the Muslim League was a weak centre in Delhi, with powerful provinces, so ensuring that Muslims would be in a strong position in Bengal and the Punjab. But this raised fears in the Congress of the 'Balkanization' of the country and even of its total disintegration. No deal was possible. Cripps found himself baffled and disillusioned yet again, not only by what he took to be Jinnah's perennial intransigence, but also by Gandhi's unhelpful stance now that the transfer of power was clearly in sight. Among ordinary people hope and fear alternated day by day. The word 'Pakistan' was used as both threat and incentive. It had been in the air since 1940 when the Muslim League had officially endorsed the vague idea of a 'homeland' for Indian Muslims. But almost to the very moment of independence neither Hindus nor Muslims really knew what the word meant. Would this Pakistan be part of an Indian union – a kind of Austria-Hungary – or part of a grouping of provinces of a more centralized state, or an independent entity? Certainly in 1946 no one would have predicted the emergence of the geopolitical absurdity that was to separate the two halves of a sovereign country by a thousand miles and cut off a large area of northeast India from the rest of the national territory.

Ultimately the Cabinet Mission returned to Britain in disarray and Wavell was left to make the best of a bad job. There was no hope of any end to the bitter 'communal recriminations' and it seemed unlikely that he could form any stable coalition government in Delhi.[3] He was soon confessing to his diary: 'For the first time in my life, I am beginning to feel the strain badly – not sleeping properly and letting these wretched people worry me.'[4] The question of India's future constitution was shelved while the results of the spring elections were put into effect. In September an Indian constituent assembly was convened and an interim government was formed. Congress dominated the cabinet; the two Muslim League ministers who participated for the time being did so in an atmosphere of mutual distrust. Congress ministers now took charge of all the major departments of state, including intelligence and police. Effectively, Congress became the government of India for internal purposes and Sardar Patel became its home minister. Significantly, he took over the intelligence department.[5]

THE KILLING BEGINS

In the meantime, a set of events occurred which made it clear that unless the Hindu–Muslim issue was quickly resolved at the constitutional level, there might be little power left to transfer to Indians, as one senior civil servant later put it. Wavell himself believed that a total breakdown of social order was in sight.[6] In August, frustrated by the Cabinet Mission's failure to reconcile Congress to sharing power with the Muslim League, Muslims in Calcutta staged mass political demonstrations against the British which spun out of control and resulted in one of the worst bouts of communal killings in Indian history. As many as 6,000 people may have been murdered and 12,000 injured in the 'Great Calcutta killings' and associated atrocities during August, September and October 1946. And day after day, for the next two years, the tally of murders in the city rose steadily. The destitution caused in Bengal by war, famine and the flight of refugees from Burma provided the dry tinder of despair and hatred. In many respects events in Calcutta were simply a continuation of the Second World War by other means. But politicians lit the conflagration. H. S. Suhrawardy, the Bengal chief minister whose lethargy during the 1943 famine had earned him much criticism, was behind the attempt to assert Muslim political influence in the face of Congress's refusal to compromise. Jinnah also bore a degree of responsibility for triggering what at times seemed more like a civil war than random riots; he called for the 'Direct Action Day' in Calcutta on 16 August that set off the killing. Officially, the purpose of this day of action was to 'end British slavery', but also, and more ominously, it was intended to 'fight the contemplated caste-Hindu domination'.[7]

Political manipulators from on high found a ready audience among ordinary people stirred to hatred of their neighbours by the corrosive effects of repeated crises and unyielding poverty. Gradually during the spring and summer of 1946, agitations in Calcutta against the British and in favour of the Indian National Army had become flashpoints of conflict between local bosses allied with the Congress, the Hindu Mahasabha (the main Hindu activist organization) and the Muslim League. The League blamed the Congress for stirring up trouble because it had done less well than the League in Bengal's elections. The Congress, for its part, staged numerous strikes and attempted to close down bazaars, including Muslim bazaars. In these straitened times, this was deeply resented by Muslim shopkeepers. As the Cabinet Mission packed up and went home, the Muslim-dominated ministry and its local supporters decided to hold their own shutdown and declared a public holiday in the city to mark Jinnah's Direct Action Day. This measure, with which the British governor, Sir Frederick Burrows, meekly complied, ensured that large numbers of people would be on the streets and that the issue of closing the bazaars and forcibly preventing people from trading would be particularly fraught. It was already a period of heightened religious sensitivity, for Direct Action Day fell in the middle of Ramadan, the Islamic month of fasting. The city was also going to be full of excitable students preparing for the annual Calcutta University examinations.

There was ample evidence of warlike preparation on both sides. In the weeks before 16 August, young members of Sarat Bose's section of the Congress were constantly marching and drilling, ostensibly in training as crowd-control volunteers for Indian National Army Day, 18 August, when Congress intended to fête INA officers recently released from jail. Muslim youth groups, such as the Muhammadan Sporting Club, were similarly mobilizing. They, like other Muslim activists, were supposedly using Direct Action Day to make the British government think again about the constitution. But the word put around by the local Muslim League politicians spelled out something different. 'We are in the midst of the rainy season,' one handbill declared. 'But this is a month of real Jehad, of God's Grace and blessings, of spiritual armament and the moral and physical purge of the nation . . . It was in Ramzan that the permission of Jehad was granted by Allah.'[8] Of course, in Islamic theology, *jihad* referred to the universal spiritual struggle against evil. Physical warfare against unbelievers was no more than 'lesser *jihad*' and could be resorted to only under special conditions. Yet when circulated among the poor and unlettered a document like this could mean only one thing: 'prepare for war.' Similarly sinister calls to the 'anti-fascist forces' to mobilize against their enemies were issued in mosques after Friday prayers on 15 August throughout Calcutta and also in Hooghly, just across the river. Some pamphlets did away with all pretence at subtlety: 'Oh, Kafir [unbeliever], your doom is not far and the general massacre will come!'[9] The suspicious and hostile Hindu press predictably denounced the prospective demonstration as 'pro-Pakistan' and 'anti-Hindu'.

On the afternoon of Saturday 16 August some 100,000 Muslims converged on the Ochterlony monument in central Calcutta to hear speeches from members of the League and Bengal government ministers. The monument, which commemorated one of the East India Company's great Kiplingesque empire-builders of the early nineteenth century, had long been the symbolic heart of British Calcutta. As the crowds flocked to it, however, they passed through predominantly Hindu quarters of the city and several of the great bazaars. When local gang-leaders tried to force traders to close their shops, trouble broke out. The League later insisted that the Muslim processions had been 'sober and disciplined', led by college students and 'Muslim girls in blue uniforms'.[10] Be that as it may, the atmosphere rapidly became menacing. One observer was Major Sim of Vickers India Co. who managed a shop in the main thoroughfare, Chowringee. Sim saw something that resembled the march of a conquering army into the city, 'with green hats and flags and every man with a lathi [heavy bamboo cane] – mostly so similar that they must have been bought especially for the occasion, and in bulk'.[11] As he watched things suddenly turned vicious. Many observers ascribed this to Hindu thugs hurling bricks down onto the Muslim marchers from the great houses that dominated the city centre. The missiles were plainly intended to maim or kill; people had apparently been stockpiling the bricks for days as a mundane but effective weapon. Then Sim saw a Muslim smash a picture of the Hindu goddess Kali. 'The crowd turned into wild beasts and tore up and looted and burned the row of little shops beneath us. We saw five people beaten to death with sticks in fifteen yards of road in the main street of the Empire's second city.' The police stood by and did nothing, probably, Sim surmised, because the chief minister, Suhrawardy, had told his subordinates not to intervene. Sim himself had a party political purpose in mind in recording these incidents. The recipient of his letter describing them was a Conservative MP, to whom Sim observed: 'Our good friends in the Labour government are responsible for quite a few dead Indians.'[12]

At this point the local political leaders lost control. Over the next three days criminals turned the city into a battlefield. The governor told the viceroy that 'it was a pogrom between two rival gangs of the Calcutta underworld',[13] with the thugs who had been released at the end of the war taking a prominent part. Bazaar toughs and gang-leaders were soon leading raids and counter-raids on Hindu and Muslim quarters, murdering whole neighbourhoods of men, women and children. Swords, iron bars and tins of kerosene were the preferred weapons. Sten guns and bombs made from chemical explosives bought or stolen from soldiers over the previous two years also came into their own. 'The swollen bodies – of young and old, men and women – were lying in heaps, folded in gunny bags in the middle of roads, on lorries, handcarts or floating in canals.'[14] Finally prodded into action, the police – a mere 500 of them, half of whom were unarmed – were hopelessly outnumbered. They drove around in their war-surplus jeeps dispersing the crowds. As soon as they had passed, the gangs emerged from the side streets and resumed the burning and killing.

There was a tinge of class hatred to these events.[15] The houses of the great Hindu Marwari merchants in the city centre proved an early target; a leading Muslim merchant was found hanging from a lamp post. But hatred of 'the enemy' overwhelmed any economic rationale. Women of both religions were murdered and mutilated. Hindu children were executed near mosques in a macabre mimicking of the slaughter of goats for the goddess Kali. A Muslim cleric, Akbar Ali, was attacked in the fashionable Park Circus area and thrown half dead into a sewer. He was one of the lucky ones; nine days later his battered body was fished alive from the Ballygunge sewerage station, almost a mile away.[16] Much of the killing showed the hand of trained fighters. The historian Suranjan Das recounts that INA men who had come to Calcutta to celebrate Indian National Army Day on 18 August were prominent in the attacks,[17] even though Sarat Bose's wing of the Congress and the INA leadership had loudly denounced communal hatred. Bose himself backed the rescue efforts of the Indian National Ambulance Corps, newly named the Azad Hind Ambulance Corps in memory of his brother. Other men of arms also took part. Hindu *darwans* or doorkeepers from Bihar and the United Provinces who had been taken on as guards for business premises fought pitched battles with Muslim toughs. People said that some officials from Suhrawardy's private office distributed kerosene and knives for the assailants by lorry; others claimed that local politicians directed the arson and murder by megaphone from the housetops. Yet there is plenty of evidence too of the eager participation of ordinary people – petty shopkeepers and artisans – in the attacks. Even the malnourished inhabitants of Calcutta's huge slums or *bustees* found the energy to murder each other. By contrast, not a single European or Eurasian in the city was reported injured over these days.

Early on the morning of Sunday 17 August, after the first day's horrendous events, the governor exerted his authority over Suhra-wardy's ministry and ordered in the troops. Soldiers of the Green Howards and Yorkshire and Lancashire regiments patrolled the city. Later a division of Nepalese Gurkhas was drafted in, but only one predominantly Indian unit was used for fear of sparking further conflict. By Monday evening 45,000 troops – four British, one Gurkha and one Indian division – were deployed in and around the city. Tanks patrolled the streets.[18] Rescue units of soldiers and civilians were deployed to try to help groups of Hindus or Muslims stranded in areas where the rival community was dominant. Often they arrived to find these people with their throats cut or burned alive in their houses. The military instituted 'Operation St Bernard' to escort workers in essential services to and from their jobs, while Government House attempted to co-ordinate the rescue of endangered civilians. Arthur Dash, a senior civil servant and long-time critic of the Bengal government, enlisted as a clerk with the rescue organization. One of his duties was to stop people jumping the queue with information about families and friends who needed to be shepherded out of murderous situations. He remembered sending one distraught man back into the line. When his turn finally came he told Dash that it was too late 'as all his family had, in the interval, been killed, and his house burnt down'.[19] For Dash, it was like the famine all over again. He saw someone being stabbed in the stomach outside the Bengal Club, the same place where he had watched the bodies of the starving fall three years before.

After three days the mass destruction and killing had been suppressed, but already 30,000 people had fled the city, some of them refugees from Burma four years earlier. Nor was there any end in sight to a more insidious, sporadic type of violence. Every day for the next two years, ten, twenty or thirty people would be murdered in the city's streets, stabbed to death in alleyways, blown to pieces in bomb attacks on shops and residential buildings or strafed in their vehicles with Sten guns. Calcutta showed how easily the fervour of anti-British demonstrations could spill over into fratricidal killings, a phenomenon that would be repeated horribly in the Punjab over the next eighteen months. As the death toll mounted, Burrows remarked sardonically that 'it was costing more in casualties to hand over Bengal than to conquer it'.[20] Fewer than 7,000 people had died at the battle of Plassey in 1757. Perhaps he could have been forgiven for thinking that power had been handed over already. When he was touring affected areas with the local army commander, General Roy Bucher, he saw three people being beaten to death on the Lower Chitpur Road, barely a hundred yards from where he and Bucher stood. The assailants were not inhibited by the presence of these representatives of the supreme authority; only when a police sergeant fired a shot did they flee.[21] Afterwards a bewildered Bucher asked Suhrawardy: 'Why is it that you Hindus and Muslims in Bengal cannot live amicably as the Hindus and Muslims do in the Army?' Suhrawardy's reply seemed as much a threat as a warning: 'General, that Hindu and Muslim amity will not last very much longer – of that I can assure you.'[22]

As in the ravaged cities of Southeast Asia in 1942, the problems did not cease when the fighting died down. Cholera, ever present in Calcutta, took over from human killers as sanitation collapsed and rubbish built up in the streets. Arthur Dash wrote in his diary that corpses 'were dotted about even in the streets of the European areas. In Indian areas they were piled up and blocked them.'[23] British authorities noted that Indians tended not to remove the bodies even if they lay outside their own houses for fear of pollution.[24] This job had to be carried out by the troops. The city was sprayed with DDT, which helped a little, but food supplies broke down and both grain and cloth had to be rationed again. As late as 28 August there were still 307 government and private relief centres feeding 190,000 people cut off in the most seriously affected parts of the city. Worse was the lingering psychological damage. Many people never again trusted their Hindu or Muslim neighbours. It was this that lay at the heart of the massive refugee problems that were to overwhelm India and Pakistan as they attained their freedom. Indirectly, it was to propel the two dominions towards three pointless and destructive wars over the next generation.

Dacca in eastern Bengal was soon to be the capital East Pakistan, but in 1946 the city still had a large Hindu minority and it quickly fell prey to Calcutta's infectious violence. The trouble was sporadic but vicious. Murderous gangs killed a handful of people every day with weapons of varying sophistication. The district magistrate recorded that: 'Occasionally acid bombs (acid contained in an electric light bulb) were used, but killing was done by knives and property was attacked with crowbars, or torches made of rags and oil helped by dry wood and straw.'[25] In September the frenzy spread to the rural areas of east Bengal, especially to villages where large numbers of Muslim immigrants had moved into India from Arakan during and after the war in Burma. Prime locations were the districts of Noakhali and Tippera in the Chittagong division which had already experienced appalling suffering in 1942. A local political boss and Muslim League member, Ghulam Sarwar, stirred up the trouble by demanding revenge for the thousands of Muslims killed in Calcutta. In this part of the countryside Muslim peasants were beginning to assert themselves, resentful at what they saw as generations of exploitation by Hindu shopkeepers, moneylenders and landlords. Once again, though, it was religious difference and not economic distress that determined the course of the disturbances, which left hundreds dead and 20,000 people homeless. Here, however, the terror hardly deserves categorization as rioting; it took the form of a highly organized programme of forced conversions of Hindus to Islam. A Muslim gang would come to a Hindu house and give its occupants twenty-four hours to convert to Islam or die. Returning at the appointed time, the gang members would force the 'converts' to eat beef, recite the Muslim confession of faith and quit their homes. These were then burnt out because, the Muslims explained, the end of the world was imminent and shelter would be unnecessary in paradise. These events were meticulously organized by local politicians and their supporters; the British district magistrate observed that 'large stocks of Muslim prayer caps had been made ready for the converts'.[26] But there is no question that many ordinary people were living in daily expectation of the apocalypse. This was a common perception up and down the crescent in Burma and Malaya where similar millenarian movements were giving legitimacy to intercommunal clashes and anti-colonial upsurges.

Help was a long time in coming; the government machine was virtually shut down for a time. Muslim clerks in the local telegraph office intercepted and destroyed messages from Hindu inhabitants of Noakhali and Tippera begging for help. When the security forces arrived, as one British subaltern remembered, it was often too late.[27] Whole villages had been plundered and dozens of people killed. In order to suppress the disturbances, the authorities eventually had to deploy 1,800 troops, 600 armed police, 130 unarmed police and even the Royal Air Force. By then the damage had been done; 50,000 people in the two districts were homeless. Thousands of Hindus from the surrounding villages fled into Dacca city, making its neighbourhoods yet more tense.[28] Another 25,000 sought shelter in Calcutta. Hindus elsewhere sought revenge. From late October into November, Hindus to the west, in Bihar, slaughtered 25,000 of their Muslim neighbours, sparking a massive migration of Muslims towards the east. By December a single abandoned US airbase in Burdwan was playing home to more than 30,000 refugees from Bihar.[29] Over the next decade as many as 4 million people would move from their ancestral homes, pursued by fear of their erstwhile neighbours. At first it was the more prosperous Hindus of east Bengal who moved off to Chandpur or Calcutta, never to return. Many had relatives and property in Calcutta and decided to cut their losses in the east. Later, poor Hindus followed them. Noakhali, even more than Calcutta, destroyed the ancient co-existence between Hindus and Muslims that had characterized much of rural Bengal. One refugee remembered: 'The change was so sudden, you see. Even a year ago we had played Holi [a Hindu festival] together with Muslim girls. But Noakhali changed everything. As young girls we began to feel insecure.'[30] The alternating waves of refugees from east and west further spread fear and hostility in the province. Hindus in the western parts of Bengal worried about the influx of Muslims fleeing from Bihar and were only too happy to see them decamp further to the east along with local Muslims.[31]

His perpetual gloom now deepening to despair, Wavell wrote home that British rule was on the point of dissolution. He was not getting much help from Indian politicians. During the Calcutta massacres Gandhi, refusing further concessions to Muslim League politicians, had thumped the table in front of the viceroy shouting, 'If India wants her bloodbath, she shall have it!'[32] Gandhi was in fact appalled by the violence and spent much of October and November touring affected villages in Bengal trying to encourage dialogue between Hindus and Muslims. But he could not help but compare the vigorous action of the British to suppress the Quit India movement of 1942 with their slowness and inaction now. In this he had neatly caught the viceroy's mood. All that could be managed, Wavell concluded, was to preserve the lives of British civilians and get the army out in some kind of order. His officials agreed. After Noakhali, John Tyson, a senior official in Bengal, recorded simply: 'I think the sooner we clear out the better.'[33] At one time Wavell contemplated a 'breakdown plan', whereby the British would roll back from one province after another, retreating to the northeast and the northwest of the country. Privately, he called this 'Operation Madhouse'. If order could not even be preserved in Bengal, the ancient core of the British Empire in the East, where could it be preserved? This thought was particularly sombre since the only force capable of pacifying the fractious colonies of the crescent was the Indian Army. But that army was now no more than a withered limb of the British state. Its regiments were worried, decimated by demobilization and made uneasy by the rise of Hindu–Muslim tension, as Suhrawardy had predicted. More seriously, the new quasi-independent Indian government had made it clear that Indian troops should not be used in Burma or Malaya, let alone farther afield. Congress was infuriated that Indian soldiers had died the previous winter in Indo-China and Indonesia putting down what its leaders regarded as fraternal national liberation movements. British rule seemed as precarious as it had done in the spring of 1942. Yet this time there was little to fight back with.

BRITAIN'S TERMINAL CRISIS IN BURMA

In Burma, too, events on the ground were spinning out of control. Dorman-Smith's departure and Knight's interregnum had given the Burmese radicals the signal for revolt. Old friends returned to stir the political pot. Out in the districts there was an ominous tide of minor revolts and clashes between different ethnic and religious groups. Ba Maw, the former Japanese-sponsored Adipadi, returned from a brief imprisonment in Tokyo, announcing on the steps of the aircraft that his government had not been a 'Jap regime' but a 'Burma regime'.[34] Sarat Bose, Netaji's brother, made a speech, closely monitored by the

CID, in which he prophesied that the British would be driven out only by the shedding of blood and urged Burmese to live up to the ideals of Netaji. A thousand people heard him speak, including 300 ex-INA men in uniform.[35] Burma's Indian population remained uncertain. Most Hindu, Sikh and Christian Indians fully identified with the AFPFL, but feared that the anti-immigrant element in Burmese politics would rise to the surface in a time of crisis. By contrast, many Indian Muslims held themselves aloof from the AFPFL, which for them still had a whiff of communalism about it from the pre-war days. In Arakan, Muslims identified with Jinnah's inchoate Pakistan, particularly after the communal riots in Calcutta in August and September. Industrial trouble spread. A few Indian radicals and workers on the partially restored oilfields heeded the call of P. C. Joshi, Secretary General of the Indian Communist Party, for a union between Burmese communists of all races and all factions in anticipation of a general Asian rising against 'monopoly capitalism and imperialism'. Large numbers of Indian postal workers struck in sympathy with their counterparts in the subcontinent who were suffering as a result of high prices. Relations between Burmese and Chinese, usually less tense than those between Burmese and Indians, also deteriorated. The nationalist government in China pledged $5 million for the rebuilding of Chinese businesses shattered by the Japanese.[36] Burmese politicians feared that this would tip the economic balance back towards the Chinese in areas where they had benefited during the war. Meanwhile, clandestine groupings such as the Black Star Society and paramilitary bodies such as the People's Volunteer Organizations hoarded the vast numbers of Allied and Japanese weapons that had fallen into their hands over the past few years.

As India's interim government took office in September, the fact that their big neighbour had already achieved a kind of independence goaded Burmese politicians to greater intransigence. Hubert Rance, the new governor, immediately noted that the Burmese were hostile and resentful because no grand British Cabinet Mission had bothered to visit Burma – 'the most devastated country in the empire'.[37] The Burmese had suddenly begun to appreciate the fragility of British power in Asia. Aung San's hungry and frustrated supporters looked on impatiently as some aspects of the old regime seemed to totter on regardless. As soon as he arrived, Rance was therefore plunged into the worst Burmese political crisis since the reoccupation of Rangoon. September 1946 saw a mass movement on a scale that appalled the authorities. It only just failed to become another 1886 or 1930 rebellion, mainly as a result of the good judgement of Aung San. Large areas of the countryside were out of control of the central authorities, principally the ones that had caused trouble throughout British rule and before: the 'badlands' of Shwebo, north of Mandalay; the impoverished middle Irrawaddy basin with its difficult lines of communication; and the old haunts in the delta of the rebel monk of the 1930 uprising, Saya San. The anti-government forces had got their hands on automatic weapons and large reserves of ammunition that had presumably been buried since the Japanese withdrawal. Two thousand police were already on strike and the number of dacoities was soaring. In one incident in a town southwest of Rangoon 17,000 bags of rice were looted in a single raid.[38] Elsewhere a Burmese district magistrate evacuated himself and his treasury from town on hearing that a small army of bandits was about to attack. Special Branch reported gloomily that 'prolonged rebellion will probably reduce the civil population to starvation'.

On the face of it, the British still had considerable strength in Burma. There were more than 10,000 British soldiers in the country in mid 1946 and they showed few signs of demoralization, let alone mutiny, unlike some of the forces in Malaya. Yet the situation was much more fragile than it seemed. In 1945 the term of service for British soldiers had been reduced from four years to three years and eight months and this meant that repatriation to Britain was proceeding apace. Later, a full-scale demobilization began, a decision that effectively turned the 'British' garrison in Burma into an Indian and West African one. Therein lay the problem: even in 1946 there were still large numbers of Japanese POWs in the county, along with a few units of the INA who had not yet been returned to India. British authority began to look stretched when West African troops conducted flag marches through the villages of southern Burma or were seen supervising Japanese soldiers building roads. Burmese villagers were wary of both groups of troops, with some reason. Their memories of the Japanese were only too recent and many Burmese were overwhelmed by the size, colour and radically different demeanour of the Africans. Not that this stopped some Burmese from exploiting the newcomers' naivety. The West African men, isolated in the countryside, began to find companions among the Burmese village girls. In some cases they proposed to them and used their meagre savings to give the girls' families 'bridewealth' in the traditional African form. These payments – between 30 and 100 rupees – signalled that the soldiers intended to marry the girls and would take them back to Africa when the time came. On more than one occasion, though, the love-smitten Africans came back to the villages only to find that the girls and their families had disappeared – along with the hard-earned bridewealth. Serious trouble flared up between Burmese villagers and the British and West African regiments in what was already a political powder keg.[39] Still, the governor was grateful to have the West African troops. They were well disciplined and rarely inclined to pick a fight with the locals. And their striking physiques did lend a little glory to Britain's shrinking power. Many of the Africans passed through a recreational camp near Rangoon. They visited the city frequently, impressing its fractious youth with the continuing reach of British rule.

The bushfire revolts and affrays in the countryside were matched in the towns by an extraordinary show of trade-union strength, all the more pointed because people were still poverty stricken from the war. The political heat was turned up as the AFPFL demanded a date for independence from the British government. Basically, this was a revolt for better conditions. British rule seemed no better than Japanese: annual inflation was soaring away and real incomes had reduced by 25 per cent. First of all the Rangoon police went on strike on 9 September, then the postal service union on 15 September. Finally, a general strike was called on 23 September. By the last week of this troubled month, nearly 100,000 key workers were on strike.[40] They included government servants, port workers, police and post-and-telegraph employees. Supplies were not coming off the ships in Rangoon harbour.[41] There was concern that the oil, which provided Burma's main foreign exchange earnings, would dry up. Worse, women and children still suffering from the malnutrition and disease of the terrible war years were once again under threat. The already spartan ration shops were running out of essential commodities such as groundnut oil. Places far upcountry, especially in the hills, could only be supplied from Rangoon and they rapidly ran out of supplies. Memories of 1942 resurfaced and the authorities planned food drops to the Karenni states and other remote points. One sign that this generation of British officials was rattled was provided by their references to the British general strike of 1926. The government's publicity offices tried to make much of the plight of children in their propaganda against the AFPFL: 'If the trains from Rangoon to Mandalay do not run our kinsmen in Upper Burma and the Shan states will suffer,' wrote Maung Tin and F. B. Arnold in a press release. Meanwhile, behind the scenes, officials tried to persuade the strikers to exempt vital provisions from their blockades.[42]

The sense of crisis radiated across the whole region. The authorities in Malaya were also facing strikes in hospitals and industrial units while the Malayan Communist Party staged a huge demonstration that drew more than 10,000 people into the streets. South East Asia Command made it clear to the cabinet that the whole of Britain's Southeast Asian empire was spiralling down to disaster. Wavell, now at his gloomiest, continued to ponder 'Operation Madhouse' and drew up a plan to save the lives of British residents in India in case of a total breakdown of order. At last Clement Attlee was obliged to look up from Britain's domestic troubles and contemplate the looming catastrophe in the East.

Field Marshal Bernard Montgomery, victor at El Alamein and now Chief of the Imperial General Staff, was also growing alarmed. He told the chiefs of staff committee on 23 September 1946 that Britain faced a critical problem if the internal situations in India, Malaya, Burma and Palestine continued to deteriorate in parallel.[43] There were simply not enough troops left for the other colonies if substantial numbers were sent to Rangoon. Britain could not count on Australian help any longer and it would have difficulty in extracting its Commonwealth troops from the occupation forces in Japan. Nor, in view of the growing Soviet menace, could it switch troops from Greece or Germany to deal with a crisis in Southeast Asia. It also had to be remembered, Montgomery warned, that India was now a virtually independent country under its own interim government. If Nehru demanded the withdrawal of Indian troops or refused them for use in the case of serious internal trouble in the country, 'we should not be able to handle the situation in Burma'.

Hubert Rance was unimaginative but hardworking. He did not have Dorman-Smith's literary flair. But he was intensely practical and, as Mountbatten's ADC in the British Military Administration, he knew a lot about Burma. Straightaway he understood that suppression of the radical nationalists was impossible. The appreciation of the situation that he wrote for the Burma Office on 15 September 1946 was clear-eyed and unsentimental. He did not like the AFPFL, distrusting its authoritarian tendencies much more than Mountbatten had done. He noted that between Dorman-Smith's departure and his own arrival it had built up its power by 'taking all the measures so profitably used by Hitler, Mussolini and Ghandi [sic]'.[44] Like many other British officials, he thought Aung San, though young and apparently indecisive, was at least sincere. Rance believed the problem was that if the British were to hitch themselves irrevocably to the AFPFL, its leftward trend might sour relations with the potentially powerful Buddhist monks, whom, perhaps mistakenly, he did not see as a radical force. Yet the alternative – the suppression of the AFPFL – really was out of the question. There were not enough British troops to go round and the hybrid Burma Army – part BNA and part old-style colonial force – would fragment on political and ethnic lines if he tried. Worse, Wavell and Auchinleck continued to tell him that there was no way he could use Indian troops to suppress Burmese nationalists.

Rance had one other option. This was to try to build up a moderate party of the old order, perhaps including some of the more conciliatory nationalists. His assessments of the available politicians were not so different from Dorman-Smith's. He quickly concluded that Sir Paw Tun was past it, but he took to the recently repatriated U Saw, as so many British did. 'I was impressed by his virility and oratory', he wrote, describing him later as 'probably the most forceful character in Burma today'.[45] In the course of conversation with Saw, Rance remarked that he was also quite impressed with Aung San, especially since he had just managed to give a speech lasting for five and a half hours. But 'U Saw was not impressed, as his record is twelve hours'. Saw held out some bait to the governor. He tried to diminish Aung

San, saying that he was sincere 'but not a strong character', controlled first by the communist Than Tun, and later by other major figures in the AFPFL. Even more to Rance's taste, Saw positioned a future independent Burma – under his rule – within the British Commonwealth. He readily accepted that free Burma would need British help. The United Nations was ineffective, he said, while Russia was ideologically purblind and the US was distant. Without British support the Burmese might wake up to find the Chinese in Mandalay one day, in Sagaing the next and Rangoon the day after: 'A hundred million Chinese in Yunnan could not be ignored.'[46] Saw tried to persuade Rance that the British overestimated the AFPFL. He said that they were powerful in Rangoon and parts of the delta but elsewhere people were thoroughly sick of them. Later, writing a memorandum for Rance, Saw took the gloves off and railed against Aung San. He had been tutored by the Japanese and hated democracy. Throughout Burma it was the 'brute force and terrorism' of the AFPFL which prevailed. Most of its members were unemployed. Hence they resorted to extorting goods and money from people by using Aung San's alternative title Bogyoke, 'a title which inspired the awe and abject submission of a great bulk of the unthinking masses'.[47] The British, he concluded, had failed in their responsibilities since their return. They should have relied on the old ministers such as Saw himself. Instead, the 'Burmese felt that the British Government have wittingly or unwittingly handed over the administration of the country to a band of traitorous fascists whose avowed policy is to gain power and ascendancy at all costs'.[48]

Though he sympathized with the spirit of such ranting, Rance was shrewd enough to see through U Saw. The AFPFL organization was much stronger than Saw's and Saw was unlikely to be able to exploit any splits within it. Saw's party, which was associated with pre-war sleaze, would certainly do poorly in an election. Rance quickly decided to back Aung San, recommend concessions to London and try to get the AFPFL to enter the Burmese cabinet. The alternative was a popular revolt, further damage to an already shattered economy and possibly even mass starvation.[49] In the meantime, one event pregnant with the future took place. Returning from a visit to his party's newspaper office, Saw was ambushed by gunmen dressed as AFPFL volunteers about half a mile from Government House on Prome Road. He narrowly escaped assassination and was badly cut around the eyes with broken glass. Next day in the bazaar, most fingers pointed to members of Aung San's party who must have known about Saw's parleys with the governor. But this was a gangsterish and prurient sort of Burma. Another strand of gossip indicted U Saw's Burmese wife, 'who was anxious to get rid of him on account of his so-called German wife from Uganda'.[50] Saw kept his counsel, bided his time and began to stockpile weapons. The consequences for Burma's future were to be no less critical than the telegrams flying between Rance and Attlee's government.

Rance's decision to work with Aung San to counter the gathering social crisis was easier said than done. The young nationalist leader had been languishing ill in bed for some time while the general strike gathered pace: 'Here I am helpless in bed, and I must remain quiet, God alone knows how long.'[51] The bruiser U Saw took this as weakness, but it seems as likely that Aung San was 'doing a Gandhi', using his apparent weakness to set the agenda. At any rate, Rance obligingly called on him at his home to discuss the political situation in secret. Rance painted a bleak scenario, not unlike the ones troubling Wavell and Gent: prolonged strikes would lead to communal and anti-British riots and the destruction of the economy. The peasant, already over-burdened, would be the great loser.[52] There were some favourable signs. Bogyoke had come to the parting of the ways with the communists over the strike. He had clearly decided that large-scale civil disobedience leading potentially to armed rebellion would not only undermine his own position but severely damage what remained of Burma's economic base. This presaged the expulsion of the communists from the AFPFL on 2 November.[53] The impending breach materially strengthened Aung San's position in Rangoon and Mandalay, though it pointed to trouble in the delta districts where communist sympathizers were numerous. But Aung San needed more concessions from the British to see off the communist threat and damp down civil disruption. Comparisons with India remained irksome. Whatever its larger failures, the Cabinet Mission had at least established that India was heading for independence within two years. In contrast, Burma was still stuck with Churchill's timescale, set out in the May 1945 White Paper, which put off independence indefinitely. Worse, the 1935 constitution, with its pitifully small franchise and bias towards Indians and Europeans, remained in force. The patience of the AFPFL could not be guaranteed to last for more than a few weeks and this would impede any attempts to call off the strikes. They could not afford to be always in danger of being outflanked on the left by communists who claimed that they had capitulated to imperialism. Rance realized that some type of dramatic gesture had to be made and it would have to be Attlee who made it.

In a sense, the British government in London made the key concession as early as 18 September when it authorized Rance to negotiate on government servants' wages, to appoint a further Burmese to the governor's council with the defence portfolio and to arrange a general election for the spring of 1947.[54] The White Paper of 1945 was thus quietly shelved. But by now, having waited for so long, Burmese public opinion demanded a far more dramatic gesture. At least Rance could now make a few gestures himself. An offer of increased wages was conveyed to key groups of workers. The governor agreed to include additional AFPFL representatives and members of U Saw's and even Ba Maw's parties in his executive council. The changes tipped the balance in favour of Aung San's supporters. Rance later judged that the AFPFL socialists had been in effective control of the government machine since October 1946.

His authority strengthened, Aung San moved to limit the industrial and political unrest. Strikes in the public sector gradually petered out. The government simultaneously moved against the continuing strikes in private companies. These were targeting the Burmah Oil Company, road transporters and saw mills. The authorities brought in military drivers and Japanese POWs to break the strikes.[55] Then the AFPFL began to exert pressure on its own affiliated unions. On 26 October 'workers demonstrated around the secretariat shouting slogans in support of the Government'. With Rance's help, Aung San had scored a significant if only temporary victory over the communists. The governor and his officials also began to bargain with the authorities in neighbouring countries to improve Burma's import position. They approached India about iron and steel supplies, Thailand about oil and, ironically, the American occupation authorities in Japan about supplies of cloth.[56] In one sense, Aung San already had the initiative. At the height of the trouble, on 8 October, Nehru sent a telegram to him saying that the interim Indian government was anxious to bring Indian troops home from Burma. But he was keen that the withdrawal should not 'upset conditions in Burma and be embarrassing to your government'. He also invited Aung San to Delhi in April 1947 to discuss military and other matters of common interest. Wavell was in no doubt about the telegram's significance. 'This was sent without consulting me', he noted.[57] Britain's erstwhile subjects in Asia were now making their political dispositions without consulting British authority. A convention established in about 1800 by Richard Wellesley, Governor General of India, was thus quietly torn up a century and a half later.

Aung San then went on to try to dissolve what remained of British control over Burma's internal affairs. On 11 November, heavily tutored by the former ICS officer U Tin Tut, he made what was, in effect, his final set of demands. He denounced the governor's remaining discretionary power over certain 'imperial' subjects as incompatible with democracy.[58] The frontier areas would now have to be brought within the remit of a Burmese cabinet. So, too, would control over affairs concerning British and Indian imports. All expenditure would have to be made subject to a vote of the lower house. The British could no longer hope to 'reserve' subjects that bore on their own interests, as they had been doing for years. As for the future shape of a popular assembly in Burma, the AFPFL made it perfectly clear that the franchise would have to be universal in the general election that was scheduled for March 1947. There was no going back to the 1935 Government of India Act and its constitution for Burma. All the old subterfuges that had guaranteed the continuation of colonial interests and their hangers-on would have to go. No longer would the Burmese be outvoted by a combination of representatives of the European and Indian chambers of commerce; those great Indian moneylenders, the Nattukottai Chettiars; and a plethora of Shans, Karens, Kachins, and so on.[59]

In all this Tin Tut, 'highly trained, intelligent and very ambitious', made it clear that his lodestar was India.[60] Burmese would never again play poor relations to the Indians. The Indians were now sending ambassadors to other countries, and in a world where nations measured each other according to international clout, that was independence. Tin Tut, who offered constitutional and financial advice to all the Burmese political parties, threatened boycotts and strikes if an agreement on independence was not reached before 31 January 1947. Rance, however, knew that boycotts and strikes would almost certainly be the precursors of armed insurrection. Aung San had only just managed to stave off that threat in October and the social situation in the country was still deteriorating. Rance bowed to force majeure, noting that 12,000 Indian troops were scheduled to leave Burma in February 1947 and there would be no replacements.[61] In the interim, these troops could not be used to put down openly nationalist risings. Timetables were now quite irrelevant. 'It cannot be argued', he wrote to the Labour government, that 'a people by assumption fit to govern themselves in 1948–49, are still unfit to begin the process in 1947–48'.[62] He urged the immediate passage of a House of Commons amending bill to expand the powers of the present government to include those formerly retained by the governor.[63] In addition, the Burmese leaders should be rapidly invited to London to discuss outstanding issues, above all financial matters and the future position of the minorities.

Rance's position was now unequivocal. The policies of Dorman-Smith were thrust aside. As 1946 drew to an end, Attlee and his colleagues realized that further equivocation was impossible in Burma, just at the moment the Indian situation was about to spin out of their control. They had to decide on quick independence for both countries and the form it would take. The AFPFL leadership was abruptly invited to London after New Year. The goal was to keep Burma within the Commonwealth and out of Soviet clutches. If possible, new agreements would safeguard British commercial interests in the country. The background to the talks in that cold, depressing London winter was an imminent conflagration in Burma. The general strike and accompanying disturbances had simmered down. Yet only Aung San's authority now stood between the British and a widespread armed uprising. Aung San himself could not afford to compromise again. As it was, he was angry with both the British and the communists because he had been forced to take strong action against the strikers. He feared that this would stand him in bad stead in any future election. Even some of the moderate AFPFL leaders who had accepted ministerial office agreed with the communists that another strike would paralyse the government and force the British to grant immediate independence. If they were to go to London, Aung San and his supporters had to be assured of total success. Any temporizing by the British would compromise them completely. It would mean handing the leadership of Burmese nationalism to one or other of the communist factions. British power was already declining rapidly, but this was a decisive moment in the history of Burma and, arguably, in that of South and Southeast Asia as a whole. If Burma had become a communist state on independence, as later happened in Vietnam, the Cold War in Asia might have taken a very different course. Certainly, with the 'cold weather' of 1946–7 approaching, the communists were in a restive mood. Their aim, like their confrères in Vietnam, was to take over and dominate a coalition of nationalist forces. If they could not do this, they would adopt the tactics of the communists in China; they would go underground and fight the nationalists, denouncing them as stooges of imperialism. Fortunately for the AFPFL, the Burmese communists split into ideological and personal factions, with neither the Vietnamese nor the Chinese model triumphing. In the longer term it was to be military nationalists who would win out.

As relations between the moderates and the communists worsened with the collapse of the strikes during October, the executive committee of the AFPFL voted to expel the communists.[64] At a critical meeting of the AFPFL supreme council on 2 November the communists accused Aung San and the moderates of becoming a 'dominion status AFPFL'. For the British, dominion status, meaning self-government within the Commonwealth and defence treaties with the UK, was a political panacea for the dissolution of empire. Burmese would join Australians and Canadians in royal processions along the Mall in London. To the Burmese, dominion status was already a swear word easily paired with 'fascism', as was everything else in the limited lexicon of Burmese nationalism. Thein Pe, the communist who had spent much of the war in India and China, launched into a laboured historical analogy. He compared Aung San with a medieval king of the Burmese city of Pagan who did not know his true friends and was eventually murdered by the national enemy, the Mons. Than Tun, the most outspoken of the communist leaders, eventually announced that the parting of the ways had come. 'Yes, all Communists must put party first and AFPFL second. Party to them meant the true welfare of the peasants, the workers and their sympathisers, who constituted the country.'[65] Justifying their own position, the AFPFL leadership accused the communists of starting a 'whispering campaign' against Aung San and, less believably, of ganging up with the British military and civil administration against the 'socialists', that is, the moderates. The only reason that the AFPFL leaders were prepared to allow the split was that most now really believed that Attlee's government would concede independence early in the new year. Moreover, they could see that the communists were splitting into personal and ideological cliques. Thakin Soe, who had done much to build up communist cells in the north of the country, had begun to accuse Than Tun and Thein Pe of collaboration with the British and of 'right-wing deviationism'. He had been suspicious of much of the leadership since they had gone along with the deal that Aung San had worked out in Kandy back in September 1945 for the absorption of the BNA into a reorganized British force. He had formed his own 'red flag', supposedly Trotskyite, communist faction that went underground and started committing acts of revolutionary terrorism. Meanwhile, Than Tun and his clique had hit back at Soe with a pamphlet which again accused him of seducing a succession of female party workers and of quoting Engels on free love in his defence. Soe certainly seems to have believed that part of his revolutionary duty was to strike heavy blows against the 'bourgeois family'. Thein Pe accused him of being 'an anarchist and opportunist in matters of morality. He had a weakness for women and no qualms about alcohol.'[66]

All the same, the AFPFL moderates were taking a chance in booting out the communists. Broad agreement with the British government there was, but ways and means were still murky. Throughout November and early December the situation remained tense. The Attlee government was disinclined to give all its bargaining chips away before the London meeting. But for his domestic audience, Aung San had to make it appear that the delegation was only going to London for a kind of lap of honour, with the AFPFL having already won every point. Disagreements surfaced over the exact form of the 'democratic' constitution Burma was to receive, Burmese control over the armed forces, the status of the frontier areas and the future of British firms in the country. The issue of whether or not Burma would remain in the Commonwealth hovered in the middle distance. Worryingly, too, representatives of business and the minority peoples were lobbying Attlee's government independently. The Burmese and their supporters in London were put on their guard in October when a Karen 'goodwill mission' arrived in town and was entertained at the exclusive Claridge's Hotel by no less a luminary than Pethick-Lawrence.[67] Against this background Rance continued to push Pethick-Lawrence and Attlee to invite representatives of the Burmese leadership to London as soon as possible, even though the composition of the delegation remained a matter of doubt.

As the AFPFL leadership considered the constitutional endgame, British intelligence warned that the situation was even worse than it had been in early October. Dacoity was rising to a new peak as the harvest operations drew to a close. The local volunteer groups, the PVOs, now numbered 15,000 units, having swelled since the Tantabin incident of the previous May. They were a handy guerrilla force in themselves and in any outbreak would certainly be joined by a good number of the 100,000 armed police who were on the point of mutiny for better pay and conditions. This was quite apart from the non-Karen elements of the BNA who would rally to their former leader Aung San if he took up arms. The local Indians and the Chinese might stay out of a rebellion, but much of the rural population would rise, especially in the Pegu region. As ever, the example of the 1930 rebellion was brought up by the intelligence chiefs: 'It took two years to put down the 1930–2 rebellion when most of the rebels were badly armed . . . and the police were co-operating with the army', a report noted.[68] In the Tathon area, communists seemed to have infiltrated the ranks of the local dacoits and were organizing them for major attacks. The Meiktila railway link was believed to be under particular threat. Internal unrest in Burma combined with a dangerous external situation. By now, a full-scale civil war had broken out between the Chinese communists and Chiang Kai Shek's nationalists. Though this had no immediate impact on Burmese politics, the rise of communism throughout Asia weighed heavily on the minds of the British and the AFPFL leadership. Equally alarming was Hindu–Muslim and Muslim–Sikh conflict in India. Burma had seen comparable 'communal' out-breaks between Buddhists and Muslims in the 1930s. In a lengthy inter-view with Reuters, Aung San deplored China's civil war and India's communalism. Events in China might lead to a Third World War, he said, while both conflicts would 'retard Asiatic unity and security'.[69]

On 13 December General Harold Briggs, the army commander in Burma, sent a particularly gloomy assessment of the situation to his superiors. For political reasons, Indian troops could not now be used, he said. Burmese troops were of 'doubtful reliability'. And the British forces were 'weak' and could not hold the situation. The evidence suggests that Briggs painted the situation to be as dire as he could because he agreed with Rance and, more distantly, Mountbatten on the need for an immediate statement about the date of independence.[70] The only alternative was the kind of warfare that was happening in French Indo-China and the Dutch East Indies. Commanders who had seen their men survive a brutal world war were extremely reluctant to throw more lives away in minor police actions designed to hold colonial territories of dubious economic value. Finally, the govern-ment decided to do what it had really known it was going to do two months or more before. On 20 December, Attlee made a speech in Parliament in which he at last disavowed the maligned White Paper and acknowledged that the government 'would hasten forward the time when Burma shall realise her independence'.[71]

Events were now moving very fast. One of the old Burma hands in Whitehall, Sir Gilbert Laithwaite, was sent to Burma to discuss the AFPFL leaders' visit to London in the new year to approve the final settlement. Laithwaite had intensive discussions with Aung San and Tin Tut and left a vivid account of them. Aung San was 'about an ordinary Burmese height, largish head, very close shaved, a straight forehead receding with a covering lock. Good small hands; a white silk Burmese coat and longyi; sandals.'[72] Though short and frail, he was 'a personality, clear headed with good controls [sic], and much in charge'. Tin Tut, the old ICS man, was much closer to and more comprehensible to the British. Educated at Dulwich College and

Queens' College Cambridge, he was an ideal negotiator, a quiet rugby-loving nationalist who could still speak to the British as an establishment insider. Mrs Tin Tut and Mrs Aung San were friends of Lady Rance and all the women were afraid of further strikes and disturbances. Tin Tut's own relationship to Aung San was 'a little like that of a family solicitor when the son of the house is up before the magistrate, he intervened from time to time to make a point or direct an argument'. Dorman-Smith's answers, said Aung San pointedly, had always been 'evasive'. The only terms on which constitutional discussions could go ahead were clear and unequivocal commitments. Laithwaite noticed that the point of reference for these Burmese leaders was always India: 'At every point there was the check back to what had happened in the case of India.'[73] Why, asked Tin Tut, had Burma occasioned fewer recent ministerial statements than India? Why had India already despatched its own diplomats to foreign countries? The Burmese were sorely aware that by October 1946 the British had effectively handed power to India. That in itself raised serious questions about future relations between India and Burma. Aung San returned to the old sore point of the position of Indians in Burma and intimated vaguely that the Burmese could not have Indians and other 'foreigners' voting on their constitution. Laithwaite's reports revealed that all participants in the forthcoming negotiations were extremely jittery. The British were worried that they faced 'another Indonesia'. Some members of the AFPFL were still quite unclear about what freedom entailed and worried about the good faith of the British. They remained afraid that any delegation to London might be arrested and incarcerated as U Saw and Tin Tut had been five years earlier.

The British saw turmoil all around them. India was convulsed by the INA trials and communal violence. Malaya was fighting off a British constitutional settlement and gripped by communist-inspired labour strife. British troops had barely extricated themselves from the unrolling civil war in the Dutch East Indies and French Indo-China. The army was 'gloomy'. The British civilian services were on the whole in favour of independence, but were now concerned about the welfare of their wives and children and their own future employment. In Burma Laithwaite said that he thought racial animosity was not too bad, but noted that there was still a diehard element in the Pegu

Club which wanted to exclude the Burmese.[74] Basically, 'there is no alternative to the AFPFL'. Of Aung San he concluded: 'I think business could be done.' Besides, the momentum towards independence was now unstoppable. Churchill had already picked up the signals. On 20 December, after Attlee had made his statement, he rose to remind the House of Commons that in the days of Lord Chatham's administration in the mid eighteenth century 'you had to get up very early to keep up with the accession of territory' to Britain. The opposite was now true: 'The British Empire seems to be running off almost as fast as the American loan.'[75] Privately, Churchill was furious that a British government was even considering parleying with someone whom he regarded as a 'quisling' and a 'fascist' such as Aung San.

For his part, Aung San knew that he had one last chance to get a complete independence package from the British. He could barely control his own supporters who were gearing up for civil disobedience, while he knew that the communists were regrouping in the delta and the Irrawaddy valley. Devastated Burma could afford no more war. But the spectre of Asian civil war in Indo-China, Indonesia, China and India hovered gruesomely before his eyes as he set off on his journey to London on a British Overseas Airways Corporation flight on the second day of 1947.

The Burma that Aung San left behind could afford no more killing. The thought appalled even the hardest of fighters in 1946. The partial peace brought by the atom bomb had allowed time for reflection. There were plenty of reminders. For one thing large numbers of Japanese POWs continued to work on the roads and act as skivvies around the countryside. In June 1945 more than 35,000 of these had been repatriated to Japan through Moulmein and Rangoon. The same number, however, remained behind and they were increasingly used as strike breakers and guards as the internal situation deteriorated. By the autumn their morale began to sag seriously; it was now fourteen months since Japan's surrender. In a token concession to their individuality, the British allowed them to make curios and art objects for sale to Allied and Burmese troops. But it was not forgotten who they were. On one occasion a fracas broke out when they tried to sell their trinkets to the civilian population and their goods were seized.[76] Several Japanese were shot dead. Sympathy for them was limited.

THE BURIAL OF THE DEAD

Shortly before Aung San and his party prepared to fly to Europe to avert civil war, a ceremony was held to commemorate some of the millions of victims of the war just ended. On 18 December 1946 a multifaith memorial service was held at Thanbyuzayat, near the Thai border, for the many thousands who had died working on the Burma–Siam railway.[77] Nearly 5,000 British, Australian and Dutch POWs lay buried there in marked graves. Hundreds of American bodies had already been repatriated through India. The graves of more than 8,000 Thai labourers could also be identified. But alongside these 15,000 known victims were the unmarked graves of anything from 30,000 to 80,000 Burmese, Chinese, Indian, Malayan and Indonesian labourers. Most of them had been forced into service. They had died of disease, starvation or as a result of Japanese brutality. In the prevailing swirl of ethnic, religious, political and racial conflict a short moment of perfect peace spread through the jungle. At one end of the commemoration ground a Buddhist tent had been erected over the officiating monks. It faced a flagstaff in the centre on which the Burmese and Allied flags flew. At the other end units of the British, Indian and Burmese armed forces were drawn up in solemn parade. In a rare display of racial and religious unity, the Christian and Buddhist commemoration ceremonies began at exactly the same moment. Alms were given to the monks and sacred libations of water were poured to the souls of the dead. As Christian hymns were played, Sir Hubert Rance presented ceremonial robes to the leading *sayadaws* or abbots. Hindu and Muslim troops saluted the dead. It was not until the next year, as the British withdrawal from Burma was imminent, that the Japanese were allowed to build a simple memorial to their own dead on the Rangoon racecourse.

In Singapore, the wartime Japanese shrines were in ruins. The sacred ashes of the Japanese war dead had been moved from the war memorial on top of Bukit Batok Hill in the centre of the island to a quiet corner of a civilian cemetery in the north, at Yio Chu Kang, which had been built by the Japanese pioneer settlers in the 1890s. It was visited by those Japanese Surrendered Personnel (JSP) remaining on the island, who erected discreet memorials to their fallen comrades. The Chinese community campaigned for them to be obliterated from the landscape altogether and replaced with a memorial to their own slain. The Singapore Chinese had yet to bury their dead. In late March, a Women's Mutual Aid Association was founded by the wives and mothers who had lost menfolk in the *sook ching* massacres; it brought together a strikingly broad cross-section of Singapore's society.[78] For those who had suffered and lost, the very landscape of the city was full of changed meanings. The Upper East Coast Road, a site of the massacres during the Japanese 'screening' of the Chinese, was a *telok kurau*, a haunted hill.[79] The absence of remains was an obstacle to the performance of rites to appease the 'hungry ghosts' of the ancestors. An atmosphere of acute psychic crisis arose. Taoist priests, according to a report in the *Straits Times*, 'peered into the underworld' and saw 'thousands of naked hungry and discontented ghosts roaming about the earth, their wrath threatening calamity to the land'. Shortly before Chinese New Year in early 1948 a high priestess, Miaw Chin, conducted a mass 'screening' of the ghosts of the dead at a massacre site, in front of thousands of bereaved relatives. She was, it was said, appointed to this task by the Goddess of Mercy, Kuan Yin. The spirits of the dead were invited to come and be fed and clothed. 'For three days and nights great piles of food, paper clothing and paper money were offered in sacrifice' and 'a thousand women asked: "How did the spirits of our men-folk fare after death?"'[80]

At this ceremony relatives burnt paper models of naked Japanese soldiers being disembowelled by devils in the court of the King of Hell. For two years after the end of the war the Japanese remained in the region as a reminder of the occupation and its suffering. The repatriation of 6 million Japanese at the end of the war was the largest concentrated population movement in history, and would increase the population of Japan by 8 per cent.[81] Yet for many it was an agonizingly slow process. There had been, at the surrender, 482,000 Japanese soldiers in the SEAC area. A year after the reoccupation there were still 116,313 Japanese to be repatriated. In the interim, 11,504 had died or gone missing.[82] The British were in no hurry to send them home. The repatriation programme – codename 'Nipoff' – was due to wind down in early 1947, but the British attempted to hold on to

80,000 Japanese as military conscript labourers until the end of 1947. This was opposed by General MacArthur, who wanted to dissolve the Japanese army by July. The British protested that repatriation would 'seriously affect the economic recovery of the countries in which they are now employed'.[83] In the event, the last JSPs in British hands were not repatriated until January 1948.

It was a dismal experience for the soldiers. They were left under their own officers, often in remote areas, and set to task building roads and repairing docks and military installations like ordinary labourers. Some units were exposed to much greater danger, being used in Burma to fight dacoits, or bandits, and in Indo-China in the front line in British action against the Viet Minh. The British established a working relationship with the prisoners of war, giving orders through Japanese commanders and holding them responsible for infractions of discipline. Japanese officers were taken time and time again for interrogation by panels investigating war crimes. There was no fraternization and British officers and men regarded the Japanese with cold racial contempt and hatred. Many Japanese testimonies exist to their physical humiliation and moral demeaning by British troops. Japanese soldiers were made to kneel in front of their captors, to beg for food and to carry out filthy jobs on under 1,600 calories a day, half the amount that should have been fed to POWs. They were given a token wage, initially no days off, and no clothing ration. On occasion sand was thrown in their rice as punishment. By the end of 1946, Red Cross reports on Japanese in central Malaya spoke of rapidly deteriorating morale. The men still had no date for repatriation in sight, they had little mail, insufficient rations, and after fifteen months of hard labour were very vulnerable to disease; routinely, only 85 per cent of the men were fit to be sent out to work.[84] On one estimate, the incidence of diseases such as amoebic dysentery and malaria was 21 per cent. A recent study gives a total death toll of JSP from various causes of 8,931; more than those who died on combat duty.[85] One account from the 9th Railway Regiment, based in Johore in Malaya, spoke of the charity of rural Chinese with whom they worked for rice and cash on their rest days. Like the British POWs before them, they boosted their morale with theatre and literary magazines. They finally embarked for Japan in September 1947. Tatsuo

Moroshoshi was a sergeant who had fought in Singapore and Burma, then served along the Burma–Thailand and trans-Sumatran railways. As he finally left for home, his officer gave a final speech: 'All of Japan, including Tokyo and all the big cities is a wide expanse of burnt ruins . . . You are the warriors for the reconstruction of our fatherland.'[86]

Japanese civilians also lingered in the region, principally at the transit camp in Jurong in Singapore. In all some 6,000 civilians passed through Singapore. Mamoru Shinozaki, the former Syonan welfare officer, found new work as an interpreter. He spent a strange period dealing with the flotsam and jetsam of the war, such as local women with children who were married to Japanese and struggled for the right to travel with their husbands. They were quietly allowed to join the camp. At Jurong, Chinese came to visit their old employers, so much so that the British laid on a bus service to the camp.[87] The British were even petitioned by Chinese men wanting Japanese wives. One offered the successful lady $59 and a bag of rice. He said he was making the application 'as it is cheaper for me to marry a Japanese wife than a Chinese one'.[88] Then there were the Japanese who were long-term residents of Malaya and who wanted to resume their life in a land which they saw as home. One case, in Malacca, involved a Japanese woman who, before the war, had been the companion of a European rubber planter. Local residents remembered her inter-cessions for them during the occupation, and with their help she was saved from internment. She was allowed to await the return of her lover, only to find that he had brought with him an Australian wife.[89] The prospect of the war-crimes trials hung over all Japanese who had worked for the military regime. The hearings in Singapore began in the middle of 1946 and continued until April 1947: 135 men were executed at Changi and 79 more in Malaya. Their remains were interred in a corner of the Japanese civilian cemetery, with a memorial to 'sacrificed men of valour'.[90]

There was a brutal coda to this story. At the end of the war, many Japanese soldiers joined resistance armies. In Indonesia perhaps 780 fought, and many died, in the revolution; but over half of them survived and created a small 'Japindo' community.[91] In Malaya esti-mates of the numbers of Japanese who crossed over to the MPAJA vary from 200 to 400. Many drifted away when it became clear that the guerrillas would not fight the British, but the hardcore remained, scattered in squatter villages, where it was comparatively easy to disguise them. The largest concentration, at least twenty or thirty of them, were in the Kuala Kangsar area of Perak, the remnants of a larger group of a hundred or so. After the demobilization of the MPAJA they were suddenly conspicuous and a burden on the Chinese families who sheltered them. The problem was referred to Lai Teck. The reply came back: 'eliminate the Kuala Kangsar Japanese'. On the pretext of a training exercise they were moved from the squatter villages in twos and threes, taken into the jungle and executed. Chin Peng would later claim that Lai Teck needed to hide their existence from the British, but he also found it hard to believe that, even in the unsettled conditions in Malaya in late 1945 and early 1946, the British could not have known about the Japanese, or been told of them by Lai Teck.[92] This incident, like so many others surrounding Lai Teck, remains obscured by shadows. But a handful of Japanese remained with the Communists, and in the years to come they would be remembered for their usefulness with machinery; one of them worked in the Party's arms factory. In 1990 two Japanese members of the MCP – Shigeyuki Hashimoto, aged seventy-one and Kiyoaki Tanaka, aged seventy-seven – were finally repatriated to Japan – the last of the Japan's wartime stragglers. The ashes of one of them were returned, at his request, to be scattered in one of the Party's final encampments in southern Thailand.

BUSINESS AS USUAL IN MALAYA

In Malaya, at last, the war seemed to be receding slightly, if only for a time. On April Fool's Day 1946 the British Military Administration officially came to at an end, although at the handover most men merely removed the insignia from their uniforms and carried on working in the same jobs. British troops remained in Indonesia. Singapore was still a massive military base, and gripes about army requisitioning rumbled on. Mountbatten left Singapore and SEAC on 30 May 1946. At a final parade he presented the people of Singapore with a Japanese gun and a Union Jack. The city fathers named a road after him. On

1 July the Singapore Cricket Club reverted to civilian use, and business began to resume as usual. British civil servants began to return from their recuperation leave, some of them prematurely perhaps. But, as O. W. Gilmour reflected after the fall of Singapore, 'Malaya seemed to have instilled an extraordinary loyalty among those who had lived and worked there and looked on it as their country.' He saw this, as many others did, as something quite unique about the colony. For these exiles, the lurid press reports after the fall of Singapore of 'whisky-swilling planters' and 'Blimp civil servants' with no roots in the country had been hard to bear.[93]

The source of this special attachment to Malaya was hard to define. There were a number of families who could trace their ancestry back over several generations. Roland Braddell, who acted as private adviser to Sultan Ibrahim and later as legal adviser to UMNO itself, was one such. A succession of scholar-administrators invested their lives in the study of the customs, language and history of Malays. For many of them, Malaya was a picturesque refuge from the industrial world. Then there was the landscape itself; luxuriant tropical tones infuse colonial *belles lettres* and memoirs. But perhaps more than this, for those who knew Malaya before the war, what bound them to it was its wealth and ease: a sense of electness, of the sharing of a unique, irrecoverable idyll. 'All golden ages are legendary', wrote Victor Purcell, 'and some are entirely mythical, but all the same I feel that Malaya's "Golden Age" of between the wars had a firm foundation in fact.'[94] But Malaya had entered a new era. 'It is very different from the "good old days",' remarked one new arrival, 'and people who suffered internment who have returned are finding it difficult to adjust themselves . . . it is not easy for us, who are used to the country in its present state, to get on with them.'[95] People who first arrived in Malaya after 1945 usually made their encounters with it on very different terms.

Before the war, the British had tended to see Malaya as 'a Tory Eden in which each man is contented with his station, and does not wish for a change'.[96] Now planters had to come to terms with the fact that their coolies would not dismount from their bicycles when a European passed by. As the *mems* began to return they were given detailed advice by the Colonial Office on the changed manner of life.

They were warned that they would have to make do with army-style camp beds, 'whilst your Kebun [gardener] or the Boy's Wife rejoice in almeirahs and other items of household equipment'. They were advised to bring out their own car; otherwise they would have to use tricycle rickshaws, 'a widely used Japanese innovation, or walk'. But there was worse. 'If you are lucky enough to have the ruins of a tennis court (most were dug up for vegetables) you are unlikely to get the labour to restore it, or even keep your garden tidy.' They were, above all, warned that they will be seen as 'useless appendages of a decadent civilisation', and would have to face criticism 'in a way that has no pre-war parallel'. The Colonial Office, faced with the problem of recruiting staff, was appalled at the frank tone of this memorandum: 'Is all the horror strictly necessary?'[97] But returning British residents discovered that they had indeed lost almost everything in the wreck of 1942. Visiting journalists, attending a cocktail party in their honour in Singapore, were shocked when one of the first guests walked across the room and claimed two of the pictures on the wall.[98]

Even before the war the British community in Malaya was becoming increasingly divided by class and income, and old Malaya families were contemptuous of birds of passage. Now these divisions became more sharply defined and instrumental. Most returning civil servants abhorred the Malayan Union and the superficial democratization of colonial life. They never forgave the governor, Sir Edward Gent, for his role in the debacle. Gent became an aloof figure: 'a slight, tense little man', wrote John Gullick, who arrived in Malaya with the BMA and was to become one of Britain's most notable scholar-administrators, 'concentrating on what he had to do and giving little attention to anything or anybody else'.[99] For his part, Gent was very open about his desire to bring the 'Heaven born' of the Malayan Civil Service back down to earth. He treated them as bureaucratic subordinates; no more, no less. The war itself was another bitter divide. An ex-POW and internees' association was soon formed. But even within it there were subtle, vicious distinctions. As the journalist Vernon Bartlett reported:

You will be told, for example, that Smith is a very decent chap, but that he was one of the ones who got away . . . You will also be told that Jones is a very decent chap, but that he was one of those who stayed on, spent his time in internment and won't let you forget it . . . Brown, you are told, is a very decent chap, but his attitude at camp was so provocative that it led to Japanese reprisals . . . Robinson you will be told, is a very decent chap, but his efforts to get milder conditions for people in the camp came very near to collaboration . . .[100]

The police force in particular was crippled by resentments. Some officers had, in the confusion of the fall of Singapore, escaped. Two of the senior men involved had served with distinction in Special Operations Executive, and one had died in an aircraft crash at the end of the war. The Colonial Office viewed the matter as closed. But internees had had a long time to brood on their resentments in the camps, and demanded that those who had escaped be called to account.[101] When some of the offenders – 'the seventeen', as they were numbered – returned, in many cases promoted, the sufferings of Changi and Sime Road seemed to have been in vain.

Men might refuse to speak to each other for years on end, but the overarching exclusivity of European life in the colony returned. The clubs reopened, and restored their old rules of membership. From 1946, the roll at Kuala Lumpur's Lake Club still comprised 40 per cent company directors, 30 per cent Malayan Civil Service and only 20 per cent planters and miners.[102] In the hotels and dance halls a more egalitarian mood reigned; ballroom dancing was a great a social leveller in places such as the Atomic in Singapore. Malcolm Mac-Donald and his new Canadian wife embraced this new democratic style. MacDonald challenged the committee of the Tanglin Club by bringing the Chinese banking tycoon Tan Chin Tuan to dine. They wrote to him to complain. He later lent his patronage to the new Island golf club to develop it as a multiracial enclave for the great and good. Golf became the defining pastime of the new elite. The agent of the government of India, S. K. Chettur, adored the MacDonalds. They had, he reported, 'no side'. But even the energetic and democratic Chettur found Singapore's informality a little *de trop*. He complained of the long queues of soldiers and their girlfriends at the cinema – 'too plebian and fatiguing' – and was most perturbed that the Indian community in Singapore after the war did not observe the niceties of 'calling', where new arrivals left their cards at the houses of leading families as a genuflection to the hierarchy: 'Social life as we understood it in Madras', he wrote, 'was unknown in Malaya.'[103] This quaint colonial ritual did not revive in post-war Malaya, but other social norms did. Ralph Hone, ex-grammar-school boy and now a rising star of the colonial service, found that his progress to a governorship of the Malayan Union, or even the governor generalship itself, was barred because, in 1945, he had divorced and remarried. Despite their disagreements, Mountbatten took up the issue with his cousin George VI, who then abolished the bar on divorcees. Hone served as Secretary General to Malcolm MacDonald, and later was awarded his governorship in North Borneo. But in his letter of appointment Hone was told that under no circumstances would he be invited to a garden party at Buckingham Palace.[104]

The old Anglo-Malay entente also revived. After the heady public displays of the BMA period, this was achieved comparatively quietly and almost behind closed doors. On 18 June the Malay political leaders and the rulers met together with Gent and MacDonald for the first time to establish the terms of their reconciliation; on 24 July the rulers and UMNO submitted their own proposals for a federal constitution. Whilst recognizing the need for strong central government and a wider citizenship, the 'individuality' of the Malay states and the 'special position' and rights of the Malay people were now acknowledged as paramount. From early August to early November an Anglo-Malay Working Committee – representing the same three parties – finalized the agreement. There was still much mistrust between them, and – as the British acknowledged – the threat of bloodshed overhung the entire proceedings.[105] Gent continued to impress on London that a clear and quick acceptance of the Malay position was necessary, even before the proposals became public and other communities were consulted. The new Malay political elites strengthened their ties to administration when the British relaxed rules that forbade government servants – in which category most of UMNO's leaders fell – to participate in politics. The Malay courts regained their equilibrium and many of the rebel commoners of UMNO took office in the state governments. In October, Dato Onn bin Jaafar became *mentri besar*, or chief minister, of Johore. His relationship with Sultan Ibrahim was never to be free from friction, but he exploited his ruler's patronage and these months marked the height of Onn's pre-eminence as 'sole spokesman' of the Malays. UMNO was not yet a political party; it remained an umbrella organization without a direct membership, and Onn's personality, projected through constant public speaking, dominated the national movement. But he became subject to increasing antagonism from those excluded from the constitutional discussions: from those in his own party, the Malay left and the non-Malays. The leaders of the Malay Nationalist Party and API also toured the *kampongs*. They never forgave Onn for his rejection earlier in the year of a greater free-Malay nation. By the end of 1946, from as far away as Mecca, Malay residents of the holy city of Islam attacked Onn as 'Indonesia's enemy No 1'.[106] A battle was beginning for the hearts and minds of the *kampong* Malays. And when the new proposals were finally made public on Christmas Eve 1946, a storm of non-Malay protest would be unleashed.

But for the British in Malaya, in dramatic contrast to Burma, the last months of 1946 were a time of consolidation. The new federal proposals kept much of the impetus towards a strong central government, whilst placing a great deal of power within the states in the hands of the rulers' chief ministers. The objective remained 'a real coherence which will make possible progressive political development', as Arthur Creech Jones, the former head of the Fabian Colonial Bureau who replaced Hall as Colonial Secretary in October, told Gent.[107] By the end of the year, Creech Jones was able to reassure the cabinet that they had achieved the substance of what they wanted to achieve in the Union. Beyond Malaya, Britain's outposts on Borneo were also coming under more direct colonial control. Vyner Brooke, the third White Rajah of Sarawak, whose private fiefdom extended some 730 kilometres along the western seaboard of Borneo, agreed to pass his rights to the crown. There were protests from his nephew and heir, Anthony Brooke, and from some of his people. With a small group of courtiers in Singapore, Anthony remained pretender to the throne, but a century of Anglo-Malay kingship had come to an end. The affairs of the British North Borneo Chartered Company were wound up, with generous compensation to its shareholders, but there was to be no relinquishing of British rights there in the face of the territorial claims of the neighbouring Philippines. With Malcolm Mac-Donald's appointment the British struggled to find a convenient short-hand for this melange of empire. The term 'Malaysia' – used from the later nineteenth century by missionaries and revived in the 1930s by an American social scientist – seemed likely to alarm the people of Borneo; any move by the British to appropriate the old notion of 'East Indies' was likely to annoy the Dutch and the French. The idea of a 'Governor General' was also something of a misnomer, as MacDonald did not, strictly speaking, govern anything. A compromise phrase, 'British South East Asia', was felt to be 'uncouth'. To Bevin it had a 'somewhat "imperialistic" ring'. But, for want of a better alternative, it stuck.[108]

There was a growing 'surfeit of Excellencies' in Singapore at this time. In addition to the Governor General of British Southeast Asia and the governors of the Malayan Union and Singapore, responsible to the colonial secretary, there was now also a special commissioner for Southeast Asia, responsible to the Foreign Office. This was further recognition of the centrality of the region, and of the way in which its nationalist politics were intertwined with each other. This post began as a plan for a resident minister, but memories of the unhappy time of Duff and Diana Cooper in Singapore before the fall, were too tender. The appointee was Miles Lampson, Lord Killearn, a senior diplomat who had recently completed eight years' service in Cairo. Killearn was also unhappy with his job title, considering it 'reminiscent of the Salvation Army', but he had a formidable brief which ranged from tackling the food emergency to acting as an honest broker in Indonesia. Killearn was a big man – 6 feet 5 inches tall and 18 stone – and was an imposing presence in every sense. He had a massive personal staff of 300, excluding a considerable number of drivers and maintenance men, which cost the British taxpayer £326,000 a year. When coupled with his strictures on the necessity for patience to people waiting for rice, this opened him up to attack. In August, the *Straits Times* printed a skit telephone call to his office:

ODATE: Hello! Is that you Killearn?
VOICE: No.
ODATE: Has he been recalled?

VOICE: Eh? well ... er ... who are you?

ODATE: Insignificant self is Odate – Siego Odate.

VOICE: What do you want?

ODATE: I wish to congratulate Killearn. You see, when I was Mayor of
Syonan, I could never reduce the rice ration to under six *kati* for men. I
was warned of trouble and black market.

But Killearn was, his driver recalled, very careful with money. He
smoked long Burmese cheroots, and at parties at Bukit Serene he
would serve cheap Thai whisky from bottles of Red and Black Label.[109]
Through Killearn's role, the idea of 'South East Asia' as a distinct
regional entity began to acquire an enduring substance.

In the Indian summer of empire, more Britons were involved in it
than at any time previously, and often in entirely new roles. The large
establishment was in part a reflection of the Labour government's
commitment to an imperialism of the welfare state. To the district
officers, planters and policemen of the pre-war era were added new
levies of doctors and midwives, social researchers and ethnographers,
welfare professionals and educationalists. British Southeast Asia
became a unique laboratory of empire. Under the aegis of Lord
Killearn, a 'Social Welfare Conference' in 1947 voiced the premise
that 'the findings of Sir William Beveridge for Great Britain are also
applicable to Southeast Asia, namely that the total resources of the
community by the redistribution of income are sufficient to make
want needless'. Social and economic research was commissioned. The
British trained a new generation of Asian technocrats. For many
women it was their first experience of administration. A social survey
of Singapore in 1947 brought to prominence a young economist, Goh
Keng Swee, who would later design Singapore's grand strategy for
economic development.[110] But it was made clear that there were no
resources for anything resembling a 'welfare state'; communities were
to be taught to help themselves. A pressing target of reform was youth.
The British believed that the region's social crisis was in large part
created by the general 'disintegration of morals' of the young during
the war, particularly in the towns. Singapore made a special claim on
the Colonial Development and Welfare Council for youth centres,
citizen's advice bureaux and community care as the British desperately

tried 'to divert energies in socially desirable channels.'[111] In the paternalistic writings of the time, radical nationalists appear as disturbed adolescents, and young communists, criminal delinquents.

The agenda of liberal imperialism was kept alive by the Labour government's particular commitment to trade unionism. Edward Gent acknowledged that the BMA's attempts to keep down inflation had been the overriding cause of strikes, and he took the unusual step of approving a back issue of strike pay for government labourers. On the basis that 90 per cent of BMA labour had struck for an average of ten days, the bill for their half pay on those days came to $270,000.[112] John 'Battling Jack' Brazier, as trade union adviser, enjoyed Gent's strong backing and Malcolm MacDonald argued that, once the constitution squabble had been resolved, labour was the dominant issue facing British Southeast Asia. But although they went to great lengths to protect Brazier's independence, his role was ambiguous and invidious. He was to be a 'guide' and 'friend' to trade unions, but in their eyes he was clearly a government official. He provided model rules for unions, and undertook to explain to employers that 'Ramasamy', a stock name for an Indian labourer, 'is waking up but so few seem to realise it'. But Brazier was unpopular with both the plantocracy and conservative officials who were unreconciled to unions in principle, and flabbergasted that an imperial functionary should be actively encouraging their formation. Brazier, it seems, was acutely sensitive about the paternalism implicit in this role; in enforcing the distinction between 'political' and 'economic' trade unionism, he was not unmindful of the history of struggle of the British labour movement, in which politics had needed at times to come to the fore in the interests of labour. He seems to have been aware that his encouragement of the moderates did not always strengthen the movement, or promote the best men. The MCP argued that establishing unions on a British model in a Malayan context often meant establishing them on communal lines. Brazier was determined to help local people 'avoid the suffering and restrictions and the bloody battles that trade unionism had had to face in other countries'. But ultimately his presence in Malaya could also legitimate repression. His deputy in Singapore, S. P. Garrett, openly chafed at the constraints of his position, and was more outspoken in his attacks on employers and closer to the General

Labour Unions. And although Brazier had some notable success with moderate unions, it was the General Labour Unions that continued to win their battles in 1946.[113]

The January general strike had brought home to both the government and the Malayan Communist Party the power of organized labour. In the later part of 1946, the Party continued to move away from its semi-open structure, and its cadres were ordered to embed themselves in the workforce. Only main party offices in Kuala Lumpur and Singapore now remained, and the 'Singapore Town Committee' became a somewhat nebulous organization.[114] The Party's leading public spokesman on the peninsula was now the editor of the *Min Sheng Pau*, Liew Yit Fan. The mood was less openly confrontational; for the Party it was a time of consolidation. But the strike weapon, as the Singapore General Labour Union argued when reviewing the events of the BMA period, was the most effective way of extending its organization. But in the wake of the 'February 15th incident' in 1946 when the British intervened to prevent marches commemorating the fall of Singapore, it resolved that it should act more cautiously and systematically: 'Only the most pressing demands of the movement should be raised, without making a comprehensive claim, in order to concentrate on one's target, secure the sympathy of the public, and make victory easy to attain.'[115] In the year after April 1946, 713,000 man days were lost through industrial action in Malaya and 1,173,000 in Singapore, where imperial strategic assets such as the Harbour Board and the Naval Base experienced prolonged strikes. Across the peninsula, in rubber and other industries, unions began to band together. Tremendous pressure was placed on the workers who stayed outside them: they complained of packing of meetings, of accusations of malpractice aimed at them, of intimidation and worse. Yet, at the same time, in a climate in which the conditions were dire and employers weak, the big unions won major successes: disputes, whatever the range of demands that they voiced, remained 'rice strikes'. The dilemma for the government, as it reintroduced registration of labour unions in July 1946, was how long it would allow these unions to continue to operate legally. To anticipate this, the General Labour Unions organized themselves into federations which had a stronger trade basis. But the government in Malaya was gaining ground: the 'laws of 1941' which the left so derided, were being reintroduced. On the industry frontier, the state was being rebuilt; land and forest offices were reopening and employers were impatient to re-establish their authority.

Meanwhile there was a constant round of rallies and parades: for the first time in early March, International Women's Day was celebrated in Singapore and Penang, followed in quick succession by the anniversary of the 1919 peace conference, the birthday of Karl Marx and May Day, a somewhat muted affair after the earlier arrests and banishments, and there were large anti-war rallies in May and June in Singapore and many peninsular towns. The memory of the war remained deeply divisive. On the first anniversary of VJ Day in Singapore, the Chinese Chambers of Commerce and the Kuomintang paraded in the morning as part of the official event. Then the left paraded in the afternoon.[116] It was a massive show of strength: a procession a mile long snaked through the city, led by veterans of the forgotten armies, of the Chinese fighters of Dalforce still demanding back pay. Some 130 other associations followed: the New Democratic Youth League, the MPAJA ex-Comrades, the trade unions, the Malayan Democratic Union and many more. A year after the end of the war, the demands were still the same: for rice, clothes and freedom, and an end to crime and violence. The parade was, as the local press pointed out, an act of thanksgiving for the end of Japanese tyranny, but it was not a sign of rejoicing. As the second colonial conquest of Malaya finally began to put down roots there, it was to be tested by a new and potentially fatal wave of opposition. Despite all the setbacks it had faced, by the end of the year the Malayan Communist Party proclaimed that its organization was larger now than during the Malayan Spring: 'This time there are more participants and there is unanimity in their actions.'[117]

7

1947: At Freedom's Gate

THE LAST DAYS OF THE RAJ

Even during the tense early months of 1947 as India, Pakistan and Burma lurched violently towards freedom, the Second World War continued to cast a long shadow. In India the issue of the INA still rankled with the British, even though all now realized that their tenure in the subcontinent was in its final stages. Wavell's original 7,600 'blacks' – men guilty of particularly treasonable or brutal acts – had been reduced by 5,500 who had been dismissed from the service with forfeiture of pay and allowances. Despite the bad publicity of the 1945 trials, in early 1946 it was still intended to bring 600 'blacks' to trial. This proved hopelessly optimistic. The military lawyers found the case against many of them difficult to prove. Continuous Congress agitation against the trials sapped Wavell's and Auchinleck's determination to proceed with them. The number proposed for trial dropped steadily, first to 300, then to fewer than 100. Finally, twenty were brought to trial in the Delhi Red Fort on charges of gross brutality. Of these, twelve were sentenced to long prison terms. In January 1947 Sarat Bose began one final push to get all the men released. He even demanded that they be given pay and allowances for the period that they were serving under the Japanese, a suggestion that particularly infuriated the British.[1] Bose tried to pressure Nehru through the Indian defence minister of the interim government, Sardar Baldev Singh. The viceroy and the commander-in-chief were both determined to resist this, even though it became a huge issue in the central legislative assembly.

The Congress leadership prevaricated. They had always been aware of the deep public hostility to the trials, even in those cases purportedly relating to 'brutality'. This was the reason Nehru and Patel had stood so firmly behind the INA prisoners in 1945. But these two men were now virtually the rulers of India. They did not want an open breach with the viceroy and commander-in-chief because it might have fostered public disturbance in a period of rising tension. Any issue could easily 'turn communal'. Some conservative Muslim clerics had long since denounced the INA as enemies of Islam because of their support for the 'godless Japanese'. A breach with the remaining British officers of the Indian Army would also be dangerous, given the pervasive fear that the security situation in the country might easily deteriorate disastrously.

Archibald Wavell had come to the end of his tenure as viceroy and almost to the end of his tether. He had been continuously involved with India and its armies since he had been commander-in-chief during the ill-fated defence of Burma in 1941. On New Year's Eve 1946 he had confided to his journal: 'It is a great strain on a small man to do a job which is too big for him, if he feels it is too big. Health and vitality suffer.'[2] He wrote to Pethick-Lawrence in early March, regretting that he was leaving India 'with the work unfinished, but if HMG feel that a younger man and a fresher mind can do it better, that is for them to decide'. The Indians would probably pull through, he thought, but 'it is force of character that is so often lacking. Perhaps they will develop it when we leave.'[3] Privately, he wrote: 'I'm glad that I have finished with politics.'[4] Most British soldiers and civil servants in India felt he had been shabbily treated, but then political hatred of the Labour government was very widespread among the remnants of the Raj's service class.

Wavell's martial paternalism and decency gave way to Mountbatten's breezy realism on 24 March. Almost straightaway a compromise was struck on the INA issue. Nehru agreed that the government would reject the demand in the legislative assembly for the release and remuneration of all the remaining 'black' prisoners, while Auchinleck agreed to allow judges of the federal court to review the evidence with a view to commuting or reducing the sentences.[5] The compromise meant that Mountbatten did not need to use his viceregal veto to overrule the Congress-dominated government, a proceeding that

Nehru had feared would cause demonstrations across the country. In return, Nehru backed Auchinleck in the assembly, a 'courageous and statesmanlike' gesture according to Mountbatten, who made little secret of his admiration and liking for the Congress leader. But the compromise went only so far. Even as independence approached in August, there was contention over eleven INA men still in jail. The Congress wanted them out before the magic date, 15 August. Auchinleck argued that this would offend the British officers who were to continue to serve in the Indian Army at least until the following spring. The solution seemed to be an amnesty, but the British would agree to this only on condition that the detainees would not be mobbed by jubilant crowds on their release.[6]

As the hot weather of 1947 set in – the last year, as it was to prove, of two centuries of British rule – a change came over the mood of the people and the politicians. Everyone seemed to adopt a more intransigent position. There was between the Congress and the Muslim League an impasse so unbreakable that by late April Mountbatten had decided that a partition of India and its Muslim-majority provinces of Punjab in the west and Bengal in the east was the only solution. Faced with troubles around the world, the Attlee government and Mountbatten decided to pull out of India as quickly as possible. Employing a mixed metaphor of woeful banality, Attlee told Mountbatten: 'I am very conscious that I put you in to bat on a very sticky wicket to pull the game out of the fire.'[7] With almost indecent haste, Attlee's government pushed legislation through the British Parliament to create two new dominions within the Commonwealth on 15 August 1947. Freedom would be granted separately to Pakistan and Hindustan-India. By 17 July secretariats for the two countries were up and running. While Hindu–Muslim conflicts increased in number all across the vast country, a myriad of apparently trivial but highly symbolic issues absorbed the time of the political leaders. The British, for instance, wanted to signal that it was dominion status within the British Commonwealth that was being conceded. They asked that a small Union Flag should be incorporated into the flags of the two countries. The Indians refused outright. Jinnah professed himself pained to have to reject the request, but reported that it would be 'repugnant to the religious feeling of the Muslims' to have a cross of

St George juxtaposed to the Prophet's crescent moon, which was to be the emblem on the Pakistan flag.[8] Similar squabbling broke out over whether the British monarch would use his signature 'George Rex Imperator', his old title as king-emperor, or simply 'George Rex'.

The Indian armed forces, to the despair of Auchinleck and his brother officers, had to be divided. The interim government's Armed Forces Nationalisation Committee had already been wrangling for months over the phasing out of British officers. Now, just before it produced its report in May, the committee had to address the frighteningly complicated issue of dividing the army between two sovereign states. The Indian members anticipated a 'loss of efficiency' when the British officers left, but simply wanted to 'get on with the job'. Naively, several members predicted that there would be no major war for ten years, only internal security operations. In fact, India and Pakistan were to be at each other's throats the moment the Union Flags came down, posing immense difficulties for the residual British element in both successor armies.[9] India got most of British India's financial assets and the new Indian army commandeered most of the military stores: Pakistan would have to beg on the international arms market. The division gave India twice as many army units, warships and aircraft as Pakistan.[10] All the same, the importance of Muslims in the old army meant that Pakistan emerged as a formidable military power. In other respects Pakistan was not so fortunate. Its territorial boundaries were a geographical absurdity with East Pakistan separated from West by 2,000 miles. This was a recipe for trouble, particularly as the commission appointed to determine the borders was working at a frantic pace and the status and options of the princely states were as yet unclear. Conflict simmered on in Bengal, where hatred had reached a peak in the massacres of the previous autumn. In the Punjab, Hindu–Muslim and Muslim–Sikh tensions escalated, even among those who had fought together as comrades through the war. Gandhi regretfully concluded that the division was ultimately not the fault of the British. Indians simply could not agree among themselves. Burmese politicians, ever watching over their shoulders, took the hint. If complete freedom, rather than 'mere' dominion status, was to be achieved, then the Burmese must stay unified.

Yet there was something else afoot in that sweltering Asian summer.

Fears for the future were mixed with pride in the coming of independence. The Indian nation was about to be reborn as a free, modern people. Sri Krishna, a journalist, reported from the 'perpetual Turkish bath' that Delhi had become:

Watching the crowded dance floors in New Delhi's clubs or hotels one wonders whether the Swadeshi [independent] Government would bring down the inflated values in the social market. Gandhi cap and Jawahar waist [coat] have become fashionable pieces of manly wear. Our women look really chic in sarees, even the Continental or American brand. No one minds the sleeveless and ever shortening blouses. Indian men and women, having achieved the freedom to dance with anybody but their wedded partners, are not likely to abandon it even for Purna Swaraj [full independence].[11]

Evidently the new India would be neither the paradise of socialist equality anticipated by Pandit Nehru nor the republic of village virtues dreamed of by Mahatma Gandhi. The future of Pakistan was, however, even more clouded. Mahomed Ali Jinnah and the Muslim League had managed to block Congress and British attempts to forge independent India in their own interests. Yet Jinnah was unable to secure anything more than a 'moth-eaten' Pakistan. The alternative, the Muslim League's submergence into a federal structure dominated by the Congress, might have been acceptable if he could have been sure of controlling his Muslim lieutenants in the Punjab and Bengal. But he could not. As a result, thousands of Muslim civil servants began to make their way on intermittent railway services to the distant western seaport of Karachi, Pakistan's capital designate. Mountbatten, who had opposed partition until the last, derisively predicted the new government would be living in a 'tent'.[12] Nehru secretly hoped that it would collapse in a few months, lacking administrative structure.

The British officers who contemplated the once unthinkable demise of the Raj were beset by mounting worries. Nehru's emotional attachment to the princely state of Kashmir seemed the most likely cause of conflict between the two new dominions. The state had a Muslim majority but was ruled by a Hindu prince; at the time, no one knew whether it was going to join India or Pakistan. Mountbatten had difficulty in stopping the prime minister designate from personally visiting Kashmir, something that might well have sparked off blood-shed there.[13] Meanwhile, the British commander of what was to become the Indian air force was stunned to learn that Nehru was contemplating sending planes to Southeast Asia to help the Indonesian nationalists against the Dutch.[14] Nehru did in fact later send Indian planes to break the Dutch embargo of its former colony. The aim was to deliver food and medicines to the nationalist forces, though some said that arms had found their way there too. In the interim All-India Radio acted as the official news station of the Indonesian Republic.[15] Nehru was also keeping a weather eye on events in Burma, where the Indian minority was vulnerable to political change. The depart-ing British disapproved of this 'meddling' in international affairs, although it was frankly unavoidable. As India became an independent nation its rulers found it difficult to distance themselves from the geopolitical interests of their British predecessor, however much they might have wished to strike a neutral pose in international affairs.

The deepest foreboding affected the officers and men of Britain's old Indian Army. They had fought together from Assam through to Rangoon, in North Africa and in Italy. They had watched comrades survive the horrors of the Second World War only to see them perish in the abortive occupation of Indonesia. Hindu and Muslim fighters from the Burma campaign watched with horror as their home villages were consumed by communal rioting. *Darbar Notes*, an army maga-zine, reported the efforts of Indian subalterns in the Punjab districts to form Hindu–Muslim peace committees.[16] At first officers noted with pleasure that only 5 per cent of the people arrested for communal crimes had military training.[17] But other men of arms – irregular troops raised during the war, princely states' armies and bandits of various sorts – actually led the ruthless communal killing that spilled out across the country. Senior British officers later acknowledged that former soldiers had probably played a more significant role in the violence than initially thought. At his prayer meetings, the frail and now deeply disillusioned Gandhi said that he feared that there was every likelihood that the partitioned armies 'would be used for making war on each other'.[18] Mountbatten too was uneasy with the whole situation. He reported to the Partition Council that the Maharaja of Patiala, who had been a key figure in the war effort, had written to him asking him to receive a deputation of Sikh officers, many of whom had served under Mountbatten in South East Asia Command.[19] Mountbatten was worried that receiving the men would compromise his supposedly impartial position and that they would use the occasion to raise the issue of the Punjab boundary, which threatened to strand their families on the wrong side of the India–Pakistan border. The Sikhs were also worried that their grants of land for wartime service would not be safe if their districts ended up in Pakistan. As the cities of the Punjab descended into a hell of communal murder, everyone feared that parts of the regular army would get involved in the fighting. In the event, the old Indian Army remained aloof from the mayhem that broke out between March and October 1947, but some former personnel took part in the violence. Officers begged their men to remain impartial as hatred grew. Every officer was sent a pamphlet, 'The army is the anchor of the country'. The forces newspaper, *Fauj Akhbar*, reported on the fine job that Indians were doing overseas. Indian troops from a variety of regiments were guarding the Japanese royal palace, for instance.[20] But the experience of war stoked the tension in many indirect but malign ways. The Radcliffe Commission, which was responsible for drawing up the boundaries between the two new dominions, divided the homeland of India's Sikh community in two. This led to what was effectively a murderous armed migration by the large Sikh community living in the Montgomery district of west Punjab to eastern parts of the province that were on the point of becoming India. The adjutant-general of the Indian army, Sir Reginald Savory, reported that this migration and concomitant Sikh violence was 'well planned, well directed and well carried out'. The Sikh connection with the army had served them excellently, he believed.[21]

Partition put the departing British into absurdly difficult situations. In theory at least, Sir Frank Messervy, who had led an Indian division at Imphal and was now commander-in-chief of Pakistan's forces, could be pitted against his old commander, Sir Claude Auchinleck, who remained head of the rest of the Indian army. With a heavy heart, Messervy set to work policing the borders of the emerging dominion of Pakistan.[22] He foresaw that old comrades from the Burma front would be trying to kill each other within a few months, as conflicts erupted over the line of the India–Pakistan border. He doubted

whether martial law would be of any use in case of a serious breakdown of order. There were simply too few officers, especially British
officers, to administer it. Yet Machiavellian diplomacy did not cease
simply because the vivisection of the subcontinent was underway. As
independence neared, defence strategists in London grasped that it
might be possible to secure an agreement with Pakistan even if India
were to withdraw from imperial defence arrangements. The Americans too were beginning to see a future for Pakistan as 'an Islamic
buffer' against Soviet communism in the Hindu Kush. It was Western
realpolitik as much as the Muslims' fear of Hindu domination that
determined that Pakistan would survive its traumatic birth.

The fury and hatred created by partition did not completely overwhelm regret and nostalgia among British officers, or indeed even
some Indian officers. As the army was split on religious grounds and
Hindus and Muslims massacred each other in the streets and on the
railways, Lieutenant Colonel Mahomed Siddiq MC, of the 7th Sikh
Regiment, wrote: 'I am a most disappointed person today . . . a fine
machine is being disintegrated to satisfy some of the so-called politicians.' He added a cry from the heart: 'I love my Sikhs, Sir!'[23] The
recipient of this letter, General Savory, was already disillusioned,
suffering from what he referred to as 'Quit India malaise'. 'What a
country . . . I want to forget India', he wrote gloomily. Other British
officers registered a profound sense of loss. W. L. Alston wrote one
of his little poems:

> Oh land of fascination!
> Deep that calls to Deep!
> Responsive to our longing,
> May you ever keep
> A corner of your heart for us,
> Who counted not the cost,
> To serve our mistress, India,
> That we have wo'ed and lost.[24]

As India's and Pakistan's 'tryst with destiny' approached the British
busied themselves with their usual rituals. There was to be no ceremonial lowering of the Union Flag in Delhi. At Lucknow, however,
where the memory of 1857, when Indian rebels besieged the British

garrison, was evergreen, a curious ceremony was played out. Every corps present at the siege was judged to be entitled to receive a flag flown from the flagstaff of the ruined Residency. As time was limited and demand high, all the flags in the Cawnpore arsenal were run up the pole, sometimes in batches of three or four at a time.

However pervasive the surrounding tension, for Indians in Delhi the emotion at the moment of independence was simply unbridled joy. Mountbatten and his staff had choreographed a ceremony in which they would salute the tricolour flag of the Indian union as the viceroy took up his new role of Governor General. But the Indian crowd surged into the specially prepared arena and threw the display into turmoil. Alston noted correctly that this represented a fine, and indeed final, example of the Indians' 'Marx Brothers-like' ability to subvert British pomposity.[25] It was perhaps the only moment of real comedy in a tragic summer. As tens of thousands more were hacked or burned to death in communal killings, Nehru rebuffed Pethick-Lawrence's breezy congratulations on India's independence: 'There is little to feel happy about in India . . . now. We have had a hard time and the forces of evil have surrounded us.'[26] For the next three or four years Nehru was plagued with doubts about whether India would survive at all.

THE CRESCENT FRAGMENTS:
BENGAL DIVIDED

In the Punjab the riots and killing that continued through the months before and after partition were marked by military precision and unbelievable sadism: in some cases whole train loads of innocents were burned alive or disembowelled. The British boundary force policing the division ordained by Sir Cyril Radcliffe's commission was too small and ineffective to make much difference. The pattern was different to the east in Bengal and Assam. The region had its share of brutal communal killings and fear had been ever present since the Calcutta and Noakhali riots of 1946, but the dismemberment of Bengal took much longer and was less dramatic than the events in the Punjab. Between mid 1946 and 1955 7–8 million people moved from east to west or vice versa. Many of these became refugees in the squalid shanty-town *bustees* of Calcutta, Dacca and other cities, putting a terrible strain on the fragile economies of the emerging dominions. These movements were like regular tidal flows rather than the abnormal waves of brutalized humanity in the west. The political repercussions were also complex. Quite apart from the simmering tension on the borders of West Bengal and East Pakistan, the peoples of northeastern India, members of recently armed and self-aware minorities such as the Nagas, Lushai and Chin, sought autonomy and looked with suspicion on the new nation-states. Local politicians agonized over the fate of what had come to be called India's 'Mongolian fringe'.[27] Hindu politicians in Assam felt they had a 'refugee problem' as poor Muslim squatters from eastern Bengal grew in numbers, allegedly enticed into the province by the local Muslim League to bolster its case for Assam to be incorporated into East Pakistan.[28] Burmese Arakan suffered not only separatist and communist movements, but also the attempts of Muslim parties to annex their populations to East Pakistan. Nowhere down the length of the crescent did relinquished or devolved British authority pass quietly into the hands of homogeneous nation-states. The divisions of colonial politics were to scarify the region for two generations.

In Bengal people came only slowly to understand the imminence of partition and even after the event most could not believe that their homeland had been irrevocably sundered into a crazy geographer's nightmare, preferring instead to believe that their Hindu or Muslim leaders would see their error and help to unite the region again. This was not entirely fanciful. In May 1947 two very different leaders had come forward to try to preserve the province's unity. Sarat Bose had always been a Bengal patriot as much as an Indian nationalist. As a young man, he had applauded the great and ultimately successful movement to reverse Lord Curzon's partition of the province into Hindu-dominated and Muslim-dominated regions. He continued to believe that partition was an imperialist ploy and promulgated a plan for a united, autonomous Socialist Republic of Bengal. Exactly what this entity's relationship was to be with the Union of India or the putative Pakistan remained unclear. But in Bose's view this was to be decided by the popular democractic assembly that would be elected after independence. Somewhat surprisingly, support for this sort of idea came from the leader of the local Muslim-dominated ministry, H. Suhrawardy. The chief minister, the local Muslim League and allied politicians were acutely aware that millions of Muslim peasants would suffer if partition actually came about. They feared, correctly, that any 'East Pakistan' without Calcutta would be an economic disaster area. The partition agitation, asserted Suhrawardy, was a move by the 'propertied classes' to serve their own interests.[29] He even managed to prevail on Jinnah to moderate his demands that Pakistan should include the whole of Bengal to see whether the unity plan got off the ground.

Bose and Suhrawardy were both to be disappointed. The majority of the middle-class Hindu politicians opposed any move that would maintain a Muslim preponderance in Bengal's politics. Their most vocal leader, Shyama Prasad Mookherjee, denounced the 'ten year communal raj' that the Muslims were said to have imposed since the 1935 constitutional reforms. Throughout the early part of 1947 the Hindu middle classes presented petitions and held public meetings to demand partition. The main Hindu organization, Hindu Mahasabha, the Bengal Chamber of Commerce, and the vast majority of local associations in which Hindus predominated pressed for separation. Mookherjee characterized the Bengali 'paradise to come' promised by Suhrawardy as simply more of the 'hell that exists in Bengal today', the result, he argued, of the chief minister's well-documented maladministration and the Muslim League's 'campaign of hatred'.[30] Bengal indeed remained a kind of hell. If the conditions of ordinary people had not been so desperate it is possible that the Bengal assembly might not have voted for partition later in the summer. By now, though, even the representatives of the poor, low-caste Hindu peasants of the east of the province who had previously shared interests with the Muslim peasantry were alarmed and apprehensive. Communist organizers tried to persuade the peasantry that it was an alliance of bosses, imperialists and landlords who were fomenting the communal rioting. They had some success in northeast Bengal.[31] Here peasants had traditionally been forced to surrender half their crop as rent to rural bosses, who often then added interest and other charges and sequestered the whole lot. A large agitation (the Tebagha movement) was fighting against this system of exploitation, provoking some clashes between peasant demonstrators and the police. Yet the dominant ideology remained that of religious difference. Communal suspicion did not dissipate. Muslim peasants were asked by lecturing clerics: 'Why agitate for a larger share of the crop when under Pakistan you would have it all?' Hindu peasants were reminded of the Noakhali killings.

On the surface the city of Calcutta looked normal. David Lean's *Great Expectations* with the young John Mills was playing at the Lighthouse. Burt Lancaster starred in *The Killers* at the Regal. But these markers of post-war cinema belied the fact that the war seemed to continue out in the side streets and *bustees*. The supply of wartime weaponry had not yet been exhausted. A score of people were murdered every other day. Arson and attacks on shops and houses with homemade bombs occurred every night. On 7 July, just six weeks before Independence, twenty-five people were stabbed to death in the city and a bomb was thrown in its main thoroughfare, Chowringee. Curfews were regularly imposed on Calcutta and other cities while magistrates banned groups marching in shirts of 'a certain colour', presumably a reference to the green and saffron hues favoured by Muslim and Hindu agitators, respectively. The refugee problem worsened. Sixty thousand Muslim refugees had fled from the revenge riots in Bihar that had followed Noakhali the previous autumn. The fear of back-street disturbances drove the poor, many of them already refugees, from their slums onto the pavements of central Calcutta. Public security was so bad that no one could be persuaded to collect the city's garbage. A photograph in the newspapers showed mounds of rubbish silting up the doors of the Calcutta Stock Exchange, the most important commercial site in Asia. At the beginning of May 7,000 tons of it lay uncollected and rotting in the city's streets.[32] Cholera returned; industrial trouble flickered on while rural Bengal endured another bad season of cyclones, floods and fears of renewed starvation.

The British were alarmed and despondent. Following the euphoria at the end of the war everything seemed to be going wrong. The economic crisis at home, the threat of communism in Europe and the collapse of empire in the East amidst bloodshed and recriminations all seemed to feed off each other. Anti-British feeling in Calcutta was stilled neither by communal violence nor by the imminence of Britain's departure. The year began badly with a riot in Calcutta about the situation in Indo-China or 'Viet-nam . . . of all things', as John Tyson, the secretary to the governor, put it.[33] In February Saraswati Puja, the festival of the goddess of learning, saw displays of more pictures of Subhas Bose than images of the deity and more Congress flags than flowers in her honour.[34]

In spite of all the arguments for and against the partition of Bengal no one actually foresaw the civil strife that would result. On 20 June the Bengal legislative assembly voted to divide the province. Soon afterwards Sir Cyril Radcliffe, fresh from carving up the Punjab, established himself and his commission in the Belvedere palace and began work on dividing the province's 25 million Hindus and 33 million Muslims whose lives had so long been intertwined. Radcliffe worked with great speed and without much local knowledge. He was dependent on maps and on the evidence given to him by the local political parties, with all their communal and factional biases.[35] Whatever he ruled, most Muslims were likely to be outraged and no one would be entirely satisfied. Mountbatten kept the details of the plan quiet until two days after independence in the hope of avoiding the massive and bloody population movements that were going on in the Punjab. 'I hope I am *not* here when the award is announced', Tyson observed.

As most people expected or feared, the division approximated to the plan of partition that the provincial Congress had been pressing for over the previous year, though it was messier than they had wanted. Given Mountbatten's distrust of the Muslim leadership and the strength of British commercial interests in Calcutta, it was to be expected that the city would be awarded to India. Not only did this leave what was to become East Pakistan without a major commercial centre, it also severed the growers of the region's main export crop, jute, from the mills and marketing infrastructure located in and around the city. The future for jute export was already far from rosy because demand for the tough vegetable fibre was declining as new synthetic fibres developed during the war usurped its role. From the very start, the eastern wing of Pakistan was destined to be a drain on the resources of the more prosperous provinces in the west; eventually it would become a millstone. Another fillip for Hindu Bengal and the new India was that two of the rulers of the local princely states, technically independent kingdoms under the crown in British constitutional thinking, opted for India rather than Pakistan. Even though both Tripura in the southeast and Cooch Behar in the northeast had near majority Muslim populations, there was little the Muslim leadership could do. The accession of Tripura to India almost severed the important port district of Chittagong from the rest of East Pakistan, while that of Cooch Behar left a huge hole in the northeast. 'Moth-eaten' was a mild description of the misshapen state that emerged from such a random dispensation.

Yet India did not win hands down. Radcliffe's rapid draughtsmanship assigned the Hindu-majority district of Khulna to East Pakistan. This was close enough to Calcutta to loose a further surge of the Hindu population to the west and further poison the relationship between the emerging dominions. If Chittagong was only joined to East Pakistan by a thread of land, India's great northeastern provinces of Assam and Manipur were equally tenuously linked to West Bengal by a thin strip squeezed between East Pakistan to the south and the independent Himalayan states of Nepal, Sikkim and Bhutan to the north. The populous district of Sylhet, formerly part of Assam, also opted for Pakistan after a plebiscite. The importance of all this was that India's northeastern section of the old British crescent was distanced even further physically and psychologically from the rest of the country. Unsurprisingly, this encouraged some local leaders, particularly among the Naga peoples, to think in terms of total independence from India. It also ensured that the Indian authorities and the Indian army became even more concerned to make their presence felt in Assam and Manipur for fear of Pakistani and, later, Chinese interference in these distant provinces. As elsewhere down the crescent, partition and the creation of new independent states sparked many small wars of secession.

In part this was because the British and Christian missionaries had always treated peoples such as the Nagas and Garos, or equally the Kachin and the Chin in Burma, differently from the Indians and Burmese of the 'plains'. Most local leaders felt that they had been conquered by the British, not by the Indians or Burmese, and they therefore saw nothing automatic about their incorporation in the post-British states. Roving British anthropologists had sought to protect their culture from 'pollution' by mainstream Hindu or Muslim society. In the case of the Nagas, American Baptist missionaries had protected them against the British civil administration and encouraged them to evolve an identity as a chosen people of God, distinct from the pagans of the Assam valley.[36] By 1947 probably a majority of Nagas were Christian. This sense of separate identity had been strengthened during the war when many of them had fought against the Japanese on the Allied side. British officers had armed them and taught them that they were independent people and owed nothing to the seditious nationalists of the plains. Naga political associations gradually came into being, some pressing for local autonomy, some for outright independence. In July 1947, just as Radcliffe was passing through Delhi en route to Calcutta, a delegation came to meet the Congress leadership and seek guarantees for an independent Nagaland. Initially Gandhi seemed to accept this, stating that Congress wanted no one to be forced into the Indian Union. But by August the Congress leaders were rattled by the prospect that riot and secession would fragment the whole subcontinent. Their position hardened, provoking some Naga leaders to issue their own declaration of independence on 14 August. In contrast to the wild celebrations elsewhere in India, very few attended the flag hoisting in Nagaland. According to Mildred Archer, art historian and wife of W. G. Archer, a local official and anthropologist, 'not a single Naga was anywhere in sight'.[37] The messianic prophetess Gaidiliu, who had led a Naga rebellion against the British in 1930, remained in prison until 1948 at the behest of the suspicious Indian authorities. Decades of conflict, sabotage and insurrection were to follow in the northeast.

The haste to partition Bengal might have made it look as if the eastern part of the province were being abandoned, but some preparations had at least to be seen to be made. The middling-sized town of Dacca was designated the capital of East Pakistan. In the eighteenth century Dacca had been a major city in the Moghul province of Bengal, but with the rise of Calcutta it had lost its importance and become an undistinguished district headquarters noted mainly for its university and periodic flooding. Already tense from minor communal incidents, the town was sadly lacking in facilities for the large number of Muslim clerks and officials who were congregating there from all over Bengal. The residence of the former Nawab of Dacca was commandeered as Government House while a British army barracks became the secretariat building and dormitory home for 3,500 disgruntled clerks.

Independence in Bengal was an even more shambolic affair than it was in Delhi. A few days before 15 August the Calcutta Corporation renamed three streets in the city centre 'Netaji Subhas Bose Street', souring the occasion for the British. C. Rajagopalachari, the moderate Madras Congressman who had been nominated governor of West Bengal, also showed little inclination to respect British traditions. He entered the splendour of the throne room of Government House for his swearing-in dressed simply in homespun *dhoti* and cap. Perhaps it was just as well. On 15 August a huge crowd waving Congress flags and shouting '*Jai Hind!*' invaded the building, stirred to action, it was rumoured, by Sarat Bose. They swarmed through the governor's quarters seizing everything from door handles to table ornaments as mementos. The police removed them only after several hours by throwing tear-gas canisters into the building. In the meantime, the outgoing governor and his family beat a hasty and ignominious retreat. As Arthur Dash recalled it, 'someone who recognised him jammed a Gandhi cap on his head and the last British Governor went out of Government House by a side door so crowned and with his wife waving the new Dominion (late Congress Party) flag. They were glad to get away.' Dash also noted that the governor's escape route was a stairway traditionally used by the low-caste sweepers who cleaned the building.[38] As the two new dominions were born, Gandhi and Suhrawardy fasted together and prayed for communal peace.[39] Years later the historian Tapan Raychaudhuri related that out in the district town of Barishal his father had kept awake throughout the night of 14 August with a gun in his hand. The disturbances he feared did not come that night, but they came soon enough.[40]

The Calcutta, Noakhali and Bihar killings had already begun the slow tide of migration across the borders of the new states. Sensing that the partition would strand them in hostile territory, hundreds of thousands more had begun to move in July and August. By 4 August

Mookherjee, the Hindu leader, was deprecating 'the mass evacuation of Hindus from the Pakistan zone'.[41] Independence and the disclosure of the Radcliffe award speeded the exchange of populations and the atrocities that accompanied it. Despite the best efforts of the Muslim League, Calcutta remained in India, so thousands of its Muslim population moved eastwards while Hindus began to stream westwards. Quite apart from the fact that many of them already had relatives and patrons in the west, the option of remaining in what Tyson called 'a rural slum' which, at one stroke of Radcliffe's pen, had been made a food deficit area did not appeal to them. The government of East Pakistan almost immediately started to beg for rice from neighbouring Arakan, but this seemed a fragile lifeline as the Burmese province was itself wracked by civil war.[42] One of the biggest problems was that the police and subordinate civil servants almost unanimously opted for the dominion where their co-religionists were in a majority because 'a Muslim who elects to serve in West Bengal tends to be looked on, at the moment, as a traitor to his religion and community', and vice versa. Poorer people threatened with minority status therefore felt that they would have no patrons who would protect their interests in the apparatus of the state and they too began to migrate. Though there was nothing on the scale of the events in the Punjab, minor communal incidents continued throughout the autumn, climaxing in late October and November as Hindus celebrated Durga Puja, the festival of Bengal's patron deity, and Muslims began their own more sombre celebration of Mohurrum. At this time tension was especially high in Dacca and Chittagong, the latter the division in which Noakhali and Tippera were situated. In Dacca religious animal sacrifice by Hindus was banned for the first time, at least in public. This was a sensible measure but it made the minority community fear for its future and only speeded the exodus. The new prime ministers of West Bengal and East Pakistan, P. C. Ghosh and Khwaja Nizamuddin, respectively, tried to stem the flow with speeches and tours across both territories. Ghosh pronounced the flight of upper-class Hindus from Pakistan 'a betrayal of the interests of poorer people'. Speaking in Comila, a district town in East Pakistan, he revealed that Muslims in Calcutta had come to him vowing to end the annual sacrifice of cows, which was deeply offensive to the Hindus, in order to ease the situation: 'I dissuaded them from doing so', he recalled, 'as I did not want the Muslims to live their lives as cowards nor do I want the Hindus in East Bengal to behave as cowards.'[43] But politicians had acted too little and too late. Rumours, especially of the abduction and rape of women, proved just as deadly as the sporadic burnings. Neighbours turned to killers. One old villager mused: 'We were under British rule for 200 years. Will Muslims prove more foreign than the British?' Arthur Dash served in East Pakistan for several months after partition. He remembered the strange world of Dacca, the new capital choked with refugees, lacking basic commodities, its schools crippled by the loss of their Hindu staff. He grew almost accustomed to the cycle of revenge killings: 'One day, for instance, you would find on your morning walk on the golf course the body of an old woman stabbed to death, lying near the sixth green. Or you are held up in your car at Nawabganj level crossing at 8am ... Just before you arrive 28 Hindu passengers had their throats cut by a gang of Muslims who had passed along the whole length of the train.'[44] Even those who tried to stay eventually lost heart and hundreds of thousands of migrants crossed the borders again in 1948, 1950–51 and 1973.

In 1946 the poet Samar Sen wrote, in Bengali:

> In Bengal, Bihar, Garmukteshwar,
> People go to the graveyard or burning ghat
> With limbless corpses on shoulders.
> Perhaps death brings amity:
> Everyone is equal after death –
> Bihar's Hindu and Noakhali's Muslim
> Noakhali's Hindu and Bihar's Muslim.[45]

TRAGEDY IN RANGOON

Burma too was poised on a knife edge. The alarming events in India weighed on the minds of Burmese politicians who had always felt a sense of inferiority as junior partners to Indians in the British Empire. Given the bull-headedness of much of the Karen leadership and the long history of frontier areas' autonomy, they feared a series of mini-partitions in their own country. There was even greater mistrust of British intentions than there was among Indian leaders. It was not entirely unjustified. The British were unable to throw off their patronizing attitude to the Burmese. Attlee wrote to Nehru: 'I like Aung San and his colleagues very much, but of course they don't have the same resources of experienced personnel as you have in India.'[46] Attlee had decided the British must leave the country, but he was concerned that the Burmese should stay in the Commonwealth and be firmly tied to Britain by defence and trade agreements. As it turned out, Burma did leave the Commonwealth, but resigned itself to commercial and defence links for some years further. The early bitterly cold weeks of January 1947 in London witnessed the denouement of the long struggle.

It had been mid December 1946 before the AFPFL accepted the invitation to attend talks on Burmese independence in London. The delegation the party sent was supposed to represent all shades of opinion but it was almost inevitably biased towards the AFPFL, now purged of communists, which dominated the governor's executive council. Aung San was there – the British government insisted on this – but so too was Tin Tut, nominally an independent, as he was the only financial expert in Burmese politics. U Saw also went, along with representatives of other small nationalist parties. Many on both the right and left of Burma's politics expected the talks to fail and the country to be plunged into full-scale civil disobedience or armed revolt in the new year of 1947. Aung San flew on ahead of the delegation to meet Indian leaders and stayed at Nehru's house in Delhi between 2 and 6 January. Nehru and Aung San had struck up a friendship when the RAF 'reds' had flown the Indian leader into Rangoon on his way to meet Mountbatten. Nehru eulogized Aung San to the Indian press. Wavell, now in his final weeks as viceroy, invited him to lunch. He was less complimentary: 'He struck me as a suspicious, ignorant but determined little tough.'[47] This underestimated Aung San's growing political sophistication. Passing through Karachi, he had arranged to meet Jinnah. Whatever deal the Muslim League leader managed to wring from independence, a large Muslim majority population would abut the northern frontier of Burma in Arakan. But when he arrived at Karachi airport, Aung San was faced with a diplomatic dilemma. Members of the Congress had arrived in a separate car from the Muslim League leaders and they both tried to whisk him off to their respective accommodations. In a Solomonic gesture, Aung San put his staff in the Congress car with half his luggage and went himself in the League car to find a neutral hotel in which to stay.[48] Aung San's speeches during his stay in India also reflected a dawning consciousness of the outside world. He remained suspicious of British intentions, replying in a non-committal way to Indian journalists' questions about whether he would resort to non-violent or armed rebellion should the London talks fail. He also alluded to the contemporary situation in Indo-China, where Ho Chi Minh's Vietnamese republic was fighting for its life against French reaction.[49] European imperialism was far from dead and this informed Aung San's demeanour at the London meetings. It was not that the Indians and Burmese saw eye to eye on everything. The end of the war had revived the Burmese fear of being 'swarmed' by Indian immigrants, as one of their delegates later put it. At his press conference, Aung San declared that 'Indian vested interests – like any vested interests – are not in favour of independence.'[50] This might easily have soured relations but for the fact that Nehru took an almost equally jaundiced view of Indian business interests and ignored the widespread clamour from those who wanted untrammelled entry to Burma again.

Before Aung San left for London, Nehru performed one final service for his Burmese friend. Despite his growing knowledge of the world, Aung San was unable to dress the part. The only clothes he had brought with him were a longyi and an old and dirty military uniform. Nehru had a new uniform properly tailored for him and it was in this that he appeared in London's January cold. Not all India's leaders were as indulgent to Aung San's bucolic ways. In Delhi the Burmese delegation also met Krishna Menon, Nehru's special foreign relations adviser and effectively now India's foreign minister, a suave left-wing negotiator with long years of political experience in Britain. The uneasy relationship of tutelage and resentment between Burmese and Indian nationalism was played out at a personal level. Kyaw Nyein, another delegate, remembered that Aung San met Krishna Menon again when they were both in London. The youthful Aung San, 'lazy as ever', had received the austere Indian intellectual stretched out on his hotel bed. Menon asked Kyaw Nyein in confidence whether Aung San could possibly be as influential as he was made out to be. He evidently felt he had been snubbed by meeting the Bogyoke prostrate in a bedroom. Kyaw Nyein mused: 'Aung San never thought about it; but he wouldn't think of meeting an Englishman in that way.'[51]

The cabinet papers record only the dry bones of the discussions.[52] But Kyaw Nyein kept a private record of the proceedings. He confirmed that Attlee and, to a lesser extent, Cripps were responsible for the sea change that had overtaken British attitudes the previous autumn. Apparently Pethick-Lawrence and William Hare, Lord Listowel, who was now in charge of Burma affairs, had been obsessed with events surrounding the Cabinet Mission to India and its consequences. Even Cripps was focused on Wavell's problems. Attlee, however, had carefully read the despatches and had come to the conclusion that no one was really in charge in Burma and that armed rebellion was only weeks away. Effectively he had taken over as secretary of state for Burma from the relatively inexperienced Listowel. During the actual meetings, however, Attlee just sat and listened, doodling on his notepad.[53] Cripps, as was his wont, did all the talking and Listowel begged off the meetings altogether in order to attend to grander Indian affairs. On the Burmese side it was Tin Tut, naturally, who did the real negotiating. Tin Tut had known Cripps since 1941, when the latter had stayed with him in Rangoon while on his way to meet Chiang Kai Shek in Chungking.

The critical point in the negotiations, according to Kyaw Nyein, was not so much British commercial interests in Burma as the status of the hill areas. At one point Cripps glanced up at the map. He said that if you looked at the hill peoples, Burma seemed to be surrounded by a scythe.[54] It was no use getting independence unless these territories and peoples were firmly welded to the new state. With these few words Cripps conceded to Buddhist Burma what three generations of British officials, commercial agents and missionaries had sought to deny it – control over the ethnic minorities. As with the Indian princes, though not the Indian Muslims, the British simply abandoned their long-term clients in the face of political reality. Ministers had already tacitly agreed that whatever clever jigsaw work might be done, nothing like a Karen state was really viable. A weak and fissiparous Burma would be dangerously exposed to Chinese incursions from the north and even to communal instability in neighbouring India. The incorporation of the hill areas and minorities would be a tricky problem, however. Both sides agreed that there should be a conference with their leaders at the hill town of Panglong once the delegation returned to Burma. The question of British participation in this remained unresolved. Aung San was deeply suspicious of the British Frontier Service officers and Tom Driberg increased his alarm by saying that even one British government representative at Panglong might encourage the more recalcitrant *sawbwas* or minority tribal leaders to hold out for too much.

Economic disagreements were significant, too, even though they seemed less pressing than the security issues. The AFPFL wanted a full-blown nationalization plan as any compromise on this might hand the communists a propaganda victory. The British cabinet wanted enterprises such as Burmah Oil to remain private. Apart from the question of profits, ministers noted that Burmah Oil was currently dependent on another British company, the Anglo-Iranian Oil Company, for marketing and distribution. The last thing anyone needed that bitter winter in a shivering and malnourished Britain and Europe was an interruption of fuel supplies.[55] Nationalization was to remain a contentious issue between the British and the Burmese for several years.

The London negotiations were a last-ditch effort and their success hung by a thread. The AFPFL was raring to go over to full non-cooperation, a general strike or even civil rebellion. Aung San had set a date of 31 January for nationwide strikes if the AFPFL had not by then been accepted as a national government. The communists, for their part, would immediately try to turn a wave of strikes into a rebellion. As British ministers contemplated acquiescence in Aung San's demands, a string of more and more alarming intelligence reports warned them of imminent trouble.[56] A British military appreciation reported widespread labour unrest and the dislocation of the administration 'affecting police and Burman elements of the services which must lead to armed conflict with which we are incapable of coping'. The Burmans were still more or less favourably disposed to the British population in Burma: 'There is just time to retain their friendship if we give up gracefully now – repeat, now.'[57] Local communist insurgency picked up ominously early in the New Year. On 16 January AFPFL, militia groups and communist supporters drove around Rangoon in lorries telling the British to 'get out'. They even did a victory lap through Burma Army headquarters. Rumours circulated that Chinese communists were dropping arms to the local reds. On 21 January, red-flag communists attacked the secretariat, hoping for a replay of events in Saigon. They were repelled by British and Burmese soldiers using fists and rifle butts.[58]

The Shan and Kachin frontier areas and the Karens of the plains were equally restive. British officers remained a problem here. Noel Stevenson, long-time advocate of the minorities, privately spoke of the British government's 'betrayal' of them. He seems to have been urging the Karen Democratic Union to adopt a tougher stand. So troublesome did he become that Rance wrote to Sir Gilbert Laithwaite, the civil service expert on Burma, that he was 'very disturbed at Stevenson's tactics during the past few weeks. Some of his telegrams to the Frontier Areas Administration are on the verge of disloyalty.' He was 'almost a fanatic where the frontier areas are concerned'.[59] Stevenson had apparently disparaged a Buddhist monk and a Burman district commissioner in the course of talks about the future of the frontier areas, rekindling the old AFPFL suspicion of British divide-and-rule tactics. Thakin Nu even complained to Rance that the British were dropping arms to the Karens as a preliminary to a full-scale revolt, a rumour that Rance had explicitly to deny.[60]

Then, on 27 January, the British government announced the successful conclusion of the negotiations for Burmese independence. A smiling Aung San, accompanied by Attlee and Tin Tut, emerged onto the steps of 10 Downing Street to speak to the world's press. Burma would be independent in January 1948.[61] New elections would be held. Arrangements for the frontier areas, the minorities and the future of British business in Burma were settled to the satisfaction of both sides. The British still hoped secretly that the AFPFL could be persuaded to stay in the Commonwealth but the issue was shelved in order to maintain the optimistic atmosphere. Aung San knew better. The night before he returned to Burma he had met Tom Driberg one last time. Driberg thought him depressed and full of foreboding, despite his public face of rejoicing. It would be best for Burma to stay in the Commonwealth, Aung San said, but he could not persuade his people.[62] A few days later at a press conference in Rangoon, Aung San announced that full elections would be held in the near future leading to the creation of an interim government. It would have the powers of a dominion government such as in Australia or Canada. He made sure to mention that the situation was exactly the same as it was in India, except that Burma did not have a minority problem like that of the Indian Muslims.[63] This must have given him great satisfaction, even if it was tinged with apprehension.

Aung San's first steps as a virtually independent political leader were remarkably sure, despite the massive problems the country faced. It is this, as much as his military exploits, which has kept his reputation high after his death. In the first place the leftist elements still within the AFPFL were less than enthusiastic about the London agreement and the communists were implacably opposed to it. Kyaw Nyein remembered acrimonious arguments in which communists asked each other: 'Why must you be afraid of Aung San? [Our] party has authority and leadership in the countryside and must assert its power over Aung San ... We want a Dictatorship of the Proletariat and not Parliamentary Socialism.'[64]

Even before he left for London Aung San had been talking of a Burma which would be 'a federation of all the races and the frontier areas'. He spoke of local governments in minority areas with their own financial independence and he was generally much more conciliatory on these issues than were the languishing parties of the right. He seems to have understood instinctively that serious civil strife was only months away unless he worked hard to keep the minorities on board. Apart from his great personal prestige, Aung San was a critical element in these negotiations because he had old links with the minorities, the Karens in particular. Not all Karens had identified with the British cause and some of their leaders in the Irrawaddy delta had come to meet Aung San in 1943 in the hope of reaching an accommodation and putting behind them the massacres of 1942. A Karen unit had fought in the old Burma Defence Army and further negotiations had taken place in 1945 at the time of its revolt against the Japanese.

Shortly before his trip to London Aung San had visited the pretty Karen Christian village of Kappali, where the Bishop of Rangoon had once lived, and soon after his return he visited the Shan states.[65] Indeed, Aung San was more prepared than most Burmese leaders to accept the cultural and political differences upon which the minorities insisted. He was not a particularly fervent Buddhist and he seems to have been genuinely concerned that the hill peoples got a democratic form of government. He was prepared to concede a large degree of autonomy to them, provided figures such as the *sawbwas* and tribal headmen were removed from the scene. In one of his speeches just after the war, Aung San recalled that a Karen soldier had once told him that the Karens and the Burmese were exactly the same under the skin. The only difference was that the Burmese preferred to play cards during their periods of leave, while the Karens would go off on fishing expeditions.

The Karen lobbyists who had caused a stir in London the previous autumn were firmly of the belief that the British government would help them to form some kind of Karen state before it finally abandoned responsibility for Burma. They were disappointed. Not only had the frontier areas' administration gradually declined in political clout after the ousting of Dorman-Smith, but the Labour government had also decided that it would make no further special representations on the part of the minorities. They had been badly shaken by the communal rioting and massacres in India the previous year and by the realization that the Punjab remained a tinderbox of Hindu–Muslim tension. Throughout the empire the idea of 'special representation' was being quietly abandoned, for the time at least. Even among Karen radicals the future remained unclear. For some time there had been talk of a country called Kawthulay, a kind of Karenistan. Yet even the most geographically challenged Karen enthusiast must have been aware that this entity, if it had ever existed, would have made the future Pakistan look a positively rational political unit. The delta Karen were scattered widely and were in a majority in only one district. Others lived some distance to the south in Tenasserim. Their distant cousins in the hilly Karenni states to the east were few in number and had had relatively little contact with the modern world.

In February Aung San and British officials convened the promised minorities conference at the hill town of Panglong high up in the northern Shan states. Leaders of the minority peoples met the AFPFL high command. One British representative was Arthur Bottomley, a Labour politician who had been part of an earlier parliamentary delegation to India.[66] Aung San met him before the conference and made it clear once again how heavily the long shadow of India lay upon these events. Burmese politicians were concerned that, now that a partition of India was a virtual certainty, the British would try something similar in Burma. Bottomley tried to persuade them that the situation on the subcontinent was quite different. The British, he said, did not want partition. It was being forced on them by the intransigence of the Muslim League and the Congress.

Inevitably, Tin Tut was at Panglong, too. As Burma's only consti-tutional and financial Mr Fixit, his forte was juggling the new consti-tution. In London he had already solicited the help of Sir Eric Machtig, a constitutional expert at the Dominions Office, in drawing up a plan for the representation of minorities in the new assembly.[67] The two men got on well. Tin Tut, once at Dulwich College, had been an old sporting rival of Machtig, who had been at St Paul's School.

The haggling at the conference was fierce. For instance, could the Kachin tribes who had always been in Burma proper, now called ministerial Burma, have the same rights as the Shan and the Chin or the Kokang Chinese way up on the northern border? When did local autonomy become virtual independence? How far could a future Burmese government in Rangoon accept this sort of autonomy when ominous clashes were already occurring beyond those borders, where Chinese nationalists and communists, Indian Hindus and Muslims, Vietnamese communists and the French were beginning to square up to each other? Superficially, a degree of agreement was reached. This was an easier matter on the northern and eastern frontiers. The Chin, Kachin and Shan wanted 'roads and schools', as one delegate said baldly. They had at least a little hope of obtaining funds for develop-ment if they stayed in some kind of united Burma after the British left. Besides, the frontier rulers were keeping a wary eye on the Chinese armies whose leaders claimed that these territories were part of their patrimony. The problem was more complex in the case of the Karens living deep in Burma, who feared for their autonomy, religion and way of life once the British had left. Whereas the representatives of the frontier areas cautiously agreed to join a new Union of Burma, the Karen majority remained unconvinced. The newly formed Karen National Union boycotted the elections to the new assembly. A delegation of its leaders waited on Rance on 25 February to tell him of the 'restiveness' of their people, arguing that the AFPFL had not offered enough. Their talk of autonomy was too vague.[68]

Aung San carefully avoided exacerbating the situation.[69] He did not denounce the Karen National Union for its boycott, merely regretted it. During the months after the Panglong meeting, he did his best to show that minority interests would be constitutionally safeguarded in an independent Burma and that the Karens in particular would have virtual autonomy within a unified country.[70] Although he had been doubtful about its wisdom, he agreed to the constitution of a Frontier Areas Commission of Enquiry, which was joined by Arthur Bottomley and J. L. Leyden, one of the less partisan of the frontier officers. The commission made recommendations about the number of seats to be reserved for these tracts in the new assembly.[71] When the report was published Thakin Nu, who had long been suspicious of its operations, signalled his approval, conceding, in his homespun way, that 'the proof of the pudding was in the eating'. Another sign of Aung San's good faith on this matter was the AFPFL's statement in May that Buddhism would not become the official faith of the new Burma. Aung San even made some disparaging remarks about political monks to keep the air sweet. This was a risky strategy as some senior figures, notably Nu, felt that the president of the new republic should automatically be a Buddhist. Certainly the priesthood had expected that Buddhism would be made the state religion.[72] Rance reported to the Burma Office that he was worried by a possible Buddhist backlash.[73] But he conceded that Aung San was 'doing everything possible to improve relations between the Burmese and people of the frontier areas, particularly the Karens'.[74] Before independence, at least, the gulf between minority leaders and the AFPFL had not become unbridgeable.

DISASTER APPROACHES

The British and the AFPFL continued to confront a situation of extreme delicacy. Communist insurgency and a fresh wave of strikes might result from the slightest hint that there were any conditions attached to the January agreement or that British business was manoeuvring behind the scenes. The country was armed to the teeth and very jumpy. Rance moved from town to town, trying to calm the situation. He had spoken at the largely Burmese Orient Club in December 1946, claiming that the country was returning to normal. In February he made an upbeat speech at the Rangoon Chamber of Commerce. The January agreement, he said, 'brings to an end the struggle of the Burmese people in their passionate and natural desire for freedom'.[75] He made an appearance at the convention of the Burmese Union of Stage and Screen and the Burmese arts and crafts exhibition, where he praised the emerging local film companies and the revival of handicrafts such as lacquer ware and basket weaving. He gave Burmese national feeling another fillip when he attended a ceremony marking the affiliation of the Burmese Olympic Committee to the international body on 8 July.

Yet, under the surface, deadly hatreds were feeding on the corruption that had spread with the military administration and the return of the old politicians. Guns were everywhere and a lot of them were not in British hands. British troops continued to return home. So did the Indians. As late as September 1947 there were still 10,000 Indian troops in Burma, but the agreement on the partition of India in April had made their withdrawal inevitable and underlined the fact that those who stayed on could not really be used in any offensive action. There were only a few thousand British troops left. Even the Japanese who had been uncomplaining cannon fodder were on the move. In February 1947 the final 35,000 POWs began to return to Japan, though it took four months to despatch them all. The British and Burmese fought one final campaign together in March. This was Operation Flush, which was designed to dislodge the 'dacoit dictatorship' in Toungoo and Yamethin districts in the heart of Burma. Gangs of bandits had been attacking trains and there was some suspicion that renegade Japanese soldiers or radical red-flag communists were training them. Led by Brigadier Charles Jerrard and Colonel Ne Win, the nationalist and future dictator, a mixed force of British, Gurkha and Burmese troops attacked the bandit strongholds.[76] This campaign was successful, but it also underlined the fragility of the post-war situation. In a very real sense order had never been re-established over much of the country: barely a year later a virtual civil war would be unrolling across these very districts. Shortly after the end of Operation Flush, the British handed over effective control of the Burma Army to the Burmese command.

Equally difficult was the situation on the frontiers. Many Burmese were convinced that British interests were playing dirty tricks among the Shan and Kachin by trying to undermine the accord which Aung San had brokered between the minorities and the future Union of Burma. While this was not official policy, the evidence suggests that some British personnel were continuing to meddle in the politics of the minorities. Meanwhile, in Arakan a communist separatist movement, led by U Seinda, was spreading vigorously.[77] A further cause for concern on Burma's borders was the continuing influx of 'unauthorized' persons into the country. These were former Indian residents who had fled in 1942 or after and were now returning to claim their property. In June the interim Burmese government rushed through an emergency immigration bill to stop the influx, claiming that it was only a temporary measure while Burma was rebuilding its shattered infrastructure. Opinion in India was not impressed and a government spokesman said that the act would fall hard on the 300,000 refugees from Burma still resident in India. Nehru had always accepted that the Burmese did not want the return of powerful Indian capitalists to their country, but ordinary refugees were a different matter. A rather tetchy relationship developed between the two countries as India edged towards independence and partition.

Aung San regularly addressed mass rallies in central Rangoon. His speeches, punctuated by wild cheering, rambled on genially about the need for national unity, the value of statistics, the wisdom of Lenin and various thinly disguised Buddhist themes concerning the baseness of luxury, and so on. On 11 June the new constituent assembly elected that spring was inaugurated. The AFPFL delegates marched down the aisle followed by colourfully dressed tribal representatives from the frontier areas.[78] Gandhi sent a message promising friendship with Burma and reminding the Burmese that the Buddha was an Indian. The city's populace was entertained with Hollywood films, now much more popular than those contemporary British productions in which moustachioed men in trilby hats addressed each other in clipped tones. Rangoon's city hall hosted an All-Burma beauty contest presided over by Aung San's wife.[79] The competition was intended to demonstrate the fitness of the body politic. The finalists were 'young, but they possess firm, neat little figures', drooled the New Times of Burma correspondent. Despite all this, politics in Rangoon and Mandalay was turning more vicious. In May Tin Tut sued the Burmese daily Bamakhit for defaming him.[80] The newspaper accused the former ICS man of getting his brother appointed as an additional judge of the High Court and using his patronage as chancellor of Rangoon University to distribute jobs to his relatives: 'one rotten fish' could undo all the good work of Aung San's government, the newspaper wrote. It was perhaps no coincidence that within a month the editor of Bamakhit had been called on to furnish security to the police that he would not print articles subversive of public order. To compound its offence against Tin Tut, the newspaper had printed stories such as 'A true red flag sheds his blood freely for the country'. A communist patriot, the paper averred, would proclaim, 'Kill me boldly in the presence of the dumb masses.'[81]

Ironically, the event that began the unravelling of Burma's politics came from within the old establishment and not from the myriad of dacoits, communists or separatists in the countryside. On 16 July 1947, three days before the most fateful date in Burma's modern history, Rance was picking up some alarming signals. The governor telegraphed London that a false demand note had led to the issue of 200 Bren guns to 'persons unknown' from the Base Ordnance Depot of Burma Command three weeks before.[82] At about the same time 100,000 rounds of small-arms ammunition and 25,000 rounds of Sten-gun ammunition had 'gone missing'. This had altered the balance of power in the capital and Aung San was so worried that he had called a tribunal to investigate the continuing leaks. Nu said that some young hotheads had concluded that the British were conniving in this leakage to strengthen the power of the opposition and put in power people who would accept dominion status.[83] The newspapers were full of rumours of nocturnal meetings and bodies of men moving around the city and surrounding villages.

The monsoon of 1947 had been particularly heavy in Rangoon. Pools of filthy water filled the streets of the dilapidated city. The third week of July was particularly unpleasant. Khin Myo Chit, the intellectual who wrote a vivid memoir of the Japanese occupation, remembered that

rain slashed mercilessly as the winds groaned and roared, and for a full week we scarcely saw the sun. The thick shroud of rain and clouds lay on us as if never to be lifted. The 19 July 1947 was a day we shall not easily forget. The rainstorm raged more fiercely on this day and the skies were darker. The terrible aspect of all nature seemed to be in keeping with the calamity which shook the whole nation.[84]

That wet morning Rance was working in Government House, expecting a report later in the day on the executive council debate that was going on some miles away in the Secretariat building. An ADC suddenly burst in to say that there had been an armed attack on Aung San and the council. Within a few minutes it was confirmed that Aung San and five members of the council had been killed. It seemed that independent Burma might die in the womb. Soon the stunning news burst on a bright summer morning at the Burma Office in Whitehall. In London it was only 8.40 a.m. when a top-secret telegraph message from Rangoon arrived: 'Attack on Executive Council in session 10.30 by three Burmans armed with Sten guns; 5 killed; Aung San wounded through chest.'[85] This was rapidly followed by another: 'A jeep with 12 Army markings – 5 men armed with Sten guns and rifles. PVO tried to stop them and was shot – he says they were men 4 Burma Rifles – sprayed Council with bullets.'[86] Aung San had actually died almost immediately after the attack. Ironically, one reason the assassins had been so effective was Burmese pride in their new army. British NCOs seconded to the Burma Army had been on guard until a couple of days earlier. But they had been replaced by PVO personnel recently recruited into the force. The assassins simply pushed past these inexperienced guards and crashed into the council chamber.

By now all Burma knew that Aung San, their hero and liberator, was dead. The city was paralysed with grief. Khin Myo Chit wrote: 'Everywhere in the city, on buses, trains and in the market places I saw men's eyes wet and women sobbing as if their hearts would break. I saw young soldiers in bedraggled uniforms standing at the foot of Bogyoke Aung San's bier, tears streaming down their faces, which they wiped with their torn, dirty caps.'[87] As the day wore on and new messages arrived in Government House and in London, the immediate sense of panic receded a little. Soon, 'the assassinated bodies, embalmed, lay in glass cases in Jubilee Hall', the meeting place where Tommy Trinder, the British comic singer, had sung to the troops, the Rangoon Theatre Club had played and British generals had addressed their officers.[88]

The British saw only confusion ahead. An official wrote to Sir Gilbert Laithwaite at the Burma Office: 'Where we go from here I don't know, or who is going to come out on top – Thakin Nu, U Saw or the Communists.'[89] Rance understood that he had to move quickly to fill the gap left by Aung San, difficult as that was. Luckily, one plausible candidate, Thakin Nu, had not been in the council chamber. The governor persuaded Nu to take on the job and he was rapidly sworn in as acting prime minister. Nu was about the only person acceptable to both the British and most of the nationalist parties. As a kind of Buddhist socialist he seemed moderate to the British compared with most AFPFL leaders and the communists. Yet the latter knew that his instinct was for fairly radical land reform and the nationalization of 'vested interests'.

Nu was a complex character. Before the war he had found it difficult to reconcile his easy, outgoing personality and sociability with the dictates of the stern Buddhism that he followed. Experience of the Japanese invasion and the fighting had heightened his religious beliefs. Although he played a part in the early organization of the AFPFL, he had soon retired to a country town to write. It was only with the greatest difficulty that Aung San had persuaded him to stand for election to the constituent assembly in the spring. Now Rance had to twist his arm even more vigorously to get him to take on the role of prime minister. He agreed to serve until independence, scheduled for January 1948, though most people clearly expected him to carry on longer. Nu quickly began to show his best asset: his capacity for conciliation. He broadcast to the nation: 'My best friend and comrade has fallen. His mantle has fallen on my shoulders.'[90] Nu gathered what remained of the nationalist leadership around him. He also recruited a young journalist and nationalist, U Thant, to act as his press adviser and personal confidant. More practical than Nu, Thant became a power behind the scenes in AFPFL politics over the next few years. Later he became a diplomat and ended his career as UN secretary general.[91]

Nu tried to coax the communists, especially his old comrade Than Tun, back into the nationalist coalition government. But this was not to be. The communists were too sure events were moving in their direction, while the AFPFL demanded that the Communist Party of Burma was dissolved before any such merger could take place. Five months before the Burmese regained their independence the troubles that would nearly destroy the young republic were clearly visible on the horizon. The minority issue and the tussle with communism were both put on hold rather than solved.

In the meantime it was essential that the British and the nationalists discover the assassins of Aung San and his colleagues. Though there was evidence that the red-flag communists had some inkling that a plot was in the air, the attack did not seem to be the signal for a leftist insurrection. By the late afternoon of the fateful day Government House in Rangoon was fairly sure that Than Tun's communists were not involved. Nu was certain that Soe's communists were also innocent. Suspicion turned quickly from the left to the right wing of Burmese politics, in particular to the former prime minister and wartime detainee, U Saw. Intelligence reports at the end of June had uncovered a good deal of night-time comings and goings around his house by 'men in singlets'.[92] On the afternoon of the assassination, British Special Branch raided his house and detained him and ten others. The police quickly discovered eighteen rifles and a Sten gun concealed in the house. Suspicion also fell on a jeep in the compound which carried no number plate. Later, when they drained an ornamental lake on the property, the police found thirty-seven complete Bren guns, fifty-nine spare barrels and eight revolvers. In another house connected with Saw's party members a further forty-four hand grenades and forty-nine detonators came to light.[93] The British had been spying on Saw for some time. One night they had seen a party in a boat on the lake. But nothing was done on this occasion because Saw had been well dressed and it was assumed that this was simply one of his evening assignations with young women. Saw and illicit arms had a long history. His Galon private army had been suspected of stockpiling arms even before the war. There was also much evidence of a growing vendetta between him and Aung San as Saw tried to re-establish himself in Burmese politics. Saw blamed Aung San for the near-fatal attack on his car he had suffered the previous September.

As suspicions about Saw grew, Rance and Whitehall had to contemplate an embarrassing possibility. A British army major commanding the ammunition depot had been observed making visits to Saw's residence over the previous month.[94] The officer commanding informed the governor that the 'previous history of this officer is unsatisfactory both as a non-commissioned officer in Burma before the war and in India during the war'. Once the possibility of any form of British involvement in the assassinations emerged, the Rangoon rumour mill went into overdrive. Spread by word of mouth to every village in the country, the accusation that the British had armed the opposition parties against the AFPFL became an article of faith. There was even a rumour that the governor had interviewed Saw and Ba Maw in an attempt to form a new government that would keep Burma in the Empire. Even today many elderly nationalists and their supporters believe that the British government connived in the murder of Aung San. Kyaw Nyein, the veteran independence fighter who had joined the delegation to London in January, was quite certain about this when he was interviewed by the historian Robert Taylor in the 1970s. Attlee, he said, had personally known about and approved of the plot against Aung San. It was an act of personal vengeance, Kyaw Nyein insisted. At the conference in London, Aung San had given Attlee his word that, in return for an immediate commitment to independence, Aung San would keep Burma in the Commonwealth. Aung San had broken his word and had thus called into question Attlee's 'personal role in history'. He had to die. But, he added, the nationalists had decided not to reveal their evidence because they feared it would delay independence.[95] While even Nu was hard pressed to believe this convoluted story, there is much circumstantial evidence to tie corrupt or rogue elements in the British armed forces and Force 136 to the plot. Privately, several British observers were unsurprised at the alleged involvement of their countrymen in graft and murder: 'After what some of our own people did during the war in the way of lining their own pockets at the expense of the lives and safety of their own kith and kin, I am prepared to believe almost anything of our race,' said one.[96] The accusation that Dorman-Smith in London knew of the plot seems implausible, but it is not entirely beyond the bounds of possibility.

Over the next week the situation remained desperately tense. Rance got little sleep. The Communist Party of Burma (the 'white flag' group) had picked up an off-the-cuff remark by Tom Driberg that the Conservatives in Britain were backing U Saw and made it an issue. Almost as vexing to the governor was the problem of what to feed that austere vegetarian Stafford Cripps during his projected visit to Burma: 'Please don't forget to let me know what can and cannot be eaten,' he pleaded with the Burma Office.[97] Laithwaite replied promptly with a list of suggestions. 'I hope this gives enough low-down on this vital subject,' he wrote, although 'I find it difficult to gauge how great the reluctance is to eat eggs.'[98] Nu did his best to calm the situation on the more important issues. He called a press conference to urge editors not to spread rumours that might 'rouse the masses'. But he also complained that not enough information was coming from the British army about who precisely was involved in the arms 'losses'. Nu's position was extremely difficult. His relations with Rance were much closer than Aung San's had been. Any direct charge by the AFPFL leadership that the British had been involved in the assassination would have compromised his own position at a time when Soe's communists were on the point of rebellion. The British had to be seen to be doing something. They arrested one Captain Vivian, an associate of U Saw, who had run a trucking business with him.[99] He had recently been seconded to the civil police as an arms adviser in the police supply department, a position that lent itself to lucrative illicit dealings. Later Captain Moore, the commandant of the Base Ordnance Depot, was also put under arrest. Moore was a drinking companion of Saw. The police already had on record a statement from Moore that Saw had told him when drunk that he had enough arms for a private army hidden in his lake. Another British officer closely associated with Saw was Major Daine, who had been seen at the house dressed in a white shirt, blue longyi and gold embroidered chappals or Indian slippers.[100] He and Saw had a mutual interest in ballistics. Daine testified that Saw was armed to the teeth and was expecting another five lorry loads of weapons from someone who seemed to be a British officer. This testimony was so embarrassing that Rance tried to have it hushed up. But it was not only the army that fell under suspicion. Kyaw Nyein, the home member and strong socialist who later indicted Attlee, said that European business firms had been secretly financing Saw in the hope of promoting a non-socialist government that would leave their interests unaffected.[101] Some credence was given to this because Mr Bingley of the British Council had apparently been in conversation with Saw about his attitude towards British firms.

The rumours created intense suspicion between the British and Nu's new government, but in the short run both parties had an interest in maintaining a smooth momentum towards independence. General Briggs, the local British commander, made a point of personally placing a wreath on Aung San's coffin. The *Burma Star*, the forces newspaper, formally denied any official British involvement in the plot. The *New Times of Burma* pointedly published a photograph of Briggs at the funeral ceremony separated by just a few column inches from a piece which denounced people spreading wild rumours, meaning those who were blaming the British government.[102] Crucially, the British were able to prove that the weapons and ammunition used in the murders were not those stolen from the Base Ordnance Depot.[103] Meanwhile, the police investigation was making some headway. A number of members of Saw's household had been forced to testify against him. Several of the assassins were supposedly identified and one was conveniently shot dead trying to escape from a police jeep which was conveying him to Rangoon.[104] The plan was evidently to concentrate minds on Saw and not to try to unravel the rest of the conspiracy for fear of where it might lead. On 24 September Saw's trial began; seventy-eight witnesses were to be examined. People in the street hooted and howled at him as he was transported to court.[105] Throughout he expected to be bailed out by his friends in Britain who included, he said, 'three ex-governors and many ex-ministers'. Dorman-Smith certainly intervened on behalf of the clever and likeable rogue who had so pleased him in 1941. But it was to no avail. Saw was sentenced to death by hanging, although the sentence was not carried out until after Burma's independence the following year. In a letter from his condemned cell to Bingley, the British Council man, he wrote: 'I took a grave risk, as advised.' On another occasion, he told his jailer that 'the governor was no use as he had already been bought by Aung San and Thakin Nu for 20 lakhs'.[106] This must have come as news to Rance, whose idea of the good life seems to have been a night out at a Gilbert and Sullivan operetta.

By mid August the vacuum left by the assassinations had been partially filled. The immediate attempt to bring the communists into government had failed. What was thought to be an auspicious day was chosen and the governor was called away from the golf course to swear in Nu and his colleagues. Rance could not find the oath of office, but luckily Tin Tut, a member of the new cabinet, had memorized it.[107] Giving up on the communists, Nu spent much of the next two months trying to assuage the Karens and other minority groups and to disarm the restive PVO bands. The task seemed all the more urgent as every day brought news of fresh massacres across northern India, where Hindus, Sikhs and Muslims were engaged in tit-for-tat killing. There was unfinished business to do with the British, too. The agreement at the start of the year between Aung San and Attlee had not tied up the loose ends of independence, especially on the financial side. The details were important especially because the communists were continuing to make political capital out of what they described as the 'rightist' AFPFL's compromise with the 'imperialists'. In September, therefore, Lord Listowel, secretary of state for Burma, visited Rangoon, while in October prime minister designate Nu flew to London for a final set of talks.[108]

Listowel's job was basically one of public relations. He took tea with Aung San's widow, Daw Khin Kyi, and her son and two-year-old daughter, Aung San Suu Kyi, and presented his condolences. He disavowed the neo-imperialist aims that the communists were imputing to the British. The hard negotiating was done by Nu and cabinet ministers in London. Nu found Attlee's government wrestling with a host of domestic industrial difficulties and worrying about the rise of communism in China and Southeast Asia. They were privately assailed by feelings of guilt about the bloodletting in India. The Conservatives were offering little support. Churchill was on the rampage about Labour's scuttling out of Burma. His father Randolph had been responsible for the conquest of the country in 1885–6; now he insulted and abused Attlee and Aung San in an 'outrageous speech' that did enormous damage in Burma, according to Gilbert Laithwaite.[109] Ministers were keen to maintain intact as many British financial interests in the country as possible. They also confirmed that a British services or military mission would remain in Burma after independence. This was ostensibly to train the Burmese army, but the real reason was that it would tie Burma, however loosely, into the Western anti-communist alliance. In September the international communist propaganda body, the Cominform, met in Poland. Andrei Zhdanov, its secretary, propounded a new militant line, calling for putsches against capitalist and imperialist governments.[110] The world was in arms again. As the year drew to an end the brief and imperfect peace after the Second World War was evaporating. In a few short months, the red armies had replaced the Axis armies as the mortal enemies of 'Western democracy'. The Cold War was about to begin, but in Asia it was to take the form of many small 'hot' wars.

On his return from London, Nu entered the Buddhist monastery at Myathabeik Hill for a brief 'religious recess', followed by a nine-day pilgrimage. He 'went to the pagodas around Keilatha Hill . . . where he practiced asceticism and is reputed to have encountered many yogis and ascetics'.[111] This was the region from which the medieval Burmese king, Anawratha, took monks when he founded the great temple city of Pagan. Nu himself went on to found a society for Buddhist meditation, aided by a group of conservative nationalist leaders and businessmen. The pilgrimage was intended to show that his agreement with Attlee was merely a technical diplomatic exercise. The real independence of Burma, Nu's actions implied, would occur when the country reconnected itself to its glorious past and recognized Buddhist contemplation and self-control as the central discipline of the new state. After his pilgrimage, he emerged into the full glare of communist hostility and anti-Western rhetoric.

Nu's opponents denounced the British services mission. They also attacked any plan to compensate the British firms that were to be nationalized on the grounds that they had exploited the Burmese people for generations. Than Tun, the communist leader, 'proud, bitter and jealous', began to plan for armed insurrection. The success of this revolution would depend on the play of interest and aspiration deep in the Burmese countryside. Here the importance of any ideology was profoundly constrained by poverty and poor education. As British rule drew to its close, not much seemed to have changed since 1886 when foreign invasion ended Burma's freedom. The peasantry was impoverished. The 'dacoit Po The' was 'ravaging, raping and murdering the inhabitants' of the district of Thayetmo.[112] From Mogaung, Balwant Singh, the district officer of Indian origin, remembered that about this time the new government decided to introduce elections for the post of village headman, previously an official appointment. This was all very well, but the practical difficulties were great. Headmanships were fine things for rich country people who could afford to spend time compiling statistics and going to see the district magistrate in return for local prestige, but most people did not have the time or resources. In many cases, the old headmen were voted back *faut de mieux*. Elsewhere, fierce factional disputes broke out between local notables. Balwant Singh remembered one case where the only suitable candidate was illiterate. He had to make out that the man was attending writing and reading classes in order to get him certified as eligible.[113]

Burma immediately after its independence seemed on the point of becoming the first of what are now called 'failed states'. Even when a kind of central control was re-established after 1952, the country rapidly became a 'failed democracy'. It never achieved India's relative stability or the early prosperity of Malaya. It remained almost as poor as East Pakistan (later Bangladesh) and the wars, civil disturbances and authoritarian rule that it suffered were even worse. The roots of the ethnic insurgencies that were to shake Burma in the years after independence lay far back in colonial history, when the British gave the minority peoples of the old Burmese Empire special administrative status and a relatively privileged position within British Burma. Yet this was not simply colonial divide-and-rule politics; many among the minority peoples never really saw themselves as part of Burma. The more immediate causes of the decline of the central state after 1948 lay in the events of the war and British reoccupation. The reconquering Allied forces had armed the Karen, the Kachin, the Chin and other minorities, but they had never really re-established control over the armed Burmese of the plains who had fought with Aung San but were excluded from the benefits of this second colonial occupation. The government, now trying to consolidate its power in Rangoon, was poverty stricken as a result of wartime damage and the collapse of Burma's once lucrative exports. Foreign firms still controlled many of the country's resources. The AFPFL leaders had neither cash nor goods with which to buy off the powerful men in the countryside. They were also split into ideological and personal factions. Very few of the newly independent countries of Asia and Africa after 1945 began their quest for stability and respect with so few advantages.

Meanwhile, Britain's Burmese days finally passed into history, marked by the usual concern with ceremonial. For some time Rance had fretted that there might be demonstrations as his governorship came to an end. He had in mind the unruly and embarrassing scenes in Government House at Calcutta.[114] Rance had little to fear. As he knew, the AFPFL membership was under tighter control than the Bengal Congress had been. In November the whole Burmese government and their wives were invited to Government House to celebrate Princess Elizabeth's marriage to the Duke of Edinburgh. Over the New Year holidays of 1947–8, the governor made his exit with decorum and a touch of bathos. He told members of the Orient Club that he would not fully realize that he was leaving 'until we see the Shwedagon disappearing as we proceed down the Rangoon river'.[115] On 4 January 1948, the day of Burma's independence, sailing far out beyond Kipling's 'old Moulmein pagoda', Hubert Rance crossed the Bay of Bengal and took ship onward from Colombo. Gilbert Laithwaite had managed to secure two tickets to a West End performance of *Annie Get Your Gun*. He presented these to the governor and his wife to celebrate their return to London.

8

1947: Malaya on the Brink

On the eve of Mountbatten's arrival in the Viceroy's House in New Delhi, at the other side of the city, in the old fort of Purana Qila, the new leaders of Asia were meeting for the first time. On 23 March 1947, standing beneath a huge illuminated map of the continent, Nehru opened the Asian Relations Conference. Those present would long remember his words: 'When the history of our present times comes to be written, this Conference may well stand out as the land-mark which divides the past of Asia from the future.' The idea for the gathering had come to Nehru during his visits to Malaya and Burma in March 1946. Although the coming of Swaraj was clouded with anxiety, Nehru and many other Indian leaders felt that they had brought Asia to the threshold of a new millennium. They believed that Congress was the exemplary nationalism for Asia and that India's civilization formed the core of what Rabindranath Tagore called the 'inner human bond' of its peoples. The Asian Relations Conference was a form of missionary outreach to other national struggles.[1] The Muslim League denounced Nehru as a 'Hindu imperialist' and boy-cotted the proceedings, but virtually every nation, or nation-of-intent, from the Levant to China was represented: there were delegations of Jews and Arabs from Palestine; commissars from Soviet central Asia; courtiers from the Kingdom of Thailand; hardened communist guer-rillas from Malaya, and polished Kuomintang diplomats. The greater number of delegates were from the lands of Britain's imperial crescent, and the official language of the meeting was English, but the largest individual contingents were from Southeast Asia. Few of the 200 delegates and 10,000 or so observers were known to each other. When Sutan Sjahrir flew in for the final days of the meeting, he apologized for the size of his retinue: Indonesians, he explained, had so few opportunities in the past to meet their fellow Asians. Sjahrir was met at the airport by his Dutch wife: such was the sum of his own years of isolation and exile that they had not seen each other since 1932. The visitors were entertained in the Viceroy's House with the full ceremonial of the Raj, but, in the words of one Irish observer, they 'felt they were witnessing the last departing gleams of its sunset splendour, not only in New Delhi, but throughout a continent'.[2]

Over the next few days the delegates surveyed their shared inheritance. Panels on social and cultural problems heard harrowing testimonies to the continuing issue of war. A session on 'economic development and social services' revealed that, from the left to the right, from Malayan communist to Indian businessman, the new generation of leaders saw a common future in planning and state intervention. But, paradoxically, it was the climactic forum on 'National Movements for Freedom' that proved to be the most divisive. The very cause that brought these men and women together – anti-colonialism – was now diminishing for some of them. In New Delhi there was no echo of the war cry of 'Asia for the Asiatics': the memory of Japanese rule was too immediate and traumatic, and leaders of new nations could ill afford to alienate the West. The crucial question of how 'free Asia' should aid nations 'struggling to be free' was left unresolved. The spiritual support offered by Nehru was far less than was sought by the Vietnamese and Indonesians. The closing session was addressed by Gandhi, who arrived following a tour of Bihar and Bengal, where he was trying to stem the tide of communal violence. 'He looked', recalled one witness from Malaya, Philip Hoalim, 'very tired and extremely frail'. The Mahatma was an inspiration, but, in the words of Abu Hanifah from Sumatra: 'We thought the idea of turning the other cheek was silly. We had then preferred the ways of Kemal Ataturk, the hero of Anatolia.'[3] Southeast Asian nationalisms shared a martial cast of mind, and the area's representatives found that they had most in common with each other. In New Delhi they witnessed at first hand the spectacle of India and China vying for influence, and it alarmed them as much as the revived imperialism of the West. The regional entity that was later to emerge, in the shape of the Association of Southeast Asian Nations in 1967, was much smaller than that envisaged in New Delhi. The summit was the high-water mark of pan-Asian solidarity, but it also signalled the beginning of its decline as a political ideal. 'We seek no narrow nationalism,' Nehru had proclaimed. But narrow nationalism was to prevail. A second meeting in China did not materialize: civil war and Cold War intervened. Purana Qila was the start of a road that led to Bandung in 1955. But the Afro-Asia Conference was to be a conclave of sovereign nation-states, and not a parliament of peoples.

THE CRESCENT FRAGMENTS:
ORPHANS OF EMPIRE

Slowly, almost imperceptibly, the great crescent had begun to fragment. The perpetual motion of peoples across frontiers that had given it unity began to still. By the end of the war, transport had ground to a halt, and borders were battle fronts. During the Japanese occupation, the largest migrations were internal: they were either forced, as in conscription for the railway projects, or took the shape of flight from troubled areas, as in the mass exodus of Chinese from the towns and mines into the forests of Malaya. By the beginning of 1947 travel, trade and remittance had resumed, and migrant communities raced to restore ties with their homelands. As many as 20,000 Indians from Malaya chose to travel back to South Asia at fares six times their pre-war level. Overseas Chinese businessmen returned to invest in the economic reconstruction of their ancestral regions. Most of them later went back to Southeast Asia but, in the longer term, the great political upheavals in India and China gave these journeys a new finality. When the communist armies entered the port cities of China, the seaboard would close to migration for two generations. Many of the later journeys from Southeast Asia would be passages into banishment or exile. Dying empires and new nations guarded their frontiers jealously. Much was lost in the process. The dream of a greater Malay nation floundered against the Dutch blockade of the Indonesian republic. Prosperous ports became backwaters. Penang, which bridged India, Burma and the Eastern world, faced the decline of its entrepôt trade, and the loss of its special status as a Straits Settlement. Fired by

'Penang patriotism', and afraid of being swamped in a Malay-dominated state, the Straits Chinese and other outward-looking traders fought to retain their British citizenship, and campaigned to secede from the new Federation of Malaya. But they could not survive alone. More enclosed state structures were being erected that placed greater importance on internal identity politics, the local defence of status and nationality, than on the pursuit of global sympathies. Wherever new 'national' boundaries were drawn, they broke up older communities that had transcended them, and left behind 'orphans of empire'.[4]

A cosmopolitan age was drawing to a close. Many of the minorities who had embodied it lost influence, and some were even confronted by the spectre of statelessness. Singapore's Jews, who numbered over 1,000 in 1941, were mostly of Middle Eastern, and specifically Baghdadi descent. They dispersed across India, Southeast Asia and coastal China in the nineteenth century, where many of them achieved prosperity and status. But in the war, the community began to break up. The story of Alfred Lelah was typical. He was born in Baghdad in 1913, and had first visited Singapore as a young child with his father. This led him to see it as a safe haven when in 1938, worried about the deteriorating relations between Arabs and Jews, he decided to leave Iraq. He created a comfortable niche for himself, trading in Japanese goods which were at the time boycotted by Chinese firms, and re-exporting them to the Middle East. Shortly before the Japanese invasion Lelah evacuated his wife and children to India, but he remained, and was interned along with the rest of the Jewish and European community. When the camps were liberated, and because he carried an Iraqi passport, Lelah was 'repatriated' via Cairo to Iraq. Before the war, in an Indian Ocean administered by the British, it would have been relatively easy for him to return to Singapore. But now Iraq lay outside the British orbit, and on arriving in Basra, Lelah was charged for his repatriation costs in local dinars and found that his immigrant status was very insecure. He struggled to reach Bombay to find his wife and children, moving through a succession of grim, isolated transit camps, and eventually secured a passage for his family from Calcutta back to Singapore. When he finally boarded the ship he destroyed his Iraqi passport. On his return, Lelah faced the full force of colonial exclusion: a British immigration officer who had been imprisoned in Changi with him refused an entry visa to his parents. His family was now homeless. They were given refuge by relatives in a house in Bencoolen Street, a Jewish quarter of the city, but they had to share it with its new occupants: the Malayan Communist Party.[5] Lelah had travelled to Iraq with a fellow internee, Jacob Ballas, who later described how their world had changed:

The Second World War showed us that we are Jews and we were pushed aside as a Jewish community by the Japanese. And we were considered enemies. When the war was over we saw and couldn't believe what had happened in Europe, the crematoriums and Auschwitz, and about Hitler and what he did to the Jewish people, which were unbelievable to us, because we'd never experienced any of these.

With this came the realization that disaster could strike anywhere, as it did in Iraq in 1948 when, in the wake of the partition of Palestine, the Jews were expelled from Baghdad.[6] Still seeking security, they dispersed again: to Sydney, Los Angeles, London and Israel. The Jews of Singapore diminished in number, but survived: Alfred Lelah re-established a booming business in Singapore's legendary travellers' bazaar, Change Alley. The community would achieve brief prominence with the rise of David Marshall, a charismatic lawyer and politician. He had been sent in the later part of the war to a coal mine in northern Japan, and on his return had busied himself in the causes of ex-prisoners of war and Jewish welfare – 'I am', he was to declare, 'both a Jew and an Asian' – and proved that it was possible for a Jew to win the political support of Chinese and other communities.[7] His spell in 1955 and 1956 as the first chief minister of Singapore was one of the final flourishes of the city's pre-war cosmopolitanism.

Between 1945 and 1950 a substantial number of the Eurasian communities of India and Burma, including many technicians, teachers and railway workers, left Asia. During the days of nationalist agitation they had identified themselves closely with the continuation of the British presence. They hoped that, at the very least, India, Pakistan and Burma would continue as dominions within the Commonwealth. As this possibility receded and ethnic conflict deepened across the crescent, they were increasingly uncomfortable. They felt betrayed by the British and suspicious of the exclusive nationalism of the incoming independent governments. Some of this anxiety was captured in fiction by John Masters' powerful novel *Bhowani Junction*, filmed in 1956 with Ava Gardner and Stewart Granger, as Hollywood's first retrospective of the Raj. Some Eurasian families packed for 'home', a mythical Britain which their ancestors had left as long as a century and a half before. But the cannier or less sentimental members of the community had sensed that racial and class prejudices were still deeply ingrained in the United Kingdom. They too left, but for Australia, New Zealand and Canada. Though these countries still maintained discriminatory immigration laws, they seemed more open and friendly and their cheerful citizen soldiery had made a positive impression in India and Burma during the war. Some 'Britasians' tried to enlist the support of Eurasians in Malaya for a colony in the Nicobar Islands, just as some of the Dutch had looked to New Guinea as a new frontier.[8] But the leaders of Malaya's 10,000 or so Eurasians saw a role for their community, perhaps above all others, in defining a new 'Malayan' nationalism. In Singapore, Gerald de Cruz and John Eber, founders of the Eurasian Progressive Association, were two of the main sponsors of the Malayan Democratic Union. De Cruz's anti-colonialism and embrace of communism was spurred by his rejection of his Indian-Irish father's slavish attachment to a colonial culture and 'an alien patriotism'.[9] The Eurasians of Malacca traced their roots to the Portuguese conquest of 1511. They petitioned the Malay sultans to be recognized as their non-Muslim subjects and as co-claimants of the status of 'sons of the soil'.[10] But two generations later, this claim had yet to be acknowledged.

As Britain's Asian empire broke apart, India came to play a much reduced role in the affairs of Southeast Asia. In the wake of Nehru's visit, Congress sent a medical mission to relieve the sufferings of local Indians: its ability to defend its own was an important test of its new authority. But, after this, the diaspora dropped out of vision. In 1942 and 1943 the Indians of Southeast Asia had been the vanguard of the freedom struggle, but these epic days soon passed into legend. INA veterans still paraded in their tattered uniforms and clung to the memory of Subhas Chandra Bose. Around this time stories first appeared in the Malayan press – rumours which would never be dispelled entirely – that he was alive and somewhere in Tibet. The British witch-hunts against the INA cast a long shadow. Many of its civilian leaders left Southeast Asia to become ambassadors for the new Indian republic, and as pre-war figureheads resurfaced, many re-affirmed their loyalty to the British Empire.[11] The community was effectively leaderless. In August 1946, on Nehru's advice, a former minister of Bose's provisional government, John Thivy, who had recently been released from a British jail, founded a Malayan Indian Congress. In its early days the new party remained firmly anchored to the subcontinent. 'Indians in East Asia', Thivy argued, 'are the Ambassadors of India.' He promoted Hindi, although the language had virtually no native speakers among Indians in Malaya, and opposed the proposals for a Malayan Union citizenship in order to safeguard dual-citizenship rights for Malaya's Indians. But as they watched the death throes of the Raj, Indian leaders in Singapore and Malaya realized they could no longer trust New Delhi. In early 1947 Thivy took further advice from Congress in India and conceded that Indians should seek their Swaraj in Malaya and adopt local citizenship. He allied the Malayan Indian Congress with the Malayan Democratic Union and other parties of the left. But Indians remained ambivalent about Malayan politics. Thivy himself stepped down as party leader in July to take up a diplomatic appointment as agent of the government of India, and the party continued to attend Congress meetings in India until 1950.[12] The labouring masses were disenchanted with an elite who claimed to speak for them, yet ignored their immediate concerns. It was an article of faith of the Penang shop and municipal workers that they would trust no man who wore trousers or spoke English.[13]

The independence of India was not an occasion for celebration in Malaya, and it left the Indian community more divided than ever and anxious about their future. The Sikhs and other minorities revived their separate associations; Indian Muslims supported a local branch of the Muslim League. At the time of the Calcutta killings there was communal violence in Singapore. The British slapped censorship on publications from India, and attributed the trouble to local gang rivalry. But on Penang, the largest centre of Indian Muslim settlement, there were protracted tensions between Hindu and Muslim workers in rival trade unions.[14] The island was home to a distinctive community of Straits-born Hindustani Muslims, or Jawi Peranakan, and many of them lent spiritual support to Pakistan. Yet Lahore was far away, and offered little hope of protection. The majority chose to identify more closely with their fellow-Muslims, the Malays. But relations between them had a history of tension. Malay nationalism in the 1920s and 1930s had asserted the precedence of Malays of 'full blood' over those of Indian or other Muslim descent. But facing bigger political challenges after the war, the Malay community was now more willing to absorb resourceful co-religionists. Jawi Peranakan leaders joined the conservative United Malays National Organization (UMNO) and, in time, became a distinct network within it. In 1947, the son of a Jawi Peranakan headmaster from neighbouring Kedah began to write a lively and acerbic column on Malay affairs for the *Straits Times*, under an Anglicized *nom de plume*, 'Che Dat'. It showed an unwavering identification with the Malay people, and an unsentimental view of the challenges they faced; Mahathir Mohamad would later become one of the Malay community's strongest defenders and most astringent critics, Malaysia's longest serving prime minister and 'father of modernization'.[15]

For the British in Southeast Asia the loss of the Raj also meant the loss of its cheap labour. Under pressure from Thivy and others in Malaya, Nehru refused to allow any more recruitment from India. When Japanese surrendered personnel were finally shipped home in early 1947, the military despaired of finding manpower to rebuild its camps and airfields. It considered looking to Mauritius, to 30,000 Maltese workers who had washed up in Cairo, and even fresh levies from Japan. In the event, around 10,000 volunteers from Ceylon were hurriedly enlisted under strict military discipline.[16] They were lured by the promise of good pay and conditions, but found themselves earning less than locals for heavy labour. On 17 September 1947 a large contingent of Ceylonese in Singapore mutinied. They refused to eat the 'coolie's food' they were given and pelted their officers with stones: 416 men were arrested. There was another revolt in April of the following year, and brawls with local Malays and Tamils in Sungei Patani and Kuala Lumpur. To local trade unionists, the use of the Ceylonese was another blatant attempt to exploit non-unionized labour: their principal employer – the RAF in Singapore – had dismissed over a thousand local workers earlier in the year.[17] Migration now was subject to new political pressures. After the Malayan Union debacle, Malay politicians refused to countenance fresh arrivals from China. In the constitutional negotiations, control over immigration policy was, Sir Edward Gent told Arthur Creech Jones, 'a matter of life and death to the Malay people'.[18] The only acceptable alternative was fellow Muslims from Java, but the British feared that they would bring with them the politics of the Indonesian revolution. For the first time, the workforce of the future would be born in Malaya itself.

In September 1947 the colonial government took a census of Malaya and Singapore, the first since 1931. It was a sign of the consolidation of boundaries and the revival of bureaucratic power. But for most people, the sudden appearance of over 13,000 enumerators with clipboards, interrogating households and placing chalk marks on dwellings, was deeply ominous. There were rumours of mass evictions and conscription, and flashbacks to Japanese screenings and massacres. The census drove home the new importance of ethnic definition and status. Where earlier censuses had made multiple distinctions in recording people's origins, the categories were now consolidated into rigid ethnic blocs: 'Chinese', 'Indians' and 'Malays'. Some sub-categories were used, but they were arbitrary and contentious. The census divided the Chinese along dialect group lines, but it made no distinction between the locally born and the China-born, which was seen as the most pertinent divide by the community itself. For official purposes, the 'Straits Chinese' did not exist. There was, for the first time, no subdivision of the category 'Malays (Indigenous Malaysians)', and it stood in sharp antithesis to 'Other Malaysians', that is people of Indonesian origin. These categories were the subject of anxious debate, and because census enumerators tallied individuals in the way they described themselves, there were choices to be made.[19] *Utusan Melayu* waged a campaign for Indonesians to identify themselves as 'Malays': the census category 'Other Malaysians' was a specious ploy to 'disunite the Malays'.[20] Malaya's political arithmetic hung in the balance: Malays now comprised 50 per cent of the peninsula's population, Chinese 38 per cent, and Indians 11 per cent. The census also showed that the Chinese community was reproducing at a far faster rate than the Malays. Women speakers from UMNO toured to remind Malay women of their duty: 'if we want to retain our identity as Malays we must have more babies'.[21] In this Malthusian mood, Malay leaders entered the final negotiations for a constitutional settlement.

The numbers game dealt a blow to those who were attempting to build non-communal solidarities. It also obscured another vitally important change: the growth in the number of women, particularly in the towns. On the peninsula, the ratio of Chinese women to men rose from 486/1000 in 1931 to 815/1000 in 1947. Malaya had evolved from being a land of pioneering males to one of rapidly extending families. For many Indians and Chinese, a land of sojourn had become a place of permanent settlement. The elderly, too, were now less likely to return to their country of origin, and most would die in Malaya. Many had no kin locally, and care for them became a pressing social need: 'We shall not forget', vowed the manifesto of the Malayan Democratic Union, 'those who in the vigour and strength of their youth played their part in Malaya.'[22] The census was a reminder that through all the tumultuous high-political watersheds of the end of empire, in the *kampongs*, mines and rubber estates, in the dockyards, factories and on the streets, the overriding need was to stabilize family life and income, to fulfil social obligations and to live with dignity. And as old and new elites jostled for position, as borders were drawn and constitutions made, the voices of the *rakyat jelita*, the common man and woman, were struggling to be heard.

MALAYA'S FORGOTTEN REGIMENTS

Among the forsaken of empire were the vast regiments of labourers on the rubber plantations of Malaya. In the words of Selangor trade unionist C. V. S. Krishnamoorthi:

Ours is a life of meek suffering toiling from the sunrise to sunset like an automaton day in and day out leading a life squalid, poverty-stricken, starving, without education, joy or any ray of hope to better ourselves and those who you consider as our dependants for whose advancement in life we are bound to God. What to do? We toil draining our life blood to produce that alluring commodity LATEX Rubber for the whole world and for the enhancement of our country's wealth, suffering mosquito and leech bites, withered by malaria, and our bones and skinny skeletons shivering in cold lack of clothing and nourishing food we lead on this existence.[23]

By 1947 rubber production had regained its pre-war peak, and the industry was once again the biggest employer in Malaya: of its 354,694 workers, 221,240 were Indian, mostly Tamils from the south. Although they worked at the heart of the industrial economy, they often lived in isolated frontier areas. The rubber industry was not solely a European creation: it was pioneered by Asian investors and, before the war, Malay smallholders produced just under a half of Malaya's rubber exports. But European estate managers saw the transformation of vast tracts of the Malayan rainforest into a model industrial garden – trees planted in geometrical lines, the ground drained and weeded – as one of the largest and most indelible monuments to British enterprise in Asia. Much of the human and epidemiological costs of this, however, had been borne by Tamil workers.[24]

The rubber plantation was one of the most all-encompassing labour regimes on earth. Its hold over the lives of its workers was captured in a documentary novel, by a Frenchman, Pierre Boulle, who worked in Malaya before and after the war. He served as an agent of the Free French in Indo-China, and this provided material for his more famous work, *La Pont de la Rivière Kwaï*. In *Le sacrilège Malais*, Boulle described a relentless routine, set in motion each morning with a ritual summons in the dark, at 4.30 a.m. precisely. Under the savage curses of the *kangany*, the Asian overseer, the men, women and children paraded with knives and shears and buckets. 'The roll call could have been held an hour later,' Boulle wrote, 'only then it would have lost its religious character and been reduced to the level of commonplace utility ... The spiritual communion in the dark was intentionally endowed with all the sacred value of holy writ.' At roll call it was the custom of some British planters, many of whom were veterans of the First World War, to hoist and salute the Union Jack. The tappers, the weeders, the pest gang, the road and drainage gang, each had their daily 'task'. For the tapper it was to cut the bark of a set number of trees – perhaps as many as 400 a day – to release the sap, and then to collect the latex that had gathered there since the last incision. This delicate process was subject to minutely governed schedules and techniques. Managers and overseers competed to achieve a 'mathematic perfection of movement that does away with every redundant gesture': it even governed bodily necessities – labourers were encouraged to urinate in their buckets to prevent the latex coagulating.[25] A large plantation of several thousand acres was an 'over-governed state' in which the European *dorai*, or master, was king: the roads, bridges, housing, school, dispensary, shop and cattle herd were all his responsibility.[26] There was virtually no aspect of labourers' lives in which the *dorai* could not intervene, including family disputes, choice of clothing and leisure activities. He was addressed by labourers as 'our mother and our father', and sometimes this was literally the case; for European bachelors, as Boulle recorded, the 'cook's wife' was a customary consolation.

Like most systems of work in Malaya, the rubber plantations were designed for single migrant men. Now they were home to families, which in many cases had to be rebuilt from the trauma of war. In 1946 there were 5,591 widows in the rubber industry; 6,795 children left with only one parent, and 2,324 orphans.[27] The 'labour lines' – terraces of one-room cottages – were often little more than 'sleeping boxes' bereft of such basic facilities as running water and privacy. They were nests of neighbourly disputes, and completely unsuited to family life. The fundamental economic reality was that a man's wages – 70 cents a day – could not support a family. After the war, women and children comprised over 40 per cent of the estate workforce. But women and children were paid at a far lower rate than men for what were often equally hard 'tasks'. A cost of living allowance brought a man's wages to $1.10, but this was far below what was paid to Chinese employed through contractors, who could expect at least $2 a day, and maybe where there was demand, $3 or $3.50. The government and employers struggled to justify such discrimination, arguing that the Tamils received free housing and, being physically weaker, were less productive. But behind these arguments lay crude racial typologies: the Chinese were a 'pushing, hard-working, independent people'; the Tamil, on the other hand, 'looks for security and a settled life, and has little ambition because of his background, going back three thousand years, which has given him his caste and position in life'.[28] Young Tamils were trapped in a cycle of poverty and low expectations. In 1947 the labour code was amended to raise the minimum age for child labour to eight years, for light agricultural and horticultural work. There were 25,000 Indian children at work on Malaya's plantations: schools on estates were of woeful quality, and few children attended them beyond the age of ten. 'It is because of their poverty', an Indian labour leader explained, 'that these workers have to send their children to work against all the laws of humanity.'[29]

Before the war, the larger European plantation companies, such as Boulle's employer, Socfin, had worked to improve workers' health and housing. But government intervention was too weak to enforce better standards on the smaller and poorer estates. Change was often dependent on the price of rubber, and was motivated less by humanitarianism than by the desire to increase workers' efficiency.[30] As with most colonial reform, improvement and social control went hand in hand: it did not enable labourers to move freely between employers or bargain collectively. By 1947, there were planters who, as prisoners of the Japanese, had worked alongside Indian labourers on the Burma–Thailand railway and knew their needs. Jacques le Doux of Johore, who spent over forty years in Malaya, recognized that in 1942 'our world came to an end'. He wrote a 'Countryman's journal' for the *Straits Times* which traced his deepening empathy with the labouring world that surrounded him.[31] But others had difficulty coming to terms with the post-war world. 'Where are the stiffs of yesteryear?', lamented a columnist in the trade rag, *The Planter*. 'The new types seemed to have lost the old joie de vivre and to have been prematurely sobered by their harrowing experiences of the last six years.'[32] Many were determined to revive their former authority, and live a life that, in the words of a *Times* correspondent, resembled 'that of an eighteenth century country gentleman enlivened by tropical variations'.[33] Planters still possessed the means to keep their labour virtually isolated. Estates were private property, subject to strict trespass laws, and labourers were wholly dependent on the management for access to their homes. Any visitor had to receive the permission of the manager to enter. Planters used all available means to obstruct unwelcome guests. To trade unionists this was a denial of a fundamental democratic right to organize: 'an attempt', in S. K. Chettur's words, 'to regiment the docile Tamil labourer in a manner that no other body of labourers on earth would dream of being subjected to'.[34]

It was difficult to see how the cycle of isolation and neglect could be ended. The links between the tappers and the management were the labour conductors and the estate clerks. Often of different ethnicity from the Tamil labourers – usually Malayalam-speaking southern Indians – they were both the natural leaders of these communities and potentially their worst oppressors. Their power had grown during the war in the absence of the European managers, and it was often abused. Clerks, it was said, had manipulated recruitment for the Japanese railway projects so as to send away the husbands and fathers of attractive women, leaving them prey to their attentions. Such abuses, the festering atmosphere of shame and vendetta, cast a long shadow over these small, insular communities. But to protest was to invite victimization or risk being turned off the estate.[35] The only focus of community life outside this hierarchy were the small Hindu temples that labourers built for themselves. Even here, the manager often acted as patron of the temple, and his clerk and conductor would sit on its management committee. But it was to a reformed Hinduism – particularly the Dravidian movement for Tamil reawakening – that many labourers turned for an improvement of their status. Its secularized 'reform marriage' was, by 1947, very popular on estates. It was a simple ceremony that did not devour the resources of the poor and, presided over by Dravidian leaders or trade unionists, it provided a rare opportunity for political speeches.[36] But the burning issue was the campaign against *toddy*, the wine of the palm tree and the coolie's comfort. Planters, who often ran the estate *toddy* shops, argued that a moderate intake of *toddy* kept labourers biddable. But to reformers, it was the root of all moral and social decay.

The largest movement was led by A. M. Samy, a lorry driver on the large Harvard estate in central Kedah. On the eve of the Japanese invasion, the European manager had set up a self-defence force on the estate, and in the interregnum Samy revived it as a *thondar pedai*, or labourers' militia. The origins of his influence are obscure. It was said that he killed a Ceylonese clerk in the war, but escaped punishment by denouncing him as pro-British. He was certainly influenced by the INA, but was not a veteran of standing, although other leaders of the movement were. His *thondar pedai* acted as stewards at religious processions, such as the parade of penitents at Thaipusam, but then began to demonstrate in the towns against liquor and to picket *toddy* shops. When, in May 1946, the workers of Harvard estate stopped work in protest at the re-opening of the estate *toddy* shop, the *thondar pedai* enforced the strike. By now Samy possessed a rag-tag army of around 1,500 young men; they dressed in old INA forage caps and tattered khaki shorts and trained by pole-fighting in mock battles. Samy branched out to form trade unions on neighbouring estates. They dispensed a rough justice through kangaroo courts: drunks were tied to trees or made to perform physical jerks; strike-breakers were fined or beaten. The rule of the unions could be every bit as arbitrary as that of the clerks and conductors, but it broke their monopoly on power. By early 1947 around 13,000 labourers in central Kedah were under Samy's sway, and he based his organization in the small town of Bedong, out of the reach of the trespass laws.[37]

On 28 February, a crowd of a thousand or so *thondar pedai* descended on Bedong, only to be confronted by the police. A labourer came forward: 'We are not anti-government,' he cried, 'we are only against the drinking of *toddy*.' He was clubbed to the ground and later died in hospital. The coroner recorded a death of 'justifiable homicide'. A series of protest strikes erupted in the area. At Bukit Sembilan estate on 3 March trouble was triggered by the dismissal of a woman activist, and the police faced orchestrated resistance. 'Women were to be in the forefront armed with pepper,' it was reported; 'Boiling water was to be kept ready; men were to be armed with sticks, stones and bottles full of sand; trees were to be cut down to make road blocks.' Sixty-six people were arrested, and all but five of them sent to jail after a trial that lasted only a day. Fearing a rescue attempt, the police closed the hearing to the public. An investigation by the Malayan Indian Congress revealed collusion and premeditation on the part of local planters and police. S. K. Chettur claimed that women were beaten, and there were allegations that two young girls were raped in custody. Conditions at Bukit Sembilan estate were particularly dire: the only supply of water came from ravines, and labourers shared it with their cattle; the managers had their water brought from town by lorry. The strikers' demands focused on wages and family needs, such as crèches, better housing and equal pay for women. But the real source of anger was the summary dismissal of workers: 'Managers feel that because we reside on the estates we are as much their property as the rubber trees.'[38] As the strikes spread across central Kedah, and also to Selangor and Johore, planters were turning dissident labourers out of estates where they had lived for ten to twenty years.[39] On Dublin estate in Kedah on 26 April, when 2,000 Indians laid down tools in protest at evictions following a secret union meeting at night in a shed belonging to the temple, 1,000 Chinese came out in sympathy. The police opened fire on demonstrators and one Chinese striker was killed. Even the mouthpiece of European business, the *Straits Times*, was appalled: 'we simply cannot have the Police firing on crowds of labourers all over the country'.[40] The wives of European planters fled to Penang.

It seemed that Indian and Chinese estate workers were forming a common front. They were the last major body of labourers that lay outside the communist-led Federations of Trade Unions. Its Indian leaders now came forward to help estate workers organize; many of them, including the president of the Pan-Malayan Federation of Trade Unions, S. A. Ganapathy, had both an INA and an MPAJA pedigree. Many Indian trade unions fought to stay independent, and the trade union adviser, John Brazier, sponsored rival unions, some backed by the Malayan Indian Congress, some led by estate clerks. Nevertheless, the Kedah disturbances on the estates were accompanied by a show of strength by the Federation. In Singapore, key municipal services, public transport and the port were paralysed. A strike at Batu Arang mine left power stations down to just three weeks' supply of coal and the railways running on skeleton services. For the last time, the Japanese were brought in. But they too now worked on a go-slow. The Singapore Federation of Trade Unions mobilized the invisible city to provide strikers with food, cigarettes and strike funds.[41] But if their resolve wavered, its underground Workers Protection Corps used secret-society methods to enforce discipline. When the secretary of the municipal workers' union opened negotiations with the government, he was stabbed. The aim of the strikes, Brazier believed, was to make the communist-backed unions the new 'labour bosses' of Singapore. He had all but abandoned his work on the island.[42] He concluded that the niceties of English collective bargaining did not translate into a Malayan context. One problem was the penchant of local petition-writers for flowery metaphors: they spoke of '"baths of blood" and "seas of fire" in what should be polite letters of requests to an employer'.[43] But Brazier's insistence that the government would only recognize 'economic' as opposed to 'political' trade unions was incomprehensible to the new leaders of labour. As S. A. Ganapathy repeatedly argued: 'The fight for a democratic constitution is a fight for better food and clothing'.[44]

On the night of 6 October an estate manager in southwest Johore, Archie Nicholson, was driving home with his wife after a dinner with a planter on a neighbouring estate when he suddenly came up against a roadblock. He decided to accelerate through it, but lost control of his car and died as it skidded and rolled into a ditch. His wife was stripped of her jewellery and beaten by four armed men, but she survived. Nicholson had been resident in Malaya since the late 1920s and was a veteran of the Burma–Siam railway. The European community was badly shaken. 'Physical fear', declared *The Planter*, 'is creating havoc amongst the inhabitants of Malaya once renowned for their complacency and general tranquillity'. The tragedy was one of many incidents of armed robbery at the time; but, in the minds of many planters, it was indistinguishable from the confrontations they were experiencing with labour agitators on their estates. After Nicholson's funeral, a delegation of planters descended on King's House for a tense audience with Gent, at which they called for the introduction of emergency measures: the death penalty, banishment, 'and particularly of flogging'. Kuala Lumpur, they said, was ignorant of the scale of the problem; only planters could take the pulse of the *ulu*, the upcountry. They demanded arms to defend themselves.[45] Gent had come to represent all that many planters detested about the post-war empire: effete officials, income tax and socialism. Whilst it remained an unwritten rule in the European clubs (in the words of Anthony Burgess) that 'the hairy legs and shorts of the visiting planter should not be juxtaposed to the pressed linen slacks of the government man', many policemen and civil servants were equally disenchanted.[46] But

Gent felt a personal obligation to uphold the Labour government's policy of encouraging trade unions and refused to capitulate in the face of pressure from employers. He dismissed them as 'alarmist'. A story did the rounds that Gent began one interview with European businessmen with the words, 'Before you tell me your troubles I want to hear what you have been doing lately to improve conditions for your workmen.'[47] Old Malaya hands in London lobbied for his immediate recall. The crisis was a full dress rehearsal for what would later come to pass.

But in 1947, the principles of liberal imperialism prevailed. In private, Gent and the Governor General, Malcolm MacDonald, like Mountbatten before them, were fighting a holding action against colleagues who were urging resort to arbitrary powers. At the height of the strikes in Singapore, the governor, Sir Franklin Gimson, demanded more authority to banish people. Without it, he warned London, 'the prestige of the government would be so damaged that it might be unable to control the situation'.[48] The pre-war legislation that regulated trade unions and societies was now revived. But throughout 1947 the legal status of the Federations of Trade Unions remained in limbo. So did that of the Malayan Communist Party. On 26 June 1947 MacDonald convened a top-secret meeting in Singapore to consider banning it. It was, perhaps, the first sally of the Cold War in British Southeast Asia. Communism, MacDonald declared, was 'Enemy No. 1'. The nearest Russians, he conceded, were in Bangkok, but their allies were at work in Malaya and Singapore among the 'gullible' Asiatic masses. They were a potential fifth column in time of war, and 'a very strong and coherent policy' was needed to counteract them. The military chiefs demanded to know why communists were still at large: 'Why was their activity not regarded as an act of sedition against the King?' The wartime agreement in the jungle between Force 136 and the MPAJA was now forgotten. In late 1946 Gent could find no record of the treaty in Kuala Lumpur; Whitehall doubted if it ever existed.[49]

MacDonald, in urging restraint, appealed to first principles. There were, he said, two types of communist. One was 'the sincere idealist ... He wanted to get the British out but was in some cases a lofty-minded Communist just as there were lofty-minded Conservatives,

341

Labourites and Liberals, and it was always part of British democratic practice that this sort of man should be given complete freedom to express his views.' Then there were the 'conspirators whose activities were always such that steps had to be taken to bring action against them'. But, MacDonald concluded, 'unless the Communist Party as a whole could be proved to be engaged in conspiracy it would be very hard to put it across to the authorities at home, who were the ultimate arbiters'.[50] He won the day, and the MCP was temporarily reprieved. But the instruments for its destruction were already in place.

THE STRANGE DISAPPEARANCE OF MR WRIGHT

In March 1947 the Malayan Communist Party demonstrated that it could bring the colonial economy to a standstill. Whilst its senior cadres remained underground, its satellites flourished.[51] Its heroic wartime struggle still exercised a tremendous hold over the imagination of the young. The MCP – itself an elite vanguard – had now around 11,800 mostly Chinese members. But it was also broadening its influence among other communities: there were 760 Indian and 40 Malay full members. Yet, at this point, the revolution suddenly seemed to stall. The strike wave petered out. In Singapore, the unions were, in a sense, victims of their own success: many of the key battles had already been won. But, equally, the conditions that had so favoured them since late 1945 – a labour shortage, weak employers – were now shifting against them. In mid-1947 there was a fall in the rubber price, and estate labourers faced cuts in wages. The employers now combined and initially refused to treat with the unions.[52] A general strike was called but, although solid in some pockets, it was not a success. On the question of wages, the interests of Chinese and Indian workers began to diverge, and the vision of a united workers' front was receding.[53] Nor was it clear that the united front with the English-educated radicals of the Malayan Democratic Union was paying dividends. Many rank-and-file members, particularly ex-guerrillas, were frustrated that the party seemed to take a back seat in the popular struggle. One Chinese writer has described the old comrades of Titi, a rural community in Negri Sembilan: 'They continued to enjoy the ecstasy of believing they were "guerrilla fighters" whilst enjoying the comforts of ordinary life at home. They still went on short camping trips, sang rousing songs, and shouted communist slogans. They assisted each other in times of difficulty.'[54] Above all, they wanted their role to be acknowledged and for the MCP to claim leadership of the workers' movement. As a letter from the Central Committee to the Penang party acknowledged, the lack of an open organization meant loss of control, and loss of control was liable to manifest itself in violence and unpopular strong-arm methods.[55]

The underground leadership of the MCP remained cloaked in secrecy, and this bred suspicion and intrigue. Rumours still circled around the Secretary General, 'Mr Wright'. In late 1946, perhaps to buy himself some time, Lai Teck travelled to Hong Kong and Shanghai on a false Chinese passport obtained for him by his deputy, Chin Peng. He returned with words of advice from the Chinese Communist Party and used them to bolster support for the united-front strategy. But Lai Teck no longer had the monopoly on contacts with international communism. In January 1947 Wu Tian Wang, Rashid Maidin and the Perak trade unionist R. G. Balan left for London as delegates for the Empire Communist Conference: it was the first time these younger leaders had been in direct contact with other movements. Wu Tian Wang presented a history of the MCP's struggle but, from the response, it was clear that its moderate aims, its calls for 'self-government', were a long way behind those of the communist parties of India, Ceylon and Burma. This news was disquieting. In Malaya, leaders read policy statements from the Chinese Communist Party (CCP) – particularly an appreciation by Lu Tingyi of Mao's own views – that seemed to contradict Lai Teck's assessment of international conditions. But still the mystique of the Secretary General endured. In mid 1946 Lai Teck effectively banished his most vocal critic, the Selangor leader Yeung Kuo, to his home state of Penang. That September Chin Peng travelled to the island to visit his wife and young daughter, who were spending time there with his mother-in-law. This marked the beginning of the unmasking of Lai Teck.

The only full account of the events that followed comes from the memoirs of Chin Peng himself, which were written with art and a great deal of hindsight, and from a long interview he gave to a panel of historians as he began to write them.[56] Evidence from contemporary sources is very fragmentary. According to Chin Peng, he and his friend Yeung Kuo met on the beach at Tanjong Bungah – then as now a popular beauty spot – where they began to voice their suspicions of Lai Teck. It was dangerous talk, but it gave them confidence to raise the issue in an oblique way at a Central Committee meeting in Kuala Lumpur in February 1947, by questioning Lai Teck on the Party finances – as much as $2 million had passed through Lai Teck's hands and was not formally accounted for – and on his 'leadership style'. Confronted by Chin Peng, Lai Teck broke down, sobbing, 'You have misunderstood me . . . you have misunderstood me.' The older men present rallied round the leader. Lai Teck claimed he was ill, and spoke of taking a holiday. The meeting was then adjourned, on Lai Teck's plea that he had urgent business in Singapore.[57] But the stakes rose when some of the MPAJA's major arms dumps in the jungle were discovered by the British. At one site near Kuala Lumpur, 213 weapons and over 16,000 rounds were lost.[58] The Central Committee reconvened in Kuala Lumpur on 6 March, but Lai Teck did not appear. Chin Peng and another committee member drove to the small house in Setapak-Gombak that the Party had provided for Lai Teck to use on his visits to Kuala Lumpur. There he had a Chinese wife, a Party member who had earlier acted as a courier for him. They took her before the Central Committee. The Secretary General had eaten his breakfast, she said, and had left in his Morris Austin car for the meeting.[59] Lai Teck was not seen in Malaya again.

At first it seemed likely that the Secretary General had been kidnapped by the British. Chin Peng maintained later that he thought otherwise, but held his tongue. Fearing liquidation as conspirators, Chin Peng and Yeung Kuo went to ground in a Chinese shophouse near the Malay quarter of Kampung Bahru, losing themselves in the coffeeshops and cinemas by day. But they did not seem to have been followed, and after a few days the pair re-emerged and, together with another leader who had been loyal to Lai Teck, were deputized to investigate the disappearance. Chin Peng followed his own line of enquiry: he travelled to Singapore, where witnesses were found among the Vietnamese émigrés. They had, it seemed, harboured suspicions of the man for a long time. When they had tried to acquire arms and men from Malaya, one of the young Vietnamese involved had recognized Lai Teck from his past life in southern Vietnam and had recalled his earlier disappearance. Then there were others who had seen him in close contact with the Japanese. These witnesses corroborated for the first time from a fresh source the stories that had been circulating since the beginning of the Japanese occupation. With this came information on Lai Teck's many business dealings and on his women. There was a Vietnamese wife in a beachside bungalow in Katong and two mistresses – a Vietnamese and a Cantonese – who were maintained by Lai Teck in Singapore; the Vietnamese girl ran a bar in the Hill Street area.[60] He had, it was later estimated, absconded with $130,000 in cash, 170 gold coins and 23 taels of gold.[61] Two months after his departure, at a party plenum meeting in May, Lai Teck was exposed and expelled from the MCP as a Japanese spy. Chin Peng was elected Secretary General. He was still only twenty-three years old. Yeung Kuo became his deputy. Yeung Kuo broke the news of Lai Teck's betrayals to his wife in Malaya, who was an old schoolfriend of his. She had just borne Lai Teck's child, but according to Chin Peng, her response was resigned: 'Then I suppose you must kill him.' The house in Katong was staked out by the MCP, and secret contacts were called upon to discover if he was in Outram prison.[62]

Few members of the Party, outside its innermost circle, knew anything about these events. The Lai Teck personality cult remained strong; too strong for his followers to accept the news of his treachery without hard evidence. After all, the Party survived on ruthless, iron discipline. In July senior leaders were sent on Lai Teck's trail. Chen Tian led a delegation to Prague to the World Federation of Democratic Youth Convention and, en route, visited Soviet officials in Paris to enquire if Lai Teck had escaped to Europe and to investigate his credentials as a Comintern representative. Chin Peng went to Hong Kong; it was the first time he had left the country. Using his cover as a businessman he travelled to Bangkok by train, arriving in early July. The city remained an important arms bazaar and haven for the Asian underground.[63] He stayed at the Vietnamese delegation – an unofficial mission of the Viet Minh – and requested help from both the Vietnamese and Thai communists in tracking down Lai Teck. Chin Peng was there two weeks, but no progress was made. Shortly before he left he was taken by a Thai communist comrade to the Cathay Pacific airline office on Suriwong Road to collect his onward ticket to Hong Kong. As he later described it, on the way back by trishaw his eyes were scanning the oncoming traffic when suddenly his attention was caught by a man on the opposite side of the street: 'He was standing with his back to us and seemingly in the middle of a transaction with a cigarette vendor. There was something about the body language. As we moved with the traffic I couldn't take my eyes off the figure. We then came to a position where I was looking directly back at the man's face. It was Lai Te[ck], all right. He was taking a first puff on a freshly lit cigarette. He raised his head and appeared to look in my direction.' Chin Peng ducked back behind the canopy of his trishaw and told his Thai companion to order the driver to turn back. By the time they had done so, Lai Teck had boarded a motorized trishaw taxi – a *tuk tuk* – and they could not keep pace with him. Chin Peng returned to the office of the Vietnamese communists in Bangkok; they mobilized their armed underground, confident of finding any renegade in the city. Chin Peng left as planned for Hong Kong.[64]

The events that followed, as Chin Peng later recalled them, read as a 'sort of fiction'. In Hong Kong Chin Peng reported to the CCP representatives on the disappearance and treachery of Lai Teck. They too, it seemed, had harboured suspicions about him, and found him evasive about his past. In his encounters with representatives of the CCP, Lai Teck had not dared to use the cover story he had employed in Malaya, that he was a Comintern agent. In Hong Kong, Chin Peng was asked to lie low whilst the CCP representatives consulted their superiors in Shanghai. He kicked his heels in a cheap hotel in Nathan Road, Kowloon, reading the Chinese and English newspapers, visiting the cinemas and travelling the Star Ferry to Hong Kong Island to kill time. It was on a return trip, scanning the advertisements and notices in the *South China Morning Post*, that he stumbled on a column of the previous day's arrivals and departures. Arriving by Cathay Pacific from Bangkok was a C. H. Chang. This sounded like 'Chang Hong', an alias of Lai Teck, under which Chin Peng had obtained a fake passport for him. 'He added a "C" in front of "H" so C.H. is Chang Hong and H. Chang is Hong Chang.'[65] Chin Peng warned his CCP contact, a worker in the office of the Chinese business daily *Hwa Sung*. This was corroborated for the Chinese Communist Party by a former Kuala Lumpur Special Branch source then resident in Hong Kong. A few days later, with tremendous audacity, Lai Teck turned up at the same office to meet the CCP representatives. His story was a characteristic double bluff: he told them he had been kidnapped by the British, captured together with his car. He was first imprisoned, then banished to Thailand. He had come to Hong Kong, he said, to report this to the CCP. The CCP representatives demanded to know what his intentions were. To go back, he said, and he asked them for money and travel documents to return to Malaya, via Bangkok.[66]

This was reported to Chin Peng, but there was little he could do about it. The CCP's position in Hong Kong was precarious: they would not sanction an assassination in British colonial territory. He gave Lai Teck a couple of days to get away, then followed him on a BOAC flight back to Bangkok. Once again, the Vietnamese underground began a search. After two days they discovered that Lai Teck was in a middle-range hotel. When the Vietnamese went to the address, they discovered that he had checked out. The next morning Chin Peng was told of this by a Vietnamese contact, and they concluded that he had 'probably found some company'. But, once again, it was Lai Teck who had calmly taken the initiative. He had contacted the Thai communists and had, in fact, left his hotel for a rendezvous with them. A few days later Chin Peng had to return to Penang. Before he left, he paid a courtesy call to Li Chee Shin, the leader of the Communist Party of Thailand. He asked about Lai Teck. Li responded quietly in Mandarin, 'He's no more.' Li would give no further details, and none would emerge until a meeting in Peking in 1950, when MCP members met one of the Thai men who had been sent to meet Lai Teck, and heard the story of his demise. Three Thai heavies, young and inexperienced, had been sent to the rendezvous, where they kidnapped Lai Teck. Their orders were to bring him to interrogation, but Lai Teck, a small, frail man, began to shout, and there was a struggle: 'They strangled him for a certain amount of time and suffocated him. He died on the spot. According to the Thai[s], they just put him in a gunny-sack, and then tossed him in the Menam River.' Chin Peng returned to Malaya to be met with the news that he had been awarded the Order of the British Empire for his wartime services. His uncle took him to a Western restaurant in Ipoh to celebrate.[67]

The crisis was kept under wraps for most of 1947. The enquiry had taken a long time; only in December was a report finalized. It was filtered through the Party hierarchy so that the new leadership could gauge reactions carefully. It was the end of May 1948 before a statement by the Central Committee was published for the Party and the world at large. The document – 'A written statement on L[ai] Teck's case' – correlates in its main themes, if not the details, with the account given by Chin Peng many years later: they are both, in a sense, authorized versions of the story. The 'Lai Teck Document' began with a short account of his rise to power in the Party in a time of 'unprepared state of thought' and of the steady loss of other leaders. 'Following a well-calculated plan he posed as a sacrosanct "hero"', it explained; 'he had held up high the "International Signboard"'. But the document reveals little about his relationship with the British, saying only that 'the possibility of his having conspired with the Imperialists was very great'. It emphasized instead his betrayals in wartime and his corruption. The document took particular pains to explain why his treachery had gone undiscovered for so long: 'very few comrades', it reported, 'had any idea of his mode of living, for he was really a "mysterious person"'.

The 'running dog' policy formulated and carried out by him was characteristically 'rightist' and traitorous to the cause of the revolution, but that policy had always been implemented as being 'leftist' or in some cases smacking of 'leftist', so it had not been easy for comrades to discover any serious mistakes or danger in it.

Above all, the 'Lai Teck Document' was written to exonerate the new Party leadership from his political errors. Lai Teck was the 'greatest culprit in the history of our Party'; but his was a case of 'individual conspiracy with the enemy'. He had recruited no accomplices and nurtured no successors. The entire Party had to accept responsibility for the deception. There was to be no general witchhunt. There was no opportunity for one. By the time the report was published, the

MCP was four weeks away from its climactic confrontation with the British.[68]

The news was met by confusion and anger, a feeling, voiced in the report, that 'our past work was done in vain, that we have to start everything all over again'.[69] A middle-ranking Perak leader described the mood on the ground: 'Some MCP veterans may be disgusted and discouraged. They will be unwilling to suffer hardships . . . we all feel that we are getting a raw deal as compared with the higher officials . . . The supreme leaders had always in the past used the slogan "Let's Struggle Together", but this was only in words and not in deeds.'[70] Lai Teck was a convenient scapegoat for the failure of the MCP after the war to convert its open-front strategy and broad public appeal into revolutionary success. Yet the unmasking of the traitor did not mean the immediate abandonment of Lai Teck's line. The advice of the Chinese Communist Party to Chin Peng in 1947 was that the decision to move to armed revolution could only be taken in the light of local circumstances. For the Party, the last months of 1947 were a time of reconstruction, of making closer contact with the masses, and reimposing its leadership on them. Supporters of Lai Teck, suspected 'rightist deviationists', were placed on probation.[71] But the decisive break with the past had yet to occur, and the united-front policy had yet to run its full course.

Questions continued to be asked within the Party. The Singapore MCP open representative at the time, Chang Meng Ching, later claimed that Lai Teck had left because the British were blackmailing him to force him to expose the hidden arms caches. Defectors from the Party in the 1950s, such as vice-president of the Pan-Malayan Federation of Trade Unions, Lam Swee, challenged the Party's account of Lai Teck's treachery, and even suggested that Chin Peng himself was behind the Batu Caves massacre of 1942, or had at least manufactured the charge that Lai Teck was responsible, in a plot to seize control of the Party. Over the long years of insurrection this was to become a staple of British and Malaysian black propaganda against Chin Peng.[72] Lai Teck's career must be set in context of the many deceptions, covert alliances and secret understandings made and later repudiated, that proved so pivotal to the course of the war and end of empire in Asia. The revolutionary underground was a fluid world which left few of those who moved in it uncompromised. Many MCP members had gone into business for the party or on their account with the spoils of war: the Party had invested $70,000 in a tin mine in Kampar; it also had stakes in the Lido Hotel in Singapore, the Lucky World Amusement Park in Kuala Lumpur and another $100,000 invested in other small business.[73] Few were immune to the glamour of insurrection; this was why, despite all the misgivings about him, Lai Teck commanded a loyal following and was, by all accounts, such a compelling presence. In 1971 Gerald de Cruz, by then a communist apostate himself, wrote of him: 'I am sure he had been involved with both the Japanese and the British authorities – what revolutionary worth his salt does not find himself in such situation from time to time with his "establishment" – and that these were raked up and exaggerated to justify the denunciation and later his assassination . . . I also recall when Rudolf Slansky was executed in Prague, he was accused of being both an American agent and an Israeli spy. Today they place flowers on his grave and say, "Sorry, comrade, it was a mistake". Perhaps they'll do the same with L[ai] Teck one day.'[74]

'BEWARE, THE DANGER FROM THE MOUNTAIN'

The British followed all this from a distance. The available sources suggest that Lai Teck did indeed stay hidden in Singapore for a few months before heading to Bangkok and Hong Kong. But then he disappeared from view. Conflicting reports surfaced from time to time. In June 1948 the Malayan Security Service reported that Lai Teck's whereabouts were unknown, but that he might yet attempt to return to power.[75] Chin Peng heard later that a British Special Branch officer had also set up a rendezvous with Lai Teck in Bangkok during his last days, one that Lai Teck was unable to keep. It is unclear how much the British ultimately gained from their association with Lai Teck, beyond a false sense of security followed by 'the confusion of darkness when . . . the light at the top of the stairs went out'.[76] Colonial intelligence had been badly damaged by the war. The Malayan Security Service had been founded only in 1939; many of its local officers were killed, or compromised by the Japanese, and its secret archive was destroyed. In 1946 it had only four European officers, as opposed to twenty-one in 1941; this climbed to thirteen by the beginning of 1948, but only one of them spoke Chinese. The head of the Security Service, John Dalley, the man responsible for arming the communists in 'Dalforce' in 1941, had made his reputation by policing Malay secret societies in the Perak river during the interwar years.[77] For much of 1947 the principal obsession of British intelligence was not the Malayan Communist Party but the Indonesian revolution.

To read the 'Political Intelligence Journal' of the Malayan Security Service was to enter a strange underworld of sinister, liminal figures: spies, subversives and deviants, peddling conspiracy and preaching violence. They took the outward form of traders, medicine men and itinerants, jumping off from Indonesia into the village-cities of Singapore, Malacca and Balik Pulau – the Malay settlement at the 'back of the island' from colonial George Town – areas that were nurseries of radical politics. The British paid their informers on a piece rate and presumably collected their intelligence from Malays who were deeply suspicious of these influences. In the overwrought imagination of colonial officials, fleeting contacts and loose social networks became a co-ordinated web of subversion that underpinned radicals groups such as the Malay Nationalist Party and its youth wing, API. It was later a serious charge against Dalley that he became too obsessed with the Malay and Indonesian underground and neglected the more obvious danger presented by the Malayan Communist Party. But the danger seemed real enough at the time. In late 1946 the armed gangs of the Sumatran social revolution – the *gagak hitam*, 'black crows' or *kerbau hitam*, 'black buffaloes' – were reported to be making their presence felt on the peninsula. Smuggling had become more sophisticated and more political. Opium sales largely financed the Indonesian Republic's diplomatic and clandestine operations. At one point the baggage of delegates to an inter-Asia women's congress in India, and that of Sutan Sjahrir himself, was found to be carrying 'black rice'. A variety of Indonesian intelligence organizations operated in Singapore, some of them the creations of self-serving fantasists. In July 1947 an Indonesian trader and a clerk were convicted of conspiracy to steal Lord Killearn's papers.[78] Official concern deepened as violence in

Indonesia again escalated in the wake of the first of the Dutch 'police actions' in July and August of 1947. The British feared it might sweep aside the fragile Anglo-Malay entente, upon which their remaining power in Asia ultimately rested.

Dato Onn bin Jaafar and other Malay conservatives played skilfully on these fears in order to push the British towards a swift and definitive settlement with the Malays. As Onn wrote privately to Gent on 17 February: 'the British must choose *now* between Malay support and cooperation or sacrificing them to political expediency'.[79] Onn remained hostile to Indonesia. As he told a UMNO meeting in early April 1946, he came from an area where the Malays were mostly of Indonesian origin. He had observed at first hand the stirring in the villages, but 'there are also', he warned, 'people who will sell the name of Indonesia to enrich themselves'.[80] But Onn faced a rising tide of criticism. Prior to the Second General Assembly of UMNO at Alor Star in Kedah in January 1947, leaflets in Arabic script circulated in the town: 'Dato Onn has sold the Sultans and the *rakyat* [people] like slaves . . . Dato Onn has become a British satellite.' Characteristically, Onn faced down the criticism in his opening speech. Malaya, he reiterated, was not yet ready for independence. There was no Malay fitted to be a minister, or an ambassador: 'Who was running the country immediately after the Japanese surrender? – The Chinese. We have been greatly endangered by the *Bintang Tiga* and by the Malay Nationalist Party. We do not care for those people. We must rise united to defend our birthright; the 2,500,000 Malays in Malaya must be united and once unity is achieved we will have no fear of foreigners.' But the weeks before and after the UMNO General Assembly saw a surge in support for the Malay Nationalist Party.[81]

These were heady days for Malay radicals. In December 1946 they converged on Malacca for the second congress of the Malay Nationalist Party. The air hung heavy with history: this colonial village was once the ancient seat of Malay civilization and the source of the nation's original sovereignty. Speakers constantly invoked its past greatness and its heroes. Malacca was, to the young Ahmad Boesta-mam, 'the Hang Jebat State', the home of the rebel. The congress was an open meeting, drawing both the committed and the curious. Rashid Maidin of the MCP figured prominently, by auctioning garlands, in a proletarian style learnt from the rallies of the Indian National Army, whereby small bids were made and a succession of winners came on stage to wear the flowers. Even the Malay policemen in attendance contributed to the cause.[82] The Party's ideologue, 'Pak Doktor' Burhanuddin, launched his personal manifesto, entitled, like Sutan Sjahrir's famous prospectus of the previous year, *Perjuangan kita*, 'Our struggle'. Its vision for the Malay nation was radically different from UMNO's narrow defence of racial primacy. 'Within Islam', Burhanuddin wrote, 'there is no space for any kind of narrow communalism.' The Malay nation, the *Melayu* nation, was a nation of believers. It was rooted in an identification with Malay history, culture and language. Membership was an act of will. In theory, this opened the possibility of non-Malay membership of this nation, should they choose it. As Ahmad Boestamam explained, 'Whoever was loyal to the country and who was willing to call himself "*Melayu*" was part of "independent Malaya". No consideration was given to the notion of "purity of blood" in anyone . . .'[83]

Flushed with success, the leaders of the movement went on a tour of northern Malaya. Recently released from prison on the strict condition of staying out of politics, the indefatigable Mustapha Hussain attached himself to Dr Burhanuddin as his unofficial secretary. He counselled him that the slogan of '*Indonesia raya*' would lead the radicals into a cul-de-sac of confrontation with the British. Certainly, the message now became more wide ranging: Burhanuddin and Rashid Maidin subtly adapted their speeches to different audiences. Burhanuddin, Mustapha Hussain observed, was beginning to make a powerful impact on religious teachers and *hajjis* – returned pilgrims from Mecca – with his gently insistent message: 'We can defeat a stronger person not only with strength but by repeated actions.' British policemen referred to Burhanuddin in Mustapha's hearing as 'the Gandhi of Malaya'. His Special Branch codename was '"Sparrow", a tiny bird that could take over huge buildings by setting up giant colonies'. At the meetings, the youths of API, in their homemade uniforms, would run alongside the cars carrying loudspeakers, and Ahmad Boestamam would rouse them to a frenzy. The tour culminated in Penang, at Balik Pulau, where, in Mustapha Hussain's words, 'a host of weathered jalopies decorated with red and white flags were already waiting . . . these ancient cars looked like blemishes against Penang's lovely buildings and mansions, all belonging to non-Malays'. Mustapha and Rashid rode in silence past the dilapidated huts of the Malays.[84]

The MNP conference in Malacca was crowned by the marriage of Ahmad Boestamam and Shamsiah Fakeh. They had been travelling together as the heads of API and AWAS. 'I suppose', Shamsiah reflected many years later, 'I married Boestamam because I was eager for his assistance in improving my understanding of political struggle.' Her political goals and personal feelings converged. The marriage failed, but it was an object lesson in the choices for women at this time, many of whom, like Shamsiah in marrying Boestamam, were entering into a polygamous union.[85] As the young Indonesian activist Khatijah Sidek said of her marriage to a politically active Johore doctor: 'I did it because in our society, one has no standing if one is unmarried, especially for the women; marriage was a sort of vehicle.'[86] The war had opened up new challenges and opportunities, and the public role and strident rhetoric of women like Shamsiah and Khatijah were deeply challenging to conservative opinion. Yet, in many cases, the wider role for women was defended on the grounds that it was an expression of women's rights under existing Malay *adat*, or custom. As Ibu Zain, a pioneer educator, told the Asian Relations Conference: 'Malay women are the most "free" in Asia. They have not known the purdah system. They work alongside their menfolk, in the paddy-fields in the villages; they trade in the "weekly markets" . . .'[87] Added to this, a new generation of young women had been educated in progressive religious schools, of which Shamsiah Fakeh and Khatijah were themselves graduates. Within the nationalist movement itself, AWAS was a potent challenge to the masculinity of the *pemuda*. In a famous incident on a march to a rally in Perak, the women invited the men to swap clothes when their enthusiasm flagged.[88]

The British were beginning to close in on the Malay left. At Malacca, Ahmad Boestamam's API had formally separated from the Malay Nationalist Party. This was recognition that it was now a force in itself. But it was also a form of political insurance so that if, or more likely when, it should collide with the British, the main party organization might survive. API became increasingly militant and martial. Its followers gathered for drills, often in places that been centres of Japanese youth training, such as Malacca. They dressed, like the Indonesian *pemuda*, in a motley of military styles: bluish RAF-type forage caps, white shirts and trousers with red shoulder tabs. But the sight of Japanese boots and leggings was deeply offensive to British observers. The Security Service believed that there were a variety of secret cells within API. Boestamam himself did little to dispel this impression, and a diagram found in a raid on MCP offices seemed to confirm it. The name itself, it was said, conveyed a secret meaning: *apuskan perentah inggeris*, 'obliterate English rule'. There were even *semut api* – literally 'fire ants': a biting local pest – organized among children in the Malay schools.[89] The military began to vet its Malay recruits, and the police feared that API was infiltrating Boy Scout troops.[90]

On 1 April Ahmad Boestamam was arrested for sedition. His public trial was one of the few attempts by the British to convict an opponent on a politically related charge. In most other cases – including Boestamam's own several months later – suspects would be detained without trial, or banished quietly and secretly. The charge related to a manifesto distributed by Boestamam in Malacca in December: the 'Political Testament of API'. It was a hastily prepared, strikingly radical document: an attack on feudalism and capitalism, and a call to restructure society, by violent means if necessary. The trial focused on its rallying cry of *Merdeka dengan darah*. This was rendered by the prosecution as 'Independence through blood'.[91] But John Eber of the Malayan Democratic Union, who acted as counsel for the defence, challenged this. Could not 'blood', in this sense, merely mean 'self-sacrifice'? The court pored over the text. When another key phrase – in Malay: *jalan chepat radical dan serantak* – was given as 'rapid and radical revolution', Eber called the Malay court translator as a witness. Under cross-examination he conceded that it could mean simply, 'go immediately and suddenly'. A senior colonial scholar-administrator, W. Linehan, was summoned; he too conceded a 'mistranslation'.[92] These slightly farcical proceedings demonstrated the calculated way in which the colonial government was now pursuing its enemies. Boestamam was found guilty and fined $1,200 with an alternative of six months in jail. The fine was paid through donations from political allies on the left, but also from the donations of the poor. The decision to stay out of jail embarrassed Boestamam politically, but he had been jailed by the British before and would soon face imprisonment again: 'I asked for a year's grace to organise and prepare API to sound the tocsin, Defeat or Fame.'[93]

British policemen and district officers felt they were being taunted by these young Malays flaunting Japanese-style uniform in areas where the government's own grip was insecure. They were also deeply worried at the undercurrents of violence in the kampongs. The police were aware of a growth in cultish religious practice; a peddling trade in talismans and charms, azimat, which were said to confer invulnerability on their wearers. Some of the rituals attached to them were heterodox within Islam, such as the insertion of gold needles beneath the skin for divine protection.[94] One exponent of this was Syed Moh'd Idris bin Abdullah Hamzah, known as Sheikh Idris, who lived in a village near the royal town of Kuala Kangsar in Perak. He was believed to hail from Indonesia, and had worked selling fruit and vegetables together with charms of goatskin and other talismans. He entranced audiences with speeches in which he suggested obliquely that he was about to reveal his true identity. Many of his followers, hearing this, believed him to be none other than the legendary holy man Kyai Salleh of Batu Pahat, who had led a jihad against the communists in 1945. They took to wearing red skull caps embroidered with the credo, 'There is no God but Allah, Mohammad is his Prophet', and red sashes and shoulder straps. Eighty of them led a public procession on the Prophet's birthday on 2 February 1947, headed by Sheikh Idris himself in a grey shirt, grey riding breeches and Japanese jackboots. Confronted by the police, Sheikh Idris sternly reminded them of the British policy of non-intervention in religious matters. The area had already been unsettled by large API demonstrations and matters soon came to a head when another medicine seller, known as Sheikh Osman, made a speech in a Malay village near Ipoh telling the Malays to prepare for a Chinese rising against them. On 31 May five of his followers were convicted at a court in Kuala Kangsar of carrying offensive weapons: krises and parang panjang. The trial took place at the time of Friday prayers, and as the convicted men were led from the court by police they were met by a crowd coming from worship at the nearby mosque. Sheikh Osman stood outside it and called: 'Orang Islam keluar orang Melayu masuk dalam' – 'Muslims come out; Malays stay inside'. To the crowd, his meaning was clear: 'Those who wish to travel the path of God, come outside; those of you who are merely Malays, stay inside'. More came outside than stayed inside. A mêlée resulted, and one of the prisoners escaped; a Malay policeman gave chase, only to be confronted by Sheikh Idris himself, brandishing a Japanese sword. A crowd of around eighty armed and uniformed Malays gathered to guard Sheikh Idris's house. The Sultan of Perak came in person to address them and order them to disperse. He made little impact. According to one report, 'weapons were insolently and suggestively fingered'. The police had lost control over the area; they did not dare to arrest Sheikh Idris or to prevent his followers from marching into Kuala Kangsar. Only when Idris agreed to surrender himself and be released on bail was peace restored. At one point the senior British official in Perak had pleaded with the crowd. A member of API countered: 'You gave the government a shock. How did you feel having one and half day's freedom in Kuala Kangsar? Of course you liked it! That is what Merdeka will be like! This is a step towards our destination.'[95]

The fragile skein of British influence had unravelled in the face of a chaotic combination of religion and politics. Sheikh Idris seemed obscurely influential; the British believed that he had the protection of the chief mufti of Perak; he had also shared a political platform with Ahmad Boestamam. His followers had openly challenged the authority of the British and that of the sultan himself, and there had been little the mostly Malay police could do about it. Against this background, on 17 July, taking advantage of a new public ordinance that prohibited military drilling, the government banned API.[96] 'The British colonialists', Boestamam later wrote, 'by their action in banning API and not banning the Malayan Communist Party, as much conceded that at that moment, API was a greater danger than the Malayan Communist Party.' The British, Boestamam believed, were wise to act. They had forestalled, by only a short time, API's plans to 'burn'.[97] But it was a heavy blow to the cause of Malay radicalism. The advent of API youths parading in uniform was a dramatic enough event in the life of the kampongs, but they had yet to enlist the support of older and more conservative rural Malays. Boestamam fell on hard times; this was a another new phenomenon: one of the first of Malaya's professional politicians was left with no alternative source of income. Some of young activists regrouped in an underground movement known as Ikatan Pembela Tanah Ayer: the League of Defenders of the Homeland, or PETA, 'The Plan'. Its leaders had stronger Malayan Communist Party connections, and they looked to the Malay peasant masses for support.

The Malay *kampongs* remained desperately poor. As administration stabilized, British doctors and officials were shocked at the conditions. The east-coast state of Trengganu was one of the worst hit areas: isolated and underdeveloped, its inhabitants were more likely to be killed by a tiger than by a motor car, and it had fewer doctors per head of the population than almost any other part of the world: one to every 75,000 people, compared one to 12,000 in China. Colonial doctors found entire communities in a state of 'semi-starvation'. A major rice-growing area, it now produced only one third of its requirements.[98] Malay infant mortality peaked in 1947 at 12.9 per cent on the peninsula as a whole; Trengganu was the worst affected state, at 17.6 per cent. This heightened the sense that the Malays were struggling for racial survival.[99] The picture elsewhere on the east coast was equally grim: one of flooding, failure of rice crops, declining fisheries and debilitating diseases such as malaria and dysentery.[100] Most of these blights could be attributed in some degree to the war. In late 1946 a Malay civil servant, Ahmed Tajuddin, conducted a survey of some of the most fertile padi lands in Krian, Perak: three quarters of the acreage had been abandoned. The peasants had sold stocks to black-marketeers, but the proceeds of sales were useless, given inflation. Now their granaries were empty and they could not feed their families. 'They lived from hand to mouth their life-long' from poultry, fishing, fruits and fishponds and collecting *atap*.[101] As the young Mahathir Mohamad wrote, padi planters 'are generally no better off than they were before the advent of British rule in Malaya'.[102]

Britain's old Malaya hands tended to see the Malay *kampong* as a timeless, rather idyllic world, and the Malays as an easygoing people whom it was their duty to protect from the rapacity of the commercial economy. But now Malays were moving to towns at a larger rate than any other community, working for wages and starting businesses. Since the 1930s much of the energy of Malay intellectuals had been directed at understanding the root causes of Malay poverty. As in Burma, the stock villain was the Chettiyar moneylender or the Chinese shopkeeper. After the war Malay newspapers carried reports that in rice-growing areas such as Kedah much of the land was mortgaged to them.[103] But it was also the case – although the British tended to keep it quiet – that in the same area the most 'ruthless ejections' of tenant farmers were by local Malay aristocrats.[104] As they toured the *kampongs*, the Malay radicals targeted the feudal class and argued that the stultifying impact of colonial protection was holding back the Malays. 'Do you know what I saw in London?' Rashid Maidin asked a Perak crowd on his return from the Empire Communists' Conference. 'At the Malaya House, I saw two paintings on exhibit. One showed the Malays as an uncivilised group of people; mere farmers of rubber, resin and *rotan*. The other one depicted a beach scene, where Malay fishermen were being received by their family members with their sarongs so high up it almost revealed their private parts. The Malay fishermen were seen eating bananas. If I had a grenade in my hand then, I would have thrown it at the paintings. How dare the imperialists portray us Malays in that manner!'[105]

At the centre of these debates was a religious school in the Krian area of Perak, the al-Ihya Asshariff at Gunong Semanggol. Founded in 1934 by Ustaz Abu Bakar al-Baqir, it was one of a network of modern *madrasahs* which had revitalized the curriculum of religious education in Malaya by including new secular subjects such as history, geography and even accounting. Many of the leading political personalities of the era had studied in these schools; Shamsiah Fakeh was one outstanding example, and Dr Burhanuddin had taught in the most renowned school, Masyhur al-Islamiah in Penang. There was a constant traffic of scholars between the *madrasahs*, and they forged strong links with the local community. Al-Ihya's school journal circulated in the surrounding villages and its students were encouraged to take part in traditional community projects such as weeding padi fields or building bridges. The region was home to politically conscious Banjarese settlers and it was a bastion of Malay Nationalist Party support. Ustaz Abu Bakar was a close friend of Dr Burhanuddin. They shared a conviction that, in the words of *Pelita Malaya*, the *ulama* were 'not free agents to give real benefit to the people. They are under the influence of the Rulers above them, who claim to be "The Shadow of God on Earth" and "The Protector of Islam", these learned men are simply as ornaments to the Royal court.'[106] On 23 March 1947 al-Ihya hosted a national conference in economics and religion. It was without precedent, and drew around 2,000 visitors to the small town of Gunong Semanggol: politicians and *ulama*, and visitors from Egypt, India and Indonesia. Welcomed by demonstrations of Malay martial arts, the delegates then reviewed the progress of the Muslim community. Two path-breaking initiatives were launched. The first was the formation of a Supreme Religious Council, which promptly demanded that the Malay rulers surrender their authority over religious matters to an elected body of *ulama*. For the first time, Islamic revival in Malaya had a tangible institutional centre. The second initiative was the creation at Gunong Semanggol of a 'Centre of Malay Economy'. It demanded 'special protective rights' for the Malays in the economy, and perhaps marked the origins of what was to be the central platform of Malaysia's post-colonial economic development.[107] A host of other, often local, initiatives sprang from this, such as 'people's schools' built by villagers, and commercial and co-operative ventures. This kind of activity was, to Dr Burhanuddin, 'the stirring of dormant Malay soul'.[108] It was also fertile ground for the Malay communists, who were well represented in these debates. A peasants' front, or *barisian tani*, was founded and led by a graduate of Masyhur al-Islamiah in Penang, Musa Ahmad. He was later to become the chairman of the MCP. The communists involved were instructed to conceal their political leanings; it was now Party policy to 'show its respect for the Malay race by giving them concessions'.[109]

This bred hostility and reaction. Conspicuous by their absence at Gunong Semanggol were the leaders of UMNO. They urged the more conservative *ulama* to boycott the conference. Dato Onn launched a stinging attack on it in a speech at Tangkak in his home state of Johore: 'We have seen the danger that came out from the jungle in 1945, and today we are going to see the danger descending from the mountain [*gunong*] under the cloak of religion.' His audience was in no doubt that he was referring in one breath to Gunong Semanggol and to the MPAJA. He would repeat this warning several times in the coming months.[110] During this period the British and UMNO worked in concert to shore up their influence in the *kampongs*, particularly through the appointment of trained and steady men as village headmen who would be a mainstay of government control. Headmen possessed considerable influence over the lives of peasants, and API complained of their obstructionism. Fearing that, after the defeat of the Malayan Union, UMNO would disintegrate, Onn began to convert it into a national institution; but only in 1949 did the leadership agree to a single direct membership, and even then some affiliates opted out of it. UMNO was run from Onn's office as chief minister of Johore, to the sultan's increasing annoyance, and from the legal practice in Ipoh of its general secretary, Haji Abdul Wahab. UMNO was, throughout its history, to rely heavily on such personal and family networks.[111] It was continually short of money, not least to meet the fees of its British legal adviser, Sir Roland Braddell. In May the Sultan of Johore bailed it out with a donation of $5,000.[112] Perhaps the strongest grass-roots movement within UMNO was its women's organization, but it struggled for recognition within the party. Dato Onn's son, Captain Hussein bin Onn, recently demobbed from the British Indian Army, led the youth wing. A painstaking, conscientious man who would serve as the third prime minister of independent Malaysia, he lacked his father's charisma. UMNO struggled to compete with API and AWAS to capture the imagination of the young. Instead, it relied on its power base in the State administrations to advance its cause.

A PEOPLE'S CONSTITUTION

In 1947, an empire was lost, and an empire regained by the British. But there remained powerful challengers to colonial authority in Southeast Asia. And whilst opposition forces seemed to be travelling different paths, by the end of the year the British and their Malay allies were haunted by the prospect that they might, against all expectations, converge. The search by ethnic minorities for belonging; the demand of trade unionists for material progress; the Malayan Communist

Party's need for allies, and the drive by the Malays for economic advancement all seemed to come together in the question of the new constitution for Malaya. A blueprint for a new Federation of Malaya had been agreed by the British, UMNO and the Malay rulers in secret talks throughout the second half of 1946. Although Malay leaders remained bitter about the Malayan Union episode – none more so than Dato Onn himself – they had defeated its most objectionable aspects. The Federation guaranteed the special rights of the Malay people. It was a return to indirect rule: new treaties with the Malay rulers, as Onn repeatedly emphasized, were an endorsement of Malay sovereignty. The new legal entity was to be termed the Persekutuan Tanah Melayu, a federation of Malay lands. The constitution enshrined a stringent legal definition of a 'Malay', but none for a 'Malayan'. There was to be no 'Malayan' nationality.[113] The constitution conceded citizenship rights to non-Malays, but whereas under the Malayan Union these would have extended to 83 per cent of the Chinese and 75 per cent of the Indians, far fewer people would now qualify.[114] For the British this was a major retreat from the idealism of the Malayan Union. But when the final proposals went to the cabinet in July, the colonial secretary, Arthur Creech Jones, viewed the future with some complacency. He believed that 90 per cent of the original strategic objectives of the Union had been secured, particularly the creation of a stronger, more cohesive central government and a common citizenship. Singapore remained outside the Federation, but this was the price of Anglo-Malay accord, and the growing divisions in policy between the two territories made the prospect of union in the future increasingly unlikely. Creech Jones reassured colleagues that the new constitution was opposed only by a 'noisy minority'.[115]

The proposals were put to a consultative committee of local dignitaries. Up until this point the British had assumed that non-Malays were, at best, indifferent to constitutional change. Support for the Malayan Union had been muted. Many non-Malays still thought in terms of dual citizenship with their country of birth; they were alienated by the exclusion of Singapore, and the left had argued that the Union was undemocratic, negotiated with 'feudal remnants' and not the people. But, as the Anglo-Malay entente deepened after mid-1946, Chinese associations mobilized to defend the Union's more liberal provisions for citizenship. It was clear that the status of non-Malays was more insecure than ever; the gateway to citizenship had narrowed and the prospects for a democratic Malaya, of which Singapore was seen as an indivisible part, had receded.[116] Leaders were incensed at the limited nature of the consultation. The two leading Chinese members of the consultative committee were H. S. Lee and a leading Perak Chinese, Leong Yew Koh, both of whom held Kuomintang military rank. As John Eber of the Malayan Democratic Union observed bitterly, 'What right have colonels in the Chinese army, owing presumably their undivided loyalty to China, to adjudicate or speak on behalf of the people of Malaya?' In late 1946, to speak for Malaya, the Malayan Democratic Union took a central role in the formation of the Pan-Malayan Council of Joint Action (later the All-Malayan Council of Joint Action, AMCJA). At its inaugural meeting in Kuala Lumpur on 19 November it rejected all existing Anglo-Malay agreements; it boycotted the consultative committee and demanded recognition as 'the *only* body that speaks for all Asiatic communities'.

The AMCJA was an attempt to draw together the various *aliran*, or flows of consciousness, within radical politics in Malaya, and all of them, at one time or another, would claim to have been its inspiration. The Malayan Communist Party, sensing that here there was political capital to be made, encouraged the initiative. Its open representative, the journalist Liew Yit Fan, attended the inaugural meeting, and although the Party never joined the AMCJA, its main satellite organizations, the New Democratic Youth League and the Federations of Trade Unions, were its largest components.[117] But equally prominent, and entirely unprecedented, was the presence of leaders of the Malay Nationalist Party. With UMNO increasingly allied to the colonial government, the Malay radicals saw that they could not go it alone: 'we shall safeguard our special rights', it announced, 'but we cannot carry on an isolated fight – isolation means defeat'. It now sought a common front against feudalism and for the popular will; in joining the AMCJA, it made an alliance of a kind that UMNO could not match.[118] This was a bold and a dangerous political undertaking: the Malay Nationalist Party immediately faced charges that it had sold out the Malay people. To counter this, it withdrew from the

AMCJA to form its own parallel coalition, the Pusat Tenaga Rakyat
– Centre of People's Power – or PUTERA. The man charged with
leading it was Ishak Haji Muhammad, a celebrated novelist and journalist. He took the view that the party should give the experiment 'a
fair trial for one or two years'. In the course of 1947 Dr Burhanuddin
lost support. The leftists within the Malay Nationalist Party were
wary of his religiosity, and impatient with his caution.[119] At the end
of the year, in a delicately arranged coup, he was replaced as party
leader by Ishak, although he remained its special adviser. Ishak represented a different stream of Malay radicalism, more secular and
socialist in outlook. He was fluent in English, which Dr Burhanuddin
was not, and as both an intellectual and a Bohemian he was more
than a match for the leaders of the Malayan Democratic Union.

The chairman of the PUTERA–AMCJA was a 63-year-old Straits
Chinese notable, Tan Cheng Lock. At first glance he appeared an
unlikely choice to lead an alliance of young radicals. He lived a world
apart from most of them, in a sprawling, antique-cluttered Chinese
mansion at 111 Heeren St, Malacca. Before the war he had been the
leading Asian on the Legislative Council of the Straits Settlements,
but had retired from public affairs, in a state of some disillusion, to
Switzerland. He spent the war in India, far removed from the social
upheaval at home. But he was remembered by the younger men
of Malayan Democratic Union as one of the first advocates of a
'Malayan' nationalism. He commanded influence within the powerful
Chinese business community, and on his return to Malaya in 1946
had been one of the first of its leaders to argue that the Union was a
first step towards self-government and that the Chinese should act in
concert to defend their position.[120] But equally important was his
status as a Straits Chinese, a member of a long-domiciled community
that had absorbed Malay culture and habitually spoke the Malay
language. As John Eber flattered him: 'the Council needs an individual
who is a Malayan as a focus ... As it is you represent *all* interests.'
Tan Cheng Lock traced his local roots to 1771 – as 'a true *anak
Malaka* [son of Malacca]' – and to a generation he would hold mythic
status as one of the first true Malayan patriots. His multiracialism
was rooted in a utopian cast of mind. His writings and speeches had
a philosophical, somewhat mystical flavour, and were peppered with

references to Nietzsche and Schopenhauer, alongside the classic Chinese philosophy he had absorbed in English translation (like many Straits Chinese, Tan Cheng Lock could neither read nor write Chinese). He shared the spiritual cosmopolitanism of many Asian thinkers of the pre-war era; like Tagore, he searched for the underlying commonalties of Asia's civilizations. But his nationalism was based on a modern democratic citizenship.[121]

We in Malaya have adopted and want to apply the dynamic conceptions of nationalism and democracy. Nationalism, if it is to be a unifying force, requires the elimination of communalism from political life. Democracy demands for its free operation an understanding of the conflicting claims of race and language and a willingness to compromise on major political issues after full and free discussion.[122]

When the Malay Nationalist Party met in Malacca, Dr Burhanuddin had called on him, and Tan Cheng Lock had promptly offered to raise $500,000 for Malay economic development. In the years to come he was to devote much of his energy into brokering an accord between the Malay political and administrative class and Chinese economic muscle.[123]

The British saw Tan Cheng Lock as a communist dupe. 'A disgruntled "failed KCMG"', the writer of one intelligence brief sneered, 'who has time and money to squander on antics which keep him in the public eye.'[124] A key role was played by the secretary of the AMCJA, Gerald de Cruz, the principal liaison with the Malayan Democratic Union, who took the lead in the organization, and the communist leadership. Certainly it was the MCP that provided much of the mass support: 300,000 from the Federations of Trade Unions alone. Yet the MCP leaders would later regret committing so far to a movement whose agenda they could not control.[125] From most accounts of its meetings, the PUTERA–AMCJA was a multivalent body, which no one party succeeding in dominating. The vital need for Malay support gave PUTERA a strong hand. This was particularly apparent in the debates on the constitution. Eber had argued from the outset that the only credible way to oppose the federal plan was to propose an alternative. Its founding principles were hammered out at a series of sub-committee meetings, the most critical in July 1947 at the office of the New Democratic Youth League in Foch Avenue, Kuala Lumpur, a building they shared with the Malayan Communist Party. The meeting, held in English, was attended by the leading figures of the movements involved and chaired by Ishak Haji Muhammad. Mustapha Hussain was witness to it. Ishak, he noted, chose careful words: 'Everyone adopted a passive attitude, a patient disposition, a peaceful mind and a united stance.' The central proposal by the Malayan Democratic Union was for a common 'Malayan' citizenship, but straightaway this ran into difficulty with the PUTERA representatives. The Malay people, they argued, would not accept the word 'Malayan'; it was a term imposed on them that did not connote the Malays. The Cambridge-educated Malayan Democratic Union leader, Lim Kean Chye, was indignant: 'We are not dogs to be led by the people. We lead the people.' This provoked an angry retort from Mustapha Hussain: 'Do not humiliate the people.' The Malays, he went on, 'slept in bus stations and train stations in order to attend this conference. Some did not even have breakfast. They drank coffee out of a pail. But you, sir (looking at John Eber), even though you were given a comfortable rattan chair, you still need a folded towel to serve as a cushion. Who among us truly needs independence, you or us?'[126]

Yet a way forward was found. The term 'Malayan' was translated as *Melayu*. To UMNO, this connoted race, but to the Malay left – in the writings of its ideologue Dr Burhanuddin, for example – it had quite a different meaning. In recent months Burhanuddin had placed less emphasis on a Greater Indonesia and more on the inclusion of non-Malays in a *kebangsaan Melayu*, a *Melayu* nation. This was open to non-Malays, if they were to embrace it wholeheartedly, to sever their links with other nations and demonstrate their love for Malaya by a 'willingness to change their *bangsa* to *bangsa Melayu*.' The *Melayu*, as PUTERA understood it, carried within it the intent 'to live and die as a Malay'. But a further question arose. Islam was a vital component of Malay history and culture. In the vernacular, to *masuk Melayu*, 'become Malay', meant also to become a Muslim. Did this mean that to truly belong the non-Malays had to accept Islam? The PUTERA spokesmen seemed to deny that it did: *Melayu* was solely a legal and political category, and freedom of religion was guaranteed in the constitution proposals. 'The content of "*Melayu*" nationality', Boestamam insisted when casting the deciding vote on the issue, 'is just and not oppressive, wide and progressive.'[127] The non-Malays, too, saw the need for an exclusive allegiance to Malaya, but saw nationality as grounded in the individual rights of the citizen; a legal category, which, in a multiracial context, had no implications for cultural conformity.[128]

The crucial, creative ambiguity was left unresolved; it was, in a sense, lost in translation. Yet the People's Constitution, as drafted largely by John Eber, went further than the British ever did in envisaging an exclusive nationality for Malaya's people. It dissolved the distinctions between nationality and citizenship – between indigenous and non-indigenous – that lay at the heart of British proposals. The people's alternative enshrined *jus soli*, and offered citizenship to all those who had lived in Malaya for eight of the preceding ten years. In effect, this made the common experience of the Japanese occupation the defining transition. The final test of loyalty was 'the country in which a man would prefer to lay his bones, and for which he is prepared to die to defend, is his home'. The People's Constitution united Malaya and Singapore in a federation where the rulers were sovereign but constitutional monarchs governed by a legislature elected through universal suffrage and, in a further concession to the Malays, for the first nine years 55 per cent of the representatives were to be of Malay descent. The Malay language would be the national language, although other tongues might be used in the new national assembly. Malay religion and custom would remain in the hands of the Malays, and a Council of Races would monitor legislation for discrimination. But these provisions failed to impress the defenders of Malay primacy within the British administration. One observed that it left the Malays like 'the unfortunate king, so well known in their history, whose "bottom was being stuck with thorns at the same time that his mouth was being fed with bananas"'.[129]

The People's Constitution received only passing attention from the British. Gent told the Colonial Office that the AMCJA commanded no support and should be ignored. 'An academic exercise', was the conclusion in London; 'a typical production of people unaccustomed to political power and responsibility, and either unaware of, or unwilling to face, the real difficulties of personal and racial animosities, and of economic rivalries, which make Malayan politics so confused and the problem of settling a stable constitution so intractable'.[130] This was an astonishing statement. To its creators, the constitution came directly out of the experience of managing difference. 'It was quite clear from the outset', Philip Hoalim argued later, 'that our partners accepted the leadership of the Malayan Democratic Union. We, for our part, put unity first on our list of priorities and fashioned a constitution which would embody this unity in practice.'[131] But the British were not interested in alternatives. After the *volte-face* on the Malayan Union the previous year, they could not back down a second time, Gent least of all. MacDonald was less convinced, but the mounting confrontation with the unions in the course of 1947 and the vital need for Malay backing settled the matter. The final version of the federal constitution that was published in July was barely amended by the consultations. Faced with the intractable opposition of the British and UMNO, the united front leaders decided to take direct action.

PUTERA–AMCJA announced a *hartal*, or stoppage, for 20 October 1947, the date of the opening of the session of the British Parliament at which the future of Malaya would be discussed. The *hartal* was a new concept in Malaya, a staple of the civil disobedience of the Indian National Congress, which Tan Cheng Lock had admired during his sojourn there. It was unprecedented too in that, through Tan Cheng Lock's mediation, the Chinese *towkays* joined the demonstrations, led by the Associated Chinese Chambers of Commerce and the clan associations. They resented chiefly the watered-down citizenship provisions of the British proposals and the exclusion of Singapore. They had lobbied London and the consultative committee to no effect. The Chinese leaders who had sat on it, H. S. Lee and Leong Yew Koh, helped broker an understanding with the PUTERA–AMCJA. The main support came from Singapore, from Lee Kong Chian, the son-in-law of the overseas Chinese leader Tan Kah Kee, who commanded the Singapore Chinese Chamber of Commerce. It was an unnatural alliance. Many businessmen refused to co-operate with communists. The Malayan Democratic Union was reluctant to work with bodies whose protest was 'strictly negative' against the colonial constitution, and which did not support the nationality proposals of the people's alternative. The combined leadership never met; it merely declared protests on the same day. But the participation of Chinese business made the *hartal* a monumental and well-financed undertaking: 400,000 copies of the manifesto and 300,000 posters were distributed, and 300 propaganda groups toured the country to prepare the ground.[132] In the words of one local writer: 'In coffee shop and government office, in rubber estate lines and bus depots, by Governors over the radio and by leader writers in the press, people talked of local issues such as self-government, citizenship and communalism in a manner that made the six-year gap between 1941 and 1947 seem sixty. People talked of Malaya as home. It bewildered many.'[133]

By all accounts, Singapore and Malaya came to a complete standstill on 20 October. 'Kuala Lumpur that day', Ahmad Boestamam wrote, 'was deserted, like a land defeated by the invincible *garuda* [the eagle of apocalyptic legend]. Only PUTERA–AMCJA were to be seen going round the town to verify that the hartal was really a complete success.'[134] The scene was repeated throughout the country: the port of Singapore was throttled, and only the remoter villages and estates were less affected, although Malay support was strong in the fishing *kampongs* of the east coast. The organizers declared the *hartal* to be 90 per cent effective: 'It was the first political strike in Malaya to be observed by all sections of the people.'[135] The British refused to acknowledge the extent of the opposition it demonstrated. The Malayan Security Service reduced participation to statistics: 5 per cent joined for 'political motives'; 30 per cent through 'Chinese defensive nationalism'; 50 per cent were 'sheep', following in fear or ignorance; 5 per cent 'disgruntled' and a further 10 per cent 'incidentals'. Yet it struggled to find evidence of intimidation anywhere.[136]

But then came the backlash. Tan Cheng Lock was now under direct attack from the British and from his own community. Many Chinese blamed him for conceding Malay majority rule in the People's Constitution, and baulked at the implications of the *Melayu* nationality. The *Straits Times* whipped up the communist bogey. From this point, Tan Cheng Lock absented himself from most PUTERA–AMCJA meetings. It was said that the outbreak of labour trouble on his own rubber estates contributed to this.[137] The alliance with Chinese

Chambers of Commerce was not to be repeated. By the end of 1947 the fastest growing political party in Malaya was the party of business, the Kuomintang. In the first days of peace it had lain low, but now it was looking to assert its position. When MacDonald convened his summit meeting on the MCP in June, those present acknowledged that, along with UMNO on the peninsula, the Kuomintang was the only effective counter-balance to the MCP. Only the Kuomintang's own reputation for violence stood in the way of open co-operation with it. MacDonald still cherished hopes that 'a centre or Centre-Left party' might emerge with which the British could treat.[138] 'Our ultimate and supreme aim', he announced in a broadcast on the eve of the *hartal*, 'is a government of the peoples of Malaya, for the peoples of Malaya and by the peoples of Malaya'.[139] But the British had now reconciled themselves to alliance with ethnic-based parties in order to hold on to their diminished Asian empire.

The British repudiated the movement that most closely resembled the multiracial 'Malayan' nationalism they had originally sought to create. But the exuberant populism of the left was anathema to them. They could not see beyond the participation of the Malayan Communist Party and its proxies in PUTERA–AMCJA, and with this the People's Constitution would be for ever tainted. It was also to be dismissed as a superficial, paper alliance.[140] But this is not how it was seen by those involved at the time. It was seen as a great experiment, of learning by doing, in which the leaders of many different communities were debating, arguing, dividing and reconciling in the name of freedom and unity. It was a moment – in the face of the competing pull of communal politics – when a popular multiracial nationalism seemed a real possibility, and, in retrospect, an historic missed opportunity, perhaps.[141] The PUTERA–AMCJA did not collapse through division or disillusionment. Despite the withdrawal of the *towkays*, in late 1947 the morale of its leaders was high. Its fate was decided for it when it became caught in the crossfire of the looming confrontation between the British and the MCP. But this would not be solely a conflict between imperialism and its enemies. Across Asia a second conflict was looming, a war that would be fought to neutralize the central political legacy of the first. In the Japanese war, a new generation had formed popular movements that threatened to overturn pre-war hierarchies. In the intoxicating air of the post-war spring, Asia's *pemuda* had seized the streets and villages, filled them with their propaganda and stood up against imperialism and feudalism. But now, in free Asia and colonial Asia, this fresh-won freedom – of youth, of women, of workers – had to contend with the re-establishment of more conservative, patriarchal forms of authority. Bosses, landlords and bureaucrats would attempt to claw back some of the ground they had lost; 1948 would be a year of confrontation.

9

1948: A Bloody Dawn

BOYS' DAY IN BURMA

Shortly before dawn on 4 January 1948 dozens of diplomats prised themselves from their beds and proceeded to don official clothing and regalia. Burma's independence and exit from the Commonwealth had finally come to pass. Terrified by the memory of the assassination of Aung San, Burma's youthful leaders had consulted numerous astrologers. They had insisted that the date should be moved from 6 to 4 January and that the proclamation itself should take place at precisely 4 o'clock in the morning to take advantage of a favourable conjunction of the stars. Later that day Thakin Nu gave a speech setting out his high hopes for the new republic. He traced the history of Burma, from its great medieval past through the humiliations of British rule and Japanese invasion. The spirit of Aung San was heavy in the air; he had made 'the last sacrifice on the altar of freedom'.[1] True to tradition in the Buddhist world, the new country's president announced a purge of Burma's religious establishment to match the prime minister's political revolution. 'Evil practices' such as 'caste, begging, pagoda and monastery slavery' would be abolished.[2] The new national flag fluttered incongruously over the neo-Gothic government house in Rangoon, where a few years earlier, as Burma fell to the Japanese, Reginald Dorman-Smith had roamed amid what he saw as the jeering portraits of his predecessors. A significant number of men and women born before 1885 had lived to see their nation free again.

That evening in Delhi Dorman-Smith's bête noire, Mountbatten, held one of his ceremonious Governor General's spectacles. He presented to the Burmese ambassador a table that had belonged to the last independent ruler of Burma, King Thibaw. General Bucher, now commander-in-chief of the Indian Army, was unimpressed by the item, which, he wrote, 'looked not unlike a very superior wash stand'.[3] He also cringed when the orderly making the presentation, 'dressed in a costume which resembled that nowadays worn by attendants at Bertram Mills Circus', became entangled in his spurs. Yet Mountbatten, with his eye for ornamental symbolism, had not failed to mark the final severing of the imperial link between India and Burma.

Out in the Shan hills of eastern Burma, where Balwant Singh, the district magistrate of Indian descent, was now posted, the ceremonies were more prosaic. Balwant Singh felt a thrill of anticipation as the Union Flag was lowered and the Burmese flag went up in that chilly early morning. Yet, he remembered,

somehow our ceremony seemed mundane and the newly liberated citizenry unconcerned. When the district commissioner, U Aung Pe, officially declared that Burma was independent, it seemed a flat statement. The ceremonies continued. As the police marched past, the district commissioner took their salute, looking to me rather odd in his silk *pasoe*, dark jacket and pink headdress. There was something awkward about the way he saluted.[4]

Later the DC laid a wreath at the local martyrs' memorial that commemorated the assassinated Aung San and his colleagues. Sports events and cart races followed. Perhaps the low-key mood reflected people's fears for the future. In this area the communists almost immediately started a movement for the non-payment of taxes, sending small armed bands to terrorize the better-off residents and levy their own punitive wealth taxes. The administration responded by forming village defence groups, a tactic that was to become common down the whole length of the crescent from the Indian border as far as Singapore. To Balwant Singh's disgust, officials also instituted a policy of burning villages whose inhabitants were suspected of collaboration with the communists and forcibly relocating others away from the influence of the insurgents.[5]

The Burmese indeed awaited independence with hope and trepidation. At this point, hope prevailed. John Furnivall, the 71-year-old left-wing agrarian expert, was the only former British official invited to return to the country as an adviser. A Fabian socialist and practising

Christian who had briefly toyed with Buddhism, Furnivall had written a number of books that denounced 'colonial capitalism' and indicted the British for exacerbating ethnic differences in Southeast Asia.[6] In the 1930s Furnivall had got to know Nu and the other nationalist leaders while he helped to run a socialist bookshop in Rangoon. Later he worked with the government in exile at Simla, advising on the reconstruction of Burma, but he was always fiercely critical of Dorman-Smith, whom he accused of promoting the return of British firms to exploit the Burmese.[7] Coming back to Burma after nearly a decade, Furnivall was struck by the changes in Rangoon: 'Rangoon is no longer an Indian city', he wrote.[8] Burmese, not Indians, now predominated among Rangoon dock workers. The Chinese, too, were more or less invisible as they had adopted traditional Burmese dress during the war. But at the same time traditional Burmese costumes were giving way to new fashions for the aspiring new nation. People wore trilby hats and pith helmets, once a symbol of the white rulers, rather than Burmese turbans.[9] Many women were to be seen on the streets in battle dress or the dull green longyis of the People's Volunteer Organization (PVOs).

Furnivall was also struck by the popular celebrations accompanying independence. Shortly after his return he went to a dramatic perform-ance, a *pyazat*: 'It ended with a scene depicting a free people dancing in a rain of gold and silver. That was a dream in which almost everyone indulged.'[10] In this drama, 'the peasants and artisans triumphed over capitalism and imperialism'.[11] Many of the monks sweeping the plat-form of the now glistening and restored Shwedagon pagoda believed equally firmly that a new age of *dharma*, or spiritual virtue, had arrived. State and religion were about to be united again. They knew that this cosmic event was to be celebrated at a ceremony at which Nu, their reluctant prime minister, would distribute great quantities of food and gifts to the serried ranks of saffron-robed monks at the pagoda. Celebrations lit up the streets in Rangoon. In Mandalay, the half burnt-out city was beginning to rise again; ugly concrete blocks sprang up from the ashes of the pretty wooden shophouses. Burmese traders looked forward to inheriting everything left by departed Indian magnates. Burmese peasants rejoiced at the prospect of the cancel-lation of their loans from the resented Chettiyar moneylenders. Edgy young soldiers and militiamen, toting their rifles on the streets and taking a cut from passing buses and taxis, confidently expected that the new government would expand the armed forces and raise their pay. Across the country, however, the peoples of the frontier areas, along with Christians, Anglo-Burmans, the few remaining British settlers, Karens, Kachins and Shans, waited tensely to see whether the new regime would honour the concessions made to them by Aung San at the Panglong conference and in other statements. No one was sure whether the millennium or an apocalypse lay ahead.

The new government got to work on 5 January with a huge head of steam behind it. Edgar Snow, an American journalist and veteran of Mao Zedong's 'long march', visited Rangoon a few weeks after independence. Snow had had his first taste of Burmese radicalism when he met Thein Pe in India in 1943 and was persuaded to write a preface to the latter's *What Happened in Burma*. On his visit to Rangoon Snow stayed with Furnivall.[12] It was from Furnivall, the British Foreign Office thought, that Snow had got the rather inflated figures of the pre-war profits of British firms that he used in an article to justify the forthcoming nationalization of British assets. An official in London remarked sourly of Furnivall that his 'socialist antipathy to British firms in Burma, acquired during his long ICS service, is well known'.[13]

Snow marvelled at the youth of the new leadership. Nu himself was 'an old man' of forty-two; the interior minister was a stripling of thirty-six.[14] Snow was charmed by the youthful enthusiasm, even naivety of his smiling hosts. It was Boys' Day all year round, he thought. The government's two-year plan for the economy was most impressive: Stalinism with a smile. Land would be given back to the tiller, as had been the case before the British invasion. Then collective farming on the Chinese model would gradually be introduced. The government would take over management of rice exports, the profit from which had gone into pockets in London, Bombay and Madras for a generation. The government would nationalize the great companies and pay off their former British and Indian owners with bonds, which meant the money would stay in Burma. Burma would become neutral in foreign affairs and a great start was to be made in March with the All-Asian Peasants Conference to be held in Mandalay. Snow put down the slightly unorthodox enthusiasm of the young Burmese rulers to the old national habit of mixing astrology, spirit worship and Buddhism. Burmese were 'competent' and pragmatic. They picked and mixed from every ideology on display. But even the amiable and left-leaning Snow worried about what the future would really bring to this small, young country wedged between two huge expansionist neighbours and perched atop the outposts of the British Empire, spruced up and given a new lease of life by its American cousin: 'It's like power and responsibility being suddenly handed to a student union, to realise the Utopia they have long demanded from their hopeless elders,' he mused.[15] Furnivall also shared these misgivings. When he first entered his new office, the Burmese minister of planning pumped the hand of the old ICS man and said: 'Now we have independence, give us a plan.' Nu, Furnivall thought, was charming and enthusiastic but 'perhaps over-prolific of ideas'.[16]

Central to the health of the new republic was indeed the genial figure of Thakin Nu. The new prime minister epitomized the Buddhist socialism that was to be the hallmark of Burma's independence. Always pining to return to the monastery, Nu was nevertheless no traditional man, but more a kind of intellectual magpie. He had been and continued to be a prolific writer and lecturer. His 1940 novel in Burmese, *Man, the Wolf of Man*, was so called after Thomas Hobbes's dictum 'Man is to man a wolf'. In it he had expatiated on the evils of colonial capitalism, asserting that the patient Burmese peasantry must be freed from debt to reach their true potential as spiritual beings. He said he had been influenced by writers as various as Sir Thomas More, G. F. Hegel, H. G. Wells and Sigmund Freud.[17] His was a modernist Buddhism which opposed the mistaken use of the doctrine of karma – cosmic retribution – which, he thought, encouraged uneducated people to be passive and accepting of exploitation. Instead, Buddhism was a science to perfect the human soul. Later, at an archaeological excavation on the site of an ancient monastery, he alluded to the discovery of penicillin and the invention of jet propulsion and the atom bomb, but pointed to the even more important and equally 'scientific' discoveries of the Buddha. At least in these early days, many Burmese saw him as an almost ideal ruler, akin to the legendary sage-king of Burmese folklore, Setkya Min. Popular dramatic performances propagated this idea. Nu saw no contradiction between Buddhism and socialism either, though, as Furnivall tartly pointed out, this was perhaps because 'although an enthusiastic Marxist, he knows little and understands less of Marxism'.[18]

Relations with the British began to become a little strained, despite the good will which had been generated by the Anglo-Burmese agreement and Listowel's visit of the previous autumn. Public opinion wanted swift action to end the legacy of colonial rule, even if Thakin Nu realized the importance of keeping foreign capital flowing into the country. The press was full of denunciations of capitalists and imperialists while more than 100,000 members of the PVOs were straining at the leash across the country.[19] The big British firms seemed the most appropriate targets. Within weeks of independence the new government served notice that it would immediately nationalize the Irrawaddy Flotilla Company and the mines. It also announced it would take over a third of all the great teak forests of central Burma which accounted for about 40 per cent of Steel Brothers' holdings.[20] This caused consternation in the City of London and Whitehall because the question of compensation was mentioned in only the vaguest possible terms. The gentlemanly capitalists of the 'square mile' were very well aware of how limited the Burmese government's resources were. Their alarm was, however, tempered with glee. Financiers and some of the more conservative civil servants noted that the anti-capitalist British government was finally being forced to recognize the importance of the resources which Britain had secured during the pre-war period of capitalist free trade: 'HMG is on something of a cleft stick', one presumably Tory official noted with satisfaction.

This attack on British firms by the Burmese government was more a matter of psychology than of leftist political economy. What was really under attack was not so much the capitalist system, but the greed and discrimination associated with it in the minds of a Buddhist people long attuned to regard themselves as underdogs, the servants of the servants. No doubt there was a drain of wealth from Burma in the pre-war period. Its handsome surplus on exports of teak, wolfram and oil to India and Britain was almost certainly outbalanced by the flow of resources abroad in the form of insurance and transport payments, and the salaries and remittances of British and Indian workers in the country. Ironically, though, it was what had stayed in the country that had caused most offence to the Burmese. After 1936 British firms operating in Burma had chosen to avoid high taxation by 'ploughing back' earnings into local projects. To a large extent, what had resulted were not new commercial enterprises which would help the Burmese but bigger salaries and perks for British expatriates and, to a lesser extent, their Anglo-Burmese, Anglo-Indian and Indian employees. In local terms the expatriates' earnings had been massive. Huge country houses with large staffs of Burmese servants had sprung up on the northern outskirts of Rangoon. Money had been 'ploughed back' into rose gardens and tropical fern houses around Maymyo, or charabancs to ferry poetry lovers to picnics at the Hampshire Falls. This had all taken place as racial segregation had become more pronounced. The old days of a nod and a wink and a cheroot had been replaced by the flagrant racism of the British nouveaux riches. To the Burmese of 1948, all these greedy interests, British and Indian, had seemed to be re-infecting the body politic under the guise of 'rehabilitation' or the slogan of keeping Burma open to 'international capital investment'.

The junior managers of the teak estates, with their carefully sequestered Burmese mistresses, at least lived alongside the people and the elephants. The Irrawaddy Flotilla Corporation, by contrast, was naked in its racial exclusiveness. The vast majority of managers had been British or Anglo-Burman; almost all its local employees were Chittagonian Indians. The IFC had a virtual monopoly of motor transport on Burma's sacred river, so the Burmese had to travel on its boats, but most could not afford or were otherwise subtly excluded from its cabin-class accommodation. It is not surprising that the IFC was marked down for expropriation so early.

'Boys' Day' was coming to a premature end, however, and Thakin Nu's leadership was quite quickly forced back into a more suppliant mode towards the British and American governments by a prolonged burst of internal disorder. One group of people who knew exactly what was about to happen were the communist leaders who had broken with the AFPFL in 1946 when Aung San had brokered his deal with Rance.[21] These red-flag communists, led by Thakin Soe, had been joined by Than Tun's 'white' communists, who had come to blows with the AFPFL more recently over the Nu–Attlee agreement made in the autumn of 1947, which they saw as a sell-out. Than Tun was a longtime associate of Nu and his rebellion shocked the prime minister. To some degree, the new 'white' militancy resulted from the changed international situation. Soviet communism was going on to the offensive and its followers in eastern Europe, India and Southeast Asia followed suit. The Indian Communist Party hosted a major conference in Calcutta in February 1948, which was attended by Than Tun along with delegates from Malay and Indo-China. But Than Tun was also over confident.[22] He predicted that the 'bones' of the AFPFL politicians would fill to the brim the Bagaya Pit near Rangoon. He was buoyed up by the huge gatherings of peasants that came out to hear the leftist leaders in February and March. Than Tun may have misinterpreted the peasants' enthusiasm for communism: they were probably just looking for some excitement, now that independence had finally dawned and the colonial policemen had retreated from the country. Another communist leader, Thein Pe, believed that Than Tun had made a fatal doctrinal error. The AFPFL was not simply an imperialist and capitalist front; it had a serious 'mass' following.[23] Than Tun and the others should have been good Marxist believers and waited for a bourgeois revolution and not allowed a workers' and peasants' putsch to go off half-cocked. The British felt that Thein Pe's moderate communism might be even more insidious than that of the white and red revolutionaries.[24]

The communist ideologues, led by Than Tun and Hari Narayan Ghosal, the latter an Indian labour organizer,[25] had scoured the history of the Russian revolution to come up with an analysis of their present situation. In a long, verbose minute, written in the unmistakable leaden language of international communism, Ghosal set out his justification for an immediate Burmese insurrection which was to take place in March 1948 at the latest.[26] He argued in retrospect that Aung San and Thakin Nu were not really leaders of a revolutionary people but representatives of a new 'Burmese bourgeoisie' that would co-operate with international imperialism. They would allow British, American and even the hated Indian businessmen to carry on exploiting the Burmese people. They doubted that the new regime would push through nationalization, but if it did they believed that even the limited compensation on offer to the likes of Steel Brothers and the Burmah Oil Company would cripple the young nation for a genera-tion. Worse, it would drive Burma to take loans from capitalist coun-tries and organizations such as the International Monetary Fund. Reactionary Tory British imperialism had now given way, they argued, to the Anglo-American 'expansionism' of the Labour Party. It amounted to much the same thing. The British would draw Burma back into the coils of their still-powerful Southeast Asian empire by manipulating the defence agreement which Nu had signed in the summer of 1947.

The communists had a point. Empire's receding shadow still fell over Burma, even when it had decided to leave the Commonwealth. The British services mission set up in the Nu–Attlee agreement reflected the last flicker of the tradition of the Indian Army. John Freeman, a future British High Commissioner in India, had negotiated a treaty with Burma in the summer of 1947. The official doctrine was that it was undesirable that Burma should go outside the British Common-wealth for arms or military advice. The Labour government wanted a 'stable and friendly' Burma.[27] It worried about an outbreak of 'anarchy' that would compromise the defence of both India and Malaya, encouraging communism and damaging British business as it struggled to recover from war. London and the Rangoon embassy both believed that the army was in a state of near chaos. As late as 1940 there had been no Burmese officers in the army and all the technicians, engineers and clerks had been Indian. Withdrawal of British and Indian expertise and experience could only lead to disaster. 'Their fighting, like their politics, is essentially medieval', haughtily minuted Peter Murray, who was in charge of the Burma desk in Whitehall.[28] The head of the services mission, Major General Geoffrey Bourne, had the difficult task of persuading the Burmese to form an efficient military force which they could also afford. He had to offer firm strategic and organizational advice without appearing to be running the show.

Bourne had some things going for him. Above all, he had good relations with the new head of the Burma Army, Major General Smith Dun. 'Four-foot' Smith Dun was the Christian Karen army officer who had fought in the first Burma campaign, staging an ultimately unsuccessful rearguard action to protect the Indian Army as it withdrew into India. To the British, who knew, from long experience, exactly how to patronize him, he had 'all the Karen's courage and loyalty', but was not very bright. A minute noted that he always allowed himself to be pushed around by political magnates. Once, when he was refused a government aircraft to fly him to Maymyo to lecture at the staff college there, Smith Dun had meekly booked himself on to a crowded passenger flight. Later, as the Karen revolt gathered pace, Smith Dun was to find his position untenable and was probably unsurprised to be sent on 'indefinite leave'.[29] It is easy to see why he succumbed to the steely ruthlessness of General Ne Win. Still, as the old Burma hand B. R. Pearn minuted in the Foreign Office, quoting Erasmus: 'In the country of the blind, the one-eyed man is king.'[30] By far the most effective parts of the army were the Karen, Kachin, Shan and Chin regiments, which were descendants of the old colonial Burmese and Indian Army units and not the nationalists' Burma Defence Army with which they had been merged by Mountbatten and Aung San.

This meeting of minds between the British and the minorities-in-arms was deeply suspect to the AFPFL, and especially to the enigmatic figure of General Ne Win, who glided to centre stage at this point of the drama. Ne Win and his socialist generals were not in the least concerned with the defence of British Asia. They were adamant that the British should be kept in a purely advisory role, not a tactical one. They still feared a British attempt to sheer off the frontier and minority areas of the country into a mini-Malaya. Above all, they wanted to use the army as a tool of nation building. Their aim was to absorb as many of the people's militias as possible into an expanded Burma Army, so that these resentful youths did not line up behind their political enemies. But in order to expand the army's payroll the politicians had to cut back on the purchase and renovation of transport. As early as February 1948 the British services mission to Burma noted that the army's strength had risen from 20,000 to 23,000.[31] The result, according to the mission, was a large and relatively immobile force, when what Burma needed was a fast-moving strike force to damp down trouble as soon as it arose. At least in British eyes, the nation-building aspect of the Burmese government's military policy also led it to favour 'less able' Burmese officers, with links to local strongmen, over tried and tested Anglo-Indian and Anglo-Burman officers who were regarded as politically suspect.

These strains made the mission's work painfully difficult. Many of the better officers of the old Burma Army reluctantly realized that help from their former imperial master was essential if the country was to stay in one piece. But they resented the tone and manner of the professional British officers. Lieutenant Colonel Maung Maung, head of the officer training school at Maymyo, barked: 'I don't need any British advisers. I am the Commandant now and I will soon get rid of all of you.'[32] Relations were further embittered by the fact that the remaining British officers occupied 90 per cent of the decent married accommodation at the major army bases. The Burmese, sporting their new national badges and epaulettes, were pushed out into leaking tents or bamboo huts as the first monsoon of independent Burma broke with patriotic violence. But, worse, there was a ghost at the feast: the Japanese. The most difficult thing of all to counteract, the British believed, was 'the legacy of Japanese influence'.[33] The Burmese admired the 'simple ruthlessness' of the Japanese. Many of the nationalist officers had been trained by them in 1941–2 and thought that the secret of Japan's success had been the deployment of lightly equipped forces with a minimum of administrative control; they believed that their own army would be highly successful if trained along these lines. Despite Britain's victorious fightback in 1944 and 1945, the Burmese thought that the British military tradition was still burdened with bumf, tied down with red tape, immobilized by protocols. After decades of colonial bureaucracy, the Burmese intensely disliked being drilled once again in spit, polish and paper.

Burmese politicians caught this mood easily. Once the communists and their other radical opponents began to accuse them of selling out to the old empire, the AFPFL began publicly to distance itself from the British mission. To the exasperation of the War Office in London, however, Nu and his colleagues freely combined public denunciations of unspecified 'scheming imperialists' with pathetic private appeals for aircraft, spare parts and ammunition, especially once the internal security situation began to deteriorate in March 1948. At the very moment when communist insurgency flared up in earnest, the Burmese minister of defence was about to make a private visit to Singapore to look at South East Asia Command's hardware with an eye to future purchases. The Burmese government was forever demanding second-hand Oxford trainer aircraft, Spitfires and, above all, ammunition.[34] The campaign of 1945 had made everyone only too well aware of the importance of fighter attacks in support of advancing troops. Thakin Nu himself had been surprised twice by British planes which came in to strafe Ba Maw's house. But ammunition was the vital need, and here was a real problem. The War Office was alarmed because the Burmese demand for 6 million rounds was merely one among dozens of requisitions from newly liberated and newly embattled countries around the world from Greece to Malaya. There were two other particular embarrassments. Much of the new Burma Army's equipment was Japanese. The British had to go cap in hand to the Americans in Japan to get them to release stores. Secondly, there was a nagging fear in the War Office that they were about to make a serious error. In China a great deal of Japanese war materiel had fallen directly into the hands of the communists or the Soviets in 1945. As summer arrived the mandarins' nightmare was that the ammunition ships, Spitfires, Oxfords and all would enter Rangoon on the very day that the provisional Soviet Republic of Burma was proclaimed and the AFPFL was abruptly replaced with the red flag.[35]

This possibility dawned on the bureaucrats surprisingly late in the day. At first the British and Burmese governments were both fairly sure that the situation could be contained. Everyone agreed that the communists were only distantly linked to Moscow and certainly did not take orders from the Comintern. Foreign ideological links, insofar as they existed, were with India's communists, who were better at discussions in coffeehouses than long marches. There had been sporadic trouble in the spring of 1947 and that had not come to very much. The only threat was that the army would itself lean to the left. When it first arrived the British mission thought this was unlikely. The Karens, Kachins and Shans were deemed to be uninterested in politics unless the government interfered in their 'racial affairs'. Men from the old colonial army in Burma were either neutral or keenly loyal to the new regime. Even the fighters from the former Burma

Defence Army were largely pro-AFPFL. There were, all the same, a few violent nationalists in the guise of communists in the 5th Burma Rifles, the training department, Burma Engineers and transport establishment.

THE GENESIS OF
COMMUNIST REBELLION

As it turned out, everything was much more fragile than the authorities thought. The youth in the villages and in the volunteer organizations were deeply frustrated. The millennium had been promised for three years, it had dawned and nothing much had changed. The towns were doing better, but there were still areas of deep misery in the countryside, hungry for basic commodities let alone consumer goods. Land reform was in train but already it seemed that the people who were getting 'peasant holdings' sequestered from the Indian, Chinese and other landholders were the hangers-on of the AFPFL village committees and not young PVO men who had fought for their country.[36] Indian moneylenders still collected their interest in the delta villages. Arrogant Europeans still patrolled the teak forests. Communist propaganda was quite effective. The young believed that Britain was still milking Burma of its resources and, worse, that the Burmese government was paying compensation to it for the nationalization of unprincipled British firms. Burma's military forces were not even its own, as could be seen by the presence of the British services mission.

Quite apart from these local resentments, a deep sense that the world was changing had trickled into even remote areas. Something called communism, which promised to get rid of landowners and capitalists, was sweeping across eastern Europe. Burmese communists joined Indian ones at their great congress in Calcutta in February 1948, perhaps the high point of radical communism in India. The Party had finally began to throw off the taint that it had collaborated with the British during the war. A violent and partly successful communist movement was pitting peasants against landlords in the southern Indian state of Telengana (to the north of the old Madras presidency) and this was shaking Jawaharlal Nehru's new polity. Burmese communists also met British communists in a conference in London that year. Meanwhile, Andrei Zhdanov and the Cominform were apparently preparing for a set of risings across Southeast Asia which would parallel the successes of communism in eastern Europe. Connections between these different groups of revolutionaries were indeed extremely indirect, but there was a general sense that the socialist world had emerged from the war in a strong position.

Back in Burma, nationalist defeats in China crept closer to the northern border and army deserters flooded into the Kachin and northern Shan states. A new charismatic name began to be heard among the youths arguing in the meeting places of small towns: Mao Zedong. There is little evidence that the Chinese communists had even the most distant relationship with the red- or white-flag communists in Burma before 1948,[37] but Burmese translations of Mao's works began to appear in large numbers in the early months of that year. Mao's military language and insistence that the peasantry could be the vanguard of revolution appealed to young people whose world had already been turned upside down once in their short lives. It meant much more than the arid, Moscow-style logic chopping of orthodox communists and their Bengali admirers. Even the British embassy began to hear rumours of Mao. They telegraphed to London asking for English translations of his works. Yet no one in London seemed to know who he was.

Hari Narayan Ghosal and his allies must have sensed this change in public mood, so rather than risk being caught off guard by an outbreak of unco-ordinated popular uprisings in the delta and the north, they began in the early weeks of 1948 to plan a co-ordinated uprising for the late spring. Ghosal adhered to what was called a 'working-class' strategy. This involved the formation in the towns of armed workers' militias. Than Tun and Ba Thein, two other leaders, favoured creating 'base areas' among the peasantry in what was rapidly becoming known as a Maoist strategy. In this 'semi-feudal' country, ignoring the peasantry was not an option. Ghosal himself addressed a mass meeting of hundreds of thousands of peasants in March 1948, promising them land and no taxes.[38] The idea was apparently to move in March and April to create a series of communist-controlled base areas which would cut the country in two and isolate Rangoon from Mandalay. Then, as the monsoon set in and the already stretched and immobile government forces became bogged down in the mud, these base areas could be linked together. A working-class rising in the Rangoon docks and the southern oil installations would accompany a *coup d'état* which would fore-shadow victory over imperialism and the Burmese bourgeoisie. As it was, the government, which was partially informed of these plans, made the first move. On 23 March several communist leaders were rounded up by the police and interrogated, but the operation was bungled and many of the most important leaders scattered into the hinterland.[39]

By 1 April the political situation in the country was very uneasy and a week later the typical signs of a Burmese insurrection were plain to see. Telegraph wires and bridges were sabotaged across the delta and police stations were under attack in a way reminiscent of the revolt against the Japanese three years earlier. Some of those more traditional symptoms of a coming uprising which generations of British officials were taught to expect had also begun to appear. People had their skin tattooed to ward off evil and insurgents tried to make themselves invulnerable to government bullets with spells.[40] The old prophecies of the 1880s about Burma's future were ransacked once again and spirit dancers at the *nat* spirit shrines mouthed apocalyptic premonitions. Villages were burned and police stations attacked across a wide range of territory in the south and the north-central part of the country. The six-month-long 'Boys' Day' party abruptly broke up in tears. James Bowker, the British ambassador, described 'a state of mind bordering on panic' in the Rangoon secretariat.[41] To add to its troubles, the government got into a long slugging match with the press about one of Burma's periodic political sex scandals. The minister of agriculture was accused of seducing a 'respectable' married woman. The minister denied this and the AFPFL leadership began attacking newspapers and encouraging mobs to destroy several newspaper offices and presses. It mattered little that the public later discovered that the woman concerned had gone through no fewer than five husbands before she was twenty-four and, in Furnivall's Victorian parlance, was 'no better than a baggage'.[42] The two years of press freedom which Burma had enjoyed effectively came to an end, never to return.

The government realized that the police were unrealiable, the volunteer brigades were hostile and the army was split down the middle. It vacillated, embarking now on a half-hearted purge of the army and pleading secretly for help from the British. At the same time, though, it confused matters by trying to improve relations with the communists in private discussions. To the annoyance of the British government, Nu again publicly denounced 'imperialists' – their identity was scarcely concealed – in an attempt to curry favour with his leftist former colleagues.[43] Yes, of course compensation would be given to British firms, the government said, but this was no different from the compensation given to Western firms by the recently installed communist government in Czechoslovakia. And Burma's debt repayment to the British was no different from the one embarked on by the communist USSR in the 1920s. Anyway, the British government was itself socialist; it had simply avoided the Soviet way of blood, pleaded Nu, once again longing for retirement to a monastery.

Though Nu's speech stirred up a flurry of pained letters from the British ambassador and even a more-in-sorrow-than-in-anger epistle from Stafford Cripps, this trimming cut little ice with the communists.[44] It also made the War Office even more suspicious about handing over military hardware to Burma. Relations between the two governments were further strained when the Burmese began alleging that British military procurement and sale in the whole of South East Asia Command was corrupt. They had been reliably informed that huge quantities of military stores, which should have gone to Burma under the Attlee–Nu agreement, were actually being sold off on the Singapore black market and were probably finding their way into the hands of Malayan and Burmese communists.[45] In Rangoon itself there were persistent rumours and allegations that the British military supply board (a civilian organization) was in cahoots with local Anglo-Burmese and Indian businessmen. Rather than selling to government, it was secretly disposing of war surplus to the highest bidder, in the best traditions of the old 'black-market administration' of 1945. Whitehall was somewhat muted in its response to these allegations because they seemed only too plausible.

Besides denouncing the British, Nu tried other ways to revive national unity and outflank the communists. In early April he masterminded a final burial ceremony for the embalmed remains of Aung San and his colleagues. Medical opinion supported the interment; the bodies, still lying in state in the Jubilee Hall, were decomposing rapidly.[46] But Furnivall understood the political motive behind the ceremony: Nu's attempt to invoke the spirit of Aung San to revive the old wartime nationalist alliance. Members of the armed forces drew Bogyoke's bier to his last resting place and some communist leaders attended the burial, but past comradeship could not hide present differences. On 8 May the final act of this older drama was played out. At dawn on this cloudy morning U Saw walked out of his prison cell wearing his usual jacket and a longyi. He chatted briefly with his guards and shook the hands of the men who were about to hang him.[47] All appeals, private and public, had failed. Dorman-Smith could do nothing for him, even though he had written a letter to him claiming that the trial was biased and had publicly declared, 'I know U Saw. I know him to be an honest man.'[48] In fact, as Furnivall noted, 'Dorman-Smith's appeal for mercy on behalf of U Saw was perhaps the most certain way of ensuring his execution', as most Burmese believed that Dorman-Smith was somehow connected with the assassination of Aung San.[49] British associates who might have taken some of the blame for murder had been quietly frog-marched off the political stage, to the relief of both governments. In his final moments, U Saw turned to Buddhist priests, saying, 'He who dares to do things, must dare bear the consequences.' Two of his Burmese associates were hanged with him. Later that day Nu hosted a rally for peasants in Fytche Square, newly renamed Bandula Park after the antique Burmese martial hero. He urged his audience to grow more food. With U Saw dead, almost the last link with the Burmese high politics of the 1930s had been severed.

A SUMMER OF ANARCHY

By early June the situation had deteriorated further. Burmese Muslims were on the point of rebellion in Arakan. To the far north sporadic rebellions among hill Karen, Shan and Kachin peoples became entwined with the politics of opium.[50] In the south, in the countryside around Pegu, rebels showed a new level of determination, fighting on during the monsoon when once they would have retired to await drier conditions.[51] They were also prepared to mount strong attacks on Burma Army units and police stations, taking heavy casualties in the process. This too was a new development. It was already, the British mission conceded, 'a small civil war'[52] and the 'Irrawaddy valley was virtually dominated by the rebels'.[53] The only thing that held the rebels back was a shortage of ammunition for their predominantly Japanese weapons. But this was true of the government forces as well. The government renewed its secret pleas to London for ammunition and attack aircraft. The War Office had already despatched an ammunition ship, but that was heading for Rangoon at a deliberately slow pace. The Burmese government fumbled on the political front too. It pronounced an amnesty and wasted fuel dropping leaflets over the countryside in imitation of Slim's psychological warfare four years earlier. The communists made an easy riposte with their argument that the government was selling the country out. There were now twenty British 'advisers' in the Rangoon War Office. Then again, the government decided to try to recruit police into the army. But 800 of the 1,200 men concerned were declared unfit 'due to VD and other causes'. In planning attacks on the rebel positions, Smith Dun always had the feeling that the descendants of Aung San's army were not really 'his' men. 'In short the whole five battalions of the ex-Patriotic Burma Force contingent . . . is not available for serious internal security purposes.'

In July, when the insurrections were making rapid headway, Nu reacted in a manner that was typical of his Buddhist beliefs and idiosyncratic politics. He knelt before an image of the Buddha in his house and made a vow of celibacy, or 'extreme purity', as he put it. Soon afterwards his wife moved out of the house and the couple separated. Perhaps Nu felt that this act of personal renunciation would help atone for the murder and destruction occurring all around him.[54] The embattled prime minister now lived alone in what was commonly called 'the concentration camp' in Windermere Park. This was a heavily fortified, barbed-wire protected enclosure patrolled by trigger-happy guards who occasionally shot dead civilians who inadvertently got too close.[55] A couple of months later a British press correspondent compared Rangoon to 'a Mexican border city expecting a raid by Pancho Villa. It is a city of non-descript uniforms, sombrero wearing gunmen with pistols lashed to their thighs, multi-guarded politicians, funk holes and fear.'[56]

By early August, large parts of the army were not merely holding aloof, but actually pulling out of the government alliance. A unit of the elite Burma Rifles was supposed to move against the communists in Hwambi. Instead, they took the opportunity to desert and tried to establish a popular-front government with the communist and militia leaderships in the district. Burmese officers posted to the south of the country were openly saying that they would not lift a finger against their former colleagues because the government was bound to fall in two or three days. Meanwhile, the insurgency crept closer to the Syriam oil storage tanks and refinery and the remaining British personnel found themselves evacuating Bassein for the second time in the decade. As the end of the year approached, the territory ruled by the formal government of Burma was effectively reduced to a couple of patches of land around Rangoon and Mandalay.

The scale of the Burmese government's problems was revealed by the case of General Zeya, the newly appointed Burmese military attaché in London. The British government could hardly hide its distaste that the appointee was a hardline nationalist and not a former Burma Army officer. Zeya had been president of the Rangoon University Students' Union in 1940–41. As one of the original Thirty Comrades who had led the march into Burma in 1942, he had duly fled to Hainan, along with Aung San, to be trained by the Japanese. But Britain's dislike of Zeya was soon rendered immaterial as Rangoon suddenly announced that he was 'unavailable' for the appointment. In fact, he was one of a large number of soldiers who had defected en masse to the communists while on counter-insurgency duty. The next time round, the Burmese government tried a little diplomacy. Zeya's replacement was to be 'Terry' Tun Hla Oung. He was deputy inspector-general of police, but it was his stewardship of the Rangoon Turf Club and his reputation as a good drinking and racing man that made him attractive to the British. An Anglophile and 'not close to the [Burmese] Socialist government', 'Terry' should, the British embassy in Rangoon suggested, be put up for membership of 'a British racing institution'.[57] The mutiny of important units of the army, including elements of the prized Burma Rifles, reflected increasing doctrinal splits within the high command.[58] The strange signals sent out by the appointment to London first of Zeya and then of his ideological antithesis, Tun Hla Oung, simply confirmed this.

KARENS AND BRITONS

The Burmese government's crises came not singly, but in threes. The moment the communist advance slackened, the military mutiny began. As soon as the government began to counter the mutiny, the Karen and other minorities became restive. To the Burmese military, which still had many connections amongst the communists, the Karen insurgency was easily the most dangerous threat to the integrity of independent Burma. Karen officers were still extremely well represented among the senior officers of the units of the old colonial Burma Army that had been merged with Aung San's forces in 1945–6. The Panglong conference the previous year had been a success, not because the anxieties of the minorities had been put to rest, but because of Aung San's personal prestige. With Bogyoke gone and the government mired in quicksand, the hard men of the Karen National Union (KNU) came to the fore again. The hill Karen of the north, the so-called Red Karens, were generally satisfied with Rangoon's agreement to the continuation of a semi-autonomous Karenni state within the Union of Burma. In the south, however, where educated Christianized Karens dominated the community, many people regarded the Union's concession of a special 'minority status' to them as insufficient. A powerful group within the KNU rejected special minority representation in local government in favour of a completely separate nation-state. This was dubbed 'Karenistan', an optimistic allusion to Jinnah's egregious creation. If the bifocal Pakistan that had emerged a few months earlier was a geographer's nightmare, the idea of Karenistan was a map-maker's hell. Only in the forested Salween tract of the south were the Karens a majority of the population. This rather backward area could hardly form the basis of a separate unit within Burma, let alone a proud new member of the Commonwealth and the United Nations, as some dreamers hoped. Elsewhere in the delta the Karens were simply too scattered to constitute a political unit, even if overall they comprised 20 per cent of the local population. The decisive point was that, unlike Karachi and Dacca in the two wings of Pakistan, Karenistan would have had no big town to act as a gateway to the world. Sleepy Moulmein was the nearest the Karens got to a capital and here they were nowhere near a majority of the population.

Political dreamers, however, are not overmuch influenced by the study of geography. Besides, there were good reasons, both long and short term, that the Karen issue should come to the boil again in the early summer of 1948. In the first place, the Karens were now acutely aware of how dependent the Burmese government was on the Karen element of the old colonial Burma Army, and in particular on Smith Dun. They saw with mounting alarm the drift of all the other elements in the army either to the communists or to mutiny. But while the government was actually militarily dependent on the Karens and other minorities, the direction of its policy belied this basic fact. Karen leaders were suspicious of Nu's oft-stated desire to compromise with the communists. They scanned the government's economic pro-gramme with dismay. It was following a slow, centralizing drift that they believed would eventually render the Panglong agreement irrel-evant. Christian Karens, in particular, were opposed on principle to 'godless communism' and believed that once Nu felt free to escape to a monastery, whatever government came to rule Burma would be hostile to them.

These political perceptions were simply surface issues, of course. What really fuelled the Karens' and other minorities' grab for the security of a separate political status was fear of their Burmese neigh-bours. It was not the political elders who dismayed them so much as the young men of the PVOs and the semi-bandit culture which permeated the delta. It was Burmese thugs, not the Japanese, who had massacred the Karens when the BIA ripped into the delta in 1942 and the raw memory of the hundreds of men, women and children slaughtered fed a much older sense of difference and alienation. Karen fears became sharper in September and October, when leftist army officers decided to raise yet another irregular force, the Sitwundan. A politically moderate Burmese officer, on the point of resignation, identified the leaders of this organization as 'dacoits or ex-dacoits or people familiar in police records. Some of them are either known criminals or political chameleons.'[59]

General Bourne of the British mission just happened to be in Smith Dun's house on 29 August 1948 when a number of the more intransigent KNU leaders were present. They regaled him with stories about the essential difference between Burmese, who were ruthless individualists, and the community-conscious Karens. Burmese politics was simply about faction and personal aggrandizement, he was told. After all, one need only look at the pre-British deeds of the old Burmese kings, who regularly disembowelled and burned alive their own relatives, to sample the Burmese idea of independence. As for Nu, 'it was his appeasement of communism which they all feared and would never accept'. Nor had they forgotten Nu's pre-war incarnation as the secretary of the Red Dragon Society, which had translated the works of Marx, Lenin and Stalin. Oliver Ba Thun, one of the most intransigent of the KNU leaders, a public school and Oxbridge-educated barrister, said that he regarded the Labour government as a bitter enemy of the Karens. In contrast he welcomed the strong support the Karens enjoyed among British Conservatives and people in America and Australia.[60] Bourne did not mention where Smith Dun himself stood on all this. Ostensibly, he remained a loyal servant of the Burmese government. Still, the Karens had to look after themselves.

Bourne's presence at this gathering was, of course, far from a matter of chance. He was helping Smith Dun reorganize and strengthen the army hierarchy as mutiny threatened. In this instance, the communists' allegations were quite correct. The long British love affair with the Karens, which had made the latter so suspect to the Japanese, continued after Burmese independence. The disgruntled Noel Stevenson had now retired from the field but other former civil officers continued to argue their case in London, convinced that the British had betrayed the Karens and other minorities. One crack-brained 'Zionist solution' was to ship the irreconcilable Karens out to North Borneo, where they could help expand rice production for the reviving Malayan economy. Some people, however, envisaged more resolute action. Force 136 still cast a long shadow over the whole of Southeast Asia. Rumours still swirled around among the Burmese about the involvement of its officers in the assassination of Aung San and his cabinet. By February Bowker, the British ambassador, had already become uneasy because Force 136 officers were still maintaining contacts with the Karens. Colonel J. C. 'Pop' Tulloch was the most active of these men.[61] He had been parachuted into Karen country in February 1945 and organized Karen levy attacks on the rear of the Japanese forces which were holding up the 14th Army's advance on Mandalay. By 1948 he had convinced himself that the Karens were fighting 'the virus of communism'. He had told Karens that if they were really in trouble members of the force would turn out to help them. As the year wore on, the Karen situation became more and more fraught and the rumours of British involvement more insistent. Nu did his best to continue Aung San's policy of conciliation, bringing in transitional measures for a form of Karen self-government in the delta while at the same time denouncing the Karenistan movement as 'undemocratic'.[62] But as the government's troubles deepened so did the determination of some KNU hardliners to go their own way.

In July something happened in London that alarmed both Whitehall and the British embassy in Rangoon. Ex Evening Standard editor Frank Owen, now at the Daily Mail, who had been selected by Mountbatten to produce the SEAC newsletter in 1943,[63] asked Esler Dening, now a Foreign Office adviser, to meet at the Carlton Bar 'someone who had been in Burma'. This turned out to be Tulloch, who was on his way out to the East and was drumming up support for the Karen cause. According to Dening, he said he 'had been connected with a Karen organisation which aimed at seizing power in Burma'. Dening was astonished to be told that the leader of this insurrection was to be none other than Smith Dun. According to his own account, he immediately told Tulloch that his was a very foolhardy course of action and that it would have 'unpleasant consequences' for him.

Tulloch said he thought that would be the answer, but that there was a lot of support around for the Karen cause. Tulloch had apparently been to see the Americans, who had expressed interest but cautiously referred him to the British Foreign Office. He had also tried to raise some money from the Burmah Oil Company in the Karen cause. All this put the Foreign Office and the Rangoon embassy in a quandary. Should they tell Nu and the Burmese government? Did they indeed have an obligation to do so under the defence agreement? Could this all be a plot within a plot to discredit Smith Dun and bring about the collapse of the socialist government? One thing that the officials were sure of was that the Karens could not really form a government in Rangoon even if they had the support of other minority groups.[64] Any such insurrection was most likely to bring the communists to power even faster.

The Foreign Office's dilemma was partly resolved by the speed of events. Soon after the meeting in the Carlton Bar, Tulloch turned up in Calcutta. In the last week of August Karen activists moved and began to take over police stations in the delta while hill Karens began to mobilize forces in Karenni. By 1 September Karen paramilitary forces were in charge of the port of Moulmein, a powerful statement of their aim of political separatism. They were joined in this insurrection by another delta people, the Mons. The Mon population was about 300,000. They were the remaining descendants of the once-dominant people of southern Burma who had been defeated, exterminated or assimilated by the Burmese after 1760. This uprising, however, was unlike either the communist insurgency or the military mutinies. At first there was little actual fighting between the Burmese forces and the Karens and Mons. The Karen delta paramilitaries simply took over the running of the towns, blockaded the roads and became a de facto government over a large part of the delta and Tenasserim.

What particularly offended the Burmese government was not so much the illegality of these acts but the open contempt displayed towards it and towards the Burmese people. The pained Nu reported a case where young Karen levies had surrounded and neutralized a Burmese government military post and then publicly urinated in the direction of the soldiers to register their disdain.[65] At this point

Rangoon had very few cards to play. Rather than redeploying its scarce troops, let alone putting at issue the loyalty of the Karen battalion, the government had to bargain for time politically. It reopened talks on the question of Karen autonomy in humiliating circumstances and hoped for the best. It also promoted Smith Dun from army commander-in-chief to commander of all the country's armed forces. This pacified the Karens under arms and persuaded them that their home villages were not likely to come under immediate assault from the Burmese. Most of them were anyway inclined to give the government the benefit of the doubt and were much more hostile to the communists than to the socialist government.

There still remained the question of Force 136. 'I think we shall have to try to stop all this Force 136 plotting', noted Peter Murray at the Foreign Office.[66] The officials then began to try to put out the fire themselves. They alerted the government of India to Tulloch's presence in Calcutta. In London, they planned to have Frank Owen rebuked. They also informed the *Daily Mail*'s owner, Lord Rothermere, of the dubious activities of his paper's editor. Rothermere, of course, loftily disavowed any intention of intervening in Burmese politics, despite his paper's sympathy with the Karens and detestation of communism. This disclaimer appeared to fall flat when the embassy reported in early September that Alexander Campbell, a *Daily Mail* reporter and close friend of Tulloch, was already in Rangoon.[67] He seemed to be in town for more than journalism and 'pays more visits to Calcutta than would seem to be justified solely by his work as a correspondent'. The Burmese police had come to this conclusion, too. On 17 September Campbell was arrested in his room at the Strand Hotel and bundled into a cell at police headquarters.[68] The Burmese police claimed that they had discovered incriminating evidence in Campbell's room, including a draft money order from Tulloch.[69]

Maung Ohn, a Burmese representative in Europe, later passed on three letters to Tom Driberg which appeared to incriminate Tulloch and Campbell. The MP was worried that capitalist forces were attempting to overthrow the fledgling Burmese government. In a curious *Boys' Own Paper* jargon, the letters from 'Skunk' (apparently Campbell) to 'Pop' and 'Ewan' paint a picture of confusion.[70] The Karen insurgents were desperately short of arms and ammunition.

Other minorities were not being too co-operative and without further aid the Karens were unlikely to try to push on to Rangoon. The funding that British business was going to provide as military help for the Karens was not forthcoming. Instead, the Karen leadership was surprised to be asked for money by the British conspirators. They refused, 'so no filthy fochre for you, Pop', one of the letters commented. Despite tantalizing references to arms on ships in Brisbane harbour and the doings of 'Oliver and the Rev.', censorship made communication with Calcutta difficult. It was nearly impossible to smuggle arms through that city because the taxis that ran to the airport were almost all driven by Indian Special Branch operatives. Tulloch's correspondent had other problems, too. He ended one letter with a query: 'Any news of that little bitch my wife when you left London?'

The arrest of Campbell coincided with several other suspicious events. The Burmese police also arrested an American pilot, who had illegally flown an old Lockheed Hudson aircraft to Mingaladon airport near Rangoon on an unspecified secret mission. Burmese troops confronting rebel Karen forces in the Karenni to the northeast claimed they had seen 'white men' fighting alongside their enemies. Secret radio messages between Calcutta and Moulmein were supposed to have been intercepted by the Indians. The Indian authorities also firmly believed that Tulloch had been planning to ship weapons from Pakistan to Burma, despite the fact that he gave an interview in Calcutta disclaiming that he was directing the Karen rebellion. By this time the government of India was also thoroughly alarmed. Armed communists had shot a soldier of the Assam Rifles shortly before and this was at a time when the Telengana communist revolt in India was still flickering. The Indians were also deeply worried about the safety of the 400,000-odd of their own citizens still living in Rangoon should the Burmese government collapse. They had already approached the British about aid and military support in this eventuality. But the ambassador had been told to politely refuse any plea for British aid. In mid September the Indian authorities asked Tulloch to leave the country, which he did under protest.[71]

Whatever the reality of Force 136 involvement in the Karen rebellions, the acid test for the Burmese government was the reaction of Smith Dun and the Karen battalions of the army. We will never know what they would have done if the communists or even a 'popular front' type government had come to power. In the event, Smith Dun, like the British and the Indians, probably decided that the incumbent Burmese government was about the best they could get. On 12 September he announced his unequivocal support for Nu. He declared to the New Times of Burma that he would 'fight all lawless elements, whether Karen or Burman' because it was essential to avert further trouble between the communities. He added in an obscure, but steely metaphor: 'You could achieve some success with bayonets, but not sit on them.'[72] In the longer view, this was to be the turning point for the government. It had held the mutineers to the north of Rangoon and within a year would begin to recapture territory to the south that had fallen under Karen control. The communist rebellion, though endemic in the delta for several years more, would make no further major political advance. In the short run, though, no one could see that the final crisis had been averted. The government was still effectively no more than the government of the city-state of Rangoon, maintaining a fitful communication with its surrogate to the north in Mandalay. Its economic problems continued to pile up.

The dissipation of the Force 136 problem did little to calm the nerves of the British either. They were now, like the Indians, deeply worried about the fate of their own subjects in Burma and also by the possible total forfeit of British economic interests in the country, which were still far from negligible. The alarm had been raised as early as June when Mr Forbes, manager of the Shan Hills Rubber Estate, had been murdered, along with his wife, by communist rebels in the vicinity of Thaton and there were several other attacks on rubber planters.[73] Though Forbes was said to have been rather unpopular locally, there had been unsuccessful attacks on other estate managers around the country and the embassy reckoned that at least twenty British subjects were seriously exposed in the interior. Then there were large numbers of Britons in Rangoon and Maymyo, not to mention the British services mission, a particular target of the communists. Questions had already been raised in Parliament about the expatriates' safety and several commentators drew disturbing parallels with contemporary assassinations in Malaya. Was this part of some region-wide communist plot?[74] The problem was that if British fears became public this tended to undermine confidence in the already battered and impecunious Burmese government. If, on the other hand, the British flexed their muscles, this played into the hands of the Burmese left. The left was correct to be suspicious. Bowker, Britain's man in Rangoon, was advocating a full expeditionary force to save British interests in the country. Somehow Reuters got wind of this and put out a report to the effect that a large British rescue force was waiting to sail from Ceylon. This had to be shamefacedly denied and, in truth, it had never been under consideration in London. The long memory of the Foreign Office recalled that the last time something like this had been attempted was in 1882 when the British had occupied an insurgent Egypt. Troops were sent in and 'they are there to this day'.[75]

As the year drew to its end the situation in Burma still seemed so grave that the Americans, acutely alert to the threat of communism, were now seriously worried. The sporadic fighting and endemic dacoities surged backward and forward across the delta, the Irra-waddy valley and the forest areas to the north. Of course, this does not mean that the country was in complete anarchy. In many places authority had simply gravitated to the level where it had always been most secure – with the village and township headmen and the chiefs and councils of the wooded and hill areas. But to the Burmese nation-alists and the old British Burma hands looking on, the worst night-mares had already come to pass. Murray noted that 'our only consolation is that we now have nothing left worth losing'. British firms had begun to leave with whatever they could still get their hands on.[76] Yet even the communists were divided and incapable of putting on a united face to negotiate with the government. A number of the saner leaders were held under Section 5 of the Preservation of Public Order Act. Because the word for 'five' and the word for 'fish' were the same in Burmese, people said they were 'eating fried fish'.[77] Many Burmese were now contemplating military rule as the only solution. The problem was that even the military seemed incapable of throwing up a strong leader.

Symptomatic of this dismal end to Burma's year of hope was the fate of Tin Tut, the redoubtable and clever former ICS officer who had fled with Dorman-Smith to Simla and re-emerged as minister and financial expert of the independent government. Tin Tut had been pushed out of the economics ministry into the Burmese Foreign Office because he was not really acceptable to the former hardline nationalists who resented his earlier connection with the British. In August he had resigned from the government altogether and had taken a commission in the army, complaining that the dictatorial socialists refused any initiative that did not come from inside their own ranks. On 17 September his car was attacked with a hand grenade as he drove through the streets of Rangoon and he died a few hours later in hospital.[78] A strong Burmese nationalist, even while within the ranks of the ICS, U Tin Tut, CBE, was almost the last of his kind. Why was he assassinated? Furnivall, by now perhaps prey to endemic Burmese political paranoia, believed that he might have been on the point of declaring a dictatorship with the help of the British services mission. Certainly many Burmese thought so: 'The Europeans and the few Burmese with any land or money were all resting their hopes in Tin Tut.'[79] This easily merged with rumours about Australian bootlegging aircraft dropping caches of arms to the Karens and the shenanigans of adventurers such as 'Pop' Tulloch. There was a strong suspicion that Aung Gyi, deputy inspector of the 'anti-rightist' and semi-criminal Sitwundan militia, was responsible for the assassination.[80]

In the long-lost pre-war days, there had been little connection between Burma and Malaya. Now events seemed to be pushing the two regions into a single frame of reference as far as the British, Americans and their communist enemies were concerned. In September Nu himself had written a rather ponderous and complacent letter to Malcolm MacDonald, British Governor General of Southeast Asia. He pointed out that they were both bulwarks against international communism and espoused a moderate democratic socialism that he claimed represented both the British and the Burmese way. As the Governor General contemplated his own equally intractable mix of ethnic conflict, communist insurrection and anti-imperialist fervour, he may well have smiled wryly.

In Burma, December was a dangerous month. The Karen delta towns had been the scene of the fiercest claims for a separate state. Here some Karens had declared independence at the very time in

January 1948 when Burma was celebrating its own freedom. By the summer, as Karen forces moved north towards Rangoon, there were once again communal murders in the villages. Attempts were made to arrange a ceasefire and several of the delta towns were handed back to the Rangoon government at one point. But the conflict was out of control. Later in the year the government attempted to disband the remaining 'loyal' Karen battalions of the army, fearing they too would mutiny. On Christmas Eve 1948, Burmese irregulars threw hand grenades into a Karen church where people were celebrating the festival. The fleeing congregation was shot down or bayoneted.[81] The insurgent Karen forces now went on the offensive, digging in at Insein, close to the capital, even after they failed to take Rangoon itself. They sang as they marched: 'Death and Life are in God's hands. Hey, why should we fear the Burmese?'[82] Increasingly, Karen officers in the regular army joined their insurgent brothers or collaborated with them privately. Massacre and counter-massacre spread across the delta region as 'ethnic cleansing' began. Meanwhile Rangoon civilians took day trips out to the front where the army allowed them to take pot shots at the Karen fighters for one rupee a bullet. Boys' Day in Burma had become a vicious dogfight. The only hope, as Furnivall put it, was that 'it is not that the rebels are strong, but the Government is weak'.[83]

INDIA RECEDES, INDIA REBORN

In early 1948 the independent government of India had sent saplings from a leafy descendant of the tree in Bodh Gaya, under which the Buddha achieved enlightenment, to celebrate Burma's own independence. Yet no more than Burma were India and Pakistan dancing in streams of gold and silver during that cold weather. Scarcely had the communal massacres died away than tension between the two dominions began to increase on the borders of the disputed state of Kashmir. Scarcely had Nehru written his first New Year message as prime minister than the aged Gandhi was shot to death by a right-wing Hindu assassin after his daily prayer meeting in Delhi. John de Chazal, one of the remaining and now increasingly disillusioned British police officials, remembered the outpouring of grief in his distant part of south India when an urn of Gandhi's ashes arrived there to be scattered, symbolizing the unity of the nation. Mourning was so intense that it reminded him of family stories of Queen Victoria's funeral. As the ashes were consigned to sacred rivers and lakes across India and even sent to Burma to be scattered on the Irrawaddy among crowds of mourning Indians and Burmese,[84] 'drums beat all night and men and boys shouted "*Gandhi-ji ki jai; Gandhi-ji ki jai* [victory to Gandhi!]" till they were hoarse'.[85] The remaining British officials and military men already knew their days in the subcontinent were numbered, some feeling that their lives' work had been for nothing. Their authority now in rapid decline, they scattered across the empire. Some went to commercial jobs in Britain, Canada or Australasia; others entered the Nigerian or Kenyan civil service or police. For them, the long tradition of the Raj came to an end with regret and resentment.

It was not only British India but also the wider British Indian empire, from the Arabian seas to the eastern shores of the Bay of Bengal, that came to an end. The year 1948 saw Indian power recede from Burma for the first time in 130 years. One of the most venerated public places in Mandalay, particularly in the year of independence when enemies were pressing in on all sides, was the pagoda that held the great image of Buddha Mahamuni. This had been taken from the kingdom of Manipur on the Burma–India border in the late eighteenth century when the Burmese king Bodhayappa had been trying to create a Buddhist empire in Southeast Asia. The raid into the northeast of the Indian subcontinent had attracted the attention of a much bigger and well-armed commercial empire, that of the East India Company. From the 1820s onward, Burma had been subject to successive waves of invasion by British troops, colonial logging companies, ruby and oil interests and, finally, Indian merchants and labourers. In 1944 and 1945 the British Indian Army had invaded the country and as late as October 1947 there had still been thousands of Indian soldiers there. That influence had now been withdrawn. Indian troops had left Burma along with the last British officers and civil servants. Up to 800,000 Indian civilians remained in the country, some like Balwant Singh in positions of authority. But India's proxy empire in Burma disappeared with the end of British rule in the subcontinent. India's new rulers were to keep a weather eye on events in their neighbouring country and even, on occasions, to intervene with money and military aid. Yet Nehru and his foreign-affairs expert Krishna Menon had no desire for a greater Indian empire. They discouraged both the Indian businessmen and labour unions which wanted to keep a hold on their smaller eastern neighbour. Pakistan retained an interest in the Muslim population of Arakan, but was keen to avoid any further ethnic and religious conflicts that might compromise its bizarre set of borders. The huge land mass of the Indian subcontinent continued to exert its gravitational pull on Burma, like a monster planet influencing a satellite moon, but empire had given way to moral and economic suasion.

In part, this was because the great subcontinent was absorbed in its own problems and because residual British influence was deployed to keep the new dominions from each other's throats. Mountbatten, the last British leader to span both India and Burma, was preoccupied with the problems that arose from partition. Some of the British who 'stayed on' accused him of 'too much pomp, overacting and creating a "Hollywood atmosphere"'.[86] But Indians enjoyed seeing newsreels where he and his wife Edwina were shown deep in discussion with Gandhi or at the recently assassinated leader's funeral. Later in the year an unofficial war broke out between India and Pakistan over Nehru's beloved state of Kashmir. The Indian Army was deployed in the mountainous country along long lines of communication to combat invasion by Muslim irregulars, who were determined to bring the Muslim-majority state into Pakistan. The remaining British soldiers and military attachés on both sides tried to prevent the situation from degenerating into full-scale war between two members of the Commonwealth.[87] Hindu, Sikh and Muslim soldiers who had been comrades in arms in the Burma campaign a mere four years before found themselves on opposite sides. Some old comrades were killed by their erstwhile friends. Major K. K. Tewari, who had fought through the third Arakan campaign and taken part in the reoccupation of Malaya, lost one of his closest comrades in the fighting.[88] This man's mutilated body could be identified only by the Japanese pistol he had in his holster and the copy of the *Bhagavad Gita*, part of the ancient Hindus scriptures, he kept in his pocket. Roy Bucher, who remained commander-in-chief of the Indian army until 1949, was put in the invidious position of treating his opposite number in Pakistan, Douglas Gracey, as an undeclared enemy. That autumn the Indian Army was also used to occupy and absorb into India the recalcitrant princely state of Hyderabad, whose royal line was Muslim. The ostensible enemy were bands of Muslim irregulars called Razakars, who opposed union with India. But a wider shadow was now falling across the whole of South and Southeast Asia. Bucher and his boss, Vallabhbhai Patel, noted the creeping advance of communism in Asia. They viewed with alarm the beginning of communist 'base areas' in the Andhra areas of Madras and nearby southeast Hyderabad. Bucher wrote that the 'greater fragmentation of India which would have occurred had Hyderabad become independent, must have resulted in Communism making more headway in this continent'.[89]

Here Bucher was anticipating a theme which President Eisenhower would coin into that masterful, if erroneous, concept of the 'domino theory' in which communist insurgency would topple one post-colonial country after another in South and Southeast Asia. By 1948 China, Vietnam and Burma seemed seriously threatened by the new political contagion. Even in India, observers espoused a kind of 'mini-domino theory'. Hyderabad might link up with Andhra and even with Kerala in the southwest, where communist parties were making electoral headway. In turn, southern Indian communism might be linked through Bengal with Arakanese and Burmese communism and on into Southeast Asia. Actually, for most of Bengal's population in 1948, the most pressing issue remained the fate of the refugees. People continued to flood across the new border in both directions, fleeing murder and arson during the great Hindu and Muslim festivals, but now scarified by local militias trying to firm up the lines of Radcliffe's notional border. Communal warfare remained endemic, yet in both north and south Bengal poor peasants were still agitating for better economic conditions, urged on by communists who claimed that Hindu–Muslim conflict was really a smoke screen behind which capitalists, imperialists and 'feudal elements' pursued their wicked ways. In the northeast of India, the leadership of a section of the Naga people, which had declared independence the previous August, remained intransigent, waiting to see how Indian administration would turn out in practice.

Against this background the city of Calcutta hosted a series of massive communist meetings. The aim was to show solidarity with the Soviet Communist Party, whose secretary Andrei Zhdanov had recently declared an international struggle against 'American neo-colonialism'. It was also designed to warn off India's tough, right-wing home minister, Sardar Patel, who was now locking up communist agitators with as much despatch as the British had once done.[90] From 19 to 26 February a South East Asia Youth Conference met in the city. Thirty thousand people marched through Calcutta alongside representatives from Malaya, Vietnam, Burma and China. A Chinese youth carried aloft the bloodstained shirt of a comrade who had died on the battlefield, in protest against 'reaction'.[91] Old conflicts between Bose supporters and hardline communists re-emerged. But the popular mood was heady. It received further fuel when the second congress of the Communist Party of India convened in Calcutta a little later. Than Tun arrived proclaiming the need for Indian and Burmese communists to link and overthrow the 'sham independence' with which the imperialists had saddled Burma and, by implication, India.[92] Malayan communists rapidly moving towards open insurrection followed the proceedings with rapt attention. It was not surprising that British and American observers looked at these events, put them together with the attempt of the USSR to starve out the city of Berlin, and decided that a worldwide communist conspiracy was afoot.

For most people in India, however, independence was far from a sham. Despite the troubles, there was widespread rejoicing and nowhere more so than in the army. Despite the bloody dawn of independence observers spoke of a 'spirit of joyous freedom'. The Indian Army in Kashmir, said the Indian attaché to the British high commissioner in Delhi, 'was as joyous and happy as a daughter-in-law who had managed to shake off her troublesome and nagging mother-in-law and set up her own house'.[93] The 'infamous libel' that the Indian Army would collapse without British officers had been disproved. Yet some homely British traditions lived on in spite of the prevailing bloodshed. General Kodandera Cariappa, appointed commander-in-chief of the Indian Army after Bucher, gave a lecture on the Kashmir operations to the 'Delhi snowball knitting party'. He later privately commented that practically all the knitters were British ladies. Nehru's independent India – high-minded, austere, supercilious – had already set its distinctive tone.

Britain's old colonial Indian Army, which had once ranged across the whole of the crescent from Bengal and Assam to Singapore, victorious in North Africa and Italy, was broken up. In November 1947, the last of the Indian legions had departed from the subcontinent. Among the last to leave were the 2 Royal Lancers – the 'Bengal Lancers' of legend – to be divided between India and Pakistan.[94] But many of the military stores went to Malaya to build up the fortress there; one third of the small island of Singapore was now given over to the military. Each service demanded two square miles of valuable land to house their radio transmitting and receiving stations. Among the baggage train were large stocks of whisky. It was shipped back to the United Kingdom: a telling augury of the end of empire. This infuriated British officers stationed in Singapore, for whom decent liquor was in short supply.[95] But Britain still looked to South Asia to defend its Eastern empire, specifically to the Gurkhas. Two regiments of these Nepalese fighters were detached from the Indian Army to become a Brigade of Gurkhas within the British one. There was trouble in their camps, between those who stayed in India and those who opted to follow their British officers. Four out of the eight battalions of troops in Malaya were Gurkhas, and a Gurkha officer, Major General Charles Boucher, was to take over the Malaya command. Many were raw recruits; some of the veterans former prisoners of war. The Gurkhas, most of them stationed in an isolated barracks near Ipoh, were ill at ease in Malaya. The only common language between gunner instructors and 2/7 Gurkha was said to be Italian: a legacy of older campaigns. 'We were', recalled one soldier, 'kept inside a camp that had wire around it like a lot of sheep . . .' They were turned out first in mid 1947, to confront the radical Malay nationalists of API in demonstrations in nearby Kuala Kangsar, when the British could not rely on their Malay policemen to do so.[96] Fifty years later Gurkhas would still serve Southeast Asian regimes as praetorians of last resort. The new arrivals in Malay were soon to experience one of the most vicious small wars of peace.

10

1948: The Malayan Revolution

Shortly after Burma's leaders received their independence, at King's House in Kuala Lumpur there was imperial pageantry of a very different kind. On 21 January 1948, the nine rulers of the Malay States, each resplendent with *kris* and hereditary regalia and flanked by their ministers, signed a treaty with the British government. These agreements superseded the Malayan Union, whose inauguration they had boycotted so dramatically two years previously, and brought into being the Federation of Malaya. The Anglo-Malay condominium that had ruled Malaya for over half a century before 1941 was now restored. But the ceremony was carefully stage-managed. Up until the final hour on the previous day, just as the treaties were sent to the printer, the leader of UMNO, Dato Onn bin Jaafar, continued to insist on prerogatives for the Malay States. He had not forgiven the British for abandoning the Malays two years previously. His master, the Sultan of Johore, was the only ruler to be absent; he pleaded his gout and sent his son on his behalf. Such was the degree of mistrust that the governor, Sir Edward Gent, sent a government doctor to verify this. But, on the day, the fifty necessary signatures were secured. 'The whole show', Gent reported to the Colonial Office, 'was accompanied by a Hollywood atmosphere of brilliant white lights and movie cameras.' This raised the temperature to 'about 150 degrees'. The ceremony dragged on most of the afternoon, much to the ire of the Sultan of Perak, who had a horse running in the 5.30 at the Selangor Turf Club.[1] This too gave the sense of the old world coming back to life. The sport of kings, the *Malaya Tribune* observed, was now 'Malaya's second industry'. An estimated $1.5m was wagered at the Singapore Turf Club's revival meeting at the end of 1947.[2]

Around such observances, the elites of Malaya began to close ranks. The previous October the wealthy *towkays* in the Chinese Chambers of Commerce had opposed the new constitution and supported a mass *hartal*. Gent was afraid that, with Malay feelings running so high, any further protests when the Federation came into effect on 1 February might result in racial war. He armed himself with a bill to outlaw *hartals*: it was, in effect, a 'shoot to kill' ordinance. There were plans afoot to arrest the leaders of the protest movement, including the head of the Singapore Chinese Chamber of Commerce, Malaya's 'rubber and pineapple king', Lee Kong Chian. But the Governor General, Malcolm MacDonald, thought this a 'serious political mistake'.[3] He drew on all his diplomatic skills to talk the *towkays* round. In private, both Lee Kong Chian and Tan Cheng Lock, the *hartal*'s figurehead, now baulked at the many-headed hydra of popular protest. They feared that any breakdown in Sino-Malay relations might prove irretrievable. They had gone as far as they would go. As a compromise, they agreed to supply placemen to serve on the new Federal Legislative Council; one of them was Tan Cheng Lock's son, Tan Siew Sin.[4] The broadest-based political movement in Malaya's history had dissolved. The left was deeply disillusioned. On 1 February, as Gent was sworn in as the first High Commissioner of the Federation of Malaya at Kuala Lumpur, within earshot of the artillery salute, the Malayan Communist Party met in secret to discuss the possibility of armed revolt.

The Federation left the Malay rulers sovereign and the States' elite entrenched in federal bureaucracies. Their powers over land and appointments were considerable: British advisers to the Malay courts complained that government files were withheld from them.[5] This was less a step to self-government than a return to the time-honoured tug-of-war of indirect rule. But Britain at least controlled a strengthened central government. As the voice of middle-class Asian opinion, the *Malaya Tribune*, put it, the Federation was a 'gentlemen's agreement under which the Malays are granted certain privileges on the understanding that they will leave all real authority in the hands of British bureaucracy'.[6] British Southeast Asia seemed extraordinarily resilient, and it was more valuable to Britain than ever before. In 1938 Malaya had accounted for 2.57 per cent of Britain's world trade; by 1951, this would rise to 9.9 per cent and the figure for Southeast Asia as a whole would be 11.36 per cent. Malaya remained the world's top producer of rubber, which brought $120m into the sterling area in 1948; the nearest commodity in value was cocoa at $50m. In 1948 the sterling area suffered an overall dollar deficit of $1,800m, but Malaya's surplus was $170m. Its nearest competitors were the Gold Coast, with a surplus of $47.5m, Gambia ($24.5m) and Ceylon ($23m). But, at the end of the year, Ceylon's contribution was lost. By 1952–3 Malaya was providing 35.26 per cent of Britain's net balance of payments with the dollar area.[7] The first British settlements in the region were founded in the wake of the fall of the first British empire of the Atlantic. Now a third British empire seemed to be emerging out of the loss of India and Burma. Soothsaying for his masters in Whitehall, W. Linehan, a senior scholar-administrator in the Malayan Civil Service, concluded that the prospect of the rise of a strong independence movement in Malaya 'within the next generation or so, appears exceedingly remote'.[8]

At the epicentre of British Southeast Asia was the new Commissioner General, Malcolm MacDonald, with his bustling court of political, economic, military and financial advisers at Phoenix Park in Singapore. He was, in the words of one Singapore civil servant, 'an influence that was pervasive yet without power'.[9] MacDonald acted as the political impresario of British imperialism in the region. He remained convinced that Britain could mould local political development after its own image. In early 1948 this seemed to be moving at a quicker pace in Singapore than in Malaya, with elections for seats on its Legislative Council due on 20 March. The island had been excluded from the Federation; it was, in theory at least, ready to join as soon as Malay political opinion would allow it to. MacDonald encouraged its leading citizens to organize themselves into a loyalist party. The Singapore Progressive Party was founded in August 1947 by John Laycock, a Yorkshire-born lawyer married to a Chinese, who recruited the respected Straits Chinese C. C. Tan, with whom he played golf. Another early member was John Ede, a Wykehamist who had taught at the school of princes, Ajmer College in India, but as Swaraj approached had taken up an offer from his old Cambridge friend, the Singapore magnate Loke Wan Tho, to run his Cathay Cinema. Ede met Laycock at the Singapore Island golf club and later married his daughter. Laycock had an orchid garden on the north of the island, and the flower became the Progressive Party's emblem. It was a genteel movement of 'people who knew people': the voice of the 'domiciled' of Singapore, or 'people who regard this country as their home'.[10] This was the political language of the old Straits Settlements, which the Progressive Party sought to revive. Only in 1955 did it commit itself to a date for independence: 1963. This was to prove uncannily accurate, but it was entirely out of kilter with the radical mood of the time. Nevertheless, the Progressive Party was a liberal political alternative where few existed, and it won five seats in the polls. The MCP and the Malayan Democratic Union did not contest their first electoral opportunity. They scorned the unrepresentative franchise, which was restricted to British subjects, of whom only 22,395 registered, 45 per cent of them Indians.[11] In retrospect, the senior figure in the Malayan Democratic Union, Philip Hoalim, felt that to stand aside was a mistake: it played into the hands of those who refused to believe in their commitment to democratic methods. They would not be given a second opportunity.

Singapore's old money seemed to be well-entrenched once again. Many leading professionals and businessmen fought shy of party politics. Loke Wan Tho – according to his sister, 'more suited to be a university professor than a business man' – was a sponsor of the Progressive Party, but preferred to exercise influence behind the scenes. Loke's father was a pioneer tin-miner and first citizen of Kuala Lumpur who had given the British government £1.5m in war loans in 1914. His sister was married to a senior colonial servant, and Loke himself was a good friend of the Commissioner General – they shared a passion for photography and ornithology (MacDonald had been known to commandeer a local fire tender to watch birds in the jungle canopy) – and co-authored a book on Angkor Wat.[12] The newer, China-born elite also aspired to new heights of influence. Lee Kong Chian was one of the first *towkays* to be fluent in English. He travelled extensively in the West and his business adopted modern management methods; he commanded enough clout to receive a personal audience from the governor of the Bank of England. Lee was son-in-law to Tan Kah Kee and also wielded influence in traditional Chinese clan associations. He had been active in the National Salvation movement and spent the war in the United States, where he lectured officers at Columbia University on China and raised money for its relief. His philanthropy was felt in education and other causes in both Singapore and China.[13] Like many of his kind, Lee Kong Chian moved comfortably between different worlds. But during the next two years the Chinese of Singapore and Malaya – like the Indians the previous year – would be confronted with an acute dilemma as to where to locate their political allegiances.

The big men of the community could not avoid being drawn into the maelstrom of civil war in China between the Kuomintang and the communists. Tan Kah Kee, now seventy three, made a final attempt to rally the Overseas Chinese behind a 'third force', the China Democratic League. But he was no longer the unifying figure he had been in the fight against Japan. Tan had become deeply pessimistic about Chiang Kai Shek's ability to return democracy to the people: it was, he said, like negotiating with a tiger for its hide. He became ever more candid in his conviction that only Mao's communists possessed the drive and moral authority to govern China, and this led him into a controversial alliance with the Malayan Communist Party. His speeches lambasted the United States for its support of Chiang. This alarmed the British and divided the Malayan Chinese. When, in May 1948, Chiang Kai Shek was elected president of China by the National Assembly, Tan Kah Kee and his supporters refused to accept the election's legitimacy and launched an anti-Chiang Kai Shek propaganda drive. The Chinese schools, which were now reopened and expanding dramatically, became a key battleground for the hearts and minds of the Chinese; powerful patrons and fiercely partisan teachers competed to politicize the students.[14] This opened a new front in the struggle between right and left in Malaya.

In the last months of the Nationalist regime in China, the Kuomintang experienced a remarkable resurgence in Malaya. Many *towkays* saw it as a route to influence. The office of the Kuomintang Overseas Department in Singapore was the centre of a region-wide web of intelligence gathering and fund raising for China. The vice-minister of overseas affairs, Tai Kwee Sheng, used monies allocated for the relief of the Overseas Chinese in Burma to finance anti-left newspapers in Malaya. The British were amazed at sums moving hither and thither and worried about the haemorrhaging of foreign exchange.[15] The Kuomintang was now attracting younger, Malaya-born, bilingual leaders; up-and-coming industrialists such as Ng Tiong Kiat in Selangor with his rubber and oil plantations and saw mills. It had become a class-based organization that transcended clan and dialect groups, and its supporters captured control of centres of Chinese social life on the peninsula such as the Chinese Assembly Hall in Kuala Lumpur and the Chinese Chambers of Commerce. Only the Singapore chamber remained aligned to Lee Kong Chian and Tan Kah Kee. As the Kuomintang vied for influence with the Malayan Communist Party, it had the advantage of being able to be more open in its organization. It had, at its peak, 219 branches and 27,690 members, excluding its Youth Corps, and mounted a direct challenge to communist domination of the trade unions.[16] In the first months of 1948, a struggle for control of the community was underway. Malaya's Cold War was growing in intensity.

A THIRD WORLD WAR?

From late 1947 the British became aware of rumours sweeping the towns and villages of Malaya that a third world war was about to begin. In some places, the Second World War had not ended. In the borderlands of north Perak there were some disquieting goings-on. The area was home to a large concentration of Chinese tobacco and ginger farmers who also had a reputation for smuggling and casual violence. 'It is clear', came reports, 'that these Kwongsi Chinese are no ordinary bandits, and that a very strange state of affairs exists astride the northern extremity of Malaya along the general lines of River Perak from Kroh through Kuala Kangsar in a SW direction.'[17] On 9 April a British police officer ventured up there with a Chinese guide to investigate. The guide shot him dead. A full-scale military operation was launched; the first occasion on which the army was called to aid the civil power. The troops went into the forest at the 74th milestone on the northern road to Grik, a frontier town close to the Thai border. After about fifty minutes' trekking through dense undergrowth they stumbled upon a sentry post. Then Chinese appeared in uniform, their leader kitted out in Japanese surplus, and fired on them with automatic guns until a bugle sounded a retreat. The British troops then charged into an empty camp. There was a kitchen, with stocks of pork and Ryvita, a barrack room and other buildings. It had held up to thirty men, and on the captured muster rolls there was even a Sikh and three or four Japanese names. In a nearby clearing they found a military training school, newly constructed, complete with desks, a blackboard and wall-portraits of Chiang Kai Shek and Sun Yat Sen. It was built to accommodate 200 to 300 men. In raids in the nearby town of Lenggong, the police pulled in one Yuin See, a Kuomintang leader with the rank of major in the Chinese army. He was, he confessed under interrogation, a member of the Malayan Overseas Chinese Self-defence Army. But, he took pains to emphasize, it was not an anti-British army. They were preparing for a new world war, which would be a battle between the communists and the rest of the world. The force, it emerged, had 800 to 1,000 members and controlled an area of some 600 square miles, where it had set up a civil administration with its own taxation and courts.[18] As Major Yuin See explained: 'The British made mistakes in 1941 when they were caught unprepared and it appears that the same thing is going to be repeated, but the Chinese cannot afford to suffer as they have suffered in 1941 and also in the period of confusion at the time of the Japanese surrender when great numbers of Chinese were massacred by the Malays.'[19]

Two years after the reoccupation, large tracts of the peninsula remained badlands which the British left largely ungoverned: tracts of jungle in which foresters feared to tread; isolated corners of rubber estates, which planters left to locals to tap for themselves. Johore – where the first British planter had been killed in August of the previous year – was particularly notorious for gang robbery, as was the Kedah border with Thailand. In the estuaries and stilted fishing villages of Perak, smuggling and piracy still thrived on a large scale, and individual gang bosses exercised an extraordinary sway. On the north Perak coast in 1947 and 1948 a young man known as 'The Leper' had a gang some fifty strong and operated three fast motor launches – former air-force rescue craft – out of the mangroves where the police could not reach him. His men – 'hunting hawks and dogs' according to one witness – raked in large sums through robbery, extortion and taxation of opium dens. One of them, 'The Crocodile', amassed tribute as the unofficial harbourmaster of the town of Matang. 'The Leper' had been a member of the Ang Bin Hoay brotherhood in Penang, but had broken away from it and set up on his own. For this reason he was seen as a homicidal upstart by the local population, and he died when a whole village at Bagan Si-Api-Api in Sumatra, where he had founded a pirate kingdom, turned on him and slaughtered him and thirty of his gang.

Even in the more settled areas, the triads amounted to a form of shadow government. On the southern outskirts of Kuala Lumpur the power of the 100-strong Green Mountain Gang was notorious, and on the adjacent coast, based on the off-shore Chinese fishing village of Pulau Ketam, the Sea Gang had around 11,000 affiliates and almost a complete grip on the docks and coastal trade of Port Swettenham. Ostensibly some of these societies had a social function: they were places where shopkeepers, traders and contractors met to drink or gamble. But some were involved in the opium and lottery business, and all of them offered protection to their members. When the Ang Bin Hoay brotherhood established itself in Kuala Lumpur, stall-holders, shopkeepers, brothel keepers, even travelling theatre companies all paid it protection money. Another similar brotherhood, known as Wah Kei, was increasingly influential among the large Cantonese population of the capital. On 23 March the two societies fought through the night in the Lucky World amusement park over control of the protection rackets. They paid off the police as a matter of form; many Cantonese detectives were members of Wah Kei, and there was nothing their European officers could do about it.[20]

The MCP challenged the ascendancy of the secret societies in many areas. Its austere doctrines were incompatible with triad ritual and unattractive to the 'opium smokers and gentlemen of leisure' who led these brotherhoods. 'The Leper' had been active in triad conflicts with the MPAJA along the Perak coast in the interregnum and, aping a hero of Chinese resistance to the Manchus, continued to send out his 'tiger generals' to target MCP sympathizers. In the Dindings area of Perak, open warfare erupted in late 1946 as gangs tried to crush leftist influence, sacking the office of the local trade union and abducting its leaders. The local police refused to protect communists.[21] By November 1947 half of the estimated 10,000 triad men in Penang were said to be Kuomintang members, and triads were a source of recruits for the secret Perak army. As the master of the Ang Bin Hoay told the police: 'The Ang Brotherhood is far less dangerous than the Third International.' In May 1948 Wah Kei chiefs met and agreed to supply information to the government to help them against the communists. In trade union disputes, Chinese employers called upon the triads to break strikes. The communists too had their own alliances with triads in old MPAJA strongholds. A faction of one triad-based association, the China Chi Kung Tong, set up in the offices of the MCP at Foch Avenue in Kuala Lumpur.[22] The extent of these connections is hard to measure, but they made disputes over land and labour lethal.

In early 1948 there were many reasons people might believe that the region was heading towards a climactic conflict. The world crisis was dramatized by Cominform secretary Andrei Zhdanov in his image of 'two camps': 'the imperialist anti-democratic camp' and the 'democratic and anti-imperialist camp'. This idea gripped people's imagination in Southeast Asia. The British saw Zhdanov's words as a Soviet directive to local communist parties to launch armed insurrections, transmitted through the Calcutta Youth Conference. But in Malaya the communists had already concluded that the hour of reckoning was at hand. The news from Calcutta was carried back to them by Lee Soong, a delegate of the Malayan Communist Party who had been chosen more because of his ability to speak English than for his seniority. But, by the time he returned, the central executive committee of the MCP had already met in Singapore on 17–21 March to resolve once and for all whether or not to prepare for war with the British. The meeting was addressed by the leader of the Australian Communist Party, Lawrence Sharkey, as he passed through Singapore on his return from Calcutta. His high standing in the international movement impressed these young inexperienced revolutionaries in Malaya. But it seems that Sharkey merely confirmed what they already knew, and counselled them to be guided by local conditions. What made the biggest impact on them was his steely advice for dealing with strike-breakers: 'We get rid of them.'[23]

The MCP saw its struggle as part of the coming world revolution, but the insurrection, when it came, was the outcome of a local crisis. Chin Peng and his comrades needed to act decisively to demonstrate their authority in the wake of the exposure of Lai Teck, the news of whose treachery had still to be broken to the rank and file. The mood in the Party had hardened. To many of the members, the United Front strategy was a blind alley. Meanwhile, the strong-arm methods adopted by employers against strikers had placed local activists in real danger. When the Central Committee met, its agenda included a copy of draft trade union legislation, stolen from a government printing office by a sympathizer. It was plain that the new law would not allow the Federations of Trade Unions to operate legally, and this was read as decisive evidence that the British were about to move against the MCP itself. The MCP leaders finally abandoned all faith in the reforms of the British Labour government. It had betrayed its true imperialist nature:

The wave of national emancipation is rising incessantly and the peoples in the colonies are ceaselessly launching their counter-attacks on the imperial-ists ... And under the many phases of the situation, an armed struggle is inevitable. For this reason, armed struggle bears a particularly important significance. In the struggles of the broad masses of the people within im-perialistic countries themselves and in their colonies, the world communists are shouldering the most glorious task in history.[24]

Chin Peng and his allies began to steel the Party for the clampdown. Although the exact timing remains unclear, it seems that from March three stages of action were anticipated. First, a campaign of industrial action would challenge the government and create a mood of crisis. Then acts of terrorism would be launched to eliminate the local enemies of the Party. The third stage would be armed revolution, led by guerrillas from the hills. The signal for full rebellion would be the banning of the MCP. But all the indications are that this final mobilization was not planned until at least September 1948. The Party desperately needed time to reverse the effects of the Lai Teck years. It was chronically short of funds, much of its rural organization had been disbanded and it needed time to respond to the groundswell of criticism from its grass-roots members. As the policy directives filtered through the ranks there was a rush of expectancy. A diary of Johore communist organizer Tan Kan later fell into the hands of the British. The entry for 9 April read: 'Our policy, since the time of the anti-Japanese campaign, has been a wrong one. We seem to have fallen into the doctrine of the rightists. Now is the time to wind up affairs. Human beings are born to struggle. It is hard to live in a colonial empire. To yield to hateful favours and to endure will not do any good, it is death. The way out is to stand united and to fight.'[25]

Rumours of war and imminent violence coursed through the countryside. British agents reported careless talk in coffeeshops in the Malay *kampongs*, initiations into invulnerability cults, the assembly of underground cells of fighters to serve the motherland. The Malayan Security Service compared them to the forces raised by Bung Tomo, the hero of Surabaya.[26] The people continued to watch closely events in Indonesia, as the struggle against the Dutch entered its final phase. The growing cleavages within the revolution culminated in an uprising by leftist troops in the central Javanese town of Madiun in August. The republican leadership of Sukarno and Hatta sent republican forces and Muslim militias to crush the rebels, and more people died in the fighting than in the battle for Surabaya itself. There was a shift to the right in Thailand also, after a military coup in November 1947. The impact of this was soon felt along its frontier with Malaya, in the Malay lands of Patani. Fearing oppression at the hands of an authoritarian regime, local Malay leaders launched an insurrection. At one point a group of over 100 fighters took sanctuary over the border, claiming that the Thai soldiers and police had been attacking their villages and raping their women.[27] The links between the historic Malay kingdom of Patani and the rest of Malaya were strong, not least as it was an important centre of religious education. In early 1948 there seemed to be an historic opportunity for Patani to reclaim its freedom, and its leaders appealed to their brethren on the peninsula to support their cause.

In this time of anxiety, Islam made its voice heard. On 13–16 March there was another gathering at the al-Ihya Asshariff at Gunong Semanggol. It now called itself the People's Congress and was attended, in one estimate, by 5,000 people. The crisis in Patani featured strongly in the speeches of those present: it fused the causes of nationalism and Islam in a powerful and urgent way. So too did events further afield in Palestine. Delegates rose to attack the partition of the Holy Land as a 'mortal affront' to the Malays.[28] The conference was led by Ustaz Abu Bakar al-Baqir and Dr Burhanuddin, and they used it to launch Malaya's first Islamic political party, the Hizbul Muslimin. Islam, they proclaimed, promised a democracy that transcended race, nation and class. They called for immediate *Merdeka*: 'the building of an Islamic society and the realisation of a *Darul Islam*, an Islamic state'. The precise shape of the Islamic order was left undefined. But the Hizbul Muslimin had a powerful appeal, and branches were soon opened, many of them in religious schools.[29] The Malayan Security Service reported that Ustaz Abu Bakar and other Malay leaders forecast that revolution was imminent in southern Thailand, that it would spread to Malaya and spell the end of British rule. There were attempts to recruit for the struggle in Patani in various places, such as the coastal villages of Pahang, where the rumour went round that the MCP was looking to aid the insurgents in order to attract the attention of the Chinese communists and pave the way for its liberating armies. The centre of this talk was the fishing *kampong* of Cherating, now a popular beach resort.[30]

Much of this was pure speculation, but it showed the multiple directions in which the mood of crisis extended. It revealed to the British that the dividing lines between the radical Malay organizations – the Hizbul Muslimin, the Malay Nationalist Party, the youth movement PETA, the peasants' front and the Malay cadres of the MCP itself – were very unclear. Their leaders appeared on the same platforms and broadcast a similar message. Malay communists took a more visible role in these events than a year previously: at Gunong Semanggol, Rashid Maidin made a strong impact with an illustrated exposition of British oppression. But as they came into the open, the Malay leaders of the MCP encountered suspicion and resistance in the villages, and had success only in certain locales, many of them of recent Indonesian settlements. In Pahang, in the Temerloh area, there was a potent tradition of anti-colonial protest dating back to a war of resistance to the British in 1891. Its heroes – Bahaman and Mat Kilau – were a vital part of the living memory of some and the folk memory of all. Here, a Malay leader of the MCP, Kamarulzaman Teh, led a *class politik kiri*, 'left-wing political class', which discussed many of the doctrinal issues of the leading thinkers of Partai Komunis Indonesia, such as Alimin and Tan Malaka. The left directed its appeal to the peasants. On 25–27 April, at the Peasants' Front's first conference at Jeram in Kedah, its leader, Musa Ahmad, publicized the widespread evictions of farmers in the area: 'We are living in a democratic era in a world of revolution . . . we are fighting to retain our human rights . . . Our greatest enemies are the capitalists.' The gathering was also addressed by an inspirational figure of the Hizbul Muslimin, Ustaz Abdul Rab Tamini: 'Have no fear,' he told the crowd. 'Let us be called Communists and so on. We are fighting for our lives . . .'[31]

In retrospect, these words ring out like a call to a defiant last stand. The MCP was warning Malay leaders of the coming repression, and they too were making preparations to move underground. In May Kamarulzaman Teh, Wahi Anuar of PETA, Musa Ahmad and Abdullah C. D. led a group of around forty Malay radicals at a 'Camp Malaya' near the village of Lubuk Kawah near Temerloh. The AWAS leader, Shamsiah Fakeh, was one of two women who attended. There they were schooled in the principles of the coming struggle, and their communist mentors tried to dissolve the conflict between Marxist principles and Islamic teachings.[32] They had disappeared from public view. Ahmad Boestamam remained at large, at Balik Pulau in Penang, tailed continually by the Malayan Security Service, who tried, unsuccessfully, to recruit him as their agent. Rashid Maidin, they reported, was often in his company, alerting him to the danger, urging him to make preparations and to talk to the MCP. But Boestamam told his remaining followers that they must not be implicated in the actions of the MCP and must maintain a clear nationalist stance.[33] The memory of the conflict between the MPAJA and the Malay *kampongs* in August and September 1945 was never far away. In March, Dato Onn warned once again of the 'danger from the mountain' and labelled the Hizbul Muslimin as 'Red'. The radicals were tainted indelibly by this, and they were opposed by elders and headmen in many *kampongs*. There were mutterings of cult resistance to the Chinese. But in the climactic months of May and June, the threat of Islamic revolution loomed large in the fevered imaginations of British secret policemen.

THE FRONTIER ERUPTS

The crucible of the coming struggles was the Kinta valley of Perak. In the nineteenth century it had been Southeast Asia's Klondike and it remained its industrial heartland. The area is formed by two granite masses: the central range of the peninsula – which rises to heights of around 2,108 metres in the north – and a spur, the Kledang range, that forms the watershed between the Kinta and Perak rivers. The valley – around 58 kilometres north to south and 45 kilometres east to west – is edged by towering limestone outcrops. This frontier region was opened up by large-scale tin mining in the hills, and modern dredging methods were first pioneered in the swamps of the coastal plain. The hillsides were edged with rubber plantations. In Kinta the delicate pluralism of rural Malaya could be seen in microcosm. Large concentrations of Chinese and Indian labour lived alongside Malay *kampongs* that stretched down to the lowlands. It was Malaya's most urbanized area: over half of the population lived in the towns or main villages. The main settlement, Ipoh, dominated the region. It was an important centre of education and printing, a place of political initiation for men like Chin Peng and Wu Tian Wang of the MCP. The Malay Nationalist Party was launched in Ipoh, and it was a centre, too, of UMNO's organization. Ipoh was built by Chinese millionaries and its markets were supplied by Chinese peasant farmers. In hard times this was a brutal juxtaposition of wealth and want. The urban world and the forest were never far apart. In the war, the dense networks of roads and estate and mining tracks, the hidden limestone caves and jungle trails, had made it an ideal terrain for guerrilla armies to operate. From Kinta the mountain forests stretched eastwards almost to the coast and connected the central spine of the peninsula from the Thai border to the badlands of central Johore in the south.[34] Kinta witnessed first blood between the British and the MCP in October 1945, when troops opened fire on demonstrators in Sungei Siput. And in June 1948 this small town would be the spark that ignited the Malayan revolution.

Kinta was home to the largest concentrations of Chinese squatters in Malaya: perhaps 94,000 out of the district's total population of around 281,500. Most of them were on mining land.[35] Numbers had risen in the war, and the British expectation was that, in peacetime, they would drift back to the towns and mines. But food and work remained scarce. The Chinese mines faced discrimination in the allocation of rehabilitation loans and many small labour-intensive mines stopped producing altogether. In 1948, the mining labour force was below a third of its 1940 level, and at the middle of the year there were up to 28,000 unemployed workers in the area. But a major change had taken place in the rural economy. When men returned to wage labour, they left their families behind in the squatter hamlets. For the first time Malaya possessed a permanent population of Chinese peasant farmers. This broke down the old ethnic division of labour whereby food growing was the preserve of the *kampong* Malays living in designated 'Malay reservations'. And whereas single males had once lived collectively in the *kongsi*, or communal hut, now a labourer usually had his own hut in which to raise his children. Between the censuses of 1931 and 1947, the proportion of children in Perak had risen from 25.6 to 39.3 per cent; the number of local-born Chinese from 31 to 65 per cent. Like Indians on the estates, the militant stance of Chinese in labour disputes was a fight for the future of their families. This phenomenon was repeated right across Malaya. There were 12–15,000 squatters on the land of Batu Arang colliery in Selangor, which, like a rubber estate, was private land. They were a direct challenge to managers' authority. Workers and squatters were, as often as not, the same people. The ability of workers to fall back on farming in the event of low wages or a strike gave them an independence and leverage that they had never possessed before.[36]

Initially, British officials showed some sympathy for these settlers. In Malay reservations and in forest reserves Chinese farmers were given a two-year reprieve and allowed to grow food. They were forced to pay charges, to take out permits, or temporary occupation licences, and occasionally long-term crops like tapioca, or commercial plantings of tobacco were pulled up. But few cases ended in eviction: Malaya needed the food these peasants grew. In the later part of 1947, however, tensions intensified as colonial regulations were reimposed in a relentless way. On rubber estates, which had been largely abandoned to food crops in the war, European companies demanded the removal of squatters to make way for replanting: they claimed that 40,000 acres were occupied. Malay politicians wanted to evict Chinese farmers from state land and Malay reservations, where Malays had exclusive call on the land. The pressure did not always come from the Malay farmers themselves. In many areas there were long-running informal agreements whereby Chinese might cultivate or tap Malay rubber smallholdings in return for a fee or part of the yield. There was little evidence of Malay land hunger in this period: official land settlement schemes found few takers. The new opportunities for young Malays lay in the towns, in the police or lower ranks of the expanding bureaucracy. Malays now constituted 17.5 per cent of the wage labour force. But land was a deeply symbolic issue for Malay politicians and bureaucrats. Under the new federal constitution, control of land was a state matter. When, under pressure from the Chinese leader, H. S. Lee, the federal government asked state governments if there was land available for the Chinese, it was told there was none to be had. In this way, Malay elites demonstrated Malay prerogatives.[37]

Many more squatters were in forest reserves. These were a prized imperial asset: Malaya accounted for 45 per cent of the timber reserves of the British Empire in 1945, and their importance rose with the loss of Burma. Foresters argued that large-scale terrace farming by squatters was responsible for soil erosion that threatened damage to the lower-lying areas where the rubber estates were situated. Planters inveighed at this 'wanton destruction'. In fact, the erosion of the thin local soil, and the imbalanced ecosystem dominated by a 'new jungle' of imported single crops, was largely the consequence of their own methods.[38] But planters were determined to get a grip on their labour forces, and ecological arguments were used to increase pressure on the rural Chinese. In mid July, in the Kroh forest reserve in Kinta, 837 peasants were rounded up in mass arrests for not taking out permits.[39] In nearby Sungei Siput large-scale prosecutions began of squatters without permits in late 1947; in December alone 151 people were charged. The bailiffs moved in. In January 1948 2,600 families in Kuala Kangsar district were given two months to quit. In May officers began pulling up crops. The peasants argued they were now wholly dependent on padi, that with layoffs on the rubber estates they had no alternative source of income, and that the planting season was already underway. But they were told to demolish their houses and move on. 'We are very much frightened and miserable', they protested, 'because we are very poor farmers, just eking out a living . . .'[40]

The squatters began to fight back: farmers evaded officials, changed their names and hid their crops under debris. They drew up petitions to point out that the Japanese and British governments had actively encouraged them to open up land for food. But they also invoked a larger principle. In the Malay States, it was a local tradition, enshrined in colonial practice, that the man who brought jungle into cultivation and maintained it had a proprietorial right to it. Peasants now asked: 'Why do the Chinese have no freedom of cultivation yet the Malays enjoy these privileges?'[41] The British saw the red ink of communist propaganda in these demands. Yet it was clear that the squatters were now firmly rooted in a complex rural economy. They exploited the forest; they took rubber on a self-tap, self-sell basis. A typical family of five worked on an average three acres of land, and supported ten other families in the towns. According to one estimate, 95 per cent of Malaya's population was dependent on squatter production in one way or another. In Perak they not only supplied rice and vegetables but 5,000 pigs a month, 12,688 fowl and 200,000 duck and hen's eggs. Yet the squatters themselves were poor: their average family income was only $150 a month.[42] Above all, they demanded to stay in areas where their families had put down roots, and where they had been living as more or less self-governing communities. 'We find it very difficult to redistribute the land again', they explained, 'for the farmers want to preserve their former allotments and disputes and fights will start [trouble] if a redistribution is forced upon them.'[43] At a mass meeting in Sungei Siput, farmers emphasized their suffering during the Japanese occupation. It was an area of counter-insurgency operations against the communists and they had been caught in the middle of it.[44] But what stiffened the government's resolve to move against the squatters was its belief that it was losing political control of these areas. Both British and Chinese employers sensed an opportunity to tame their industrial labour.

When forest officers began to tear up crops, the protests turned violent. One official, D. Speldewinde, described an incident when he entered a squatter area in Changkat Jong with some Malay assistants to pull up some illegal tapioca plants:

The young man made a speech and ended in Malay, saying, 'We were not afraid of the Japs and we are not afraid of the British. Don't you think you can do these things to Chinese and get away with it . . . All of a sudden this young Chinese shouted, '*pak ung mor*' [Beat up the 'red hair'] and about thirty of them dived in surrounding tapioca bushes and each seized a spear and came towards us on the run. Two of the forest workers ran away and then we were surrounded. All I could do was to take a *parang* and prepare to defend myself.

Some older men intervened and saved Speldewinde and his men. The young firebrand was later arrested. It turned out he was president of the local peasants' union.[45] The membership of Chinese rubber-workers' unions and peasants' unions overlapped. They shared the same offices and framed their demands in similar terms. When evictions of squatters occurred at the same time as dismissals and evictions from rubber estates, the situation for the rural Chinese became desperate and the mood explosive. The situation in Perak came to a head with a new wave of strike action, led by the MCP Indian labour organizer R. G. Balan. He toured estates raising the tempo of protest: European managers, he said, would be nothing but coolies in their own country, but in Malaya they lived in luxury and obtained beautiful cars by exploiting the workers. Once again, estate managers sent their wives and families to the towns for safety.[46] By May there were calls for resistance to the police. Workers were told to grow food and maintain strikes as long as possible. They were told not to fear arrest; this would add pressure to the government, who would have to build jails to house them and buy food to feed them. The disputes moved to the larger estates, where living conditions were better, and their political motives were clear. At the Lima Blas and Kelapa Bali estates in Slim river strikes escalated when a manager refused to employ some fifty-four Indian and twenty-four Chinese labourers. Police and soldiers were moved in to support the evictions. The trouble spread across the Sungei Siput area. In Johore there were attacks on labour bosses with revolvers and knives. The manager of the Chan Kang Swee estate was forced to flee. His labourers began to tap and sell rubber for themselves and blocked entry and exit to the estate. When the police arrived they initially had to withdraw. When they returned with a magistrate they faced a large hostile crowd armed with spears, *parangs* and *changkols*. Eight labourers were killed and thirty more arrested. In a dispute on Sagil estate in Johore, the manager was knocked unconscious and was about to be decapitated when the police arrived.[47]

Singapore was also again hit by strikes. As in the previous year, the centre of the conflict was the Singapore Harbour Board. But the struggle was becoming more violent. The previous year communist-backed unions had managed to take over the system of labour contracting. In early 1948 the management decided to deal directly with labourers and a strike broke out. At one point the chairman of the board was approached by a Chinese businessman and asked if he wanted the help of secret-society men to fight the strikers. He refused the offer, but soon afterwards had to leave Singapore under the shadow of a death sentence from the MCP. Hand grenades were thrown at working stevedores. The strikes divided workers; the Kuomintang backed rival associations and the communist trade unions acted as if they were fighting for survival.[48] In the midst of this, the government banned the annual May Day parade, and the annual conference of the Federations of Trade Unions voiced a militant defiance. On 15 May the MCP Central Committee convened for a final time. Practical preparations for insurrection were set in motion: guerrilla bands were to be established on a state-by-state basis, a nucleus that could be expanded later. Party workers in the towns were told to avoid arrest, to withdraw to the countryside and lose themselves in the squatter settlements. The new directives were couched in defensive terms. They did not lay plans for a *coup d'état*. Instead, the MCP was waiting for the repression that would provide it with the legitimacy and the popular support that would carry it forward into revolution. The coming crackdown on organized labour would give it an opportunity to demonstrate leadership. The biggest obstacle to the Party's control over the labourers were the *kong chak*, 'labour thieves', or contractors, and the 'running dogs' who supplied information to the police. They were now to be eliminated. At this point there was no general order to kill Europeans. However, the broad terms of the directives gave discretion to local cadres.[49]

Between 17 May and 7 June twelve managers and one foreman were murdered; all were Asian except one European mining superintendent who, during a robbery, proved to be too slow in opening a safe where wages were kept. On 12 June in central Johore, three Kuomintang leaders were shot dead in their homes. Gent was under siege from delegations of planters: they were at a loss to understand why he did not act more decisively to protect them. In a speech to the Legislative Council on 31 May the chief spokesman for expatriate business, Aubrey Wallich, blamed the communists for the violence. Gent now telegraphed London to warn of 'the imminence of [an] organized campaign of murder by Communist agitators'. On 31 May the new trade union legislation finally came into operation, and the Federations of Trade Unions were outlawed on 13 June. But officials remained bitterly divided over the necessity for more extreme measures. Some years later, John Dalley, the head of the Malayan Security Service, revealed that as early as September 1947 he had recommended operations against 'uniformed armed Communists training and encamped in the jungle' in Johore. He gave a figure of potential men-and-women-in-arms of 5,000; it was, he said, 'given to me by the Secretary General of the Communist Party!' The police denied that the problem existed, and Gent had backed them. By December, Dalley was 'desperate'. He wrote a memorandum listing 'Gent's omissions and commissions' and sent it to MacDonald and to Gent himself. Gent never mentioned it to Dalley. In April and May he again flatly refused to countenance repressive measures.[50]

Malcolm MacDonald now concluded that Gent's useful time was at an end. The governor's future had been in doubt since the beginning of the year. On a visit to London in May, MacDonald pressed for his recall, and Attlee was informed of it. Ironically, MacDonald's main argument related not to the issue of communism but to the fact that Dato Onn and other Malay leaders 'dislike him and distrust immensely'. The overriding reason for the seeming inertia in dealing with the strikes and violence was the fact that MacDonald's own argument of the previous June still held: the Labour government would not permit the banning of the MCP unless there was conclusive evidence for its conspiracy to overthrow the local government. The Malayan Security Service had issued dire prognostications about the

MCP – and equally about the Kuomintang and 'Indonesian' influences – but it had given little in the way of a hard assessment of communist intentions.[51] As one watcher of the skies in Whitehall, J. B. Williams, commented on 28 May after reading intelligence reports, the effect was 'almost of melodrama. It conjures up pictures of hordes of people burrowing mole-like in the interstices of Malayan society or scurrying hither and thither on their mischievous errands, so that one may almost wonder whether that society is not about to rock to its fall'. But, Williams concluded, nothing 'would lead us to suppose that any serious trouble is brewing in Malaya. The threat, such as it was, came from 'mere bandits' rather than the communists whose 'immediate threat is but slight'.[52] Two weeks later, on 14 June, the British government received Dalley's own assessment: 'There is no immediate threat to internal security in Malaya, although the position is constantly changing and is potentially dangerous.'[53] This gave no firm indication that the MCP had ordered an armed revolt. But no such command had, in fact, been issued: it was contingent on the actions of the British themselves.

CALLS TO ARMS

Two days later, on the morning of 16 June, at 8.30 a.m., three young Chinese appeared on bicycles at the office of 50-year-old Arthur 'Wally' Walker, manager of Elphil estate in Sungei Siput. One came to the door and greeted him respectfully, 'Tabek, Tuan', 'Greetings, sir'; the two others went round the side and fired two shots into the back of his head, killing him instantly. A terrified Indian estate clerk witnessed the affair. Around half an hour later, on Phin Soon estate, the two planters there, 55-year-old John Allison and his 21-year-old assistant, Ian Christian, were surrounded by a dozen Chinese, taken onto their veranda and made to sit on chairs. Both men were then executed. The Chinese shouted to the watching labourers in Malay: 'We are out only for the Europeans. These men will surely die today. We will shoot all Europeans.' Walker and Allison had been prisoners of the Japanese. Christian, a former Gurkha officer, had been in the country for only a few weeks. A few days earlier he had approached his old comrades in the Gurkhas stationed nearby and borrowed an old Luger. The Gurkhas had promised to go pig shooting on the estate the next weekend as a deterrent to trouble.[54] Years later Chin Peng reflected on the killings: 'From the revolutionary's point of view at the time, I saw no validity in the killing of Christian. The deaths of the other two were acceptable.'[55] They had been implicated in the bitter disputes in Sungei Siput over evictions from estates and forest reserves. Now labourers took their revenge. The murders were a consequence of the orders that had been issued in May, and perhaps could have occurred in any number of places, but they were unplanned by Party leaders. The spark that lit the Malayan revolution came from below, and caught both the British and the communists unawares and unprepared.

Gent responded by declaring a state of Emergency in Perak and parts of Johore, and it was extended to the entire peninsula two days later. It was seen as a temporary measure, but it would last for twelve years. It did little to stem the tide of criticism. On 17 June the *Straits Times* ran a headline: 'Govern or get out'. Gent was very near breaking point.[56] He clashed with MacDonald at a conference at Kuala Lumpur on 22 June, over whether troops should be committed for static guard duty on mines and estates – as favoured by MacDonald – or in going after the main 'troublemakers' – as advocated by Gent. He was now accused of indecision and blamed for earlier lapses. The local military commanders reported that all soldiers had lost faith in him and Mac-Donald demanded his immediate recall. On 26 June Creech Jones telegraphed Gent to tell him to come home at the earliest opportunity. He was offered the face-saving formula to return on 'health grounds', but he declined to take it.[57] At a final meeting at Bukit Serene, Mac-Donald's residence in Johore Bahru, Gent requested the use of MacDonald's private office. He asked Dalley to follow him: 'There he produced from an attaché case the memorandum I had written on his omissions and commissions and went through it paragraph by paragraph, admitted it all and asked me if we could continue to be friends. As we shook hands on it, I felt quite emotional but my main feeling was one of relief, feeling that when he reached London he would give full support to all-out action.'[58]

Gent left Singapore on the night of 28 June. Old Malayan hands gloated. John Falconer, the British resident commissioner in Malacca, wrote to his wife on 2 July: 'It appears certain now that Gent will not be coming back, I feel rather sorry for Lady Gent who is left behind to clear up and say goodbyes. No doubt she regards her husband as a wonderful fellow and I'm sure he's always been a clever little boy. He has not done this country any good – on the contrary, much harm – though doubtless with good intentions.'[59] But Gent never had the opportunity to defend his actions. As his York freighter plane approached London on 4 July it collided with another aircraft. All that survived was Gent's silver cigarette case. He was mourned by many leaders of the Asian community, who recognized his liberal intentions and were dismayed by what looked like a triumph for British businessmen. To Tan Cheng Lock, it smacked of conspiracy. He protested at Gent's recall immediately to the Colonial Office, and, after his death, his son, Tan Siew Sin, told the Federal Legislative Council that Gent was disliked because, 'in the eyes of his country-men, he committed the unpardonable sin of treating Asians as if they were human beings . . .'[60] Gent saw it as his duty as proconsul to uphold the higher principles of Labour's imperial policy. He was reluctant to concede that this policy had failed by capitulating to special interests and governing through repressive powers. In his quiet way, Gent embodied the contradictory life and strange death of liberal imperialism in Malaya.

Neither side was ready for war. In June 1948 the MCP was at only an early stage of mobilization. It called up ex-MPAJA men and women, many of them well entrenched in civilian life. In Perak, by mid June, only one in five of the old comrades had responded to the call to arms. Some remained in the towns and villages as workers. 'Others', admitted a captured Perak leader, 'have good jobs and do not want to go.' But over time, new recruits were found, and the new army's strength would rise to at least 3,000. There were few large units; the strategy was to mix fighters up with villagers. This was to prevent their isolation and increase their opportunities for action. It was also a recognition that, unlike the anti-Japanese war, this would be a protracted struggle and the Party had to remain as close to the people as possible. Privately, Chin Peng thought in terms of ten years. The guerrilla groups began to move to hill hideouts. Many were wartime sites, but those from which British Force 136 officers had been excluded. As well as the mobile standing army there were auxiliaries drawn from the squatters and townsfolk. The main handicap to mobilization was lack of funds. The squatters were poor, and were not always able to feed party workers. A spate of robberies of payrolls in May and June was to make up the deficit.[61] As Chin Peng acknowledged, the Party was relying on the period between July and September to complete these tasks, and many of the key tactical decisions were yet to be made. 'Now in retrospect', Chin Peng reflected many years later, 'I think we were very inexperienced. At that time we were very young.'[62] This chaotic state of affairs would continue for the rest of the year and into 1949. It was only in December that the Party would issue its declaration of intent: the establishment of a People's Democratic Republic of Malaya. Even this, Chin Peng conceded, was perhaps a mistake: 'Our battle-cry should have been: Independence for Malaya and all Malayans who want independence.'[63]

The most compelling evidence for the Party's lack of readiness was the loss of so many of its senior cadres. Arrests had begun before the Sungei Siput murders. R. G. Balan was picked up on 30 May; on 9 June the editor of the Min Sheng Pau, Liew Yit Fan, was arrested together with many other journalists; so too was the cause célèbre of the February 1946 protests, Soong Kwong. On 20 and 21 June the British launched Operation Frustration, which dragged many more into the net including Rashid Maidin in Perak. Chin Peng's deputy, Yeung Kuo, had been visiting his wife and newly born daughter in Penang. On hearing the news of the Emergency he left his family home and made his way back to Kuala Lumpur by bus. In the confusion he managed to go underground in the Ampang area, but his wife was arrested and later banished to China. On 16 June Chin Peng was visiting a mine less than forty miles away from Sungei Siput, at Kampar. The Party had made a substantial investment in the business, but the owner was not sharing the profits. 'After some persuasion' he agreed to pay out, and Chin Peng had gone to collect the cash. The night after the Sungei Siput killings he narrowly avoided arrest and, together with a female worker from the mine, had to pose as a young married couple in order to navigate the police road blocks back to a safe house in Ipoh, where he was effectively trapped and out of action for some weeks.[64]

On 16 July a British police patrol located some suspects in an isolated hut two miles southeast of Kajang in Selangor. As they approached, a woman gave the alarm. Three men ran from the hut. The police opened fire and two of them were killed. One of them – shot in the forehead – was the military commander of the MPAJA, Liew Yao: he was thirty years old, a former schoolteacher, and just two years previously he had led the Malayan contingent at the Second World War victory parade in London. The police moved into the hut and arrested six women and tied them up outside, then set fire to the hut. Suddenly there was a counter-attack by a party of thirty to fifty guerrillas. Five of the bound women were killed in the crossfire: one of them was Liew Yao's wife. Four more guerrillas died in the shoot-out. The attackers dispersed only when the police began to shout in Malay, 'Here come the Gurkhas!'[65] A number of papers were recovered, including a diary. It described the arrests on 20 June, and Liew Yao's retreat into a rubber estate: 'the first time sleeping in the open after Jap[anese] surrender. It gives thoughts for future policy, for improvements to the *Vanguard* newspaper and military training.' On the night of 22 June the author reached an old haunt: 'Met an old woman who was my neighbour. I saw her kind face in the moonlight: her presence always gives me fortitude and the feeling the people are always with us. Her eldest son was in the MPAJA and he died a heroic death. Her other sons have grown up, and the older of the two has joined up. She is the mother of the people.' He met an armed section the next day, 'enthusiastic and friendly youths more or less twenty years, and full of energy. They have a bright future!' The next days were spent fining Kuomintang elements and recruiting school students. On 29 June he witnessed a British raid on a hamlet at Sungei Jelok. 'Well! Treat it as a practice for retreat.'[66]

There was another diary, this written by a woman, Tung Lai Chong of Amoy Street in Singapore's Chinatown. The entry for 6 July reads:

At about 2 p.m. I received a note from Wah requesting me to go up immediately. I am happy and only feel a bit uneasy when I think of mother. However, there is no time for me to hesitate now. Nothing can change my mind except to say sorry to mother as I must fulfil my promise to serve for the freedom of the people in Malaya. So, at about 4 p.m., after my meal, I bid goodbye to my house people. At five, I reach the paradise of liberty. Henceforth, I have to lead a camp life. It is a hard one, but I have confidence in it. I can endure the hardship. At night, we have to sleep in the open air.

There were three women with her. 'We love each other', she reported the next day, 'and the boys do try their best to help us.' On 8 July they heard that the area was 'occupied by the enemy', and they removed to the rubber estates. On 10 July three of the gang went out to 'hit the "dogs"'; they struck one down. The group moved to a safer place. The last entry was for 13 July: 'Many of our comrades say that I am losing weight. Yes, it is true. I think it is because of the effect of the kind of life I am leading now. I have no worry here, except at night, when we fear that the enemy might come and attack us.' It is very probable that Tung Lai Chong perished with Liew Yao in the firefight on 16 July.[67]

The man who led the attack on Liew Yao, with his 'killer squad' of twenty Chinese detectives dressed in black, was Superintendent Bill Stafford, a former stoker with the Royal Navy in the Far East, who had turned policeman in Hong Kong, and had been parachuted behind the lines many times during the Burma war. His trademark was the revolver slung under each armpit, and he was photographed in *Time Life*, complete with bandoleer and Sten gun. He slept in a mirrored room with a handgun under his pillow. His maxim was 'the only good communist is a dead communist'. To the Chinese he was *Tin Sau-pah* – 'The Iron Broom'. He had found Liew Yao on a tip from his barber.[68] Police methods were tough. There were reports of beatings and the settling of old scores. One member of the Singapore Special Branch, Ahmad Khan, described the interrogation of one of the first suspects to be pulled in, an Indian. He had been grilled for a month in Kuala Lumpur, then Ahmad Khan was sent for. After spending twenty-fours hours with him in Kuala Lumpur, he took him to the isolated hill town of Kuala Kubu Bahru to unnerve him and break him down. A successful interrogator, he maintained, found out all there was to know about a suspect: 'his attachments, whether he loves his mother or father or wife . . . Whether he is a truly family man or is not interested in family life. Whether he is a drunkard. Whether he likes money. You have to find out first the weak points in him. Then you can later press him on his weak points.' Then 'mentally you overpower him . . . 72 hours I worked without sleep, without proper food, without a wash, 72 hours continuously.' The man broke and a series of offensive operations were mounted on the back of it.[69] It was to become a curiously intimate war. The MCP lost a number of key leaders in this way, and, as in the time of Lai Teck, double agents were played back into the ranks of the guerrillas.

Operation Frustration was a catalyst to MCP recruitment. For ex-MPAJA members who fell into the hands of the police the likelihood of banishment to China was very strong. It was a widely held belief, supported by evidence from the newspapers, that those banished were immediately arrested and killed by the Kuomintang regime. Sympathizers reasoned that it was better to die fighting in Malaya. The mood of terror deepened as the British moved in on the squatter communities. When the British began to interrogate guerrillas in large numbers, they discovered that over 50 per cent of them had gone into the jungle through fear of arrest by the security forces.[70] The fact of colonial suppression – 'the criminal war created by the British Imperialists' – lay at the heart of MCP justifications for violence. In the words of one of its first manifestos: 'Only through such a war can democracy and freedom be achieved, the livelihood of the people be improved and the national economy developed . . . It is a national revolutionary, a progressive and sacred war.'[71] At 'Camp Malaya' at the village of Lubuk Kawah in Pahang, the Malay leaders assembled there faced a stark choice. Shamsiah Fakeh argued that she went into the forest because there seemed no further opportunity for democratic and open politics through which to continue her struggle. It was a choice between the forest and a British jail: 'all other roads were already closed'.[72]

The British had effectively removed an entire political generation from the scene. The arrests extended well beyond the MCP and its satellites. Ahmad Boestamam knew from the moment he heard the news of the Emergency that he would be taken in. He was working cutting scrub on a rubber holding in his home village in Perak when he was arrested on 1 July. His detention would last seven years. The arrest of the president of the Malay Nationalist Party, Ishak Haj Muhammad, became a new *cause célèbre*. As he wrote from jail, 'I wish to say that since the Emergency started; I felt that I have been used and I am still being used as a scapegoat to instil fear and create prejudice towards the Malay Nationalist Party, and consequently to discourage thousands of Malays from trying to assert their rights in the land of their forefathers and thereby continue to be a mute and maltreated community.'[73]

Other voices were silenced: the leaders of the Hizbul Muslimin, including Ustaz Abu Bakar and Ustaz Abdul Rab Tamini, were also arrested, and some religious schools had to close because of a shortage of teachers. A further sweep in Krian the following year saw 107 more arrests of Malays. This distorted political life for many years. Many saw in this the hidden hand of Dato Onn. As Boestamam put it: 'A vacuum naturally resulted in the Malayan political arena. This vacuum was quickly filled by UMNO, the one organization that remained legal at the time . . .'[74] Years later there were those on the Malay left who argued that the communist Emergency was manufactured by the British to allow for a crackdown on the radical Malay nationalism that was perhaps a much more potent long-term threat to British interests.[75]

Some of the well-to-do radicals of the Malayan Democratic Union were forewarned of their arrest. Philip Hoalim was told by a Chinese legislative councillor in Kuala Lumpur to take a long cruise around the world. He now realized that some of his colleagues were deeply involved with the communists. To protect its surviving members, the MDU was dissolved in late June. Two of its younger activists were boyhood friends from Johore, and students in the elite Raffles' College. William Kuok Kock Ling came from a prosperous and well-connected family – his younger brother, Robert, would become the richest man in Southeast Asia – but he had been active in the Malayan Democratic Union from the outset. Dato Onn, a friend of his family, warned him that he was to be picked up, and advised him to leave the country. 'This is my country,' Kuok responded, and took to the forest. His friend James Puthucheary had an early and dramatic political awakening, as a middle-class volunteer in the Indian National Army. He fought at Imphal, and there witnessed the price of anti-colonial struggle: he was the only one of his platoon to survive. After the war he had hidden in Bose's Calcutta home for several months and taken in the heady mood of liberation in the city. But when he returned to Malaya in 1948 he was faced with a three-way choice between exile, detention and the underground. His friends invited him to join them in the jungle. As he explained in a political testimony in 1957, written in a British jail: 'One is always drawn by the desire to fight colonialism and the urge to join up with those who are fighting hardest is irresistible. It often appears that to refuse to join such allies is to be dishonest to one's anti-colonial principles. But in such an alliance one is always tormented by the fundamental differences one has with one's allies.'[76] William Kuok was killed by the security forces in 1953 – as Lim Hong Bee wrote many years later – 'his body desecrated by men who could probably not tell the difference between Dostoevsky and a doughnut or an iambic from a tropical itch'.[77] Some of those caught up in the white terror of 1948 and after would survive to play a part in national life. But many did not. The Emergency extorted a high toll in political talent. For this reason, many felt an enduring resentment at what the MCP had done. The Party, as much as the British, had refused to allow a free trade unionism to strengthen and mature. It had betrayed the political hopes of the Malayan Spring. In Hoalim's words: 'Now the precipitate action of the Communist Party to violence had brought to an end our effort for national unity and democracy for a new Malayan nation, as it was plain that the Emergency would not allow genuine democratic activity to continue until the Communists had been defeated. How long this would take was uncertain.'[78]

STEN GUNS AND *STENGAHS*

For some time the British remained unsure as to what exactly they were fighting in Malaya. The first written report to the cabinet on 1 July blamed 'gangsters' for the violence. 'The trouble is almost certainly Communist-instigated,' Creech Jones argued, 'though direct connection between the gangsters and the Communist Party cannot always be traced.' This remained the position when the cabinet first discussed the crisis on 13 July. It was not until 19 July that the Labour government, at Malcolm MacDonald's urging, accepted that the MCP should be banned. On 23 July the MCP, the MPAJA Ex-Comrade's

Association, the New Democratic Youth League and PETA were all outlawed. But even at this stage Attlee personally amended the parliamentary statement to make it clear that the decision was taken on the basis of MacDonald's personal assessment, in order to distance his ministers from it. Creech Jones believed that success in Malaya was 'a vital step in the "Cold War" against communism in the East' and MacDonald's public statements spoke of the 'hand of Moscow and the rule of gun and knife'. But the search for hard evidence of a Moscow-directed 'plot' dragged on for many years.[79]

The British were also unsure as to what to call the guerrillas. MacDonald caused panic by referring to them as 'insurgents' in a radio broadcast. This threatened the insurance cover for the estates and mines; they were protected against 'riot and civil commotion', but not 'rebellion or insurrection'. Above all, officials were desperate to avoid any words 'which might suggest a genuine popular uprising'.[80] The Gurkhas in the front line called the guerrillas alternately 'Congress', or *daku*, dacoit.[81] The British settled on 'bandit'. This had a 'fine minatory ring', but it was also an ambiguous term. The Japanese had described the MPAJA as 'bandits' during the war. It conferred on the MCP the glamour of the people's resistance and invoked the Robin Hood figures of Chinese folklore. The rhetoric of Cold War brushed aside these semantic niceties. By 1952 the guerrillas were termed 'Communist terrorists' – 'CT' in more clinical usage – and it was axiomatic that the Malayan Emergency was an arm of the global Soviet conspiracy. But the underlying anxiety persisted. In the words of a senior mandarin, Sir Thomas Lloyd: 'The dividing line between the terrorist and the fighter for freedom is not always so clear in the minds of the outside world or the people of the terrorists' own country.'[82]

In June 1948 Malaya was not well defended. The acting head of government, Sir Alex Newboult, an old Malayan hand, was chronically short of manpower. There were ten infantry battalions in Malaya, but the Gurkha units that had been shipped to Malaya in 1947 were under strength and not fully trained. There were very few British troops: a battalion of the King's Own Yorkshire Light Infantry, the 26th Field Regiment of the Royal Artillery and 1 Battalion Seaforth Highlanders; with 1 Battalion of the Devonshire Regiment in Singapore. The commanding officer in Malaya, General Ashton Wade, saw that his forces were inadequate and petitioned the Commander-in-Chief Far East, Neil Ritchie, for two infantry divisions. Ritchie demurred: 'I can't possibly ask Monty [then Chief of the Imperial General Staff] for anything like that', he told Wade. 'He's hard put enough as it is with events in Germany and elsewhere.'[83] The entire British army was overstretched. With 400,000 men in arms there was difficulty in supplying a single brigade for Malaya, but such was the gravity of the situation that the elite Guards brigade was sent, troops who had been originally earmarked for Germany. This was the first time the Guards would see service in the empire in peacetime. However, the troops were not available for operations until early December. In the interim, MacDonald gently enquired about the possibility of troops from Australia. It was out of the question, he was told: the Australian trade unions who had so successfully blockaded supplies for the British intervention in Indonesia would never allow it.[84]

The police and planters formed the front line. Yet there were only around 12,000 police available in Malaya in mid 1948. Virtually none of them had received any training since the Japanese occupation, and they were sent on operations in peacetime khaki and heavy boots, with Lee Enfield rifles dating from around 1917. The force moved at a slow pace. Police headquarters still closed at six each evening and for the weekends. Rural police stations began to fortify themselves, but they had no wireless communications and a number were overrun in the first weeks of fighting. The telephone lines were immediately declared insecure, and planters' wives were hurriedly trained to operate the exchanges. The British turned to the Malay community for more recruits. Within the first month of the Emergency 25,000 men came forward to join a special constabulary. This voluntary, uniformed force was overwhelmingly Malay, and it bore some of the heaviest casualties of the war: thirty-seven were killed in 1948, just eight fewer than died serving with the regular police. In addition to this, by October, there were 12,000 more auxiliary police, again mostly Malay 'kampong guards'. In late 1951 the number had risen to nearly 100,000. Their level of training varied; most units were short of guns and few men had fired them. When the weapons were fired many failed to go off, not least because the ammunition, five rounds per man, was mostly stamped '34 or '36. Most of these guards went to European estates; the government would not risk giving arms to the Chinese businesses.[85] The Kuomintang office in Singapore urged young Chinese to join the police and in Kuala Lumpur Chinese *towkays* offered to form special police units. But it would be many months before the British agreed to harness the military resources of the Kuomintang to the anti-communist cause in Malaya.[86] Meanwhile Malay political leaders demanded a return for their community for their commitment.

One of the first acts of the Labour government was to turn to veterans of Britain's other imperial emergency: Palestine. This was a controversial move. In his last days, Gent had opposed it: his local officers had been confident that they had enough police to meet the challenge. But a former commissioner of police in Palestine, Nicol Gray, was sent to inspect policing in Malaya and was persuaded to stay on as commissioner of police there. His appointment, and the over 500 Palestine police sergeants who came with him, added further divisions to a police force torn by the resentments of war and internment. There were resignations and retirements, including that of John Dalley. The new arrivals placed the local system of apostolic succession in promotions in jeopardy and challenged old methods. Nicol Gray's paramilitary approach was deeply unpopular and the Palestinian sergeants acquired a brutish reputation. In the disdainful words of one senior Malay official, 'They kept Chinese women as mistresses and spent most of their time drinking.'[87] It was true that they broke many of the codes of pre-war empire and this exposed the class snobbery of colonial society. Once again, European clubs in Singapore excluded men in uniform. These tensions were later satirized in the tragicomic form of Nabby Adams in the 1959 novel *Time for a Tiger*. The Somerset Maugham epoch was giving way to the Anthony Burgess era. The new arrivals were welcomed by the planters, not least for their training of special constables. Many lost their lives. They were part of a broader influx of new blood into colonial society. Many new police recruits were recently demobbed national servicemen who had seen a glimpse of the colonial good life and were determined to enjoy it themselves. Others were adventurers who had not settled to peace and civilian life: 'There were infantry officers, Air Force pilots, Royal

Navy frogmen, Commandos, Paras and Force 136; all ranks from Lt/
Col down . . .'[88] Their conditions of life were a long way from what
was promised; they were often cooped up in fenced compounds in
remote areas, often without electricity or company, and the casualty
rate was high. One of the basic rules of self-preservation was to 'Go
to the biggest village in your area and run up a large bill for food and
grog with the largest Chinese shopkeeper, always keep your account
in debit. He, the shopkeeper, might see you as an investment and do
his best to keep you alive.'[89]

Colonial society armed itself. Most planters were veterans of at
least one war, and some had special forces experience. Managers
purchased large stocks of war materials on the open market and
created elaborate defences of trenches, barbed wire, floodlights and
traps of broken glass. One cook took the Emergency so seriously that
he served only military rations of bully beef and tea. The wealthier
estates hired small private armies. American miners played a leading
role in armament. At Kampar in the Kinta valley, Ira Phelps, a Mor-
mon employee of Pacific Tin, made armour from the remains of
Japanese tanks on local battlefields to create Dodge weapons carriers.
There were plenty of carbines available to the police, but precious
little ammunition for them. Most of what existed had been acquired
from the communists themselves. Pacific Tin offered to make clip
magazines for the police in return for the arming of its British and US
engineers. The chairman of Anglo-Oriental flew in guns from Sydney
and Bangkok on Pan-Am. This gave a boost to the underground arms
trade with Indonesia.[90] The unvarying routine of estate life became
more disciplined than ever, although individual managers had to constantly vary their movements to reduce the risk of ambush on the
dangerous estate roads. Many believed that a popular manager would
not be shot, but often popular men were killed by gangs passing
through. By 1949, 745 planters and miners had honorary police rank.
This gave them unprecedented powers over their workforce. One
planter in Pahang later recounted firing in the dark at a moving light
to enforce a curfew: 'The next day, to my horror, we found that an
elderly estate labourer had been seriously wounded. He had been
breaking the curfew to collect some stored *samsu* [distilled *toddy*]
from a cache in preparation for his daughter's wedding celebrations

the following day.'[91] The upcountry clubs were a strange vista of Sten guns and *stengahs*, the staple whisky and soda.[92] 'Those were the days is heard frequently in up-country clubs', reported *The Times*, 'as the pistol-belt is buckled around the expansiveness of middle age, and the sten gun is disentangled from handbags and children's toys'. Some of the older planters disliked it, 'as much as they did the carrying of parcels in the streets of pre-war London'.[93] But it became an indelible image of the war, especially as glamorized by Jack Hawkins and a rather over-dressed Claudette Colbert in the 1952 movie *The Planter's Wife*.

The European business lobby capitalized on this attention to argue for more men and stronger measures for Malaya. Morale was soon strained by MCP attacks on Europeans. In Selangor, in July, there were ambushes of planters' families as they evacuated, in which a child died. This may well have been a reprisal for the five Chinese women who were killed with Liew Yao earlier in the same week. In one incident, on 7 August at Telok Sangat in southeast Johore, the European manager, H. M. Rice, was shot in front of his wife and daughter while watching a cinema show on his estate. His body was burned in the cinema hall. His special constables were unable to resist up to sixty armed fighters. The Malay workforce was paraded and told by the guerrillas that they need not be afraid of Europeans any more. Rice's wife and daughter fled into the jungle; six constables and estate workers were injured. The isolation was enervating. Although Telok Sangat was a mere eight miles from Changi on Singapore island as the crow flew, the nearest town in Johore, Kota Tinggi, was two hours away by river.[94] Other attacks occurred on estates very close to Kuala Lumpur. Planters in the old FMS Bar in Ipoh ran a sweepstake on who would be next. Planters were departing on home leave with no intention of returning, the industry warned that production would break down, and that all control over their labour forces would be lost. Thirteen European planters were killed between May and October 1948, but only five between November and April 1949, and none in the six months following that. In early August 1948 forty KMT members were killed by the MCP. Chinese businessmen asked the British if they could arm themselves, as did the Europeans, but to no avail. As one later remarked, 'I too could have been a hero with such protection.'[95] Throughout the Emergency it was Malayans who, least well-defended, suffered most of the casualties.

To restore its authority and to boost public confidence, the government's first response to the Sungei Siput murders was to arm itself with draconian powers. The Emergency Regulations allowed for detention without trial for up to one year, later extended to two. All but capital offences were to be tried *in camera*. The death penalty was reinstated for possession of arms, including possession of fireworks, which guerrillas might turn into explosives. The police were given powers to impose curfews and controls on movement and food. All newspapers had to obtain a government permit. Even cinema was restricted: gangster films were withdrawn on the grounds that they glamorized violence, and also, it was reported, *A Tale of Two Cities*, because it portrayed a revolution.[96] These actions marked the final end of the Malayan Spring. Over fifty years later many of the measures still remained on the statute book. One of the most far-reaching initiatives was the registration of the population. For many it was a first direct contact with government – literally so, in the taking of fingerprints. But also it gave citizens individual identities: for the first time it recorded the names and numerous aliases customarily adopted by the Malayan Chinese. The task was accomplished surprisingly quickly; by the end of the year a twenty-mile belt along the Thai frontier was registered – significantly it was Chinese only who were registered first – and the entire island of Penang.[97] Less than three years after its virtual collapse, the state was taking on unprecedented new functions.

These were dangerous powers and in the early days of the Emergency they were wielded with uncompromising ferocity. As J. B. Williams in the Colonial Office warned in mid August, there was a real danger of 'allowing our regime to become purely one of repression. This was, after all, the final tragedy of our rule in Palestine.'[98] But it was again to Palestine that London looked for leadership in Malaya. Even before Gent's departure there had been a good deal of discussion of his successor in private. Among the names canvassed was the recent chief secretary in Palestine, Sir Henry 'Jimmy' Gurney. When consulted by Creech Jones, MacDonald had not been impressed. He felt that local opinion would demand an old Malaya hand or a major public figure; certainly this was the view of the planting community

('Give us Monty'). But Gurney had proved his ability to work with the military and was respected for his even-handed approach to communal issues. This was precisely the problem for Malay leaders when the news was broken to them: the constant analogy with Palestine troubled them deeply and they feared Gurney would treat the Chinese as a kind of Jewish Agency. Creech Jones prevailed, but Gurney did not arrive until 1 October. A slight man of fifty, he had more panache than his predecessor – even at the height of the Palestine crisis, he was a contributor to *Punch* magazine – but possessed a mandarin manner which alienated many people. He was overshadowed by the vivacity of MacDonald, who had no direct responsibility for fighting the communists, and the martial drive of his successor, General Gerald Templer, who was given far more powers than Gurney. But two lessons of the Middle East shaped Gurney's approach in Malaya: a need to prevent the deterioration of the ethnic situation that could create 'another Palestine' and the need to keep the war in Malaya a civilian conflict. He resisted firmly calls for martial law.[99] A religious man who understood the power of communism, Gurney's first months in Malaya were overshadowed by the heavy hand of oppression.

The army chiefs were confident that the threat could easily and quickly be countered. Even MacDonald forecast that the Emergency might be over by September. The new military commander, a Gurkha officer from India, Major General Charles Boucher, was ebullient. 'I can tell you', he announced, 'this is by far the easiest problem I have ever tackled. In spite of the appalling country, and ease with which he can hide, the enemy is far weaker in technique and courage than either the Greek or Indian reds.'[100] He fought communism as if it were a set of skirmishes on the North West Frontier. In particular large 'sweeps' were set in train to dislodge guerrillas, followed through with air-force raids to break morale and to flush the enemy into the open. These were unsuccessful. Commanders were later to learn that it needed a thousand hours of patrolling to eliminate one guerrilla.[101] The British did, however, begin to experiment with specialist private armies. Veterans of Force 136 – many of whom had returned to Malaya as district officers, policemen and planters – formed themselves into what were called 'Ferret Forces'. The leading figures were John Davis and Richard Broome, the 'Dum' and 'Dee' who during the war had liaised with Chin Peng, a man who was, Davis remarked, 'my greatest ally and who has always, I believe, remained a good friend'.[102] These kinds of forces had the merit of being easy to dissolve should they become controversial. The use of Dyak trackers from Sarawak caused a press sensation; the reaction of the *Daily Worker* was hysterical: 'The Labour Government policy requires for successful operation the participation of man-eating, primitive savages...' Eventually in Malaya, as Broome later put it, 'the whole army became "ferretized"'.[103] The objective was to bring the guerrillas out of the jungle and to a fixed battle. In 1954 this strategy would also be pursued by the French against the Viet Minh, and culminate in defeat at Dien Bien Phu, but the communists in Malaya were never put to this test.

Men like Davis and Broome drew upon their deep knowledge of the MPAJA but, in general, British understanding of Chinese society in Malaya was either very rudimentary or very out-of-date, and distorted by racial prejudice. A stock view was that the Chinese were a busy and conspiratorial people, more interested in money than in politics, and responsive chiefly to intimidation and force. As a specialist of the old Chinese Protectorate put it: the heart of Chinese society was 'the secret society complex'.[104] These sage saws were drawn upon by the new high commissioner, Henry Gurney, and shaped his approach to countering terrorism. In one of his first despatches to Creech Jones, Gurney wrote that 'it is universally agreed here that the support which [the communists] get is almost wholly through intimidation and cannot by any stretch of the imagination be described as "popular"... The truth is the Chinese are accustomed to acquiesce to pressure.'[105] The British continually played down the political roots of the rebellion. This encouraged the view, prevalent in mid 1948, that a show of force against 'bad hats' would be enough to restore the situation. The cannier officials were aware that the government had no understanding of what the ordinary Chinese men and women were thinking. Many lamented the demise of the Protectorate and the local knowledge that had been lost in the war. Eighteen months into the Emergency, of the 256 Malayan Civil Service officers, only 23 had passed the Chinese-language exams and 16 were learning it. The main consequence of this, a group of Chinese specialists in Singapore argued, was that the Chinese were still almost wholly disconnected from government and possessed a deep-rooted aversion to authority and avoided it when they could. 'They are bewildered and because the British have failed once they are afraid that they may fail again.'[106]

This had tragic consequences. Under the terms of the Emergency Regulations, aversion or evasion implied guilt. Few military operations took Chinese interpreters with them. In November the rules were amended to allow a chief police officer to declare 'special areas' in which anyone called to stop and be searched, and who failed to do so, might be shot.[107] The designation of the war as an 'anti-bandit campaign' did not help understanding. In the lexicon of empire, 'banditry' was a catch-all word for evil; it criminalized the communists, and the Chinese community as a whole, and this did not encourage officials, soldiers or policeman to reflect on the social and political issues that were at stake, or to make distinctions between degrees of guilt and innocence.[108] It encouraged in professional soldiers contempt for the adversary, and a tendency to underestimate his tenacity and intelligence. For the conscript, it was a recipe for fear and perplexity. As one recalled: 'No one appeared to be quite sure of the size of the problem or where the danger was coming from. Many of us couldn't tell the difference between Malays and Chinese and it was all very confusing.'[109] This was the first time British regular forces had engaged in jungle fighting in the Malayan terrain. (The war of 1941–2 had not been a forest campaign.) It was, for many, a nightmarish experience. The British soldiers in the front line were often ill trained and inexperienced, and they were up against hardened, bloodied veterans. Chin Peng described his first close encounter with British troops, at Ayer Kuning in Perak in July. His own men had been strafed from the air and, with a Dakota circling above, the troops were searching and burning the long grass to draw out the communists. 'They were', he remarked, 'very white and very young.' They never discovered Chin Peng, who slipped by them during a cloudburst.[110]

THE ROAD TO BATANG KALI

Chin Peng was in Ayer Kuning to pick up an escort to take him to safety. He had spent the first days of the Emergency holed up in a house in Ipoh. Hidden in the back of a biscuit delivery van, he moved to a village in the Sungei Manik area of Perak to meet with Perak units to discuss the situation. The communist high command was non-existent. His deputy, Yeung Kuo, was in Selangor and plans for a Central Committee meeting had to be set aside. The MCP's military objectives were, as Chin Peng admitted, very vague at this stage. The immediate goal was to create a command post in Pahang as a prelude to the creation of two 'base areas', one in the north and one in the south. But while he was with the Perak commanders, word came by courier from the other senior Party leaders that they now recommended concentrating resources in a fully 'liberated area' in the north. This was a classic Maoist strategy based on the fabled Yenan liberated area in China. As a result, Chin Peng's party, including eighty Malays and twenty Indians, moved out of the area to Bidor and then into the Cameron Highlands. He was back in the neutral jungle of his Force 136 days.

MCP units had mobilized on a state-by-state basis, as planned, but, lacking common objectives, many now launched operations on their own initiative. The most dramatic was a dawn attack by five groups of guerrillas on Batu Arang colliery on 13 July. Five men – including three Kuomintang figures – were identified and killed, the Kuala Lumpur train was held up and its passengers robbed. Demolition parties damaged excavation equipment and generators. Around fifty fighters were involved and the whole incident lasted less than an hour. The government was deeply alarmed when the mine demanded compensation.[111] This set the pattern for the first weeks: labour contractors and others were executed and there were arson attacks on industrial buildings. There were also assaults on remote police stations. One incident at Langkap in Perak involved around 100 fighters. It was the most intense firefight of the Emergency, in which the guerrillas loosed over 2,000 rounds of ammunition.[112] Although there were incidents in most states, Kajang in Selangor, the area where Liew Yao had been killed, was a centre of activity. These attacks gave a sense of an impressive underground organization, but made overall co-ordination of the campaign difficult.

But at a key crossroads of the central range there took place an incident that would prove to be a decisive military encounter of the Emergency. Ulu Kelantan was an isolated area of Chinese settlement high upriver in the northeastern state of Kelantan, one of the oldest Chinese settlements in Malaya. During the war it had been a battle-ground for rival Kuomintang and MPAJA forces. The area was a plausible site for a liberated area for the MCP. It backed onto the Thai frontier, and there was a profitable cross-border traffic to be taxed. It was not easily accessed by the British: the east-coast railway had gone out of action in the war and services had not been re-established. Yet, with the jungle communication network the Party had constructed during the war, it had the potential to be a command centre for the various units working in the different states.[113] The guerrilla commanders began to focus their thoughts on the small town of Gua Musang, and it began to seem like an insurgent's El Dorado. It was the railhead of the old east-coast line, but to reach it from the state capital, Kota Bahru, was forty-four miles by road, and then eight to ten hours by river. A major operation was planned. The main forces were to come from battalions from the 'model' 5th Perak Regiment of the MPAJA, now renamed the Malayan Peoples' Anti-British Army. A large party of guerrillas moved across the watershed in north Pahang to create a 12th Regiment in west Kelantan. And with other units from Perak, there were around 600–700 guerrillas concentrated in Kelantan, including men who were to become the MPABA's chief commanders.[114] Such a large concentration of men could not be kept together for long; the problems of supplying it were immense.

But they had anyway arrived too late. The Battle of Gua Musang had already between fought and lost. Local MCP men in the nearby Party stronghold of Pulai had seen the opportunity. In Gua Musang itself there was a garrison of only fourteen men in a reinforced police post and they had no radio contact with the outside world. A village headman in Pulai had been given a bicycle by the government to get a message quickly to Gua Musang in the event of trouble with communists in the Pulai area, but when the attack came, in early July, many villagers from Pulai joined it, including the headman himself. They had been told that Kuala Lumpur had fallen to the communists and that this was merely a mopping-up operation. They first captured the police inspector, but he managed to escape to the police post to rally its defenders. He was persuaded to surrender when it was suggested to him by his sergeant that grenades could be lobbed into the post from a huge limestone outcrop that towered over the town. The defenders were then each given $20 and a cup of coffee by the victorious guerrillas. The first British army relief party was pushed back, but the second forced the guerrillas to retire into the jungle, together with villagers. The final attack was supported by RAF Spitfires. The villagers believed that they were from liberating Chinese armies, until they were strafed by them.[115] The communists had held their liberated area for five days.

Once again, the leadership's plans had been pre-empted from below. The large units had to break up, and many of the Perak units slipped back over the watershed to operate in Kinta, around Ipoh and Sungei Siput. Now that an orthodox strategy was denied it, at least for a time, the MCP changed tactics. For much of the rest of the year the characteristic operations were small scale, often led by the MCP's 'special mobile squads' in urban and semi-urban areas. They were brutal affairs. The first attacks occurred in Ipoh: on 1 October a Kuomintang newspaper in Ipoh, *Kin Kwok Daily News*, was attacked with a grenade. It landed on a reporter's table and killed him instantly. Most of the victims were Chinese contractors and businessmen. There were also attacks on the night trains from Kuala Lumpur and, increasingly, rubber estates were the targets of specialized industrial sabotage. Trees were slashed with knives to put them out of production. On the night of 18–19 November, in Tapah alone 30,000 trees were destroyed. Planters estimated that most would take up to seven years to recover. The cost was measured in tens of thousands of dollars.[116] Another campaign was against national registration. The 'body-stealing cards', as they were called, hit the MCP hard, as they damaged their units' ability to move freely. Slogans appeared in public places: 'Photographers will be killed. Authenticators will suffer.' Photographic shops were raided and negatives and prints stolen and destroyed. The purpose of the cards, the MCP announced, 'is to tie up people tightly, thus enabling them to burn, kill, drive out, rape and make fun of the people at their pleasure'. It instructed people to 'Use your identity cards as joss paper.'[117]

But it was in the squatter settlements that battle was joined most fiercely. The British saw entire peasant communities as supporters of the guerrillas. Operations against them began in Sungei Siput on 20 and 29 October, when 456 squatters were evicted and their houses burned behind them. In Tronoh in the same month over 700 people were forced into town when their homes were destroyed. The rebel town of Pulai in Kelantan was razed to the ground. The management of Batu Arang, with the help of the British army, managed finally to evict 5,000 squatters from their land. In justifying these actions to Creech Jones, Gurney argued that the squatters 'have no part whatsoever in the community life of Malaya. They do not speak the Malay language and remained completely Chinese in outlook. By no stretch of the imagination can they lay claim at present to belong to the country.'[118] Suspects were summarily detained. An over-large quantity of rice, drinking cups or torch batteries were sufficient grounds for arrest.[119] The military applied a 'callus test' to find those whose hands did not seem hardened by toil. Gurney argued that the displaced squatters of Sungei Siput were offered alternative land in the Dindings, that they were in fact 'resettled'. One of the few journalists to write about this in any depth was Harry Fang of the *Malaya Tribune*. Of the 5,350 squatters moved from the area, only 2,000 made it into camps. He found 1,073 of them at Sungei Batu – only 360 of them men – living in tents, given two meals a day and charity handouts. They had been offered two acres of jungle, but only eighty accepted. Several months later many of them were washed out by floods. 'He and his father', he wrote of two squatters, 'have lived in fear almost all their lives: fear of sudden death; fear of starvation. They do not think in terms of citizenship: its duties and responsibilities. They think in terms of their plot of vegetables; their poultry and pigs. They ask for nothing except the right to go on living.'[120]

The military thinking behind these operations appeared to date from the Boer War. To the Chinese, it was the method of the Japanese fascists. A particularly brutal 'punitive action' occurred at Kachau, four and a half miles from Semenyih in Selangor. It was a notorious area in the occupation; a base for MPAJA operations. It had recently witnessed the murder of a European manager of a nearby estate, a Malay barber had been killed at work in the centre of the village, and in the two days before the operation a mine and an estate were raided and set alight. On the morning of 2 November the villagers were paraded and given two hours to remove their belongings. The village of 61 houses was burned and 400 people were made homeless. There was, Gurney reported, a 'complete and voluntary exodus of the squatters from the surrounding area'. It was, he concluded, 'admittedly drastic', but, he argued, the squatters had abetted the bandits.[121] 'On the same analogy', responded the Chinese consul, 'it would seem permissible to burn the whole of Kuala Lumpur or even the State of Selangor because some terrorist outrages had occurred in the State.'[122]

The Malayan Communist Party responded in kind, burning huts where farmers had been seen to co-operate with the police. The Chinese community was in crisis. Its leaders were no longer able to give any protection to their people. As Tan Cheng Lock pleaded to the minister of state in the Colonial Office, Lord Listowel, the Chinese were 'placed between two *millstones* between which they stand to be crushed, or to put it bluntly between the devil and the deep blue sea. Should they give information or actively co-operate with the government against the Malayan Communist Party, they or their families would simply be slaughtered by the guerrillas, whilst government would be unable to protect them'.[123] By the end of the year the number of detainees had swelled to 5,097, and in November a new Emergency regulation, 17C, allowed for banishment of non-Federal citizens if their appeals were rejected, together with their dependants.[124] It was suddenly unclear whether the rural Chinese had any future in Malaya or where else there would go. MacDonald spoke in terms of wholesale banishments to relieve tensions: to China, to North Borneo, even to a remote outpost of the old Straits Settlements in the southern Indian Ocean, Christmas Island.

The full ferocity of counter-terror was exposed in a small settlement of Chinese rubber tappers at Batang Kali in Selangor. The story took twenty-one years to surface and, even today, the picture remains incomplete. The first newspaper reports on 13 December announced that, on the previous day, twenty-six bandits had been surprised and captured by a platoon of 2 Battalion Scots Guards. When the bandits tried to escape, they ran into the guns of the soldiers and, according to a police officer, 'Everyone was killed'. It was heralded as the government's greatest success of the Emergency. Then there was a curious silence until 3 January 1949, when a further statement was issued by the federal government to the effect that, after an investigation into the incident, it was to take no further action. More details emerged which implied that the people killed were labourers suspected of supplying the guerrillas. The men and women in the settlement had been separated, and the men held overnight on 11 December in a *kongsi* hut and interrogated. Fearing an ambush by the communists, the Scots Guards hid watchers around the clearing in which the hut was found. The next morning the labourers in the hut, seeing only a few soldiers around, had made a break for freedom. The hidden guards, seeing the Chinese men run and not knowing what was happening, had called on them to halt, then, acting under standing orders, had finally opened fire.[125] Many questions were asked about this incident at the time, by the Chinese press and by the *Straits Times*. Not least, how had so many guerrillas died leaving none injured, and at the hands of a small platoon of British troops? And how was it that the Scots Guards could have been so certain that they were guerrillas? According to one journalist's account, Gurney called in one of the senior writers of the *Straits Times* to ask why the paper would not let the matter rest.[126] The enquiry into the incident, which was undertaken by the Attorney General of Malaya, Sir Stafford Foster-Sutton, was never made public. In Britain, questions about Batang Kali were raised by the *Daily Worker*, which was now a tenacious opponent of the campaign in Malaya. When asked about it by Creech Jones, Gurney denied knowledge of the operation. He assumed, in his reply, that the reference was to the earlier controversial action at Kachau.[127]

The story resurfaced in the wake of the My Lai massacre in Vietnam in 1968 and a comment by a Labour MP, George Brown, that 'there are an awful lot of spectres in our cupboard, too'.[128] On 1 February 1970, the *People* published a front-page story under the headline: 'Horror in a nameless village'. In it, men from the Scots Guards came forward with a new version of events, and alleged that the twenty-five Chinese – some accounts say twenty-four – had not been running away. The story caused a sensation. Over the next few days British witnesses were grilled by the media. On 3 February 1970 Alan Tuppen, who was eighteen in 1948, was interviewed by Leonard Parkin on ITN's *News at ten*

PARKIN: Did you fire?

TUPPEN: I fired, yes.

PARKIN: And hit someone?

TUPPEN: Yes.

PARKIN: Did you remember how many?

TUPPEN: No I don't remember.

PARKIN: Can you tell me this: do you believe now that these men were trying to escape?

TUPPEN: Now, no, but even then there must have been a shadow of doubt. But I don't think they were trying to escape.

PARKIN: Would you have been in a position at that time to know whether they were trying to escape, whether they'd left somewhere else?

TUPPEN: Well, the thing is if they came with us, this is a point I should remember, I know, but I don't remember. If they came with us, well, that's another story.

PARKIN: Can you tell me this: did you and the others fire in cold blood here?

TUPPEN: Yes.

PARKIN: Why didn't you tell the story to the enquiry?

TUPPEN: Well, this is another thing I can't remember, but it seems as though a story was concocted after this incident in the barrack room or somewhere, and I can't remember any concoctions at all going on but, it must have gone on. Obviously we all told the same story.[129]

Other men corroborated aspects of Tuppen's account, and said that they had been told that the men would be shot, and given the option of falling out. One man who said he did fall out, Victor Remedios, was left to guard the women and children who were in a lorry nearby. When shooting started, he told a BBC radio interviewer, 'they were all screaming, shouting and screaming'. On returning to the village: 'we found all these bodies round the streams like and blood all over the place'. He said that they were more or less threatened into lying at the enquiry.[130]

These were to be the only public testimonies from those involved.

On 4 February the then Secretary of State for Defence, Denis Healey, told the House of Commons that there was a direct conflict of evidence and that he was considering whether the matter should be referred to the Director of Public Prosecutions. In the enquiries that followed many confused and contradictory versions of events emerged. In particular, there was debate as to whether the Chinese labourers were walking or running; as to whether the huts in the clearing were set on fire or not. One version, which was reported by an official historian who had access to government papers, was that the Scots Guards were accompanied by a guerrilla supporter under arrest who was identifying those who were supplying the communists with food. On first arriving in the rubber estate the troops encountered two Chinese carrying rice, who were shot. The larger incident, it was suggested, occurred when the huts were burned and this set off an ammunition cache, or more likely detonators used for fishing, which cause the soldiers to panic and open fire with automatic weapons at close quarters. There were tales too that, during the night before the incident, one man had been separated from the rest of the Chinese and put through a bizarre ordeal with a gun at his head. The trigger was pressed several times, but the gun did not fire. Variants of this story circulated at the time, among journalists and the villagers themselves: one suggested that shots were fired in the air, so as to terrorize the captives in the hut as they were contemplating what might be their fate.[131]

Enquiries within the Scots Guards in 1970 revealed that the soldiers were without an officer. A lance-sergeant was in command, accompanied by a Malay special constable and a Chinese interpreter. They were, for the most part, only a few weeks in Malaya; for some it was their first patrol. They were 'drivers, sick men and at least one member of the Corps of Drums'. It was, the colonel commanding the regiment in 1970 commented, 'most unusual' for an officer not to be present. There were no standing orders for the jungle patrols at the time; although there was a standing government statement that those running must expect to be shot.[132] Few contemporary records of the event seemed to have survived. 'It would appear that there was NO military inquiry, at least NO inquiry amounting to an "Army Court of Inquiry" though the Adjutant remembers writing a form of summary.'[133] This did not survive; nor was correspondence from Kuala

Lumpur forthcoming. The sole communication from Malaya that surfaced, from Sir Alex Newboult to an official in the Colonial Office, dealt with the subject in oblique but chillingly defiant terms:

One of the difficulties of the situation is that we have a war of terrorism on our hands and we are at the same time endeavouring to maintain the rule of law. It is an easy matter from one's office and home to criticize action taken by the security forces in the heat of operations and working under jungle conditions but not so easy to do the job oneself. Rightly or wrongly we feel here that we must be conservative in our criticism of the men who are undoubtedly carrying out a most arduous and dangerous job . . . we feel it is most damaging to the morale of the security forces to feel that every action of theirs, after the event, is going to be examined with the most meticulous care.[134]

No original report to the Colonial Office could be traced. The two European police officers involved in the case were later killed. The Attorney General of Malaya, Foster-Sutton, it appeared, had visited the site with police officers and two of the Scots Guards: he saw the corpses, and took the view that the wounds in the backs of the dead Chinese supported the soldiers' story that they were trying to escape. There was no other formal enquiry. Foster-Sutton told the BBC in 1970 that, 'having satisfied myself that the statements were true, I made a statement to the press'. He remembered seeing some women about the huts, but did not interview them. The affair, he concluded, was 'a *bona fide* mistake'.[135]

The official records relating to Batang Kali were, it seems, destroyed, under the terms of Section 6 of the Public Records Act, 'as not being worthy of permanent preservation'. This was the fate of most files relating to law and order during the Malayan Emergency. The 'report' by the Attorney General was never found. It was either kept in Malaysia as a so-called 'legacy' document, or destroyed when Malaya attained its independence. In 1970, the affair had passed the time limit still to be regarded as a military matter, and was referred to the Director of Public Prosecutions, who passed the available information to Scotland Yard. An investigation in the United Kingdom ensued, led by the man who hunted down the Great Train Robbers, Chief Superintendent Frank Williams. But in June 1970, following a change of government in London, his planned visit to Malaysia was called off. There was, the Director of Public Prosecutions told the new Conservative Minister of Defence, 'substantial conflict among the soldiers who were present'. In light of the lapse of time, given what he saw as the unequivocal nature of contemporary statements and the unlikelihood of new evidence coming to light, he did not ask the police to pursue the case.[136] On 9 July 1970, the Conservative Attorney General told the House of Commons that the Director of Public Prosecutions would not take the matter any further. The file was closed, or rather it had been closed a long time before 1970.[137]

The charges resurfaced in a 1993 BBC documentary, *In cold blood*, which claimed that Frank Williams had, in fact, secured sworn testimony by a Scots Guardsman to the cold-blooded shooting. In the wake of this, in Malaysia, witnesses came forward: the Malay policemen; a male survivor, Chang Hong; and two women who had witnessed the shooting from the lorry. Chang Hong had fainted and survived among the dead bodies. He was later arrested and released, and his escape may explain the discrepancy in numbers. The survivors filed a police report, and the Malaysian Chinese Association, a party of the ruling coalition, petitioned the British government to reopen the case. The women – and indeed the oral tradition of the village – spoke of harrowing scenes; of how the men were led out of the hut in small groups of four or five; how they were then told to turn round and were shot in the back. They described the mutilated bodies, left for days in the sun. One of the women who came forward, Foo Mooi, saw her husband killed.[138] In 2004 the matter was raised again after Chin Peng had published his own account of events. He alleged – on the basis, it seems, of what he had heard on the Party underground – that Batang Kali was 'a premeditated massacre'. The following year a veteran Malaysian opposition leader, Lim Kit Siang, took up the case of the by then 77-year-old Chang Hong and two eyewitnesses, Tan Moi, 73, and Foo Mooi, 86. The Malaysian government's own investigation, begun in 1993, was completed in 1997, but has yet to be published. Again it was argued that no legal redress was now possible. But Lim Kit Siang argued that this was no longer the main issue. 'No one expected any one of the Scots Guards responsible for the Batang Kali massacre 56 years ago to be identified, let alone to be prosecuted.

The issue, however, is whether there was a massacre of the 24 innocent rubber tappers and the righting of such a 56-year historic wrong and injustice.'[139] Chin Peng's charge met with a storm of protest from veterans of the Scots Guards: their collective memory was that, in the words of Major General Sir John Acland, 'there was a very strong feeling in the battalion that nothing wrong happened'.[140] But neither had the incident been properly explained.

When the story re-emerged in 1970, the prime minister of Malaysia was Tunku Abdul Rahman, a Malay aristocrat who in 1949 was a director of public prosecutions in the government legal service. 'I thought it not fair to rake up the old wounds', he remarked. 'It is sad that such a thing happened but war is war . . . Why not bring up all the atrocities committed by the Japanese during the occupation? There are millions of them.'[141] Although much of what happened at Batang Kali remains obscure, the incident reveals a great deal about the public memory of these events: of the resistance to a full post-mortem on empire in Britain; of the divisiveness of the Emergency in contemporary Malaysia; of how the voice of the peasant communities caught up in this violence has been silenced over the years. By the end of 1948 the Malayan public were becoming conditioned to them being reported in clinical, statistical forms, as 'kills' of 'bandits', or later, 'CTs'. Very rarely does any account of the precise circumstances emerge from the newspapers or the official record, still less of the individuals involved.

The Batang Kali killings were a direct consequence of the way the British had chosen to fight their war in Malaya. As Gurney explained to Creech Jones a few days after the event, the Chinese 'are as you know notoriously inclined to lean towards whichever side frightens them more and at the moment this seems to be the government'.[142] By all accounts, the incident in the clearing was exceptional in its scale. But it was part of a continuing succession of killings on the estates, in the villages and along the roadsides. In Gurney's own testimony, in January 1949, 'the army are breaking the law every day'. British policemen were troubled at the numbers of people killed while 'running away' and of reports of bullets being placed on corpses to justify this. Scandal was never far away.[143] There are personal testimonies to the arbitrary fashion in which some people died and some were spared. A Gurkha soldier recalled a routine ambush on an estate in Johore:

'Two men walked about ten yards in front of us, carrying sickles, wearing pants, but with no headgear. They wore *rubber shoes*. As I did not see any weapons I did not open fire but Dalbir did, killing them both.' The Gurkhas ended up in court, but were acquitted. Their officer told them to stick to their story.[144] The culture within the military was such that British units kept competitive tallies of 'kills'; in military memoir, hunting metaphors abound. The desecration of corpses alleged at Batang Kali was widespread. Heads were taken, and not necessarily by Dyaks: British soldiers removed them to avoid carrying bodies from the forest. Bodies were routinely placed on public show to cow local people. The *Daily Worker* caused a sensation in April 1952 when it published pictures of Royal Marine Commandos posing with heads as trophies. In Whitehall it was admitted that 'a similar action in wartime would be a war crime.'[145]

The Emergency was a war, by any other name, and like all wars it made little distinction of guilt or innocence in its victims. It is impossible to make a full reckoning now. In the various conflicts that tore apart the crescent in the years after 1945, most of the fallen were not front-rank protagonists. They were townsfolk, farmers and tribals caught up in conflicts that were not always their own and which they did not always understand. In Malaya, many of the 'bandits' were merely couriers, helpers and bystanders, villagers, students; and – although the figures were rarely broken down in this way – a striking number were young women, like the five who died with Liew Yao. On the government side, the heaviest casualties were borne by the police and special constables. It was small businessmen and contractors, and increasingly villagers themselves, upon whom the revolutionary fury of the communists fell. In Malaya in late 1948, a cycle of terror and counter-terror was in motion: in fighting terms, it was deadlock. It was unclear to both sides how it might be broken. And the violence of the conflict was to be found not only in the casualty lists from 'the shooting war', but in the growing trauma of arrests and detentions, the removals and deportations which tore apart the lives of individuals, families, and whole communities. In the coming years, hundreds of thousands of people would be ensnared by this crisis. This too has dropped from historical memory; a forgotten story of a forgotten war.

I I

1949: The Centre Barely Holds

BRITAIN, INDIA AND THE COMING OF THE COLD WAR

By the early months of 1949 the Cold War had firmly announced itself. The aggressive and expansionist young communist regime in China loomed over the northern rim of Burma, into which country several hundred thousands of Chinese nationalist troops had fled. Pandit Nehru's government in India had beaten off the rural communist challenges in Bengal and also in Telengana. But, in recognition of the new balance of power in the world, India had moved closer to the Soviet Union in both international affairs and its development plans. The shrinking 'red on the map' of the British Empire was being replaced by the new red on the map of communist Europe and Asia. The United States, having begun to dislodge the Dutch from Indonesia, reluctantly found itself financing the French government in its struggle with the communist-led Viet Minh in Indo-China. The Americans worried that the greatest danger of the spread of communism in Asia was its effect 'within the Atlantic community itself'.[1] The Dutch had already told Field Marshal Montgomery that they could not meet their obligations to NATO because of the drain of war in Indonesia. The CIA thought that the policies being pursued in Asia by the Dutch and the French were a disaster. They were more sanguine about Malaya because the only visible alternative to British rule was 'Chinese domination, which would be unacceptable not only to Malaya but to us'.[2]

Whitehall, too, was shaken by a new sense of uncertainty about the world situation. The British had acquired their own atomic bomb, but the situation in Europe was extremely threatening, with the new communist powers building up a large arsenal in the east while sophisticated communist parties were winning votes in the west. The country itself faced yet another sterling crisis and the Americans were loath to bail the British out. Resources were scarce and Southeast Asia had resumed its traditional position as the poor man's problem, ranking well below the defence of western Europe and the security of Middle East oil. None the less, the British were determined to cling on in Malaya: the Singapore naval base and Malaya's rubber and tin were just too important to the economy in these years of austerity. By the end of 1948 the Emergency was costing $300,000 Straits dollars a day. Elsewhere, the best that could be managed was a holding operation. The chiefs of staff were clear that British policy outside Malaya should be 'defensive'.[3] Nevertheless, communist domination of the new and fragile Union of Burma would be dangerous. It would threaten East Pakistan and India and 'would provide an opportunity for the infiltration of Malaya'. It would interfere with Commonwealth air routes and provide Britain's potential enemies in China and Russia with air and naval bases in Southeast Asia. According to the British, Burma's rice exports were down to a third of what they had been before the war because of the government's doctrinaire land reform policy and the impact of the rebellions. But the country was still one of the biggest rice exporters in the world. The disruption of the rice trade would lead to further hardship across the region and hardship was a breeding ground for communism.[4] The basic problem, the British thought, was leadership. Aung San might have provided it but Nu was 'not big enough'.[5] The Americans concurred. The Burmese government was 'weak, unpredictable and highly unstable'.[6] It was vulnerable to indirect pressure from the Indian Communist Party and direct military pressure from the Chinese.

James Bowker, British ambassador in Rangoon, was clear that the best thing the Burmese government could do to allay the 'communist threat' would be to 'put its own house in order' by reaching some sort of accommodation with the Karen rebels and the rebellious People's Volunteer Organizations (PVOs).[7] Yet the Burmese remained deeply suspicious of British intentions and Nu himself complained that the Rangoon embassy and 'Pop' Tulloch, the Karens' most passionate supporter in Britain, were somehow still plotting in the background. In a letter to Nu, Attlee felt compelled to disavow any connection with 'malicious persons'.[8] The British were keen to maintain their services mission in a low-key mode and provide some military assistance. The Treasury was less happy about finding the money for a large loan which Nu and some of the cabinet were contemplating. Would this not be throwing good money after bad, given that Burma's acute balance of payments problem was itself the result of the ill-advised leftist measures that had been undertaken a year or more before? There were some signs, the old hands recognized, that the Burmese leadership was now moderating its policies. R. B. Pearn, a former professor in Rangoon University, had often taken a dim view of the Burmese capacity to organize things. His gibe that the Burmese were a 'primitive people', made six years before among the peaks of Simla, had provoked a scornful comment from Tin Tut about the second-class Oxbridge graduates who found jobs in Burma. Now Pearn was a member of the Foreign Office research department and secretly gloated over the difficulties of another old bête noire of his, J. S. Furnivall.

Early in 1949 Furnivall gave a lecture in Rangoon which the Foreign Office interpreted as a coded warning to Nu to take a more positive line towards Attlee's government and foreign capital. Furnivall told his audience that the country's problems were psychological first, economic second and only thirdly financial. The vision of 'a free people dancing in a rain of gold and silver' which he had seen at that *pyazat* or dramatic performance twelve months or more before was the real problem.[9] People had expected independence immediately to improve their standard of living. When it led instead to a financial crisis and severe restrictions on the import of hard-currency consumer goods, they looked around for someone to blame. People said that everything was the fault of Churchill and Dorman-Smith skulking menancingly in London; or it was the fault of foreign capitalists whose grip on Burmese resources was still ferocious; or it was the enemy in their midst, the Christians, the Karens or the Anglo-Burmese. Furnivall's analysis, intelligent but too little and too late, then toppled over into academic wishful thinking.[10] He outlined a plan for Burma which involved military-agricultural colonies expanding rice cultivation along the lines of nineteenth-century Dutch Java, an area of scholarly interest for him. He thought that a foreign financial expert, probably not British, should be allowed to run the economics ministry, while foreign troops might be brought in to secure internal order. On reading this, Pearn wrote acidly that Furnivall was 'as woolly-minded as ever'.[11] No Burmese government could possibly bring in foreign troops and survive.

In retrospect, Furnivall's speech did in fact mark something of a turning point. Over the next few months Nu edged closer to Western interests and moderated his government's leftist economic policies. A new charter was approved which allowed foreign companies to operate in the country for up to ten years, with the reasonable expectation that they would be able to make profits and repatriate a proportion of them. The land nationalization policy was loosened; it was anyway beginning to create large numbers of small private owners – a new rural elite, rather than the peasant co-operative that had been envisaged. The government made strenuous efforts to meet the requirements that the British Treasury had hedged around the offer of a large sterling loan. Insofar as they gave a thought to Burmese matters amid labour unrest, sterling crises and the onward march of international communism, Attlee and Cripps, who was now Chancellor of the Exchequer, began to take a rosier view of the Burmese government.

Britain was, at least physically, distant from Burma's problems, but the Republic of India had inherited that acute sense of menace about the security of its borders which had long plagued the British Raj. As if to symbolize this, Jawaharlal Nehru lived in Parliament Street, New Delhi, in the very house that had once been occupied by the commander-in-chief of the old colonial army. Nehru's moments for reflection were few in the early months of 1949, though the anniversaries first of Gandhi's assassination and next of Subhas Chandra Bose's birthday punctuated his heavy workload. Linked by an accident of chronology, the memories of India's apostle of non-violence and the warrior martyr were to march in unlikely companionship into India's future. Nehru's education as a world statesman had been brutal. Less than five years earlier he had been writing Indian history in a British jail. On his release he had plunged into a final vigorous campaign to push the British out. Cripps and Attlee had assented and he mended battered personal friendships with them, but the price of independence and political stability was partition and the bloodletting that accompanied it. Although by 1949 the worst massacres had ceased and the flood of refugees into India had abated, the sub-continent remained tense. Thousands still crossed the borders of East Pakistan and West Bengal as poverty and communal tension drove people to seek security with their co-religionists. In the west, fighting with Pakistan over the Muslim-majority state of Kashmir had reached a deadlock. Pakistani fighters had clawed their way to unofficial rule over half of the state, which they called Azad Kashmir (Free Kashmir), but they could make no further headway. Neither country was pre-pared to give way, even though internal food and financial crises meant that neither could afford the burden of war.

Historians sometimes write as if a sturdy and reliable British Raj had been transformed overnight into an equally dominant Indian secular state. Nothing can be further from the truth. Like the Raj, the Indian Union had feet of clay and that clay was only hardening as troubles poured down on the new state in 1947 and 1948. In April Thakin Nu wrote to Nehru to plead for financial and military aid to halt his country's disintegration; already Rangoon was in control of only little more than a third of the old British Burma. Nehru replied frankly: India was itself on the rack. Partition, the influx of refugees and war with Pakistan had reduced India's military competence drasti-cally. There was no way in which India could equip ten battalions of Burmese troops to fight the rebels. Military supply, communications and control had all been compromised by the division of the old colonial army. It was no longer the great fighting force it had once been. India itself was scouring the world for military spare parts at knockdown rates. So great was the military and financial burden, Nehru wrote, that 'it would not have been surprising if that new state [India] collapsed under the burden'.[12] The international scene was now even more dangerous: 'The whole of Asia is in a state of turmoil and revolution.' Nehru insisted that he did not fear revolution but he worried that constant war would irrevocably diminish the people's standard of living, which it had been the main aim of the national movements to improve: 'We have barely escaped disaster ourselves in the last year and a half.' This was why India had stayed in the

Commonwealth and was about to renew its membership, despite the political taint of association with the British. This was also why Lord Mountbatten had been asked to stay on as Governor General and the 'steel frame' of the old Indian Civil Service had largely been maintained.

Nehru had good cause for concern. The Dutch had only just begun to pull back from their 'police action' against Indonesian nationalists, influenced by the stance of the US government and perhaps marginally by the fierce denunciations of Dutch policy at the Asian summit in New Delhi in March. About the same time, Chiang Kai Shek was driven from power in China and the French launched a massive attack against the Viet Minh forces in their 'liberated zones' west of Hanoi. It was not clear whether revived imperialism or rogue communism was the greater danger to the new Asia. With all the naivety of a refined left-wing academic, Nehru had admired the scientific and social progress of Stalin's Soviet Union, oblivious of the mass murder which had sustained it. But he was much more cautious about communism nearer home. As far as communist China was concerned, it was a question of wait and see. He was not in a rush to recognize the new government of Mao Zedong and only did so some time after Burma's own recognition. He worried about the possibility of Chinese communist incursions into Indian territory and privately conceded that India might have to fight them off. He was beginning to develop an amicable relationship with China's new foreign minister, Chou En Lai, but demurred about taking a strong leadership role in South and Southeast Asia in case that might be seen in Beijing as a hostile move against China.

If Nehru was ambivalent about Chinese communism at this stage, he was downright hostile to Indian, Malayan and Burmese communists, regarding the Burmese variety in particular as 'freebooters and terrorists'.[13] The background for this attitude was the situation in India itself. Communist insurrectionists did not have much of a track record in India. There had been agitation in north Bengal in the 1930s, but the Communist Party of India had lost ground when, under orders from Moscow, it had backed the British war effort. But Soviet bosses alone were not to blame for Indian communism's failings. Indian communists excelled at ranting in coffee shops, but did not seem to be the stuff of the vanguard of the proletariat. Their leadership rallied mass support only in exceptionally propitious circumstances, such as the old state of Hyderabad, especially its alienated Telugu-speaking tract of Telengana. Here the Nizam of Hyderabad's regime seemed to offer a textbook illustration of Marxist 'feudal despotism'. Young revolutionaries had seized on peasant grievances and begun to organize rural soviets and people's courts in classic style. When Hyderabad was absorbed into the Indian Union in 1948, the situation actually deteriorated. So-called *razakars*, bands of toughs who had been recruited by the Nizam as a kind of 'Black and Tan' force to put down the communist rebellion, joined in a mêlée of looting and assassination of landlords. The trouble seemed likely to spread into other parts of the Indian Union. Delhi took tough action against the rebels and an Indian press, tamer in many respects than that which had operated under the British, denounced the revolutionaries and bandits.[14]

Events at home warmed Nehru to Nu's position on communist insurgency in Burma. The Indian prime minister's attitudes were also informed by his fears for the more than 800,000 Indians still living under Nu's government.[15] He did not seek a 'Greater India' and had at this point deliberately distanced himself from the overseas imperial ambitions of the Raj. But since the Burmese refugee tragedy of 1942 he had worried about Indians overseas, a fear that was reinforced by a spate of vicious riots against Indians in South Africa after the white supremacists of the National Party took power there in 1948. Early in 1949 Nehru gave the go-ahead for the army to evacuate 4,000 Indians from the Karen stronghold of Insein, a mere six miles from Rangoon.[16] Next on his list of potential victims were the 30,000 Indians in the rich sugar-growing Ziawadi estate in southern Burma.[17] This was an old colony of farmers from Bihar that the British had settled there several generations earlier. They were now prosperous cash-crop growers and moneylenders who attracted the hostility of the local communists. Nehru believed that the rebels had not yet targeted Indians, but he was not confident that would remain the case. Not only would systematic assaults on Burma's Indians inflame public opinion at home, a new influx of refugees would add to the horrendous problem of housing and feeding the millions who had fled from Pakistan. Nehru pointedly thanked Nu for averting a large-scale migration of the many Sikhs and north Indian settlers who lived around Myit-kyina, the airfield town in the north of the country which had been the scene of so many tragic events during the Japanese occupation.[18]

THE CENTRE BARELY HOLDS

Nehru's aim was to get the Burmese government and the Karens to negotiate, thus freeing up the government to deal with the communist menace. He was convinced that a simple military solution would not work. He pointed out to Nu that, in Malaya, even after eight months the powerful and well-equipped British army had yet to make much headway against a similar group of 'freebooters' and self-styled communists. Yet the situation in Burma seemed to deteriorate further. The communists refused to lay down their arms, despite strenuous efforts by Nu to conciliate them. Worse, the much larger bands of insurgent PVO men seemed unwilling to fall in behind the government again, even though he offered to incorporate them into the national army and initiate a 'leftist unity programme'. Nu regarded the revolt of the white-flag communists of the PVO the previous year as a stab in the back, but more dangerous yet was the Karen situation. After their initial uprising in 1948, Karen leaders had held their ground and had begun to negotiate with the government through non-political intermediaries. They were awaiting further government commissions on the status of an autonomous 'Karenistan' and also a resolution of the issue of the military service of the Karen defence volunteers. Newly instituted discrimination against Karen volunteers for the army must be halted, they insisted. Between November 1948 and January 1949, however, the negotiations collapsed. Karen National Defence Organizations (KNDOs) renewed their assault on Rangoon, occupying dozens of delta villages, driving out or killing headmen and destroying government property. Where they were in a weaker position in the lower Irrawaddy district, the KNDOs made common cause with communist insurgents and helped them to capture a number of towns and cities. Stung by the unexpected coalition between Karens and communists, the government bitterly assailed the Western commentators who had so often claimed that Karen autonomy would help form a bulwark against communism in Southeast Asia. On the contrary, Karens 'cooperated fully with both red and white flag communist insurgents to further their interests of a separate state. They invariably released all communist prisoners from the jails overrun by them to increase the difficulties of the government.'[19] To add to the government's woes, the ministerial services union decided to strike for more pay and better conditions on 4 February 1949. Though most of the police stayed at work, government offices across the country ground to a halt. Within a few days the Karen forces were back in Insein, just north of Rangoon. Nu's government again seemed likely to be the first of the post-colonial governments to fall victim to a coup.

Karen rebel forces remained dangerously close to the capital and the rice harvest seemed in danger. The crisis spurred the government to greater piety. The day officially beginning the Buddhist season of fasting was set aside as a national day of prayer and supplications for peace were chanted in Rangoon and throughout the country. When the Buddha had chanted those prayers thousands of years earlier, war had come to a stop. Relics were paraded through the countryside and Nu visited monasteries, giving alms to the monks and propitiating the *nats*. Divine aid was slow in coming, though. Nu called the months of February, March and April 1949 'the bleakest months . . . all of us were kept in a terrible state of suspense'.[20] There were said to be 10,000 rebels in the field under communist or Karen leadership and probably half of these were deserters from the army, police and other services. Even the leaders of the hitherto-loyal PVOs (known as the yellow-band or yellow-flag PVOs to distinguish them from the white-flag communists of the rebellious PVOs) resigned from the government, threatening a new crisis. Nu's government still controlled little territory beyond the cities of Mandalay and Rangoon.

Yet the important point was that the Burmese government did continue to control the cities. Rangoon, in particular, was vital, for it was through that city that rice exports flowed out to the rest of the world and it was on the rice revenues that the government now depended for most of its income. Ironically, the Karen rebels who could easily have disrupted rice exports from their forward position at Insein did not do so, probably because they too were dependent on income from rice. In fact, as had been clear after the Japanese invasion of 1942, he who controlled Rangoon controlled Burma. This was perhaps the main reason Nu's government survived.

Another reason was that some foreign aid became available, but in a form surreptitious enough for the Burmese government to disavow accusations that it was drifting towards the Western alliance. In Rangoon and Mandalay there was still a good deal of suspicion about British aid to the Karens. This was understandable in view of the previous year's shenanigans and the constant support voiced for the minorities in the British press by former Force 136 officers and other Britons who had served in Burma. Nu was not so worried about losing power to the Karen rebels, whom he saw as less hardline than the communists. The real problem was that a Karen advance against Rangoon might spark a Soviet intervention on the communist side. It was not a far-fetched fear. This was the year in which the USSR attempted to starve out its former allies from Berlin, a blockade that was broken only by high-risk relief sorties flown by Allied pilots. But how could Burma be assisted without handing a propaganda victory to the communists? Both the British and the Indians thought that an initiative by the Commonwealth would be easier for the Burmese government to swallow than one started by either the former colonial master or its huge neighbour.

The Commonwealth leaders duly met in New Delhi, where they drew up a plan and issued a joint declaration stating their willingness to help negotiate a peace treaty in Burma.[21] But they had already overplayed their hand. Nu's government had no option but sharply to reject these overtures.[22] The military under General Ne Win, now increasingly influential, would allow no further concessions to the Karens. The ranting about 'imperialist machinations' on the Burmese left would have become even louder if Nu had accepted Commonwealth mediation. Nu remained suspicious of the British because of the pro-Karen activities of the rogue British officers the year before. Nehru tried to reassure him that the British government had no more interest in Karen separatism than did the Indians. At a press conference in Delhi he made a careful distinction between 'the imperialists', meaning the ex-Force 136 types on the fringes of Dorman-Smith's and Churchill's circles, and the British government itself, which, he said, merely wanted stability and the resumption of Burma's full rice exports to India and Britain. But even as Nehru tried to reassure the Burmese of Britain's good intentions, the Dutch were in the midst of their 'police action' against the nationalist regime in Indonesia; there was good reason to think that 'imperialism' was far from dead. At the same time, the international situation seemed to be going the way of the communists. Burma was, as Nu later said in one of his homely metaphors, 'a tender gourd among the spiky cactuses'. If Nehru had been ready then to head up a bloc of non-aligned South and Southeast Asian nations, Burma might have taken shelter under its umbrella, but Nehru was still wary of antagonizing China, where the communists were carrying all before them.

Any deals, therefore, between the Burmese government and non-communist powers had to be private ones. Burma's new foreign minister, E Maung, and General Ne Win went to London and negotiated a shipment of 5,000 rifles from the British government under the aegis of the defence agreement. More significantly, Nu flew to Delhi and persuaded India to furnish a large consignment of small arms, ammunition, and, it was thought, covert military advice.[23] Having pleaded lack of military supplies, the Indian government finally scratched together something for the Burmese, though Nehru insisted that the whole negotiation remained strictly secret in case the communists or the minorities vented their anger on Indian expatriates. India's ambassador in Rangoon was M. A. Rauf, a Muslim businessman who was close to those AFPFL members who represented Indian interests in Burma. To him Nehru wrote sternly: 'We shall give them something, though not nearly as much as they want. This too must be kept completely secret.'[24] Actually, India seems to have been quite generous with its low-key military aid. Six years later Nu let slip in one of his wordy speeches that India had given two batches of 5,000 small arms to its neighbour. The first batch had immediately fallen into rebel hands when the white-flag PVO revolted, but Nehru considered the situation critical enough to replace it with another consignment.[25] Moreover, India, Britain and Japan, which was now firmly in the Western camp, stepped up their purchases of Burmese rice, despite the fact that prices were soaring on the world market as a result of the demand generated by the Korean War. The war had disrupted

Korea's production and sent hundreds of thousands of Allied troops into the region, putting pressure on food supplies. Britain and India also gave Burma the facilities for a large loan. India had little cash and Britain was stretched as warfare erupted in Malaya and Korea, but the loan was negotiated by releasing the frozen 'sterling balances' that Britain owed India as a result of debts accumulated during the Second World War. Though not much of this loan was actually taken up, it buttressed Burma's credit on the international market at a critical time. For a time, American aid was also forthcoming, though right-wing US commentators berated the administration for supporting a 'red' government and Burmese opinion was uneasy. Ever mindful of the need to keep a balance, Nu's became one of the first non-communist governments to recognize communist China. This also helped with domestic interests because the large Chinese minority in Burma, mainly small businessmen, wanted to keep the borders open regardless of the ideology of the men in power in Beijing.

New arms, new money and control of a good rice crop kept the government's head just above water in Rangoon and Mandalay. Out in the countryside the political struggle ebbed and flowed from day to day. In the first three months of 1949, the authority of the government showed little sign of reviving. Two-thirds of the country was still subject to the sorties of insurgent groups – communists, rebellious PVOs, mutinying soldiers and police, cattle rustlers and the Karens. Government authority survived only where a resolute district officer held on supported by small numbers of loyal troops and backed by local headmen and notables. One such defiant officer was Balwant Singh, the Sikh civil servant who always stood out from his Burmese charges because of his height. The leading townspeople of Yamethin in the Shan states had persuaded him to stay on even after Karen rebels had swept through the town looting its stores and severing its road and rail links to the outside world. Balwant Singh established what he called the 'City State of Yamethin' and held this against successive bands of communists, minority group rebels and bandits for more than two months, with little idea of what was going on elsewhere in the country.

This was a very personal war. When PVOs of doubtful allegiance arrived in Yamethin demanding weapons, the townspeople clinging to their remaining small arms and Bren guns met them warily. A powerful local resident said: 'We have our arms and we intend to keep them, and use them. No one will force us to give them up.'[26] The speaker sat down, smiling widely with his betel juice-stained lips. Another man, a local lawyer, warned the insurgents: 'The armed men here are mostly the sons of the town. They belong to it and are here to defend it. The town fully supports the SDO [Balwant Singh] and the armed men under him.' At this the PVO band decided to forgo a fire fight and themselves retreated smiling. These were times of confusion and uncertainty. Balwant Singh and his supporters listened to the radio news from Rangoon, which always put a brave spin on events, but critical local news was scarce: 'As an alternative we turned to what is normal in the East – spirits, mediums, soothsayers and astrologers.'[27] Balwant Singh considered that these authorities' predictions had a good chance of being true, and besides, the mediums provided the sort of service that would fall to psychiatrists in the West. A palm-reader made a good stab at predicting his career, while the abbot of the local monastery broke the rules to allow a medium to go into a trance within the walls. The medium, guided by the *nats*, gave useful advice about the morale of the Yamethin armed forces. Meanwhile, most people began to wear invulnerability charms, as Burmese country people often did during times of crisis. Balwant Singh himself was given a couple of charms and put them on: 'Courage was not a natural commodity with me, and I needed all the outside help I could get.' All the same, he sensed that the crisis was past its worst.

J. S. Furnivall had spent part of the year lecturing on Southeast Asian history and politics in Chicago. On his return in the middle of the year he also felt a change of mood. The opposition was split and the splits were widening. In August he wrote to a correspondent in England, the Burmese linguist C. W. Dunn, that the communists were now even more at odds because Than Tun had argued for bringing in the Chinese to resolve the civil war.[28] This his communist colleagues flatly rejected. Meanwhile the Christian Karens, themselves worried that the communists might win, were beginning to drift back towards the government.[29] So, by the end of 1949, Burma's crisis was beginning to pass. The country would be battered by insurrection and violence for years to come. But it would neither disintegrate nor become communist. Yet the savage civil war had already put the army into a strong position within the new state, a position which it would consolidate over the next decade.

THE BATTLE FOR THE *ULU*

Across the region, men in arms once more dictated political futures. Fresh levies from Europe began the long journey east. The Grenadier Guards came straight from ceremonial duties at Buckingham Palace and Windsor Castle. They sailed from Liverpool in August 1948 in an old wartime troopship; it was a four-week journey through the last outposts of the British Indian Ocean. They were met with the usual jeers – 'Get your knees brown!' – as they passed the British garrison at Great Bitter Lake on the Suez Canal. But now there was no period of acclimatization in Bombay; the troubled situation in Egypt made it difficult to give men shore leave at Port Said. On arrival in Malaya the men were plunged into an exotic tropical world, and a war for which they were unprepared. They were issued with unfamiliar gear – mosquito nets, jungle green and jungle boots with canvas tops and rubber soles – and had to acclimatize quickly to the heat and humidity; the 'bashers', (*bashas*) or open-sided huts, and squat toilets, and the terrors of the undergrowth: the snakes, scorpions, centipedes and fire ants. Within two weeks they were on long marches in the forest with tattooed Iban 'head-hunters', a first taste of the *ulu*, a Malay word for upriver which now became British military argot for the back of beyond. Between 1 January 1949 and 30 May 1950, 4,500 national servicemen were despatched to Malaya.[30] By October 1950 twenty-one infantry regiments, two armoured car regiments and one commando brigade were deployed: a total of 50,000 men. This was more British soldiers than were in Malaya at the time of its fall to the Japanese.

Not all of them were fighting men. The military remained a massive consumer of men and materiel, a provider for thousands of locals who worked in the naval bases or the NAAFI. The sharply finessed black-market scams of the BMA period were revived; in one case, in

1953, six soldiers were convicted of stealing two bulldozers, a tractor, and a three-ton truck, together with a generator, cutting plant and six winches.[31] New cantonments were thrown up at Nee Soon and Ulu Pandan in Singapore, and at Port Dickson and Sungei Besi, just outside Kuala Lumpur. For many men, they were a comfortable billet. 'There's too many vested interests in this Emergency,' one Kuala Lumpur lawyer was overheard to gripe. 'In fact, it's no Emergency at all. It is a racket to find jobs for British officers.'[32] The rankers at Nee Soon had a chorus:

> We're a shower of bastards,
> Bastards we are . . .
> We'd rather fuck than fight,
> We're the pay corps cavalry![33]

Leslie Thomas, who arrived in early 1950, christened himself and his comrades 'the virgin soldiers': 'idle, homesick, afraid, uninterested, hot, sweating, bored, oversexed and under-satisfied'.[34] For them, barracks life was 'as peaceful as a suburb'; its ennui only occasionally disturbed by transit of men from the jungle war: 'The garrison soldiers would examine them with curiosity, at a distance, as though looking for bullet holes . . . There was a dullness about the infantrymen's eyes, a redness about their faces, so that they looked like labourers or country boys.'[35]

For a colonial society still obsessed by prestige, there was the perennial problem of how to keep in line thousands of poor whites whose very presence transgressed the racial code. Handbooks of military Malay marked out the boundaries: 'By a Malay, or by a Malay speaking Asian, the European male is addressed as "TOO-AN" . . . Master.'[36] But the new arrivals discovered that few of the expatriates they were there to protect would have anything to do with them socially. The planters upcountry were more hospitable, but most of the clubs in Singapore were barred to men in uniform. A functional Britannia Club was built opposite the opulent Raffles Hotel, to keep soldiers out of trouble. But the native city had a compelling lure. Kuala Lumpur was invaded by serviceman as never before. Police lieutenants held wakes for fallen colleagues at Nanto's on Batu Road; they would put up nearby at the Coliseum Hotel, which was, and still is, famous for its baked crab and steak. The bars and cafés thrived. As one Gurkha on military police detail remarked of British soldiers, 'I had a lot of working to do to keep them apart on a Saturday night from their drunken fights and away from the brothels in Kuala Lumpur. I couldn't understand why they were so worthless.'[37]

The soldiers lived at a remove from the locals. Leslie Thomas was later to recall that he did not once eat Chinese food during his tour of Malaya. Local businessmen catered to English tastes. The local stout, brewed by Carlsberg, was increasingly popular, and remains an enduring legacy of empire. For Alan Sillitoe, an RAF signaller, an evening out in George Town was 'a meal of rice with an egg on top at the Boston café, then to see a film such as "Cato" or "Watch on the Rhine", followed by an evening with taxi-dancing Eurasian girls at the City Lights'.[38] The cabarets were a rare opportunity to talk to local girls and to practise 'bazaar' Malay; the men paid 30 cents a ticket to dance with them for five minutes. The new sensation was the *joget modern*, a mixture of the samba, rumba and conga fused with the swaying local sound of the *ronggeng*. In Kuala Lumpur there were three *joget* 'parties', the 'Sentosa', the 'Lucky' and the 'Chendramata Joget' in Bukit Bintang amusement park. The star turns became famous; Rose Chan's python dance was legendary. But the cabarets generated great moral unease. Girls as young as twelve were to be found working in them. Welfare officers campaigned to raise the minimum age to fifteen, in the hope that a girl would then be 'quite robust to stand any strenuous job and is quite matured mentally to understand the tricks and traps laid out by a man in his attempt to spoil her morality'. It was at least, the argument went, an alternative to prostitution.[39] The best-selling Malay novelist of the day, Ahmad Lufti, combined frank accounts of the fall of young women with a sharp moral and religious commentary. His novels were pornographic to some, but they portrayed an acute sense of the vulnerability of women who had since the war been forced to consort with soldiers, of 'a courage stemmed from the torments of the devil'.[40] Suicide was on the rise in Singapore, and an incidence of 31.2 per 1,000 was estimated in the entertainment industry, not least among dance hostesses.[41]

The war had now retreated from the towns, and the enemy was largely unseen. For British and Gurkha troops, the campaign was a succession of long, exhausting 'jungle bashes', broken by sudden, furious combat. In the dense undergrowth, adversaries might not spot each other until they were almost face to face. A Gurkha, Jasbahadur Limbu, described an encounter with a guerrilla: 'We looked at each other. He did not have his weapon ready, but mine was. He smiled at me and I smiled at him. I then shot him dead . . .'[42] But direct skirmishes constituted only 10 per cent of incidents in the early stages of the Emergency.[43] The most deadly encounters were ambushes on the roads. An incident in Sungei Siput on 31 December 1948 was typical: a troop of A Squadron of the 4th Hussars, in three vehicles, was attacked by around seventy guerrillas. Of the nineteen British soldiers, seven were killed and nine wounded. In what was a chaotic firefight, the Hussars' radio malfunctioned and they could not call for assistance. As the survivors tried to escape they saw the guerrillas firing lethal rounds into the wounded they had left behind.[44] In 1949 the guerrillas killed 229 and wounded 247 security forces personnel. This sowed fear and dismay, but the communists failed to convert it into more substantial gains. On 1 February, in an attempt to claim patriotic legitimacy across all communities, the guerrilla force was renamed the Malayan National Liberation Army (MNLA).[45] Its commanders still looked to create a 'liberated area' in the Pulai and Gua Musang region. Two fighting units around 200 strong, and one more 100 strong, were concentrated in the old resistance stronghold of the Cameron Highlands, where there were ready supplies from Chinese vegetable farmers who had colonized its elevated valleys. It was also Malaya's most popular hill station; but now the roads up to it were designated 'red routes' and the few intrepid golfers needed military escorts to reach the fairways. At the same time the other large concentrations of guerrillas in Johore pressed northwards towards Tasek Bera in Pahang, a large inland lake that nestles at the southern end of the central range. This was the dead centre of the peninsula: a point from where the MNLA could launch diversionary attacks on the main north–south railway, and its northeastern branch line, while the northern force created a 'little Yenan' at the railhead at Gua Musang. In Party annals these treks would be known as 'the little Long Marches'.

Both operations were aborted. Gurkha operations unsettled the Gua Musang area, and there was no repeat of the occupation of mid 1948. The tropical rainforest is sparse in natural provender and commanders faced acute difficulties in keeping large units together for more than a short period of time. The communists turned to the aborigines, the Orang Asli, for supplies, but they had little to give and the big battalions had to be broken up. The convergence on Tasek Bera failed for the same reason. Smaller bands of guerrillas were pushed deeper into the jungle interior and further from the villages. In the meantime Chin Peng had left the Cameron Highlands in December 1948 to fulfil his original objective of creating a Party military HQ in central Pahang. With a five-man bodyguard, he moved into the Kuala Lipis region, travelling about sixty miles as the crow flies towards Raub; but, finding his way blocked by the security forces, he then swung to the east and south to a place known as 'Ten Milestone Village', on the road just east of Mentekab. But such was the tortuous nature of forest communications that he arrived there only in May 1949. Half an hour's trek from the road, a camp had been prepared for him, and he was reunited with his old friend and deputy, Yeung Kuo. The following month the full MCP Central Committee assembled for the first time since the declaration of the Emergency. A year had passed. The goal still remained a liberated area, but Party leaders now acknowledged that attacks on the British would have to be smaller in scale. The mood, however, was confident: 'The more difficult or complicated the situation becomes', Central's new directive read, 'the more our attacks should be positive and active in the sense of holding the initiative.' And whilst Chin Peng was on the move, Chiang Kai Shek had fled to Taiwan and the armies of the Chinese Communist Party had entered Shanghai. The East was red.[46]

From February 1949 until the second half of the year there was a lull in the fighting, as the MCP began to build up its mass organization, the Min Yuen. Local units took on a multiplicity of forms, but their functions were similar. There were the unarmed 'self-protection units' – the collectors of food and subscriptions, the couriers and propagandists in the villages and towns; an armed 'protection corps' for industrial sabotage and small ambushes, and a spectrum of smaller Min Yuen committees or cells of sympathizers.[47] Shopkeepers, *kongsis* and contractors would pay a cess to the Party; labourers would make subscriptions. A Min Yuen cadre was a higher grade position than that of a guerrilla fighter; a higher percentage of them were full Party members. This remained, in the words of a captured leader, 'a highly coveted honour and not lightly bestowed'. They were more or less in the full-time service of the Party, and were a more regular presence in the villages than any government official. In the village of Semenyih in Selangor, for example, the man in charge of the area adopted various disguises, sometimes as a rubber tapper, sometimes as a coffee-shop worker, even dressing as a coolie woman.[48] The British saw all rural Chinese as potential supporters of the MCP.

It was only by the early 1950s that the British began to collect detailed data on who the communists actually were. These surveys were based on intensive interrogations and were conducted for 'psychological warfare' purposes, rather than to gather social information. But there are few alternative sources on the background of the fighters. A study of internees at one of the largest rehabilitation camps, Taiping, in 1952 revealed that a high proportion of the Chinese – 36.5 per cent – were of the Hakka dialect group. This was a community of manual labourers, well known for their traditions of self-help and self-government and, throughout Chinese history, for making rebellion. But otherwise the sample was a fair cross-section of the Chinese population in Malaya.[49] A survey of 104 surrendered communists in 1953 revealed that 85 per cent were workers, 61 per cent of them rubber tappers, who were a particularly rich source of recruits because their work gave good cover on the borders of the jungle. Forty per cent of those interviewed had aided the communists before joining up; but two-thirds said that fear of arrest or conscription was their primary motive for taking to the jungle. Not only the Emergency Regulations but the repeated arrests of MPAJA men since 1945 weighed heavily in their decision.[50] A more in-depth interrogation of twenty-five surrendered guerrillas revealed that all but two had been born in Malaya, or had left China before they were sixteen. Most were too young to have served in the war. Their connections to the MCP came through the New Democratic Youth League or the trade unions, where they had been approached individually, and then drawn into performing tasks for the Party. The report concluded that they came from 'a section of society that was very poorly structured'. The British writer was here thinking in terms of formal social institutions; there seemed to be little social life for the young beyond the village coffee shop or the workplace. He saw the recruits as disaffected with life, and the appeal of the Party in its ability to formulate their grievances for them and give them scope to act.[51] A young American scholar, Lucien Pye, was also given access to sixty detainees. He saw them as upwardly mobile young people (their mean age was twenty-three) who were more educated than their peers. But in these uncertain times they saw their advancement in terms of aligning themselves to a group, in following opinion-makers and in each becoming 'a party faction man'. They seemed desperate to align themselves to anyone who looked to possess power, and were hungry for any extra knowledge that might help them to anticipate how larger events might affect them. The mood of obsessive secrecy within the MCP suggested that it possessed a 'secret doctrine' to light the way forward. Pye saw the Emergency as a disorder of modernity, a rebellion of those who had been exposed to its upheavals, but 'have not yet found their place in it'.[52]

The British, for the most part, saw the MCP's hold on its supporters in terms of the 'secret society complex', and people's motives for joining the rebellion as stemming from confusion or anomie. They tended to play down the ideological commitment of guerrillas, and this impression was reinforced by the fact that those captured tended to plead that they acted under compulsion of one kind or another. But as one woman fighter, Huang Xue Ying, was later to recall, the role of the cadres in rural communities was very wide-ranging, particularly among the young. These confident young men and women represented a dramatic broadening of horizons, in which the revolutionary mood of the times was transmitted through the villages. In the early days of the campaign the MCP placed great emphasis on political education. In peacetime this had taken the form of organized outings, night classes and public readings of newspapers and pamphlets. In Huang Xue Ying's words:

At that time I hardly understood a word; so it was like playing music to the bull, so to speak. They taught us that women were the most oppressed class . . . they awakened our consciousness. They told us they wanted to improve our lives, we all had to work hard. Those with money must contribute money, those who had none, could contribute their labour . . . I joined the guerrillas because I knew they were good people. My family life was hard; I had no chance to study. The Communists taught me a lot. I felt that this was the path I should take to have a different future. These comrades were loving to us and very concerned about us.[53]

The British never really understood the village and small-town loyalties around which the MCP mobilized. Its recruits were not necessarily rejecting traditional family or community life. Often, they sought to strengthen it where it was under threat. Where families, communities and livelihoods were insecure, the tight networks of kinship and friendship in the villages and workplace took on a compelling significance, and the MCP's cadres were able to enmesh themselves in this. The threat of coercion was never far away, but equally, by this time, two generations of squatters had identified themselves with the MCP's resistance to the Japanese and to colonialism. This was sealed by a succession of personal tragedies as families became separated by killings, arrests and deportations.[54] Now that the MCP was pushed out of the towns, and the trade unions decimated, all its hopes were placed in the squatters. The expectation was that, in the wake of guerrilla actions and government operations, production from mines and estates would begin to break down. The ranks of the squatters would swell, and so too would their support for the rebellion. Led by the MNLA, the people would then take over the industrial areas, and run them on a co-operative basis. The old practice of 'self-tap, self-sell' would become the powerhouse of the insurrection.[55] The guerrillas believed that the first removals of squatters had played into their hands: 'It allows the people to see how heartless government is. The bandits realise that government cannot remove all squatters.'[56] This was a crucial assumption, and on this the success of the revolution rested.

The British army was determined to keep on the offensive, and continued to make big 'sweeps' in areas where the guerrillas were believed to operate. General Boucher had such scant information on the MNLA that he had little alternative. For example Operation Leo in October 1949 launched twenty-four platoons from a 'start line' into 74,000,000 square yards of jungle, with aircraft bombing and strafing ahead of them, in a systematic attempt to box guerrillas into a confined area. But there was no contact; the insurgents slipped easily between the government units.[57] The 'yo-yoing' style of patrolling along ridges favoured by the army and the general low visibility were disorienting for troops; maps were notoriously inaccurate – they dated from around 1928 and did not always show crucial features like tributary rivers. The MNLA jungle camps were well camouflaged, even from the air; *atap* lean-to huts were hidden beneath the forest canopy, and scattered over an extended area so that no more than one building could be seen on the ground at a time. Chin Peng's camp near Mentekab housed around 300 men and women; it was ringed by a mini-stockade, and was quickly evacuated when security forces attacked it by air and land. The trails to the camps were well guarded; paths were strewn with dried foliage that would snap underfoot, and British troops were soon observed and easily heard. They were soon smelt too, by their cooking fires and hair oil. Nor was large-scale bombing – by 1950 this involved Lincolns with 1,000lb pounds bombs – as effective in Malaya as it had once been against Iraqi villagers. Gullies provided natural cover, and many bombs exploded in the trees; the biggest danger was from falling branches. It did not break morale, which was its main purpose. Instead, it seems to have even raised a mood of defiance, not least when bombs hit civilians. In one incident in Johore in early 1950, five children were killed in their schoolhouse. Although the army could harry the guerrillas from place to place, it could not bring them to battle. The shooting war had reached stalemate.

The *ulu* remained a fearsome place for British soldiers, and the stories they swapped of the Burma campaign did not diminish its horrors. They were ill equipped: the much-vaunted jungle boots were said to last six days, and they let in sand and leeches. In the early days troops wore 1943-issue webbing, and the standard-issue Aertex underpants rode up and withered in the heat to create embarrassing rashes. Most of the campaign was conducted not in the primary rainforest, where the high canopy restricts the light and there is little undergrowth, but in disturbed, secondary jungle, *belukar*, which was often impassable – a dense mass of shrubs, bushes and spiky creepers. To move off a path meant hacking with 'tree-basher' machetes that soon blunted. The Gurkha units viewed 5,000 yards in one day as good going; often progress fell to a mere 2,000 yards.[58] A patrol through the clean, regular lines of rubber trees was no less enervating in its way. Over time, commanders and their troops became grounded in jungle lore but the first interrogations of captured guerrillas made it clear that the British were not staying in the jungle long enough to worry the MNLA. The exceptions to this were the 'Ferret Forces', which were a vital sign of the presence of government in some areas. But even here contacts were few and far between. One unit, in twenty-four days of operations in Perak in September 1948, made sixty-nine day patrols and eleven night patrols; they met guerrillas on nine occasions, wounding two and capturing seven others. Ferret Force was dissolved in November 1948: it was unpopular with the regular army, and its skilled personnel were needed elsewhere. Tensions between the police and the army remained high. In the first year of the Emergency there was little co-operation in intelligence matters, and although the army was acting in support of the civil power, police were not always present on its operations. This was one reason some soldiers felt unconstrained by civil considerations in the screening of squatters. Under relentless pressure, Gurney insisted that martial law should not be declared. The irony of this was that soldiers were less restricted than they might have been under the law of war. 'It is most important', Gurney stressed, 'that police and soldiers who are not saints, should not get the impression that every small mistake is going to be the subject of a public enquiry or that it is better to do nothing at all than to do the wrong thing quickly.'[59]

The police continued to act as a paramilitary force. One young lieutenant stationed in Campbell Road, Kuala Lumpur, described his first encounter with a jungle squad of Chinese detectives, of which by the end of the year there were 230: 'All wore black shirts with black shorts or long trousers, and trilby hats, always inclined to the right. The style of headgear was probably copied from actors seen in countless American B pictures shown nightly in the Cattle Shed, an affectionate name for the open-cinema in the Lucky World Amusement Park.'[60] The chief of police, Nicol Gray, was under increasing attack for his methods, not least from his own officers. Gurney accused the Old Malaya contingent of a campaign of 'deliberate disloyalty' against

Gray, and lambasted them in turn for neglecting to tackle the corruption which was rampant in the force.[61] Some of the bitterest disputes were over intelligence and its uses. The British were engulfed by an information panic. The Malayan Security Service was dissolved and its functions devolved to the Special Branch, but it had, in 1948, only twelve officers and forty-eight inspectors; most of them expatriates or Malays. Only 5 per cent of the police force was Chinese, and even the translation of captured materials was a problem.[62] But from this, lessons were being learnt. A police mission visited Malaya at the end of 1949: it recommended a return to normal police training and methods and, above all, the need to recruit Chinese into the force.[63] Slowly, some of the key elements of a counter-insurgency programme were being identified, if not yet fully implemented.

The new state arm of 'public relations' moved to the heart of counter-terrorism. In 1949, 51 million information leaflets were produced, many of them dropped in the jungle; government spokesmen toured villages, in the manner of local story-tellers. But the message was indistinct. The early leaflet campaigns were mercenary in their appeal – 'Give information to the police. Get good rewards. Live happily with your family' – or platitudinous in their tone – 'Communism is the enemy of honest workers'.[64] Visual propaganda was often brutal: photographs of dead guerrillas were circulated, notably of Liew Yao. But this could be counter-productive. Broadcasting the acts of terror of the MNLA merely seemed to increase its notoriety; it added to the mood of menace, to a sense that the government was losing its grip.[65] The British dismissed communist propaganda as semi-literate and crude. As Chin Peng admitted, 'Our pronouncements were largely unadorned and straightforward. What you read was what you got.'[66] Yet they often possessed what the voice of the colonial government lacked: an ability to appeal directly to rural communities, in their own idiom. Detained communists spoke of 'propaganda' as a positive and empowering force: 'After you have had their fierce propaganda, you can't do without it. It gives you so much strength, you feel weak when you don't have it.'[67] Despite the difficulties, the MCP ran a network of underground presses, roughly cyclostyled productions such as the *Humanity News* in Perak, the *Vanguard Press* in Selangor, the *Battle News* and *Combatant News* at Pahang, and other ephemeral titles. They served as internal newsletters for isolated jungle units and their supporters, but they also reached out to the general population. The message was often effectively wrapped around recent local events. Allegations of rape were common and these fed popular rumour and fear of the security forces; the MCP constantly evoked memories of Japanese atrocities. One report just after Chinese New Year in 1949 was typical: 'The British and Indian soldiers came to Chin Lin San to create a disturbance. They were like beasts. They raped every female in the village from 13 to 45 years of age . . .' Paper notices were pinned to trees or scattered at the scene of an assassination: 'Tonight this Conductor Maniam has been shot dead by a gun of the people. Everyone of you, Brothers and Sisters! Think deeply for what reason he has been shot dead.' And from deep inside the forest, the Party still attempted to respond directly to speeches and broadcasts by 'the white monkey leader', Malcolm MacDonald.[68]

Gurney felt that the time was right to increase the psychological pressure on the guerrillas by announcing an amnesty on 6 September. The terms, however, were vague. They stated that those who surrendered and had 'managed to avoid becoming assassins or committing the other more dastardly crimes' would not face the death penalty. To fighters in the jungle this appeal seemed naïve, and it was mistrusted. Above all, as one captured guerrilla reported, 'it does not clearly state what punishment you will get for which offence'.[69] The amnesty encouraged the communists to keep its recruits well blooded; few guerrillas seemed to qualify for leniency and, in the last months of 1949, only 155 of them came forward. They presented the British with an acute dilemma. In the court of the public opinion, the colonial government could not seem to be lenient, but equally it had to offer some incentive to people to come out of the jungle. The British, at this stage, could only advertise their intentions indirectly.[70] In the twelve years of the Emergency, 226 people were executed, most of them in the early period.[71] Capital offences required a public trial and these proved to be deeply controversial. It was dangerous to give Asian nationalists an opportunity to defend themselves in open court, and in full view of world opinion. The conviction in Kuala Lumpur of the former president of the Pan-Malayan Federation of Trade Unions, S. A. Ganapathy, on a charge of possessing arms led to

Nehru's personal intervention and put India's continuing membership of the Commonwealth in jeopardy.[72] The World Federation of Trade Unions called it 'murder'. The British were shocked when the keynote speaker at a conference of local moderate trade unionists, orchestrated by the trade union adviser, John Brazier, paid tribute to Ganapathy: 'His sincere services to the workers for a long time cannot be forgotten. In appreciation of these services it is but right to express our sympathy to him in his dark days.'[73] But Ganapathy's plea for clemency was refused by the Sultan of Selangor, and on 5 February 1949 he was executed.

It was better to detain and deport suspects in private. In January 1949 the notorious Emergency Regulation 17C was amended to require detainees' families to leave with them. A new provision, 17D, allowed for collective detention – an old tool of empire first employed against the Boers. Between January and October 1949 it was used sixteen times against a total of 6,343 people. The detainees had a right to appeal to committees of review, but the rule was that, in the event of doubt, a person was to stay in detention. Between April and December 1949 162 appeals were heard and sixty people released. This was felt to be 'too lenient' and the procedure was strengthened by the creation of a Review Commission, which was so constituted, the British Cabinet was told, that 'there can be no danger that instructions issued to it by the Federation Government will not be fully implemented'.[74] By May 1950 7,644 individuals were held and another 3,076 were under collective detention orders.[75] By mid January 1952, a total of 26,741 detention orders had been signed.[76] Officers were recalled from the UK to assist in screening. The facilities were overwhelmed; some were hastily erected and others, such as St John's Island in Singapore and Pulau Jerejak off Penang, were former quarantine stations. The clinical language used to describe the process disguised a brutal reality. Families were irrevocably divided. In January 1949, at the Malacca camp, British observers found elderly persons and parentless children awaiting 'repatriation' to a homeland with which they had lost all connection.[77] Of the individual detainees around 1,000 were Malay. In August 1948, the young Indonesian leader, Khatijah Sidek, was arrested and sent to Sime Road, where the European women had been detained during the war. She was seven

ung San and Attlee, London, January 1947

ung San and family, 1947

The Mountbattens in Delhi, eve of independence, August 1947

Celebrating independence in Calcutta, August 1947

Ending the Burmese days: Rance and Burma's president, January 1948

Communist suspect, Malaya, c. 1949

Bren gun and stengah: rubber planter in Malaya, 1949

Chinese peasants being arrested by Malay policemen, April 1949

Dyak trackers in Malaya, *c.* 1949

The Sultan expects: the ruler of Selangor inspects Malay special constables on a rubber estate, 1949

Hearts and minds: a propaganda leaflet drop, 1948

Imperial twilight: drinks party at Malcolm MacDonald's residence, Bukit Serene, 1949

Fighting during the Karen insurgency, 1949

The quiet man: Ne Win (*left*) in London for military training, 1949

The man with the plan: Templer with the Home Guard, Kinta, 1952

Bandung spirits: Nasser, Nu and Nehru celebrating the Burmese Water Festival, 1955

Chin Peng at Baling, December 1955, with his old Force 136 ally, John Davis.

months pregnant, and struggled on the diet of wild rice with scraps of vegetables and fish. She shared a cell with forty other women, mostly girls from the Chinese high schools. She cajoled them into sharing any extra food, such as biscuits brought in by visitors: 'Before we ate, we each had to make a speech, and then we sang national songs – Malay, Indian, Indonesian and Chinese. Then we shouted the Malay word *Merdeka* and repeated it in Indian and Chinese, before eating the biscuits.'[78]

In early 1950, Mountbatten's old confidant, Tom Driberg, visited Taiping camp, from which local journalists had been barred. Here the British experimented with a 'rehabilitation' programme for communists and their sympathizers. Driberg described it as 'a kind of Wilton Park, or rather Macronissos of Malaya'; this was a reference to the controversial conditions of internment in wartime Britain, and to a notorious island camp used in the Greek insurrection. It was, Driberg wrote, 'a disgrace to the British Commonwealth, to the Federation of Malaya and to the Labour Government'.[79] He took up allegations of assault on detainees. The conditions, the deputy commissioner of police frankly admitted, were 'now worse than that experienced by internees under the Jap regime'.[80] In Klang there had been protests: 'Various forms of obstruction were practised including sitting down, refusing to identify their possessions and generally adopting an attitude of complete indifference. Under certain conditions these persons had to be assisted to their feet and a certain degree of compulsion used.'[81] In July 1950 there was a week-long hunger strike by 1,370 detainees in Ipoh, and when the Johore notable Wong Shee Fung visited Majeedi camp, ostensibly to inspect conditions, he was nearly scragged by inmates: two of them were shot. Many saw the camps as 'nurseries of communism'. The new secretary of state, James Griffiths, felt there was a serious risk of a mass breakout. By the end of 1951 conditions at Taiping had improved, but Tanjong Bruas, in Malacca, was dirty and neglected; it was, in the eyes of the former head of the UK Prison Service, 'a most distressing encampment'.[82] There were more riots in Ipoh in June 1955, in which wardens opened fire, killing three people. It spread to the rehabilitation centre, where women were among those to resist the longest. The wardens, the coroner, concluded, 'lost their heads'.[83]

In February 1949 the first 1,074 detainees were embarked on two ships for China.[84] They had lost almost everything: family, home, goods, crops, pigs and fishponds. Privately, Gurney hoped to 'repatriate' as many as 2,000 people a month.[85] But the system of appeals proved burdensome, and collective detentions had to be put on hold, although they continued in some key areas. The British then experimented with 'voluntary repatriation', but there were few takers. The whole business was a scandal waiting to erupt, and there was a small rebellion of civil servants against the policy.[86] Nevertheless, by the middle of March 1951 10,140 people had been sent to China and 104 more to India and Indonesia. Banishments came to a standstill in 1950 with the fall of Nationalist China. But they resumed again in 1951 through the port of Hoihow on Hainan island; by April 1952 the total had risen to 13,317. A Norwegian vessel was used for the work; at one time the captain was arrested, and a British official had to buy him out of jail. The cost for each detainee was equivalent to a first-class berth on a P&O liner to Colombo.[87] A British policeman accompanying one batch described their arrival at a port under Kuomintang control:

When the launch came alongside, the soldiers who were armed to the teeth, swarmed abroad. Since, as far as I was concerned, the banishees were my responsibility until formal handover was completed, I posted sentries outside the doors where the formalities were being carried out, and mounted a Bren gun covering the top of the gangplank. The atmosphere was tense . . . Rumour had it that the KMT gave the ex-[Communist Terrorists] the choice of donning their uniforms and proceeding to the front or else.[88]

At ports such as Swatow, each adult was given twenty-five Straits dollars and $10 for each child, as well as a blanket, a pair of trousers, a pullover and a pair of rubber shoes for the children.[89] British reports admitted that the vast majority were women and children. On one occasion, a nine-month pregnant woman was shipped; families were put in different ships or sent to the wrong location; in the words of the deputy chief secretary, 'far from their homes and in a war-torn China where some may be left to starve and not reach their villages at all'.[90] The new Chinese government took up their cause: 'The inhuman tortures which were used by the Japanese fascist pirates during their rule in Malaya are also being employed.'[91] There were mounting protests. After the communist takeover the *Nan Feng Jin Pao* carried lurid reports of children abandoned, of sexual harassment and beatings, including the case of Chen Chin Chu a teacher in Perak, who at the time of her arrest was two months pregnant and had to leave behind four children with no one to care for them. She alleged that her baby was killed by the British: 'When I was giving birth to my girl, the British imperialists did not give me anything to eat for a whole day, and after the baby was born I was only given a small piece of bread every day. The most cruel thing was that many female prisoners had to give birth to babies in the corridor of the hospital, and the British imperialists even forced them to drown their own babies in a cess pit.'[92]

This was one of the last official interventions by China in Malayan affairs. The fall of Kuomintang China was a moment of decision for the local Chinese. Tan Kah Kee played a significant and symbolic role in the new People's Political Consultative Conference. His overt support for Mao so exasperated the British that they considered arresting him, or depriving him of his British citizenship. But they drew back from this: Tan Kah Kee's status was now effectively that of a minister within the new regime. When he left for China in late May there were persistent rumours that he had been deported.[93] These events left the Malayan Chinese divided and uncertain. When the Double Tenth national-day celebrations arrived there was a ban on public meetings. A battle of the flags broke out in the towns. In Chinatown in Singapore the banner of the People's Republic was openly on sale but, on the day, only fifty 'five star' flags were seen in the city, mostly in trade union offices and schools; only fifty-two were counted in Penang; none in Kuala Lumpur, Ipoh or Taiping. Possession of this kind of paraphernalia was now dangerous. There were muted celebrations by one of the last vanguards of leftist influence, the Mayfair theatrical troupe in Singapore, which put on a rousing play called *The Volunteers' March*. Its signboard was tarred. By contrast, a cocktail party by the consul of the nationalist regime in Taiwan was attended by 600 representatives of Chinese associations.[94] But below the surface there was considerable elation at the communist victory. It boosted the MCP's cause in the countryside and kept alive a sense of expectancy, so much so that Party propaganda had to dismiss as 'wishful thinking and completely divorced from reality' rumours that a victorious Red Army was about to sweep into Malaya.[95] The colonial regime was in a bind. The whole logic of Britain's economic and strategic interests demanded that the new People's Republic of China be recognized. But Gurney believed that the arrival of communist Chinese consuls would be a 'suicidal folly', equivalent to reinforcing the guerrillas by an entire division. He made the issue a resigning matter, and prevailed.[96]

Gurney was becoming increasingly impatient with the Malayan Chinese. He believed that the insurrection was financed by payment of protection money on a massive scale, and that this practice reached into the highest echelons of the business community. He chose first a softer target: a number of Chettiar businessmen were arrested, many of them absentee owners of rubber estates. In 1949 the British estimated that they had lost control of a quarter of an estimated million acres of estate land. Their payments to the MNLA varied from $50 to $5,000 a month and a cess on the rubber produced. There was a small exodus of Chettiars as they closed their estates and moved their persons and their capital back to India. They were still counting their losses in Burma and smarting from the British anti-INA witchhunts of 1945. Remittances abroad by Asians rose from US$16m in 1949 to US$130m in 1951.[97] But Gurney's real target was the Chinese *towkays*: the individual sums estimated to be changing hands here were astronomical: $100,000 a month or higher. The guerrillas in the jungle were awash with cash: 'Our people said at that time', recalled Chin Peng, 'we had . . . a haversack full of money . . . but we can't get a bit of food.'[98] Gurney saw this as all one with 'the whole vast racket of black-marketing, smuggling and commercial corruption that go to make up Chinese business methods . . . To these people banditry pays, because the police tend to go off looking for the bandits and have not so much time for the supervision of rubber dealers, or, as Lord Mancroft puts it, issuing dog licences.' Gurney now looked for 'one or two really big *towkays*' to prosecute as an example. The son of Tan Cheng Lock, Tan Siew Sin – still a federal legislative councillor and a future finance minister of Malaya – was pulled in. But, Gurney wrote, 'though he appears shaken we have not yet enough evidence to pick him up'.[99]

Gurney was well aware of the fragile, divided state of the Chinese community, and this stayed his hand somewhat. In early 1948, at a dinner to celebrate his CBE in the New Year's honours list, H. S. Lee had called for a unified body of all Malayan Chinese. But he had then been away from the country for nine months of the year, and nothing had happened. The subject arose again at a dinner party with Gurney on 15 December 1948. Now the high commissioner actively encouraged the mostly English-educated Chinese leaders on the Legislative Council to take the initiative. But it was a delicate undertaking. The obvious choice of figurehead was Tan Cheng Lock. He had ruminated on the creation of a 'Malayan Chinese League' since the war, but as an anglophone Straits Chinese, he did not command the large personal following of the China-born magnates. Yet the depth of the crisis, and their sudden isolation from China, drew the big men of the Chinese community together as never before, and on 27 February 1949 a Malayan Chinese Association (MCA) was formed. Tan Cheng Lock saw its role as educating the Chinese in a 'Malayan' consciousness. But, as a quid pro quo, he argued, the British must acknowledge the Chinese stake in Malaya. As he told the MCA in October: 'A state which is incompetent to satisfy different races condemns itself; a state which labours to neutralise, to absorb, or to expel them, destroys its own vitality; a state which does not include them is destitute of the chief basis of self-government.'[100] Tan saw multiracialism as the natural state of man, but in terms of practical politics the MCA was a communal counterpart to UMNO.[101] Its core following – by the end of December 1950 a paper membership of 170,000 – was summoned up by the Chinese-speaking, China-born leaders who commanded the Chambers of Commerce and the clan associations. The MCA was the Kuomintang resurrected in all but name, led by nationalist stalwarts such as H. S. Lee in Selangor and Lau Pak Khuan in Perak. The MCA included some of the wealthiest men in Southeast Asia and, over time, they used it to restore their traditional patronage networks. For example, businessmen now began a concerted campaign to get control of school management committees and oust left-wing influence. In such places, some of the most crucial battles of the insurrection were fought.[102]

A stated aim of the MCA was 'to promote and assist in the maintenance of peace and good order'. Gurney insisted on this: he had originally wanted to use the word 'collaborate', but this had evil connotations with the Japanese occupation.[103] Gurney saw an opportunity for the state to make a direct connection with its Chinese subjects. The number of 'Chinese affairs officers' grew in number, and MCA leaders were co-opted onto 'Chinese Advisory Committees'. These were the scene of bitter exchanges: businessmen complained of their lack of protection compared to the European mines and estates, and that when they gave information no action was taken.[104] The 'distrust and dislike' of the police was universal. But, crucially, the MCA was now able to press the cause of squatters and detainees.[105] More controversially, some MCA representatives began to embed themselves in screening operations. They selected squatter representatives who would then become MCA representatives in their villages. In turn, the government tried to give special priority to the security of MCA areas.[106] Some major figures in the MCA wanted to go further. Leong Yew Koh, a former colonel in the Chinese nationalist army, suggested that 10,000 men be recruited to Malaya from the Kuomintang armies in Taiwan or from those interned in northern Vietnam.[107] Tan Cheng Lock rose in the esteem of the British, after their execration of him a year earlier for leading the united front. Gurney, Malcolm MacDonald recollected, had called him 'gaga' (Tan was sixty-six years of age). But now both men recognized Tan's skill in bringing the various factions together and interceding for the community. At a meeting with Gurney at the beginning of April, Tan petitioned for some squatters at Kajang, south of Kuala Lumpur, as 'good and blameless people'. Gurney asked him if he was leaving to return to Malacca that evening, and 'he said no, he thought that it was too late in view of possible dangers on the road. I asked him where the dangers lay, he said "Kajang". Let it be to his credit that he also laughed.'[108] Within a few days, on 10 April, Tan Cheng Lock was seriously injured, along with the leader of the Perak mine owners, Cheong Chee, by a grenade attack on the Perak MCA office at the Ipoh Chinese Chamber of Commerce. Tan, the British reported, 'displayed a brilliant sense of occasion, and some may even suspect that he has enjoyed himself immensely'. His journey back to Malacca was a triumphal progress. He was met at each stage with well-wishers and special escorts to protect him. He kept his bloodied shirt as a memento. But his health never recovered from the injury.[109] This was one of several attacks on MCA targets; in December, at the funeral of the mother of Cheong Chee, another grenade killed three mourners and injured Lau Pak Khuan and Leong Yew Koh. They 'knelt before the British bandits, wagging their tails to beg for pity . . .', announced the MNLA: 'shameless "country-selling" thieves. They are racial traitors.'[110]

But the British had now found a way to hurt the communists. As plans for the mass deportations of squatters looked like collapsing in late 1948, the government began to think in more radical terms: the resettlement en masse of the rural Chinese on the peninsula. A federal committee on squatters was set up in late 1948, and reported in January 1949. Approaching the issue more as one of efficient administration rather than security, it argued that squatters should be settled where they stood. This was a dramatic shift in policy: it proposed giving land wholesale to Chinese peasants for the first time. But the plan ran into a quagmire of opposition from the State governments, in whom control over land was vested. Some Malay bureaucrats argued that squatters should be evicted and left entirely to their own devices. After pressure from the central government, and with large financial incentives, a number of trial initiatives were launched, but they were driven solely by the strategic imperative to remove people from the jungle fringes. One was at Titi, in Negri Sembilan, an area that was virtually an autonomous communist republic during and after the war. It was a site of massacres of villagers by the Japanese, but the district officer, C. E. Howe, looked to emulate some of their methods: 'The Japs put barbed wire around Titi and Pertang, garrisoned these towns with troops and made all Chinese of the locality live within the defended areas . . .', he observed. 'Could we not try the same idea?' He immediately had an answer from the local guerrillas, who spread rumours of mass repatriation and extermination camps. The newly formed branch of the MCA was enlisted to help manage the scheme, but its leaders had nocturnal visits from communist guerrillas and all of them withdrew or left town 'on urgent business'. But at the end of the year the army and police moved in and more than 600 families were uprooted from outlying villages into the town area. Where some tried to remain in their homes they were forcibly ejected and their huts burnt. The resettled farmers had to camp in the streets and build their own shelter with discounted timber. Much of the promised aid did not materialize. They received little help from their new neighbours, who tried to make money out of them. Titi was now a rural ghetto. The process was taken inexorably to its conclusion when much of the surrounding countryside was declared a 'no human area'.[111]

Another early scheme was a colony of around 326 detainees from Majeedi detention camp near Johore Bahru, who were settled at Mawai. There were only ten men aged between twenty and forty among them. The people had no agricultural or household equipment. The MCA had opposed the scheme: it was built on poor soil, close to the jungle's edge, and they doubted it could be defended. But they gave $100,000 as a token of good faith to support it. In 1951 it was closed. The people, said Tan Cheng Lock, 'were being treated like cattle'.[112] Perhaps as few as 5,000 Chinese were resettled by the end of 1949. But it was the prelude to a vastly more ambitious programme. In Kinta alone 94,000 squatters, that is a third of the population and half of the country folk, were targeted for resettlement. In the peninsula as a whole, by 1954 572,917 people were resettled in 480 'New Villages' and 560,000 more would be 'regrouped' on towns and rubber estates. This was the largest planned population relocation in recorded history.

Resettlement was accompanied by a host of new restrictions on persons and on movement: there was a standing curfew from 6 a.m. to 6 p.m. which could be extended to all hours if there was trouble; there was no travel except in restricted areas, and no bicycles on public roads after 7 p.m. 'Food restriction' areas imposed strict controls on commodities.[113] The impact of this was immense. To begin with, not all of those moved were squatters; many had been legitimately occupying land. Squatters who had lost their crops struggled to find work, and when they did it was hard to reach it under curfew conditions. It divided and scattered families, and broke up old communities: the Chinese of Pulai were resettled three times. Reciprocal relations with *kampong* Malays were severed. As a Malay writer, Keris Mas, described it in his short story, 'A row of shophouses in our village':

We are to be shifted. We, our families, our livestock, our rice, our loves and our hatreds. Everything.

They say we have been helping the terrorists, helping our young men in the jungle. The shops are the pride of our village, yet they accuse us of setting fire to them so that we would distract the security forces from their pursuit of our boys in the jungle last night.

We are as powerful to meet their accusations as a beautiful woman in the hands of a terrible giant. We have lost all that we love best, all that we have lived for.[114]

In the new settlements people often had little in common, not even a shared language. The trauma of removal did not encourage the formation of new community ties, whether through dialect associations, clubs or temples. Social trust was deeply damaged. In this state of anomie, other forms of assistance and protection reasserted themselves, in particular, the triads. In Titi, a society known as the New Kongsi was quickly established. It provided *ang pow*, gifts of money wrapped in red envelopes, for the resettled people, and helped in the construction of houses or by lending money and goods. It then moved into gambling and illegal lotteries. The police, however, had other worries, and the triads were, at least, a potential check on the communist underground.[115]

As the MLNA moved back from the squatter areas, it moved closer to the forest dwellers, the Orang Asli. These shy peoples became the object of the imperial gaze as never before. In 1947, the census officials had tried to count the Orang Asli, at least those who were two to ten miles away from roads, rivers or villages. But some communities remained forest nomads in inaccessible areas, such as the Negrito of Ulu Kelantan. The official count was 34,737 Orang Asli, of whom 29,648 were designated 'nomads'.[116] The larger communities of the north and central parts of the main range were the Senoi peoples – the Semai and the Temiar – who followed shifting cultivation around a cycle of sites, but who also traded with other communities. Before the war, as with the much larger 'hill tribes' of Burma, a few British officials and ethnographers build up a close and protective relationship with the Orang Asli. They were fascinated by their 'primitive socialism' and, in the case of the Senoi, by their peaceful 'non-violent' way of life. The chief authority was H. D. 'Pat' Noone, a Cambridge-trained anthropologist who became the first Protector of Aborigines in Perak. He took a Temiar wife, and during the Japanese occupation went to ground with them in the forest. The leaders of Force 136, John Davis, Richard Broome and Spencer Chapman, met him from time to time. But Noone had tended to go his own way, protected by his Temiar bodyguards. He had helped the communists during the war to liaise with the forest communities, and even imparted ethnographic techniques to them. The MCP's connection with the Orang Asli kept its resistance alive during one of the grimmest periods of the war. But Noone broke with the MCP in mid 1943, and nothing more was heard of him after the later part of that year; it was assumed that he had perished from malaria.[117]

The loss of Noone cast a long shadow over British relations with the forest peoples. Not everyone accepted that he was dead. One of the last men to see him was Lau Mah, the principal MPAJA liaison with the Orang Asli. In mid 1946 he visited London as part of the Malayan contingent for the victory parade, and Noone's father interviewed him over tea at the Savoy. It seemed that he had nothing to add to what Force 136 had reported. In late 1948 Lau Mah was again a senior commander of the MNLA forces in the Kelantan–Perak watershed. The same year, the High Court in London ruled that Noone was deceased, but the Royal Anthropological Society demanded a search for him, not least to try to recover his valuable ethnographic notebooks. In Malaya there were persistent rumours of a white man at large in the jungle, and that it might be Noone still co-operating with the MCP in order to protect the Temiar. It was conceivable that he had survived. In October 1949 the Gurhkas stumbled upon one of their own men, Nakam Gurung, who was living quietly in the jungle. He had been there since 1941, when, ill with malaria, he had been left behind in the British retreat down the peninsula; he had been living off a small plot of vegetables and raising some pigs ever since. He was discharged with seven years' back pay.[118] But the Temiar had placed an impenetrable taboo over the entire affair of Noone, even over his name. After a long search his wife, Anjing, was found in August 1950, but she was very ill, and just as friends of Noone reached her, she died and took any secrets she possessed with her. It took several years for Noone's brother Richard, now his successor as government adviser on Aborigines, to lift the taboo and piece the story together. Noone had been killed by a Temiar companion who was in love with his wife. But what precipitated the break between them was anger at the danger which Noone had brought to the community by involving it in political struggles beyond the forest.[119]

This episode marked the beginning of a cycle of violence through which the Orang Asli were brought into the mainstream of Malaya's political struggles, and forced to take sides in them. In July 1949 MNLA guerrillas attacked a Semai settlement at Kampong Krikit in Perak; two Semai women were killed, and others abducted. Some of the Semai had been serving as Special Policemen at a nearby mine, and the guerrillas wanted food and weapons from them. This normally peaceable community took bloody revenge on a neighbouring Chinese settlement at Bukit Pekan: fourteen Chinese were killed and thirteen more wounded.[120] Another incident involved a group of Semai who had taken work at the Boh Tea plantations in the Cameron Highlands. As they trekked from their settlements and approached the estate they met guerrillas who warned them that police were in the area and moved them on. For reasons that are unclear, perhaps because they were suspected of spying for the authorities, the Semai were taken to a hut and the men tied up. From the testimony of a small boy who escaped, it appears that thirty-four of them – men, women and children – were strangled and buried in a rough fashion nearby. Some days later, the boy reached safety and reported the incident to the estate manager. More time elapsed before the army investigated and unearthed the bodies. There were testimonies to similar incidents, but it is not clear if the full extent of the violence ever came to light.[121] In the Boh estate massacre, a notorious Semai guerrilla known as Bah Pelankin was at the scene. He had a brutal reputation and terrorized the area; the Orang Asli never referred to him by name, but as 'The One'. These incidents were all the more shocking because they seemed to challenge the Semai's status as 'the most peaceful society known to anthropology'. The psychological trauma experienced by these communities was profound.[122] Some communities managed to stay out of the way of the war, but for most its consequences were irreversible. After

1950 the British recruited Orang Asli into a Perak Special Areas Constabulary and the MNLA organized leagues of young Orang Asli based on an understanding of forms of social organization gleaned from Noone's earlier fieldwork.

The military saw the Orang Asli as a vital link in the MNLA's chain of supply. Resettlement of them began even before large numbers of Chinese were moved. The fragments of evidence that survive from this suggest that it was a hasty and largely unplanned process whereby forest peoples were uprooted and sent to concentrated settlements in lowland areas. The effects were catastrophic. The Orang Asli were confronted with an unfamiliar diet, and exposed to diseases to which they had no natural resistance. They succumbed to the heat, to malaria, to infection and to mental depression, and died at a shocking rate. When 1,485 Semai from the Ulu Bertam area of the Cameron Highlands were settled at Bukit Betong in Pahang, they were, it was reported 'dying off like flies'; 213 deaths occurred to only thirty-eight births in the fifteen months after November 1949. Amongst Temiar resettled on the Plus river there were sixty-four deaths and only eight births in a four-month period. At Semenyih, sixty died within two and a half months. Not only was the restriction of camp life profoundly disturbing for a forest people who had always been free to roam, but it was a ritual practice within many communities to move whenever a death occurred. Now they were tormented by the unsettled spirits around them. There are no reliable statistics for the total number of Orang Asli who died in the camps. It seems that the British did not think to tally them fully. The higher estimates suggest that 5–7,000 of 25,000 resettled Orang Asli perished.[123]

The Orang Asli lacked any kind of voice. Only two them, it was said, spoke English. There were 'Protectors of Aborigines' in some states, but all but one were part-time. In Perak it was seen as a job for the game warden. At the end of 1949 another Cambridge anthropologist, Peter Williams-Hunt, was appointed as federal adviser on Aborigines. He had few real powers, but he tried to instil into military commanders an understanding and respect for these forest communities. He wrote a series of memoranda on how to conduct contacts, which counselled soldiers to talk to them in an unhurried way, 'rather as if one is dealing with semi-trained animals'.[124] But he was in an invidious position. His welfare responsibilities sat uncomfortably with his role in prosecuting a war. In one of his first interventions in resettlement matters he urged soldiers to be sensitive to the religious beliefs attached to houses; but this was juxtaposed with the advice, 'Let the aborigines destroy their own houses. They might as well get some fun out of the evacuation.'[125] British soldiers saw him as 'a strange character' and 'a bit of a crank'. They were fascinated by his relationship with his Semai wife; his accounts of the sexual practices of the hill people were an inspiration for salacious doggerel ('When Temiar stay up too late / They're somewhat apt to fornicate . . .').[126] But Williams-Hunt exercised an impressive personal sway over the Orang Asli. His reputation in the community would survive his death in 1953, from a fall in the forest, and the newborn son he left behind would emerge as an Orang Asli leader in the 1980s.

The paternalism of Old Malaya survived in curious places and, in a sense, was strengthened by the Emergency. On the rubber estates the planters, backed with arms and police powers, reclaimed their fiefdoms largely unchallenged. The trade unions were devastated, particularly among Chinese workers. Activists lived in fear of arrest and the moderate trade unionists faced MCP reprisals. On some estates managers relied on the old system of temple committees, and when trade unions revived, they were chiefly a vehicle for Tamil ethnic consciousness. Management took full advantage of the weakness of labour. In Singapore the major employers reduced wages in a way that would not have been possible before June 1948. There were only three strikes on the island in 1949. Special Branch openly attended union meetings and the RAF police terrorized trade unions on their bases in Singapore.[127] But this was not merely a story of reaction. A retired planter such as 'Tuan Djek' would take up the plight of squatters in his newspaper column. District officers continued to nurse their 'parishes' in the old way. Christopher Blake had arrived in Malaya with the British Military Administration; in November 1948 he was sent to one of the most isolated districts in Malaya, the borderlands with Thailand in upper Perak. The area had a mythic status in colonial lore. Its district officer from 1895 to 1925 was an Anglo-Irish adventurer, Hubert Berkeley. He epitomized the Malay Civil Service tradition of protection by encouraging Malay settlement in the *ulu* and keeping the modern world at bay. He lived, in effect, as a white rajah, surrounded by a small army of liveried Malay retainers. The story goes that when his superior, the British Resident of Perak, attempted to visit, he would find the road blocked. When forced himself to visit the state capital, Berkeley would descend with a procession of elephants. His spirit still permeated the district at all levels 'as if they had lived in some kind of Arcadia'. Some of the elephants survived, as did his monogrammed crockery and thunderbox, as well as several unusually fair-skinned Malays (it was said that he had exercised *jus prima noctis* on young girls from the local orphanage). Berkeley was survived by his great friend Jimmy Kemp, who had, extraordinarily, made it through internment and still, at the age of ninety-one, worked his own mine. Blake took to consulting Kemp on land use and tin. But more than this, in fighting the Emergency, he also drew on 'the spirit of Berkeley' for small-scale initiatives – such as a fish-drive and agricultural show – to restore local confidence.[128]

The sharp brutality that marked counter-insurgency in 1948 and 1949 was slowly being blunted. The scruples of the Labour government were never wholly allayed. The plight of labour was kept alive by their brother trade unions in Britain and by a concerted campaign by international bodies. The Attlee administration in London and MacDonald in Singapore had to take it seriously. By the end of 1949 a new national body modelled on the British Trades Union Congress was established under close British tutelage. It was a shadow of the old Federations of Trade Unions[129] but, driven by the needs of the Emergency, social initiatives took on a new urgency. Welfare state imperialism acquired new teeth. Over the coming years even private initiatives – the British wives in the Women's Institutes, Scouting and Guiding, Christian mission work revived in the resettlement areas – were harnessed to counter-insurgency. It would create a police state with a paternalist veneer that would become the hallmark of British counter-insurgency and would later be called 'winning hearts and minds'. Or, in the words of a senior police officer, asked in 1954 what was the biggest difference between the Emergency then and five years earlier: 'Less beating up.'[130]

FREEDOM AND REVOLUTION

In years to come the Malayan Emergency would be seen as the first, and perhaps the only, real victory in the Cold War in Asia. Military analysts and historians were to pore over these events to try to discern a turning point, a moment when crucial lessons were learnt and decisive moves made. In early 1949 the Labour government was asking the same question. Attlee chaired a ministerial meeting at the beginning of April and demanded an assessment from MacDonald. He was worried that there was an ongoing struggle with no sense of a turning point being reached. He was under renewed pressure from businesses employing Europeans, and there was a 'growing sense of anxiety' among the relatives of national servicemen. There were rumours of a new wave of attacks on Europeans in April, but these were kept quiet.[131] Gurney could give no guarantee that a turning point had been reached. The main danger was that the MCP would slip back into civilian life, and an illusion of order be created. He was working not for a partial military victory, but to create a longer-term guarantee of order. He repeatedly demanded more police: 'the lesson has not apparently been learned that the answer to Communist terrorism equipped with modern arms is not the soldier but the policeman'. This was the only way in which a conviction of lasting victory might be achieved, as the people of Malaya knew full well that the troops would eventually leave. Yet, in private, Gurney told Creech Jones that he felt that 'the main turning point had occurred about two months ago, but it was not obvious at the time'.[132] In May Gurney was confident enough to place some of the lessons learned in a paper on the 'Organisational lessons of the Emergency'. Certainly, in 1949, many of the elements of the Malayan model – the civil direction, population control, food denial – were beginning to roll into place.[133]

Yet the Emergency was not – as invariably presented, then and since – a British victory. Nor is the history of Malaya in this period solely the history of the Emergency. The forest war erupted out of a series of conflicts within Malayan society that had their origins in the Japanese war, and it was upon these that the fate of the revolution ultimately rested. Although the MNLA in the forest claimed to fight for the 'nation', there were other 'nations of intent' being voiced, other parallel struggles for freedom underway. These too were at their defining hour, and their course could no longer be dictated by the British. The main thrust of colonial high policy between 1945 and 1948 had been to weld Malaya more closely to the British Empire. There was vague talk about self-government – it was written into the federal constitution – but it was clear that the British were thinking in terms of twenty-five years. Now the British seemed cut adrift by events. But there was a remarkable underlying continuity to political aims and a quickening of political vision. In early 1949 there was talk that the British were preparing to abandon Malaya to its fate. This reached the ears of the deputy leader of the opposition, Anthony Eden, who was visiting the country at the time. This provoked Attlee to stand in the House of Commons on 13 April and announce that Britain would not leave Malaya until the insurrection was defeated. But this was also a public commitment to self-government, and it was no longer a distant prospect, but a fact of life. This was no sudden political decision to withdraw; but there was a change of mindset; an acknowledgement that Britain had lost the ability to dictate the pace of events. By mid 1950, MacDonald acknowledged, it was clear that Malay politicians were now thinking of fifteen years, 'and there is now a tendency that the transition to self-government will have to be speeded up'. He also recognized that it would 'inevitably be accelerated by factors over which we shall have little or no control'.[134] In such circumstances it was vital that Britain's local allies were firmly secured, but this entailed a concession of initiative to them which became a slow but steady haemorrhaging of power.

The clearest sign that the British had recognized the inevitable in Malaya was their obsession with placating Dato Onn bin Jaafar. In 1949 the turbulent and temperamental Malay leader still seemed to command the open political scene. Britain's reliance on UMNO had grown during the Emergency. The party was strengthened by the arrest of its opponents; the police provided a good living for tens of thousands of young Malays and gave UMNO 'a larger ready-made well-controlled audience which would not otherwise had been readily available'.[135] In the face of reports of Malays taking to the jungle, it was ultimately Britain's final line of defence in Malaya. But the British could not take the mercurial Onn for granted. In 1948 there were a series of clashes between the British and the Malay State administrations, principally over land for Chinese squatters. In the middle of the year Onn looked set to resign from the Legislative Council. In December 1948 his frustrations spilled over during a visit to London. As a senior mandarin, John Paskin, told Gurney: 'I don't think any of us were quite prepared . . . for the degree of bitterness, under which he still labours, at what was done in 1945/6 . . .' Stopping just short of an ultimatum, Onn made it clear that the British had yet to prove themselves; he demanded tangible evidence of Britain's 'special responsibility towards the Malays'. 'We have', the British were told, 'reached the stage when only deeds and not merely assurances would tell'. He suggested a gift of £10m as restitution to the Malays, for their development. The Emergency had raised Onn's ire: Britain's 'first thought is, "What will the Chinese think about it?", whereas it ought to be, "What will the Malays think about it?" '[136] Yet despite Onn's 'disconcerting quirks', Whitehall was convinced that 'he has the makings of a statesman'; that he was 'capable of a broader vision, and was a man with whom (except on the subject of our "misdeeds" of 1945/6) one could reason'.[137] Throughout 1949 Onn continued to snipe at the 'authoritarian' federal administration and his 'Jekyll and Hyde' personality infuriated Gurney. But the British had made it clear that a solution to what they now termed the 'communal issue' was a condition of political development, and Onn seemed the man most likely to deliver it.

The first steps came at the end of 1948, with Onn's return from London. Inspired by his attendance at the World Conference on Moral Rearmament, a well-connected Straits Chinese schoolteacher, Thio Chan Bee, attempted to apply its principles to inter-ethnic tensions in Malaya. This was not a new idea. Civic movements like Rotary and Kiwanis were taking root among the middle classes. Onn himself had encountered Moral Rearmament on a sojourn at the World Trade Fair in San Francisco in 1939, where he had run the Johore pavilion. The industrialist Lee Kong Chian had attended a Moral Rearmament conference in the United States on the recommendation of President Truman himself. It chimed too with recent speeches of Malcolm MacDonald, who agreed to act as honest broker. Thio Chan Bee used his offices to bring Onn and Tan Cheng Lock and their followings together for the first time. The meeting was carefully choreographed. Eleven Chinese leaders met beforehand at the Singapore Garden Club, where even the issue of whether Tan Cheng Lock should bring himself to thank the host for dinner was a matter for discussion. They then travelled to Onn's residence in Johore Bahru, where many of the leading Malays of the south were gathered. Onn and MacDonald met them at the door. The meeting was tense: the leading Malayans were strangers to each other. Tan Cheng Lock broke the ice by reciting Malay *pantuns*, playful lyrical quatrains. The discussion then became open and frank. It hinged on a key issue: 'The Chinese have economic power. The Malays now have political power. If the Chinese will help the Malays to rise economically, then surely the Malays must share with the Chinese their political power.' The meeting was secret, but a more formal gathering was arranged at the wedding of a Malay notable in Penang in January. It was the first time that Malays had crossed the threshold of the Chinese Corner Club in Northam Road.[138]

The meetings continued for the rest of 1949, and into the following year. Those attending became known as the Communities Liaison Committee, and membership was broadened to include a Ceylonese lawyer, E. E. C. Thuraisingham. It had no official standing, nor were its proceedings ever made public, but it began a process whereby the core issues of state would be ironed out, *in camera*, by representatives of the two main ethnic communities.[139] The first crucial meetings in 1949 were dominated by Malay resentment at the Chinese stranglehold on Asian commerce in Malaya. In a testy meeting in Kuala Lumpur in late February, the Chinese leaders sat through a strongly worded attack by the Perak leader of UMNO, Abdul Wahab. Historically, he argued, the Malays were well represented in the economy, but they had lost commercial control. He inveighed against 'the use of strangulation methods' by Chinese businesses: the lending of money to 'infiltrate' the economy; the use of syndicates to control prices, short weights and 'systematic corruption'. 'The Malays,' he said, 'who used to be a proud race, were forced to begging and the ultimate results of all this would be discontent, jealously and hatred.' The response of Tan Cheng Lock was measured: 'Not only the Malays are suffering,' he said. 'There are many Chinese suffering.' But he enunciated a clear principle: 'In the common interest of Malaya, it is of paramount importance that the non-Malays shall make every endeavour to co-operate amongst themselves and with the Malays to improve the economic position of the Malays so that they, the Malays, can take their rightful and proper place and share fully in the economic life of Malaya.' The debate centred on quotas for the Malays in key sectors: transport for Malays to get their goods to market, and bus routes, a symbolic area where Malays had once been leading entrepreneurs, but had been dislodged since the war. This approach would have an enduring legacy for the post-colonial development of Malaya. It defined the 'new paternalism' of the elite: the combination of a bureaucratic and communal approach to economic problems with a capitalist vision for Malaya's future.[140]

The Committee also reopened the debate on the meaning of citizenship and nationality that had proved so incendiary in 1947. In August 1949 the following questions were posed: 'Is the ultimate aim a United Malayan Nation?' 'What is meant by the "special position" of the Malays?' 'Should there be equality of status, privilege and opportunity between federal citizens (in due course to Malayan nationals)?' As Tan Cheng Lock argued, 'I do not say that the special position should not be upheld, but in what direction? Is there going to be inequality as between the citizens themselves or are they to be on an equal footing?' Onn responded that it was not so much the equality of citizenship that was at stake, but the principle that 'the Malay's allegiance to this country came before anybody else'. A Chinese might have a physical home in Malaya and also a spiritual home elsewhere, but for the Malays the two were inseparable. Malay leaders questioned whether a Chinese, in principle, could place his spiritual loyalty in Malaya, and even if this were conceded, how could it be done without jeopardizing the position of the Malays? But Onn now went further than he had ever gone before in conceding a nationality for non-Malays: 'The Malay feeling has changed, and they do accept the principle provided that [the non-Malays] are prepared to give undivided loyalty.'[141] In subsequent meetings the basis of common nationality was hammered out. A proposal began to emerge, based on a technical provision of the Nationality Bill of the State of Johore, whereby a subject of the ruler automatically became a federal citizen. Could this, it was suggested, be extended more widely to Chinese? One obstacle was the rulers themselves. As the legal adviser to UMNO, Roland Braddell, put it: 'The other rulers would not have it at any price . . . They were Muhammadan rulers and they wanted Muhammadans. He did not know if the rulers ever heard of the idea of nationality.'[142]

In mid August thousands of Malays descended on the royal town of Kuala Kangsar for the installation of the 33rd Sultan of Perak. Significantly, a representative of the Chinese squatters was invited for the first time to attend the ceremony. The Perak line was traced back to the last Sultan of Melaka, deposed by the Portuguese in 1511. The state regalia included the *kris* of the Malay hero Hang Tuah and a sword said to have belonged to Alexander the Great. It was a striking display of the *daulat*, or the aura of a sultan.[143] But Onn was increasingly impatient with the rulers. The next month, at a speech to the UMNO general assembly at Arau in Perlis, Onn floated proposals for a Malayan nationality without consulting them, and reminded them that he had saved their thrones in 1946. This angered them deeply, especially the Sultan of Kedah, whose state was a rival centre of Malay politics. The rulers retaliated by opposing a tentative proposal from the British to appoint a Malay deputy high commissioner, who would most likely be Onn himself; they refused to accept a commoner elevated to a status above them. Onn resigned shortly afterwards as chief minister of Johore. In the face of this obstruction, Onn's latent radicalism resurfaced. He told UMNO's youth wing at a rally at Butterworth on 26 August that 'the days of feudal rule are over. We are in the age of democratic and constitutional rule.'[144] But Onn was finding it difficult to reconcile his reputation as the sole spokesman of the Malays with his conviction that the political struggle must now be broadened to include others. He was losing patience with UMNO, and saw it as too narrow for his ambitions. He was moving ahead of Malay opinion.

At a meeting in Penang over 29–31 December, from which Onn was absent, other senior Malay leaders rounded on the citizenship proposals. 'Our Malay friends', Tan Cheng Lock complained to a colleague, 'seem to think that the Chinese are born criminals or inherently wicked, that whatever we do in this country is inherently wrong.' But the situation was saved by a formula in Tan's words: 'Only when the Chinese acknowledge the same sovereigns as the Malays do, can they demonstrate their wish to be the equals of the Malays.'[145] On the basis of this, the principle of *jus soli* was conceded by Malay leaders. These resolutions were never enshrined in any binding agreement; they remained a private understanding among the elite. Yet the 'communal bargain' that emerged set the terms of political debate for many years to come. It encouraged the British to move forward with a draft development plan: the first of a series of five-year plans. They also set up a rural development agency for the Malays, which Onn would head. It did not eradicate, or even much reduce Malay poverty, but it gave a clear sign to the UMNO leaders of the rewards of patronage that were to be reaped. By the end of the year, the British were laying plans for a system of Asian shadow ministers, or 'Members'. The lineaments of the post-colonial order were coming into relief.

THE GENERATION OF 1950

This fragile alliance of ethnic interests was not the 'multiracial' nationalism that British idealists had wanted to fashion. This now seemed much further away than it had in 1945, and Gurney, for one, was deeply pessimistic that a truly 'Malayan' consciousness would ever emerge: its future lay in education and in the young. Not least of the battles of the Emergency was the struggle for the imagination of the new generation; the men and women who were to lead Malaya to independence. But this was also the generation that had been exposed to the full force of Japanese cultural warfare, to the mystique of patriotic resistance and the general assault on the corrupt, colonialist mentalities. The British tended to portray radical nationalists as emotional adolescents and communists as vicious delinquents. They recoiled at the indiscipline and hostility 'already noticeable in everyday street contact between Europeans and Chinese of the urchin variety or coolies who now often go out of their way to be rude without the least provocation.'[146] The schools themselves – the large Chinese high schools of Singapore and Penang in particular – were dominated by over-age students who had missed out on formal education during the war. Their schooling had been on the streets, in petty trade and politics. Most were old beyond their years, and resented that the only path to advancement in a colonial world was the English language. They did not see their future as becoming clerks in British companies. Often with the connivance of teachers, classmates set up study cells and circulated clandestine political writings. They devoured the patriotic literature of the National Salvation movement, but also Russian authors – Pushkin, Gogol, Tolstoy, Gorky – in cheap Chinese translations. It was, as one activist was later to recall, 'an eclectic mix of romantic, naturalist and realist writers, who wrote of oppression, struggle and freedom. It was a heady literary diet, quite different from the staple fare most English-educated students were exposed or accustomed to.'[147] In their spare time students remained part of the labour force, in which they were seen as something of an elite. Student broadsheets and hustings were schools for activism, and their leaders were the natural vanguard of a new wave of radical trade unionism. In 1955, when Singapore island was once again crippled by strikes, the governor struggled to explain to the colonial secretary why the British government was being held hostage by children.[148]

In no small way, the future of Britain's interests in the region was staked on the creation of a new elite in its own image: anglophone, Anglophile in outlook and committed to the Commonwealth connection. As a step towards this, on 8 October 1949 the new University of Malaya was opened. It was built as a symbol of 'national belonging' and pride. Significantly, Singapore was chosen as its site, rather than the neighbouring Malay capital of Johore Bahru, as was originally suggested. Malcolm MacDonald was its first proud chancellor, and the economic architect of the second colonial occupation, Sir Sydney Caine, soon arrived as its vice-chancellor. Within a year 645 students were registered at the new Dunearn Road campus.[149] It attracted a new generation of British educators to Malaya – 'pale young colonial men', wrote one of them, 'graduates of technical colleges, brought up on the W. E. A. and the Arts Councils, who have read all the appropriate Penguins and Pelicans'.[150] Many of them voiced a commitment to 'Malayan' culture. C. Northcote Parkinson, the first Raffles Professor of History, led research on Southeast Asia's past (and drew on his experience of colonial bureaucracy to formulate his famous 'Parkinson's Law': work expands to fill the time available for its completion). Under the influential Dean of Arts, E. H. G. Dobby, geography became a defining discipline, with surveys of the padi landscapes of Malaya and rapidly changing settlement patterns. Excavations resumed at sites such as the enigmatic Hindu remains of the Bujang valley in Kedah, and projected an ancient past for the new Malayan nation. Young local scholars cut their teeth in these endeavours; the economist Ungku Abdul Aziz, who had been schooled in wartime Japan, and the leading Malay literary figure of his generation, Za'ba, bristled in the hierarchical expatriate atmosphere. A highly coloured memoir of the campus by the English don Patrick Anderson captures well the missionary purpose and manifest contradictions of instilling a national culture through the English literary canon. So too, in a different way, do the travails of the dissolute schoolmaster, Victor Crabbe, in Anthony Burgess's Malayan Trilogy. As John Wilson, Burgess taught at the elite Malay College Kuala Kangsar and, in his spare time, published translations of Shakespeare in Malay. But these writings also give a sense of a social and intellectual world that was evolving out of the reach of the colonial opinion makers, and against which, in Anderson's words, 'the whites seem no more than photographs, acutely defined in terms of surface personality, but isolated and ephemeral'.[151]

The first post-war intake of students revived the platform of the Malayan Democratic Union.[152] In 1949 student publications from Raffles College, which along with King Edward VII Medical College was the core of the new university, attacked 'the opiate atmosphere' of colonial education and the cultural model of nationalism that was being thrust upon them by the British. The Malayan Democratic Union had explicitly warned against the creation of 'a miniature replica of Oxford or Cambridge' and demanded 'a focal point of Malayan cultural activities taking its bearing from the rich traditions of our people and the needs of their future development'.[153] Poetry and prose in English attempted to give expression to the polyglot world of the colonial city; as one early literary journal, New Cauldron, put it, it was 'a courageous attempt at synthesis between the conflicting currents'. Writers in English absorbed and tropicalized a wide range of influences from Palgrave's Golden Treasury to W. H. Auden and T. S. Eliot – 'a very clever gentleman, of course', the student poet and later historian, Wang Gungwu, mused to Patrick Anderson, 'but we in Malaya perhaps require something . . . a little more direct . . . and a little more explicit'.[154] Wang and his friends were later to experiment with a hybrid poetic language they called 'EngMalChin'. They also recognized that if such a synthesis was not possible, 'then we must start from scratch . . . with Malay as a basis'.[155] But as their critics pointed out, they themselves were 'cut off by intellectualisation from the mass of the common people', and inherited from the British the dilemma of how to impose a new national culture from on high.

As predicted, the first generation of undergraduates was to have an enduring, but also diverse, influence on the intellectual life of Malaya. But it was an unrepresentative group: only 10 per cent of the first cohort to enter the new campus were Malay. The university's much-vaunted meritocratic admissions policy disadvantaged Malay families who – through cultural pride or, more often, lack of choice – did not send their children to English-language schools. This point was driven home by 'C. H. E. Det', the future prime minister, Mahathir Mohamad, who was now a medical student, in his newspaper column, and it later became an argument for mandatory Malay 'quotas' in higher education. The Chinese-educated remained unreconciled to colonial curricula. However, radical students such as James Puthucheary kept alive contacts with Malay intellectuals. The principal channel for this after 1948 was the newspaper *Utusan Melayu*, which remained the vanguard of Malay anti-colonial opinion. Its editor, A. Samad Ismail, never placed himself in the foreground of Malay radicalism, but was at the centre of a network of correspondents from upcountry towns, and a web of cosmopolitan friendships. These began to include the new generation of activists from the Chinese schools and trade unions. The coming man was Lim Chin Siong. In 1949, aged sixteen, after a childhood spent mostly in rural Johore, he entered Tan Kah Kee's foundation, the Chinese High School in Singapore. Within two years he would take the lead in student protests and be expelled for subversion. With a personal mythology grounded in the patriotic resistance to Japan, a trenchant anti-colonialism and a charismatic oratory rooted in the demotic Hokkien dialect of the urban working class, Lim Chin Siong would come to personify the politics of this new generation. He led popular campaigns in defence of Chinese culture, and against registration for national service ('Listen friends, only dogs have licences and numbers'). The British dismissed these student activists as Chinese 'chauvinists', but Lim Chin Siong also won the respect and trust of the Malay left for his advocacy of Malay as a national language rather than English. 'He appeared in the sky of history', eulogized the Malay 'people's laureate', Usman Awang, 'as a shining star in the sky of time.'[156] The united front had dissolved, but its trans-ethnic patriotic vision was never lost, or wholly defeated.

The underground remnants of the Singapore Town Committee of the Malayan Communist Party tried to reconnect to this world. Under Ah Chin, the son of a Penang hawker, it was in tenuous contact by dead-letter boxes and couriers with the Party leadership in south Malaya, and was ordered to undertake acts of sabotage and arson to create economic chaos and tie up British resources. A young woman from a wealthy Perak family, Ah Har, was given responsibility for re-establishing links with the intellectuals. Only three of the Malayan Democratic Union leaders had taken to the jungle in late June 1948. Many of the older members, such as Philip Hoalim, repudiated the movement, but others remained sympathetic to the MCP's claims to be at the forefront of national struggle. The key figure was thirty-year-old Eu Chooi Yip, who took a leading role in the formation of an 'Anti-British League'. He was one of the most able activists of his time: Tan Cheng Lock had even invited him to be the organizing secretary of the Malayan Chinese Association. Eu Chooi Yip began to recruit from Malayan Democratic Union members, many of whom were already steeped in socialism, and to lead them to Marxism. Two important recruits to the Anti-British League were P. V. Sharma, a Brahmin schoolteacher who had championed the employment rights of Asian educators in relation to their expatriate counterparts, and John Eber. After the climactic events of May 1948 Eber had taken a eight-month holiday in Australia and New Zealand; when he returned he continued to lobby the Colonial Office for immediate self-government but, convinced that the British saw independence as far distant, he too threw in his lot with the Anti-British League. From a loft in Eber's house Eu Chooi Yip produced *Freedom News*, perhaps the most sophisticated propaganda mouthpiece of the MCP. The League made inroads into the University of Malaya, and even among junior civil servants. In the Chinese schools activists such as Lim Chin Siong were equally receptive. By January 1951 thirty-six League members were groomed for admission to the MCP itself.[157] But this incipient united front never reached the breadth of organization that was achieved between 1945 and 1948. Special Branch smashed the organization in 1951 with another spate of arrests, including John Eber, James Puthucheary and A. Samad Ismail. After their release two years later, P. V. Sharma went into exile in India and Eber went to London. Eu Chooi Yip remained underground in Singapore and then Indonesia, only to return to Singapore in the early 1990s. In London, another Malayan Democratic Union leader in exile, Lim Hong Bee, had, with the help of ex-national serviceman friends, become an unofficial roving representative for the MCP. At a 'Malayan Forum', the radicals debated the nation's future with a new breed of anti-communist student leaders of whom the Fabian-inclined Cambridge-trained lawyer Lee Kuan Yew was the most prominent. Lee had been absent during most of the struggles of the past three years in Malaya. He returned after 1950 to a much narrower political arena and tempered his anti-colonialism accordingly. Over the next twelve or so years, Lee Kuan Yew and his friends were to ally themselves with Chinese-educated leaders such as Lim Chin Siong in order to harness mass support. But this also marked the beginning of a new and desperate struggle for control of the independence movement on the island that would last over a decade. During it, Lee Kuan Yew employed the spectre of communism and the methods of colonial counter-insurgency to prevail. In defeat, and in long years of detention and exile, Lim Chin Siong and a great many of his generation were to carry 'an unerasable Communist stigma'.[158]

In 1949, of the Malay radicals, the only leader of consequence who remained outside jail was Burhanuddin al-Helmy. At its fourth and final annual conference in January 1949, Dr Burhanuddin spoke of the Malay Nationalist Party as 'fighting a cold war with the authorities'.[159] Mustapha Hussain remained at liberty, but on strict police conditions. He brokered a meeting between Burhanuddin and Special Branch to ease the tension. But Pak Doktor and the Malay Nationalist Party were under notice and Mustapha Hussain was already an example of how hard life could be for a former detainee. He ran a stall selling noodles and sweet tea at the Sunday market in Kampong Bahru in Kuala Lumpur. His former students were embarrassed to meet him in the street. But he learnt how to tailor his dishes to the tastes of the different communities who patronized his stall, and it became a popular haunt for politicians, journalists, cabaret artistes, dancing girls and European policemen. Next door, a former leader of AWAS, Aishah Ghani, also owned a restaurant. Mustapha Hussain's stall was watched by the Special Branch, but his high-profile patrons seem to have given him some protection. This was all one with the curious intimacy that grew up between the secret police and their prey. The trade union adviser John Brazier even brought a visiting Labour MP, Woodrow Wyatt, to eat there, and to talk politics with Mustapha: it turned out that he had read Wyatt's *Theories and Practices of Socialism*. Visiting nationalists from Burma and India also sought him out. 'Is there another place', he wrote, 'apart from the Left Bank in Paris, where so many artists and performers from all walks of cultural pursuit gather at a dilapidated stall?' Then there were other, more unwelcome visitors. On a busy Saturday night in 1949 a young man known to Mustapha rushed into his shop, thrust a note into his hand and promptly disappeared into the crowd. The paper was wrapped in wax, the message written in Arabic script in red ink: 'You are required to set up a third force as soon as possible. *Benzin* will be sent' (literally 'petrol' or, in Indonesian slang, money). It was signed 'IBHY': Ibrahim Haji Yaacob, the lost leader of the Malay radicals who had fled to Indonesia in August 1945 in a Japanese plane. No *benzin* came and Mustapha did nothing. Ibrahim was now a wealthy Jakarta businessman. Too many of Mustapha's comrades were in detention, and he himself, as he put it, 'still had one foot in the drain'.[160] But it was to Indonesia and into the hands of Ibrahim Haji Yaacob that the leadership of the Malay Nationalist Party passed when it was finally dissolved on the peninsula in early 1950. Ibrahim himself did not return to Malaya until shortly before his death in 1979.

In the invisible city, the embers of radicalism still smouldered. There was, from around this time, a large influx of Malay migrants to the towns, particularly to Singapore. The island was at least a haven from the full weight of the oppressive Emergency Regulations; it remained the principal centre for publishing and entertainment, and it was in these fields that many of the new arrivals found employment. The poet Usman Awang was one of the Malay policemen on duty to witness the triumphal rally of the Malay Nationalist Party in Malacca in December 1946; he threw up his job and drifted into the world of letters in Singapore. The novelist and short-story writer Keris Mas, who succeeded Ahmad Boestamam as leader of Malay Nationalist Party youth, now worked beside A. Samad Ismail at *Utusan Melayu*. The short-story form was easily adapted to newspaper columns, and at a time when events could not be fully reported, fiction became an important way of representing actuality. Where overt political propaganda was dangerous, writers were encouraged to engage more deeply with social themes. They adopted a symbolic and allusive literary language; in the words of the poet Masuri S. N., 'parcels so wrapped up that it became difficult to grasp their message'. They learnt how a national culture might flourish under conditions of strict censorship. In this way, the anti-colonial, anti-feudal message of the Malay Nationalist Party found an outlet. Young writers quietly forged a new language, purged of status terms, in which the people were addressed as equals. They coined new borrow-words to modernize and urbanize the Malay language; to create a language that was *realistik* and showed *inisiatif*.[161] Poets and storytellers – emulating Chairil Anwar and his Indonesian *pemuda* contemporaries – created 'art for society', and the following year Keris Mas and other writers in Singapore took the lead in forming an Angkatan Sasterawan 50 – Generation of 1950 – that would, over time, play a crucial role in defining a national culture.

This was the quiet beginning of a second wave of independence struggle, one that would carry on beyond the formal transfer of power: the decolonization of the mind. The impact of this movement stretched beyond print to performance. In these years the theatre took a scripted form and the Malay cinema became a new vehicle for exploring social and national agendas. It was the invisible city brought to life; the life of the streets and the urban villages featured heavily in the new films. Most dramatically of all, the Malay cinema became a new vehicle for exploring social and political themes. It reached beyond its language stream and built on the hybrid, polyglot style of the Malay opera. Malay movies spun tales of the wartime underground and brought the urban fantasy of the Worlds, the entertainment parks, to life: indeed, the cabaret was a staple backdrop for early social dramas. The Shaw brothers' film *Nighttime in Singapore*, directed by B. S. Raghans – a graduate of the Indian National Army's wartime propaganda school in Penang – had settings at the Padang and the New World. In *Seruan Merdeka*, Bachtiar Effendi – a leading 'culture warrior' for the Japanese during the war – played a police informer.[162] The Shaw brothers and Loke Wan Tho ran rival racing stables, and rival film studios with their own small galaxies of stars. Politics retreated into popular culture. But this urban world was beginning to vanish almost at the moment it came to life on the silver screen. Ever since the anarchic days of the British Military Administration, the authorities had been cleaning up the streets. After 1948 the uniform flats of the Singapore Improvement Trust would remap dramatically the urban landscape of Singapore. It was an ambitious programme of urban regeneration, but it was executed in much the same way as the resettlement of squatters on the peninsula, as an emergency measure, and, for much the same reasons, as a strategy of social control.[163] The cosmopolitan world of the village-city – which had moulded Malaya's politics for a generation – began to recede.

The generation of 1950, born into a world of radically expanding horizons, came of age in a time of shrinking political opportunities. Keris Mas, in his famous story 'A would-be leader from Kuala Semantan', captured one of central political dilemmas of his generation. In it a young radical, Hasan, confides his doubts as to whether or not to join the struggle in the jungle.

He hated violence, yet violence was everywhere, inside the jungle and out. He loved freedom, yet he was pursued by circumstances which imposed upon him and his society. He was committed to only one thing, truth. And a man without freedom has no way of obtaining truth.

'Perhaps I am a coward!' – once more the explosion of Hasan's thoughts shattered the stillness of the night.

Perhaps he's a coward . . . the explosion reverberated inside my head.

'Is it cowardly to hate violence?' asked Hasan finally. The words vanished into the night.

I had no conclusion of my own with which to reply.

Kuala Semantan, in Pahang, was a centre of MCP support among the Malays. In 1949, for a brief moment, Malay support for the insurrection seemed to be growing and party propaganda attacked the 'white man' instead of the capitalist and promised *Merdeka*.[164] Villages along the Pahang river, around Temerloh, were dangerous badlands, and infused with the memory of the heroes of the first British conquest. This was the worst nightmare of the British. For the first time a recording of the voice of a Malay sultan, the ruler of Pahang, was broadcast to calm the area.[165] On 21 May a new regiment of the MNLA was formed: the 10th Regiment, under the command of Abdullah C. D., as political commissar. The Malay radicals who had taken to the jungle rallied under its banner. It was seen as a major triumph by the Party: a goal 'realised for the first time in the twenty years of Malaya's revolutionary struggle ... This solid fact has also smashed to smithereens all those anti-revolutionary arguments concerning the backwardness of Malayan peasants.'[166] Abdullah C. D. was ordered by Chin Peng to mobilize recruits, and managed to raise nearly 500 Malays by early 1950. The British need for information was now 'desperate': 'the reign of terror established by Malay banditry', it was reported from the area, 'is quite extraordinary': they even took the unprecedented step of paying money to those Malays whose property was destroyed for helping the British.[167] A camp near Jerantut was broken up by military action – led by Chinese ex-Force 136 personnel – and the remnants were dispersed in much smaller numbers. It was a serious setback. The alliance of the Malay peasant and the Chinese worker failed just at the time the feudalists and the capitalists, in the shape of UMNO and the MCA, were coming together. There were other centres, in Jenderam in Selangor, the site of the Peasants' Congress in May 1948, where at least eighteen villagers joined the MNLA, eleven of whom died in the jungle.[168] The 10th Regiment remained a demon to haunt the British.

But the MNLA was locked in the jungle fastness, and coming to terms with the fact that its fight would drag on for many years. 'Throughout the history of the world', it warned, 'one can never find a simple and easy revolutionary struggle. So revolutionary wars, in particular, must necessarily be full of difficulties, obstructions and dangers.'[169] By the end of 1949, the number of incidents began to rise again. As Chin Peng later acknowledged: 'If I had to pick a high point in our military campaign, I suppose it would be around this time. But it would be a high point without euphoria and it would be short lived.' The MNLA turned increasingly towards smaller-scale operations against remote rural targets. With reinforcements from Johore, the Pahang guerrillas launched exploratory raids on isolated police stations. But even this strength was insufficient to make an impact on fixed positions.[170] There were some dramatic incidents, but the MCP never gained the initiative in the 'shooting war'. Its defeats and reverses in 1948 and 1949 proved fatal. The diminishing food supplies meant that its units were steadily broken into ever smaller contingents. As the effects of resettlement began to bite, conditions in the forest deteriorated sharply. The Party leadership's core strategic assumption was that the squatters would swell the ranks of the revolution. But already relations between the party and the rural people had deteriorated from what they had been during the war. Then, the MPAJA had acted as protectors of communities from the Japanese. They enabled them to eke out a living in the face of shortages and sudden violence. Chin Peng, for one, had assumed that the forced movement of people by the British would fail, just as similar schemes by the Japanese had failed. The central strategic assumption of the revolution was that the villages would rise in resistance to the British. But the MNLA could offer them little protection from an equally tenacious and better-equipped regime. Peasant resistance was futile, the Malayan revolution foundered on a false premise. As the Emergency dragged on, the communists became an increasing liability to their most natural supporters, and there was little prospect that this burden could be lifted. The British watched the borders closely, and despite their propaganda to the contrary, there was virtually no infiltration in support of the MCP by land or sea. Chin Peng was in contact with the Chinese Communist Party by a secret postal service in code. Some cadres who were suffering from tuberculosis were sent to China for medical treatment; the expectation was that they could brief their Chinese comrades, receive instruction and then return to Malaya. But none made their way back until the late 1950s. The Malayan revolution – unlike the revolution in Vietnam – had to fall back entirely on its internal resources, and had already begun to eat its own.

The Party leadership was now facing open criticism. Two critics in the southern leadership sparked what became known as the 'South Johore incident'. Siew Lau was a schoolteacher and intellectual. In 1949 he produced a pamphlet, 'The keynote of the Malayan revolution'. He argued that the Party had misunderstood and misapplied Mao's tenets of 'New Democracy'. They had not built up a wide enough coalition of support across all communities. The lack of Malay support had 'doomed the revolution from the start'. There was no coherent programme of land distribution of the peasantry. He attacked the 'buffalo communists' on the Central Committee, and his polemic came with a call for elections for a new committee. Siew Lau went as far as to hold a meeting in November to discuss his ideas. The Party leadership demanded that he recant. Siew Lau tried to escape with his wife and some followers to Sumatra, but was caught and executed. 'Siew Lau', the leadership pronounced, 'had proved himself impossible.' Another figure involved was Lam Swee, a former vice-president of the Singapore Federation of Trade Unions. Chin Peng later argued that his alienation was as much the consequence of ambition as of doctrinal dissent. The following year Lam Swee became one of the most high-profile surrenders to the British. Both these incidents were the subject of early attempts at black propaganda by the British against the Party.[171] But ordinary rank-and-file members were voicing similar complaints at the arrogance and privileges of the high command, leaders of which ordinary Party members had only the haziest notion. The party's once formidable apparatus for political education went into steep decline. As one early defector put it: 'I was treated like a coolie.'[172] By February 1953 986 communists had taken advantage of amnesty terms. In such circumstances, the mood of paranoia and betrayal that had so dogged the Party since the war became deeper still.

The last year of a troubled decade ended with the beginning of a series of long marches for the Malayan Communist Party. It drew on legends of the Japanese war to sustain morale. Within the jungle, songs and commemorations kept the dream alive, such as the marking of the legendary 1 September 1942 Batu Caves massacre, with a '91' oath to reaffirm loyalty. It was a morality tale of strength in adversity that encouraged a belief in the inevitability of victory, a faith that sustained the MNLA, even when it suffered severe reverses.[173] But its leaders knew that there was no road back: it was too late to break up the army and return to civilian life. They pressed ahead, hoping that some sudden shift in conditions within Malaya would occur, that a new wave of labour unrest might paralyse the country and allow them to take over. But neither this nor a dramatic widening of Malay support materialized. The Party's 1 October 1951 directives – the product of two months of self-criticism by Chin Peng and his small politburo – openly acknowledged that the initial campaign of terror, the slashing of rubber trees and the destruction of identification cards, had hit hardest the Party's own sympathizers. The MCP still looked to rebuild its political base, to attempt to recapture influence in the towns and revive the united front. But its fighting units began to withdraw into the deep jungle interior. Chin Peng and his dwindling headquarters was harassed from near Mentekab through a series of camps northwards to Raub, then to the Cameron Highlands and eventually, in the last weeks of 1953, compromised by betrayals from comrades in the pay of the Special Branch, he passed over the Thai border. The area around the Betong Salient remained the redoubt of the Malayan revolution until December 1989, when a peace treaty was finally signed in the Thai town of Haadyai. 'I never admit that's a failure', Chin Peng said later. 'It's a temporary setback . . .' But by this point guerrilla morale was deteriorating in many places, and more defections occurred. From this position the MCP could prolong the war indefinitely, but it could not win it. 'I don't think there was any opportunity of our success,' reflected Chin Peng. 'Without foreign aid, we could not defeat the British army, even if we expanded our forces to 10,000 . . . the most was to continue to carry out the guerrilla warfare.' The Party was now fighting for honour and for posterity, awaiting a general Asian uprising that would never come.

Epilogue: The End of Britain's Asian Empire

In 2007, as the 'Asian century' begins and the economies of the crescent from India to Singapore are booming, it is difficult to imagine the scale of suffering and conflict that occurred during and after the Second World War in Asia. For much of the region, August 1945 was at best a hiatus in the fighting, and for many people the worst was yet to come. The continuing toll remained heaviest on civilians; the number of deaths from war-related famine in India, Indo-China and south China alone was close to 6 million. Millions more were driven from their homes and countries during the war and the numerous petty but lethal conflicts that surged on for decades in its aftermath. With the fall of Japan, the Great Asian War entered a new phase: it became a struggle against Western imperialism and its allies; a war for national freedom and for a new ordering of society. What gave the years from 1945 to 1949 their peculiar epochal quality was a sense of being part of a great acceleration in time, of living at a moment of unprecedented change. The days of Japanese occupation had a millennial edge to them; but any promise of peace and righteousness was soon destroyed by repression, exploitation and hunger. The fall of Japan came when many societies were at their lowest ebb: battle scarred, battle hardened, at war with one another. But as the Malay radical Mustapha Hussain had earlier reflected, 'although the Japanese Occupation was described as one of severe hardship and brutality, it left something positive, a sweet fruit to be plucked and enjoyed only after the surrender'.[1] Now history seemed open, at a juncture when the peoples of colonial Asia could shape their own future as they had not been able to do within living memory.

As the British sought to regain their Asian empire, they were confronted by myriad mutinies against old patterns of authority. This was Asia's revolutionary moment when many previously disempowered groups in society – women, the young, workers and peasants – took the political initiative, for a time, as they tried to rebuild their communities, salvage their livelihoods and regain their dignity. They joined movements that were fired by radical ideologies – social democracy, religious revival, Marxism and Maoism – and these doctrines reacted with each other in a dangerous alchemy. It was, to use the phraseology of the Indonesian *pergerakan*, or movement, an age in motion, a world upside-down. New leaders addressed an often bewildered people in exhilarating new language. In the words of the Malay radicals:

The People's Constitution of PUTERA is based on elections, *kedaulatan rakyat* [sovereignty of the people], and moves towards social justice, and egalitarianism, without upper and lower classes in the *bangsa* [nation] except according to the capability, intelligence and industry of the individual. We hope in this matter the *rakyat* no longer have any doubts, but instead have more faith in the struggle and loyalty to their respective movements. Because of this we appeal once more, struggle onwards with a fiery spirit, but with a cool head until the sacred aims that we aspire to are achieved. Remember, comrades, that the world is changing fast and we cannot live with the understandings and feelings that we had in the year 1941. We are now in the year 1947 in the atomic age, the old era has passed.[2]

For many, this sense of possibility, this call to be the agents of historical change, was irresistible.

Everywhere men and women were still in arms. During the Second World War the Allies and the Japanese had armed and militarized many ethnic minorities whose identities had previously conformed only loosely to the labels applied by colonial administrators and anthropologists. Karens, Kachins, Shans, Chins, Nagas and, in Malaya, the Orang Asli all now possessed weapons, military know-how and identifiable enemies to rally against. Many of the local soldiers who took part in these actions had been displaced by the ending of the international war and were hungry for combat and special operations. Militant nationalists, communists and Islamists were still continuing to fight for their vision of the good society among the ravaged and hungry peasant communities and impoverished townspeople. The aims of the radicals and ethnic leaderships were constrained by their limited range, but the war also left its imprint on the aims and conduct of the leaders of the dominant emerging nationalities. Coercion, summary execution and assassination were the orders of the day. And unlike western Europe, where the American military blanket had established stability and a respite from war, the returning colonial powers in Southeast Asia had triggered or participated in a host of further conflicts. Where the colonial powers had been forced to withdraw, as in India, Indonesia and Burma, the creation of national states seemed like the continuation of war by other means.

Yet whilst these struggles – these forgotten wars – were by no means over by 1949, there was by the end of the decade a palpable sense that one era of conflict was coming to an end and another beginning. The freedom struggles in Asia were being eclipsed and overtaken by another global confrontation. By 1949, with the Berlin airlift and signing of the North Atlantic Treaty, the battles lines were drawn in Europe for the Cold War. As the Iron Curtain came down, eastern and western Europe settled to a superficially peaceful period of stand-off and suspicion under the shadow of the atomic bomb and the Red Army. After 1949 American Marshall Plan aid and, later, the initiatives of the European Economic Community began to spread a fragile prosperity, at least in the west of the continent. In Asia, by contrast, the political and economic future was much less predictable. By 1949 some struggles, at least, seemed to have been resolved. The new regime in Beijing had reunified most of China, and in New Delhi Nehru governed the world's largest popular democracy. Yet these massive political achievements spawned new and equally vicious wars. China's Red Army, unlike its Soviet counterpart, had not imposed a peace on the countries beyond its borders, and within them Mao Zedong's communists began their programme of liquidating China's landlords. To the west the leaderships of India and Pakistan began a pointless series of wars over the possession of the Muslim-majority state of Kashmir. The revival of the Japanese economy and the cease-less toil of the hardy Indian and Chinese business communities saw a slow trickle of the lifeblood of trade back into cities such as Singapore and Kuala Lumpur. But most of Asia's people remained desperately poor. And with the looming confrontation on the Korean peninsula, Asia was to experience the Cold War at its most heated.

The Cold War brought new violence to the end of empires as the local struggles in Southeast Asia were now seen as a part of a global chain of conflicts between the two power blocs. Reduced in political might and fearing the spread of communism, the waning colonial powers – Britain, France and the Netherlands – redeployed the weapons of the Second World War in the guise of counter-insurgency campaigns in those territories where they retained a fragile hold. As a result the hopes for liberal democracy that had sustained for decades colonial nationalists and European liberals alike were largely dashed. The advocates of social revolution were now fighting for their lives. The Malayan Emergency saw a retreat by the British government from a liberal, late colonialism towards a police state. By the end of the next decade soldiers and their associated ideologues were poised to take power in Burma, Indonesia and Pakistan. Even in India, the republic's fragility in its early years resulted in a dangerous slowing down of radical political and economic change. National and social revolutions had either run into obstacles or been only partially accomplished. The old bureaucracies lived to fight another day.

In the midst of this, Britain's Asian empire survived. But, increasingly, the United States was taking over key strategic responsibilities in parts of Asia which for a century had fallen to the Pax Britannica. Not yet an empire itself, America was now the arbiter of others. American economic pressure on the Dutch forced them to withdraw from most of Indonesia. This was dictated by Cold War logic, to prevent the Indonesian revolution lurching to the left, and the same logic led to the United States' commitment to support British colonial rule while it was containing communism in Malaya. A major review of Britain's long-term policy in Southeast Asia for the cabinet in October 1949 continued to see a British role there as indispensable to world peace, but it also acknowledged that 'no plans will, however, be really successful without American participation'.[3] On these terms, the British imperial presence endured in Malaya until 1957, in Singapore for five years after this, and in Hong Kong for another forty years.

But these were insular outposts and no longer a great territorial empire. By 1949 British Asia – the great crescent of land that four years earlier had linked Suez to Sydney in one overarching, cosmopolitan swathe – had collapsed. Its last great proconsul, Louis Mountbatten, had finally left the region. The old Indian Army was dismantled. The new sovereign nations of India, Pakistan and Ceylon (though not Burma) remained in the British Commonwealth of Nations. But this was a fragile, racially divided entity, and many more concrete linkages in the region were severed. The route from India to China, via the Burma Road, was closed, and these two emerging Asian superpowers squared up to each other along the line drawn in the Himalayas by the Victorian soldier Sir Henry McMahon. A world of travel and movement was finally stilled. After the last traumatic crossings in the wake of partition in south Asia and the revolutionary struggles in the southeast and east of the continent, most movements thereafter would be within borders. The 'George Washington of the Overseas Chinese', Tan Kah Kee, had returned to China and would die in Beijing in 1961. Never again would the Overseas Chinese act as a unified force. The new Indian republic still looked to play a role in the region, but this too was increasingly shaped by Cold War concerns. In 1950 Nehru again visited Singapore, bringing with him his daughter, Indira. More so than in 1946, the British welcomed his visit; he arrived in the wash of Anglo-Indian naval manoeuvres in the Bay of Bengal, and the British hoped he would voice support for their counter-insurgency. Nehru's reception by the locals was warm, but it was a faint echo of the triumphant progress of 1946. His speeches signalled the changes: 'Indians in Malaya', he announced, 'should not look to India for any help; neither is India in a position to render any because she has her own problems to solve and her own population to look after.'[4] Nehru told a rally in Jalan Besar, where he had spoken in 1946: 'We have seen plenty of killing and become rather callous but this method of terrorism is degrading to the whole human race and reduced men to the level of beasts.' 'In the present day', he explained, 'governments have to deal with all kinds of violence and force and inevitably they have to deal with that with force.'[5]

FREEDOM, SLOWLY AND GENTLY

The British war in Malaya would drag on until 1960 and eventually claim the lives of 6,697 CTs 'communist terrorists' (not all of whom were combatants), 1,865 members of the security forces, most of them Malay policeman, and 2,473 civilians, most of them Chinese.[6] The fury of counter-terror did not abate. In the second year of the Emergency veterans of clandestine warfare or colonial police operations in the Middle East and Africa continued to gravitate to Malaya. On the recommendation of Field Marshal Slim, Colonel 'Mad Mike' Calvert, who had been second-in-command to Orde Wingate in Burma, was sent in 1950 to review the situation. On an early foray into the forest he was welcomed by a grenade, lobbed at him with the pin still in. To it was attached the message: 'How do you do, Mr Calvert'. The Emergency remained a very personal war. 'I went to the brothels and picked up the gossip of the gutter', he recalled, and after six months he delivered a tough-minded report. British troops, he concluded, lacked aggression. One Scots Guards officer was allegedly heard to say that it was not his job 'just to chase bare-arsed niggers around South East Asia'. Calvert recommended the formation of a deep-jungle penetration force, which included Orang Asli.[7] From this the Special Air Squadron was revived as 'The Malayan Scouts (SAS Regiment)'. They adopted a Malay *kris* as their emblem, but the ethos and philosophy was that of the Chindits: informal, unorthodox and hard living. By September 1950 the Malayan Scouts camp at Dusun Tua was filled with ex-Chindits, volunteer national servicemen and unruly elements from other units of which their commanding officers were trying to rid themselves. It even attracted a group of French foreign legionnaires who had deserted en route to Indo-China. Still the foe was elusive; one eight-week training mission from October 1950 brought no contact with the insurgents, and the unit attracted press criticism and the hostility of other units over its lax discipline, wild parties and the wearing of beards. New drafts for the SAS from the United Kingdom were appalled, and Calvert was recalled.[8] In late 1951 the force was reorganized by Lieutenant Colonel John Sloane and many of the locally recruited men were sent back to their units. But from this a highly specialized form of warfare evolved, fought by shock troops, in which guerrilla warfare was met with its own methods.[9]

This was not a war which the British could win alone: in mid-November 1951, there were deployed in Malaya seven British infantry battalions, eight Gurkha battalions, three 'colonial' battalions and the Malayan Scouts, two Royal Armoured Corps regiments, one Royal Marine commando brigade, four battalions of the Malay Regiment, ten RAF squadrons, two Royal Australian Air Force squadrons and a small naval contingent. This reliance on imperial auxiliaries remained controversial and nearly collapsed when Nepalese communists campaigned to dissuade young men from joining the Gurkhas and Indian opposition parties in the Lok Sabha pressurized Nehru to end the use of the 'sacred soil' of India to recruit for the war in Malaya.[10] The British looked further afield. Calvert had preferred Australian and Rhodesian recruits, in whom he felt the frontier spirit of empire still burned. He even travelled to apartheid South Africa to seek new drafts of men. But white troops were expensive. Instead, the first African units of the King's African Rifles arrived in 1951 and would rotate in Malaya for the next few years. But for the Mau Mau rebellion, more of these *askaris* would have been sent. Most had joined for the improved pay and allowances, but they had a tough time in Malaya. It was fallaciously assumed that Africans were 'natural' jungle fighters, but the conditions were entirely new to them. So too was the diet. They were supplied from Australia with an 'African' maize meal, *posho*, which was often too roughly or finely ground for their taste. They were viewed with suspicion on all sides. In the field they were put to the task of 'shamba bashing' – the destruction of food crops in the jungle – and the communists put it about that they were cannibals. The *askaris* were poorly paid compared to the Gurkhas and Fijian soldiers, the latter mostly volunteers from the poor lesser islands. The Africans were given large bonuses to make up the difference, but they still chafed at their humiliating, inferior khaki uniforms: which had no collar, pockets, belt loops or fly. 'They were insulting', one veteran would recall, '. . . and brought us no respect'. When the Maasai education officer who led the protests against the uniforms was threatened with court martial his *askaris* promised him that they would 'take care' of any difficult officers on the next jungle patrol. The scragging of officers was not unheard of in the Burma campaign. Veterans of 3 King's African Rifles were later to attribute their sympathy with the Mau Mau to their experience of the anti-colonial struggle in Asia.[11]

Despite these reinforcements, there were times during the MNLA's flurry of small-scale raids in 1950 and 1951 when the British felt that they were losing the war. There was little co-ordination between the army and police, the chief police officer and the director of intelligence were not on speaking terms, the morale of European civilians was breaking and the rural Chinese seemed entirely indifferent to the government. In 1950 there was an attempt on the life of the governor of Singapore, Sir Franklin Gimson, at Happy World amusement park, where he was adjudicating a boxing competition. The grenades failed to explode and he escaped with a bruised leg. But on 6 October 1951 the MNLA scored its most dramatic success. In the early afternoon a guerrilla unit ambushed a Rolls-Royce bearing a crown insignia and the Federation flag, driving behind a police Land Rover on the narrow winding ascent up to the colonial playground of Frazer's Hill. It seems that the attack was unplanned and that the guerrillas did not know that they had stumbled on the most valuable prey of all, the high commissioner himself. Sir Henry Gurney faced the attack with courage and presence of mind, drawing fire away from his wife, who survived the attack by crouching in the car, which was riddled with thirty-five bullet holes. Gurney was shot in the head and the body and died almost instantly. His escort was stranded further down the road due to a mechanical fault. Gurney was the last colonial governor to be killed in office, and his death was another augury of the passing of liberal imperialism.[12] The news broke in the middle of a general election campaign in Britain, and in December the new Conservative colonial secretary, Oliver Lyttelton, toured Malaya to assess the situation for himself. When he visited Ipoh on 5 December to meet planters he was protected by 350 policemen and troops and driven from Ipoh airfield in a closed armoured car with an escort of six others. There a Chinese tin miner, Foo Yin Fong, told him that the Chinese villagers distrusted the police, who treated them with no respect, and that the resettlement officers 'paid little attention to Chinese customs and feelings, and appeared not to regard them as human beings'.[13] On his return Lyttelton delivered a stinging verdict on the failings of administration in Malaya. This was reinforced by a minute from Montgomery: 'We must have a plan,' he told Lyttelton. 'Secondly, we must have a man.'[14]

The man with the plan was General Sir Gerald Templer, a former director of military intelligence with experience of civil affairs on a large scale in crisis-ridden post-war Germany, during which he had famously sacked Konrad Adenauer as mayor of Cologne.[15] He was not the first choice. Slim, for one, had ruled himself out as being 'too old to go flipping around in an Auster aircraft in the trying climate of Malaya'. There were rumours that Montgomery himself had been asked to go. Malcolm MacDonald, in Singapore, was alarmed at the prospect of 'military dictatorship'. Templer was, and remains, a controversial figure. In some accounts he is credited with a mastery of the crisis that has few parallels in British colonial history. The historian C. Northcote Parkinson saw in him a Shakespearean hero. His most savage critic was the architect of the Malayan Spring, Victor Purcell, who was also a history don, at Cambridge, who returned to Malaya in 1953 as an adviser to the Malayan Chinese Association. He wrote a series of articles and a polemical book, *Malaya: communist or free?*, in which he accused Templer of authoritarian, even quasi-fascist methods: 'a terrifying mixture of crassness and voodoo'.[16] Their feud was bitter and personal, although Purcell was merely articulating what many Chinese leaders such as Tan Cheng Lock thought but felt unable to say directly and publicly. From this Templer emerges perhaps more plausibly as a useful if limited man, favoured by fortune and riding the tide of achievement of his predecessors; in the words of one Malayan civil servant, 'a *facile princeps*'.[17] Templer embodied Britain's counter-insurgency in a way that Gurney had been unable to do. In his hands – as both high commissioner and director of operations – was concentrated more power than had been possessed by any British general since Oliver Cromwell. He used it to create a new integrated system of command and a functioning intelligence system, to cut through red tape, official parochialism and jealousies and to facilitate new specialist initiatives. He was constantly in the field, where his presence was likened to the charismatic dynamism of Marshal de Lattre de Tassigny in Indo-China, and he took strong stands against diehard employers and colonial prejudice.[18] In a hallmark incident, he threatened to run the committee of the elite Kuala Lumpur Lake Club out of town when they barred the Sultan of Selangor, as an 'Asiatic', from attending a St George's day function in his own realm.

But Templer was a blunt instrument. One of his first actions following his arrival in March 1952 was to direct personally a draconian collective punishment operation against the town of Tanjong Malim, the scene of heavy guerrilla activity where recent government casualties had included a hero of 'the wooden horse' POW escapade, Lieutenant R. M. C. Codner. Templer would descend on truculent resettlement areas to parade and berate their inhabitants. In one famous incident he began, 'You are all bastards.' A Chinese interpreted: 'His Excellency says that none of your parents were married.' 'Well', continued Templer, 'I can be a bastard too.' 'His Excellency says his parents were also unmarried.'[19] But as he himself admitted, Templer was building on the foundations of the work of Gurney and others. The key component of the campaign – resettlement on a mass scale – had been begun in earnest in Gurney's time by Sir Harold Briggs, who was pulled out of retirement after his campaigns in Burma to become the first director of operations. He developed a plan to 'roll up' Malaya from the south.[20] This began in, as those responsible admitted, an experimental and 'rough and ready' fashion in June 1950 in Johore. As one European resident put it: 'This fair land is now, it would appear, in danger of becoming infested with a series of untidy, shabby shanty towns: a succession of inferior Butlin's camps but lacking the amenities.'[21] The programme was largely completed by the end of 1952. What Templer achieved was co-ordination of Emergency work with the everyday business of government. He also possessed a stronger mandate from Whitehall, and a clearer appreciation of the impending advance of self-government. This added a new dynamism to local politics that had been paralysed by the Emergency. Again, there was little new in the letter of Templer's statements on the transfer of power delivered on his installation in Kuala Lumpur; the commitment was already there. But Templer set about executing it with the briskness of a country solicitor winding up a heavily entailed estate.[22]

The counter-insurgency regime created by the British in Malaya was perhaps the most ambitious undertaking of any colonial state. In the 'New Villages' – which became the new official euphemism – health services, sports halls and village councils were introduced; propaganda acquired a new relevance and the official vernacular embraced new terms such as 'community development' – a vague catch-all for a miscellany of initiatives in leadership training, by which, in the words of one official, the people were to be 'suitably instructed towards their own emancipation'.[23] A favoured keyword of Templer himself was 'service'; it began with a scheme to make the police appear more friendly to the community, inspired, it was said, by the scene in *The Wizard of Oz* where a lion is made brave after receiving a medal for courage. Templer had been a keen Boy Scout, from which experience he seems to have drawn many of his ideas; his wife, Peggy, lent her patronage to the Women's Institutes, in which elite wives brought their home skills to the New Villages and *kampongs*. Purcell felt 'service' to be a particularly pernicious substitute for the development of democratic institutions. All this entailed a massive expansion of government outside the counter-insurgency campaign; from local government and town-and-country planning to the electricity grid and the road network. This resulted in an infrastructure that few countries in Asia could match. It also created a strong – and potentially over-bearing – state: the number of its employees grew from 48,000 in 1948 to 140,000 in 1959. Equally, the ravages of war and occupation were repaired to a degree that Burma never experienced. But the idea that 'winning hearts and minds' was a carefully prepared strategy is a myth. The classic manual was written – by Robert Thompson, an ex-Chindit, Chinese affairs officer and later secretary for defence in Malaya – only after the Emergency had ended.[24] At the time the strategy was an 'agglomeration of trifles', and it proceeded mainly by trial and error. Many of the 'after-care' measures, as they were termed, arrived in fits and starts some time after the worst effects of resettlement – the uprooting, banishments, loss of income, exposure to corruption and exploitation – had already been experienced by rural Chinese. As the novelist Han Suyin wrote of a New Village in Johore, where she set her novel *And the Rain my Drink* . . .:

The dirt road was a new gash across the jungle. There, at the edge of a foetid mangrove swamp, between the thrusting mangrove spikes like a field of spears for miles . . . was the 'New Village', spreading itself into the swamp. Four hundred beings, including children, huddled there, foot deep in brackish mud. There were some *atap* huts with zinc roofs, obviously brought from elsewhere. I shall never forgot the pale and puffy faces: beri-beri, or the ulcers on their legs. Their skin had the hue of the swamp.[25]

The routine harassment of women and men by strip-searching during the daily food searches as people left the village of Semenyih became a public scandal; the official report painted a picture of proud and individualistic cultivators, goaded by the daily indignity almost beyond endurance.[26] The military still dealt in crude racial stereotypes, and Templer's personal endorsement of a thinly disguised soldier's fiction, *Jungle Green*, with its racist language, caused a storm among the Chinese community. The charge that the British were, at bottom, 'playing the race card' was never dispelled.[27] But 'hearts and minds' was the subject of a carefully orchestrated campaign of press coverage, not least to offset the mounting criticism, and it began to attract international attention. Malaya would eventually become a textbook case, to be applied beyond its borders from Vietnam – where Thompson led a British advisory mission – and, into the twenty-first century, to Iraq and Afghanistan.

The British would take the credit for defeating communism in Malaya, but if the essence of 'hearts and minds' lay in creating a sense of security and confidence, that allowed people to pursue their livelihoods with reasonable freedom and in reasonable safety, and in the absence of intimidation, and so encourage them to identify with government initiatives, other factors were crucial. The British in Malaya were rescued by the economy. By 1951 the cost of maintaining and operating forces was £48.5m. The extra cost to the federal government was £13.8m and its total costs came to £29m out of a budget of £66m.[28] This was a crippling burden, and it was entirely fortuitous that the British were able to meet it through the windfall of the Korean War boom in Malaya's raw materials. This was a time of relative prosperity for some. Little of it was enjoyed by labourers; wage increases were absorbed by price inflation and undercut by the recession that followed the boom. The chronic poverty in which communism flourished diminished only slightly. But above all, Asian business revived. The profits of Chinese *towkays* were increasingly reinvested in Malaya, in rubber estates and in shares in locally registered companies. The leading Chinese bank, the Overseas Chinese Banking Corporation, was on a par with the European concerns and held two-thirds of the total deposits of Chinese banks in Malaya. Tan Cheng Lock was a director both of OCBC and of the colonial concern Sime Derby.[29] This was important because much of the burden of counter-insurgency – for relief and after-care – fell on Malayans, and the decisive shifts in the conflict came within Malayan society itself. This was chiefly the process whereby the Chinese consolidated their stake in the country and the Chinese leadership, now gathered together in the Malayan Chinese Association, consolidated its grip on the community. In this the British, of course, played a role; in encouraging Chinese enlistment in the police, in the vital struggle to give land title to resettled farmers. But often the British were bystanders.[30] Obscure battles for control in the New Villages, or over village councils or in the Chinese schools, became key. The resources of the Chinese community were gradually amassed behind the government. In Perak the Kuomintang guerrillas were mobilized into a Kinta Home Guard. The Emergency was also fought by Malay officials as they sought to recover their authority in troubled Malay *kampongs*. But Malay wrath at the administrative attention showered on the erstwhile supporters of the communists was only partially assuaged by the expansion of rural health services and development funds. Malay policemen continued to bear the brunt of the casualties and they particularly resented another key aspect of the strategy: the rewards – sometimes thousands of dollars – paid to surrendered guerrillas who turned coat and informed on their comrades. 'Why should they risk their necks to help the [surrendered communists] get rewards greater than anything they were ever likely to come by?'[31] It was a battle to reconstruct communities, and for the elite to restore the networks and patron–client relationships that had been so damaged in the Japanese occupation. This was done increasingly on an ethnic basis. Above all, the fate of the rebellion in Malaya was decided by the continuing rapprochement between Malay administrative power and Chinese economic muscle.

Independence in Malaya was won by the alliance of conservatively inclined ethnic-based parties that had begun to form through the Communities Liaison Committee in 1949. The British still believed that something more was needed; a more authentic 'united Malayan nation' in Templer's brief – and they still pinned their hopes on Dato Onn bin Jaafar to create it, although Lyttelton was less enamoured by him than were his predecessors. In 1950 and again in 1951, Onn argued that UMNO should open its doors to non-Malays. He was ultimately rejected by his party, and amid much lamenting stepped down as leader. He launched an Independence for Malaya Party the same year, with the backing of Tan Cheng Lock and other liberal Chinese. The idea behind it was that it would present a unified front for independence, and that the ethnic parties would dwindle into welfare bodies. MacDonald and Gurney had high hopes for it. But Onn's refusal to embrace the cause of immediate independence, his insistence that the Malays still needed colonial protection, did not win over popular Malay opinion, nor that of the non-Malays, many of whom still mistrusted him. His was an elite patriotism grounded in the public service, and his principal allies included many of the chief ministers of the Malay States. Even the British began to lose patience with Onn. As Templer told him in April 1953, in the presence of US presidential candidate Adlai Stevenson, one of the first of a growing number of visiting American observers: 'You are going to be forced to take independence.' To which Onn's response, to Stevenson in private, was: 'I want independence, but I want to keep it.'[32] Onn first refused, and then accepted in 1953 a KBE; he was given official standing and patronage as the first Member for Home Affairs and head of the Rural and Industrial Development Agency. But he never again commanded the support of his countrymen, and ended his career in the political wilderness.

The logic of Malayan politics was moving in a different direction. Against all expectation, UMNO – which had never been a strong organization – revived. The contest for a new leader pitched the old veteran Mustapha Hussain, against a 48-year-old prince of Kedah, Tunku Abdul Rahman. Both were unlikely candidates. Mustapha's standing was unexpected, even to himself, because he was still on hard times selling *mee* (noodles). Few of the Malay radicals outside jail had such leadership experience, and they searched for a voice, but they did not prevail. The Tunku's name had been canvassed by the former Labour minister David Rees-Williams, and some questioned his nationalist credentials. Yet during the war, as a district officer, he had distinguished himself in welfare work for Malay victims of the Burma–Siam railway, and afterwards flirted with the Malay radicals in Kedah. Many observers, not least British officials, underestimated his political acumen and also his tenacity.[33] He possessed a strong sense of the original sovereignty of the Malay people. 'Who are these "Malayans"?' he asked in his first speech as UMNO leader. 'This country was received from the Malays and to the Malays it ought to be returned. What is called "Malayans"; therefore let the Malays alone settle who they are.'[34] The Tunku was no intellectual; he was remembered during his time at Cambridge chiefly as 'Prince Bobby' at the Huntingdon races, for canvassing for the Liberal Party in his Riley sports car, for clocking up twenty-three traffic offences in sixteen years of study, and for being responsible for the proctors' ruling in Cambridge University that banned the use of motor cars by undergraduates. But he surrounded himself with younger, energetic men – such as the Pahang notable Abdul Razak bin Hussein – and when Malay radicals began to be released from detention between 1953 and 1955 many joined UMNO, giving new vitality to its grass roots. It also held the loyalty of much of the growing army of state servants, school-teachers and policemen. When the Conservative government seemed to be back-pedalling on elections and the transfer of power in 1954, the Tunku threatened non-cooperation. The British blinked and came to terms. But, in the knowledge that a condition of self-government was that the ethnic communities would create a unified political front, the Tunku had also built a fresh understanding with the Malayan Chinese Association, on the basis of the Communities Liaison Committee 'bargain'. It became a political force when an electoral alliance was mooted by local leaders to contest the first Kuala Lumpur municipal elections in February 1952. Both UMNO and the MCA now reorganized as political parties and soon became a formal, well-financed and enduring electoral alliance, the basis of Malaysia's government to this day.

Not all the ex-detainees were reconciled to UMNO. Khatijah Sidek was released from jail in Singapore and banished to Johore Bahru.

With a baby, born in jail, to support and another on the way, she opened a restaurant there, serving fiery Minangkabau food from her home in Sumatra. She called it the Merdeka Restaurant. She joined UMNO's women's wing, the Kuam Ibu. It had a reputation as a movement led by the wives of the aristocracy and elite, but Khatijah now drew in the commoners. She learnt that they feared the word *Merdeka* [freedom]: 'Perhaps someone will say to you: "Whoever says *Merdeka* will go to jail, or will be beaten,"' she told them. 'But I have just said *Merdeka* very loud and very clearly, and the police are there, yet they are not arresting me.' She taught, in the manner of the Indonesian revolution, the cry *Merdeka* to the mothers, and for the mothers to pass it on to their children. Yet many in the party mistrusted her and the Tunku warned her not to be so free with the word. She noted that the Malays 'even softened the word *Merdeka* itself into *Merde-heka*, making it longer and softer, unlike *Merdeka*, which is short and sharp'. When she began to campaign for more representation for women within the party, she was expelled from UMNO. 'They only wanted independence slowly and gently, and perhaps did not really want to be so independent at all.'[35] Her political journey would eventually lead her into the Islamic opposition, but it too was an uncomfortable home for her. By the mid 1950s the various *aliran*, or streams of consciousness, within Malay radicalism had begun to drift apart. In the wake of religious riots, an Islamic Party was founded by leading *ulama* who felt that the mainstream national leaders had failed to defend the Muslim community. It drew in many who supported the Hizbul Muslimin in 1948, but also began to recruit from the more traditional religious schools and bureaucracies of the impoverished rural heartlands of northern and eastern states, peasants and village religious leaders. Shortly after his release from detention in 1955 Dr Burhanuddin looked to realize his Islam-centred philosophy of nationhood by taking up the leadership of the party. After seven years in prison Ahmad Boestamam formed a new secular, socialist party, the Partai Rakyat and there was a further attempt to rally non-Malay support for a 'democratic, secular state' in a new Labour Party.[36] But Boestamam and other survivors of the non-Malay left never regained the political prominence they had achieved from 1945 and 1948, nor did they build a trans-ethnic movement that was able to compete with the support mobilized on racial lines within the Alliance. When the first federal elections were held in 1955 the Islamic Party won the only opposition seat. Candidates of the UMNO–MCA Alliance – now extended to included the Malayan Indian Congress – were returned for the remainder on a landslide. Onn was defeated in his native Johore. People were casting their vote for freedom. It was an overwhelmingly Malay election. Of the 1,280,000 registered to vote, 84 per cent were Malays, 11 per cent Chinese and 5 per cent Indians. Of the 600,000 Chinese eligible to register, only 140,000 did so: one eighth of the total Chinese population. Nevertheless, under the alliance formula, seventeen non-Malay candidates were successful and it won an overwhelming 79.6 per cent of the popular vote.[37] Tunku Abdul Rahman now formed a ministry, if not a government.

The end of empire is not a pretty thing if examined too closely. What redeemed it, in the eyes of the British, was the idea only. In their vision for Malaya they looked to atone for the humiliation of 1942, and they saw late-colonial rule as 'the completion of a stewardship'. But they failed in the core objective that had shaped policy since 1942: to form a 'Malayan' nationalism that was organic and multiracial. In asking, 'Who are these "Malayans"?', Tunku Abdul Rahman gave a different answer. Whilst there could be a Malayan nation based on clearer defined citizenship rights for non-Malays, the core of the nation, the bearers of its original sovereignty, were the Malays. The British now prepared to devolve power to a coalition of ethnic parties. This was a long way from what they wanted to see. But it was a political solution they were willing to take. In any case, Malcolm MacDonald's idealism now had a less receptive audience in the Conservative government in London; it was felt he had spent too long living on the equator to be able to see things clearly. In 1955, as the transfer of power approached, he left the region, though not for good; he was still to serve as high commissioner in India. It was left to the last of Britain's Asian supremos, Sir Robert Scott, who had himself been present at the fall of Singapore, to anoint the successor regime: 'Tunku Abdul Rahman has an overwhelming Parliamentary majority', he told the prime minister, Anthony Eden; 'the local forces and police are largely Malay, and for his own ends he will keep legal powers to detain without trial ... He gives the impression of aiming at an old-fashioned Muslim dictatorship, with some democratic trappings, ready if need be to deal ruthlessly with Chinese who give trouble.'[38]

But in 1955 few could argue that Malaya was 'not yet ready' for independence. Of their Asian subjects, it was the Malay rulers who perhaps had the most to lose from the severance of the colonial connection. One of the first public functions of the new chief minister, with six of his colleagues, was to represent the government at the diamond jubilee of Sultan Ibrahim of Johore. When Ibrahim succeeded his father in 1895, the Malay States had not yet entirely submitted to British rule. He had inherited from his father a vigorous, reforming monarchy, and in accepting British 'protection', he still retained many of his privileges and even his own armed forces. The sultan had spent little time in Malaya since the war, having been mostly away in Europe. He had returned briefly in 1951 only to complain of the 'most damnable' noise of RAF flights over his palace, and had requested them to avoid his capital altogether; it reminded him too much of 1941. Less than six weeks after his return he set sail again for England.[39] But in 1955 he was met with a splendid gathering; the crowds that streamed across the causeway from Singapore were so immense that traffic could not cross. The sultan gave a speech in his trademark mixture of English and Malay. He spoke in forthright tones, striking the floor with the end of his sword as he did so. 'I don't like it at all,' he said. 'My head is disturbed. I say if I remain here, I shall probably go mad – thinking of my people.' He continued:

It is easy to say I want independence. I want to be happy. I can buy slaves. I myself do not buy slaves. But I know there are people who buy human beings. It is not that we do not want to ask for *Merdeka*. We too, do not want to ask for *Merdeka*? We ask for it – Then we ask for independence. But what? Why do we want independence? Where are our warships? Where is our army? Where are our planes which can repel an invading army?[40]

The speech caused an uproar and the ministers did not attend the rest of the functions. It showed that, in so many ways, the formal transfer of power was only a beginning.

The semi-elected government now entered the strange twilight phase of unequal power-sharing with the British. In Singapore a coalition led by the Labour Front of David Marshall achieved a similar status. On arriving to begin work, both of the new chief ministers found that the British had not seen fit to provide them with offices. Marshall – who horrified the governor of Singapore with his trade-mark open-necked bush jacket and the bare feet and sandals of some of his ministers – only prevailed when he threatened to set up shop 'under the old apple tree' outside the government offices in Empress Place. It was here that he introduced his ministers to the people.[41] But however constrained the new regimes were, across the Thai border the MCP leadership realized that they placed in jeopardy the legitimacy of their claims to fight for the nation. Through intermediaries, Chin Peng sued for peace. The fighting units drew back, and with a small bodyguard Chin Peng, the Malay leader Rashid Maidin and another veteran of the wartime resistance, Chen Tian, were met at the jungle fringe by an old Force 136 comrade, John Davis. On 28–29 December 1955 a meeting took place in the frontier town of Baling, in a school-house commandeered for the purpose. It was a condition of the gather-ing that Chin Peng would not be allowed to speak to the press, who scrambled for a first glimpse of the man on whom the British had already placed a $250,000 reward. A young Malay correspondent of *Utusan Melayu*, Said Zahari, was a witness: 'In the midst of the flashing lights of photographers' cameras, I saw apprehensive looks on the faces of the communist leaders. Chin Peng and Rashid Maidin looked straight and stiff, while Chen Tian turned rapidly to the left and to the right as if to avoid the cameras.'[42] Malaya and Singapore were represented by Tunku Abdul Rahman, David Marshall and Tan Cheng Lock, ill and frail after his injury in the MNLA bomb attack six years earlier.

The talks focused on the MCP's desire to return to the *status quo ante bellum*: on its right to function as an open political party and the question of whether the communists who laid down their arms would be able to return to Malaya without detention. 'If you demand our surrender', Chin Peng insisted, 'we would prefer to fight to the last man.' On this issue the talks broke down. But Chin Peng had also been given the impression that when the Tunku had negotiated inde-pendence from the British the talks might be reopened. The ability of the Tunku to negotiate on matters of internal security – the defining moment of the slow transfer of power – and Chin Peng's apparent pledge to lay down arms when this was conceded, dominated proceedings, as was symbolized by Chen Tian's theatrical scrutiny of the tape recorders running in an adjoining room. In agreeing to meet, the Tunku sought to boost his own reputation in relation to the British and with regard to Chin Peng. In both of these aims he was successful. In secret, the British had pondered the various contingencies should – against all advice – the Tunku seek to make a separate peace with Chin Peng. They had concluded that they could not afford to break with him. But this, it seems, was never his intention. As the Tunku walked away from the schoolroom Said Zahari asked him if he was disappointed. 'No, I'm not. I never wanted it to be a success.' These remarks were never reported.[43] Perhaps more than any other event, the Baling talks cemented the Tunku's reputation with the British as a safe pair of hands in which to transfer power. After them Chin Peng was delivered back to the jungle by John Davis. They camped and talked over 'the good old days'. In vain Davis offered to come in with him and continue talking.[44] Directly afterwards the Tunku, brandishing Chin Peng's offer to lay down arms to an independent government, flew to London for the crucial negotiations for independence. He was met at the airport to be assured by the men from the Colonial Office that he was to be granted independence 'on a silver platter'. But the negotiations with the communists were never reopened.

FREEDOM FROM FEAR?

In early June 1950, almost at the midpoint of the twentieth century of the Christian era, the Buddhist prime minister of Burma, U Nu, began a course of meditation, the origins of which lay 2,000 years before the birth of Christ. Nu retreated into a hallowed meditation centre and vowed not to emerge until he had attained a certain stage in *vipassana* meditation, the Buddhist discipline that taught self-purification and equanimity. 'Until then', he told his ministers, 'do not send for me even if the whole country is enveloped in flames. If there are flames, you must put them out yourself.'[45] When told of U Nu's practice of spending three of four hours a day in solitary prayer,

Nehru remarked: 'That seems to me as good a way of governing Burma as any.'[46] But one of the main components of the state of consciousness which Nu believed that he had attained that summer was 'freedom from fear'. As the Korean War entered a critical phase and the threat of global nuclear conflict grew ever closer, this was no easy goal. By the middle of the year, Allied forces in Korea seemed on the verge of conquering the whole peninsula and a major war with China and the Soviet Union loomed. In Britain Attlee broadcast to the nation of further preparations for war in Korea and also against Russia, 'if another world war is to follow'.[47] In Delhi, Nu's closest foreign friend, Jawaharlal Nehru, urged the US to draw back, arguing that war solved nothing. In his alarm, he seemed to be conjuring up again the non-violent maxims of the late Mahatma Gandhi. Attacked by the Americans for appeasement of totalitarianism, Nehru was equally suspect in China and Russia for his suppression of Indian communists.[48]

In Burma itself, however, fear was retreating a little. The tide of war in the country was beginning to turn in the government's favour and Burma's positioning on the new map of Southeast Asia was becoming slightly clearer. In 1950 the Chinese communists finally defeated Chiang Kai Shek's resistance on the mainland and the Viet Minh communists established a critical hold on the northwest of Vietnam. Yet 1950 was also the year when the hopes of the Malayan communist insurrection began to fade and Burmese communists lost their tactical advantage. In Burma the Karen and other minority revolts also surrendered their initial gains. The outcome of the Cold War in Asia seemed to be very evenly balanced. In the south of the region the British continued to provide a military presence that protected its capitalist economy, but further north the outcome remained uncertain. The leaders of the huge new Republic of India looked on with concern. Early in the year Nu was able to write with satisfaction to Nehru that a major Karen stronghold in the Irrawaddy delta had been retaken. He thanked the Indian prime minister for his moral and material support.[49] Nehru, for his part, was grateful to Burma for its rice exports at a time when India was suffering food shortages. Revived Japanese purchases and the backwash of the Korean War were pushing up prices throughout Asia. Nehru visited

Burma to cement his quiet alliance in the middle of the year. J. S. Furnivall was impressed by Nehru's moral courage, if not by his appearance: 'He is such a small and apparently un-aggressive, unassuming little man that it is difficult to imagine how he came to be so important.'[50]

The period 1950 to 1953 was one of reconsolidation in Burma. The government's authority began to reassert itself, even if many of the failures which would eventually drive Burma to the margins of the new world order were also present: corruption, an arbitrary military and botched measures of economic development. One sign of the changing mood was the attempt of the Communist Party of Burma (CPB) to compromise with the Rangoon government. After their striking successes of 1949, the red-flag communists of the CPB and their Karen allies had abandoned their policy of trying to take and hold the towns. They now became more 'Maoist' in their strategy, basing themselves in villages and eliminating landlords. They were never again to seize the initiative. The government may have been weak, and its army underpaid and undersupplied, but it had kept its hold over Rangoon, the sole remaining financial prize in the country. It had done so because foreign financial and military aid, particularly small arms, had reached it in large quantities. Even in 1948 and 1949 Burma had never collapsed into total anarchy. In most districts notables and important men still held sway. They were generally suspicious of the communists and hostile to the Karens and other minority group rebels. Provided the government directed some cash, some local offices and, best of all, arms to them, they were prepared to come back into Rangoon's fold.[51]

Under the surface of the government's resurgence, however, the balance of power was shifting irrevocably towards the military, though Nu hardly noticed it as he flew around the world on missions of peace and sanctity in the early 1950s. The army had appropriated more and more of the country's diminished wealth. It benefited from the feeling that Burma was a threatened country in the midst of an armed camp, with the Chinese, the rump of the British Empire or even India greedily surveying the remains of its assets of oil, timber and rice. It benefited from the feeling that Nu's botched land reforms had helped few but clients of the AFPFL leaders. The military gradually came to dominate the villages and to control the ministries and the police force. The first coup against the civilian government finally came on 26 September 1958. Nu returned to power briefly in the early 1960s but his grip was never firm. A second coup occurred in 1963 and Nu went into a long exile. Ne Win and his family were to hold power in Burma for much of the next forty years. The consequence was that a country once fabled for its natural wealth and promise isolated itself increasingly from the world. Burma fell further and further behind its Southeast Asian neighbours, suffering international sanctions and continuing local rebellions. Only the new wealth spilling into the country from a booming China in recent decades seems capable of ending its long stagnation.

The mid 1950s were a time of high tension across the whole of what had once been British Asia. The tenth anniversary of the climacteric of the Second World War in the region did not witness that era of peace and prosperity that many Asians had envisaged when they had still been under the yoke of Japanese occupation and colonial rule. For one thing, full-scale armed conflict had only temporarily ceased in Indo-China and the bloody denouement there spread waves of apprehension across the whole region. Indo-China had been at war every day since General Gracey's ill-fated intervention had come to an end in the early months of 1946. At Dien Bien Phu, in April 1954, the French suffered an epochal defeat at the hands of Viet Minh forces supplied with artillery and modern weapons by the Chinese and Russians. The Western fight against communist advance seemed to be deeply compromised, at least on this front. An American officer, Colonel Edward Lansdale, made a series of momentous journeys there during the course of 1954 and 1955.[52] On 1 June 1954 he landed in Saigon, which was on the point of becoming the capital of a vivisected South Vietnam under the peace accords signed between the French and the Viet Minh in Geneva. He was part of a network of deadly expertise linking anti-communist special operations forces across Southeast Asia. A specialist in sabotage and psychological warfare, Lansdale had been an adviser to the cabal of right-wing strongmen who ran the Philippines. At the beginning of the 1950s he had helped the authorities put down the so-called Huk rebellion, a peasant uprising which the US government feared would drag the Philippines into the communist camp. Lansdale drew heavily on the British experience of counter-insurgency in Malaya while he was working in the Philippines and Vietnam. United States senators made the British colony a port of call on fact-finding visits to Asia. After Adlai Stevenson, who had a close shave when his helicopter crash-landed, came vice-president Richard Nixon, on whom Templer impressed the need to wean Russia and China apart, and John and Robert Kennedy, who did not impress hardened American residents with their lack of sympathy for the British imperial cause.[53] But the traffic went in both directions. Malayan officials had flown in to visit the villages where disarmed Huk rebels were settled, gathering information for their own 'New Villages' on the peninsula.[54]

Lansdale's journey to Saigon signalled the beginning of the era of deep US involvement in Vietnam. The looming conflict was also marked in fiction by Graham Greene's novel *The Quiet American*, published in 1955.[55] Greene, himself a former British agent, had been living in Saigon in 1952 when a series of bomb attacks rocked the French colonial city. The authorities blamed the communists, but Greene suspected a plot between right-wing Vietnamese militias and the CIA. He was probably right. A *New York Times* reporter just happened to be on the spot at the vital moment. Photographs of people maimed in the attack were speedily published under a headline blaming Ho Chi Minh for the violence. By 1955 Lansdale was certainly working hard to put in place a third force to take over from the French as a bulwark against the communists. In that year he helped organize a coup which placed the city of Saigon in the hands of the future dictator of South Vietnam, Ngo Din Diem. This final act of the unending war, the American struggle with North Vietnam, would run its bloody course to 1975. Meanwhile General Douglas Gracey, who had reinstalled the French in Saigon in 1945 and managed another post-colonial armed struggle between India and Pakistan in Kashmir, retired from his post as commander-in-chief of Pakistan's army.

FLAWED MEMORIES

At the height of the crescent's forgotten wars, few had the time or the inclination to ponder the tidal wave of war and change that had swept over them since 1941. By 1955, the tenth anniversary of the formal end of the Second World War, the mood was changing. This was a year when the rhetoric of the Bandung Conference – of development, non-alignment and peace – concealed both the onrush of aggressive nationalism and the slow expansion of the crescent's new capitalism. Yet it was also the year of memory, when people began to take stock of events in that terrible year a decade before: the year of the atom bomb, the fierce campaign of the 14th Army, the death of Subhas Chandra Bose and Aung San's revolt against the Japanese. A whole series of commemorative ceremonies were held. In Rangoon and Mandalay, people celebrated Independence Day, Aung San's birthday and Union Day with particular fervour that year. Ominously, people noted that the highlight of that year's Independence Day festivities was the 'participation of a larger number of armed forces personnel in the march past before the President of the Union'.[56] As yet 'Army Day', the celebration of that momentous event in April 1945 when Aung San had led his Burma Defence Army into the jungle to fight the Japanese, had not assumed the significance in the calendar of Independence Day. As the Burmese army became increasingly autonomous and powerful, the meaning of this festival became a source of debate and controversy. Ceremonies to mark the tenth anniversary of the end of the war were more muted in India. But Subhas Chandra Bose's birthday saw celebrations across the subcontinent, particularly in Calcutta. The veterans of the Indian National Army, still uncertain of their status in independent India, drilled and marched with particular pride. The simplest ceremony of all was held on 6 August 1955 at 8 a.m. in the city of Hiroshima. At the exact moment the bomb had fallen ten years before, the mayor of the city, himself a survivor, released 500 doves into the air and inaugurated a new peace centre.[57] The press across the world reflected on the folly of nuclear war while peace campaigners denounced the great powers in speeches and newspaper articles. Sir William Slim, now

Governor General of Australia, interpreted the world scene in another way. Ten years on from the end of the war, he observed, an authoritarian power once again overshadowed Asia. He was referring, of course, to China.

The most poignant acts of commemoration related to the physical remains of the fallen. Parties of former soldiers still moved across former battlefields seeking and memorializing their lost comrades. For the armies of Britain's former empire, the task was organized by the Commonwealth War Graves Commission. Monuments were built at Imphal, Kohima and other major battle sites, but individual graves were also identified and tended in remote and isolated countryside. The task required tact and diplomacy. Disputes arose between the British, Australians, Canadians and Americans. Indian soldiers' groups debated the appropriateness of forms of burial or cremation, depending on the assumed religion of the fallen. The Japanese, still regarded with cold indifference by their conquerors, had been allowed to build a monument to their dead at Rangoon racecourse only very late in 1947. But slowly thereafter, as the country was rehabilitated and the war crimes trials ceased, Japan began to press for the proper burial of its war dead. For many Japanese the recovery of a dead soldier's remains for burial on home soil was crucial to the continuity of families and their chain of ancestry. On his visit to Tokyo in 1955 Nu offered Burmese co-operation in the recovery of the bodies of the more than 85,000 Japanese soldiers who had perished on Burmese soil.[58] The government formed a survey mission to plan the recovery and repatriation of the dead. For years afterwards towns and cities in Japan were host to sad little ceremonies as urns and caskets were returned from Burma. More gruesome tales went the rounds. The activities of guerrilla levies and special forces in north Burma, the Philippines and Borneo had led to an upsurge of head-hunting among the tribal peoples. Quiet negotiations went on to have severed heads returned to the military authorities and properly disposed of. Soldiers' groups were particularly active along the Burma–Siam railway, of course, and 1955 saw a series of memorial services hosted by the Thai and Burmese governments and the British Burma Star Association. The huge numbers of Thai, Burmese, Malayan and Burmese civilians who had perished on the railway were also commemorated, but most remained without named graves. Their bodies had simply been thrown into huge lime pits.

Many people's memories were very personal, almost picaresque. When he was in northern Burma the writer Norman Lewis met a cheerful Burmese former soldier who had served in the forces fighting alongside the Japanese. He took Lewis to a tree where, he said, Chinese soldiers had tried to hang him as a traitor following his capture. Laughing heartily he explained how the Chinese were too 'weak from semi-sickness and starvation' to hoist him off the ground. His proposed execution, according to Lewis, degenerated into 'a lurid Disney-like farce' with the Chinese attempting to pinion him while hoisting him into the air. Eventually he escaped, but the memory was not so easily defeated. It is unlikely that Lewis was the only person he took back to his hanging tree to marvel at the wound on the branch where the rope had rubbed it raw.[59] There were also grander, public memorials. In Mandalay, nursing nuns at a hospital had vowed to construct a miniature Lourdes if the building was spared during the wartime bombing. At the end of the war a Japanese POW camp had been stationed near the hospital and the commanding officer had despatched some of the inmates to do the sisters' bidding. The POWs set to work enthusiastically and on Mandalay Hill, traditional home of votive shrines, they created a miniature mountain landscape with a meandering stream and a delicate Oriental bridge – to Lewis's eye it was Lourdes as it might have appeared on a willow-pattern plate. The Japanese captain himself carved the statue of the Virgin, which bore a striking resemblance to Kwannon, the Japanese goddess of mercy.[60]

Religion played an important part in people's reconstruction of the past. The Burmese intellectual Khin Myo Chit had passed through an atheist and communist phase in her youth. She had been disgusted by the corruption and selfishness she discovered while hiding in a monastery during the Japanese invasion of 1942. In the straitened circumstances of newly independent Burma, however, she redis-covered a simpler and heartfelt Buddhism, as she recovered from a mental breakdown with the help of her meditation master. She became a 'lay sister' in a monastery, replicating in her own life the prime minister's tilt towards Buddhism and illustrating how Nu's revivalism was more than a simple political tactic.[61] Several Allied soldiers, too, recounted how they had to dig deep into their reserves of Christian faith to find forgiveness for the brutality of their Japanese captors. But as early as ten years after the war, soldiers on both sides were beginning tentative meetings for the purposes of reconciliation and creating a true record of the terrible events they had witnessed. For their part, the Japanese were also haunted by what they had seen in Southeast Asia. The author of the *Harp of Burma*, a bestselling novel in post-war Japan, was a former soldier who drew on his wartime experiences to tell of a disillusioned man whose battered faith in the search for enlightenment is reinvigorated by the earnest folk Buddhism of Burma. His hero becomes a wanderer, a kind of forest monk, typical of the region, moving from village to village playing his Burmese harp and telling fables.

Other vivid fictional recreations of the Second World War sparked controversy. In 1954 the first English translation appeared of Pierre Boulle's novel *Le Pont de la Rivière Kwaï*. The French author, himself a former prisoner of the Japanese, depicted a group of British POWs being forced to build a bridge on the Burma–Siam railway. The fictional senior British officer, Colonel Nicholson, after a protracted and painful battle with his Japanese jailer about officers' honour and dignity, becomes obsessed with the creation and perfection of the bridge, at the same time as British special forces are doing all they can to destroy it. At first sight it seemed an odd thing for a Frenchman to write a novel about the hidebound British military mentality, although his story undoubtedly served as a good illustration of the futility of war. But Boulle had worked on rubber plantations in Malaya before and after the war and had had ample opportunity to observe the waning British Empire at close hand. Or perhaps his novel represented a kind of transposition of his views on the glorious folly of de Lattre de Tassigny and the defenders of Dien Bien Phu to the British, whose decolonization in the region had been generally more circumspect and less bloody. In 1957, just after Britain and France's occupation of the Suez Canal, the controversy about the book was revived by David Lean's film version. The British public had long been sensitive about cinematographic portrayals of the Burma war and its aftermath. In 1945 a Warner Brothers' film, *Objective, Burma!*, which depicted

Errol Flynn as an American paratrooper recapturing Burma without the benefit of a single British ally, had caused such offence in the United Kingdom that it was withdrawn from release until 1952. Now, the American financiers of the Lean film insisted on inserting a brave American individualist into a story carefully crafted by Boulle to juxtapose the honourable but purblind orthodoxy of 'Colonel Nicholson' with the unorthodox but ultimately futile heroics of 'Major Warden', the 'Force 316' agent. This was only a few years after the American General Joseph Stilwell's dismissive and foul-mouthed reflections on the British war effort were made public and Lean's film was given a very mixed reception in Britain. In retrospect, though, it was simply another marker on the road that transformed Britain from an imperial nation at war into a consumer society increasingly suspicious of class, deference and moral homilies.

It was not only the British who were stirred up by dramatic re-creations of the Second World War. In 1955, the Hollywood film *The Purple Plain* reached Burma. It starred Gregory Peck and a young Burmese actress, Win Min Than, and told the story of a Canadian special operations executive soldier lost in the fastnesses of Burma during the latter stages of the war. Many Burmese were unimpressed. For one thing it had been shot in Ceylon (as had Lean's film). But what they really objected to was its cultural crassness. One scene showed people wearing shoes in a pagoda; another showed a Burmese boy killing a lizard. This, it was said, was 'a gross slander on the character of Burmese children'.[62] Worst of all, the Peck character was seen sleeping beside the Burmese maiden, 'without being married'. This 'suggested that Burmese women were immoral'. Government censors debated whether to ban the film, but in the end it was released so that Burmese people could criticize it in full knowledge of its contents. The horrors and compromises of the Second World War were still fresh in the minds of both Asians and Europeans.

Memory changed over time; different themes would come to the fore at different periods, in ways that reflected how societies sought to fashion their public history. For Singapore, as its new prime minister Lee Kuan Yew argued in opening a memorial to civilians, in 1961, it was 'through sharing such common experiences that the feeling of living and being one community is established'. In Malaysia, nationhood perhaps demanded that much be forgotten. Memories would often speak to contemporary anxieties.[63] They were reawakened by the reappearance of the Japanese. Their presence in the region – as long-term residents – predated the war and the logic of Japanese interests drew them at a very early stage after it, and in exactly the strategic areas – Malayan iron mining, for example – in which they had made such a pronounced investment before 1941. In 1951 the wartime administrator of Singapore, Mamoru Shinozaki, returned to the island, or at least to its harbour, where, unable to land, he received guests on board a freighter. Later Shinozaki was to lead the way in confronting the past with a memoir, published in English in Singapore, of his wartime experiences: *Syonan: My Story*. It acknowledged the atrocities of the *sook ching* massacres, but also highlighted his role and his contribution to the welfare of Singapore's people. These returns generated considerable anger in the Chinese press. But, with the encouragement of key figures such as Malcolm MacDonald, they persisted. In April 1952 the first senior Japanese to visit MacDonald arrived at Bukit Serene with a letter from the Japanese prime minister. The visitor was nervous. The cook at Bukit Serene wept – his parents and sister had been murdered by the Japanese in China – but, it was observed, he did his duty.[64] By 1954 the flagship Japanese departmental store, Echigoya, where a pre-war generation of Asian clerks had bought their cheap office ducks and toys for their children, reopened, as did the Singapore Japanese Association, which had been such a prominent feature of the island's social scene before the war. The old Japanese expatriate community began to return as 'advisers', often exploiting their wartime connections. Some still saw Malaya as their home, and a sense of rootedness began to return with the refoundation of the Japanese School.[65] The economic consequences of this were immense. By 1972 Southeast Asian countries purchased nearly 12 per cent of total Japanese exports and supplied 16 per cent of total imports. By 1979, 35.4 per cent of Japan's total manufacturing investment and 43 per cent of investment in mining was in Southeast Asia.[66] 'Even after the war', one Japanese historian has observed, 'many Japanese businessmen and entrepreneurs still thought of Indonesia as a sort of second Manchuria'.[67] The old wartime battlefields and shrines in Singapore island – with the remains of both the Japanese war criminals and war victims, Kempeitai and conscript labourers – began to be visited in large numbers by a new and ubiquitous presence: the Japanese tourist.

A FLAWED INHERITANCE

If in 1955 people's memories of the Second World War were still raw, with much suppressed or forgotten, the present was in some ways a disappointment of those dreams of independence which had entranced them a decade before. As India struggled with the problems of statehood, Nehru was personally in a more optimistic mood in 1955. It was only with the resurgence of severe economic difficulties in the late 1950s and the conflict with China in his last years that his outlook darkened. But in objective terms the problems that faced independent India remained vast. If famine did not reappear as frequently as it had under the Raj, the country's food problems seemed no nearer solution and tens of millions continued to live in the direst poverty while the first flush of wealth from the new industrialization faded. Perhaps, indeed, Nehru's very adherence to a Soviet model of gargantuan 'socialist industry' had worsened the poverty of the countryside. Political problems were equally pressing in New Delhi. Once the British left, India's fractious politicians set about fighting over the spoils of office. The Punjab's Sikhs and people in the south who did not speak Hindi, the new national language, vociferously demanded special status within the constitution. Refugees from East and West Pakistan had not been fully absorbed into India's massive, ramshackle cities. On the frontiers, particularly in the northeast, militant groups such as the Nagas, who had been armed and radicalized by the war, continued to fight the central government in Delhi. India's 'most dangerous decades' were looming.

India's pre-eminent problem was the continuing fight with Pakistan over the Kashmir, a Muslim-majority state that Nehru had insisted in 1947 must belong to India. Both countries diverted vital resources to their armed forces, distorting development almost as much as military priorities had done under the Raj. The diplomatic stand-off led to sporadic armed clashes on the borders and, though it did not erode

India's resolutely civilian political order, the army became more and more visible in the politics of Pakistan. General Ayub Khan came to believe that he could do a better job than quarrelling politicians of bringing India to book over Kashmir and holding his fissiparous country together. Ironically, the legacy of Mahomed Ali Jinnah, that consummate political schemer and master artisan of constitutions and resolutions, was to be decades of military rule in Pakistan. Nowhere were the tensions which undermined the new, uncertain and divided state more evident than in East Pakistan, located at the apex of the former crescent of British Southeast Asia. The Bengali-speaking politicians of East Pakistan chafed under what they saw as the semi-colonial domination of their leaders in the western capital of Islamabad. Refugees continued to surge across the borders in both directions, Hindus to the west, Muslims to the east, creating new pools of privation in the poverty-stricken countryside and declining cities. Even on Pakistan's and India's most easterly frontier with Burma, conflicts between Muslim and Buddhist, Hindu and Muslim, separatists and centralizers continued to kill hundreds and terrorize remote villages.

Many of the acute problems that faced the new nations could be traced directly to the nature of British rule and the corroding, radicalizing effect of the Second World War. They represented the other face of freedom from the beaming crowds and proud processions on independence days. They were also testament to the continuing role of the great Western powers in Asia and the coming of age of the new leviathans, the USSR and China, which were determined to play their own Great Game for South and Southeast Asia. As Nehru leaned towards the USSR, shunned by the anti-communist USA, so the Soviet leadership flattered his wishes and the Soviet security services began to infiltrate the country. Communist China, for its part, fresh from its great success in bolstering Ho Chih Minh in Vietnam, began to play politics in Burma, Pakistan, and Indonesia, though it was impotent to affect the course of the war to the south in Malaya. The Cold War gave new life to old fantasies of imperial dominance. British anti-communism and American suspicion of India caused them tacitly to support the emerging 'state of martial rule' in Pakistan, Burma, Indonesia, and the 'softer' authoritarianism of Malaysia and Singapore.

Britain and the USA retained the largest economic and political stakes in the region. Both countries still counted the new states as important partners in trade. Even though India, Pakistan and Burma had erected high tariff barriers against foreign goods, the whole organization of the world economy continued to put them at a massive disadvantage which would persist until the early twenty-first century. Writing from Changi jail in 1959, James Puthucheary, once again a detainee, penned a classic analysis: *Ownership and Control in the Malayan Economy*. It argued that the British still dominated 'commanding heights and much of the valleys' of the Malayan economy, and that the British had removed much of the sting of this by bringing in Malay directors and Chinese investors. As is now acknowledged, 'crony capitalism' – the scourge of modern corporate Asia – cut its teeth in the British and Japanese periods.[68] The imperial past still shaped borders. The exclusion of Singapore from the Malayan federation was to be briefly reversed in 1963, when, with North Borneo and Sarawak, it joined the Federation of Malaysia. Although this experiment was not predetermined to fail, the reasons for Singapore's departure in 1965 – the alarm of Malay elites that its volatile Chinese politics would upset the delicate balance of power on the peninsula – was foreshadowed by events in 1946 and 1947. The political compromises of the transfer of power were to unravel as ethnic tensions rose, and in 1969 Malaysia experienced race riots on a scale it had not seen since 1945. It would face the need for a second, deeper decolonization in which the state would affirm the centrality of the Malay language and culture and drive forward the ethnic distribution within the economy. In Singapore the new independent regime of the People's Action Party would also have to seek new ways to reconstruct Singaporean society and shift the course of national development.

In Burma it was a combination of unending internal conflict and foreign intervention which led to the rise and seemingly endless rule of the military in a country which had once been one of the brightest hopes for Asian prosperity. Burma had all but become one of the first 'failed states', as piously categorized by Western political scientists. The wars of the minorities against Rangoon were again partly the legacy of colonial rule, even though the Labour government itself had decided that Burma must be kept together in order to repel Chinese influence. The British and Americans, of course, had never actively sought to bolster General Ne Win's rise to power but, as in the case of Ayub Khan of Pakistan, Western politicians were relieved enough when non-communist strongmen came to control poor and conflict-ridden countries. It was not even that Ne Win and the other Burmese generals were entirely *personae non gratae* amongst the post-war Western leaders, despite the harsh words traded by both sides. Britain (and India) had helped to arm Burma in 1949 and 1950 when the government in Rangoon seemed about to fall to the Karen–communist alliance. Ne Win was more than once seen in the company of Malcolm MacDonald. He even dallied in the Commissioner General's Malayan swimming pool. Thus it had ever been since the days of Thucydides the Athenian, that democracies at home consorted with dictators and became tyrannies abroad, though still cloaking their interests in the rhetoric of 'spreading democracy'.

As they faced the future, not all the auguries for the crescent and its neighbours were so poor, of course. Independence had given a huge moral boost to the peoples of India, Pakistan and Burma. The sense of release from the grip of European colonialism was palpable, perhaps not least because it had shown some of its worst sides just before and during the early stages of the Second World War. Open racism, economic exploitation and neglect by the European powers reached their high point in the Depression and during the first phase of the war. After 1945 newly independent governments set limits to the privileges of European business in South and Southeast Asia, though nationalization proceeded quite slowly even in Burma. Still, reading the newspapers and memoirs of this period, it becomes apparent that fears for the future were mixed with a sense that the new nations possessed limitless capacity for growth and development. The stilted, sanctimonious yet aspiring language of the Bandung generation amply illustrates this. Even in the surviving enclaves of British government in the crescent, officials paid more attention to the improvement of the health and education of their remaining subjects. Malcolm MacDonald regarded his greatest act to have been the creation of the University of Malaya. A new, high-thinking and Christian imperialism seemed to be taking shape beneath a blanket of counter-insurgency and press censorship. In Malaya and Singapore at least, decolonization was seen as major success story, as their later prosperity seemed to affirm. Yet it must be remembered that the achievements of colonial rule, such as relatively stable and independent institutions of state, were not solely, or primarily, a colonial legacy. From the first collapse of colonial power in 1941 these institutions had been shaped by Asian initiative. In these tense and violent days of the mid 1950s the seeds of the Southeast Asian miracle were sown by Chinese and Indian entrepreneurs, Malay educationalists and returning Japanese businessmen. Now the new promise has spread to India and Vietnam while China reaps the rewards of its state-directed capitalism. Moreover, the darker underside of the colonial story has rarely been told. The maladministration and graft of the military administration; the wild and unchecked fury of white terror in the first years; the extra-judicial killings of young men and women; the grotesque atrocity exhibitions of the mutilated slain; the violence to family life and livelihoods of hundreds of thousands of farmers and labourers during resettlement; the insidious small tyrannies of a vast and largely unaccountable bureaucracy; the racism and arrogance of empire – all this must be set in the balance.

Merdeka was lived by an entire generation. But many people in what had been British Asia felt that it had not been realized wholly; that is in the cry of Tan Malaka for 'one hundred per cent *Merdeka*' that was raised in the Solo valley in late 1945 and taken up right across the region. The *Merdeka* that was achieved fell something short of this. The achievements of independence were substantial, but new regimes showed themselves willing to adopt the paternalistic methods of colonial rule, and they were eager to retain its authoritarian instruments. It was not always the case. In his constitutional talks for Singapore in April and May 1956, David Marshall rejected a formula for self-government which still gave the British control over internal security, and the power to suspend the constitution. He had become increasingly nervous at the continuing shadow of powers of detention without trial. He denounced the independence he was offered as a 'three quarters rotten *Merdeka*'. But for all his clear-sightedness of what was at stake, Marshall paid dearly for not taking what was on offer. Within weeks he was swept out of office. In the longer term it was Lee Kuan Yew – the Fabian-inclined, Cambridge-educated lawyer

– who was prepared to compromise with the British and their security state. It seemed that the democratic niceties of the formal transfer of power were not so important as knowing how to wield it effectively. For Marshall the liberal traditions of Western rule were worth fighting for. His ally in this, the charismatic radical Lim Chin Siong, saw the matter from the perspective of the popular movement for a New Democracy, to which he was heir. 'The people ask for fundamental democratic rights', Lim Chin Siong had thundered, in an early speech to the Legislative Council, 'but what have they got? They have got only the freedom of firecrackers after seven o'clock in the evening. The people ask for bread and they have been given stones instead.' At the heart of the issue was that so long as these discretionary powers hung over society – in whoever's hands – Singapore would still be unfree, and *Merdeka* would be unrealized.[69]

In arguing to keep these authoritarian instruments, in particular powers of detention without trial, Lee Kuan Yew pleaded historical necessity, the continuing threat of communism and communalism. This was to become one of the powerful legacies of the end of empire in British Asia. In the aftermath of its revolutionary hour, and scale of the violence it unleashed, not only was communism all but obliterated, but in the process so too were a panoply of other alternatives. Liberalism never recovered from the shocking blows to civil society during these years of upheaval. The internationalist vision of the radicals evaporated. The post-independence elites saw it as a dangerous thing; it was, in Lee Kuan Yew's striking phrase, 'anti-national'. In this new atmosphere many of the great figures of the popular movements faced long periods of imprisonment, exile or exclusion. But the vanquished also were struck out of national narratives, and almost vanished from historical memory itself. For many of them the post-independence years were a long struggle to be heard; in the words of Ahmad Boestamam: 'to give a true picture of how a path to the summit was cut and who were its pioneers, so that in time to come it will not be "the cow that gives the milk but the bull too that gets the credit"'.[70] In Britain, much was also forgotten, not least the many horrors of the post-war campaigns in Malaya, Indonesia and Vietnam. In 2005 British veterans of the Emergency were refused permission from the British government to wear their campaign medal from the Malaysian government, the Pingat Jasa Malaysia, in recognition of their sacrifice in conflicts in which 519 British troops were killed.

In 1998, fifty years after the outbreak of the Malayan revolution, Chin Peng began a series of journeys. At this point his countrymen had seen only four images of him: at the victory parade in January 1946 when Louis Mountbatten pinned the Burma Star on his jungle fatigues; a grainy photograph on the poster that offered a quarter of million dollars for him, dead or alive; then there was Chin Peng at Baling, looking like a young clerk on his day off in baggy trousers and a short-sleeved shirt; then nothing for thirty-four years until he appeared at the Haadyai peace talks of 1989, an elderly man now, a little overweight, in a smart business suit, but entirely composed in the full glare of the world's media. There, in fluent Malay, he had pledged allegiance to the King of Malaysia, and his deputy Abdullah C. D. urged Malaysians to unite in the cause of social justice. But in June 1998, on the fiftieth anniversary of the Emergency, Chin Peng appeared in London. This excited some comment in the British press, but was unreported in Malaysia, and the subject of only a short notice in the Singapore *Straits Times*. There he travelled to the Public Record Office at Kew; where, in a curious circumlocution of history, the insurgent entered the imperial archive. Surrounded by dozens of other visitors researching their family histories, Chin Peng began a paper trail through his own past. He took pencil notes from the newly opened files of Special Operations Executive; of missions of which he had been a part during the war; of the first agreements in the Malayan jungle between the Malayan Communist Party and South East Asia Command, signed by the traitor Lai Teck; and other names, other betrayals. It began a short odyssey of meetings and interviews with writers and scholars in London, Canberra and, eventually, even Singapore, many of them adversaries, retired policemen and soldiers. Some years later, with the heavy editorial hand of a retired correspondent of the *Daily Telegraph*, his memories would be woven into a memoir entitled *My Side of History*.

Even to his own followers Chin Peng was something of a myth. He had not been seen in the camps of the MCP since he had escaped overland to Beijing in 1960. In his absence, the party had fought a second Emergency, and continued to recruit in small numbers from the poverty and disillusions of independence. It had faced fissures and a brutal internal 'cleansing'. Now small communities of aged fighters, their families and more recent arrivals lived in 'friendship villages' along the Malaysian border, established by the Thai government under the patronage of the Crown Princess. The remnants were still bound by a keen sense of the MCP's history – the landmarks of its struggle celebrated in commemoration and song. In Hong Kong histories began to appear, in Chinese, of the resistance struggle and, in Malay, of the role of the 10th Regiment, and eventually in Malaysia itself other memoirs of the forgotten wars began to appear. For younger Malaysians and Singaporeans they were something of a revelation. At the heart of Chin Peng's story, as with many others, was a demand for recognition as a fighter for his nation's freedom; a claim for a place in the narrative of the nation. With this lay the possibility of return, the issue which had broken up the Baling talks in 1955, but seemed to have been conceded in the Haadyai agreement of 1989. A number of old fighters, including veterans of the Malay 10th Regiment, had quietly come home. But now, it was asked, could Chin Peng – with his lack of repentance for armed struggle, with his long revolutionary's exile in China and Thailand – be considered a citizen of Malaysia? Permission to return was refused and Chin Peng – seeking to fulfil his obligation to honour his parents' graves – was forced in 2004 to challenge the government of Malaysia in the Malaysian courts with breaking the Haadyai agreement. He has yet to have his day in court. As this controversy rumbled on, in 2005, a Malay writer and film-maker, Amir Muhammad, born after the Emergency had ended, shot a documentary that traced, through interviews and music, a voyage from Chin Peng's childhood home of Sitiawan and other parts of Perak to the veterans' villages in south Thailand. Chin Peng himself did not appear. The film, *Lelaki Komunis Terakhir*, 'The Last Communist', was released in the wake of the sixtieth anniversary of the ruling party, UMNO. Its old veterans warned that 'old wounds will bleed again', and the film was eventually banned in Malaysia. 'I don't believe', mused the minister responsible, 'Malaysians have reached a level where they are ready for it.'[71] The Last Communist's claim for his side of history, was only one of many – of friends and fellow-travellers;

victims and vanquished – that were yet to be heard. For many individuals and for whole societies – in the struggles of everyday life and in the perpetual play of memory – the great, terrible Asian war was not yet at its end.

Notes

PROLOGUE: AN UNENDING WAR

1. Haruko Taya Cook and Theodore F. Cook, *Japan at war: an oral history* (New York, 1992), p. 306.

2. Stuart Ball (ed.), *Parliament and politics in the age of Churchill: the Headlam Diaries, 1935–51* (Cambridge, 1999), p. 473.

3. John W. Dower, 'The bombed: Hiroshimas and Nagasakis in Japanese memory', in Michael J. Hogan (ed.), *Hiroshima in history and memory* (Cambridge, 1996), pp. 116–42.

4. John W. Dower, *Embracing defeat: Japan in the wake of World War II* (London, 1999), p. 45.

5. Dr Constantine Constantinovich Petrovsky interview, OHD, SNA.

6. The Committee for the Compilation of Materials on Damage Caused by the Atomic Bombs in Hiroshima and Nagasaki, *Hiroshima and Nagasaki: the physical, medical and social effects of atomic bombings* (New York, 1981), p. 478; Rinifo Sodei, *Were we the enemy? American survivors of Hiroshima* (Boulder, 1998).

7. Petrovsky interview.

8. Brian MacArthur, *Surviving the sword: prisoners of the Japanese, 1942–45* (London, 2005), pp. 420–1.

9. Hugh V. Clarke, *Twilight liberation: Australian POWs between Hiroshima and home* (Sydney, 1985), pp. 63–95, 121.

10. The best account of the campaign remains Louis Allen, *Burma: the longest war 1941–45* (London, 1984).

11. Datuk Mohd Yusoff Hj. Ahmad, *Decades of change (Malaysia – 1910s–1970s)* (Kuala Lumpur, 1983), pp. 283–4.

12. Sheila Allan, *Diary of a girl in Changi, 1941–45* (2nd edn, Roseville, NSW, 1999), p. 137.

13. The title of a vivid early memoir by N. I. Low & H. M. Cheng is *This Singapore (our city of dreadful night)* (Singapore, 1946).

14. See Chin Kee Onn, *Malaya upside down* (Singapore, 1946), pp. 199–202.

15. Cheah Boon Kheng, *Red star over Malaya: resistance and social conflict during and after the Japanese occupation of Malaya, 1941–1946* (Singapore, 1983), pp. 130–1. This is a classic study.

16. Romen Bose, *The end of the war: Singapore's liberation and the aftermath of the Second World War* (Singapore, 2005), p. 101. He quotes a figure of 300 suicides.

17. Carl Francis de Souza interview, OHD, SNA.

18. Takao Fusayama, *Memoir of Takao Fusayama: a Japanese soldier in Malaya and Sumatera* (Kuala Lumpur, 1997), pp. 147–50.

19. Nicholas Tarling, *Britain, Southeast Asia and the Onset of the Cold War, 1945–1950* (Cambridge, 1998), p. 26.

20. Mountbatten to H. R. Hone, 1 February 1944, in A. J. Stockwell (ed.), *British documents on the end of empire: Malaya, part I* (London, 1995), p. 73.

21. Nicholas J. White, *Business, government and the end of empire: Malaya, 1945–1957* (Kuala Lumpur, 1996), pp. 64–5.

22. Paul H. Kratoska, *The Japanese occupation of Malaya, 1941–45* (London, 1998), p. 32.

23. M. E. Dening, 'Review of events in South–East Asia, 1945 to March 1946', 25 March 1946, in Stockwell, *British documents: Malaya, part I*, p. 211.

24. Richard J. Aldrich, *Intelligence and the war against Japan: Britain, America and the politics of secret service* (Cambridge, 2000), pp. 172, 186–7, 330.

25. S. Woodburn Kirby, *The war against Japan*, vol. V, *The surrender of Japan* (London, 1969), pp. 77–82.

CHAPTER I 1945: INTERREGNUM

1. Bengal press adviser's report for the first half of August 1945, L/P and J/5/142, OIOC.

2. Rajmohan Gandhi, *Patel: a life* (Ahmedabad, 1990), p. 341.

3. Penderel Moon (ed.), *Wavell: the viceroy's journal* (London, 1973), entry for 7 August 1945, p. 162.

4. Bengal press adviser's report for the second half of August 1945, reporting the *Dainik Basumati*, L/P and J/5/142, OIOC.

5. Reuter report 18 November 1945, CASB weekly intelligence reports for Burma, f. 211, Clague Papers, Mss Eur E252/55, OIOC.

6. Angelene Naw, *Aung San and the struggle for Burmese independence* (Copenhagen, 2001).

7. Robert H. Taylor, *Marxism and resistance in Burma, 1942–45: Thein Pe Myint's 'Wartime Traveler'* (Athens, OH, 1984), introduction; Joseph Silverstein (ed.), *The political legacy of Aung San* (Ithaca, 1972).

8. Abu Talib Ahmad, *The Malay Muslims, Islam and the Rising Sun: 1941–45* (Kuala Lumpur, 2003), pp. 10–11.

9. Firdaus Haji Abdullah, *Radical Malay politics: its origins and early development* (Petaling Jaya, 1985), p. 67.

10. Mustapha Hussain, *Malay nationalism before Umno: the memoirs of Mustapha Hussain, translated by Insun Mustapha and edited by Jomo K. S.* (Kuala Lumpur, 2005), p. 313.

11. Cheah Boon Kheng, 'The Japanese occupation of Malaya, 1941–45: Ibrahim Yaacob and the struggle for *Indonesia Raya*', *Indonesia*, 28 (1979), pp. 85–120.

12. Gandhi, *Patel*, p. 348.

13. S. A. Das and K. B. Subbaiah, *Chalo Delhi! An historical account of the Indian independence movement in East Asia* (Kuala Lumpur, 1946), pp. 221–2.

14. Leonard A. Gordon, *Brothers against the Raj: a biography of Indian nationalists Sarat and Subhas Chandra Bose* (New York, 1990), p. 539.

15. SEATIC (Southeast Asian Translation and Interrogation Corps) intelligence bulletin, 17 May 1946, interrogation of Ono Ishire, formerly Hikari Kikan Rangoon, WO203/6312, TNA.

16. Karuppiah N. interview, OHD, SNA.

17. Gandhi to Amrit Kaur, 24 August 1945, *Collected works of Mahatma Gandhi*, vol. 81 (Ahmedabad, 1980), p. 161.

18. Karuppiah interview.

19. Joya Chatterji, *Bengal divided: Hindu communalism and partition, 1932–1947* (Cambridge, 1994).

20. *New Times of Burma*, 23 October 1945.

21. Mamoru Shinozaki, *Syonan – my story: the Japanese occupation of Singapore* (Singapore, 1979), p. 24.

22. David L. Kenley, *New culture in a new world: the May Fourth Movement and the Chinese diaspora in Singapore, 1919–1932* (London, 2003), ch. 7.

23. *Reynolds News*, 10 June 1945.

24. Ibid., 15 April 1945.

25. S. R. Rahman, 'The new storm over Asia', ibid., 4 November 1945.

26. Francis Wheen, *Tom Driberg: his life and indiscretions* (London, 1990), p. 2.

27. Ibid., p. 211.

28. John H. McEnery, *Epilogue in Burma, 1945–48: the military dimension of British withdrawal* (Tunbridge Wells, 1990), p. 74.

29. Hussain, *Malay nationalism before Umno*, p. 288.

30. 'The AJUF in Perak', WO208/3928, TNA.

31. Innes Tremlett, 'Memorandum by Head of Malaya Country Section Force 136 on resistance forces in Malaya on the eve of the Japanese capitulation, 15 August, 1945', WO203/4403, TNA.

32. The biographical details that follow are taken from Yoji Akashi, 'Lai Teck, Secretary General of the Malayan Communist Party, 1939–1947', *Journal of the South Seas Society*, 49 (1994), pp. 57–103.

33. By the Singapore communist Ng Yeh Lu, quoted in C. F. Yong, *The origins of Malayan Communism* (Singapore, 1997), p. 188.

34. Anthony Short, *The communist insurrection in Malaya, 1948–60* (London, 1976), p. 41.

35. Akashi, 'Lai Teck'.

36. James Wong Wing On, *From Pacific War to Merdeka: reminiscences of Abdullah C. D. Rashid Maidin, Suriani Abdullah and Abu Samah* (Petaling Jaya, 2005), p. 33.

37. Interviewed by James Wong Wing On, ibid., p. 7.

38. John Davis to SACSEA, 21 August 1945, HS1/114, TNA.

39. Chin Peng, *My side of history* (Singapore, 2003), pp. 111–12.

40. Dorothy Thatcher and Robert Cross, *Refugee from the Japanese* ([1959] Kuala Lumpur, 1993), p. 156.

41. 'Operational report by Major T. A. Wright, Sergeant Orange, PLO', n.d., HS1/117, TNA.

42. J. P. Hannah, 'MPAJA personalities 5th (Perak) Independent Regiment', HS1/107, TNA.

43. Ah Yeow [Liew Yao] to Major D. K. Broadhurst, 16 June and 21 July 1945, Broadhurst Papers, SNA.

44. M. E. Dening to Foreign Office, 3 September 1945, in A. J. Stockwell (ed), *British documents on the end of empire: Malaya, part I* (London, 1995), p. 123.

45. Chin Peng, *My side of history*, pp. 120–1; C. C. Chin and Karl Hack (eds.), *Dialogues with Chin Peng: new light on the Malayan Communist Party* (Singapore, 2004), pp. 106–10.

46. John Davis interview, OHD, SNA; Commander Force 136 to HPD SACSEA, 19 August 1945, HS1/114, TNA.

47. Col. L. F. Sheridan to Edward Gent, 27 August 1945, ibid.

48. Quoted in Cheah Boon Kheng, *Red star over Malaya: resistance and social conflict during and after the Japanese occupation of Malaya, 1941–1946* (Singapore, 1983), p. 137.

49. Richard Gough, *Jungle was red: SOE's Force 136 Sumatra and Malaya* (Singapore, 2003), p. 147.

50. Khoo Salma Nasution and Abdur-Razzaq Lubis, *Kinta Valley: pioneering Malaysia's modern development* (Ipoh, 2005), pp. 290–1; Wong, *From Pacific War to Merdeka*, pp. 10, 19.

51. 'Operational report by Maj. H. H. Wright, Carpenter State PLO', 28 December 1945, HS1/107, TNA.

52. Yoji Akashi, 'The Anti-Japanese movement in Perak during the Japanese occupation, 1941–45', in Paul H. Kratoska (ed.), *Malaya and Singapore during the Japanese occupation* (Singapore, 1995), pp. 113–16.

53. 'Operational report by Maj. H. H. Wright', HS1/107, TNA.

54. Chin Peng, *My side of History*, pp. 123–5.

55. I. D. Ross, 'Operational report Funnel Blue PLO', 19 October 1945, HS1/107, TNA; Michael Stenson, *Class, race and colonialism in West Malaysia: the Indian case* (Queensland, 1980), p. 101.

56. Netaji Centre, Kuala Lumpur, *Netaji Subhas Chandra Bose: a Malaysian perspective* (Kuala Lumpur, 1992), pp. 228–9.

57. For example, Datuk Mohd Yusoff Hj. Ahmad, *Decades of change (Malaysia – 1910s–1970s)* (Kuala Lumpur, 1983), p. 293; Laurence K. L. Siaw, *Chinese society in rural Malaysia* (Kuala Lumpur, 1983), p. 74.

58. 'Operational report D. R. W. Alexander, Sergeant GLO', 5 December 1945, HS1/107, TNA. Chin Peng, who visited the National Archives in Kew, later endorsed Alexander's report; Chin Peng, *My side of history*, p. 128; Ho Thean Fook, *Tainted glory* (Kuala Lumpur, 2000), pp. 240–2.

59. 'Operational report by Maj. H. H. Wright, Carpenter State PLO', 28 December 1945, HS1/107, TNA.

60. Shinozaki, *Syonan – my story*, p. 97; Heng Chiang Ki interview, OHD, SNA.

61. N. I. Low, *When Singapore was Syonan-to* ([1947] Singapore, 1995), pp. 130–1.

62. Mustapha Hussain, *Malay nationalism before Umno*, p. 288.

63. The most thorough and balanced account of the conflict is Cheah, *Red star over Malaya*, ch. 8. For Malay religious anxieties, Abu Talib Ahmad, *The Malay Muslims, Islam and the Rising Sun*, esp. chs. 4 and 5.

64. Syed Naguib al-Attas, *Some aspects of Sufism as understood and practised by the Malays* (Singapore, 1963), pp. 47–8, 100.

65. 'Sabilu'llah and invulnerability', supplement to Malayan Security Service, Political Intelligence Journal, No. 9/1947, 15 June 1947, Dalley Papers, RHO; A. J. Stockwell, *British policy and Malay politics during the Malayan Union experiment, 1945–1948* (Kuala Lumpur, 1979), p. 150, and n. 21.

66. 'Report on incidents of banditry, Langkap area', 25 September 1945, HS1/107, TNA.

67. Cheah, *Red star over Malaya*, p. 225.

68. J. K. Creer, 'Report on experiences during Japanese occupation of Malaya', 3 November 1945, Heussler Reports, RHO.

69. Chin Peng, *My side of history*, pp. 110–11.

70. Wilfred Blythe, *The impact of Chinese secret societies in Malaya: a historical study* (London, 1969), pp. 327–38.

71. Mahmud bin Mat, *Tinggal kenangan: the memoirs of Dato' Sir Mahmud bin Mat* (Kuala Lumpur, 1997), pp. 271–88; Gough, *Jungle was red*, p. 163.

72. Tunku Abdul Rahman, *As a matter of interest* (Petaling Jaya, 1981), pp. 162–3.

73. Pamela Ong Siew Im, *One man's will: a portrait of Dato' Sir Onn bin Ja'afar* (Penang, 1998), pp. 170–1.

74. Anwar Abdullah, *Dato Onn* (Petaling Jaya, 1971), p. 111.

75. Cheah, *Red star over Malaya*, pp. 225–30.

76. S. Chelvasingham-MacIntyre, *Through memory lane* (Singapore, 1973), p. 128.

77. Rahman, *As a matter of interest*, pp. 160–1.

78. John Tan Boon Liang, *A bamboo flower blooms* (New York, 1984), pp. 215–16.

79. O. W. Gilmour, *With freedom to Singapore* (London, 1950), pp. 74–9; Romen Bose, *The end of the war: Singapore's liberation and the aftermath of the Second World War* (Singapore, 2005), pp. 2–11.

80. Gilmour, *With freedom to Singapore*, pp. 89–93, 150.

81. Note by Lt Cdr W. E. Machin, HQ British East India Fleet, 13 September 1945, ADM1/25907, TNA.

82. S. Woodburn Kirby, *The war against Japan*, vol. V, *The surrender of Japan* (London, 1969), pp. 266–9.

83. Chin Peng, *My side of history*, p. 130; Alan Stripp, *Codebreaker in the Far East* (Oxford, 1989), p. 176.

84. Capt. G. P. Brownie, quoted in Gough, *Jungle was red*, p. 158.

85. R. W. Holder, *Eleven months in Malaya: September 1945 to August 1946* (Kuala Lumpur, 2005), p. 24.

86. Chin Peng, *My side of history*, p. 129.

87. Gough, *Jungle was red*, p. 161.

88. Gilmour, *With freedom to Singapore*, pp. 101–2.

89. Holder, *Eleven months in Malaya*, pp. 37–8.

90. Frank Gibney (ed), *Senso: the Japanese remember the Pacific War: letters to the editor of Asahi Shimbun* (London, 1995), pp. 226–7.

91. 'Report on RAPWI in Malaya and Singapore', 7 January 1946, BMA/ADM/2/34.

92. Arshak Catihatoer Galstaun interview, OHD, SNA.

93. A. J. F. Doulton, *The Fighting Cock: being the history of the 23rd Indian Division, 1942–1947* (Aldershot, 1951), p. 222.

94. Madelaine Masson, *Edwina: the biography of the Countess Mountbatten of Burma* (London, 1958), p. 150.

95. Dato Haji Mohamed Yudof Bangs interview, OHD, SNA.

96. Gilmour, *With freedom to Singapore*, p. 96.

97. Sheila Allan, *Diary of a girl in Changi, 1941–45* (2nd edn., Roseville, NSW, 1999), pp. 137–47.

98. Sjovald Cunyngham-Brown, *Crowded hour* (London, 1975), pp. 147–9.

99. Letter to his wife, 10 September 1945, John Lowe Woods, *An Irishman in Malaya* (Peterhead, 1977), p. 136.

100. Gilmour, *With freedom to Singapore*, p. 100.

101. 'Appendix A: The psychological state of RAPWI', Lt. Col. R. F. Tredgold, 'Psychiatry in ALFSEA', March 1946, WO222/1319, TNA; Robert H. Ahrenfeldt, *Psychiatry in the British army in the Second World War* (London, 1950), p. 235.

102. 'Appendix D: Talks to groups of repatriates', Lt Col. R. F. Tredgold, 'Psychiatry in ALFSEA', March 1946, WO222/1319, TNA.

103. Bose, *The end of the war*, pp. 116–24.

104. Note by Lt Cdr W. E. Machin, HQ British East India Fleet, 13 September 1945, ADM1/25907, TNA; Low, *When Singapore was Syonan-to*, pp. 132–3.

105. Wong, *From Pacific War to Merdeka*, pp. 21–2.

106. Chelvasingham-MacIntyre, *Through memory lane*, pp. 128–9.

107. L. F. Pendred, Director of Intelligence, 'The visit of Pandit Nehru to Malaya', 30 March 1946, CO717/149/8, TNA.

108. Kevin Blackburn and Edmund Lim, 'The Japanese war memorials of Singapore: monuments of commemoration and symbols of Japanese imperial ideology', *South East Asia Research*, 7, 3 (2001), pp. 321–40; Gilmour, *With freedom to Singapore*, pp. 118–19.

109. Kevin Blackburn, 'The collective memory of the *sook ching* massacre and the creation of the civilian war memorial of Singapore', *Journal of the Malaysian Branch of the Royal Asiatic Society*, 73, 2 (2000), p. 76.

CHAPTER 2 1945: THE PAINS OF VICTORY

1. T. L. Hughes to H. Stevenson, 15 August 1945, fortnightly reports f. 24, Clague Papers, Mss Eur E252/55, OIOC.

2. Slim to HQ ALFSEA, 15 May 1945, in Hugh Tinker (ed.), *Burma: the struggle for independence, 1944–1948*, vol. I: *From military occupation to*

civil government, 1 January 1944 to 31 August 1946 (London, 1983), p. 250.

3. Loyal resolution by leading Burmese monks at Rangoon victory celebrations, 15 June 1945, Governor of Burma's Papers, M/3/1736, OIOC.

4. The naming of Aung San's forces is extremely confusing, to say the least. The Burma Independence Army (BIA) of 1941–2 became the Burma Defence Army (BDA) shortly after the Japanese invasion. On 'independence' in 1943 it became the Burma National Army (BNA). In July 1945, along with other armed elements, it became part of the Burma Patriotic Forces (PBF), though many of its personnel were stood down and became members of the People's Volunteer Organizations (PVOs or, in Burmese, PYTs). To avoid alphabet soup we have continued to refer to the predominantly Burman forces of the PBF as BNA. For a comprehensive account using Burmese-language material, see, Mary P. Callahan, *Making enemies: War and state building in Burma* (Ithaca, 2004).

5. Maung Maung, *To a soldier son* (Rangoon, 1974), p. 77.

6. Ibid., p. 79.

7. Ibid., pp. 74–5.

8. 'Twelfth Army report upon the state of civil affairs departments and conditions in Burma, 16 October 1945', WO203/2269, TNA.

9. *Rangoon Liberator*, 27 September 1945, copy in Governor of Burma's Papers, M/3/1693, OIOC.

10. Ibid.

11. Fortnightly intelligence report, civil censorship, no. 2, Burma and Malaya, 23 August 1945, R/8/41, OIOC.

12. 'Report on the general feelings of the people in the Rangoon area', c. July–August 1945, in fortnightly reports, Clague Papers, Mss Eur E252/55, OIOC.

13. Balwant Singh, *Independence and democracy in Burma, 1945–52: the turbulent years* (Ann Arbor, 1993), p. 14.

14. Gordon S. Seagrave, *Burma surgeon* (London, 1944), and *Burma surgeon returns* (London, 1946).

15. Gordon S. Seagrave, *My hospital in the hills* (London, 1957).

16. Ibid, p. 36.

17. Comments of Sir William Slim, SAC meeting, 5 September 1945, WO/203/5240, TNA; Angelene Naw, *Aung San and the struggle for Burmese independence* (Copenhagen, 2001), p. 135.

18. Naw, *Aung San*, p. 135.

19. Minute by S. Brooke-Wavell, RAF Public Relations Officer on Than Tun, November 1945, Tom Driberg papers, S3, 23, Christ Church, Oxford.

20. Aung Sang to Mountbatten, 25 September 1945, Dorman-Smith Papers, Mss Eur E215/14, OIOC.

21. Dorman-Smith to Leo Amery, 25 June 1945, L/PO/9/10, OIOC.

22. Maurice Collis, *Last and first in Burma, 1941–48* (London, 1956), p. 243.

23. Meeting between the governor of Burma and representatives of organizations and communities in Burma, WO203/5238, TNA; Tinker, *Burma*, vol. I, pp. 339–40.

24. U Ba U, *My Burma: the autobiography of a president* (New York, 1959), pp, 176, 183.

25. 'Victory dinner, 15 September 1945', menu in Tom Driberg Papers, S3, 1, Christ Church, Oxford.

26. Naw, *Aung San*, p. 141.

27. Mountbatten to Dorman-Smith, 1 August 1944, Dorman-Smith Papers, Mss Eur E215/28, OIOC.

28. Sir R. MacDougall to Dorman-Smith, 20 October 1944, Dorman-Smith Papers, Mss Eur E215/15, OIOC.

29. Joseph Silverstein (ed.), *The Political Legacy of Aung San* (Ithaca, 1976); Gustaaf Houtman, *Mental culture in Burmese crisis politics* (Tokyo, 2002), pp. 181–9.

30. Callahan, *Making enemies*, pp. 109–11.

31. Aung San to Mountbatten, 25 September 1945, Dorman-Smith Papers, Mss Eur E215/28, OIOC.

32. Tom Driberg, *Ruling passions* (London, 1979), p. 215.

33. Driberg's column in *Reynolds News*, 14 October 1945.

34. Ibid.

35. Francis Wheen, *Tom Driberg: his life and indiscretions* (London, 1990), p. 216.

36. Driberg, *Ruling passions*, p. 216.

37. *Reynolds News*, 14 October 1945.

38. Extract from a letter from Tom Driberg, SEAC to Dorman-Smith, 4 October 1945, Dorman-Smith Papers, Mss Eur E215/28, OIOC.

39. A/C Allen, A. G., 346 Wing, SEAF, to Driberg, 19 December 1945, Tom Driberg Papers, S3, 5 (miscellaneous), Christ Church, Oxford.

40. Col. John Ralston, 2 Area Singapore, to Driberg, 25 November 1945, Tom Driberg Papers, S3, 1, 25, Christ Church, Oxford.

41. Kyin Hla to Driberg, 28 September 1945, Tom Driberg Papers S3, 1, 16, Christ Church, Oxford.

42. See Christopher Bayly and Tim Harper, *Forgotten armies: Britain's Asian empire and the war with Japan* (London, 2004).

43. Montagu Stopford to Mountbatten, 26 December 1945, Mountbatten Papers (microfilm), 8, OIOC.

44. Letter of Aung San in *Rangoon Liberator*, 5 October 1945, Governor of Burma's Papers, M/3/1694, OIOC.

45. *Rangoon Liberator*, 27 October 1945, ibid.

46. Naw, *Aung San*, pp. 142–9.

47. Ibid, p. 143.

48. See, e.g., 'Karen memorial', memorandum presented by H. N. C. Stevenson and T. L. Hughes, February 1946, FO643/39, TNA, printed in Tinker, *Burma*, vol. I, pp. 650–1.

49. San C. Po, *Burma and the Karens* (London, 1929).

50. Jonathan Falla, *True love and Bartholemew: rebels on the Burmese border* (Cambridge, 1991), p. 25.

51. Callahan, *Making enemies*, pp. 86–113.

52. Peter Clarke, *The Cripps version: the life of Sir Stafford Cripps* (London, 2002).

53. Lady Pethick-Lawrence to Vijaya Lakshmi Pandit, 5 September 1945, Pethick-Lawrence Papers, Box 5/83, Trinity College, Cambridge.

54. Krishna Menon to Pethick-Lawrence, 31 March 1954, ibid., 5/91.

55. Pethick-Lawrence to Huxley, 29 November 1943, ibid., 5/61.

56. Nehru to Cripps, 3 December 1945, ibid., 5/64.

57. Gandhi to Pethick-Lawrence, 12 January 1946, ibid., 5/66.

58. Intelligence report quoting soldiers' letters, no. 172, 16 February 1945, appendix A, L/WS/1/1433, OIOC.

59. Personal communication from Eric Stokes, 1979.

60. Provincial officers and Intelligence Bureau conference on INA, 19–20 November 1945, L/WS/1/1577, OIOC.

61. Appended to above, ibid.

62. *Statesman*, 5 October 1945.

63. W. L. Alston 'My day and age': this was a compilation of memoirs and contemporary letters etc., 8005–151, box 10, National Army Museum.

64. Note from Deputy Director of Military Intelligence (S), f. 112, L/WS/1/1577, OIOC.

65. Conference of provincial officers, ibid.

66. *Amrita Bazaar Patrika*, 2 November 1945.

67. *Statesman*, 23 July 1947.

68. Governor of Bengal to viceroy, 22 August 1946, 'Calcutta riots 1947', L/P and J/8/655, OIOC.

69. *Amrita Bazaar Patrika*, 24 October 1945.

70. *Amrita Bazaar Patrika*, 3 November 1945.

71. *Amrita Bazaar Patrika*, 22 November 1945.

72. *Amrita Bazaar Patrika*, 2 November 1945.

73. *Amrita Bazaar Patrika*, 6 November 1945.

74. *Amrita Bazaar Patrika*, 27 October 1945.

75. S. N. Arseculeratne, *Sinhalese immigrants in Malaysia and Singapore, 1860–1990: history through recollections* (Colombo, 1991), p. 337.

76. 'INA in Siam', WO203/2462, TNA.

77. Attachments to WO203/4673, TNA.

78. Girishchandra Kotari interview, OHD, SNA; Arseculeratne, *Sinhalese immigrants*, p. 338.

79. Memo, 15 October 1945, WO203/4203B, TNA.

80. Penderel Moon (ed.), *Wavell: the viceroy's journal* (London, 1973), statement of the governor of North West Frontier Province, entry 24 November 1945, p. 188.

81. Ibid., entry 5 November 1945, p. 182.

82. V. S. Kulkarni and K. S. N. Munshi, *The First Indian National Army trial* (Poonah, 1946), p. i.

83. Ibid., pp. xv–xviii.

84. Ibid., p. 58.

85. Ibid. p. 47.

86. Conference of provincial officers, L/WS/1/1577, OIOC.

87. For instance, Sir Dalip Singh, K. N. Katju and J. N. Sapru; Kulkarni and Munshi, *First Indian National Army trial*, p. 171.

88. Moon, *Wavell*, p. 191.

89. D. K. Palit, *Major General A. A. Rudra: his services in three armies and two world wars* (Delhi, 1997), pp. 282, 284.

90. Wavell to Pethick-Lawrence, 17 October 1945, CAB119/191, TNA; Cabinet Defence Meeting, minutes of meeting on 19 October 1945, CAB121/698, TNA.

91. S. K. Chettur, *Malayan adventure* (Mangalore, 1948), pp. 12–30.

92. Wavell to Mountbatten, 4 December 1945, WO203/4203B, TNA.

93. Malaya Command to SACSEA, 7 January 1946, WO203/4303B, TNA.

94. Chettur, *Malayan adventure*, pp. 31–60.

95. Mustapha Hussain, *Malay nationalism before Umno: the memoirs of Mustapha Hussain, translated by Insun Mustapha and edited by Jomo K. S.* (Kuala Lumpur, 2005), pp. 295–327.

96. F. S. V. Donnison, *British military administration in the Far East* (London, 1956), p. 304. See the discussion by Abu Talib Ahmad, *The Malay Muslims, Islam and the Rising Sun: 1941–45* (Kuala Lumpur, 2003), pp. 133–6.

97. Mamoru Shinozaki, *Syonan – my story: the Japanese occupation of Singapore* (Singapore, 1979), p. 107.

98. Herman Marie de Souza interview, OHD, SNA.

99. Cited in Romen Bose, *A will to freedom: Netaji and the Indian independence movement in Singapore and Southeast Asia, 1942–45* (Singapore, 1993), p. 49.

100. T. T. Hui to unnamed official, 8 November 1945, on NARA/XL30328, SNA.

101. Wee Kim Guan, letter, 13 May 1946, BMA HQ S.DIV/151/45, SNA.
102. Examples from *New Democracy*, 6 October, 1945.

CHAPTER 3 1945: A SECOND COLONIAL CONQUEST

1. Cited in Robert Pearce, *Attlee* (London, 1977), p. 122.
2. Ibid, p. 281.
3. Note on the paper 'Religion in the army' by R. Savory, 7603–93/90, National Army Museum, London.
4. Sir Donald Cameron, 'Give an account of Thy Stewardship', 15 May 1942, CO875/19/13, TNA.
5. Wavell cited in Rajmohan Gandhi, *Patel: a life* (Ahmedabad, 1990) p, 433.
6. Penderel Moon (ed.), *Wavell: the viceroy's journal* (London, 1973), entry for 31 August 1945, p. 170.
7. Harold Macmillan, *Tides of fortune* (London, 1969), p. 246, cited in Nicholas Owen, 'The Conservative Party and Indian independence, 1945–47', *Historical Journal*, 46, 2 (2003), p. 411.
8. Victor Purcell, *The memoirs of a Malayan official* (London, 1965), p. 293.
9. Ralph Hone to E. V. G. Day, 21 February 1945, BMA/ADM/239, ANM.
10. Chua Ai Lin, 'Negotiating national identity: the English-speaking domiciled commmunities in Singapore, 1930–41', MA thesis, National University of Singapore, 2001.
11. Captain L. D. Gammans, 'Post-war planning in South-East Asia', *British Malaya*, November 1942.
12. Ralph Hone, *Report on the British Military Administration of Malaya, September 1945 to March 1946* (Kuala Lumpur, 1946).
13. Amy and Richard Haggard, 'An account of the British Military Administration of Upper Perak, Malaya – 1945/46: being memories based on diaries and letters', 4 April 2000, RCS, CUL.
14. Melanie Chew, *Of hearts and minds: the story of Sembawang* (Singapore, 1998), p. 58.
15. O. W. Gilmour, *With freedom to Singapore* (London, 1950), p. 117.
16. Nicholas J. White, *Business, government and the end of empire: Malaya, 1945–1957* (Kuala Lumpur, 1996), p. 75.
17. Sydney Caine to Lord Keynes, 19 March 1945, in A. J. Stockwell (ed.), *British documents on the end of empire: Malaya, part I* (London, 1995), pp. 90–1.
18. Arthur Alexander Thompson interview, OHD, SNA; J. Pickering, 'Monthly report for January 1946, Refugees and Displaced Persons Branch, Peninsula Division', BMA/ADM/2/28, ANM.

19. T. N. Harper, *The end of empire and the making of Malaya* (Cambridge, 1999), pp. 41, 66; 'A report on the damage resulting from the war and the Japanese occupation', 10 December 1946, CSO/6929, SNA.

20. S. K. Chettur, *Malayan adventure* (Mangalore, 1948), p. 22. For the figures see Michiko Nakahara, 'Labour recruitment in Malaya under the Japanese occupation: the case of the Burma–Siam railway', in Jomo K. S. (ed.), *Rethinking Malaysia* (Kuala Lumpur, 1997), pp. 215–45.

21. J. Pickering, 'Monthly report for December 1945, Refugees and Displaced Persons Branch, Peninsula Division', BMA/ADM/2/28, ANM; 'Monthly report for January 1946', ibid.

22. For example, Lau Siew Foo (Malayan Security Service) and J. C. Bary, 'A brief review of Chinese affairs during the period of the Japanese occupation', BMA/ADM/8/1, ANM.

23. R. W. Holder, *Eleven months in Malaya: September 1945 to August 1946* (Kuala Lumpur, 2005), pp. 91–2. These images are in the collection of the Imperial War Museum; see, for example, Christopher Bayly and Tim Harper, *Forgotten armies: Britain's Asian Empire and the war with Japan* (London, 2004), illustration no. 24.

24. Jan Ruff-O'Herne, *50 years of silence* (Sydney, 1994), p. 131. For pioneering work on the Malayan case, Nakahara Michiko, 'Comfort women in Malaysia', *Critical Asian Studies*, 33, 4 (2001), pp. 581–9.

25. Minutes of the inaugural meeting of the Singapore Social Welfare Council, 26 July 1946; H. R. Horne, 'Girls' training school', 26 September 1946, BMA/CH/27/45, SNA.

26. V. Purcell, minute, 25 March 1946, BMA/ADM/2/46, ANM.

27. Harper, *The end of empire*, pp. 42–4, 97, 229–30.

28. Nutrition Unit Visit to Mersing, BMA/HQ S.DIV/466/45; Matthews to Purcell, 22 September 1945, BMA/CH/7/45, SNA; Nutrition Unit, BMA, Malaya, 'Final Report', BMA/DEPT/1/13, ANM.

29. Sudarajulu Laksmana Perumal interview, OHD, SNA.

30. 'Monthly report on labour, December 1945', BMA/DEPT/2/1, ANM.

31. Pickering, 'Monthly report for December 1945'; 'Monthly report for January 1946'.

32. R. E. Vine, 'Memorandum on the medical aspects of the use of opium and allied drugs in Malaya', 5 December 1944; War Office to ALFSEA, 18 April 1945, BMA/DEPT/1/14 Pt 1, ANM.

33. *Nanyang Siang Pau* [Singapore], 23 November 1945; Pook Luk, 'Broadcasting station', *Nanyang Siang Pau*, 27 November 1945. Citations from the Chinese, Malay and Tamil press come from the translations in a variety of 'Chinese Press Summaries' and 'Vernacular Press Digests' prepared by the colonial government and to be found in the Singapore National Archives, the

National Library of Singapore, the Arkib Negara Malaysia and the library of SOAS, London. The translations were selective and made in haste, but in some cases they form the only extant record of these journals.

34. Chang Cheng Yean interview, OHD, SNA.

35. Heng Chiang Ki interview, OHD, SNA.

36. 'The Civilians' to Victor Purcell, 9 December 1945, BMA/CH/7/45, SNA.

37. Ralph Hone to F. S. V. Donnison, 25 March 1953, Hone Papers, RHO.

38. Wilfred Blythe, *The impact of Chinese secret societies in Malaya: a historical study* (London, 1969), pp. 338–44.

39. D. F. Grant diary, 17 June 1946, DF/370/45, ANM.

40. J. P. Mead, 'Renewed collection of forest revenue', 19 October 1945, DF/90/45, ANM.

41. Ang Keong Lan interview, OHD, SNA.

42. Haggard and Haggard, 'An account of the BMA of Upper Perak'.

43. Peter Bates, *Japan and the British Commonwealth Occupation Force, 1946–52* (London, 1994), p. 105.

44. Hone to F. S. V. Donnison, 1 May 1952, Hone Papers, RHO; H. T. Pagden, 'Unrest in Malaya', in letter to O. H. Morris of the Colonial Office, 12 October 1948, CO537/3757, TNA.

45. Charles Gamba, *The origins of trade unionism in Malaya* (Singapore, 1960), pp. 46–7; Arshak Catihatoer Galstaun interview, OHD, SNA.

46. *Nanyang Siang Pau*, 20 November 1945.

47. Victor Purcell to Maj. General G. N. Wood, 28 December 1945, WO203/5302, TNA.

48. *Kin Kwok Daily News* [Ipoh], 12 December 1945.

49. *Sin Chew Jit Poh* [Singapore], 19 November 1945.

50. Dr Benjamin Chew interview, OHD, SNA.

51. Victor Purcell to CCAO, 31 October 1945; H. S. Lee to Purcell, 29 October 1945, BMA/CH/31/45, SNA.

52. James to Purcell, 13 November 1945, BMA/CH/31/45, SNA.

53. Gay Wan Guay interview, OHD, SNA.

54. *Straits Times* [Singapore], 20 December 1945; HQ SACSEA, 'Discipline: Singapore Island', 12 January 1946, WO203/4362, TNA.

55. *Kung Pao* [Singapore], 18 April 1946.

56. B. Dean, *The theatre at war* (London, 1956), p. 490.

57. Brig, E. H. A. J. O'Donnell to Norman Collins, BBC, 21 September 1945; Minister of Food to First Lord of the Admiralty, 5 September 1945, WO32/11479, TNA.

58. Holder, *Eleven months in Malaya*, pp. 55–66.

59. *Malaya Tribune* [Kuala Lumpur], 9 December 1945.

60. For a rare historical study, Haryati Hasan, 'Malay women and prostitution in Kota Bahru, Kelantan, 1950s–1970s', *Journal of the Malaysian Branch of the Royal Asiatic Society*, 78, 1 (2005), pp. 97–120.

61. Memo: V. D.' DA & QHG 14th Army, 15 October 1945; C. E. C. Davis, 'Report on the VD situation in Singapore, 4 March 1946'; 'Special meeting held at HQ SACSEA to consider methods to combat VD in SEAC, 7 December 1945', BMA/DEPT/1/2, AMN.

62. Acting Commissioner of Police, Malayan Union, 'Suppression of brothels – reasons against', n.d. [November 1946], SCA/28/46, SNA.

63. Singapore City Committee Malayan Communist Party to Civil Affairs Department, 23 October 1945, BMA/CA/8/45, SNA.

64. *Min Sheng Pau* [Kuala Lumpur], 18 October, 11 December, 1945.

65. *New Democracy*, 27 October 1945.

66. Maj. General G. N. Wood (25 Indian Division) to Victor Purcell, 24 December 1945; Purcell to Wood, 28 December 1945, WO203/5302, TNA.

67. *Min Sheng Pau*, 22 October 1945.

68. *New Democracy*, 22 January 1946.

69. 'BMA Monthly Report for February 1946', WO220/564, TNA; Mubin Sheppard, *Taman Budiman: memoirs of an unorthodox civil servant* (Kuala Lumpur, 1979), pp. 144–5; Datuk Mohd Yusoff Hj. Ahmad, *Decades of change (Malaysia – 1910s–1970s)* (Kuala Lumpur, 1983), p. 325.

70. Gilmour, *With Freedom to Singapore*, pp. 133, 152, 155.

71. Chin Kee Onn, *Malaya upside down* (Singapore, 1946), pp. 190–8.

72. Wong Yunn Chii and Tan Kar Lin, 'Emergence of a cosmopolitan space for culture and consumption: the New World Amusement Park – Singapore (1923–70) in the inter-war years', *Inter-Asia Cultural Studies*, 5, 2 (2004), pp. 279–304.

73. M. S. Daud, 'Popularity of the "Bangsawan" is declining', *Malaya Tribune*, 18 July 1948.

74. *Sin Chew Jit Poh*, 22 October 1945.

75. *New Democracy*, 4 October 1945.

76. *Modern Daily News*, 10 October 1945.

The 'Eight Principles' are:

(1) Support the Democratic Alliance of Soviet Russia, China, Britain and America. Support the new International Peace Organization.

(2) Materialize the Malayan Democratic polity. Establish organs of peoples' wish for the whole of Malaya as well as the respective States by universal suffrage of the various nationalities and Anti-Japanese organizations of Malaya.

(3) Abolish the political structure formed by the domination of the Japanese Fascists in Malaya. Abolish all Japanese laws and decrees.

(4) Practise the absolute freedom of speech, publication, organization, public meeting and belief. Assure the legal position of all parties and organizations.

(5) Relinquish the old system of education and exercise democratic education with the respective national languages. Expand national culture.

(6) Improve the living conditions of the people; develop Industry, Agriculture and Commerce; relieve the unemployed and refugees; increase wages universally and practise the '8 hours' work system'.

(7) Reduce the prices of goods to the level; stabilize the living conditions of the people; punish corrupt officials, profiteers and hoarders.

(8) Treat the Anti-Japanese armies kindly, and help the families of the fallen warriors.

(Cheah Boon Kheng, *Red star over Malaya: resistance and social conflict during and after the Japanese occupation of Malaya, 1941–1946* (Singapore, 1983), appendix D, 'Statement of the Selangor State Committee, The Communist Party of Malaya', 27 August 1945, pp. 308–9.)

77. Victor Purcell, 'Malaya's Political Climate IV: 10–30 November 1945', WO203/5302, TNA.

78. 'Number of cases receiving relief and amount of cash issued', 11 October 1945, BMA/CA/48/45, SNA.

79. Cheah Boon Kheng, *The masked comrades: a study of the Communist United Front in Malaya, 1945–48* (Singapore, 1979), pp. 24–5.

80. *Modern Daily News* [Penang], 25 December 1945.

81. *Sin Chew Jit Poh*, 6 October 1945.

82. See the testimonies in Agnes Khoo, *Life as the river flows: women in the Malayan anti-colonial struggle* (Petaling Jaya, 2004).

83. Tai Ngo, 'To our sisters', *Kin Kwok Daily News* [Ipoh], 3 November 1945.

84. A. F. P. Hulsewe, 'Survey of current Chinese periodicals in Malaya', *Chinese Press Summary*, 60 [Jan. 1946], pp. 13–18.

85. Victor Purcell, 'Malaya's Political Climate II: 1–19 October 1945', WO203/5302, TNA.

86. Ibid.

87. Purcell, *Memoirs of a Malayan Official*, p. 353.

88. Quoted in Gamba, *The origins of trade unionism in Malaya*, p. 19.

89. *Min Sheng Pau*, 26 October 1945.

90. 'Report on Labour troubles in Singapore', 27 October 1945; 'Labour sitrep Singapore', 27 October 1945, BMA/DEPT/2/15, ANM; *New Democracy*, 23 October 1945.

91. Michael Stenson, *Industrial conflict in Malaya: prelude to the communist*

revolt of 1948 (London, 1970); Leong Yee Fong, *Labour and trade unionism in colonial Malaya* (Penang, 1999). For Brazier, see Gamba, *The origins of trade unionism*, p. 101.

92. Under the name Wee Mong Cheng, Ng Yeh Lu embarked on a successful business career; he became an office bearer in the Singapore Chinese Chamber of Commerce, and between 1973 and 1980 Singapore's ambassador to Japan and Korea, C. F. Yong, *The origins of Malayan Communism* (Singapore, 1997), pp. 190–2, 253. Also Yoji Akashi, 'Lai Teck, Secretary General of the Malayan Communist Party, 1939–1947', *Journal of the South Seas Society*, 49 (1994), pp. 57–103.

93. *Kin Kwok Daily News* [Ipoh], 27 November 1945.

94. Victor Purcell, 'Malaya's Political Climate V: 1–20 December 1945', WO203/5302, TNA.

95. 'Appendix I: Lai Teck, Communist leader', in CO537/3737, TNA.

96. Mamoru Shinozaki, *Syonan – my story: the Japanese occupation of Singapore* (Singapore, 1979), pp. 101–2; Yoji Akashi, 'The Anti-Japanese movement in Perak during the Japanese occupation, 1941–45', in Paul H. Kratoska (ed.), *Malaya and Singapore during the Japanese occupation* (Singapore, 1995), p. 118.

97. We have here drawn on the detective work of Cheah Boon Kheng, *Red star over Malaya: resistance and social conflict during and after the Japanese occupation of Malaya, 1941–1946* (Singapore, 1983), pp. 244–7.

98. Quoted in Charles B. McLane, *Soviet strategies in Southeast Asia: an exploration of Eastern Poicy under Lenin and Stalin* (Princeton, 1966), p. 306.

99. US Army, Kuala Lumpur, 'Interview with Communist leaders', 15 October 1945, NARA/XL26313, SNA. Lim Cheng Leng, *The story of a psy-warrior: Ta Sri Dr C. C. Too* (Batu Caves, 2000), pp. 67–9.

100. *Shih Tai Jit Poh*, 21 October 1945; *Min Sheng Pau*, 24 October, 1945.

101. Purcell, 'Malaya's Political Climate V'.

102. The following report is complied from notes taken by William McDougall of United Press during an interview with 'Wu Tain Want' [Wu Tian Wang], spokesman of the Singapore City Committee of the Malayan Communist Party, 23 September 1945, NARA/XL27129, SNA.

103. OSS, 'Activities of Liu Yau', 31 August 1946, NARA/A-71322, SNA.

104. Hu Ti Jun, 'A letter to the British Advisor of Malayan Affairs (The Parkerton Open Letter)', in Foong Choon Hon (ed.), *The price of peace: true accounts of the Japanese occupation* (Singapore, 1991), p. 288.

105. War Office to ALFSEA, 27 June, 1946; Chief Secretary to HQ Malaya District, 20 April 1950, WO32/17642, TNA.

106. Ho Thean Fook, *Tainted glory* (Kuala Lumpur, 2000), pp. 252–9.

107. Purcell, *Memoirs of a Malayan official*, pp. 352, 357.

108. Mary Turnbull, 'British planning for post-war Malaya', *Journal of Southeast Asian Studies*, 5, 2 (1974), pp. 239–54.

109. H. M. Cheng, 'Re: Malayan Nationality', 5 December 1945, BMA/CH/68/45, SNA.

110. Purcell, 'Malaya's Political Climate II'.

111. Mountbatten to Oliver Stanley, 19 July 1944, in Stockwell, *British documents: Malaya, part 1*, pp. 82–3.

112. Report by H. C. Willan, 7 October 1945, ibid., pp. 140–2. For the Sultan's tiger kills, A. Locke, *The tigers of Trengganu* (London, 1954), p. 149.

113. A. J. Stockwell, *British policy and Malay politics during the Malayan Union experiment, 1945–1948* (Kuala Lumpur, 1979), p. 40.

114. Sir Harold MacMichael to Sir George Gator, 22 October 1945, in Stockwell, *British documents: Malaya, part I*, pp. 171–5.

115. Notes by Sir Harold MacMichael, 30 November–3 December 1945, ibid., pp. 181–6.

116. Badlishah's letter to Yang di-Pertuan Besar [ruler] of Negri Sembilan, in Ismail bin Haji Salleh, *The Sultan was not alone: a collection of letters written by Sultan Badlishah in his effort to repeal the Malayan Union policy imposed by the British Government on Malaya in 1946, and other supporting letters and documents written by others* (Alor Setar, 1989), p. 2; 'Extract from letter from an official in Malaya', 6 January 1946, Maxwell Papers, BAM Papers, CUL.

117. *Warta Negara*, 11 December 1945.

118. *Majlis* [Kuala Lumpur], 12 December 1945.

119. *Utusan Melayu* [Singapore], 2 November 1945.

120. Ahmad Boestamam (trans. William R. Roff), *Carving the path to the summit* (Athens, OH, 1979), pp. 22–7.

CHAPTER 4 1945: THE FIRST WARS OF PEACE

1. Bengal press adviser's report for the first half of August 1945, L/P and J/5/142, OIOC.

2. Dirk Bogarde, *Cleared for take-off* (London, 1995), pp. 100–110.

3. As reported in John Coldstream, *Dirk Bogarde: the authorised biography* (London, 2005), p. 164.

4. Dirk Bogarde, *Backcloth* (London, 1985), pp. 125–35.

5. M. E. Dening, 'Review of events in South-East Asia 1945 to March, 1946', 25 March 1946, in A. J. Stockwell (ed.), *British documents on the end of empire: Malaya, part I* (London, 1995), p. 211.

6. Peter Bates, *Japan and the British Commonwealth occupation force, 1946–52* (London, 1993).

7. George Rosie, *The British in Vietnam: how the twenty-five year war began* (London, 1970), p. 15.

8. David Marr, *Vietnam 1945* (Berkeley, 1995), p. 135.

9. Cited in Rosie, *The British in Vietnam*, p. 25; there is a recent reassessment of these events in John Springhall, 'Kicking out the Vietminh: how Britain allowed France to reoccupy south Indochina', *Journal of Contemporary History*, 40, 1 (2005), pp. 115–30.

10. Marr, *Vietnam*, p. 458.

11. E.g. 'A short note on Indochina', intelligence summary appended to orders of 20th Indian Division, Gracey Papers, 4/1, LHCMA.

12. Paul Mus, *Le destin de l'union française de l'Indochine à l'Afrique* (Paris, 1955), cited in Susan Bayly, 'French anthropology and the Durkheimians in Indochina', *Modern Asian Studies*, 34, 3(2000), p. 603, n. 49.

13. Germaine Krull, 'Diary of Saigon, following the Allied occupation in September 1945', WOS special file RG 59, lot file 59 D 190, Box 9, US National Archives, Washington, DC. We are grateful to Professor Christopher Goscha for making this available.

14. SACSEA, 'Note on relations with surrendered Japanese forces', Gracey Papers, 4/1, LHCMA.

15. 'Medical History of Allied Forces in French Indo China', September 1945–February 1946, Gracey Papers, 4/7, LHCMA.

16. Marr, *Vietnam*, p. 526.

17. Krull, 'Diary of Saigon', p. 3.

18. Ibid., p. 8.

19. Ibid., pp. 1–2.

20. Gracey's minute in SACSEA to Cabinet, 23 September 1945, 'Indo China Intelligence', WO203/4431, TNA.

21. Krull, 'Diary of Saigon', p. 18.

22. Ibid., p. 19.

23. 12th Army to SACSEA, 27 September 1945, enclosing despatch from McKelvie, dateline Saigon, 25 September 1945, WO203/4431, TNA; cf. Krull, 'Diary of Saigon', p. 20.

24. Leclerc to French Minister of War, 24 September 1945, in SACSEA to Cabinet, 24 September 1945, WO203/4431, TNA.

25. See Christopher Goscha, 'Belated Asian allies: the technical and military contribution of Japanese deserters (1945–50)', in Marilyn B. Young and Robert Buzzanco (eds.), *A companion to the Vietnam War* (Oxford, 2002), pp. 37–64.

26. *Reynolds News*, 30 September 1945.

27. Francis Wheen, *Tom Driberg: his life and indiscretions* (London, 1990), p. 221.

28. Driberg regularly received copies of the nationalist 'Viet Nam news'

and other publications and notices of nationalist activities in France and Indo-China; see Tom Driberg Papers, S3, 1–3, Christ Church, Oxford.

29. Minutes of a meeting between General Gracey and Vietnamese representatives, 10 October 1945, Gracey Papers 4/18, LHCMA.

30. Gracey to Slim, 13 October 1945, WO203/4431, TNA.

31. SACSEA to Saigon Control Commission, 24 September 1945, ibid.

32. Mountbatten to Driberg, 4 October 1945, Driberg Papers, Christ Church, Oxford, cited in Wheen, *Tom Driberg*, p. 219.

33. Slim to CIGS, 6 October 1945, 'The future of Indo China', CAB 121/741, TNA.

34. Political report 13 September to 9 November 1945, Saigon Control Commission, Gracey Papers, 4/8, LHCMA.

35. Gracey to Leclerc, 12 December 1945, Gracey Papers, 4/11, LHCMA.

36. 'Medical History', Gracey Papers, 4/7, LHCMA.

37. 'To Indian Soldiers', leaflet, Gracey Papers, 4/20, LHCMA. There were also leaflets directed to British and French soldiers, some in Vietnamese and some in French. The catalogue of Gracey's papers also refers to pamphlets in Hindi but we were unable to locate any of these.

38. 'Appeal to the Indian Officers and soldiers among the British troops', Gracey Papers, 4/20, LHCMA.

39. *Reynolds News*, 30 September 1945.

40. Everard to M. E. Dening, 30 October 1945, 'Indians in French Indo China, etc.', WO203/5650, TNA.

41. Appendix to report, apparently by M. S. Aney, agent of the government of India, 'Report on conditions of Indians in French Indo China', early 1946, WO203/6217, TNA.

42. Viceroy's telegram enclosed in SACSEA to Cabinet, 2 September 1945, WO203/4431, TNA.

43. *Times of Saigon*, 1 December 1945, WO203/4584, TNA.

44. *Times of Saigon*, 15 January 1946, ibid.

45. Gracey to Slim, 5 November 1945, Gracey Papers 4/11, LHCMA.

46. Krull, 'Diary of Saigon', p. 21.

47. Andrew Roadnight, 'Sleeping with the enemy: Britain, Japanese troops and the Netherlands East Indies, 1945–46', *History*, 87, 286 (2002), pp. 245–68, p. 248.

48. Sir John Anderson to Prime Minister, 8 August 1945, CAB126/76, TNA.

49. P. S. Gerbrandy, *Indonesia* (London, 1950), p. 26.

50. Frances Gouda, *Dutch culture overseas: colonial practice in the Netherlands Indies, 1900–1942* (Amsterdam, 1992), p. 237.

51. This is evoked wonderfully in Takashi Shiraishi, *An age in motion: popular radicalism in Java, 1912–26* (Ithaca, 1990).

52. For this, see Peter Carey, 'Myths, heroes and war', in Peter Carey and Colin Wild (eds.), *Born in fire: the Indonesian struggle for independence: an anthology* (Athens, OH, 1986), pp. 6–11.

53. Harry J. Benda, *The Crescent and the Rising Sun: Indonesian Islam under Japanese occupation, 1942–1945* (The Hague, 1958).

54. Goto Ken'ichi, 'Modern Japan and Indonesia: the dynamics and legacy of wartime rule', in Peter Post and Elly Touwen-Bouwsma (eds.), *Japan, Indonesia and the war: myths and realities* (Leiden, 1997), pp. 14–30.

55. Burton Raffel (trans. and ed.), *The Voice of the Night: complete poetry and prose of Chairil Anwar* (1993).

56. Benedict R. O'G. Anderson, *Java in a time of revolution: occupation and resistance, 1944–46* (Ithaca and London, 1972), pp. 2–10.

57. Ali Sastroamijoyo, *Milestones on my journey: the memoirs of Ali Sastroamijoyo, Indonesian patriot and political leader* (St Lucia, 1979), p. 120.

58. Two classic accounts are G. McT. Kahin, *Nationalism and revolution in Indonesia* (Ithaca, 1952), and A. J. S. Reid, *The Indonesian national revolution, 1945–50* (Sydney, 1974).

59. J. D. Legge, *Sukarno: a political biography* (Harmondsworth, 1972), pp. 181–202.

60. Tan Malaka (trans. and intro. Helen Jarvis), *From jail to jail*, vol. III, ([1948] Athens, OH, 1991), p. 100.

61. For more about this remarkable figure, see Rudolf Mrázek, 'Tan Malaka: a political personality's structure of experience', *Indonesia*, 14 (1972), pp. 1–47; Anderson, *Java in a time of revolution*, pp. 269–83. For the Bose comparison: C. W. Watson, *Of self and nation: autobiography and the representation of modern Indonesia* (Honolulu, 2000), p. 74.

62. Richard Aldrich, *Intelligence and the war against Japan: Britain, America and the politics of secret service* (Cambridge, 2000), pp. 315–16.

63. Abu Hanifah, *Tales of a revolution: a leader of the Indonesian revolution looks back* (Sydney, 1972), p. 191.

64. Bogarde, *Backcloth*, p. 167.

65. William H. Frederick, *Visions and heat: the making of the Indonesian revolution* (Athens, OH, 1989), p. 200.

66. Idrus, 'Surabaja', trans. S. U. Nababan and Benedict Anderson, *Indonesia*, 5 (1968), p. 1.

67. Rudolf Mrázek, *Sjahrir: politics and exile in Indonesia* (Ithaca, 1994), pp. 669–70.

68. A. J. F. Doulton, *The Fighting Cock: being the history of the 23rd Indian Division, 1942–1947* (Aldershot, 1951), p. 230.

69. William H. Frederick, 'The man who knew too much: Ch. O. van der Plas and the future of Indonesia, 1927–1950', in Hans Antöv and Stein

Tønesson (eds.), *Imperial policy and South East Asian Nationalism* (London, 1995), p. 53.

70. Laurens van der Post, *The admiral's baby* (London, 1996), p. 225.

71. F. S. V. Donnison, *British military administration in the Far East* (London, 1956), pp. 413–24.

72. Frederick, 'The man who knew too much', p. 51.

73. Van der Post, *The admiral's baby*, p. 220.

74. Anthony Reid, 'Pictures at an exhibition', in Antöv and Tønesson (eds.), *Imperial policy*, p. 15.

75. Yong Mun Cheong, *H. J. van Mook and Indonesian independence: a study of his role in Dutch–Indonesian relations, 1945–48* (The Hague, 1982), pp. 8–23.

76. As shown in a new and detailed study of the campaign, published since this account was completed: Richard McMillan, *The British occupation of Indonesia, 1945–1946: Britain, the Netherlands and the Indonesian Revolution* (London, 2005), revised from his 'The British occupation of Indonesia, 1945–46', unpublished PhD dissertation, London University, 2002.

77. Alberic Stacpoole, 'Christison, Sir (Alexander Frank) Philip, fourth baronet (1893–1993)', *Oxford dictionary of national biography*, Oxford, 2004; http://www.oxforddnb.com/view/article/51563, accessed 12 Sept. 2005.

78. Christison to Mountbatten, 13 October 1945, CAB119/191, TNA. See also Kahin, *Nationalism and revolution in Indonesia*, pp. 141–2.

79. SACSEA to Chiefs of Staff, 15 October 1945, CAB119/191, TNA.

80. 'Report on morale of British, Indian and Colonial troops of ALFSEA, November 1945–January 1946', WO203/4539, TNA.

81. Testimony of William H. Maaskemp, in Jan A. Krancher (ed.), *The defining years of the Dutch East Indies, 1942–1949: survivors' accounts of Japanese invasion and enslavement of Europeans and the revolution that created free Indonesia* (London, 1996), p. 84.

82. Abu Hanifah, *Tales of a revolution*, pp. 194–8. See also McMillan, *British occupation of Indonesia*, pp. 156–64.

83. Anthony Reid, *The blood of the people: revolution and the end of traditional rule in Northern Sumatra* (Kuala Lumpur, 1979), p. 167.

84. Kahin, *Nationalism and revolution*, pp. 142–4.

85. Roadnight, 'Sleeping with the enemy'.

86. Takao Fusayama, *A Japanese memoir of Sumatra: love and hatred in the liberation war* (Ithaca, 1993), pp. 102, 136–7; Reid, *The blood of the people*, pp. 166–9, 195.

87. Dening to Foreign Office, 3 October 1945, CAB119/191, TNA.

88. Dening to Cabinet, 24 October 1945, CAB121/698, TNA.

89. SACSEA to Cabinet, 14 October 1945, CAB119/191, TNA.

90. SACSEA to chiefs of staff, 16 October 1945, ibid.

91. We have here drawn chiefly on Frederick, *Visions and heat*, pp. 263–9, and Anderson, *Java in a time of revolution*, pp. 151–66.

92. Idrus, 'Surabaja', p. 1.

93. Timothy Lindsey, *The romance of K'tut Tantri and Indonesia: text and scripts, history and identity* (Kuala Lumpur, 1997), p. 146. For K'tut Tantri's own highly coloured version, *Revolt in paradise* (New York, 1960), pp. 176–98.

94. Idrus, 'Surabaja', p. 23.

95. Quoted in Frederick, *Visions and heat*, p. 255.

96. Doulton, *The Fighting Cock*, p. 253. For recent accounts see John Springhall, '"Disaster in Surabaya": the death of Brigadier Mallaby during the British occupation of Java, 1945–46', *Journal of Imperial and Commonwealth History*, 24, 3 (1996), pp. 422–43; McMillan, *British occupation of Indonesia*, pp. 31–46.

97. Foreign Office to Dominion governments, 6 November 1945, CAB121/698, TNA.

98. SACSEA to Cabinet, 2 November 1945; ARNEI to SACSEAC, 3 November 1945, CAB121/698, TNA.

99. 'Indonesian version of Brig. Mallaby's death', WO203/2455, TNA.

100. For the Mallaby controversy see J. G. A. Parrott, 'Who killed Brigadier Mallaby?', *Indonesia*, 20 (1975), pp. 87–111; Springhall, '"Disaster in Surabaya"'. Richard McMillan continues the debate in *British occupation of Indonesia*, pp. 46–52. McMillan's account is more sympathetic to Mallaby than previous studies.

101. SEAC to Cabinet, CAB121/698, TNA.

102. This was certainly the view of Mallaby's deputy, Major Lewis Pugh; see David Jordan, '"A particularly exacting operation": British forces and the battle of Surabaya, November 1945', *Small Wars and Insurgencies*, 11, 3 (2000), p. 109.

103. D. Wehl, *The birth of Indonesia* (London, 1949), pp. 65–7.

104. AFNEI to ALFSEA, [?]16 November 1945, WO203/2650, TNA.

105. Idrus, 'Surabaja', p. 13.

106. Christison to Sir Archibald Nye, 23 November 1945, CAB121/698, TNA.

107. Mrázek, *Sjahrir*, p. 308.

108. Anderson, *Java in a time of revolution*, pp. 2–10; Reid, *The Indonesian national revolution*, pp. 54–7. For a thoughtful discussion see William H. Frederick, 'Shadows of an unseen hand: some patterns of violence in the Indonesian revolution, 1945–1949', in F. Columbijn and T. Lindblad (eds.), *Roots of violence in Indonesia: contemporary violence in historical perspective* (Singapore, 2002), pp. 143–72.

109. Robert Cribb, *Gangsters and revolutionaries: the Jakarta People's Militia and the Indonesian revolution, 1945–1949* (Honolulu, 1991).

110. Abu Hanifah, *Tales of a revolution*, p. 175.

111. Ibid.

112. SACSEA to Chiefs of Staff, 22 December 1945, CAB121/699, TNA; Wehl, *Birth of Indonesia*, pp. 77–80.

113. Raymond ('Turk') Westerling, *Challenge to terror* (London, 1952), pp. 41–57.

114. Mrázek, *Sjahrir*, pp. 274–83.

115. Martha Gellhorn, 'Java journey', in *The face of war* (Harmondsworth, 1991). Mrásek, *Sjahrir*, pp. 209–18.

116. Frances Gouda with Thijs Brocades Zaalberg, *American visions of the Netherlands East Indies/Indonesia: United States foreign policy and Indonesian nationalism, 1920–1949* (Amsterdam, 2002), p. 126.

117. Woodman's file has been released to the National Archive, KV2/1609, TNA.

118. John Coast, *Recruit to revolution: adventure and politics in Indonesia* (London, 1952), pp. 1–25.

119. Dening to SACSEA, 9 November 1945, CAB121/698, TNA.

120. Aldrich, *Intelligence and the war against Japan*, pp. 356–7.

121. Danilyn Fox Rutherford, 'Trekking to New Guinea: Dutch colonial fantasies of a virgin land, 1900–1942', in Julia Clancy-Smith and Frances Gouda (eds.), *Domesticating the empire: race, gender and family life in French and Dutch colonialism* (London, 1998), pp. 255–71.

122. Testimony of Hendrik B. Babtist in Krancher, *The defining years of the Dutch East Indies*, pp. 151–3.

123. S. Woodburn Kirby, *The war against Japan*, vol. V, *The surrender of Japan* (London, 1969), pp. 334–6. Christison to Sir Archibald Nye, 23 November 1945, CAB121/698; SACSEA to Cabinet, 3 December 1945, CAB121/699, TNA.

124. *The Times*, 29 December 1945.

125. Doulton, *The Fighting Cock*, pp. 290–1.

126. Bogarde, *Backcloth*, p. 175; Coldstream, *Dirk Bogarde*, pp. 176–9. The milieu is captured in Bogarde's first novel, *A gentle occupation* (London, 1980).

127. Van der Post, *The admiral's baby*, p. 279.

CHAPTER 5 1946: FREEDOM WITHOUT BORDERS

1. 'Vernacular Press Digest, No. 4', 24 November 1945, SNA.

2. 'Peace or Destruction', *New Demcracy*, 22 November 1945.

3. *Utusan Melayu*, 30 November 1945.

4. We have used the account of the Australian Communist Party leader John Lockwood, *Black Armada: Australia & the struggle for Indonesian independence 1942–49* (Sydney, 1975).

5. Margaret George, *Australia and the Indonesian revolution* (Melbourne, 1980), p. 36.

6. Batavia to Foreign Office, 6 November 1945, CAB121/698, TNA.

7. Christopher E. Goscha, *Thailand and the Southeast Asian networks of the Vietnamese revolution, 1885–1954* (London, 1999), ch. 5.

8. C. C. Chin and Karl Hack (eds.), *Dialogues with Chin Peng: new light on the Malayan Communist Party* (Singapore, 2004), pp. 126–7.

9. Suryono Darusman, *Singapore and the Indonesian revolution, 1945–50* (Singapore, 1992), ch. 3; Twang Peck Yang, *The Chinese business elite in Indonesia and the transition to independence, 1940–1950* (Kuala Lumpur, 1998).

10. Yong Mun Cheong, *The Indonesian revolution and the Singapore connection, 1945–1949* (Singapore, 2003), p. 118.

11. *New Democracy*, 14 January 1946.

12. 'Report on RAPWI in Malaya and Singapore', 7 January 1946, BMA/ADM/2/34, ANM.

13. Wim Willems, 'No sheltering sky: migrant identities of Dutch nationals from Indonesia', in Andrea L. Smith (ed.), *Europe's invisible migrants* (Amsterdam, 2003) pp. 33–60.

14. Quoted in Frances Gouda with Thijs Brocades Zaalberg, *American visions of the Netherlands East Indies/Indonesia: United States foreign policy and Indonesian nationalism, 1920–1949* (Amsterdam, 2002), p. 126.

15. Malayan Security Service, Political Intelligence Journal [MSS/PIJ], 15 July 1946, Dalley Papers, RHO; Commissioner of Police, 'Dutch–Malay fracas', 6 July 1946, CSO/2206/46, SNA.

16. Mustapha Hussain, *Malay nationalism before Umno: the memoirs of Mustapha Hussain, translated by Insun Mustapha and edited by Jomo K. S.* (Kuala Lumpur, 2005), pp. 318–19.

17. We have here drawn on Yong, *The Indonesian revolution and the Singapore connection*, ch. 3.

18. Khatijah Sidek, *Memoirs of Khatijah Sidek: Puteri Kesateria Bangsa* (Kuala Lumpur, 2001 [1960]), pp. 71–2.

19. Firdaus Haji Abdullah, *Radical Malay politics: its origins and early development* (Petaling Jaya, 1985), pp. 52–3.

20. Ahmad Boestamam (trans. William R. Roff), *Carving the path to the summit* (Athens, OH, 1979), p. 40. We are also grateful to Dr Syed Husin Ali for his recollections. For Bose's influence on Boestamam, see A. J. Stockwell, *British policy and Malay politics during the Malayan Union experiment, 1945–1948* (Kuala Lumpur, 1979), p. 46.

21. Shamsiah Fakeh, *Memoir Shamsiah Fakeh: dari AWAS ke Rejimen Ke-10* (Bangi, 2004), pp. 34–3; MSS/PIJ, 15 July 1946.

22. Farish A Noor, *Islam embedded: the historical development of the Pan-Malaysian Islamic Party PAS (1951–2003)*, vol. I (Kuala Lumpur, 2004), pp. 113–16.

23. 'Temubual dengan Saudara Abdullah C. D., tokoh nasional tanahair kita', an interview which appeared in the publication *Suluh Rakyat* in 1988.

24. Han Suyin, 'An outline of Malayan Chinese literature', *Eastern Horizon*, 3, 6 (June, 1964), pp. 6–16; *My house has two doors* (London, 1980), p. 71.

25. 'Fu-sheng', 'A new understanding is indispensable to the Malayan Overseas Chinese', *New Democracy*, 9 December, 1945.

26. Victor Purcell, 'Malaya's Political Climate VII: 12 December 1945–7 January 1946', WO203/5302, TNA.

27. 'Pa-Jen' [Hu Yuzhi], 'The emancipation of the Chinese intelligentsia in Malaya', *Feng Hsia*, 21 January 1946.

28. Speech by Hu Yu-chih [Hu Yuzhi], 'Twofold mission of the democratic movement', *Min Sheng Pau*, 12 October 1945.

29. T. J. Danaraj, *Japanese invasion of Malaya and Singapore, memoirs of a doctor* (Kuala Lumpur, 1990), pp. 153–4.

30. Lee Kuan Yew, *The Singapore story* (Singapore, 1998), pp. 89, 138.

31. Yeo Kim Wah, *Political development in Singapore, 1945–55* (Singapore, 1973), pp. 88–98.

32. 'The Malayan Democratic Union manifesto', in Charles Gamba, *The origins of trade unionism in Malaya* (Singapore, 1960), pp. 433–7.

33. Lim Hong Bee, *Born into war: autobiography of a barefoot colonial boy who grew up to face the challenge of the modern world* (London, 1994), p. 373.

34. Charles B. McLane, *Soviet strategies in Southeast Asia: an exploration of eastern policy under Lenin and Stalin* (Princeton, 1966), pp. 308, 318.

35. 'A manifesto to the people of different races for the realisation of democratic policies, issued by the Central Executive Committee of the Malayan Communist Party on 5 February, 1946', *New Democracy*, 8 February 1946.

36. Purcell, 'Malaya's Political Climate VII'.

37. Chin Peng, *My side of history* (Singapore, 2004), pp. 157–8.

38. McLane, *Soviet strategies in Southeast Asia*, pp. 310–12. McLane was one of the few scholars to be given access to the Special Branch's four-volume, *Basic paper on the Malayan Communist Party* (1950).

39. *Min Sheng Pau*, 8 March 1946.

40. *Sin Chew Jit Poh*, 18 January 1946.

41. Manicasothy Saravanamuttu, *The Sara saga* (Singapore, n.d. [1969]), p. 132; *New Democracy*, 29 January 1946.

42. René Onraet to Hone, 6 March 1946, CO537/1579.

43. P. A. B. McKerron, 'Minute of the meeting of the local civil labour employment committee, Fort Canning, 5 January 1946', BMA/DEPT/2/4, ANM.

44. Diary 29 January 1946 to 1 February 1946, in Philip Ziegler (ed.), *Personal diary of Admiral the Lord Mountbatten: Supreme Allied Commander, South-East Asia, 1943–1946* (London, 1988), p. 289.

45. 'SAC's 316th Meeting', 9 February 1946, Hone Papers, RHO.

46. Mountbatten to chiefs of staff, 11 February 1946, CO537/1579.

47. Khong Kim Hoong, *Merdeka: British rule and the struggle for independence in Malaya* (Kuala Lumpur, 1984), p. 60. See also, John Springhall, 'Mountbatten versus the generals: British military rule of Singapore, 1945–46', *Journal of Contemporary History*, 34, 4 (2001), pp. 335–52.

48. Mountbatten to Brazier, 9 March 1946, CO537/1579, TNA.

49. Mountbatten to Stanley, 26 March 1946, ibid.

50. Hone to Gater 13 March 1946, ibid.

51. Ralph Hone to F. S. V. Donnison, 25 March 1953, Hone Papers, RHO.

52. Hone to Gator, 2 April 1946, CO537/1579, TNA.

53. Victor Purcell, *The memoirs of a Malayan official* (London, 1965), pp. 353–6.

54. 'Crisis in Malaya', *New Democracy*, 21 February 1946.

55. Mountbatten to George Hall, 4 January 1946, in A. J. Stockwell (ed.), *British documents on the End of Empire: Malaya, part I* (London, 1995), p. 191.

56. Summarized by Hone to Chinese Consul, Singapore, 8 March 1946, CO537/1580, TNA.

57. Amy and Richard Haggard, 'An account of the British Military Administration of Upper Perak, Malaya – 1945/46: being memories based on diaries and letters', 4 April 2000, RCS, CUL.

58. James de Vere Allen, *The Malayan Union* (New Haven, 1967), pp. 34–6.

59. Sultan of Johore to G. H. Hall (Colonial Office), 15 February 1946, RCS, CUL.

60. Johore Malays to Sultan Ibrahim, 22 February 1946, Maxwell Papers, RCS, CUL.

61. George Maxwell, 'The enigma of Ibrahim of Johore', n.d., ibid.

62. For these debates see Ariffin Omar, *Bangsa Melayu: Malay concepts of democracy and community, 1945–50* (Kuala Lumpur, 1993).

63. See the seminal essay by Kassim bin Ahmad, *Characterization in Hikayat Hang Tuah: a general survey of character-portrayal and analysis and interpretation of the characters of Hang Tuah and Hang Jebat* (Kuala Lumpur, 1966), p. 43.

64. John Coast, *Recruit to revolution: adventure and politics in Indonesia* (London, 1952), p. 41; Donna J. Amoroso, 'Dangerous politics and the Malay nationalist movement, 1945–47,' *South East Asia Research*, 6, 3 (1998), p. 259.

65. Quoted in Amoroso, 'Dangerous politics', p. 259.

66. O. W. Gilmour, *With freedom to Singapore* (London, 1950), p. 186.

67. Henry Barlow, *Swettenham* (Kuala Lumpur, 1995), p. 727.

68. 'Notes of a discussion at the Colonial Office on 26 February 1946 on the White Paper on Malayan Union', ibid.

69. *The Times*, 16 April 1946.

70. MacDonald to Hall, 21–22 June 1946, in Stockwell, *British documents: Malaya, part I*, pp. 252–5.

71. *Pelita Malaya*, 6 May 1946.

72. Firdaus Haji Abdullah, *Radical Malay politics: its origins and early development* (Petaling Jaya, 1985), pp. 82–4; Amoroso, 'Dangerous politics'; Boestamam, *Carving the path*, p. 49.

73. Lt. Col. R. F. Tredgold, 'Psychiatry in ALFSEA', March 1946, WO222/1319, TNA.

74. 'HMS *Northway*: minutes and findings of a Board of Enquiry', 20 October 1945, ADM116/6422, TNA.

75. MSS/PIJ, 31 May 1947.

76. MSS/PIJ, 31 May 1946.

77. *New Democracy*, 30 January 1946.

78. David Duncan, *Mutiny in the RAF: the Air Force Strikes of 1946*, The Socialist History Society, Occasional Papers Series, no. 8, London, 1998.

79. R. D. Heanly, 'Final Report on SIB investigation of RAF Mutinies in India', 21 May, 1946; Tom Driberg to William Attwood, 11 April 1946; minute 23 July 1946, AIR20/11516, TNA.

80. *The Times*, 14 August 1946.

81. *The Times*, 11 October 1946.

82. Stopford to Roberts, 9 October 1946, WO203/6249; Roberts to Stopford to Roberts 11 October 1946, WO203/6249, TNA.

83. Montgomery to All Commanders at Home and Overseas, 15 October 1946, WO32/16169, TNA.

84. Brigadier K. T. Darling to Montgomery, 24 May 1946, WO32/16169, TNA.

85. Quoted in Robert H. Ahrenfeldt, *Psychiatry in the British army in the Second World War* (London, 1950), p. 210.

86. Brian Aldiss, *The twinkling of an eye, or my life as an Englishman* (London, 1998), p. 201.

87. *Northern Star*, 6 May 1946; *Straits Echo*, 13 May 1946.

88. G. B. Folliot, OSPC Island, memorandum, 3 January 1947, FO371/69629, TNA; *Sunday Gazette*, 17 February 1946.

89. Aisha Akbar, *Aishabee at war: a very frank memoir* (Singapore, 1990), p. 229.

90. Stokes to Jessie Muirhead, 24 June 1945, Stokes Papers, Centre of South Asian Studies, Cambridge.

91. Patrick French, *Liberty or death: India's journey to independence and division* (London, 1997), pp. 222–3.

92. Dash Diaries, February 1946, Mss Eur C188/6, f. 74, OIOC.

93. Sir Arthur Dash, Bengal Diary, vol. 9, p. 67, Centre of South Asian Studies, Cambridge. This is an extended version of the contemporary diary in the India Office Collection.

94. Intelligence Report, 26 January, 1946, L/PO/9/15, OIOC.

95. Report by Thakin Than Tun on AFPFL Congress, 17–23 January 1946, L/PO/9/15, OIOC.

96. See, e.g., Karen Memorial presented by H. Stevenson and T. L. Hughes, 2 February 1946, in Hugh Tinker (ed.), *Burma: the struggle for independence 1944–48*, vol. I: *From military occupation to civil government, 1 January 1944 to 31 August 1946* (London, 1983), pp. 650–2.

97. Dorman-Smith, memoir, Mss Eur E215/32b, f. 272, OIOC.

98. Dorman-Smith to David Monteath, 5 April 1946, Laithwaite Papers, Mss Eur F138/72, OIOC.

99. S. K. Chettur, *Malayan adventure* (Mangalore, 1948), pp. 84–5.

100. F. V. Duckworth, 'The visit of Pandit Nehru to Malaya, 18 March to 26 March 1946', 4 April 1946, CO717/149/8, TNA.

101. Chettur, *Malayan adventure*, pp. 78–80.

102. *Tamil Nesan*, 22 June 1946; *Jananayakam*, 24 June 1946.

103. L. F. Pendred, Director of Intelligence, 'The visit of Pandit Nehru to Malaya', 30 March 1946, CO717/149/8, TNA.

104. Saravanamuttu, *The Sara saga*, pp. 133–4.

105. Cabinet meeting, London, 13 March 1946, in Tinker, *Burma*, vol. I, p. 686.

106. Note on political matters by Major E. G. Robertson, 25 August 1946, Clague Papers, Mss Eur E252/54, OIOC.

107. Dorman-Smith to Pethick-Lawrence, 6 January 1946, Dorman-Smith Papers, Mss Eur E215/10, OIOC.

108. Dorman-Smith to Pethick-Lawrence, 22 January 1946, ibid.

109. Dorman-Smith to Pethick-Lawrence, 6 and 22 January 1946, ibid.

110. 'Ralph Michaelis's Independent Newsletter Reports from Burma', 13 December 1945, Laithwaite Papers, Mss Eur F138/72, f. 41, OIOC.

111. The fullest discussion of this whole incident from both the British and Aung San's side can be found in the papers of Sir Hubert Rance, 'Prosecution of Aung San', Mss Eur F169/1, OIOC. This is essentially Dorman-Smith's file, with a note by Sir Henry Knight passed on to Rance.

112. *Reynolds News*, 24 March 1946, cited in Angelene Naw, *Aung San and the struggle for Burmese independence* (Coperhagen, 2001), p. 238, n. 72.

113. B. Fase to Tom Driberg, 9 March 1946, Tom Driberg Papers, S3, 2, 25, Christ Church, Oxford.

114. Mountbatten to government of Burma, 27 March 1946, Rance Papers, Mss Eur F169/1, OIOC.

115. Cabinet Mission, Delhi, to Cabinet, London, 18 April 1946, L/PO/9/15, OIOC.

116. Pethick-Lawrence to Attlee, 7 April 1946, Pethick-Lawrence Papers, Box 1/72, Trinity College, Cambridge.

117. Dorman-Smith memoirs, Mss Eur E215/32b, ff. 264–6, OIOC.

118. Ibid., f. 266.

119. Government of Burma to Burma Office, 13 May 1946, 'Prosecution of Aung San', Rance Papers, Mss Eur F169/1, OIOC.

120. Ibid; also 'Humble petition of Ma Ahma, wife of the late Abdul Raschid, residing at Paung', M/5/102, OIOC, reproduced in Tinker, *Burma*, vol. I, p. 728.

121. Dorman-Smith Papers, Mss E215, 32 a/b, f. 218, OIOC.

122. GB to BO, 13 May 1946; Aung San's rejoinder to the charges in the Legislative Council was printed in the *Hanthawaddy* newspaper c. 4 April 1946.

123. Ibid.

124. Naw, *Aung San*, p. 156, citing *Hanthawaddy* newspaper.

125. Appreciation by G. Appleton, 27 March 1946, Rance Papers, Mss Eur F 169/1, 'Prosecution of Aung San', OIOC.

126. Dorman-Smith Papers, Mss Eur E215/32, f. 64, OIOC.

127. Ibid., f. 207.

128. *Report of the Tantabin Enquiry Committee* (Rangoon, 1947), pp. 1–36. There is an unpaginated copy in the Library of the School of Oriental and African Studies, University of London.

129. Kyaw Win to an associate, 17 May 1946, ibid. p. 5.

130. Ibid., pp. 7–12.

131. Aung San to T. L. Hughes, 22 May 1946, M/4/2619, OIOC.

132. Attlee to Pethick-Lawrence, 7 May 1946, in Tinker, *Burma*, vol. I, p. 773.

133. Pearce to Dorman-Smith, 18 August 1946, Dorman-Smith Papers, Mss Eur E215/15, OIOC.

134. Tom Driberg, *Ruling passions* (London, 1978), pp. 215–16.

135. Aung San to Driberg, 12 June 1946, Driberg Papers, S3, Christ Church, Oxford.

136. Naw, *Aung San*, p. 166, citing Maurice Collis, *Last and first in Burma, 1941–48* (London, 1956), p. 280.

137. Dorman-Smith to John Humphrey Wise, 8 November 1946, Dorman-Smith Papers, Mss Eur E215/16, OIOC.

138. Ibid.

139. U Thein Pe Myint, 'A critique of the communist movement in Burma', 1973, Mss Eur C498, f. 12, OIOC.

140. *Burma and the insurrections*, Government of the Union of Burma Publications, September 1949 (Rangoon, 1949), p. 3; Thein Pe, 'A critique', f. 19.

141. M. E. Dening, 'Review of political events in South-East Asia 1945 to March 1946', 25 March 1946, in Stockwell, *British documents: Malaya, part I*, p. 218.

142. Clyde Sanger, *Malcolm MacDonald: bringing an end to empire* (Montreal and London, 1995).

143. John Falconer to Hugh Bryson, 3 October 1969, Heussler Papers, RHO.

144. Ibid., p. 80. The description of the palace is by Han Suyin, a frequent guest of MacDonald's.

CHAPTER 6 1946: ONE EMPIRE UNRAVELS, ANOTHER IS BORN

1. Nicholas Mansergh (ed.), *Constitutional relations between Britain and India: the transfer of power 1942–47*, vol. VII, *The Cabinet Mission* (London, 1977), introduction.

2. Maulana Azad to Wavell, 13 June 1946, ibid., p. 914.

3. Wavell, note of 29 June 1946, ibid., p. 1085.

4. Penderell Moon (ed.), *Wavell: the viceroy's journal* (London, 1973), entry for 24 October 1946, p. 363

5. Patrick French, *Liberty or death: India's journey to independence and division* (London, 1997), pp. 247–9.

6. Moon, *Wavell*, entry for 27 August 1946, p. 341.

7. Joya Chatterji, *Bengal divided: Hindu communalism and partition, 1932–1947* (Cambridge, 1994), pp. 230–40; Suranjan Das, *Communal riots in Bengal, 1905–1947* (Delhi, 1991), p. 165.

8. Extract in 'Calcutta riots 1946–7', L/P and J/8/655, OIOC.

9. Cited in Das, *Communal riots*, p. 168.

10. Press release of Working Committee of the Bengal Provincial Muslim League, 6 September 1946, 'Calcutta riots 1946–7', L/P and J/8/655, OIOC.

11. Sim to Col. F. J. Erroll MP, n.d. August 1946, extract in 'Calcutta riots 1946–7', ibid.

12. Ibid.

13. Governor Bengal to viceroy, 22 August 1946, entry Monday 19 August, ibid.

14. Das, *Communal riots*, p. 171.

15. This paragraph follows Das, *Communal riots*, the most authoritative secondary account of these events. This narrative itself is largely based on the 10-volume, *Calcutta disturbances commission of enquiry: minutes of evidence* (Calcutta, 1946).

16. *Statesman*, 26 August 1946.

17. Das, *Communal riots*, pp. 183–4.

18. *Statesman*, 24 August 1946; the newspaper's coverage of these events was collected in the 'Great Calcutta Killing, August 1946–September 1946', copy in Stephens Papers, Centre of South Asian Studies, Cambridge.

19. Dash, Bengal diary, vol. IX, p. 80, Centre of South Asian Studies, Cambridge.

20. Moon, *Wavell*, entry for 3 November 1946, p. 370.

21. Diary entry for 17 August, 'Report on the disturbances in Calcutta commencing August 16 1946 issued by HQ Eastern Command', Bucher Papers, 7901–87 A, National Army Museum.

22. Diary entry for 18 August, ibid.

23. Dash diaries, August 1946, ff. 74–80, Mss Eur C188/6, OIOC.

24. Governor Bengal to viceroy, 28 August 1946, 'Calcutta riots 1946–7', L/P and J/8/655, OIOC.

25. 'Record of life in the Indian Civil Service 1930–47', F. O. Bell Papers, Centre of South Asian Studies, Cambridge.

26. A retrospective account; Edward McInery to J. H. Habbakuk, 14 February 1976, McInery diary, Mss Photo Eur 148, OIOC.

27. Personal communications to the authors, 2001, from Professor F. M. L. Thompson.

28. Secret report on the political situation in Bengal for the second half of

September 1946 by chief secretary to government of Bengal, J. M. G. Bell Papers, 2, Centre of South Asian Studies, Cambridge.

29. 'Note on recent experiences', late 1946, J. M. G. Bell Papers, 3, Centre of South Asian Studies, Cambridge.

30. Manju Bandyopadhyay, cited in Sandip Bandyopadhyay, 'The riddles of partition: memories of the Bengali Hindus', in Ranabir Samaddar (ed.), *Reflections on partition in the east* (Calcutta, 1997), p. 68.

31. J. Tyson to his family, 30 November 1946, Tyson Papers, Mss Eur E341/41, OIOC.

32. Moon, *Wavell*, entry for 27 August 1945, p. 341.

33. Tyson to his family, 17 November 1946, Tyson Papers, Mss Eur E341/41, OIOC.

34. Counter-Intelligence summary, Burma Command, fortnight to 15 August 1946, f. 11, L/WS/1/744, OIOC.

35. Ibid., f. 21.

36. Counter-Intelligence summary, fortnight to end July, 1946, f. 35, ibid.

37. Note by Rance, 15 September 1946, in Hugh Tinker (ed.), *Burma: the struggle for independence 1944–1948*, vol. II: *From general strike to independence, 31 August 1946 to 4 January 1948* (London, 1984), p. 19.

38. SACSEA to Cabinet, 17 September 1946, L/PO/9/15, OIOC.

39. John H. McEnery, *Epilogue in Burma, 1945–48* (Tunbridge Wells, 1990), p. 56.

40. See daily progress reports of general strike, 24–30 September 1945, 'The strike of September 1946', Arnold Papers, Mss Eur F145/38 OIOC.

41. Mr Binns's press release and note 'immediate' by F. Donnison, 21 September 1946, ibid.

42. Appeal by Maung Tin and F. B. Arnold, c. 23 September 1946, ibid.

43. Note by Montgomery, 23 September 1946, L/PO/9/15, OIOC.

44. Note by Rance, 15 September 1946, in Tinker, *Burma*, vol. II, p. 22.

45. 'His Excellency's interview with U Saw', 12 September 1945, L/PO/9/15, OIOC.

46. Note by Rance, 'Interview with U Saw', 12 September 1946, in Tinker, *Burma*, vol. II, p. 17.

47. Memorandum of U Saw to Rance, October 1946, Laithwaite Papers, Mss Eur F138/72, OIOC.

48. Ibid.

49. SACSEA to Cabinet, 21 September 1946, L/PO/9/15, OIOC.

50. Rance To Pethick-Lawrence, 21 September 1946, in Tinker, *Burma*, vol. II, p. 56.

51. Aung San to Rance, 17 September 1946, L/WS/1, 669; reproduced in Tinker, *Burma*, vol. II, p. 33.

52. Rance to Pethick-Lawrence, 19 September 1946, ibid. pp. 47–8.

53. *The Burman*, 3 November 1946, clipping, FO/643/38 (G6/G546), TNA, reproduced in Tinker, *Burma*, vol. II, p. 105.

54. Cabinet India and Burma Committee, 18 September 1946, ibid. pp. 36–9.

55. Progress Report for October 1946, Government of Burma Commerce and Supply Department, Arnold Papers, Mss Eur F145/24, OIOC.

56. Ibid.

57. Wavell reproducing Nehru to Aung San, 8 October 1946, in Tinker, *Burma*, vol. II, p. 78, citing Mansergh, *Transfer of Power in India*, vol. VIII, p. 682.

58. 'Hon. Aung San's proposal for the immediate grant of a fuller measure of self-government to the people of Burma', 11 November 1946, R/8/36, OIOC.

59. Rance to Pethick-Lawrence, 13 November 1946, in Tinker, *Burma*, vol. II, pp. 139–40

60. Rance to Pethick-Lawrence, 13 November 1946, R/8/36, OIOC.

61. Rance to Pethick-Lawrence, 12 November 1946, ibid.

62. Rance's memorandum on the need to accelerate the progress of constitutional advance for Burma, 12 November 1946, ibid.

63. Rance to Pethick-Lawrence, 13 November 1946, in Tinker, *Burma*, vol. II, pp. 139–44.

64. Angelene Naw, *Aung San and the struggle for Burmese independence* (Copenhagen, 2001), pp. 177–81.

65. Extract from *The Burman*, 3 November 1946, 643/38, TNA, cited in Tinker, *Burma*, vol. II, p. 105.

66. Thein Pe, 'A critique of the communist movement in Burma', a note to Indian communsists, 1973; Mss Eur C498, OIOC.

67. Invitation to reception 22 October 1946, Tom Driberg Papers, S3, 2, 51, Christ Church, Oxford; cf. ibid., no. 54, conversation between Tom Harrisson (Mass Observation) and Karen representatives, passed on to Driberg.

68. Combined civil and military intelligence for December 1946, ff. 70–4, Rance Papers, Mss Eur F169/5, OIOC.

69. 'Reuter interview with Bogyoke Aung San, 16 December 1946', in Tinker, *Burma*, vol. II, p. 194.

70. John H. McEnery, *Epilogue in Burma, 1945–48* (Tunbridge Wells, 1990), pp. 75–90.

71. Hansard, House of Commons debates, vol. 431, col. 2343–5, cited in Tinker, *Burma*, vol. II, p. 209.

72. Laithwaite to Monteath, 17 December 1946, Laithwaite Papers, Mss Eur F138/72, OIOC.

73. Ibid.

74. Laithwaite to Monteath, 20 December 1946, ibid.

75. Excerpt from Hansard, House of Commons debates, 20 December 1946, col. 2343; clipping in Laithwaite Papers, Mss Eur F138/72, OIOC.

76. McEnery, *Epilogue in Burma*, pp. 95–6.

77. 'Memorial service for the men who died in captivity at work on the Burma–Siam Railway, 1942–5, December 18 1946', Laithwaite Papers, Mss Eur F138/72, OIOC.

78. Fujio Hara, *Malayan Chinese and China: conversion in identity consciousness, 1945–57* (Singapore, 2003), p. 32.

79. Charlie Cheah Fook Yong, OHD, SNA.

80. Kevin Blackburn, 'The collective memory of the *sook ching* massacre and the creation of the civilian war memorial of Singapore', *Journal of the Malaysian Branch of the Royal Asiatic Society*, 73, 2 (2000), pp. 76–7.

81. Beatrice Trefalt, *Japanese army stragglers and memories of the war in Japan, 1950–1975* (London, 2003), p. 25.

82. 'Jap nationals in SEAC area', 19 September 1946, WO208/3909, TNA.

83. SEALF to SCAP, 1 March 1947, WO208/3910, TNA.

84. 'Japanese Surrendered Personnel in Central Malaya', December 1946, WO 208/3910, TNA.

85. Kazuo Tamayama, *Railwaymen in the war: tales by Japanese railway soldiers in Burma and Thailand, 1941–1947* (Basingstoke, 2005), pp. 274–5.

86. Ibid., pp. 233–7.

87. Mamoru Shinozaki, *Syonan – my story: the Japanese occupation of Singapore* (Singapore, 1979), pp. 102–4.

88. Enclosures on BMA/CH/43/46, SNA.

89. Wee Hock Chye, *Comfort homes and early years* (Kuala Lumpur, n.d.) pp. 45–7.

90. Kevin Blackburn and Edmund Lim, 'The Japanese war memorials of Singapore: monuments of commemoration and symbols of Japanese imperial ideology', *South East Asia Research*, 7, 3 (2001), p. 336.

91. Kenichi Goto, *Tensions of empire: Japan and Southeast Asia in the colonial and postcolonial world* (Singapore, 2003), p. 196.

92. Chin Peng, *My side of history* (Singapore, 2003), pp. 146–7; C. C. Chin and Karl Hack (eds.), *Dialogues with Chin Peng: new light on the Malayan Communist Party* (Singapore, 2004), p. 96.

93. O. W. Gilmour, *With freedom to Singapore* (London, 1950), pp. 16–18.

94. Victor Purcell, *Memoirs of a Malayan official* (London, 1965), p. 303.

95. Letter of 7 July 1946, in Amy and Richard Haggard, 'An account of the British Military Administration of Upper Perak, Malaya – 1945/46: being memories based on diaries and letters', 4 April 2000, RCS, CUL.

96. E. T. Campbell in 1931, quoted in Margaret Shennan, *Out in the midday sun: the British in Malaya, 1880–1960* (London, 2000), p. 114.

97. 'Notes for women proceeding to Malaya: 21st May 1946'; minute 8 June, 1946, CO717/149/2, TNA.

98. Vernon Bartlett, *Go East, old man* (London, 1948), p. 103.

99. J. M. Gullick, 'My time in Malaya', June 1970, Heussler Papers, RHO.

100. Bartlett, *Go East, old man*, p. 103.

101. A. H. Dickenson to Gent, 22 December 1945; W. S. Morgan, minute, 25 October 1945, CO273/673/7, TNA.

102. Nicholas J. White, *Business, government and the end of empire: Malaya, 1945–1957* (Kuala Lumpur, 1996), p. 82.

103. S. K. Chettur, *Malayan adventure* (Mangalore, 1948), p. 178–87.

104. Philip Warner, 'Hone, Sir (Herbert) Ralph (1896–1992)', *Oxford dictionary of national biography*, Oxford University Press, 2004; http://www.oxforddnb.com/view/article/51132, accessed 3 May 2005.

105. Gent to Sir George Cator, 5 November 1946, A. J. Stockwell (ed.), *British documents on the end of empire: Malaya, part I* (London, 1995), pp. 271–4.

106. A. J. Stockwell, *British policy and Malay politics during the Malayan Union experiment, 1945–1948* (Kuala Lumpur, 1979), ch. 5; Malayan Security Service, Political Intelligence Journal [MSS/PIJ], 31 December 1946, Dalley Papers, RHO.

107. Creech Jones to Gent, 1 May 1946, CO537/1529, TNA.

108. Nicholas Tarling, '"Some rather nebulous capacity": Lord Killearn's appointment in Southeast Asia', *Modern Asian Studies*, 20, 3 (1986), pp. 559–600.

109. Charles Gamba, *The origins of trade unionism in Malaya* (Singapore, 1960), p. 67; Ronald Milne interview, OHD, SNA.

110. Office of the Special Commissioner in South East Asia, 'Social Welfare Conference, Singapore 19–23 August 1947: Minutes', SCA/5/47, SNA.

111. 'Youth Welfare in Singapore, 10 July 1947', ibid.

112. Gent to Creech Jones, 1 October 1946, CO537/1579, TNA.

113. Gamba, *The origins of trade unionism in Malaya*, pp. 100–113.

114. 'Malayan Communist Party policy', Supplement No. 9 to MSS/PIJ, 31 July 1948; HQ Malaya Command, Weekly Intelligence Review, 2 April 1946, CO537/1581, TNA.

115. Singapore General Labour Union, 'An account of experiences derived from strikes', printed in MSS/PIJ, 31 May 1946.

116. MSS/PIJ, September, 1946.

117. Gamba, *The origins of trade unionism in Malaya*, p. 196; *Min Sheng Pau*, 5 December 1946.

CHAPTER 7 1947: AT FREEDOM'S GATE

1. Viceroy (Wavell) to Secretary of State, 21 January 1947, 'INA and Free Burma Army', L/WS/1/1578, OIOC.

2. Penderel Moon (ed.), *Wavell: the viceroy's journal* (London, 1973), entry for 31 December 1946, p. 403.

3. Wavell to Pethick-Lawrence, 1 March 1947, Pethick-Lawrence Papers, Box 5/73, Trinity College, Cambridge.

4. Moon, *Wavell*, entry for 27 March 1947, p. 433.

5. Mountbatten to Secretary of State, 20 March 1947, L/WS/1/1578, OIOC.

6. Viceroy's personal report, 1 August 1947, in Nicholas Mansergh (ed.), *The transfer of power in India*, vol. XII, *The Mountbatten viceroyalty: princes, partition and independence, 8 July–15 August 1947* (London, 1983), p. 455.

7. Attlee to Mountbatten, 17 July 1947, ibid., p. 215.

8. Discussion between Jinnah and Mountbatten, 12 July 1947, ibid., p. 122.

9. 'Report of the Armed Services Nationalisation Committee' and minutes, papers of Major-General D. A. L. Wade, 8204/797-2, NAM.

10. *New Times of Burma*, 13 July 1947.

11. Sri Krishna, special correspondent, Delhi, draft article 4 July 1947, papers of Lady Edwina Mountbatten, MB Q4, Southampton University Library.

12. Ayesha Jalal, *The state of martial rule: the origins of Pakistan's political economy of defence* (Cambridge, 1990), p. 29.

13. Viceroy's Personal Report, 1 August 1947, in Mansergh, *Transfer of power in India*, vol. XII, p. 452.

14. Ibid.

15. Benjamin Zachariah, *Nehru* (London, 2004), p. 200.

16. *Darbar Notes*, no. 6, December 1946, L/WS1/1654, OIOC.

17. Personal memorandum by Lt. Gen. R. A. Savory, 4–9 May 1947, ibid.

18. Discussion between Mountbatten and Gandhi, early July 1947, in Mansergh, *Transfer of power in India*, vol. XII, p. 50.

19. Meeting of Partition Council, 10 July 1947, ibid., p. 51.

20. *Fauj Akhbar: Indian Forces Weekly*, 3 May 1947, 7403-28, NAM.

21. Note on 'The Sikhs' by Lt. Gen. R. A. Savory, endorsed by Auchinleck 29 September 1947, Savory Papers, 7603/93-92, NAM.

22. Jalal, *State of martial rule*, p. 43.

23. Lt. Col. Siddiq to Lt. Gen. R. A. Savory, 27 August 1947, Savory Papers 7603/93-83, NAM.

24. W. Alston Papers, vol. X, 8005/151-11, NAM.

25. Ibid., entry for 15–16 August 1947.

26. Nehru to Pethick-Lawrence, 20 October 1947, Pethick-Lawrence Papers, Box 5/76, Trinity College, Cambridge.

27. *Statesman*, 5 May 1947.

28. *Statesman*, 10 May 1947.

29. *Statesman*, 1 May 1947.

30. *Statesman*, 2 May 1947.

31. *People's Age* (Bombay), 20 April, 18 May 1947.

32. *Statesman*, 6 May 1947.

33. John Tyson to his family, 16 January 1947, Tyson Papers, Mss Eur E341/41, OIOC.

34. John Tyson to his family, 2 February 1947, ibid.

35. Joya Chatterji, 'The fashioning of a frontier: the Radcliffe line and Bengal's border landscape, 1947–52', *Modern Asian Studies*, 33, 1 (1999), pp. 185–243.

36. An excellent brief account of Nagas and Naga nationalism can be found in Julian Jacobs with Alan Macfarlane, Sarah Harrison and Anita Herle, *Hill peoples of northeast India, the Nagas: society, culture and the colonial encounter* (Stuttgart, 1990), esp. pp. 151–70.

37. Mildred Archer, 'Journey to Nagaland, an account of six months spent in the Naga Hills in 1947; entry for 23 8 1947', typescript in Archer private collection cited in Jacobs, *The Nagas*, ch. 14, n. 24.

38. William Saumarez Smith, 'Seventy four days in 1947', p. 27, Mss Eur C409, OIOC; Dash, Bengal Diary, vol. IX, p. 106, Centre of South Asian Studies, Cambridge.

39. *Statesman*, 15 August 1947.

40. Tapan Raychaudhuri, *Romonthon Atharba Bhimratipraptar paracharit charcha* (Calcutta, 1993), p. 98, cited in Sandip Bandyopadhyay, 'The riddles of partition: memories of the Bengali Hindus', in Ranabir Samaddar (ed.), *Reflections on partition in the East* (Calcutta, 1997), p. 68.

41. *Statesman*, 4 August 1947.

42. *Statesman*, 8 September 1947.

43. *Statesman*, 30 October 1947.

44. Dash, Bengal Diary, vol. X, p. 6, Centre of South Asian Studies, Cambridge.

45. Samar Sen, 'Birthday', translated by Subhoranjan Das Gupta, 'Poems on a divided world', in Samaddar, *Reflections on partition*, p. 201.

46. Attlee to Nehru, 17 July 1947, Mansergh, *Transfer of power in India*, vol. XII, p. 214.

47. Angelene Naw, *Aung San and the struggle for Burmese independence* (Copenhagen, 2001), p. 186, citing Wavell to Pethick-Lawrence, 4 January 1947, in Mansergh, *Transfer of power in India*, vol. XI, p. 503.

48. Naw, *Aung San*, p. 188.

49. *Dawn* [Karachi], 6 January 1947.

50. *New York Times*, 6 January 1947, cited in Uma Shankar Singh, *Burma and India 1948–62* (Delhi, 1979), p. 43.

51. Dr R. H. Taylor, 'Interview with U Kyaw Nyein', 19 November 1976, Mss Eur D1066/2, OIOC.

52. See CAB 133/3, TNA; the key documents are printed in Hugh Tinker (ed.), *Burma. The struggle for independence 1944–48*, vol. II: *From general strike to independence, 31 August 1946 to 4 January 1948* (London, 1984), pp. 271–84 and following.

53. Taylor, 'Interview with U Kyaw Nyein'.

54. Ibid.

55. Cabinet India–Burma Committee meeting, 22 January 1947, L/WS/1/1578, OIOC.

56. E.g. summaries in Rance to Pethick-Lawrence, 9 January 1947, in Tinker, *Burma*, vol. II, pp. 242–3.

57. Central intelligence staff Singapore telegram, 5 January, military appreciations 1946–7, Rance Papers, Mss Eur F169/5, OIOC.

58. John H. McEnery, *Epilogue in Burma 1945–48* (Tunbridge Wells, 1990), p. 173.

59. Rance to Laithwaite, 28 January 1947, Rance Papers, Mss Eur F169/4, OIOC; Rance to Pethick-Lawrence, 22 January 1947, Tinker, *Burma*, vol. II, p. 328.

60. Rance to Laithwaite, 28 January, 1947, Rance Papers, Mss Eur F169/4, OIOC.

61. Naw, *Aung San*, pp. 188–9; 'Bogyoke Aung San speaks to press conference,' 3 February 1947, M/4/2590, OIOC.

62. Tom Driberg, *Ruling passions* (London, 1978), p. 217.

63. Naw, *Aung San*, pp. 191–2.

64. Taylor, 'Interview with U Kyaw Nyein'.

65. Naw, *Aung San*, p. 198.

66. Narrative of Arthur George Bottomley, Mss Eur E362/2, OIOC, reproduced in part in Tinker, *Burma*, vol. II, pp. 841–8.

67. Ibid., p. 842.

68. 'Note of a meeting of a Karen deputation with the Governor on Tuesday 25 February, 1947, ibid., pp. 437–8.

69. Pethick-Lawrence to Rance, 3 April 1947, Rance Papers, Mss Eur F169/2, OIOC.

70. Aung San to the frontier peoples, *Times of Burma*, 15 June 1947.

71. 'Frontier Areas Commission of Enquiry; Recommendations and Observations', 24 April 1947, R/8/33, OIOC.

72. *New Times of Burma*, 5 June 1947.

73. Rance to Burma Office, 29 May 1947, Rance Papers, Mss Eur F169/2, OIOC.

74. Rance to Listowel, 3 June 1947, ibid.

75. Rance Papers, Mss Eur F169/6, OIOC.

76. McEnery, *Epilogue in Burma*, pp. 98–9.

77. *New Times of Burma*, 14 June 1947.

78. *New Times of Burma*, 11 June 1947.

79. *New Times of Burma*, 3 June 1947.

80. *New Times of Burma*, 31 May 1947.

81. *New Times of Burma*, 4 June 1947.

82. Governor of Burma to Secretary of State, 16 July 1947, Rance Papers, Mss Eur F169/13, OIOC.

83. Ibid.

84. Khin Myo Chit, 'Memoir', f. 105, Mss Eur D1066/1, OIOC.

85. Governor of Burma to Secretary of State, 19 July 1947, 12.00 hours, Rance Papers, Mss Eur F169/13, OIOC.

86. Governor of Burma to Secretary of State, 19 July 1947, 16.25 hours, ibid.

87. Khin Myo Chit, 'Memoir', f. 105.

88. McEnery, *Epilogue in Burma*, p. 110.

89. G. E. Crombie to Laithwaite, 19 July 1947, Laithwaite Papers, Mss Eur F138/74, OIOC.

90. *New Times of Burma*, 22 July 1947.

91. June Bingham, *U Thant of Burma: the search for peace* (London, 1966), pp. 164–6.

92. Governor of Burma to Secretary of State, 20 July 1947, Rance Papers, Mss Eur F169/13, OIOC.

93. Governor of Burma to Secretary of State, 22 July 1947, 12.45 hrs, ibid.

94. Governor of Burma to Secretary of State, 20 July 1947 15.25 hrs, ibid.

95. Taylor, 'Interview with U Kyaw Nyein'.

96. G. E. Crombie to Laithwaite, 23 July 1947, Laithwaite Papers, Mss Eur F138/74, OIOC.

97. Rance to Laithwaite, 29 July 1947, ibid.; in the event it was Lord Listowel, the new secretary of state, and not Cripps who visited the country.

98. Laithwaite to Rance, 6 August 1947, ibid.

99. R. E. Gibson, Govt Burma, to R. E. McGuire, Burma Office, 24 July 1947, Rance Papers, Mss Eur F169/13, OIOC.

100. J. A. Moore's statement, Governor of Burma to Secretary of State, 28 July 1947, ibid.

101. Governor of Burma to Secretary of State, 28 July 1947, second telegram, ibid.

102. *New Times of Burma*, 28 July 1947.

103. McEnery, *Epilogue in Burma*, p. 112.

104. Governor of Burma to Secretary of State, 2 August 1947, Rance Papers, Mss Eur F169/13, OIOC.

105. Maung Maung, *A trial in Burma: the assassination of Aung San* (The Hague, 1962), p. 27.

106. Governor of Burma to Secretary of State, 27 August 1947, Rance Papers, Mss Eur F169/13, OIOC.

107. Richard Butwell, *U Nu of Burma* (Stanford, 1963), p. 88.

108. See 'Lord Listowel in Burma', correspondence and press releases, Laithwaite Papers, Mss Eur F138/74, OIOC.

109. Laithwaite to Rance, 7 November 1947, ibid.

110. Frank N. Trager, *Burma from kingdom to republic* (London, 1966), p. 97.

111. *Sangayama Monthly Bulletin*, 1, 6 October 1953, p. 10; cited in Gustaaf Houtman, *Mental culture in Burmese crisis politics: Aung San Suu Kyi and the National League for Democracy* (Tokyo, 1999), p. 205.

112. Rance to Laithwaite, 12 November 1947, Laithwaite Papers, Mss Eur F138/74, OIOC.

113. Balwant Singh, *Independence and democracy in Burma, 1945–52, the turbulent years* (Ann Arbor, 1993), p. 58.

114. Rance to Laithwaite, 17 November 1947, Laithwaite Papers, Mss Eur F138/74, OIOC.

115. 'Speech to Orient Club, 27 December 1947', Rance Papers, F169/6, OIOC.

CHAPTER 8 1947: MALAYA ON THE BRINK

1. T. A. Keenleyside, 'Nationalist Indian attitudes towards Asia: a troublesome legacy for post-Independence Indian foreign policy', *Pacific Affairs*, 55, 2 (1982), pp. 210–30.

2. For the conference, Nicholas Mansergh, 'The Asian Conference', *International Affairs*, 23, 3 (July 1947), pp. 295–306; Philip Hoalim, *The Malayan Democratic Union: Singapore's first democratic political party* (Singapore, 1973), pp. 20–24. For Sjahrir's role, Rudolf Mrázek, *Sjahrir: politics and exile in Indonesia* (Ithaca, 1994), pp. 334–9.

3. Abu Hanifah, *Tales of a revolution: a leader of the Indonesian revolution looks back* (Sydney, 1972), p. 236.

4. Mohamed Noordin Sopiee, *From Malayan Union to Singapore separation: political unification in the Malaysia region, 1945–65* (Kuala Lumpur, 1974),

pp. 56–71; Clive J. Christie, *A modern history of Southeast Asia: decolonisation, nationalism and separatism* (London, 1996), pp. 39–47. Robert Cribb and Lea Narangoa, 'Orphans of empire: divided peoples, dilemmas of identity, and old imperial borders in East and Southeast Asia', *Comparative Studies in Society and History*, 46, 1 (2004), pp. 164–87.

5. Alfred Lelah interview, OHD, SNA; 'A profile of the late Mr Albert Abraham Lelah', *The Scribe* [Journal of Babylonian Jewry], 70 (October 1998), http://www.dangoor.com/70012.html. For the refugees in India, Joan G. Roland, *The Jewish communities of India: identity in a colonial era* (New Brunswick, 1998), p. 222.

6. Jacob Ballas interview, OHD, SNA.

7. Chan Heng Chee, *A sensation of independence: a political biography of David Marshall* (Singapore, 1984).

8. Manicasothy Saravanamuttu, *The Sara saga* (Singapore, n.d. [1969]), p. 134. MSS/PIJ, May 1946.

9. Gerald de Cruz, *Rojak rebel: memoirs of a Singapore maverick* (Singapore, 1993), pp. 68–73.

10. *Malaya Tribune*, 28 November 1947.

11. Rajeswary Ampalavanar, *The Indian minority and political change in Malaya, 1945–1955* (Kuala Lumpur, 1981), pp. 18–19.

12. For Thivy, Michael Stenson, *Class, race and colonialism in West Malaysia: the Indian case* (Queensland, 1980), pp. 141–51; 'Draft proposals for an All-Malaya Indian Organisation (MIC) to be inaugurated at the All-Malayan Indian Conference, Kuala Lumpur 1–4 August 1946', Thivy Papers, Perpustakaan Universiti Malaya. See also S. Arasaratnam, 'Social and political ferment of the Malayan Indian community, 1945–55', *Proceedings of the First International Conference Seminar of Tamil Studies, Kuala Lumpur April 1966* (Kuala Lumpur, 1966), pp. 141–55.

13. Malayan Security Service, Political Intelligence Journal [MSS/PIJ], 15 April 1947.

14. MSS/PIJ, 30 June 1946, 31 August 1947, John Dalley Papers, RHO; Ampalavanar, *The Indian minority and political change in Malaya*, pp. 25–32.

15. See Halimah Mohd Said and Zainab Abdul Majid, *Images of the Jawi Peranakan of Penang; assimilation of the Jawi Peranakan community into the Malay society* (Universiti Pendikikan Sultan Idris, 2004), pp. 53–57, 104–7; Khoo Boo Teik, *Paradoxes of Mahathirism: an intellectual biography of Mahathir Mohamad* (Kuala Lumpur, 1995), p. 81–8.

16. 'British Defence Committee in South East Asia, 10th meeting', 12 March 1947, CO537/2503, TNA.

17. MSS/PIJ, 30 September 1947; UK High Commission Ceylon to

Commonwealth Relations Office, 10 April 1948; FARELF to War Office, 13 April, 28 April, 4 May, 14 May 1948; 'Aide Memoire', DO35/2406, TNA. Charles Gamba, *The origins of trade unionism in Malaya* (Singapore, 1960), p. 208.

18. Gent to Creech Jones, 11 May 1947, in A. J. Stockwell (ed), *British Documents on the End of Empire: Malaya, part I* (London, 1995), p. 335.

19. M. V. del Tufo, *Malaya: a report on the 1947 census of population* (London, 1949); Charles Hirschman, 'The meaning and measurement of ethnicity in Malaysia: an analysis of census classifications', *Journal of Asian Studies*, 46, 3 (1987), pp. 555–82.

20. *Utusan Melayu*, 18 November 1946.

21. *Malaya Tribune*, 13 November 1947.

22. Gamba, *The origins of trade unionism*, p. 436.

23. C. S. V. K. Moorthi, President of Selangor Estate Workers' Trade Union, 24 March 1947, Thivy Papers.

24. R. Shlomowitz and L. Brennan, 'Mortality and Indian labour in Malaya, 1877–1933', *Indian Economic and Social History Review*, 29 (1992), pp. 57–75.

25. Pierre Boulle, *Sacrilege in Malaya* ([1958] Kuala Lumpur, 1983), pp. 35–6, 44.

26. For a first-hand description of a planter's work see Margaret Shennan, *Out in the midday sun: the British in Malaya, 1880–1960* (London, 2000), pp. 176–81. For the quotation, Henri Falconnier, *The soul of Malaya* ([1931] Singapore, 1985), p. 52.

27. Gamba, *The origins of trade unionism*, pp. 32–3, and for general conditions on estates, pp. 252ff.

28. 'Report: Work on the plantations', FS13622/49, ANM.

29. 'Special meeting of the Malayan Union Labour Advisory Board . . . 3 July 1947', MU Labour/167/47, ANM.

30. We are grateful to Dr Emma Reisz for her comments. See also, J. Norman Palmer, 'Estate workers' health in the Federated Malay States in the 1920s', in P. Rimmer and L. Allen (eds.), *The underside of Malaysian history: pullers, prostitutes and plantation workers* (Singapore, 1990), pp. 179–92.

31. Stephen Dobbs, *Tuan Djek: a biography* (Singapore, 2002).

32. Scorpio, 'ITBA', *The Planter*, 22, 9 (September 1947), p. 235.

33. 'Planters in Malaya', *The Times*, 9 October 1951.

34. S. K. Chettur, *Malayan adventure* (Mangalore, 1948), pp. 249–50.

35. Ravindra K. Jain, 'Leadership and authority in a plantation: a case study of Indians in Malaya (c. 1900–42)', in G. Wijeyewardene (ed.), *Leadership and authority: a symposium* (Singapore, 1968), pp. 163–73; P. Rama-samy, 'Indian war memory in Malaysia', in P. Lim Pui Huen and Diana

Wong (eds.), *War and memory in Malaysia and Singapore* (Singapore, 2000), pp. 90–105.

36. Arasaratnam, 'Social and political ferment of the Malayan Indian community, 1945–55', pp. 141–55.

37. This paragraph and the next is drawn from '[Draft] Summary of reports regarding recent disturbances on estates in South Kedah', in Gent to Creech Jones, 8 April 1947, CO537/2173, TNA; K. Nadaraja, 'The Thondar Pedai movement of Kedah, 1945–47', *Malaysia in History*, 24 (1981), pp. 95–103; Leong Yee Fong, *Labour and trade unionism in colonial Malaya: a study of the socio-economic and political bases of the Malayan labour movement, 1930–1957* (Pulau Pinang, 1999), pp. 164–7, and Gamba, *The origins of trade unionism*, pp. 252–303.

38. Gamba, *The origins of trade unionism*, p. 284.

39. Brazier to Commissioner for Labour, 19 September 1947, LAB/158/47, ANM; For example, 'Trade dispute Rengo Malay Estate, 12 November 1947', LAB/139/47, ANM.

40. Quoted in Gamba, *The origins of trade unionism*, p. 296.

41. Gimson to Creech Jones, 4 March 1947, CO537/2171, TNA; *Malaya Tribune*, 14 February 1947.

42. Minutes of sixth Governor General's conference in Singapore, 11 March 1947, in Stockwell, *British documents: Malaya, Part I*, pp. 303–6.

43. Labour Report for October 1947, LAB/54/47, ANM.

44. *Malaya Tribune*, 16 October 1947.

45. Chin Peng, *My side of history* (Singapore, 2004), pp. 195–6; 'Lawlessness and insecurity', *The Planter*, 23, 10 (October, 1947), pp. 240–44.

46. Quoted in Nicholas J. White, *Business, government and the end of empire: Malaya, 1945–1957* (Kuala Lumpur, 1996), p. 82.

47. Ibid., p. 103; Norman Cleaveland, *Bang! Bang! in Ampang* (San Pedro, CA, 1973), p. 54.

48. Gimson to Creech Jones, 2 March 1947 and 20 March 1947, CO537/2171, TNA.

49. Gent to J. J. Paskin, 20 September 1946; Paskin to Gent, 4 October 1946, CO537/1522, TNA.

50. 'Report on the Special Conference on the threat of Communism in Malaya and Singapore, 1947', 26 June 1947, Dalley Papers, RHO.

51. Michael Stenson, *Repression and revolt: the origins of the 1948 communist insurrection in Malaya and Singapore* (Athens, OH, 1969).

52. C. W. Lyle, 'Selangor Protest Committee', 16 July 1947, LAB/158/47, ANM.

53. Returns on LAB/562/47, ANM. See also Leong, *Labour and trade unionism in Malaya* pp. 168–73.

54. Laurence K. L. Siaw, *Chinese society in rural Malaysia* (Kuala Lumpur, 1983), p. 86.

55. MSS/PIJ, 15 October 1947.

56. They were also written with access to British documents and 'as told' to a retired *Daily Telegraph* journalist, Ian Ward, and his wife and collaborator Norma Miraflor. Chin Peng discusses the relationship briefly in his preface to *My side of history*, pp. 4–5.

57. Ibid., pp. 167–74.

58. MSS/PIJ, 31 March 1947.

59. There is a discrepancy here over the dates. Chin Peng, in his memoirs, gives the date as late January, and the subsequent meeting at which the dossier of evidence was presented as 6 March. However, this must be an error. Most other sources give the date of Lai Teck's disappearance as 6 March and of the meeting to expel Lai Teck as May, and we have followed them. The March date was also given by Chin Peng when questioned directly in an earlier interview: Chin Peng, *My side of history*, pp. 171–9; C. C. Chin and Karl Hack (eds.), *Dialogues with Chin Peng: new light on the Malayan Communist Party* (Singapore, 2004), pp. 124–6. See also Anthony Short, *In pursuit of mountain rats: the communist insurrection in Malaya* (Singapore, 2000 [1975]), pp. 40–41. We are grateful to C. C. Chin for clarification of this point.

60. Chin Peng, *My side of history*, pp. 178–9.

61. 'The Wright (@ Lye Teck) Document: "A written statement on Lye Teck's case issued on 28 May 1948 by the MCP Central Committee"', supplement to MSS/PIJ, 31 July, 1948.

62. Chin Peng, *My side of history*, pp. 179–84.

63. Christopher E. Goscha, *Thailand and the Southeast Asian networks of the Vietnamese revolution, 1885–1954* (London, 1999), ch. 5.

64. Ibid., pp. 187–8.

65. Chin and Hack, *Dialogues with Chin Peng*, p. 130.

66. Chin Peng, *My side of history*, pp. 188–9.

67. Ibid., pp. 187–91; Chin and Hack, *Dialogues with Chin Peng*, pp. 106–10.

68. 'The Wright (@ Lye Teck) Document'; MSS/PIJ, 31 July 1948.

69. Ibid.

70. 'Interrogation of a Perak prisoner, MCP area representative, political', Supplement No. 7 to MSS/PIJ, 15 July 1948.

71. Short, *In pursuit of mountain rats*, p. 44; C. C. Chin, 'In search of the revolution: a brief biography of Chin Peng', in Chin and Hack, *Dialogues with Chin Peng*, pp. 355–8.

72. Yoji Akashi, 'Lai Teck, Secretary General of the Malayan Communist

Party, 1939–1947', *Journal of the South Seas Society*, 49 (1994), pp. 57–103; Chin Peng, *My side of history*, p. 159; Lim Cheng Leng, *The story of a psy-warrior: Tan Sri Dr C. C. Too* (Batu Caves, 2000), pp. 113–25.

73. 'Malayan Communist Party policy', supplement no. 9 to MSS/PIJ, 31 July 1948.

74. Michael Stenson, *The 1948 Communist revolt in Malaya: a note on historical sources and interpretation with a Reply by Gerald de Cruz* (Singapore, 1971), p. 29–30.

75. Short, *In pursuit of mountain rats*, p. 41; 'Malayan Communist Party Affairs 25 April 1984 to 26 June 1948', Appendix A to MSS/PIJ, 30 June 1948.

76. Short, *In pursuit of mountain rats*, p. 40.

77. Malayan Security Service, 'Report on BMA Period', 3 April 1946, SNA; Leon Comber, 'The Malayan Security Service (1945–1948)'; *Intelligence and National Security*, 18, 3 (2003), pp. 128–53.

78. Robert Cribb, 'Opium and the Indonesian revolution', *Modern Asian Studies*, 22, 4 (1988), pp. 710–22; Young Mun Cheong, *The Indonesian revolution and the Singapore connection, 1945–1949* (Singapore, 2003), pp. 101–37.

79. Onn to Gent, 17 February 1947, in Stockwell, *British documents: Malaya, part I*, p. 294.

80. *Majlis*, 2 April 1946.

81. 'Report on UMNO General Assembly, 10–12 January 1947', in Gent to Creech Jones 27 January 1947, Stockwell, *British documents: Malaya, part I*, pp. 292–3.

82. Ahmad Boestamam (trans. William R. Roff), *Carving the path to the summit* (Athens, OH, 1979), pp. 82–5. Mustapha Hussain, *Malay nationalism before Umno: the memoirs of Mustapha Hussain*, translated by Insun Mustapha and edited by Jomo K. S. (Kuala Lumpur, 2005), pp. 330–31.

83. Quoted in Farish A Noor, *Islam embedded: the historical development of the Pan-Malaysian Islamic Party PAS (1951–2003)*, vol. I (Kuala Lumpur, 2004), pp. 113–16.

84. Hussain, *Malay nationalism before Umno*, pp. 334–9.

85. Shamsiah Fakeh, *Memoir Shamsiah Fakeh: dari AWAS ke Rejimen Ke-10* (Bangi, 2004), pp. 40–45.

86. Khatijah Sidek, *Memoirs of Khatijah Sidek: Puteri Kesateria Bangsa* (Kuala Lumpur, 2001 [1960]), p. 160.

87. *Malaya Tribune*, 17 March 1947; Wazir Jahan Karim, *Women and culture: between Malay adat and Islam* (Boulder, 1992), pp. 96–100.

88. Boestamam, *Carving the path to the summit*, pp. 61–2; MSS/PIJ, 30 April 1947.

89. MSS/PIJ, 31 March 1947; Gent to Creech Jones, 24 February 1947, CO537/2151 TNA.

90. *Utusan Melayu*, 14 August 1947.

91. This pamphlet has recently been republished, in facsimile form, in Ahmad Boestamam, *Memoir Ahmad Boestamam: merdeka dengan darah dalam api* (Bangi, 2004).

92. *Malaya Tribune*, 20 March and 21 March 1947; Firdaus Haji Abdullah, *Radical Malay politics: its origins and early development* (Petaling Jaya, 1985), pp. 98–101.

93. Boestamam, *Carving the path to the summit*, p. 90–91.

94. A. J. Stockwell, *British policy and Malay politics during the Malayan Union experiment, 1945–1948* (Kuala Lumpur, 1979), pp. 149–50.

95. 'Sabilu'llah and invulnerability', supplement to MSS/PIJ, 15 June 1947.

96. 'Activities of the organisation known as API for the information of the Secretary of State', enclosure to Gent to Creech Jones, 1 July 1947, CO537/2151, TNA.

97. Boestamam, *Carving the path to the summit*, p. 126.

98. 'Annual Medical Report, 1949', SUK Tr/118/50.

99. 'Infant mortality rates per 1000 births', 7 May 1949, FS/13157/47, ANM.

100. 'Annual Report on the social and economic progress of the people of Kelantan for the year 1947', FS/9358/48, ANM.

101. Ahmed Tajuddin, 'Economic survey of the padi planters in Krian South', 22 November 1946, Coop/1045/46, ANM.

102. Mahathir bin Mohamad, *The early years, 1947–1972* (Kuala Lumpur, 1995), p. 59.

103. For example, *Utusan Malaya*, 24 November 1947.

104. See enclosures in FS/2255/48, ANM.

105. Hussain, *Malay nationalism before Umno*, pp. 335–6.

106. *Pelita Malaya*, 6 April 1946.

107. Firdaus, *Radical Malay politics*, pp. 30–44.

108. *Malaya Tribune*, 2 June 1947.

109. 'Malayan Communist Party Policy', supplement no. 9 to MSS/PIJ, 31 July 1948.

110. MSS/PIJ, 30 June 1947.

111. We have drawn here on A. J. Stockwell, 'The formation and first years of the United Malays National Organization (U.M.N.O.), 1946–1948', *Modern Asian Studies*, 11, 4 (1977), pp. 481–513.

112. MSS/PIJ, 15 May 1947.

113. Ariffin Omar, *Bangsa Melayu: Malay concepts of democracy and community, 1945–50* (Kuala Lumpur, 1993), pp. 106–10; Tan Liok Eee, 'The rhetoric of bangsa and minzu: community and nation in tension, the Malay

peninsula, 1900–1955', Centre of Southeast Asian Studies, Monash University, Working Paper no. 52, 1988, pp. 18–20.

114. K. J. Ratnam, *Communalism and the political process in Malaya* (Kuala Lumpur, 1965), pp. 75–84.

115. 'Malayan policy', Cabinet memorandum, 28 June 1947, in Stockwell, *British documents: Malaya, part I*, pp. 352–8.

116. See M. R. Stenson, 'The Malayan Union and the historians', *Journal of Southeast Asian History*, 10, 2 (1969), pp. 344–54, and Wong Lin Ken, 'The Malayan Union: a historical retrospect', *Journal of Southeast Asian Studies*, 13, 1 (1982), 184–91. For a full discussion see Albert Lau, *The Malayan Union controversy, 1942–48* (London, 1991).

117. For the origins of AMCJA, Yeo Kim Wah, 'The anti-Federation movement in Malaya, 1946–48', *Journal of Southeast Asian Studies*, 4, 1 (1973), pp. 31–51.

118. *Malaya Tribune*, 21 December 1947. This was the reasoning of Ahmad Boestamam, *Carving the path to the summit*, pp. 98–9.

119. Quoted in Sopiee, *From Malayan Union to Singapore separation*, p. 41; Hussain, *Malay nationalism before Umno*, p. 365.

120. Tan Cheng Lock to representative Chinese leaders throughout Malaya, 9 July 1946, SCA/161/46, SNA.

121. See K. G. Tregonning, 'Tan Cheng Lock: a Malayan nationalist', *Journal of Southeast Asian Studies*, 10, 1 (1979), pp. 25–76; for his thought, we have drawn on his daughter's memoir: Alice Scott-Ross, *Tun Dato Sir Cheng Lock Tan: a personal profile* (Singapore, 1990).

122. 'Public meeting under the auspices of the Pan-Malayan Council of Joint Action: Speech at Kuala Lumpur on 23 December 1946', in Tan Cheng Lock, *Malayan problems from a Chinese point of view* (Singapore, 1947), p. 134.

123. Hussain, *Malay nationalism before Umno*, pp. 333–4.

124. 'The hartal of 20 October 1947', supplement to MSS/PIJ, 31 October 1947.

125. Wu Tian Wang in the *MCP Review*, of June 1948, quoted in Sopiee, *From Malayan Union to Singapore separation*, p. 47. Chin Peng in his memoirs suggests that it was 'not exactly a communist front but . . . firmly under our influence', *My side of history*, p. 199, but on other occasions he has suggested that control was weak; personal communication, June, 1998.

126. Hussain, *Malay nationalism before Umno*, pp. 341–7.

127. Quoted and discussed in Ariffin Omar, *Bangsa Melayu*, pp. 115–16; Boestamam, *Carving the path to the summit*, p. 110.

128. For this, see the seminal essays by Tan Liok Eee, 'The rhetoric of bangsa and minzi', and Muhammad Ikmal Said, 'Ethnic perspectives on the left in Malaysia', in Joel Kahn and Francis Loh Kok Wah (eds.), *Fragmented*

vision: culture and politics in contemporary Malaysia (Sydney, 1992), pp. 254–81.

129. Malayan Democratic Union, 'Memorandum on counter-proposals for future constitution, for consideration of PMCJA' (signed by John Eber), SP13/A/5, Tan Cheng Lock Papers ANM. *The People's Constitutional Proposals for Malaya 1947 drafted by PUTERA–AMCJA* (Pusat Kajian Bahan Serjarah Kontemporari Tempatan, Kajang, 2005), quotes on p. 35 and p. 100.

130. O. H. Morris, minute, 13 November 1947, reprinted in *The People's Constitutional Proposals for Malaya 1947*, pp. i–ii.

131. Hoalim, *The Malayan Democratic Union*, pp. 18–20.

132. Yeo, 'The anti-Federation movement', pp. 43–5.

133. Tregonning, 'Tan Cheng Lock', pp. 54–5.

134. Boestamam, *Carving the path to the summit*, p. 110.

135. 'Minutes of the Third Delegates Conference of the PUTERA and AMCJA held at Kuala Lumpur at the premises of the New Democratic Youth League, Selangor Branch, at 7 Foch Avenue (3rd Floor) at 11am on Monday November 3rd 1947', Tan Cheng Lock Papers, SP13/A/7, ANM.

136. 'The hartal of 20 October 1947', supplement to MSS/PIJ, 31 October 1947.

137. Tregonning, 'Tan Cheng Lock', pp. 53–5.

138. 'Report on the Special Conference on the threat of Communism in Malaya and Singapore, 1947', 26 June 1947, Dalley Papers, RHO.

139. *Malaya Tribune*, 6 October 1947.

140. Sopiee, *From Malayan Union to Singapore separation*, pp. 41, 48–9.

141. For this see *The People's Constitutional Proposals for Malaya 1947 drafted by PUTERA–AMCJA*.

CHAPTER 9 1948: A BLOODY DAWN

1. Cited in Frank N. Trager, *Burma: from kingdom to republic* (London, 1966), p. 108.

2. *Burma's Independence Celebrations* (Copygraph London Ltd, 1948), p. 15.

3. Roy Bucher to Miss Elizabeth Bucher, 5 January 1948, Bucher Papers, 7901/87–5, National Army Museum.

4. Balwant Singh, *Independence and democracy in Burma* (Ann Arbor, 1993) pp. 67–8.

5. Ibid., pp. 74–5.

6. Notably, J. S. Furnivall, *Netherlands India: a study of a plural economy* (London, 1939), which compared British administration in Burma and Malaya unfavourably with Dutch Indonesia; see also Julie Pham, 'Furnivall

and Fabianism: reinterpreting the plural society in colonial Burma', *Modern Asian Studies*, 39, 2 (2005), pp. 321–48.

7. J. S. Furnivall to C. W. Dunn, 9 April 1948, Furnivall Papers, PP/MS 23, vol. I, SOAS.

8. Furnivall to Dunn, 11 January 1948, ibid.

9. Furnivall to Dunn, 28 March 1948, ibid.

10. Furnivall in *New Times of Burma*, 10 April 1949.

11. Furnivall to Dunn, 11 January 1948, Furnivall Papers, PP/MS 23, vol. I, SOAS.

12. Marginal notes in FO371/61595, TNA.

13. P. J. Murray, note 20 August 1948, FO371/69518, TNA.

14. Edgar Snow in *Saturday Evening Post*, 29 May 1948, FO371/69515, TNA.

15. Ibid.

16. Furnivall to Dunn, 11 January 1948, Furnivall Papers, PP/MS 23, vol. I, SOAS.

17. Richard Butwell, *U Nu of Burma* (Standford, 1963), pp. 73–84.

18. Furnivall to Dunn, 4 July 1947, Furnivall Papers, PP/MS 23, vol. I, SOAS.

19. The estimate is in Mary Callahan, *Making enemies: war and state building in Burma* (Ithaca, 2004), p. 121.

20. 'Nationalisation of British assets in Burma', FO371/69491, TNA.

21. Security service report on communism in Burma, March 1948, FO371/69515, TNA.

22. Trager, *Burma*, pp. 97–8.

23. Thein Pe Myint, 'Critique of the communist movement in Burma', 1973, Mss Eur C498, OIOC.

24. Dossier on Thein Pe including his manifesto of 19 March, enclosed in Bowker to Foreign Office, FO371/69517, TNA.

25. Ghosal was a student labour activist at Rangoon University in 1940–1. He had been evacuated to India during the war and worked as a war correspondent for *People's War*, the Indian Communist Party journal, and was a close aide of P. C. Joshi, the party's Secretary General. He returned to Burma in 1945 and later went underground. Intelligence report, received 13 May 1948, FO371/69515, TNA.

26. 'On the present political situation in Burma', January 1948, enclosed in Bowker to Foreign Office, 20 July 1948, FO371/69516, TNA.

27. British Services Mission, preliminary report, 9 February 1948, p. 3, L/WS/1/1705, OIOC.

28. Note by Peter Murray, 'Establishment of British Services Mission in Burma', and report by Major General G. K. Bourne, 9 February 1948, FO371/69481, TNA.

29. Smith Dun, *Memoirs of the four-foot Colonel: General Smith Dun, first commander in chief of independent Burma's armed forces* (Ithaca, 1980), pp. ii–vii.

30. Notes by R. B. Pearn, 26 November 1948, on minutes by Bowker and Bourne, FO371/69486, TNA.

31. British Services Mission, preliminary report, 9 February 1948, pp. 4–6, L/WS/1/1705, OIOC.

32. Rangoon to London, 15 May 1948, minute by Bourne, FO371/69482, TNA.

33. Ibid.

34. Rangoon to London, 9 April 1948, FO371/69481, TNA.

35. Peter Murray, minute, 14 September 1948, FO371/69484, TNA.

36. Furnivall to Dunn, 29 February 1948, Furnivall Papers, PP/MS 23, vol. I, SOAS.

37. 'Effect of Communist Party advance in China on communists in Burma', Rangoon to FO, 4 December 1948, FO371/69522, TNA.

38. Bertil Lintner, *The rise and fall of the Communist Party of Burma* (Ithaca, 1990), p. 11.

39. Thein Pe Myint, 'Critique of the communist movement in Burma', 1973, Mss Eur C498, ff. 26, OIOC.

40. Rangoon to London, 26 May 1948, FO371/69515, TNA.

41. Bowker to Foreign Office, FO371/69481, TNA.

42. Furnivall to Dunn, 28 March, 9 April 1948, Furnival Papers, PP/MS 23, vol. I, SOAS.

43. Bowker to Foreign Office, 12 April 1948, FO371/69515, TNA.

44. Nu to Cripps, 7 October 1948, Cripps–Nu correspondence, CAB127/151, TNA.

45. Rangoon to Foreign Office, 3 July 1948, FO371/69483, TNA.

46. Furnivall to Dunn 12 April 1948, Furnivall Papers, PP/MS 23, vol. I, SOAS.

47. Maung Maung, *A trial in Burma: the assassination of Aung San* (The Hague, 1962), p. 68.

48. Clipping from the *Sunday Despatch*, 15 February 1948, Laithwaite Papers, Mss Eur F138/74, OIOC.

49. Furnivall to Dunn, 12 April 1948 with some additions 2 May, Furnivall Papers, PP/MS 23, vol. I, SOAS.

50. See Bertil Lintner, *Burma in revolt: opium and insurgency since 1948* (Boulder, 1994).

51. Report of British Mission, Rangoon to London, 30 June 1948, FO371/69483, TNA.

52. Ibid.

53. Rangoon to London, 14 August 1948, FO371/69484, TNA.

54. Butwell, *U Nu of Burma*, p. 62.

55. *News Chronicle*, 27 August 1948.

56. *News Chronicle*, 23 September 1948.

57. P. Murray, Foreign Office, to Major A. K. Rugg-Price, FO371/69486, TNA.

58. For a detailed account of these events and the Karen insurgency see Callahan, *Making enemies*, pp. 124–42.

59. Ibid., p. 127.

60. Bowker to Foreign Office, 'Karen movement and British complicity', 12 September 1948, FO371/69509, TNA.

61. Bowker to Foreign Office, 19 June 1948, ibid.

62. Bowker to Foreign Office, 28 February 1948, ibid.

63. Christopher Bayly and Tim Harper, *Forgotten armies: Britain's Asian empire and the war with Japan* (London, 2004), p. 336.

64. Note by P. J. Murray, 16 September 1948, FO371/69509, TNA.

65. 'Translation of speech by the Honble Thakin Nu, Prime Minister of Burma, delivered in Parliament on 14 June 1949', CAB127/151, TNA.

66. Note by P. J. Murray, 16 September 1948, FO371/69509, TNA.

67. Bowker to Foreign Office, 15 September 1948, ibid.

68. Bowker to Foreign Office, 18 September 1948, FO371/69510, TNA.

69. Bowker to Foreign Office, 21 September, ibid.

70. Anon to 'Pop', 2 September 1948; 'Skunk' to 'Ewan', 14 September 1948, Tom Driberg Papers, S3 (miscellaneous), Christ Church, Oxford.

71. Bowker to Foreign Office, 13 September 1948, FO371/69510, NA; cf. Furnivall to Dunn, 14 December 1948, Furnivall Papers, PP/MS 23, vol. I, SOAS.

72. Bowker to Foreign Office, 13 September 1948, FO371/69510, TNA.

73. Rangoon to Foreign Office, 'Burma insurrection', 13 July 1948, FO371/69516, TNA.

74. 'Red star over Asia', *News Chronicle*, 27 August 1948.

75. Note, September 1948, FO371/69519, TNA.

76. Murray to Laithwaite, 25 October 1948, Laithwaite Papers, Mss Eur F138/74, OIOC.

77. Bowker to Foreign Office, 11 November 1948, FO371/69522, TNA.

78. Bowker to Foreign Office, 18 November 1948, FO371/69519, TNA.

79. Furnivall to Dunn, 21 September 1948, Furnivall Papers, PP/MS 23, vol. I, SOAS.

80. Callahan, *Making enemies*, p. 132.

81. Jonathan Falla, *True Love and Bartholomew: rebels on the Burmese border* (Cambridge, 1991), p. 26; cf. Callahan, *Making enemies*, p. 132.

82. Falla, *True Love*, p. 27.
83. Furnivall to Dunn, 24 December 1948, Furnivall Papers, PP/MS 23, vol. I, SOAS.
84. Furnivall to Dunn, 28 March 1948, ibid.
85. John de Chazal, memoir, p. 4, Mss Eur D1041/3, OIOC.
86. Military adviser to UK High Commission in India to London, 30 March 1948, L/WS/1/1187, OIOC.
87. Correspondence appended to situation report, 28 November 1950, FO371/84243; prime minister Pakistan to prime minister UK, 20 July 1948, DO35/3163, TNA.
88. K. K. Tewari, *A soldier's voyage of self discovery* (Auroville, 1995), p. 46.
89. Roy Bucher to Miss Elizabeth Bucher, 24 September 1948, Bucher Papers, 7901/87-5, NAM.
90. *People's Age*, 1 February 1948.
91. *People's Age*, 29 February 1948.
92. *People's Age*, 14 March 1948.
93. Military adviser to UK High Commission in India to London, 6 May 1948, L/WS/1/1187, OIOC.
94. Ashton Wade, *A life on the line* (Tunbridge Wells, 1988), pp. 147-9.
95. Andrew Gilmour, *My role in the rehabilitation of Singapore, 1946-53* (Singapore, 1973), p. 16.
96. J. P. Cross and Buddhiman Gurung, *Gurkhas at war in their own words: the Gurkha experience, 1939 to the present* (London, 2002), pp. 178-80; Ahmad Boestamam (trans. William R. Roff), *Carving the path to the summit* (Athens, OH, 1979), p. 95.

CHAPTER 10 1948: THE MALAYAN REVOLUTION

1. Gent to H. T. Bourdillon, 22 January 1948, A. J. Stockwell (ed.), *British Documents on the End of Empire: Malaya, Part I* (London, 1995), pp. 372-3.
2. *Malaya Tribune*, 13 November 1947.
3. Gent to Creech Jones, 30 December 1947, 4 January 1948, CO537/3667, TNA.
4. Thio Chan Bee, *The extraordinary adventures of an ordinary man* (London, 1977), pp. 70-74.
5. Simon C. Smith, *British relations with the Malay rulers from decentralization to independence, 1930-1957* (Kuala Lumpur, 1995), pp. 97-9, 118-19.
6. Editorial, *Malaya Tribune*, 15 December 1947.
7. A. J. Stockwell, 'British imperial strategy and decolonization in South-east

Asia, 1947–57', in D. K. Basset and V. T. King (eds.), *Britain and South-East Asia* (University of Hull Centre of Southeast Asian Studies, Occasional Papers, no. 13, 1986), pp. 79–90, at pp. 81–2.

8. 'Note: W. Linehan', 2 March 1948, CO537/3746, TNA.

9. Christopher Blake, *A view from within: the last years of British rule in South-East Asia* (Castle Cary, 1990), pp. 84–5.

10. John Ede interview, OHD, SNA.

11. *Malaya Tribune*, 24 September 1947; Yeo Kim Wah, *Political development in Singapore, 1945–55* (Singapore, 1973), pp. 254–66.

12. Lady Percy McNiece interview, OHD, SNA.

13. Lee Kam Hing and Chow Mun Seong, *Biographical dictionary of the Chinese in Malaysia* (Kuala Lumpur, 1997), pp. 88–90.

14. Yong Ching Fatt, *Tan Kah Kee: an Overseas Chinese legend* (Singapore, 1987), pp. 312–18; Chui Kwei-chiang, 'The China Democratic League in Singapore and Malaya, 1946–48', *Review of Southeast Asian Studies*, 15 (1985), pp. 1–28.

15. 'KMT party funds: their sources and investments', supplement to Malayan Security Service, Political Intelligance Journal, [MSS/PI], 31 August 1947.

16. C. F. Yong and R. B. McKenna, *The Kuomintang movement in British Malaya, 1912–1949* (Singapore, 1990), ch. 8.

17. Lt. Col. T. N. Glazebrook to C.H. Tarner, MI2, 20 April 1948, WO208/3929, TNA.

18. 'The KMT guerrillas, North Perak' supplement no. 4 of 1948 to MSS/PIJ, 31 May 1948; Wilfred Blythe, *The impact of Chinese secret societies in Malaya: a historical study* (London, 1969), pp. 388–91.

19. 'Statement of Yuin See', appendix A to supplement no. 4 of 1948 to MSS/PIJ, 31 May 1948.

20. Blythe, *The impact of Chinese secret societies*, pp. 368–78, 392–9.

21. Ibid, pp. 380–83; Charles Gamba, *The origins of trade unionism in Malaya* (Singapore, 1960), pp. 230–31.

22. MSS/PIJ, 15 May 1947; 'Politico-Triad activities in Malaya', supplement no. 2 to MSS/PIJ, 15 January 1948.

23. Anthony Short, *In pursuit of mountain rats: the communist insurrection in Malaya* (Singapore, 2000 [1975]), pp. 52–3; Chin Peng, *My side of history* (Singapore, 2004), pp. 202–5.

24. 'Translation of a cyclostyled pamphlet marked "Passed at the 4th Plenary Conference of the MCP Central Executive Committee held from 17–21 March 1948', supplement to MSS/PIJ, 30 June 1948.

25. 'Malayan Communist Party policy', supplement No. 9 to MSS/PIJ, 31 July 1948.

26. For example, MSS/PIJ, 6 March 1948.

27. Clive J. Christie, *A modern history of Southeast Asia: decolonisation, nationalism and separatism* (London, 1996), pp. 183–6; Gurney to Creech Jones, 10 November 1948, CO537/3685, TNA.

28. *Straits Echo*, 20 March 1948.

29. Firdaus Haji Abdullah, *Radical Malay politics: its origins and early development* (Petaling Jaya, 1985), pp. 44–7.

30. MSS/PIJ, 31 May 1948.

31. *Straits Times*, 26 April 1948; MSS/PIJ, 15 May 1948.

32. Shamsiah Fakeh, *Memoir Shamsiah Fakeh: dari AWAS ke Rejimen Ke-10* (Bangi, 2004), pp. 53–4; Ibrahim Chik, *Ibrahim Chik: dari API ke Rejimen Ke-1* (Bangi, 2004), pp. 64–6.

33. MSS/PIJ, 31 May 1948.

34. We have drawn here on the richly descriptive and sumptuously illustrated study by Khoo Salma Nusution and Abdur-Razzaq Lubis, *Kinta Valley: pioneering Malaysia's modern development* (Ipoh, 2005).

35. Ooi Jin Bee, 'Mining landscapes of Kinta', *Malayan Journal of Tropical Geography*, 4 (1955), p. 52.

36. For this, see Francis Loh Kok Wah's seminal work, *Beyond the tin mines: coolies, squatters and New Villagers in the Kinta valley, c. 1880–1980* (Singapore, 1988), pp. 66–85.

37. T. N. Harper, *The end of empire and the making of Malaya* (Cambridge, 1999), pp. 96–101.

38. For a contemporary assessment see E. H. G. Dobby, 'Some aspects of the human ecology of South-East Asia', *Geographical Journal*, 108, 1/3 (1946), pp. 40–51.

39. State Forest Officer to Resident Commissioner, Perak, 3 July 1947, ibid.

40. Farmers of Bekor Sakai Reserve and Keledong Saiong Forest Reserve to Resident Commissioner, Perak, 3 January 1948, Pk.Sec/2777/47, ANM.

41. Petition of Chin Wong Peng and others, 'Cultivation in Kg Bahru, Kuala Selangor', 29 August 1946, MU/1437/46, ANM.

42. Harry Fang, 'Who are the squatters?', *Malaya Tribune*, 5 February 1949.

43. Farmers of Pokang (Kampar) to the District Forest Officer, 14 June 1947, Pk.Sec/1006/48, ANM.

44. District Officer Kuala Kangsar, memo, 16 March 1948, Pk.Sec/690/48, ANM.

45. 'Pulling out tapioca in Comp. 16 Bikam and Comp 2. Changkat Jong Forest Reserves', 12 May 1948, Pk.Sec 830/48, ANM.

46. Labour Department monthly report, April 1948, MU4181/47, ANM.

47. Labour Department monthly report May 1948, ibid.

48. Gamba, *The origins of trade unionism*, pp. 323–7.

49. 'Interrogation of a Perak prisoner, MCP area representative, political', supplement no. 7 to MSS/PIJ, 15 July 1948.

50. John Dalley to Hugh Bryson, 7 June 1967; 3 July 1965, BAM, II/19, RCS, CUL.

51. A. J. Stockwell, '"A widespread and long-concocted plot to overthrow government in Malaya"? The origins of the Malayan Emergency', *Journal of Imperial and Commonwealth History*, 21 (1993), pp. 66–88.

52. J. B. Williams, minute, 28 May 1948, CO537/3755, TNA.

53. J. D. Dalley, 'Internal Security – Malaya – 14 June 1948', CO537/6006, TNA.

54. H. James and D. Sheil-Small, *A pride of Gurhkas: the 2nd King Edward VII's Own Goorkhas, 1948–71* (London, 1971), p. 7.

55. Chin Peng, *My side of history*, pp. 214–15.

56. J. M. Gullick, 'My time in Malaya', Heussler Papers, RHO.

57. Short, *In pursuit of mountain rats*, p. 118–19.

58. Dalley to Hugh Bryson, 3 July 1965, BAM, II/19, RCS, CUL.

59. Jean Falconer, *Woodsmoke and temple flowers: memories of Malaya* (Edinburgh, 1992), p. 136.

60. Quoted in Gamba, *The origins of trade unionism*, p. 346.

61. 'Interrogation of a Perak prisoner, MCP area representative, political', supplement no. 7 to MSS/PIJ, 15 July 1948.

62. C. C. Chin and Karl Hack (eds.), *Dialogues with Chin Peng: new light on the Malayan Communist Party* (Singapore, 2004), p. 136.

63. Chin Peng, *My side of history*, p. 238.

64. Ibid., pp. 209–22.

65. *The Times*, 16 July 1948.

66. 'Document B.12: Translation of a diary found among the papers of Lau Yiew', supplement no. 7 to MSS/PIJ, 15 July 1948.

67. 'Document B.18: Translation from a pocket book in the possession of Lau Yiew', ibid.

68. Noel Barber, *The war of the running dogs: how Malaya defeated the communist guerrillas, 1948–1960* (London, 1971), pp. 56–7.

69. Ahmad Khan interview, OHD, SNA.

70. Kumar Ramakrishna, *Emergency propaganda: the winning of Malayan hearts and minds, 1948–1958* (Richmond, 2002), p. 30.

71. J. N. McHugh, *Anatomy of communist propaganda* (Kuala Lumpur, 1949), p. 12.

72. Shamsiah Fakeh, *Memoir Shamsiah Fakeh*, p. 59.

73. Ishak Haji Muhammad to Chief Secretary, 28 June 1949, Tan Cheng Lock Papers, TCL/3/187, ISEAS.

74. Ahmad Boestamam (trans. William R. Raff), *Carving the path to the*

summit (Athens, OH, 1979), p. 144. Ali Mohamed, 'PAS' platform: development and change, 1951–1986', PhD thesis, Universiti Malaya, 1989, p. 27.

75. For example, Said Zahari, *Dark clouds at dawn* (Kuala Lumpur, 2001), pp. 280–81.

76. Dominic Puthucheary and Jomo K. S. (eds.), *No cowardly past: James J. Puthucheary, writings, poems, commentaries* (Kuala Lumpur 1998), pp. 5–6, 162.

77. Lim Hong Bee, *Born into war: autobiography of a barefoot colonial boy who grew up to face the challenge of the modern world* (London, 1994), p. 368.

78. Philip Hoalim, *The Malayan Democratic Union: Singapore's first democratic political party* (Singapore, 1973), pp. 25–6.

79. Stockwell, ' "A widespread and long-concocted plot to overthrow government in Malaya" '; Philip Deery, 'The terminology of terrorism: Malaya, 1948–52', *Journal of Southeast Asian Studies*, 34, 2 (2003), pp. 231–47.

80. Andrew Gilmour, *My role in the rehabilitation of Singapore, 1946–53* (Singapore, 1973), p. 29; Nicholas J. White, *Business, government and the end of empire, Malaya, 1945–1957* (Kuala Lumpur, 1996), p. 116; J. D. Higham, minute, November 1948, CO537/4762, TNA.

81. J. P. Cross and Buddhiman Gurung, *Gurkhas at war in their own words: the Gurkha experience, 1939 to the present* (London, 2002), p. 178.

82. Sir Thomas Lloyd to Gimson and Newboult, 23 August 1948, CO537/3758, TNA.

83. Ashton Wade, *A life on the line* (Tunbridge Wells, 1988), pp. 147–9.

84. Cabinet Defence Committee meeting, 3 November 1948, CO537/3643, TNA.

85. Short, *In pursuit of mountain rats*, pp. 124–33.

86. Yong and McKenna, *The Kuomintang movement*, p. 217.

87. Datuk Mohd Yusoff Hj. Ahmad, *Decades of change (Malaysia – 1910s–1970s)* (Kuala Lumpur, 1983), p. 341.

88. Brian Stewart, *Smashing terrorism in the Malayan Emergency: the vital contribution of the police* (Kuala Lumpur, 2004), pp. 189–90.

89. R. Cole, 'It aint 'arf 'ot', http://members.tripod.com/Askari_MB/id47.htm.

90. Norman Cleaveland, *Bang! Bang! in Ampang* (San Pedro, CA, 1973) pp. 55–63.

91. Stewart, *Smashing terrorism in the Malayan Emergency*, pp. 49–50.

92. John Strawson, *A history of the SAS Regiment* (London, 1984), p. 160.

93. 'Planters in Malaya', *The Times*, 9 October 1951.

94. *The Times*, 9 August 1948.

95. Chui Kwei-chiang, *The response of the Malayan Chinese to political and military developments in China, 1945–9* (Singapore, 1977), pp. 71–2;

Richard Stubbs, *Hearts and minds in guerrilla warfare: the Malayan Emergency, 1948–1960* (Singapore, 1989), p. 77.

96. *The Times*, 26 July 1948.

97. Short, *In pursuit of mountain rats*, pp. 142–3.

98. J. B. Williams, minute, 19 August 1948, in CO537/3746, TNA.

99. A. J. Stockwell, 'Gurney, Sir Henry Lovell Goldsworthy (1898–1951)', *Oxford Dictionary of National Biography* (Oxford, 2004), http://www. oxforddnb.com/view/article/33611, accessed 12 Sept. 2005.

100. Quoted in Barber, *The war of the running dogs*, p. 36.

101. Short, *In pursuit of mountain rats*, pp. 136–9.

102. Quoted in Charles Allen, *Tales from the South China Seas* (London, 1983), p. 294.

103. Broome to Heussler, 27 August 1981, Heussler Papers, RHO.

104. Note by W. L. Blythe, Heussler Papers, RHO.

105. Gurney to Creech Jones, 8 October 1948, CO537/3758, TNA.

106. Memorandum by T. P. F. McNeice, G. C. S. Atkins and G. W. Webb, in Gimson to Sir Thomas Lloyd, 8 December 1948, in A. J. Stockwell (ed.), *British documents on the end of empire: Malaya, part II* (London, 1995), pp. 83–87. See Stubbs, *Hearts and minds in guerrilla warfare*, p. 78.

107. Gurney to Creech Jones, 26 November 1948, CO537/3758, TNA.

108. Stubbs, *Hearts and minds in guerrilla warfare*, p. 69, and more generally the discussion on pp. 69–77.

109. R. Cole, 'A signalman remembers', http://members.tripod.com/Askari_MB/id51.htm.

110. Chin Peng, *My side of history*, pp. 230–31.

111. Gurney to Creech Jones, 30 October 1948, CO717/152/52146/73/49, TNA.

112. Yuen Yuet Leng, *Operation Ginger* (Kuala Lumpur, 1998), pp. 8–9. We are grateful to Dato Seri Yuen – a Special Branch Officer in Perak at the time of the Emergency – for making this available to us.

113. S. M. Middlebrook, 'Pulai: an early Chinese settlement in Kelantan', *Journal of the Malayan Branch of the Royal Asiatic Society*, II, 2 (1933), pp. 151–6.

114. Yuen, *Operation Ginger*, p. 8

115. Short, *In pursuit of mountain rats*, pp. 102–4.

116. Gurney to Creech Jones, 26 November 1948, CO537/3758, TNA.

117. McHugh, *Anatomy of communist propaganda*, pp. 46–47.

118. Gurney to Creech Jones, 2 December 1948, CO537/4240, TNA.

119. 'Perak State Intelligence Sitrep for 24hrs ending 9am', 5 November 1948, 16 November 1948, Pk.Sec3216/48, ANM.

120. Harry Fang, 'Who are the squatters?', *Malaya Tribune*, 5 February

1949; 'The eviction at Sungei Siput', *Malaya Tribune*, 7 February 1949; DSW/ER/4159/1/53, ANM.

121. Gurney to Creech Jones, 3 January 1949, CO537/4750, TNA.

122. Consul General of China to the Chief Secretary, 5 November 1948, ibid.

123. Tan Cheng Lock to Lord Listowel, 24 July 1948, Tan Cheng Lock Papers, SP13/A/12, ANM.

124. Federation of Malaya, Dept of Public Relations, *Communist banditry in Malaya: the Emergency, June 1948–December 1949* (Kuala Lumpur, 1950), p. 7.

125. *The Times*, 4 January 1948.

126. Barber, *The war of the running dogs*, pp. 80–81.

127. Gurney to Creech Jones, 3 January 1949, CO537/4750, TNA.

128. See the account in Short, *In pursuit of mountain rats*, pp. 167–9, and also Stubbs, *Hearts and minds in guerrilla warfare*, p. 74.

129. Transcript: ITN, *News at ten*, 3 February 1970, DEFE13/843, TNA.

130. Transcript: Radio 4, *The world this weekend*, 1 February 1970, ibid.

131. Short, *In pursuit of mountain rats*, p. 168.

132. Lt.-Col. A. Fletcher, '2SG Malaya – December 1948', 17 February 1970; Fletcher to HQ London District, 4 March 1970, DEFE70/101.

133. Ibid.

134. Newboult to Higham 1 January 1949, WO296/41, TNA.

135. Transcript: Radio 4, *World at one*, 2 February 1970, ibid.

136. DPP to Sir James Dunnett, MoD, 29 June 1970, DEFE13/843, TNA.

137. For the paper chase described here, see Tony Stockwell, 'Colonial atrocities: uncovering cover-ups', *PROphile*, 16, 1 (April 2005), pp. 1–6. We are grateful to Professor Stockwell for making this available to us.

138. Jonathan Kent, 'Past lessons for occupying forces', 17 July 2004, http://news.bbc.co.uk/1/hi/programmes/fromourowncorrespondent/3897147.stm.

139. 'MCA Ministers should honour the MCA pledge a decade ago to secure justice for the 56-year Batang Kali Massacre by asking Cabinet to make public the finding of police investigations into the massacre completed in 1997', Media statement by Lim Kit Siang, 17 July 2004, http://www.dapmalaysia.org/all-archive/English/2004/ju104/lks/lks3143.htm.

140. Kurt Bayer and Graham Ogilvy, 'Veterans' fury at "Malay massacre" claim', *Scotland on Sunday*, 14 December 2003.

141. Reuters wire report, 4 February 1970, DEFE13/843, TNA.

142. Gurney to Creech Jones, 19 December 1948, CO537/3758, TNA.

143. Quoted in Stubbs, *Hearts and minds in guerrilla warfare*, p. 75; Short, *In pursuit of mountain rats*, pp. 168–9.

144. Cross and Gurung, *Gurkhas at war*, p. 204.

145. *Daily Worker*, 28 April 1952; see the discussion in CO1022/45, TNA.

CHAPTER 11 1949: THE CENTRE BARELY HOLDS

1. Central Intelligence Agency internal memo 208, 26 August 1949, p. 12, US declassified documents.

2. Ibid., p. 18.

3. 'Review of Present Far East Defence Policy' by chiefs of staff, January–February 1949, FO 371/75679, TNA.

4. Woodrow Wyatt to Cripps, 23 January 1949, CAB127/151, TNA.

5. Murray to Laithwaite, 23 June 1949, Laithwaite Papers, Mss Eur F138/74, OIOC.

6. CIA memo, 26 August 1949, p. 17, US declassified documents.

7. Bowker to Foreign Office, 27 January 1949, FO371/75679, TNA.

8. Attlee to Nu, 4 August 1949, following a series of complaints from Nu to Cripps, 20 April, 24 June 1949, CAB127/151, TNA.

9. Furnivall in *Times of Burma*, 10 April 1949.

10. Bowker to Foreign Office, 26 April 1949, FO371/75691, TNA.

11. Minute by B. R. Pearn on press cutting, 'Establishment of National Economic Council by Burmese Government', FO371/75691, TNA.

12. Nehru to Nu, 14 April 1949, in S. Gopal (ed.), *Selected works of Jawaharlal Nehru*, 2nd Series, vol. X (Delhi 1990), p. 410. This correspondence is located in the Jawaharlal Nehru Papers and the Krishna Menon Papers, Nehru Memorial Library, New Delhi.

13. Ibid., p. 413.

14. E.g., *Hindustan Times*, 9 January 1949.

15. Nehru to M. A. Rauf, 10 April 1949, in Gopal, *Selected works of Nehru*, X, p. 408.

16. Answer in Nehru's Press Conference, 6 March 1949, ibid., p. 400.

17. Nehru to M. A. Rauf, 15 April 1949, ibid., pp 417–18.

18. Ibid. and fn.

19. Government of the Union of Burma, *Burma and the insurrections* (Rangoon, September 1949), p. 31.

20. Richard Butwell, *U Nu of Burma* (Stanford, 1963), p. 105.

21. Nehru to Commonwealth Relations Office, 21 February 1949, 'Commonwealth Conference on Burma', FO371/75686, TNA.

22. William C. Johnstone, *Burma's foreign policy: a study in neutralism* (Cambridge, MA, 1963), pp. 59–60.

23. Uma Shankar Singh, *Burma, 1948–1962* (Bombay, 1979), p. 57.

24. Nehru to M. A. Rauf, 15 April 1949, Gopal, *Selected works of Nehru*, X, p. 417.

25. Transcription of a speech to AFPFL conference by U Nu, 24 September

1955, enclosure in Rangoon to London, 12 October 1955, 'Corruption in the Burma civil service, etc.', FO371/117030, TNA.

26. Balwant Singh, *Independence and democracy in Burma, 1945–52* (Ann Arbor, 1993), p. 106.

27. Ibid., p. 109.

28. Furnivall to Dunn, 14 August 1949, Furnivall Papers, PP/MS 23, vol. I, SOAS.

29. Furnivall to Dunn, 5 September 1949, ibid.

30. Ken Sutton, 'A Guardman's tale', www.nmbava.co.uk/a_guardsmans %20man%20tale.hml; Kumar Ramakrishna, *Emergency propaganda: the winning of Malayan hearts and minds, 1948–1958* (Richmond, 2002), p. 235.

31. *The Times*, 12 August 1953.

32. George Edinger, *The twain shall meet* (New York, 1960), p. 40.

33. Leslie Thomas, *In my wildest dreams* (London, 1984), p. 183.

34. Leslie Thomas, *The virgin soldiers* (London, 1967), pp. 13.

35. Ibid., p. 15.

36. J. N. McHugh, *A handbook of spoken 'bazaar' Malay* (Singapore, 1956 [1945]), p. 7.

37. J. P. Cross and Buddhiman Gurung, *Gurkhas at war in their own words: the Gurkha experience, 1939 to the present* (London, 2002), pp. 221–2.

38. Alan Sillitoe, *Life without armour* (London, 1995), p. 118.

39. Che Abdul Khalid, 'Joget Modern in Kuala Lumpur', 21 May 1952; minute, 2 June 1952, DCL Selangor/115/52, ANM.

40. Virginia Matheson Hooker, *Writing a new society: social change through the novel in Malay* (St Leonard's, NSW, 2000), pp. 153–9.

41. H. B. M. Murphy, 'The mental health of Singapore: part one – suicide', *Medical Journal of Malaya*, 9, 1 (1954), p. 21.

42. Quoted in Cross and Buddhiman Gurung, *Gurkhas at war*, p. 186.

43. John Coates, *Suppressing insurgency: an analysis of the Malayan Emergency, 1948–54* (Boulder, 1992), p. 62.

44. John Branchley, 'The ambush of 4 Troop, A Squadron, 4th Hussars', www.nmbva.c.uk/The%20ambush.htm.

45. This was mistranslated at the time as the Malayan *Races* Liberation Army. C. C. Chin and Karl Hack (eds.), *Dialogues with Chin Peng: new light on the Malayan Communist Party* (Singapore, 2004), p. 149.

46. 'Translation of a printed MCP booklet entitled "Present day situation and duties"', 1 November 1949, FO371/84481, TNA; Chin Peng, *My side of history* (Singapore, 2004), pp. 243–4, 253.

47. Federation of Malaya CID Intelligence Report, August–September 1952, appendix A: 'MCP Auxiliary Organisation', CO1022/187, TNA.

48. 'Statement of 'Liew Tian Choy', 4 October 1949, B. P. Walker Taylor Papers, RHO.

49. Review of Chinese Affairs, May 1952, CO1022/151, TNA. Discussed in T. N. Harper, *The end of empire and the making of Malaya* (Cambridge, 1999), pp. 159–60.

50. P. B. Humphrey, 'Some further items of psychological warfare intelligence as obtained from surrendered Communist terrorists in Malaya: I. Overt reasons', 26 November 1953, WO291/1777, TNA.

51. P. B. Humphrey, 'A preliminary study of entry behaviour among Chinese Communist terrorists in Malaya', June 1953, WO291/1764, TNA.

52. Lucian W. Pye, *Guerrilla communism in Malaya: its social and political meaning* (Princeton, 1956), esp. pp. 133–90.

53. Huang Xue Ying, oral testimony in Agnes Khoo, *Life as the river flows: women in the Malayan anti-colonial struggle* (Petaling Jaya, 2004), p. 186. See also the discussion in Richard Stubbs, *Hearts and minds in guerrilla warfare: the Malayan Emergency, 1948–1960* (Singapore, 1989), pp. 88–90.

54. This is a striking theme of the testimonies in Khoo, *Life as the river flows*.

55. This is extrapolated from a statement in papers found on a dead Johore commander; Anthony Short, *In pursuit of mountain rats: the communist insurrection in Malaya* (Singapore, 2000 [1975]), pp. 104–6.

56. Statement of 'Liew Tian Choy'.

57. Coates, *Suppressing insurgency*, p. 150.

58. As described in Alan Hoe and Eric Morris, *Re-enter the SAS: the SAS and the Malayan campaign* (London, 1994), pp. 30–31.

59. BDCC (FE), 16th meeting, 28 January 1949, CO537/4773, TNA.

60. Brian Stewart, *Smashing terrorism in the Malayan Emergency: the vital contribution of the police* (Kuala Lumpur, 2004), pp. 24–5.

61. Gurney to Creech Jones, 6 October 1949, CO717/162/52745/19/49, TNA.

62. Karl Hack, 'British intelligence and counter-insurgency in the era of decolonisation: the example of Malaya', *Intelligence and National Security*, 14, 2 (1999), pp. 127–9.

63. A. J. Stockwell, 'Policing during the Malayan Emergency, 1948–60: communism, communalism and decolonization', in D. Anderson and D. Killingray, *Policing and decolonization: politics, nationalism and the police* (Manchester, 1992), pp. 105–28.

64. Emergency propaganda leaflets, RHO.

65. For this assessment see the important study by Ramakrishna, *Emergency propaganda*, pp. 72–84.

66. Chin Peng, *My side of history*, p. 4.

67. Pye, *Guerrilla communism*, p. 187.

68. J. N. McHugh, *Anatomy of communist propaganda* (Kuala Lumpur, 1949). See also the interesting essay by Rui Xiong Kee, 'Exploring the "communist" in the communist insurrection in Malaya', Standford University, Program in Writing and Rhetoric, *The Boothe Prize essays, 2004* (Standford, 2004), pp. 37–49, http://pwr.stanford.edu/publications/Boothe%20book%202004.pdf.

69. 'Third further statement of Liew Thian Choy', 10 October 1949, B. P. Walker Taylor Papers, RHO.

70. 'Surrender policy', Arthur Young Papers, RHO.

71. Short, *In pursuit of mountain rats*, pp. 383–4.

72. Simon C. Smith, *British relations with the Malaya rulers from decentralization to independence, 1930–1957* (Kuala Lumpur, 1995), p. 125.

73. Charles Gamba, *The origins of trade unionism in Malaya* (Singapore, 1960), p. 418.

74. 'Cabinet – Malaya Committee: Detention procedure, memorandum by the Secretary of State for the Colonies', 10 July 1950, CO717/199/1, TNA.

75. 'Detention in the Federation of Malaya'; *Straits Budget*, 5 April 1950, CO717/199/1, TNA.

76. Federation of Malaya, monthly newsletter no. 36, 16 December 1951 to 15 January 1952, CO1022/132, TNA.

77. Frank Brewer, 'Malaya – Administration of Chinese affairs, 1945–57', in Heussler Papers, RHO.

78. Khatijah Sidek, *Memoirs of Khatijah Sidek: puteri kesateria bangsa* (Kuala Lumpur, 2001 [1960]), pp. 89–90.

79. Tom Driberg, 'In detention', *Reynolds News*, 12 November 1950.

80. Quoted in Short, *In pursuit of mountain rats*, p. 193.

81. F. D. Marrable, Officer Superintending Police Circle Klang to Superintending Klang Camp, 10 October 1950, CO717/199/2, TNA.

82. N. R. Hilton, 'Detention camp – Tanjong Bruas, visited on 1 December 1951', CO1022/326, TNA.

83. Sir Donald MacGillivray to Alan Lennox Boyd, 6 June 1955, CO1030/145, TNA; *Straits Times*, 16 June 1955, 16 July 1955.

84. Ramakrishna, *Emergency propaganda*, pp. 65–6.

85. Gurney to Sir Thomas Lloyd, 20 December 1948, in A. J. Stockwell, ed., *British documents on the end of empire: Malaya*, part II (London, 1995), p. 91.

86. Short, *In pursuit of mountain rats*, p. 191.

87. Federation of Malaya, monthly newsletter, 16 January to 15 February 1951, CO717/199/2; ibid., 16 March to 15 April 1951, CO1022/137, TNA; A. H. P. Humphreys. 'The communist insurrection in Malaya', A. H. P. Humphreys Papers, RHO.

88. P. A. Collin, 'Escorting banishees to China', in Stewart, *Smashing terrorism in the Malayan Emergency*, p. 234.

89. 'Malaya: detention, repatriation and resettlement of Chinese', 31 January 1951, CO717/199/2, TNA.

90. Quoted in Short, *In pursuit of mountain rats*, p. 191.

91. British Embassy Peking to Foreign Office, 14 March 1951, CO717/199/2, TNA.

92. *Nan Feng Jih Pao*, 6 May 1951.

93. C. F. Yong, *Tan Kah-Kee: the making of an overseas Chinese legend* (Singapore, 1989), pp. 328–31. See also enclosures on FO371/84480, TNA.

94. Chui Kwei-chiang, *The response of the Malayan Chinese to political and military developments in China, 1945–9* (Singapore, 1977), pp. 82–4.

95. McHugh, *Anatomy of communist propaganda*, p. 20.

96. Short, *In pursuit of mountain rats*, pp. 215–16.

97. Harper, *The end of empire*, pp. 203–4.

98. Chin and Hack, *Dialogues with Chin Peng*, p. 162.

99. Gurney to Creech Jones, 28 February 1949, CO537/4750, TNA.

100. Tan Cheng Lock, *One country, one people, one government: Presidential address by Tan Cheng Lock at a meeting of the General Committee of the MCA held in Penang on 30 October, 1949* (Kuala Lumpur, 1949), p. 2.

101. K. G. Tregonning, 'Tan Cheng Lock: a Malayan nationalist', *Journal of Southeast Asian Studies*, 10, 1 (1979), pp. 60–61.

102. Tan Liok Ee, *The politics of Chinese education in Malaya, 1945–1961* (Kuala Lumpur 1997), pp. 104–5.

103. Gurney to J. D. Higham, 10 February 1949, CO/537/4242; Pan-Malayan Review of Political Intelligence, no. 5 of 1959, CO537/4671, TNA.

104. 'Minutes of the Second Meeting of the Emergency Chinese Advisory Committee held at the Perak State Council Chamber, Ipoh on 11 June 1949', SP13/A/21, ANM.

105. 'Malayan Chinese Association', PR/261/51, ANM.

106. 'Minutes of the First Meeting of the Emergency Chinese Advisory Committee held at the Council Chamber, Kuala Lumpur on 5 April 1949', SP13/A/21, ANM.

107. Heng Pek Koon, *Chinese politics in Malaysia: a history of the Malaysian Chinese Association* (Singapore, 1988), p. 89.

108. Gurney to Paskin, 4 April 1949, CO537/4761, TNA.

109. Monthly Review of Chinese Affairs, April 1949; Pan-Malayan Review of Political Intelligence, no. 11 of 1949, CO537/4671, TNA.

110. Khoo Salma Nusution and Abdur-Razzaq Lubis, *Kinta Valley: pioneering Malaysia's modern development* (Ipoh, 2005), p. 308; McHugh, *Anatomy of communist propaganda*, p. 48.

111. Laurence K. L. Siaw, *Chinese society in rural Malaysia* (Kuala Lumpur, 1983), pp. 93–103.

112. Tan Cheng Lock to Mentri Besar, Johore, 30 October 1951, CO1022/27, TNA.

113. The literature on resettlement is extensive. The key studies are, K. S. Sandhu, 'Emergency resettlement in Malaya', *Journal of Tropical Geography*, 18 (1964), pp. 157–83; 'The saga of the "squatter" in Malaya: a preliminary survey of the causes, characteristics and consequences of the resettlement of rural dwellers during the Emergency between 1948 and 1960', *Journal of Southeast Asian History*, 5 (1964), pp. 143–77; J. W. Humphrey, 'Population resetlement in Malaya' (PhD thesis, Northwestern University, 1971); Francis Loh Kok Wah, *Beyond the tin mines: coolies, squatters and new villagers in the Kinta valley, c. 1880–1980* (Singapore, 1988). For a summary of the impact see Harper, *The end of empire*, pp. 176–92.

114. Keris Mas (trans. Harry Aveling), 'A row of shophouses in our village', in *Blood and tears* (Petaling Jaya, 1984), pp. 113–14.

115. Judith Strauch, 'Chinese new Villages of the Malayan Emergency, a generation later: a case study', *Contemporary Southeast Asia*, 2 (1981), pp. 126–39; Siaw, *Chinese society in rural Malaysia*, pp. 108–16.

116. Protector of Aborigines to Asst Superintendent of Census, 9 May 1947, DO Temerloh/467/46, ANM.

117. For a fuller account, see Christopher Bayly, and Tim Harper, *Forgotten armies: Britain's Asian empire and the war with Japan* (London, 2004), pp. 267–8, 348–50.

118. Tony Gould, *Imperial warriors: Britain and the Gurkhas* (London, 1999), p. 329–30.

119. For the search for Noone, see his brother's account, Richard Noone, *Rape of the dream people* (London, 1972).

120. Reported in *Malay Mail*, 15 July 1949.

121. *Malay Mail*, 22 August 1949; for a discussion see John Leary, *Violence and the dream people: the Orang Asli in the Malayan Emergency, 1948–1960* (Athens, OH, 1995), pp. 74–83.

122. Robert Knox Dentan, 'Bad day at Bukit Pekan', *American Anthropologist*, 97, 2 (1995), pp. 225–31.

123. Ivan Polunin, 'The medical natural history of the Malayan aborigines', *Malayan Medical Journal*, 8, 1 (1953), pp. 55–174; P. D. R. Williams-Hunt to Del Tufo, n.d., FS/12072/50, ANM.

124. P. D. R. Williams-Hunt, *An introduction to the Malayan Aborigines* (Kuala Lumpur, 1952), p. 93.

125. 'Evacuating Malayan Aborigines', *Malayan Police Journal*, March 1950, reprinted in Leary, *Violence and the dream people*, pp. 219–30.

126. Anthony Crockett, *Green beret, red star* (London, 1954), pp. 185–9.

127. Gamba, *The origins of trade unionism*, pp. 352–73.

128. Christopher Blake, *A view from within: the last years of British rule in South-East Asia* (Castle Cary, 1990), pp. 94–117.

129. Leong Yee Fong, *Labour and trade unionism in colonial Malaya: a study of the socio-economic and political bases of the Malayan labour movement, 1930–1957* (Penang, 1999), pp. 236–45.

130. J. B. Perry Robinson, *Transformation in Malaya* (London, 1956), p. 79.

131. 'Meeting of ministers on Malaya', 2 April 1949; Creech Jones to Mac-Donald, CO537/4751, TNA.

132. Gurney to Creech Jones, 11 April 1949, CO537/4751, TNA.

133. Gurney to Creech Jones, 30 May 1949, CO537/4773, TNA.

134. 'Minutes of the Fifteenth Conference held under the chairmanship of HE the Commissioner-General . . . on 7 June 1950 at Bukit Serene, Johore', CO537/5970, TNA.

135. Appendix B, 'The attitude of the Malay public towards the Malayan Communist Party', 5 April 1949, CO537/4751, TNA.

136. Paskin to Gurney, 22 December 1948, CO537/3746, TNA.

137. Sir Thomas Lloyd to Gurney, 5 January 1949, ibid.

138. Thio Chan Bee, *The extraordinary adventures of an ordinary man* (London, 1977), pp. 62, 66–7, 75–87; *Malay Mail*, 10 January 1949.

139. One of the few academic discussions is Heng, *Chinese politics in Malaysia*, pp. 147–56.

140. 'Notes of discussions of the Communities' Liaison Committee held at Kuala Lumpur, 18 and 19 February 1949', TCL/23/2, ISEAS.

141. 'Notes of discussions of the Communities' Liaison Committee held at Kuala Lumpur 13 and 14 August 1949', TCL/23/7, ISEAS.

142. 'Notes of discussions of the Communities' Liaison Committee held at Penang 29, 30 and 31 December 1949', TCL/23/8, ISEAS.

143. *The Times*, 18 April 1949.

144. *Malay Mail*, 27 August 1949.

145. Tan Cheng Lock to Yong Shook Lin, 19 January 1950, Tan Cheng Lock Papers, SP13/1/19, ANM.

146. MSS/PIJ, 15 November 1947.

147. Tan Jing Quee, 'Lim Chin Siong: a political life', in Jomo K. S. and Tan Jing Quee (eds.), *Comet in our sky: Lim Chin Siong in history* (Kuala Lumpur, 2001), p. 61.

148. Sir John Nicoll to Alan Lennox-Boyd, 26 February 1955, CO1030/360, TNA.

149. A. J. Stockwell, 'Knowledge and power; university and nation in the

new Malaya of 1938–62', paper delivered at 'Asian Horizons' conference, Singapore, 1–3 August 2005.

150. Patrick Anderson, *Snake wine: a Singapore episode* (Singapore, 1980 [1955]), p. 221.

151. Ibid., p. 155.

152. Yeo Kim Wah, 'Student politics in University of Malaya, 1949–51', *Journal of Southeast Asian Studies*, 23, 2 (1992), pp. 346–80.

153. *Malaya Tribune*, 14 April 1947.

154. Anderson, *Snake wine*, p. 127.

155. G. I. Puthucheary, 'Building the Malayan nation', *The Undergrad: unofficial organ of Raffles College Students' Union*, 1, 2 (24 January 1949), and other issues, 1, 3 (12 February 1949); 1, 4 (16 March 1949).

156. Cheah Boon Kheng (ed.), *A. Samad Ismail: journalism and politics* (Kuala Lumpur, 1987); Said Zahari, *Dark clouds at dawn* (Kuala Lumpur, 2001), p. 172.

157. Yeo Kim Wah, 'Joining the communist underground: the conversion of English-educated radicals to communism in Singapore, June 1948–January 1951', *Journal of the Malayan Branch of the Royal Asiatic Society*, 67 (1994), pp. 29–59.

158. For this see T. N. Harper, 'Lim Chin Siong and "the Singapore Story"', in Jomo K. S. and Tan, *Comet in our sky*, pp. 1–56; Zahari, *Dark clouds at dawn*, pp. 275–9.

159. *Malaya Tribune*, 4 January 1949.

160. Mustapha Hussain, *Malay nationalism before Umno: the memoirs of Mustapha Hussain, translated by Insun Mustapha and edited by Jomo K. S.* (Kuala Lumpur, 2005), pp. 360–67.

161. A. Samad Said, '1948: Dawn of a new literary era', *Between art and reality: selected essays* (Kuala Lumpur, 1994), pp. 57–71.

162. Oswald Henry, 'Singapore makes Malay movies', *Malaya Tribune*, 24 December 1947.

163. Gregory Clancey, 'Towards a spatial history of emergency: notes from Singapore', Asia Research Institute, National University of Singapore, Working Paper 8, 2003.

164. Federation of Malaya, Political Report for January 1949, CO537/4763, TNA.

165. *Malaya Tribune*, 29 March, 1949.

166. 'Translation of a printed MCP booklet entitled "Present day situation and duties"', 1 November 1949, FO371/84481, TNA.

167. W. C. S. Corry to W. E. Rigby, 9 May 1949, BA Pahang/99/49, ANM.

168. Firdaus Haji Abdullah, *Radical Malay politics: its origins and early development* (Petaling Jaya, 1985), pp. 24–6.

169. 'Translation of a printed MCP booklet entitled "Present day situation and duties"', 1 November 1949, FO371/84481, TNA.

170. Chin Peng, *My side of history*, p. 262.

171. A document, purporting to be from the Malayan Communist Party, Johore–Malacca Border Committee, *Death of a heretic* (Singapore, 1951).

172. 'Yap Sang, 14 October 1949', B. P. Walker Taylor Papers, RHO.

173. Federal War Council Joint Intelligence Advisory Committee, 'The potential of the Malayan Communist Party', 24 October 1950, FO371/84482, TNA.

EPILOGUE: THE END OF BRITAIN'S ASIAN EMPIRE

1. Mustapha Hussain, *Malay nationalism before Umno: the memoirs of Mustapha Hussain, translated by Insun Mustapha and edited by Jomo K. S.* (Kuala Lumpur, 2005), p. 313.

2. From *Utusan Melayu*, 23 August 1947, translated and quoted in Ariffin Omar, *Bangsa Melayu: Malay concepts of democracy and community, 1945–50* (Kuala Lumpur, 1993), p. 116.

3. 'The United Kingdom in South-East Asia and the Far East', October 1949, and cabinet conclusions on 'South-East Asia and the Far East', in A. J. Stockwell, ed., *British documents on the end of empire: Malaya, part II* (London, 1995), pp. 158–70, 173.

4. Rajeswary Ampalavanar, *The Indian minority and political change in Malaya, 1945–1955* (Kuala Lumpur, 1981), p. 27.

5. George C. Thomson, 'Political Assessment of the visit of Pandit Nehru to Singapore', 29 June 1950, FO371/101233, TNA.

6. Anthony Short, *In pursuit of mountain rats: the communist insurrection in Malaya* (Singapore, 2000 [1975]), pp. 507–8.

7. Michael Calvert, *Fighting mad* (Shrewsbury, 1996), pp. 202–5.

8. David Rooney, *Mad Mike: a life of Michael Calvert* (London, 1997), pp. 134–45.

9. Tony Geraghty, *Who dares wins: the story of SAS, 1952–92*, 3rd edn (London, 1992), pp. 327–55.

10. *The Times*, 13 August 1953; Raffi Gregorian, *The British army, the Gurkhas and Cold War strategy in the Far East, 1947–1954* (Basingstoke, 2002), p. 175.

11. Timothy Parsons, *The African rank-and-file: social implications of colonial military service in the King's African Rifles, 1902–1964* (Oxford, 1999), pp. 39, 93, 109, 166, 199, 212. Malcolm Page, *A history of The King's African Rifles and East African Forces* (London, 1998), pp. 190–95.

12. Short, *In pursuit of mountain rats*, pp. 304–5. For the absence of planning see Chin Peng, *My side of history* (Singapore, 2004), pp. 287–9.

13. *The Times*, 6 December 1951.

14. A great deal has been written about these reappraisals. For Lyttelton's report see, 'Malaya': Cabinet memorandum by Mr Lyttelton, 21 December 1951, in Stockwell, *British documents: Malaya, part II*, pp. 319–533. Also, Short, *In pursuit of mountain rats*, pp. 322–44; Richard Stubbs, *Hearts and minds in guerrilla warfare: the Malayan Emergency, 1948–1960* (Singapore, 1989), pp. 136–40.

15. John Cloake, *Templer: tiger of Malaya* (London, 1985).

16. Victor Purcell, *Malaya: communist or free?* (Stanford, 1955), p. 16.

17. R. W. I. Bland to Heussler, 21 August 1969, Heussler Papers, RHO.

18. For ongoing controversy, see Karl Hack, '"Iron claws on Malaya": the historiography of the Malayan Emergency', *Journal of Southeast Asian Studies*, 30, 1 (1999), pp. 99–125, who also argues for an early change of direction, and Kumar Ramakrishna, who restates the pivotal importance of Templer in '"Transmogrifying Malaya": the impact of Sir Gerald Templer (1952–54)', *Journal of Southeast Asian Studies*, 32, 1 (2001), pp. 79–92.

19. Robert Heussler, *British rule in Malaya, 1942–57* (Singapore, 1985), p. 186.

20. For the coercive side of the population control from a counter-insurgency perspective, see also Hack, '"Iron claws on Malaya"', pp. 115–23.

21. Johore Council of State, 4 October 1950, Sel.Sec/151/149, ANM.

22. We are grateful to Simon Winder for suggesting this image.

23. D. W. Le Mare, 'Community development', INF/18677/533, ANM.

24. Sir Robert Thompson, *Defeating communist insurgency: experiences from Malaya and Vietnam* (London, 1966).

25. Han Suyin, *My house has two doors* (London, 1980), p. 79.

26. Federation of Malaya, *Report on the conduct of food searches at Semenyih in the Kajang District of the State of Selangor* (Kuala Lumpur, 1956).

27. For this see Frank Furedi, 'Britain's colonial wars: playing the ethnic card', *Journal of Commonwealth and Comparative Politics*, 28, 1 (1990), pp. 70–89.

28. Ministry of Defence 'Malaya: defence costs', 13 November 1951, CO1022/34, TNA. This was first brought to light by Richard Stubbs, *Counter-insurgency and the economic factor: the impact of the Korean War prices boom on the Malayan Emergency* (ISEAS Occasional paper no. 19, Singapore, 1974).

29. Nicholas J. White, *Business, government and the end of empire: Malaya, 1945–1957* (Kuala Lumpur, 1996), pp. 51–3.

30. For an extended discussion of the 'domestication' of the Malayan Chinese, see T. N. Harper, *The end of empire and the making of Malaya* (Cambridge, 1999), chs. 5 and 6.

31. Roy Follows, *Jungle-beat: fighting terrorists in Malaya, 1952–61* (London, 2000), p. 97.

32. W. Johnson (ed.), *The papers of Adlai E. Stevenson*, vol. V: *Visit to Asia, the Middle East, and Europe, March–August 1953* (Boston, 1974), pp. 148–9.

33. Abdul Aziz Ishak, *The architect of Merdeka: Tengku Abdul Rahman* (Singapore, 1957).

34. Quoted in Harper, *The end of empire*, p. 322.

35. Khatijah Sidek, *Memoirs of Khatijah Sidek: Puteri Kesateria Bangsa* (Kuala Lumpur, 2001 [1960]), pp. 118, 124–5.

36. Miss P. G. Lim, 'Radio broadcast on behalf of the Labour Party of Malaya', 1 July, 1955, CO1030/313, TNA.

37. Francis G. Carnell, 'The Malayan elections', *Pacific Affairs*, 28, 4 (1955), pp. 315–30.

38. Sir Robert Scott to Anthony Eden, 23 October 1955, CO1030/245, TNA.

39. *The Times*, 3 October 1951.

40. 'HH the Sultan of Johore's speech', in MacGillivray to Lennox-Boyd, 19 September 1955, CO1030/374, TNA.

41. Chan Heng Chee, *A sensation of independence: a political biography of David Marshall* (Singapore, 1984), pp. 93–4.

42. Said Zahari, *Dark clouds at dawn* (Kuala Lumpur, 2001), p. 285.

43. Ibid., p. 282.

44. Chin Peng, *My side of history* (Singapore, 2004), pp. 387–95.

45. Cited in Gustaaf Houtman, *Mental culture in Burmese crisis politics* (Tokyo, 2001), p. 267.

46. Peking to Rangoon, 4 July 1952, FO4371/101276, TNA.

47. C. W. Dunn to J. S. Furnivall, 30 August 1950, Furnivall Papers, PP/MS 23, vol. I, SOAS.

48. 'A voice above the battle', interview with Nehru, *Picture Post*, 49, 4 October 1950, pp. 13–15.

49. S. Gopal (ed.), *Selected works of Jawaharlal Nehru*, Second Series (Delhi, 1984), vol. XIV, Part I, p. 501, n. 4.

50. J. S. Furnivall to C. W. Dunn, 17 June 1950, Furnivall Papers, PP/MS 23, vol. I, SOAS.

51. Mary Callahan, *Making enemies: war and state building in Burma* (Ithaca, 2004), pp. 137–44.

52. H. Bruce Franklin, 'By the bomb's early light; or the Quiet American's war on terror': http://rutgers.edu/~hbf/Quietam.htm.

53. Cloake, *Templer*, p. 297; Norman Cleaveland, *Bang! Bang! in Ampang* (San Pedro, CA, 1973), pp. 140–42.

54. John A Nagi, *Learning to eat soup with a knife: counterinsurgency lessons from Malaya and Vietnam*, new edn (New York, 2005).

55. Norman Sherry, *Life of Graham Greene, 1939–1955* (London, 1994).

56. *New Times of Burma*, 5 January 1955.

57. *The Nation*, 7 August 1945.

58. *The Nation*, 21 July 1955.

59. Norman Lewis, *The golden earth: travels in Burma* (London, 1952), p. 139.

60. Ibid., p. 90.

61. Khin Myo Chit, Memoir, Mss Eur D1066/1, OIOC, fos. 138 ff.

62. *New Times of Burma*, 18 March 1955.

63. P. Lim Pui Huen and Diana Wong (eds.), *War and memory in Malaysia and Singapore* (Singapore, 2000); William H. Frederick, 'Reflections in a moving stream: Indonesia memories of the war and the Japanese', in Remco Raben (ed.), *Representing the Japanese occupation of Indonesia: personal testimonies and public image in Indonesia, Japan and the Netherlands* (Amsterdam, 1999), pp. 16–35.

64. J. C. Sterndale Bennett to Sir Esler Dening, Tokyo, 12 April 1952, FO371/101233, TNA.

65. Junko Tomaru, *The postwar rapprochement of Malaya and Japan, 1945–61: the roles of Britain and Japan in South-east Asia* (London, 2000).

66. Shoko Tanaka, *Post-war Japanese resource policies and strategies: the case of Southeast Asia* (Ithaca, 1986), ch. 3.

67. Masashi Nishihara, *The Japanese and Sukarno's Indonesia: Tokyo–Jakarta relations, 1951–1966* (Kyoto, 1976), pp. 211–12; Hikita Yasuyuki, 'Japanese companies' inroads into Indonesia under Japanese military administration', in Peter Post and Elly Touwen-Bouwsma (eds.), *Japan, Indonesia and the war: myths and realities* (Leiden, 1997), p. 152.

68. James Puthucheary, *Ownership and control in the Malayan economy* (Singapore, 1960); Nicholas White, 'The beginnings of crony capitalism: business, politics and economic development in Malaysia, c. 1955–70', *Modern Asian Studies*, 28, 2 (2004), pp. 389–417.

69. See T. N. Harper, 'Lim Chin Siong and "the Singapore Story"', in Jomo K. S. and Tan Jing Quee (eds.), *Comet in our sky: Lim Chin Siong in history* (Kuala Lumpur, 2001), pp. 1–56.

70. Ahmad Boestamam (trans. William R. Roff), *Carving the path to the summit* (Athens, OH, 1979), p. 3.

71. http://www.thestar.com.my/news/story.asp?file=/2006/5/10/nation/14195479&sec=nation; also Amir Muhammad's lastcommunist.blogspot.com. However, fresh memoirs by MCP leaders such as Rashid Maidin, Abdullah C. D. and Suraini Abdullah (Eng Ming Chin) were beginning to appear in Malaysia as this book was completed.

Bibliography

MANUSCRIPT SOURCES
National Archives of Singapore

Oral History Department, interviews, OHD:
Ang Keong Lan
Jacob Ballas
Dato Haji Mohamed Yudof Bangs
Chan Cheng Yean
Cheah Fook Yong, Charlie
Dr Benjamin Chew
Carl Francis de Souza
John Ede
Arshak Catihatoer Galstaun
Gay Wan Guay
Ahmad Khan
Heng Chiang Ki
Karuppiah N.
Alfred Lelah
Lady Percy McNiece
Sudarajulu Laksmana Perumal
Dr Constantine Constantinovich Petrovsky
Arthur Alexander Thompson

D. K. Broadhurst Papers

Institute of Southeast Asia Studies, Singapore

Tan Cheng Lock Papers

Arkib Negara Malaysia, Kuala Lumpur

Tan Cheng Lock papers, SP13

Perpustakaan Universiti Malaya, Kuala Lumpur

J. A. Thivy Papers

Oriental and India Office Collection, British Library

Arnold Papers, Mss Eur F145
Burmese Politics Collection, Mss Eur D1066/2
Dash Papers, Mss Eur C188
Donnison Papers, Mss Eur B357
Dorman-Smith Papers Mss Eur E215
Clague Papers, Mss Eur E252
Khin Myo Chit, 'Many a house of life hath held me', Mss Eur D1066/1
Memoir of P. E. S. Finney, Mss Eur D1041/4
Laithwaite Papers, Mss Eur F138
McInery Diary, Eur Photo 148
Pearce Papers, Mss D947
Rance Papers, Mss Eur F169
Saumarez Smith, W., 'Seventy four days in 1947', Mss Eur C409
Thein Pe Myint, 'Note to Indian Communists 1973, a critique of the Communist movement in Burma', Mss Eur C498, fo. 8
Tyson Papers, Mss Eur E341
Walton Papers, Mss Eur D545
Wavell Papers, Mss Eur D977

Centre of South Asian Studies, Cambridge

F. O. Bell Memoir
H. W. Bell Papers
J. G. E. Bell Papers
Benthal Papers
Dash Papers
P. D. M. Lingeman Memoir

Ian Stephens Papers
E. T. Stokes Papers

Cambridge University Library

United States Declassified Documents, State Department, Central Intelligence
Agency, etc.

Royal Commonwealth Society Library, Cambridge University Library

British Malaysia Association:
H. Bryson Papers
Amy and Richard Haggard, 'An account of the British Military Adminis-
tration of Upper Perak, Malaya – 1945/46: being memories based on
diaries and letter', 4 April 2000
Sir George Maxwell Papers

Trinity College, Cambridge

Pethick-Lawrence Papers

Liddell Hart Centre, King's College, London

Gracey Papers
Messervy Papers

National Army Museum, London

Alston Papers
Bucher Papers
Fauj Akhbar
Savory Papers
Wade Papers

School of Oriental and African Studies, University of London

Furnivall Papers

Southampton University Library

Mountbatten and Edwina Mountbatten Papers

Rhodes House Library, Oxford

John Dalley Papers/Malayan Security Service, Political Intelligence Journals, 1946–8
Robert Heussler/Malayan Civil Service Papers
Sir Ralph Hone Papers
A. H. P. Humphreys Papers
B. P. Walker Taylor Papers
Sir Arthur Young Papers

Christ Church, Oxford

Tom Driberg Papers

OFFICIAL PAPERS
National Archives of Singapore

British Military Administration Headquarters, Singapore, 1945–6: BMA/ HQ
British Military Administration Chinese Affairs, Singapore, 1945–6: BMA/CA
Social Welfare Department/Chief Secretary's Office, Singapore, 1945–7: SCA

Microfilm collection:
Files from National Archives and Records Administration, United States (NARA)
From series: XL

Arkib Negara Malaysia, Kuala Lumpur

Federal records:
British Military Administration Administrative, 1945–6: BMA/ADM
British Military Administration Departmental, 1945–6: BMA/DEPT
Malayan Union Secretariat: MU
Labour, Malayan Union: LAB
Director of Forests: DF
Director of Co-operation: Coop

State records:
British Adviser, Pahang: BA Pahang
Deputy Commissioner of Labour, Selangor: DCL Selangor
District Office, Temerloh: DO Temerloh
Information Department: INF
State Secretariat, Perak: Pk.Sec
State Secretariat, Selangor: Sel.Sec
State Secretariat, Trengganu: SUK Tr

Oriental and India Office Collection, British Library

Burma Miscellaneous: L/PO/4 and 9
Burma Office Papers: M/3
Governor of Burma's Office: R/8
Information Department: L/I/1
Judicial and Public Department: L/P and J/4, 5 and 8
Reforms Series: R/3
War Staff Files: L/WS/1 and 2

The National Archive, Kew, London

Admiralty: ADM1, 116
Air Ministry: AIR20
Cabinet Office: CAB119, 121, 126
Colonial Office: CO273, 537, 717, 875, 1022
Dominions Office: DO35
Foreign Office: FO371, 4371
GCHQ: KV2

Ministry of Defence: DEFE13
Prime Minister's Office: PREM4
Special Operations Executive: HS1
War Office: WO32, 106, 203, 208, 222, 291, 296, 325

NEWSPAPERS AND PERIODICALS

Amrita Bazaar Patrika (Calcutta)
Dawn (Karachi)
The Democrat (Singapore)
Eastern Times (Lahore)
Greater Asia (Rangoon)
Hindustan Times (New Delhi)
Leader (Allahabad)
Malay Mail (Kuala Lumpur)
Malaya Tribune (Singapore)
The Nation (Rangoon)
New Times of Burma (Rangoon)
New York Times
News Chronicle (London)
Picture Post (London)
The Planter (Kuala Lumpur)
Rangoon Times
Reynolds News (London)
Statesman (Calcutta)
Straits Echo (Penang)
Straits Times (Singapore)
Sunday Gazette (Penang)
The Times (London)
Times of Burma (Rangoon)
The Undergrad (Singapore)

Vernacular press translations:
Kin Kwok Daily News (Ipoh)
Kung Pao (Singapore)
Majlis (Kuala Lumpur)
Min Sheng Pau (Kuala Lumpur)
Modern Daily News (Penang)
Nanyang Siang Pau (Singapore)
New Democracy (Singapore)

Northern Star (Ipoh)

Pelita Malaya (Kuala Lumpur)

Shih Tai Jit Poh (Ipoh)

Sin Chew Jit Poh (Singapore)

Warta Malaya (Singapore)

Utusan Melayu (Singapore)

BOOKS, ARTICLES AND OFFICIAL PUBLICATIONS

A. Samad Said, *Between art and reality: selected essays* (Kuala Lumpur, 1994)

Abdul Aziz Ishak, *The architect of Merdeka: Tengku Abdul Rahman* (Singapore, 1957)

Abu Talib Ahmad, *The Malay Muslims, Islam and the Rising Sun: 1941–45* (Kuala Lumpur, 2003)

Ahmad Boestamam (trans. William R. Roff), *Carving the path to the summit* (Athens, OH, 1979)

Ahrenfeldt, Robert H., *Psychiatry in the British army in the Second World War* (London, 1950)

Aisha Akbar, *Aishabee at war: a very frank memoir* (Singapore, 1990)

Akashi, Yoji, 'Lai Teck, Secretary General of the Malayan Communist Party, 1939–1947', *Journal of the South Seas Society*, 49 (1994), pp. 57–103

Akashi, Yoji, 'The Anti-Japanese movement in Perak during the Japanese occupation, 1941–45', in Paul H. Kratoska (ed.), *Malaya and Singapore during the Japanese occupation* (Singapore, 1995)

Aldiss, Brian, *The twinkling of an eye, or my life as an Englishman* (London, 1998)

Aldrich, Richard, *Intelligence and the war against Japan: Britain, America and the politics of secret service* (Cambridge, 2000)

Allan, Sheila, *Diary of a girl in Changi, 1941–45*, 2nd edn (Roseville, NSW, 1999)

Allen, Charles, *Tales from the South China Seas* (London, 1983)

Allen, James de Vere, *The Malayan Union* (New Haven, 1967)

Allen, Louis, *The end of the war in Asia* (Brooklyn, 1979)

Allen, Louis, *Burma: the longest war* (London, 1984)

Amoroso, Donna J., 'Dangerous politics and the Malay nationalist movement, 1945–47', *South East Asia Research*, 6, 3 (1998)

Ampalavanar, Rajeswary, *The Indian minority and political change in Malaya, 1945–1955* (Kuala Lumpur, 1981)

Anderson, Benedict R. O'G., *Java in a time of revolution: occupation and resistance, 1944–46* (Ithaca and London, 1972)

Anderson, Patrick, *Snake wine: a Singapore episode* (Singapore, 1980 [1955])

Anwar Abdullah, *Dato Onn* (Petaling Jaya, 1971)

Arasaratnam, S., 'Social and political ferment of the Malayan Indian community, 1945–55', *Proceedings of the First International Conference Seminar of Tamil Studies, Kuala Lumpur, April 1966* (Kuala Lumpur, 1966), pp. 141–55

Ariffin Omar, *Bangsa Melayu: Malay concepts of democracy and community, 1945–50* (Kuala Lumpur, 1993)

Ayer, S. A., *Unto him a witness: the story of Netaji Subhas Chandra Bose in East Asia* (Bombay, 1951)

Ba Maw, *Breakthrough in Burma: memoirs of a revolution, 1939–46* (New Haven, 1968)

Ba Than, U, *The roots of the revolution* (Rangoon, 1962)

Ba U, U, *My Burma: the autobiography of a president, with a foreword by J. S. Furnivall* (New York, 1959)

Ban Kah Choon, *Absent history: the untold story of Special Branch operations in Singapore, 1915–1942* (Singapore, 2001)

Barber, Noel, *The war of the running dogs: how Malaya defeated the communist guerrillas, 1948–1960* (London, 1971)

Bartlett, Vernon, *Go East, old man* (London, 1948)

Bates, Peter, *Japan and the British Commonwealth occupation force, 1946–52* (London, 1993)

Bayly, Christopher and Harper, Tim, *Forgotten armies: Britain's Asian empire and the war with Japan* (London, 2004)

Bayly, Susan, 'Anthropology and the Durkheimians in colonial Indochina', *Modern Asian Studies*, 34, 3 (2000), pp. 581–622

Benda, Harry J., *The Crescent and the Rising Sun: Indonesian Islam under Japanese occupation, 1942–1945* (The Hague, 1958)

Bingham, June, *U Thant of Burma: the search for peace* (London, 1966)

Blackburn, Kevin, 'The collective memory of the *sook ching* massacre and the creation of the civilian war memorial of Singapore', *Journal of the Malaysian Branch of the Royal Asiatic Society*, 73, 2 (2000), pp. 71–90

Blackburn, Kevin and Edmund Lim, 'The Japanese war memorials of Singapore: monuments of commemoration and symbols of Japanese imperial ideology', *South East Asia Research*, 7, 3 (2001), pp. 321–40

Blake, Christopher, *A view from within: the last years of British rule in South-East Asia* (Castle Cary, 1990)

Blythe, Wilfred, *The impact of Chinese secret societies in Malaya: a historical study* (London, 1969)

Bogarde, Dirk, *Backcloth* (London, 1986)

Bogarde, Dirk, *Cleared for take-off* (London, 1995)

Bose, Mihir, *The lost hero* (London, 1983)

Bose, Romen, *A will to freedom: Netaji and the Indian independence movement in Singapore and Southeast Asia, 1942–45* (Singapore, 1993)

Bose, Romen, *The end of the war: Singapore's liberation and the aftermath of the Second World War* (Singapore, 2005)

Boulle, Pierre, *Sacrilege in Malaya* (Kuala Lumpur, 1983 [1958])

Brown, J. M., *Gandhi: prisoner of hope* (New Haven, 1989)

Burma Frontier Areas committee of enquiry, Cmnd. 7138 (1947)

Burma's independence celebrations (Copygraph Ltd, London, 1948)

Butwell, Richard, *U Nu of Burma* (Standford, 1963)

Callahan, Mary P., *Making enemies: war and state building in Burma* (Ithaca, 2004)

Calvert, Michael, *Fighting Mad* (Shrewsbury, 1996)

Carey, Peter, 'Myths, heroes and war', in Peter Carey and Colin Wild (eds), *Born in fire: the Indonesian struggle for independence; an anthology* (Athens, OH, 1986), pp. 6–11.

Carnell, Francis G., 'The Malayan elections', *Pacific Affairs*, 28, 4 (1955), pp. 315–30

Chan Heng Chee, *A sensation of independence: a political biography of David Marshall* (Singapore, 1984)

Chatterji, Joya, *Bengal divided: Hindu communalism and partition, 1932–1947* (Cambridge, 1994)

Cheah Boon Kheng, 'The Japanese occupation of Malaya, 1941–45: Ibrahim Yaacob and the struggle for Indonesia Raya', *Indonesia*, 28 (1979), pp. 85–120

Cheah Boon Kheng, *The masked comrades: a study of the Communist United Front in Malaya, 1945–48* (Singapore, 1979)

Cheah Boon Kheng, *Red star over Malaya: resistance and social conflict during and after the Japanese occupation of Malaya, 1941–1946* (Singapore, 1983)

Cheah Boon Kheng (ed.), *A. Samad Ismail: journalism and politics* (Kuala Lumpur, 1987)

Chelvasingham-MacIntyre, S., *Through memory lane* (Singapore, 1973)

Chettur, S. K., *Malayan adventure* (Mangalore, 1948)

Chew, Melanie, *Of hearts and minds: the story of Sembawang* (Singapore, 1998)

Chin, C. C. and Karl Hack (eds.), *Dialogues with Chin Peng: new light on the Malayan Communist Party* (Singapore, 2004)

Chin Kee Onn, *Malaya upside down* (Singapore, 1946)

Chin Peng, *My side of history* (Singapore, 2003)

Christie, Clive J., *A modern history of Southeast Asia: decolonisation, nationalism and separatism* (London, 1996)

Chui Kwei-chiang, *The response of the Malayan Chinese to political and military developments in China, 1945–9* (Singapore, 1977)

Chui Kwei-chiang, 'The China Democratic League in Singapore and Malaya, 1946–48', *Review of Southeast Asian Studies*, 15 (1985), pp. 1–28

Clancey, Gregory, *Towards a spatial history of Emergency: notes from Singapore* (Asia Research Institute Working Paper Series no. 7, Singapore, 2003)

Clarke, Hugh V., *Twilight liberation: Australian POWs between Hiroshima and home* (Sydney, 1985)

Clarke, Peter, *The Cripps version: the life of Sir Stafford Cripps* (London, 2002)

Cleaveland, Norman, *Bang! Bang! in Ampang* (San Pedro, CA, 1973)

Cloake, John, *Templer: tiger of Malaya* (London, 1985)

Coast, John, *Recruit to revolution: adventure and politics in Indonesia* (London, 1952)

Coates, John, *Suppressing insurgency: an analysis of the Malayan Emergency, 1948–54* (Boulder, 1992)

Coldstream, John, *Dirk Bogarde: the authorised biography* (London, 2005)

Comber, Leon, 'The Malayan Security Service (1945–1948)', *Intelligence and National Security*, 18, 3 (2003), pp. 128–53

Committee for the Compilation of Materials on Damage Caused by the Atomic Bombs in Hiroshima and Nagasaki, *Hiroshima and Nagasaki: the physical, medical and social effects of atomic bombings* (New York, 1981)

Connell, John, *Auchinleck: a biography of Field Marshal Sir Claude Auchinleck* (London, 1959)

Collis, Maurice, *Last and first in Burma, 1941–48* (London, 1956)

Cook, Haruko Taya and Theodore F. Cook, *Japan at war: an oral history* (New York, 1992)

Cribb, Robert, 'Opium and the Indonesian revolution', *Modern Asian Studies*, 22, 4 (1988), pp. 710–22

Cribb, Robert, *Gangsters and revolutionaries: the Jakarta People's Militia and the Indonesian revolution, 1945–1949* (Honolulu, 1991)

Cribb, Robert and Lea Narangoa, 'Orphans of empire: divided peoples, dilemmas of identity, and old imperial borders in East and Southeast Asia', *Comparative Studies in Society and History*, 46, 1 (2004), pp. 164–87

Crockett, Anthony, *Green beret, red star* (London, 1954)

Cross, J. P. and Buddhiman Gurung, *Gurkhas at war in their own words: the Gurkha experience, 1939 to the present* (London, 2002)

Cunyngham-Brown, Sjovald, *Crowded hour* (London, 1975)

Danaraj, T. J., *Japanese invasion of Malaya and Singapore, memoirs of a doctor* (Kuala Lumpur, 1990)

Darusman, Suryono, *Singapore and the Indonesian revolution, 1945–50* (Singapore, 1992)

Das, S. A. and K. B. Subbaiah, *Chalo Delhi! An historical account of the Indian independence movement in East Asia* (Kuala Lumpur, 1946)

Das, Suranjan, *Communal riots in Bengal, 1905–1947* (Delhi, 1991)

de Cruz, Gerald, *Rojak rebel: memoirs of a Singapore maverick* (Singapore, 1993)

Dean, B., *The theatre at war* (London, 1956)

Deery, Philip, 'The terminology of terrorism: Malaya, 1948–52', *Journal of Southeast Asian Studies*, 34, 2 (2003), pp. 231–47

del Tufo, M. V., *Malaya: a report on the 1947 census of population* (London, 1949)

Dentan, Robert Knox, 'Bad day at Bukit Pekan', *American Anthropologist*, 97, 2 (1995), pp. 225–31

Dobbs, Stephen, *Tuan Djek: a biography* (Singapore, 2002)

Dobby, E. H. G., 'Some aspects of the human ecology of South-East Asia', *Geographical Journal*, 108, 1/3 (1946), pp. 40–51

Donnison, F. S. V., *British military administration in the Far East 1943–46* (London, 1956)

Doulton, A. J. F., *The Fighting Cock: being the history of the 23rd Indian Division, 1942–1947* (Aldershot, 1951)

Dower, John W., 'The bombed: Hiroshimas and Nagasakis in Japanese memory', in Michael J. Hogan (ed.), *Hiroshima in history and memory* (Cambridge, 1996), pp. 116–42

Dower, John, *Embracing defeat: Japan in the wake of World War II* (London, 1999)

Driberg, Tom, *Ruling passions*, with a postscript by Michael Foot (London, 1977)

Dun, Smith, *Memoirs of the four-foot Colonel: General Smith Dun, first commander-in-chief of independent Burma's armed forces* (Ithaca, 1980)

Edinger, George, *The twain shall meet* (New York, 1960)

Falconer, Jean, *Woodsmoke and temple flowers: memories of Malaya* (Edinburgh, 1992)

Falconnier, Henri, *The soul of Malaya* (Singapore, 1985 [1931])

Falla, Jonathan, *True Love and Bartholemew: rebels on the Burmese border* (Cambridge, 1991)

Farish A. Noor, *Islam embedded: the historical development of the Pan-Malaysian Islamic Party PAS (1951–2003)*, vol. I (Kuala Lumpur, 2004)

Fay, Peter Ward, *The forgotten army: India's armed struggle for independence, 1942–1945* (Ann Arbor, 1993)

Federation of Malaya, Dept of Public Relations, *Communist banditry in*

Malaya: the Emergency, June 1948–December 1949 (Kuala Lumpur, 1950)

Federation of Malaya, *Report on the conduct of food searches at Semenyih in the Kajang District of the State of Selangor* (Kuala Lumpur, 1956)

Firdaus Haji Abdullah, *Radical Malay politics: its origins and early development* (Petaling Jaya, 1985)

Follows, Roy, *Jungle beat: fighting terrorists in Malaya, 1952–61* (London, 2000)

Foong Choon Hon (ed.), *The price of peace: true accounts of the Japanese occupation* (Singapore, 1991)

Frederick, William H., *Visions and heat: the making of the Indonesian revolution* (Athens, OH, 1989)

Frederick, William H., 'The man who knew too much: Ch. O. van der Plas and the future of Indonesia, 1927–1950', in Hans Antöv and Stein Tønesson (eds.), *Imperial policy and South East Asian nationalism* (London, 1995), pp. 34–62

Frederick, William H., 'Reflections in a moving stream: Indonesian memories of the war and the Japanese', in Remco Raben (ed.), *Representing the Japanese occupation of Indonesia: personal testimonies and public image in Indonesia, Japan and the Netherlands* (Amsterdam, 1999), pp. 16–35

Frederick, William H., 'Shadows of an unseen hand: some patterns of violence in the Indonesian revolution, 1945–1949', in F. Columbijn and T. Lindblad (eds.), *Roots of violence in Indonesia: contemporary violence in historical perspective* (Singapore, 2002), pp. 143–72

French, Patrick, *Liberty or death: India's journey to independence and division* (London, 1997)

Furedi, Frank, 'Britain's colonial wars: playing the ethnic card', *Journal of Commonwealth and Comparative Politics*, 28, 1 (1990), pp. 70–89

Furnivall, J. S., *Netherlands India: the study of a plural economy* (London, 1939)

Furnivall, J. S., *Colonial policy and practice* (Cambridge, 1957)

Fusayama, Takao, *A Japanese memoir of Sumatra: love and hatred in the liberation war* (Ithaca, 1993)

Fusayama, Takao, *Memoir of Takao Fusayama: a Japanese soldier in Malaya and Sumatra* (Kuala Lumpur, 1997)

Gamba, Charles, *The origins of trade unionism in Malaya* (Singapore, 1960)

Gammans, Captain L. D., 'Post-war planning in South-East Asia', *British Malaya*, November 1942

Gandhi, Mohandas, *Collected works of Mahatma Gandhi* (Delhi, 1958–), vol. LXXXI

Gandhi, Rajmohan, *Patel: a life* (Ahmedabad, 1990)

Gellhorn, Martha, *The face of war* (Harmondsworth, 1991)

George, Margaret, *Australia and the Indonesian revolution* (Melbourne, 1980)

George, T. J. S., *Krishna Menon: a biography* (London, 1964)

Geraghty, Tony, *Who Dares Wins: the story of SAS, 1952–92*, 3rd edn (London, 1992)

Gerbrandy, P. S., *Indonesia* (London, 1950)

Ghosh, K. K., *The Indian National Army: second front of the Indian national movement* (Meerut, 1969)

Gibney, Frank (ed.), *Sensō: the Japanese remember the Pacific War: letters to the editor of Asahi Shimbun* (London, 1995)

Gilmour, Andrew, *My role in the rehabilitation of Singapore, 1946–53* (Singapore, 1973)

Gilmour, O. W., *With freedom to Singapore* (London, 1950)

Gopal, S. (ed.), *Selected works of Jawaharlal Nehru*, 2nd series, vol. X (Delhi, 1990)

Gordon, Leonard A., *Brothers against the Raj: a biography of Indian nationalists Sarat and Subhas Chandra Bose* (New York, 1990)

Goscha, Christopher, *Thailand and the Southeast Asian networks of the Vietnamese revolution, 1885–1954* (London, 1999)

Goscha, Christopher, 'Belated Asian allies: the technical and military contribution of Japanese deserters (1945–50)', in Marilyn B. Young and Robert Buzzanco (eds.), *A Companion to the Vietnam War* (Oxford, 2002), pp. 37–64

Goto Ken'ichi, 'Modern Japan and Indonesia: the dynamics and legacy of wartime rule', in Peter Post and Elly Touwen-Bouwsma (eds.), *Japan, Indonesia and the war: myths and realities* (Leiden, 1997), pp. 14–30

Gouda, Frances, *Dutch culture overseas: colonial practice in the Netherlands Indies, 1900–1942* (Amsterdam, 1992)

Gouda, Frances, with Thijs Brocades Zaalberg, *American visions of the Netherlands East Indies/Indonesia: United States foreign policy and Indonesian nationalism, 1920–1949* (Amsterdam, 2002)

Gough, Richard, *Jungle was red: SOE's Force 136 Sumatra and Malaya* (Singapore, 2003)

Gould, Tony, *Imperial warrior: Britain and the Gurkhas* (London, 1999)

Government of Burma, *Report of the Tantabin incident enquiry committee* (Rangoon, 1947)

Government of Burma, *Burma and the insurrections* (Rangoon, 1949)

Greenwood, Alexander, *Field-Marshal Auchinleck* (Brockerscliffe, Durham, c.1981)

Gregorian, Raffi, *The British army, the Gurkhas and Cold War strategy in the Far East, 1947–1954* (Basingstoke, 2002)

Hack, Karl, 'British intelligence and counter-insurgency in the era of decolonisation: the example of Malaya', *Intelligence and National Security*, 14, 2 (1999), pp. 124–55

Hack, Karl, '"Iron claws on Malaya": the historiography of the Malayan Emergency', *Journal of Southeast Asian Studies*, 30, 1 (1999), pp. 99–125

Halimah Mohd Said and Zainab Abdul Majid, *Images of the Jawi Peranakan of Penang; assimilation of the Jawi Peranakan community into the Malay society* (Perak, 2004)

Han Suyin, 'An outline of Malayan Chinese literature', *Eastern Horizon*, 3, 6 (June, 1964), pp. 6–16

Han Suyin, *My house has two doors* (London, 1980)

Hanifah, Abu, *Tales of a revolution: a leader of the Indonesian revolution looks back* (Sydney, 1972)

Harper, T. N., *The end of empire and the making of Malaya* (Cambridge, 1999)

Harper, T. N., 'Lim Chin Siong and "the Singapore Story"', in Jomo K. S. and Tan Jing Quee (eds.), *Comet in our sky: Lim Chin Siong in history* (Kuala Lumpur, 2001), pp. 1–56

Haryati Hasan, 'Malay women and prostitution in Kota Bahru, Kelantan, 1950s–1970s', *Journal of the Malaysian Branch of the Royal Asiatic Society*, 78, 1 (2005), pp. 97–120

Headlam, Cuthbert, *Parliament and politics in the age of Churchill: the Headlam Diaries, 1935–51*, ed. Stuart Ball (Cambridge, 1999)

Heng Pek Koon, *Chinese politics in Malaysia: a history of the Malaysian Chinese Association* (Singapore, 1988)

Heussler, Robert, *British rule in Malaya, 1942–57* (Singapore, 1985)

Hirschman, Charles, 'The meaning and measurement of ethnicity in Malaysia: an analysis of census classifications', *Journal of Asian Studies*, 46, 3 (1987), pp. 555–82

Hoalim, Philip, *The Malayan Democratic Union: Singapore's first democratic political party* (Singapore, 1973)

Hoe, Alan and Eric Morris, *Re-enter the SAS: the SAS and the Malayan campaign* (London, 1994)

Holder, R. W., *Eleven months in Malaya: September 1945 to August 1946* (Kuala Lumpur, 2005)

Hone, Ralph, *Report on the British Military Administration of Malaya, September 1945 to March 1946* (Kuala Lumpur, 1946)

Hooker, Virginia Matheson, *Writing a new society: social change through the novel in Malay* (St Leonard's, NSW, 2000)

Houtman, Gustaaf, *Mental culture in Burmese crisis politics* (Tokyo, 2002)

Hudson, Lionel, *The Rats of Rangoon: the inside story of the fiasco that took place at the end of the war in Burma* (London, 1987)

Ibrahim Chik, *Ibrahim Chik: dari API ke Rejimen Ke-1* (Bangi, 2004)

Idrus, 'Surabaja', translated by S. U. Nababan and Benedict Anderson, *Indonesia*, 5 (1968), pp. 1–28

Ismail bin Haji Salleh, *The Sultan was not alone: a collection of letters written by Sultan Badlishah in his effort to repeal the Malayan Union policy imposed by the British government on Malaya in 1946, and other supporting letters and documents written by others* (Alor Setar, 1989)

Jacobs, Julian, *Hill peoples of northeast India: the Nagas. Society, culture and the colonial encounter* (Stuttgart, 1990)

Jain, Ravindra K., 'Leadership and authority in a plantation: a case study of Indians in Malaya (c. 1900–42)', in G. Wijeyewardene (ed.), *Leadership and authority: a symposium* (Singapore, 1968), pp. 163–73

Jalal, Ayesha, *The state of martial rule: the origins of Pakistan's political economy of defence* (Cambridge, 1990)

James, H. and D. Sheil-Small, *A pride of Gurkhas: the 2nd King Edward VII's Own Goorkhas, 1948–71* (London, 1971)

Johnson, W. (ed.), *The papers of Adlai E. Stevenson*, vol. V: *Visit to Asia, the Middle East, and Europe, March–August 1953* (Boston, 1974)

Johnstone, William C., *Burma's foreign policy: a study in neutralism* (Cambridge, MA, 1963)

Jordan, David, '"A particularly exacting operation": British forces and the battle of Surabaya, November 1945', *Small Wars and Insurgencies*, 11, 3 (2000), pp. 89–114

Kahin, G. McT., *Nationalism and revolution in Indonesia* (Ithaca, 1952)

Kassim bin Ahmad, *Characterization in Hikayat Hang Tuah: a general survey of character-portrayal and analysis and interpretation of the characters of Hang Tuah and Hang Jebat* (Kuala Lumpur, 1966)

Keenleyside, T. A., 'Nationalist Indian attitudes towards Asia: a troublesome legacy for post-independence Indian foreign policy', *Pacific Affairs*, 55, 2 (1982), pp. 210–30

Khan, Shah Nawaz, *The INA and its Netaji* (Delhi, 1946)

Khatijah Sidek, *Memoirs of Khatijah Sidek: Puteri Kesateria Bangsa* (Kuala Lumpur, 2001 [1960])

Khong Kim Hoong, *Merdeka: British rule and the struggle for independence in Malaya* (Kuala Lumpur, 1984)

Khoo, Agnes, *Life as the river flows: women in the Malayan anti-colonial struggle* (Petaling Jaya, 2004)

Khoo Salma Nusution and Abdur-Razzaq Lubis, *Kinta Valley: pioneering Malaysia's modern development* (Ipoh, 2005)

Kirby, S. Woodburn, *The war against Japan*, vol. V: *The surrender of Japan* (London, 1969)

Krancher, Jan A. (ed.), *The defining years of the Dutch East Indies, 1942–*

1949: survivors' accounts of Japanese invasion and enslavement of Europeans and the revolution that created free Indonesia (London, 1996)

Kratoska, Paul H., *The Japanese occupation of Malaya, 1941–45* (London, 1998)

Keris Mas (trans. Harry Aveling), *Blood and tears* (Petaling Jaya, 1984)

K'tut Tantri, *Revolt in paradise* (New York, 1960)

Kulkarni, V. S. and K. S. N. Munshi, *The first Indian National Army trial* (Poonah, 1946)

Lau, Albert, *The Malayan Union controversy, 1942–48* (London, 1991)

Leary, John, *Violence and the dream people: the Orang Asli in the Malayan Emergency, 1948–1960* (Athens, OH, 1995)

Lee Kam Hing and Chow Mun Seong, *Biographical dictionary of the Chinese in Malaysia* (Kuala Lumpur, 1997)

Lee Kuan Yew, *The Singapore story* (Singapore, 1998)

Legge, J. D., *Sukarno: a political biography* (Harmondsworth, 1972)

Leong Yee Fong, *Labour and trade unionism in colonial Malaya: a study of the socio-economic and political bases of the Malayan labour movement, 1930–1957* (Penang, 1999)

Lim Cheng Leng, *The story of a psy-warrior: Tan Sri Dr C. C. Too* (Batu Caves, 2000)

Lim Hong Bee, *Born into war: autobiography of a barefoot colonial boy who grew up to face the challenge of the modern world* (London, 1994)

Lindsey, Timothy, *The romance of K'tut Tantri and Indonesia: text and scripts, history and identity* (Kuala Lumpur, 1997)

Lintner, Bertil, *The rise and fall of the Communist Party of Burma* (Ithaca, 1990)

Lintner, Bertil, *Burma in revolt: opium and insurgency since 1948* (Boulder, 1994)

Lockwood, John, *Black armada: Australia and the struggle for Indonesian independence 1942–49* (Sydney, 1975)

Loh Kok Wah, Francis, *Beyond the tin mines: coolies, squatters and New Villagers in the Kinta valley, c. 1880–1980* (Singapore, 1988)

Low, N. I., *When Singapore was Syonan-to* (Singapore, 1995 [1947])

Low N. I. and H. M. Cheng, *This Singapore (Our city of dreadful night)* (Singapore, 1946).

MacArthur, Brian, *Surviving the sword: prisoners of the Japanese, 1942–45* (London, 2005)

Mahmud bin Mat, *Tinggal kenangan: the memoirs of Dato' Sir Mahmud bin Mat* (Kuala Lumpur, 1997)

Malaka, Tan (trans. and intro. Helen Jarvis), *From jail to jail*, vol. II (Athens, OH, 1991 [1946]); vol. III (Athens, OH, 1991 [1948])

Malayan Communist Party, Johore-Malacca Border Committee, *Death of a heretic* (Singapore, 1951)

Mansergh, Nicholas, 'The Asian Conference', *International Affairs*, 23, 3 (July 1947), pp. 295-306

Mansergh, Nicholas (ed.), *Constitutional relations between Britain and India: the transfer of power, 1942-7*, vol I, *Quit India, 30 April to 21 September 1942* (London, 1971); vol. VII, *The Cabinet mission* (London, 1977)

Marr, David, *Vietnam 1945* (Berkeley, 1995)

Masson, Madelaine, *Edwina: the biography of the Countess Mountbatten of Burma* (London, 1958)

Masters, John, *The road past Mandalay* (London, 1962)

Maung Maung, *A trial in Burma: the assassination of Aung San* (The Hague, 1962)

Maung Maung, *To a soldier son* (Rangoon, 1974)

Maybury, Maurice, *The heaven-born in Burma* (Castle Cary, 1985)

McEnery, John H., *Epilogue in Burma, 1945-48: the military dimension of British withdrawal* (Tunbridge Wells, 1990)

McHugh, J. N., *A handbook of spoken 'bazaar' Malay* (Singapore, 1956 [1945])

McHugh, J. N., *Anatomy of communist propaganda* (Kuala Lumpur, 1949)

McLane, Charles B., *Soviet strategies in Southeast Asia: an exploration of Eastern Policy under Lenin and Stalin* (Princeton, 1966)

McMillan, Richard, *The British occupation of Indonesia, 1945-1946: Britain, the Netherlands and the Indonesian revolution* (London, 2005)

Middlebrook, S. M., 'Pulai: an early Chinese settlement in Kelantan', *Journal of the Malayan Branch of the Royal Asiatic Society*, 11, 2 (1933), pp. 151-6

Mohd Yusoff Hj. Ahmad, Datuk, *Decades of change (Malaysia – 1910s-1970s)* (Kuala Lumpur, 1983)

Moon, Penderel (ed.), *Wavell: the viceroy's journal* (London, 1973)

Mrázek, Rudolf, 'Tan Malaka: a political personality's structure of experience', *Indonesia*, 14 (1972), pp. 1-47

Mrázek, Rudolf, *Sjahrir: politics and exile in Indonesia* (Ithaca, 1994)

Muhammad Ikmal Said, 'Ethnic perspectives on the left in Malaysia', in Joel Kahn and Francis Loh Kok Wah (eds.), *Fragmented vision: culture and politics in contemporary Malaysia* (Sydney, 1992), pp. 254-81

Murphy, H. B. M., 'The mental health of Singapore: part one – suicide', *Medical Journal of Malaya*, 9, 1 (1954), pp. 1-45

Mustapha Hussain, *Malay nationalism before Umno: the memoirs of Mustapha Hussain, translated by Insun Mustapha and edited by Jomo K. S.* (Kuala Lumpur, 2005)

Nadaraja, K., 'The Thondar Pedai movement of Kedah, 1945-47', *Malaysia in History*, 24 (1981), pp. 95-103

Nagi, John A. *Learning to eat soup with a knife: counterinsurgency lessons from Malaya and Vietnam*, new edn (New York, 2005)

Nakahara, Michiko, 'Labour recruitment in Malaya under the Japanese occupation: the case of the Burma–Siam railway', in Jomo K. S. (ed.), *Rethinking Malaysia* (Kuala Lumpur, 1997), pp. 215–45

Nakahara, Michiko, 'Comfort women in Malaysia', *Critical Asian Studies*, 33, 4 (2001), pp. 581–9

Nasradin Bahari, 'Cherpen2 terjemahan didalan majalah Mastika, 1946–59', *Bahasa*, 7 (1965), pp. 56–93

Naw, Angelene, *Aung San and the struggle for Burmese independence* (Copenhagen, 2001).

Netaji Centre, Kuala Lumpur, *Netaji Subhas Chandra Bose: a Malaysian perspective* (Kuala Lumpur, 1992)

Nishihara, Masashi, *The Japanese and Sukarno's Indonesia: Tokyo–Jakarta relations, 1951–1966* (Kyoto, 1976)

Noone, Richard, *Rape of the dream people* (London, 1972)

Nu, U (Thakin) (ed. and trans. J. S. Furnivall), *Burma under the Japanese: pictures and portraits* (London, 1954)

Nu, U (Thakin), *Saturday's son* (Bombay, 1976)

Oatts, Balfour, *The jungle in arms* (London, 1962)

Ong Siew Im, Pamela, *One man's will: a portrait of Dato' Sir Onn bin Ja'afar* (Penang, 1998)

Ooi Jin Bee, 'Mining landscapes of Kinta', *Malayan Journal of Tropical Geography*, 4 (1955), pp. 1–58

Overy, Richard, *Why the Allies won* (London, 1995)

Owen, Nicholas, 'The Conservative Party and Indian independence, 1945–47', *Historical Journal*, 46, 2 (2003), pp. 403–36.

Page, Malcolm, *A history of The King's African Rifles and East African Forces* (London, 1998)

Palit, D. K., *Major General A. A. Rudra: his services in three armies and two world wars* (Delhi, 1997)

Palmer, J. Norman, 'Estate workers' health in the Federated Malay States in the 1920s', in P. Rimmer and L. Allen (eds.), *The underside of Malaysian history: pullers, prostitutes and plantation workers* (Singapore, 1990), pp. 179–192

Parrott, J. G. A., 'Who killed Brigadier Mallaby?', *Indonesia*, 20 (1975), pp. 87–111

Parsons, Timothy, *The African rank-and-file: social implications of colonial military service in the King's African Rifles, 1902–1964* (Oxford, 1999)

Pearce, Robert, *Attlee* (London, 1997)

Pearn, B. R., *The Indian in Burma* (Ledbury, Herts, 1946)

The People's Constitutional Proposals for Malaya 1947 drafted by PUT-ERA-AMCJA (Pusat Kajian Bahan Serjarah Kontemporari Tempatan, Kajang, 2005)

Pham, Julie, 'Furnivall and Fabianism: reinterpreting the plural society in colonial Burma', *Modern Asian Studies*, 39, 2 (2005), pp. 321–48

Po, San C., *Burma and the Karens* (London, 1929)

Polunin, Ivan, 'The medical natural history of the Malayan aborigines', *Malayan Medical Journal*, 8, 1 (1953), pp. 55–174

Prasad, B., *Official History of the Indian armed forces in the Second World War*, 4 vols (Delhi, 1954–65), vol. I: *The reconquest of Burma*

Purcell, Victor, *Malaya: communist or free?* (Stanford, 1955)

Purcell, Victor, *The memoirs of a Malayan official* (London, 1965)

Puthucheary, James, *Ownership and control in the Malayan economy* (Singapore, 1960)

Puthucheary, Dominic and Jomo K. S. (eds.), *No cowardly past: James J. Puthucheary, writings, poems, commentaries* (Kuala Lumpur 1998)

Raffel, Burton (trans. and ed.), *The voice of the night: complete poetry and prose of Chairil Anwar* (1993)

Ramakrishna, Kumar, ' "Transmogrifying Malaya": the impact of Sir Gerald Templer (1952–54)', *Journal of Southeast Asian Studies*, 32, 1 (2001), pp. 79–92

Ramakrishna, Kumar, *Emergency propaganda: the winning of Malayan hearts and minds, 1948–1958* (Richmond, 2002)

Ramasamy, P., 'Indian war memory in Malaysia', in P. Lim Pui Huen and Diana Wong (eds.), *War and memory in Malaysia and Singapore* (Singapore, 2000), pp. 90–105

Ratnam, K. J., *Communalism and the political process in Malaya* (Kuala Lumpur, 1965)

Reid, A. J. S., *The Indonesian national revolution, 1945–50* (Sydney, 1974)

Reid, Anthony, *The blood of the people: revolution and the end of traditional rule in northern Sumatra* (Kuala Lumpur, 1979)

Reid, Anthony, 'Pictures at an exhibition', in Hans Antöv and Stein Tønesson (eds.), *Imperial policy and South East Asian nationalism* (London, 1995)

Roadnight, Andrew, 'Sleeping with the enemy: Britain, Japanese troops and the Netherlands East Indies, 1945–46', *History*, 87, 286 (2002), pp. 245–68

Robinson, J. B. Perry, *Transformation in Malaya* (London, 1956)

Roland, Joan G., *The Jewish communities of India: identity in a colonial era* (New Brunswick, 1998)

Rooney, David, *Mad Mike: a life of Michael Calvert* (London, 1997)

Ruff-O'Herne, Jan, *50 years of silence* (Sydney, 1994)

Rutherford, Danilyn Fox, 'Trekking to New Guinea: Dutch colonial fantasies of a virgin land, 1900–1942', in Julia Clancy-Smith and Frances Gouda (eds.), *Domesticating the empire: race, gender and family life in French and Dutch colonialism* (London, 1998), pp. 255–71

Said Zahari, *Dark clouds at dawn* (Kuala Lumpur, 2001)

Samaddar, Ranabir, *Reflections on partition in the East* (Delhi, 1997)

Sandhu, K. S., 'Emergency resettlement in Malaya', *Journal of Tropical Geography*, 18 (1964), pp. 157–83

Sandhu, K. S., 'The saga of the "squatter" in Malaya: a preliminary survey of the causes, characteristics and consequences of the resettlement of rural dwellers during the Emergency between 1948 and 1960', *Journal of Southeast Asian History*, 5 (1964), pp. 143–77

Sanger, Clyde, *Malcolm MacDonald: bringing an end to empire* (Montreal and London, 1995)

Saravanamuttu, Manicasothy, *The Sara saga* (Singapore, n.d. [1969])

Sastroamijoyo, Ali, *Milestones on my journey: the memoirs of Ali Sastroamijoyo, Indonesian patriot and political leader* (St Lucia, 1979)

Scott-Ross, Alice, *Tun Dato Sir Cheng Lock Tan: a personal profile* (Singapore, 1990)

Seagrave, Gordon S., *Burma surgeon* (London, 1944)

Seagrave, Gordon S., *Burma surgeon returns* (London, 1946)

Seagrave, Gordon S., *My hospital in the hills* (London, 1957)

Shamsiah Fakeh, *Memoir Shamsiah Fakeh: dari AWAS ke Rejimen Ke-10* (Bangi, 2004)

Shennan, Margaret, *Out in the midday sun: the British in Malaya, 1880–1960* (London, 2000)

Sheppard, Mubin, *Taman Budiman: memoirs of an unorthodox civil servant* (Kuala Lumpur, 1979)

Shinozaki, Mamoru, *Syonan – my story: the Japanese occupation of Singapore* (Singapore, 1979)

Shiraishi, Takashi, *An age in motion: popular radicalism in Java, 1912–26* (Ithaca, 1990)

Shlomowitz, R. and L. Brennan, 'Mortality and Indian labour in Malaya, 1877–1933', *Indian Economic and Social History Review*, 29 (1992), pp. 57–75

Short, Anthony, *In pursuit of mountain rats: the communist insurrection in Malaya* (Singapore, 2000 [1975])

Siaw, Laurence K. L., *Chinese society in rural Malaysia* (Kuala Lumpur, 1983)

Sillitoe, Alan, *Life without armour* (London, 1995)

Silverstein, Josef (ed.), *The political legacy of Aung San* (Ithaca, 1976)

Singh, Balwant, *Independence and democracy in Burma, 1945–52: the turbulent years* (Ann Arbor, 1993)

Singh, Uma Shankar, *Burma and India 1948–62* (Bombay, 1979)

Slim, Sir William, *Defeat into victory* (London, 1955)

Smith, Felix, *China pilot: flying for Chiang and Chennault* (London, 1995)

Smith, Simon C., *British relations with the Malay rulers from decentralization to independence, 1930–1957* (Kuala Lumpur, 1995)

Sodei, Rinifo, *Were we the enemy? American survivors of Hiroshima* (Boulder, 1998)

Sopiee, Mohamed Noordin, *From Malayan Union to Singapore separation: political unification in the Malaysia region, 1945–65* (Kuala Lumpur, 1974)

Springhall, John, ' "Disaster in Surabaya": the death of Brigadier Mallaby during the British occupation of Java, 1945–46', *Journal of Imperial and Commonwealth History*, 24, 3 (1996), pp. 422–43

Springhall, John, 'Mountbatten versus the generals: British military rule of Singapore, 1945–46', *Journal of Contemporary History*, 34, 4 (2001) pp. 335–52

Springhall, John, 'Kicking out the Vietminh; how Britain allowed France to reoccupy south Indochina,' *Journal of Contemporary History*, 40, 1 (2005), pp. 115–30

Stenson, Michael R., 'The Malayan Union and the historians', *Journal of Southeast Asian History*, 10, 2 (1969), pp. 344–54

Stenson, Michael R., *Repression and revolt: the origins of the 1948 Communist insurrection in Malaya and Singapore* (Athens, OH, 1969)

Stenson, Michael R., *Industrial conflict in Malaya: prelude to the Communist revolt of 1948* (London, 1970)

Stenson, Michael R., *The 1948 communist revolt in Malaya: a note on historical sources and interpretation with a reply by Gerald de Cruz* (Singapore, 1971)

Stenson, Michael R., *Class, race and colonialism in west Malaysia: the Indian case* (Queensland, 1980)

Stewart, Brian, *Smashing terrorism in the Malayan Emergency: the vital contribution of the police* (Kuala Lumpur, 2004)

Stilwell, Joseph W., *The Stilwell papers*, ed. Theodore H. Wright (London, 1949)

Stockwell, A. J., 'The formation and first years of the United Malays National Organization (U.M.N.O.), 1946–1948', *Modern Asian Studies*, 11, 4 (1977), pp. 481–513

Stockwell, A. J., *British policy and Malay politics during the Malayan Union experiment, 1945–1948* (Kuala Lumpur, 1979)

Stockwell, A. J., 'British imperial strategy and decolonization in South-east Asia, 1947–57', in D. K. Basset and V. T. King (eds.), *Britain and South-East Asia* (University of Hull Centre of Southeast Asian Studies, Occasional Paper no. 13, 1986), pp. 79–90

Stockwell, A. J., 'Policing during the Malayan Emergency, 1948–60: communism, communalism and decolonization', in D. Anderson and D. Killingray, *Policing and decolonization: politics, nationalism and the police* (Manchester, 1992), pp. 105–28

Stockwell, A. J., ' "A widespread and long-concocted plot to overthrow government in Malaya"? The origins of the Malayan Emergency', *Journal of Imperial and Commonwealth History*, 21 (1993), pp. 66–88

Stockwell, 'A. J., Gurney, Sir Henry Lovell Goldsworthy (1898–1951)', *Oxford Dictionary of National Biography*, Oxford University Press, 2004 (http://www.oxforddnb.com/view/article/33611, accessed 12 Sept 2005)

Stockwell, A. J., 'Colonial atrocities: uncovering cover-ups', *PROphile*, 16, 1 (April 2005), pp. 1–6

Stockwell, A. J., ed., *British documents on the end of empire: Malaya*, 3 Vols (London, 1995)

Strauch, Judith, 'Chinese New Villages of the Malayan Emergency, a generation later: a case study', *Contemporary Southeast Asia*, 2, 2 (1981), pp. 126–139

Strawson, John, *A history of the SAS Regiment* (London, 1984)

Stripp, Alan, *Codebreaker in the Far East* (Oxford, 1989)

Stubbs, Richard, *Counter-insurgency and the economic factor: the impact of the Korean War prices boom on the Malayan Emergency* (ISEAS Occasional paper no. 19, Singapore, 1974)

Stubbs, Richard, *Hearts and minds in guerrilla warfare: the Malayan Emergency, 1948–1960* (Singapore, 1989)

Syed Naguib al-Attas, *Some aspects of Sufism as understood and practised by the Malays* (Singapore, 1963)

Tamayama, Kazuo, *Railwaymen in the war: tales by Japanese railway soldiers in Burma and Thailand, 1941–1947* (Houndmills, 2005)

Tan Boon Liang, John, *A bamboo flower blooms* (New York, 1984)

Tan Cheng Lock, *Malayan problems from a Chinese point of view* (Singapore, 1947)

Tan Cheng Lock, *One country, one people, one government: presidential address by Tan Cheng Lock at a meeting of the General Committee of the MCA held in Penang on 30 October, 1949* (Kuala Lumpur, 1949)

Tan Liok Eee, *The rhetoric of bangsa and minzu: community and nation in tension, the Malay peninsula, 1900–1955* (Centre of Southeast Asian Studies, Monash University, Working Paper no. 52, 1988)

Tan Liok Ee, *The politics of Chinese education in Malaya, 1945–1961* (Kuala Lumpur 1997)

Tanaka, Shoko, *Post-war Japanese resource policies and strategies: the case of Southeast Asia* (Ithaca, 1986)

Tarling, Nicholas, ' "Some rather nebulous capacity": Lord Killearn's appointment in Southeast Asia', *Modern Asian Studies*, 20, 3 (1986), pp. 559–600

Tarling, Nicholas, *Britain, Southeast Asia and the onset of the Cold War, 1945–1950* (Cambridge, 1998)

Taylor, R. H., *The state in Burma* (London, 1987)

Tewari, K. K., *A soldier's voyage of self-discovery* (Auroville, 1995)

Thatcher, Dorothy and Robert Cross, *Refugee from the Japanese* (Kuala Lumpur, 1993 [1959])

Thein Pe Myint, 'Wartime traveller,' translated by R. H. Taylor in his *Marxism and resistance in Burma 1942–5: Thein Pe's wartime traveller* (Athens, OH, 1984)

Thio Chan Bee, *The extraordinary adventures of an ordinary man* (London, 1977)

Thomas, Leslie, *The virgin soldiers* (London, 1967)

Thomas, Leslie, *In my wildest dreams* (London, 1984)

Thompson, Sir Robert, *Defeating communist insurgency: experiences from Malaya and Vietnam* (London, 1966)

Tinker, Hugh (ed.), *Burma: the struggle for independence, 1944–1948*, vol I: *From military occupation to civil government, 1 January 1944 to 31 August 1946* (London, 1983); vol. II: *From general strike to independence, 31 August 1946 to 4 January 1948* (London, 1984)

Tomaru, Junko, *The postwar rapprochement of Malaya and Japan, 1945–61: the roles of Britain and Japan in South-east Asia* (Houndmills, 2000)

Toye, Hugh, *The springing tiger: a study of a revolutionary* (London, 1959)

Trager, Frank N., *Building a welfare state in Burma 1948–56* (New York, 1958)

Trager, Frank N., *Burma from kingdom to republic: a historical and political analysis* (London, 1966)

Trager, Frank N., *Burma. Japanese military administration: selected documents 1941–5* (Philadelphia, 1971)

Trefalt, Beatrice, *Japanese army stragglers and memories of the war in Japan, 1950–1975*, (London, 2003)

Tregonning, K. G., 'Tan Cheng Lock: a Malayan nationalist', *Journal of Southeast Asia Studies*, 10, 1 (1979), pp. 25–76

Tunku Abdul Rahman, *As a matter of interest* (Petaling Jaya, 1981)

Turnbull, Mary, 'British planning for post-war Malaya', *Journal of Southeast Asian Studies*, 5, 2 (September 1974), pp. 239–54

Twang Peck Yang, *The Chinese business elite in Indonesia and the transition to independence, 1940–1950* (Kuala Lumpur, 1998)

van de Ven, Hans J., *War and nationalism in China, 1925–45* (London, 2003)

van der Post, Laurens, *The Admiral's baby* (London, 1996)

Wade, Ashton, *A life on the line* (Tunbridge Wells, 1988)

Warner, Philip, 'Hone, Sir (Herbert) Ralph (1896–1992)', *Oxford Dictionary of National Biography*, Oxford, 2004 (http://www.oxforddnb.com/view/article/51132, accessed 3 May 2005)

Watson, C. W., *Of self and nation: autobiography and the representation of modern Indonesia* (Honolulu, 2000)

Wavell, Archibald (ed. Penderel Moon), *Wavell: the viceroy's journal* (London, 1973)

Wee Hock Chye, *Comfort homes and early years* (Kuala Lumpur, n.d.)

Wehl, D., *The birth of Indonesia* (London, 1949)

Westerling, Raymond ('Turk'), *Challenge to terror* (London, 1952)

Wheen, Francis, *Tom Driberg: his life and indiscretions* (London, 1990)

White, Nicholas J., *Business, government and the end of empire: Malaya, 1945–1957* (Kuala Lumpur, 1996)

Willems, Wim, 'No sheltering sky: migrant identities of Dutch nationals from Indonesia', in Andrea L. Smith (ed.), *Europe's invisible migrants* (Amsterdam, 2003), pp. 33–60

Williams-Hunt, P. D. R., *An introduction to the Malayan aborigines* (Kuala Lumpur, 1952)

Wong Lin Ken, 'The Malayan Union: a historical retrospect', *Journal of Southeast Asian Studies*, 13, 1 (1982), pp. 184–91

Wong Wing On, James, *From Pacific war to Merdeka: reminiscences of Abdullah C. D., Rashid Maidin, Suriani Abdullah and Abu Samah* (Petaling Jaya, 2005)

Wong Yunn Chii and Tan Kar Lin, 'Emergence of a cosmopolitan space for culture and consumption: the New World amusement park, Singapore (1923–70) in the inter-war years', *Inter-Asia Cultural Studies*, 5, 2 (2004), pp. 279–304

Woods, John Lowe, *An Irishman in Malaya* (Peterhead, 1977)

Yasuyuki, Hikita, 'Japanese companies' inroads into Indonesia under Japanese military administration', in Peter Post and Elly Touwen-Bouwsma (eds.), *Japan, Indonesia and the war: myths and realities* (Leiden, 1997)

Yeo Kim Wah, 'The anti-Federation movement in Malaya, 1946–48', *Journal of Southeast Asian Studies*, 4, 1 (1973), pp. 31–51

Yeo Kim Wah, *Political development in Singapore, 1945–55* (Singapore, 1973)

Yeo Kim Wah, 'Student politics in University of Malaya, 1949–51', *Journal of Southeast Asian Studies*, 23, 2 (1992), pp. 346–80

Yeo Kim Wah, 'Joining the communist underground: the conversion of English-educated radicals to communism in Singapore, June 1948–January 1951', *Journal of the Malayan Branch of the Royal Asiatic Society*, 67 (1994), pp. 29–59

Yong, C. F., *Tan Kah-Kee: the making of an overseas Chinese legend* (Singapore, 1989)

Yong, C. F., *The origins of Malayan communism* (Singapore, 1997)

Yong, C. F. and R. B. McKenna, *The Kuomintang movement in British Malaya, 1912–1949* (Singapore, 1990)

Yong Mun Cheong, *H. J. van Mook and Indonesian independence: a study of his role in Dutch–Indonesian relations, 1945–48* (The Hague, 1982)

Yong Mun Cheong, *The Indonesian revolution and the Singapore connection, 1945–1949* (Singapore, 2003)

Yuen Yuet Leng, *Operation Ginger* (Kuala Lumpur, 1998)

Zachariah, Benjamin, *Nehru* (London, 2002)

Ziegler, P., *Mountbatten: the official biography*, paperback edn (London, 2001)

Ziegler, P. (ed.), *Personal diary of Admiral the Lord Mountbatten: Supreme Allied Commander, South-East Asia, 1943–1946* (London, 1988)

UNPUBLISHED MANUSCRIPTS AND MISCELLANEOUS ONLINE SOURCES

Amir Muhammad's blog: lastcommunist.blogspot.com

Branchley, John, 'The ambush of 4 Troop, A Squadron, 4th Hussars'; www.nmbva.c.uk/The%20ambush.htm

Chua Ai Lin, 'Negotiating national identity: the English-speaking domiciled communities in Singapore, 1930–41', (MA thesis, National University of Singapore, 2001)

Cole, R. 'A signalman remembers': http://members.tripod.com/Askari_MB/id51.htm

Cole, R. 'It aint 'arf 'ot': http://members.tripod.com/Askari_MB/id47.htm

'Daripada buruh menjadi pejuang kemerdekaan yang ulung', typescript of interview with Rashid Maidin from *Suluh Rakyat*, 1989

Franklin, H. Bruce, 'By the bomb's early light; or the Quiet American's war on terror': http://rutgers.edu/~hbf/Quietam.htm

Humphrey, J. W., 'Population resettlement in Malaya' (PhD thesis, Northwestern University, 1971)

Kent, Jonathan 'Past lessons for occupying forces', 17 July 2004: http://news.bbc.co.uk/1/hi/programmes/fromourowncorrespondent/3897147.stm

Lim Kit Siang, media statement of 17 July 2004: http://www.dapmalaysia.org/all-archive/English/2004/ju104/lks/lks3143.htm

'A Profile of the Late Mr Albert Abraham Lelah', *The Scribe* (Journal of Babylonian Jewry), 70 (October 1998): http://www.dangoor.com/70012.html

Rui Xiong Kee, 'Exploring the "communist" in the communist insurrection in Malaya', Stanford University, Program in Writing and Rhetoric, Boothe Prize essays, 2004 (Stanford, 2004), pp. 37–49: http://pwr.stanford.edu/publications/Boothe%20book%202004.pdf

Stockwell, A. J., 'Knowledge and power; university and nation in the new Malaya of 1938–62', paper delivered at 'Asian Horizons' conference, Singapore, 1–3 August 2005

Sutton, Ken, 'A Guardsman's tale: www.nmbava.co.uk/a_guardsmans%20man%20tale.html

'Temubual dengan Saudara Abdullah C. D., tokoh nasional tanahair kita', typescript of interview from *Suluh Rakyat*, 1988.

Index